MW00781632

ARAB ORTHODOX CHRISTIANS UNDER THE OTTOMANS 1516–1831

Arab Orthodox Christians Under the Ottomans 1516–1831

By Constantin A. Panchenko

Translated by Brittany Pheiffer Noble and Samuel Noble

Foreword by His Beatitude Patriarch John X of Antioch and All the East

Holy Trinity Seminary Press
Holy Trinity Monastery
Jordanville, New York
2016

Printed with the blessing of His Eminence,
Metropolitan Hilarion First Hierarch
of the Russian Orthodox Church Outside of Russia

Arab Orthodox Christians Under
the Ottomans 1516-1831
© 2016 Holy Trinity Monastery

HOLY TRINITY
SEMINARY PRESS

An imprint of

HOLY TRINITY PUBLICATIONS
Holy Trinity Monastery
Jordanville, New York 13361-0036
www.holytrinitypublications.com

ISBN: 978-1-942699-07-1 (hardback)
ISBN: 978-1-942699-08-8 (paperback)
ISBN: 978-1-942699-10-1 (ePub)
ISBN: 978-1-942699-11-8 (Mobipocket)

Library of Congress Control Number: 2016931933

The Russian language edition was published by
the INDRIK Publishing House in 2012, Moscow
ISBN 978-5-91674-226-8

Cover image: The 7th Ecumenical Council, Icon of the
eighteenth-century Aleppo School © Our Lady of Balamand
Patriarchal Monastery, www.balamandmonastery.org

The publication was effected under the auspices of the Mikhail
Prokhorov Foundation TRANSCRIPT Programme to Support
Translations of Russian Literature

All rights reserved.
Printed in the United States of America

CONTENTS

FOREWORD

The Church of Antioch has faced many challenges throughout its two thousand year history, but through such hardship firm and unshakeable faith in the Lord is produced. As much as this was the case in the past it is true today, when our Antiochian people in the Middle East are enduring countless trials that cause some to even call into question their continued existence in the land of their ancestors.

I am grateful to Dr Constantin Panchenko for his great labors in revealing to the world more fully the history of our people in the Middle East, drawing on sources both previously known and unknown to us, many of which have only survived in archives in Russia. He recounts to us the observations of many believers who visited our Antiochian lands in previous centuries, as well as those of delegations from our Antiochian Church to the Russian lands, Georgia, Wallachia, and other places stretching back to the late fourteenth century. His expertise in the field of archeology has also been brought to bear on the unfolding narrative.

The picture that all these present to us is sometimes stark in its bleakness. Nevertheless, we see that despite schism, natural disasters, and civil strife, our Church has survived and remains deeply rooted in its Middle Eastern homeland. In all these things, it has refused to succumb to the catacombs of darkness. We are reminded of the teaching of the holy apostle Paul that "we have this treasure in earthen vessels, that the excellence of the power may be of God and not of us" (2 Cor 4:7).

This monograph fills an important lacuna in the wider history of the Christian Church as it unfolds the presence and extent of indigenous Arabic-speaking believers in the Levant. In particular, it amplifies the nature of their relationship with other non-Arabic-speaking Orthodox, with other Christians, and also with

Muslim believers who have been present with us in the Middle East for fourteen hundred years. These are matters of great complexity and a fuller understanding of them will help to shape our understanding of the takfirism against which we now struggle.

I am particularly heartened that Dr Panchenko's book reveals the history and extent of the monastic life and its main centers in our Patriarchate. We read not only of Balamand and Saydnaya, St George Humayra, and Maaloula, but also of many other communities, some of which have been revived in our own times. It is in our monasteries that theology should be leavened with the leaven of humility and become incarnate as love and prayer.

Finally, I wish to express my thanks to the husband and wife team of Samuel and Brittany Noble for their work in translating Dr Panchenko's work into English and to Holy Trinity Monastery for preparing it for publication. This will serve to make it available to a wider international audience, both scholarly and churchly. May God richly reward them and all those who come to know more of our Antiochian Church through reading this work.

John X
Greek Orthodox Patriarch of
Antioch and All the East

INTRODUCTION

Over the past two decades, society's attention increasingly has returned to the forgotten world of the Christian East—the whole constellation of bright and now nearly endangered cultures of the Christian peoples of Southwest Asia and Northeast Africa.[1]

The foremost place among these communities is occupied by the Orthodox Arabs of the Syro-Palestinian region, descendants of the ancient Aramaic population of the Near East, who preserve their own particular culture and identity, despite having lived for almost a millennium and a half under the domination of the surrounding Muslims. The fate of Orthodoxy in Syria and Palestine—from the Arab conquest of the seventh century up to the present—still largely remains a blank spot in Russian historiography.[2] At the same time, Russian scholarship has in the past greatly contributed to the study of the Christian East and now, it seems, it should be especially interested in the history of Arab Orthodoxy, as Russia and the Orthodox communities of the Levant have their roots in the same Byzantine (or Eastern Christian) civilization, and over the centuries, the destinies of our nations have been closely intertwined—in both the seventeenth and the nineteenth centuries.

Scholars who turn to the Christian East are always attracted to its earliest stages, the first steps of Christian preaching in Syria and Iran, the ascetics and martyrs, the scribes and theologians at the time of the Late Roman Empire or the Ecumenical Councils, and the flowering of Middle Eastern Christianity in the age of the Arab Caliphate. Much less has been written about the Late Medieval and the Early Modern periods, which are perceived by many researchers as the time of deepest decline for the Christian peoples of the East. It is all the more interesting, then, to turn to such "dark ages," as they are fraught with unexpected discoveries. The years of a nation's decadence and decline are no less worthy of study than those of its flourishing. To understand properly the history of any civilization, one should be equally familiar with all the stages of its life. Moreover, the first centuries of Ottoman rule did not languish on the sidelines of history. On the contrary, they witnessed a distinct cultural—and to some extent demographic and political—rise that is worthy of close study.

The story of Arab Orthodoxy, of course, is not entirely or even primarily the chronicle of church life and theological tracts left by scholarly monks. The history of each Middle Eastern Church is 90 percent the history of the nation that it brings together. In circumstances in which the Orthodox societies of the Levant did not have their own statehood and aristocracy, the Church took upon herself the role of being the cultural, sociopolitical, and to some degree economic center of Arab Christian life. Thus, the history of the Orthodox Church in Greater Syria[3] goes far beyond the scope of purely religious events and incorporates elements of cultural history, geopolitics, historical ethnography, diplomacy, sociology, the dynamics of political-military conflict, and the vicissitudes of interethnic contact: in other words, the entire way of life of the Arab Christians.

In the present work, the author has sought to give a maximally complete picture of the various aspects of the life of Middle Eastern Orthodoxy in the Ottoman period, to outline its demographics and the ethnosocial structure and processes that took place in this environment, especially the nature of Greco-Arab relations in the Near East, to show the interactions of the Orthodox of Syria and Palestine with their coreligionists within and outside the Ottoman Empire and their coexistence with other Christian confessions and Ottoman rule. Special attention is given to the schism in Middle Eastern Orthodoxy in the eighteenth century and the separation of the Melkite Uniate Church from the Patriarchate of Antioch. In this work, the major outlines of the material and spiritual culture of the Orthodox East are taken into consideration.

It should be mentioned that by the terms *Orthodox East* and *Middle Eastern Orthodoxy*, we have in mind, in geographic terms, Egypt, Greater Syria, and Eastern Anatolia. That is, the territories of the patriarchates of Jerusalem, Antioch, and Alexandria. At the same time, the focus of this monograph is on the first two of these local churches. The Patriarchate of Alexandria is excluded from consideration because the local Orthodox Church was in full decline and barely numbered a few thousand parishioners, half of whom were recently arrived Greeks. In only a few cases shall we refer to the Monastery of St Catherine on Mount Sinai, whose history in the Ottoman period is perhaps more related to Modern Greek studies than Middle Eastern studies.

The four-century period of Ottoman domination over the Arab East (1516–1918) is clearly divisible into two parts. The first constitutes the sixteenth through the eighteenth centuries, the period of the rise of the Sublime Porte, the apogee of Ottoman power, and the beginning of its decline, when the empire still remained independent and was building relationships with its ethnic and religious minorities on the basis of their submission and interests. Although the Christian East felt a certain influence emanating from Western Europe, as a whole, it maintained its traditional way of life and developed under the influence of internal (or more precisely, intra-imperial) impulses. The second period, the nineteenth and the beginning of the twentieth centuries, is a time of pivotal reforms in all areas of the life of Ottoman Turkey, including in the sphere of interconfessional relations, which came to be largely determined by European diplomacy and so took on an altogether different nature. Western and Russian influence on the Middle East took on a more powerful character and contributed to a radical transformation of the characteristics of the communities of the region, spreading among them secular and nationalist views and the formation of new models of identity. For the Levant, the line between these two eras undoubtedly appears to be the year 1831, which was marked by the Egyptian invasion of Syria. The present work is devoted to the first of these periods, the era between 1516 and 1831.

The Ottoman era in the history of Middle Eastern Orthodoxy is reasonably well reflected in the sources. A number of chronicles were kept in the milieu of the Greek clergy of the Patriarchate of Jerusalem, as well as of the Arab scribes of the Church of Antioch. The historiographical tradition of the Palestinian Greeks, arising with the works of Patriarch Dositheus (r. 1669–1707), were continued in the eighteenth century with the writings of the Patriarchs Chrysanthos (r. 1707–1731) and Parthenius (r. 1737–1766), while at the beginning of the nineteenth century, they experienced a veritable flourishing associated with the name of Maximus Simais (d. after 1810), Procopius Nazianzen (1776–1822), Neophytus of Cyprus (d. after 1844), and others. The chronicles of the Orthodox Arabs were revived in the seventeenth century with the efforts of the Patriarch Macarius of Antioch (r. 1647–1672) and his son the Archdeacon Paul of Aleppo (1627–1669). In the following century, the tradition of chronicles was continued by the Damascene priest Mikhail Breik (d. after 1781) and a series of anonymous authors, whose works were included in a chronicle of the Beiruti compiler ʿAbdallah Trad (d. 1824).[4] Here, mention must also be made of the geographic literature of Arab Christians, featuring descriptions of travels and of foreign countries. The central place among works of this genre is indisputably occupied by the great work of

Paul of Aleppo, *The Journey of Macarius*, about the patriarch of Antioch's journey to Russia in the middle of the seventeenth century.

Alongside the Orthodox chronicles, the historical writings of the Arab Uniates are of considerable importance: the anonymous chronicle of 1782–1840 "The History of Events in Syria and Lebanon," the chronicles of the Aleppan Ni'ma ibn al-Khuri Tuma (mid-eighteenth century), and the Lebanese monk Hanania al-Munayyir (1756–after 1830).

A significant amount of various official documents of the eastern patriarchs have been preserved, especially all their correspondence with the heads of other local churches and foreign governments. Part of these materials has been published at different times. In addition to these, this work has utilized unpublished documents from the Russian State Archive of Ancient Acts (RGADA), the Archive of the Foreign Policy of the Russian Empire (AVPRI), and so on. The author also relied on Arab Christian manuscripts from the collection of the Institute of Eastern Manuscripts RAN and the Russian National Library (St Petersburg). Of particular interest in the context of the issues studied here are the colophons left by scribes in the Arabic manuscripts of the sixteenth through early twentieth centuries. These notes usually are given in the catalogs of the various manuscript collections, which also were used in this study.

In the sixteenth to eighteenth centuries, a number of pilgrims, travelers, and scholars visited the Middle East. The descriptions of their travels vary in terms of size and value and contain information on the ethnoreligious situation, topography, and economy of the region. Of the works of Russian authors, it is important to mention the texts of Vasily Poznyakov (active 1559–1560), Arseny Sukhanov (active 1561–1562), Ivan Lukyanov (active 1701), Vasily Grigorovich-Barsky (active in the 1720s), Melety (active 1794), and Porphyry Uspensky (active in the 1840s). Among the most informative texts of European travelers are those of the Polish aristocrat Mikołaj (Nicholas) Radziwiłł (active 1559–1560), the English merchant Henry Maundrell (active 1697), and the French scholar Constantin-François de Chassebœuf, who wrote under the name Volney (active 1783–1784).

CHAPTER I

The Historical Context: Orthodox Christians Under Muslim Rule from the Sixth to the Fifteenth Century

I do not cry for the king of this world ... but I cry and weep for the believing people, for how the Almighty, holding the whole world in his palm, despised His flock and He forsook his people for their sins.
—Antiochus Strategos, 631

THE ARAB CONQUEST: CHRISTIANS IN THE CALIPHATE

The seventh century, the time of the Arab conquests, was the most dramatic landmark in the history of the Christian East. Boundaries between civilizations that had remained immutable for seven centuries were swept away within nine years. The global crisis of Late Antique civilization—depopulation, deurbanization, the decline of the economy and culture, exacerbated by epidemics of the plague, and natural disasters in the sixth century—predestined the Byzantine Empire's inability to resist the Arab invasion. Justinian's ambitious reign had undermined the empire's last strength. The short-lived success of the Persian conquests at the beginning of the seventh century demonstrated Byzantium's political and military weakness. The Persian occupation struck a powerful blow to Greco-Roman culture and the Christian Church, leading to the breakdown of the administrative and economic structures of the Middle East. In the confrontation with Persia, the empire completely exhausted its military and economic resources. The spiritual unity of the state was undermined by schism in the Church, the confrontation between Orthodoxy and Monophysitism, and the two centuries of futile attempts to overcome it. The Aramaic and Coptic East, the stronghold of Monophysitism, was oppressed by the authority of the *basileus* in Constantinople. The Emperor Heraclius's attempt to reconcile the warring confessions on the basis of a compromise Monothelete dogma only worsened the situation, pushing part of the Orthodox away from the emperor. As a result, the Muslims who invaded Palestine did not meet any serious resistance from the army or the population.

Arab troops first crossed the Byzantine frontier in late 633; then, by 639, the Arabs already had conquered Syria and stood at the edge of the Anatolian Plateau; and in 642, the Byzantine army left Egypt. Byzantium lost half its territory and lands inhabited by millions of Christians; their holy places and the most famous monasteries and patriarchal sees all came under Islamic rule.[1]

Heretics who were persecuted in Byzantium clearly preferred the authority of the Muslim caliphs, for whom all Christian confessions were equal. The Orthodox of the Middle East ("Melkites"[2]) perceived the Muslim conquest far more negatively, but they were not exposed to special persecution by Arab authorities. It should be added that when the Monothelete heresy dominated in Constantinople, the Orthodox of Syria and Palestine were also in opposition to the Byzantine emperor. First of all, one can speak of Patriarch Sophronius of Jerusalem (d. 637), to whom later tradition attributes a key role in shaping Muslim–Christian relations in the Caliphate, including the apocryphal "Pact of 'Umar."[3]

From the beginning, the Muslim religion took a relatively tolerant attitude toward the "People of the Book" (Christians and Jews), as well as toward several other categories of non-Muslims. The Arabs gave their Christian subjects the status of *dhimmis*[4]—people under the protection of Islam. *Dhimmis* enjoyed freedom of religion and general internal autonomy in exchange for political loyalty and the payment of a poll tax, the *jizya* (in reality, the *jizya* was as a rule paid collectively on behalf of the residents of a village or quarter). Christian communities in the Caliphate were ruled by their own ecclesiastical hierarchies, which held many of the prerogatives of secular authorities, in particular the right to collect taxes, conduct trials of coreligionists, and decisions with regard to marriage and matters of property.[5]

In the seventh and eighth centuries, Christians still made up the majority of the population in the lands of the Caliphate from Egypt to Iraq. At the same time, Islamization was a major concern for Christian communities. Islam, the religion of the victorious conquerors, had high prestige. Most often, Christians converted to Islam under the influence of social and economic pressure. The lower classes sought to get rid of the burden of the poll tax and wealthy people wanted to raise their status and succeed in society. Mixed marriages,[6] the children of whom according to *sharia* became Muslims, were one of the most significant factors in eroding Christian communities, especially during the first Islamic century. Other factors, including forcible conversion to Islam, extermination, and ethnic cleansing were typical for the era of the Caliphate. Birth rates among Muslims and Christians appear to have been comparable. In any case, at the beginning of the era of the Crusades, Christians still accounted for about half the population in Syria and Egypt.[7]

Because of their level of education, some *dhimmis* managed to obtain a high social position in the Caliphate. Non-Muslims had a strong position in trade and finance, practically monopolized the practice of medicine, and almost completely filled the ranks of the lower and middle levels of the administrative apparatus. Christian, including Orthodox, doctors and administrators were of great importance at the caliph's court. Masterpieces of Arab architecture of the late seventh and early eighth centuries were created by Christian craftsmen according to Byzantine techniques. The Umayyad period is considered the last flowering of Hellenistic art in the Middle East.[8] The Russian Arabist N. A. Ivanov somewhat shockingly, but not without reason, described the Umayyad Caliphate as "an Eastern Christian society under the rule of Muslims."[9]

The Fading Inertia of Byzantine Culture in the 7th and 8th Centuries

The Arabs had no experience managing a developed urban society and gladly made use of the services of former Byzantine officials in their tax administration. Before the eighth century, bureaucratic documents in Syria and Egypt were written in Greek. Until the late seventh century, many areas of the Caliphate, such as Upper Mesopotamia, remained under the control of local Christian elites. The territory of Egypt was divided into smaller administrative districts managed by governors from among the Christian Copts. This system was convenient both for farmers and the lower bureaucracy, allowing them to understate the actual volumes of agricultural products and to withhold taxes on newly plowed land. During the first half-century of Arab rule, Egypt prospered and was completely loyal.[10]

Archeological research in Palestine and Jordan in recent decades gives a picture of almost universal Christian presence in the cities of the Middle East in the seventh and eighth centuries, with Byzantine traditions of urban development, crafts, daily life, and culture remaining intact. Ecclesiastical organization and other forms of self-government were preserved in Christian communities. Churches were built and renovated and were decorated with mosaics almost indistinguishable from their Byzantine counterparts. The Arab conquest itself hardly left a material trace, and archaeologists have not found any destruction or fires. Several churches in Transjordan were consecrated in the second half of the 630s, right in the middle of the Muslim invasion. The Christian communities demonstrated their creativity and capacity to develop.[11]

The best-preserved architectural monuments of Umayyad Christianity include Umm al-Jimal in northeastern Jordan where fourteen churches and two monasteries were active in the seventh century; two dozen churches and seven monasteries were close by. At the beginning of the seventh century, there were more than fifteen churches in Jerash (Gerasa), to which only one mosque was added in the Umayyad period. Many churches in northwest Jordan were rebuilt during the era of the Caliphate and continued to be used until the Mamluk era. In the village of Samra near Jerash, the mosaics of three churches date back to the beginning of the eighth century. Hundreds of Christian funerary *stelae* with inscriptions in Greek and Aramaic have also survived. In the village of Gadara in Wadi Yarmouk, a Greek inscription decorated with a cross was found from the year 662. It was about the restoration of public baths by the local Christian administrator, John, at the behest of the Caliph Mu'awiya. In Madaba, there are Greek inscriptions mentioning the bishops and construction activity up to 663. In Ramla, which was founded by Arab governors in 717 as the new capital of Palestine, the Christians built two churches.[12]

Archaeological data about the relative prosperity of Christians is supported by the testimonies of Western pilgrims who visited the Holy Land—the bishops Arculf (ca. 680), Willibald (720s), and to some extent Bernard (860s). They describe the ornate Church of the Holy Sepulchre in Jerusalem, the golden lamps over the Lord's Tomb, the golden cross crowning the Edicule,[13] and the churches and monasteries in the various holy places of Palestine, including Bethany, Mamre, the Ascension Mount, and the place of the Baptism in the Jordan, where later pilgrims no longer noticed any traces of a Christian presence.[14]

Along with this, in the seventh and early eighth centuries, aspects of the decline of Middle Eastern Christian society are already noticeable. Many churches, monasteries, and villages—including seats of dioceses—ceased to exist, either after the devastating earthquake at the beginning of the seventh century, or after the Persian or Arab invasion. In some cities, churches were abandoned or converted into mosques and commercial facilities. Thus, in Fahl (Pella), the capital of the Arab province of Palestine, the neglect of the churches contrasted with the prosperity of the rest of the city. The clearest features of degradation and extinction appeared along the borders of the desert. Under the Umayyads, population density plummeted in central Transjordan. Toward the end of the seventh century, villages in the Negev were abandoned, including Beersheba, Elusa, and Nessana, famous for its papyrus archives preserving Greek and Arabic documents, the last of which date to the 680s.[15]

The Early Umayyads: "Byzantium After Byzantium"

The situation of Middle Eastern Orthodoxy under Arab rule was determined by a complex combination of internal and external factors, including the relationships between the Melkites and Byzantium and between the Byzantium and the

Caliphate, as well as the struggle between various ethnoreligious groups in the Caliphate for influence in the Muslim administration.

In the first couple of decades after the Arab conquest of Byzantium's eastern provinces, the Melkites of Syria and Egypt underwent a profound crisis. Church structures were in a state of almost complete collapse, with all three patriarchal thrones vacant.

The last Melkite patriarch of Alexandria, Peter, escaped from Egypt with the departing Byzantine troops. After Peter's death in 654, a successor was not elected for him. With the arrival of the Arabs, the Monophysite Copts retaliated for their long-term persecution by the Byzantine emperors. The Coptic patriarch Benjamin, who had long been hiding in the desert to escape persecution, solemnly returned to Alexandria. The Monophysites seized Orthodox churches and monasteries and some Egyptian Christian sects, including part of the Melkites, joined the Coptic Church. After the death of the last Melkite bishops, the remnant of the Orthodox community in Egypt was led by priests ordained in Syria who formally adhered to Monotheletism.[16]

In Palestine, the patriarchal throne was vacant after the death of Sophronius in the spring of 637. A significant proportion of the bishops rejected Monothelete dogma and tried to rely on the support of Rome, the last stronghold of orthodoxy, and opposed Monothelete Constantinople. The Pope of Rome, appointed from among the Palestinian bishops *locum tenentes* for the patriarchal see, would rule the Palestinian church for the next three decades.[17]

Continuity in the Patriarchate of Antioch was interrupted from approximately 609 to 611 and was not restored during the war with Persia, after which came the Monothelete troubles. In 639/640, however, Macedonius, a Monothelete, was ordained Patriarch of Antioch in Constantinople, but he and his successors tried to direct the affairs of the Church of Antioch from Byzantium without taking the risk of appearing in Arab-controlled territory. That segment of the Melkites of Syria who shared Monothelete dogma obeyed the patriarch of Antioch residing in Constantinople. Those who remained faithful to Orthodoxy acknowledged the supremacy of the *locum tenens* of the patriarchal see in Jerusalem.[18]

With the coming to power of the Umayyad Caliphate in 661, the political center of the state moved to Damascus and the Arab rulers found themselves in a densely Christian environment. In Damascus, there formed an Orthodox center of influence, including a group of high-ranking Melkite officials who had a marked impact on the religious policy of the Caliphate. At the court of Muʿawiya (661–681), a tolerant ruler who respected Christian culture, several influential

Christians were known, the most notable of whom was the Orthodox Sarjoun (Sergius) ibn Mansur, the caliph's secretary for Syria and manager of his personal finances.[19] In the absence of Melkite patriarchs, leadership of the community was assumed by the Orthodox secular elite, led by Sarjoun. Around 668, Mu'awiya restored the throne of the Melkite patriarchs in Jerusalem;[20] however, even after that, Sarjoun's influence at the caliph's court—and thus also in the Melkite community—remained unquestioned.

Hagiographic tradition says that Sarjoun ibn Mansur was the father of the greatest Christian theologian and writer, John of Damascus (676–748), who bore the family name Mansur.[21] Sarjoun himself is also sometimes considered in the literature to be son of the semilegendary governor of Damascus Mansur, who handed the city over to the Arab commander Khalid ibn al-Walid in 636.[22] Although sources do not offer clear evidence of kinship between Mansur and Sarjoun, it is sufficiently obvious that within the Orthodox community (as well as in other Christian ethnoreligious groups in the Caliphate) a hereditary quasi-aristocracy had formed that occupied prominent positions in the civil administration and church hierarchy.

During the period of Monothelete dominance in the Byzantine Empire, the Orthodox of the Caliphate perceived the Byzantine emperors as heretics and the Arabs did not consider their Melkite subjects to be a Byzantine "fifth column." The Russian scholar Vasily Bartold already drew attention to the fact that, despite Mu'awiya's frequent wars with Byzantium, the Middle Eastern Orthodox were not subject to any harassment.[23] However, the balance of power dramatically changed in 681 after the Sixth Ecumenical Council in Constantinople, when Monotheletism was anathematized and religious unity between Byzantium and the Orthodox of Syria and Egypt was restored. The defeated Monothelete creed suddenly took on new life in the land of the Caliphate. A significant proportion of the Middle Eastern Aramaean Melkites continued to adhere to this belief. It became for them a means to preserve their ethnic and cultural identity and to avoid being absorbed into Greek Orthodoxy and Syrian Monophysitism. The Syro-Lebanese Monothelete community developed into the Maronite subethnicity, receiving its name, according to one version, from the name of its first spiritual center, the Monastery of St Maroun on the Orontes or, in another version, from Yuhanna Maroun, the legendary founder of the Maronite church organization at the turn of the seventh to the eighth century. During this period, there were repeated clashes between the Orthodox and the Maronites in various areas of Syria and Lebanon. Polemic with Maronite doctrine became one of the areas of Melkite theology in the eighth and ninth centuries. Thanks to the Byzantine–Arab peace treaty of 685, the Orthodox were able to win the authorities of the Caliphate over to their side and to use them in the fight against Monotheletism. Relying on Arab military force, Sarjoun ibn Mansur brought about the submission of the Syrian heretics.[24] In 745, Patriarch of Antioch Theophylact bar Qanbar, who enjoyed the support of the Caliph Marwan, once more attempted military action. According to some authors, in 745, after a wave of Melkite–Maronite conflicts at the Monastery of St Maroun, Aleppo, and Manbij, the Maronites created an autonomous church headed by a patriarch. It was only later that the mythologized historiography of that community granted the laurels of "founding father" to Yuhanna Maroun.[25]

Christians of various denominations actively fought for access to administrative positions to influence the caliphs. For example, there is a well-known debate between Maronites and Jacobites in 660 in the presence of Mu'awiya, who acted as arbitrator.[26] During the reign of the Caliph 'Abd al-Malik (685–705), a Monophysite group led by Athanasius bar Gumoye from Edessa played a prominent role in the state. The caliph made Athanasius tutor and secretary to his younger brother 'Abd al-'Aziz, the governor of Egypt. For two decades, Athanasius governed the richest province on his behalf, collecting taxes and amassing an enormous fortune. For obvious reasons, Sarjoun ibn Mansur could not get along with a rival of such stature. After the death of 'Abd al-'Aziz around 704, when Athanasius returned to his homeland with a huge caravan of property, Sarjoun remarked to the caliph, "bar Gumoye has ransacked all the cellars of Egypt."[27] 'Abd al-Malik contented himself with confiscating half of Athanasius' wealth.

Athanasius' example demonstrates the extent of the prosperity of the region's Christian elite at the courts of the emirs in the Caliphate's provinces. In Egypt, alongside influential Monophysites, Orthodox courtiers of 'Abd al-'Aziz are known to have received from him the right to build a church in Hulwan for their coreligionists.[28] Although the patriarchal throne of Alexandria continued to be vacant, towards the end of the seventh century an Orthodox ecclesiastical organization with its bishops was somehow reconstituted in Egypt. Egyptian Melkites participated in church life in Byzantium: at the Sixth Council the Patriarchate of Alexandria was represented by the priest Peter, who signed the conciliar acts with the title "Vicar of the Apostolic See". He also attended the Council in Trullo of 691 as a bishop.[29]

The Late Umayyads: Pressure Mounts

At the turn of the seventh to the eighth century, the internal structure of the Caliphate underwent important changes and the position of Christians at the caliphal court was shaken. ʿAbd al-Malik emerged the winner of a long civil war and started large-scale reforms to strengthen the Arab–Muslim state. First, he began by minting coins with Islamic symbols. A new census of the territory was carried out, in which previously Byzantine and Persian inventories had been used in the administration. Individual taxation was introduced, which was painfully felt by the *dhimmis*. It was in the course of these reforms that the language of state records transitioned to Arabic (700–705), something that later Muslim authors portrayed as an attempt to put an end to the monopoly of Christian scribes, led by Sarjoun, in the administrative structures.[30] This change, however, did not much alter the status of *dhimmi* officials, who for the most part had mastered Arabic.

Much more painful for the Melkites was the Caliph al-Walid I's (705–715) seizure of the Cathedral of St John the Baptist in Damascus in 707. The Umayyad Mosque was built on its site, designed to eclipse the beauty of the Christian churches in its splendor.[31] In their own times, Muʿawiya and ʿAbd al-Malik had also attempted to obtain the cathedral, but the Christian elites managed to fend them off by referring to the guarantee of the security of *dhimmis*' property given by Khalid al-Walid when he captured Damascus. The new caliph, however, paid no attention to Khalid's decree. Similarly, during the construction of a mosque in Ramla, Muslims seized columns that had been prepared by the Christians of neighboring Lydda for one of its churches.[32]

During the reign of the Caliph ʿUmar II (717–720) came the first targeted religious persecutions against Christians. The cause was the growing discontent among Muslims caused by the *dhimmis*' wealth, prosperity, and influence. Umar introduced restrictions for Christians in dress, forbade the building of new churches, and encouraged *dhimmis* to convert to Islam. Muslim tradition attributes him with expelling Christian officials from service. Such "purges" of infidels from the administrative apparatus were carried out during each persecution. It did not, however, achieve tangible results because for a long time not enough educated Muslims in the Caliphate were able to replace Christians in public service.[33] In 724, under the Caliph Yazid, a campaign against images of living things in churches swept through the Middle East.[34]

In this period, the Orthodox community was already led by Sarjoun's successors, including John of Damascus, who inherited from his father the post of caliphal secretary. He was certainly a witness to these persecutions and, moreover, at the end of the 720s John himself fell into disfavor and went to a monastery.[35]

Soon, however, Arab–Melkite relations entered into a new, more favorable phase. When the doctrine of iconoclasm prevailed in Byzantium in 726, it provoked a sharp rejection from Middle Eastern Orthodox. It was here, in the late

720s and early 730s, that John of Damascus formulated the first profound justi-
fication for the veneration of icons and Middle Eastern bishops anathematized
the emperor Leo the Isaurian.[36] Byzantine monks, fleeing iconoclast persecution,
came to Palestine. On the day of Pentecost 764, the three Eastern patriarchs, by
prior agreement each in their own city anathematized Bishop Cosmas of Epiphania, who had joined the iconoclasts.[37] The acts of the Seventh Ecumenical Council
preserved the epistle of Patriarch Theodore of Jerusalem (d. after 767) to the patriarchs of Alexandria and Antioch, justifying the veneration of relics and icons.

The Seventh Ecumenical Council in 787, which restored the veneration of
icons, was attended by representatives of the three Eastern patriarchs, the syncellus John, and the abbot Thomas, who actively supported the council's decisions.[38]

From the beginning of the iconoclast turmoil, the Umayyad Caliph Hisham
(724–742) no longer had any reason to see his Melkite subjects as supporters of
Byzantium. This seems to be behind the restoration of the Orthodox patriarchal
sees of Alexandria (731) and Antioch (742).[39]

Thus, by the middle of the eighth century, Orthodox ecclesiastical structures
in the regions of Egypt and Syria were completely restored and mechanisms
developed for the self-government of the Orthodox community, which upheld its
interests before the Muslim authorities. The laity did not play as much of a role in
the management of the community as it had during the era of Sarjoun and John of
Damascus. In the Orthodox community during the eighth to tenth centuries, however, one can clearly observe a merger of the secular elite with the theocratic church
hierarchy and the "migration" of influential laymen to bishops' posts. Sarjoun's
adopted son Cosmas became bishop of Mayouma. In the ninth century, two descendants of Mansur held the See of Jerusalem: Sergius (844–860) and Elias (880–909).
Influential physicians repeatedly became patriarchs of Alexandria, such as Poli-
tianus (767–801) and the famous historian Eutychius (Saʿid ibn Batriq, 934–940).
Members of the class of *kuttab* (scribes) ascended to the throne of Antioch, such as
Elias I (905–932/4), Theodosius II (935–942), and Christopher (960–967).[40]

Arab authorities repeatedly interfered in the election of patriarchs, seeking
the election of their protégés and sometimes even Christian officials in the administration of the caliphate who had not previously held any spiritual dignity. The
Muslims were primarily concerned with ensuring the loyalty of the Melkite bishops. For this reason, the Syrian monk Stephen was made the first Patriarch of
Antioch in 742, although he did not know Greek and was in no way connected
with Byzantium.[41]

The political sympathies of the Melkite bishops, balancing between the
two empires, could differ quite a lot. On the one hand, around 757, Patriarch

Theodore of Antioch (751–773) was exiled to Transjordan for alleged contacts with Byzantium.[42] On the other hand, some bishops cooperated with the Muslim authorities so long as it did not affect their religious beliefs. Patriarch Job of Antioch (811/2–842) went the furthest of all down that path. Around 821, by order of the caliph, he crowned the Byzantine rebel Thomas the Slav with the imperial diadem (for which he was excommunicated by the Synod of Constantinople), and in 838, he accompanied the Arab army in the campaign against Amorium and persuaded its besieged garrison to surrender.[43]

At the same time, for the majority of Melkites, even those absolutely loyal to the Muslims, there was a longstanding characteristic attitude toward Arab rule as something that God allowed to take place for the time being, a feeling of belonging to the Byzantine world, and the perception that the Emperor of Constantinople was their true lord and protector.

The Culture of the Melkites

In the seventh and eighth centuries, the cultural creativity of the Syro-Palestinian Christians continued. The eastern half of the Byzantine Empire that had been captured by the Arabs was still part of a common cultural space with the rest of Byzantium. The contribution of the Middle Eastern Melkites to general Byzantine culture was comparable to what was created within the empire itself.

Mosaics of Palestinian and Transjordanian churches of the eighth century represent rare examples of Byzantine fine art contemporary to the iconoclastic era, which did not leave similar monuments in Byzantium.

The Sinaite monks John Climacus (d. ca. 650) and Anastasius of Sinai (d. ca. 700) had a tremendous impact on Eastern Christian theology. Andrew of Crete (660–740), the great composer of Byzantine church poetry, spent the first half of his life in the Middle East and was a monk of Mar Saba (the Lavra of St Sabbas the Sanctified) and secretary to the *locum tenens* of the See of Jerusalem. There, at Mar Saba and in Jerusalem, John of Damascus, the greatest Christian thinker of the eighth century and the last of the fathers of the church, spent the most productive years in his life. The Damascene's foster brother, Cosmas of Mayouma, also a monk of Mar Saba and then bishop of Mayouma (near Gaza), left an enormous poetic heritage. Living at the turn of the eighth to the ninth century, the Sabbaite monks Stephen the Younger and Leontius composed a number of hagiographical works about the Palestinian martyrs and ascetics of their time.

The chronicles of Syrian Melkites had a direct influence on the development of Byzantine historiography. The anonymous Melkite chronicle of 780 was extensively used by Theophanes the Confessor in his *Chronography*.[44] In contrast to the self-contained, sealed-off classical culture of Byzantium, the Melkites, who lived at the crossroads of civilizations, were more open to cultural contacts. This resulted both in their polemics with people of other faiths and their translating into Greek works of Syriac literature.

Although most of the Orthodox of the Holy Land were not Greeks, but rather Hellenized Aramaeans, as well as Arabs in Transjordan and the Negev, the language of Christian literature was predominantly Greek. The liturgy was conducted in Greek with Syriac translation, when necessary. Within the Patriarchate of Antioch, liturgical services were conducted in Syriac and Orthodox literature existed in Syriac. It included not only liturgical texts and translations from Greek but also original works. Mention can be made of the anti-Monophysite treatises of George, bishop of Martyropolis, and his disciples Constantine and Leo, who successively held the episcopal see of Harran at the end of the seventh and beginning of the eighth centuries or the anonymous Aramaic *Life of the Sixty New Martyrs of Jerusalem* composed in the middle of the eighth century.[45]

The theme of suffering for the faith held a special place in the literature and consciousness of the Caliphate's Christians. Images of the martyrs were important symbols of identity. The history of the Churches of Antioch and Jerusalem in the eighth and early ninth centuries was adorned by the deeds of several such martyrs. Acquaintance with their biographies paradoxically confirms the relative tolerance of Muslim authorities and their compliance with the rules of *shari'a* regarding *dhimmis*. Many of the Christians executed by the Arabs were Byzantine prisoners of war who did not belong to the category of *dhimmis*, such as the Sixty New Martyrs of Jerusalem in 724, the Forty Martyrs of Amorium in 845, or the Byzantine monk Romanos the New (d. 778), who moreover was charged with espionage.[46] Some of the zealots wanting to be found worthy of a martyr's crown themselves publicly denounced the Islamic faith and the "false prophet" Muhammad, which, of course, was severely punished according to Muslim law (Peter, metropolitan of Damascus, who, however, was not executed but rather exiled in 743, and Peter of Capitolias, murdered in 744).[47] Islam punished apostasy just as radically: executed for this were Christopher, a monk of Mar Saba and a convert from Islam in 799 or 805, and St Anthony/Rawh, a Muslim noble who converted to Christianity and tried to win over others. Under 'Abd al-Malik, Michael, a monk of Mar Saba, was executed on false charges of apostasy. On account of the same slanderous accusation, Elias the New from Baalbek was martyred either in 779 or, according to a different estimate, in 795.[48]

Among the martyrs of the early Arab period is the interesting figure 'Abd al-Masih al-Najrani al-Ghassani (d. in the 860s or, according to another account, the 750s). A Christian who converted to Islam and took part in the raids on Byzantium, he repented of his past, returning to Christianity and becoming a monk on Sinai. Desiring to die for Christ like other voluntary martyrs, ʿAbd al-Masih went to Ramla to denounce Islam before the Arab governor. At the last moment, however, the monk did not have sufficient strength of will and he left the city. Human weakness, no stranger to ʿAbd al-Masih and something that the author of his *Life* does not attempt to hide, distinguishes this figure from the stereotyped hagiographic heroes abundantly represented in Byzantine literature. In the end, the monk nevertheless acquired a martyr's crown when one of the Muslims recognized him and accused him of apostasy.[49]

These examples show the high intensity of religious feeling among Middle Eastern Melkites in the seventh and eighth centuries. The same can be said for the monastic movement, not much inferior to that of the Early Byzantine era. Stories about the Sinaite fathers—contemporaries of John Climacus—suggest that the early Byzantine monastic tradition was maintained unchanged.[50] On the basis of the written sources, the total number of Palestinian monasteries was quite large, but a precise count cannot be given. Alongside the monasteries in cities and densely populated rural areas, the remote monasteries of the Judean Desert and the Jordan Valley attracted the attention of pilgrims and hagiographers. Central among these was Mar Saba, about 15 kilometers to the east of Jerusalem. Along with Mar Saba should be mentioned the lavras of St Euthymius the Great, St Theodosius the Great, St Chariton (Mar Kharitun), and others along the same mountain range between Jerusalem and the Dead Sea. Among the monasteries along the Jordan, the best known were the Monastery of St John the Baptist, where at the beginning of the eighth century there were as many as twenty monks,[51] the Monastery of St Gerasimus, and the Monastery of St George of Koziba in the Wadi Qelt. Among the monks of the Judean Desert mentioned in the sources are natives of Palestine, Transjordan, Egypt, and southern Syria. Syriac-speaking monks had a separate community with its own presbyter in Mar Saba. The main source for the history of Palestinian monasticism in the eighth century is the *Life* of the famous ascetic, Stephen the Wonderworker the Elder (725–794), written by his disciple Leontius at the beginning of the ninth century.

In his youth, Stephen spent five years in a narrow cave, almost never leaving it. Several times for the entirety of Lent the hermit went into the desert near the Dead Sea, where he fed only on the tips of reeds. During the last thirty years of his life, he received the gifts of conversing with God, healing the sick, and predicting the future. There were monks who claimed to have seen Stephen walking on the water of the Jordan and the Dead Sea with his hands lifted up to heaven, glowing radiantly. An interesting event in Stephen's *Life* is a conversation he had with a Christian from Transjordan, whom the ascetic encouraged to become a monk and go out into the desert. "Now it is possible for people to please God in the world as well as in the desert," Stephen's companion replied to him.

> It seems preferable to me to suffer evil with God's people who are in great distress and affliction … than to pay attention to oneself in silence and not help anyone … Now life in the world is more difficult and sorrowful … for we see that monks enjoy great tranquility and rest, while those in the world are in great distress and misfortune.[52]

Perhaps the person saying this was unwittingly exaggerating, but nevertheless the perception among laypeople in the Caliphate of the monastic life as quiet and comfortable is quite remarkable.

At the same time, relations within the monastic community were not always sunny. There are mentions of conflicts in Mar Saba. According to the hagiographer of St Stephen the Wonderworker, "Some novices, deceived by demons, rebelled at the end of the service and beat some of the elders with sticks and maliciously laid hands on the venerable … abbot himself."[53]

There is significantly less information about Syriac monasticism. Its main center, as during the Byzantine period, remained the Monastery of St Symeon the Stylite (Mar Sam'an) in the desert 70 kilometers northwest of Aleppo.

The 'Abbasid Revolution

The most important internal milestone in the history of the Caliphate was the coming to power of the 'Abbasid dynasty in 750 after a bitter civil war. Egypt briefly became the last refuge of the defeated Umayyads. Taking advantage of the collapse of power structures, the local Christians started a revolt.

The insurrection was primarily caused by economic oppression by the Arab governors. After 'Abd al-Malik's reforms, officials became more exacting with regard to tax collection. Peasants were prevented from migrating or attempting to take shelter from taxation in monasteries. Christian grassroots administration was replaced by Muslim governors. The authorities imposed civil servants who were responsible for collecting taxes. The fiscal apparatus became more efficient, and so oppression of Coptic peasants increased. In response, starting in 725, the Christians repeatedly rebelled.[54] These uprisings were not religious in nature and the Church, concerned about preserving its privileges and property, did not try to lead the popular unrest. Nevertheless, in 750 both patriarchs—Coptic and Orthodox—joined the revolt. In one of the battles, the patriarchs were captured, but the Orthodox primate Cosmas managed to get ransomed. Finally, ʿAbbasid troops invaded Egypt and defeated the Umayyads.[55]

Under the new dynasty, the political center of the state moved from Damascus to Mesopotamia. The displacement of trade routes and centers of economic activity painfully affected the well-being of Middle Eastern Christians. Unlike under the Umayyads, Melkites did not play a serious role at the ʿAbbasid court. Among the Christian denominations in Baghdad, the Nestorians were dominant. In 912, they foiled an attempt by the Melkites to gain a foothold in the ʿAbbasid capital, achieving the expulsion of the Orthodox metropolitan of Baghdad. Among the heads of all the Christian churches, only the Nestorian catholicos was allowed to have a residence in the Caliphate's capital.[56]

With the coming to power of the ʿAbbasids, the moral climate in the government changed and many Muslim caliphs attempted to demonstrate their piety, which adversely affected the position of peoples of other faiths. Contrary to remarks by Bartold about the caliphs' tendency to patronize the Melkites during their conflicts with heretical Byzantine emperors, the greatest of the ʿAbbasid caliphs, al-Mansour (755–775), severely persecuted Orthodox Christians in his domains at the same time as the iconoclast persecution under the Emperor Constantine V Copronymus (743–775) in Byzantium. The death of the two monarchs, which occurred in the same year, was welcomed in the Melkite Chronicle: "These two terrible beasts, who for so long had plagued the human race with equal ferocity, died by God's merciful providence."[57]

Generally speaking, under the early ʿAbbasids, persecution broke out only sporadically. The caliph al-Mahdi (775–783) demanded that the last Bedouin Christians from the tribe of Tanukh in northern Syria convert to Islam. Their leader refused and was executed. The Tanukhid women, however, retained their religion, and churches were active in the tribe's territory for some time. Several Christians were martyred in Emesa (Homs) in 780. In 807, many churches in Syria were destroyed at the order of Harun al-Rashid.[58] In general, the position of Middle Eastern Christians did not depend so much on the policies of the caliphs as on the mood of the governors, some of whom subjected Christians to extortion and destroyed their churches, whereas others allowed them to renovate their places of worship and to erect new ones.[59]

The First Crisis of the Christian East

Starting in the middle of the eighth century, there was an increasing number of crises in the life of Middle Eastern Melkites. The catastrophic earthquake in January 749 led to the destruction of many cities and monasteries that were never restored. Inhabitants abandoned Gerasa, Gadara, Umm al-Jimal, and other cities. A number of villages were simply abandoned but not destroyed.

At the same time, hundreds of towns and villages on the rocky hills between Apamea and Aleppo, in the region archaeologists call "the country of the dead cities," were abandoned. These cities had once thrived on account of the export of olive oil through Antioch to all corners of the Pax Romana. The rupture of old ties and the decline of Antioch forced farmers to abandon the highly specialized economy of olive cultivation and to return to subsistence farming. Wheat could not grow in the arid hills and residents left their homes to go down into the valleys.[60]

From the beginning of the ʿAbbasid era, church construction declined, the quality of mosaics decreased, and the language of inscriptions deteriorated; thus, local Christians lost their knowledge of Greek.[61] The traces of iconoclastic damage, discovered in many Jordanian churches, also have been associated by historians with this period of time. No doubt, the Christians destroyed images of living creatures, sometimes carefully replacing them with new mosaics. In the most famous of these mosaics, the image of a bull was removed and replaced with an inanimate date palm. In this case, because of the negligence of the workmen, hooves and a tail hang from the bottom of the palm trunk. The motivations for these acts are rather vague, but it seems that those who vandalized the mosaics were not inspired by the theories of the Byzantine iconoclasts, but rather by Islamic (or a broader Semitic?) rejection of images of living beings. Clearly, there was either pressure on Christians from the Muslim environment or major shifts in the attitudes of these Christians during in the ʿAbbasid era.[62]

By the turn of the eighth to the ninth century original literary activity by Christians almost ceased, writers and saints disappeared, and Greek fell into disuse. Both literary and material sources themselves, by which we can judge the subsequent life of Middle Eastern Christians, disappeared or radically changed. Joseph Nasrallah called the three hundred years from the ninth to the eleventh centuries the "great lacuna" in the history of Palestinian monasticism.[63] These words can be applied to almost the entirety of the Orthodox Middle East during the High Middle Ages.

It can be argued with reasonable certainty that the crisis in Middle Eastern Christian society did not occur immediately following the earthquake of 749, although the latter did deal a severe blow to the ecclesiastical and secular structures of the Melkite community. There are several examples of construction activity by Christians of Transjordan in the second half of the eighth century. Archaeologists have discovered inscriptions marking the renovation of churches in Umm al-Rasas in 756 and Madaba in 767.[64] By the end of the eighth century, however, such activities came to naught.

The decline of the Christian community was compounded by the general political instability of the Caliphate and the inability of authorities to maintain order and stability. The most striking evidence of this kind is the narrative of Stephen the Sabaite concerning the martyrdom of Sinaite monks killed by the Saracens in 796. It gives a vivid picture of the bloody chaos in Palestine at the end of the eighth century when the Bedouin tribes of Mudar and Yemen fought each other. Many villages were looted and burned, whereas the villagers discarded everything and fled to the cities, which, however, were not much of a safe haven. Hordes of bandits ravaged Gaza, Ashkelon, and Eleutheropolis. In March 797, a band of rebellious Bedouin captured Mar Saba and, to extort the monastery's treasures from the monks, tortured to death twenty of its inhabitants.

The crisis of Palestinian monasticism was perhaps largely associated with the rampaging nomadic element in the Judean hills and multiple devastations of the monasteries at the turn of the eighth to the ninth century. Although the monks said with fervor that they should not "fear those who kill the body, but are unable to kill the soul,"[65] the common human instinct for self-preservation was not alien to them. Even contemporaries, who believed that Stephen the Wonderworker was the last of the great ascetics, felt the nascent decline of the monastic movement. "At the present time," wrote Leontius, Stephen's biographer, "monastic struggle has weakened in the ten years since the earthquake [of 749?] and it will grow weaker and weaker because laziness and carelessness will increase."[66]

Sinaite monasticism entered a period of decline at the same time as Palestinian monasticism. In the Early Arab period, almost all the cells and monasteries on Mount Horeb, towering over the Sinai Monastery of the Burning Bush (St Catherine's), were abandoned. Medieval ceramics have been found at only three of fifteen sites from the Byzantine period. The monasteries in the Umm Shomer mountains to the south of Mount Sinai likewise went derelict. Traces of a later presence are found only in four of the eleven Byzantine monasteries. The very quality of the construction of churches and cells deteriorated sharply—the rectangular Byzantine buildings of hewn stone were replaced by rougher structures with rounded corners built of unhewn stones.[67]

Disasters occurred repeatedly for Palestinian Christians in 809 and 813, during the civil war that engulfed the Caliphate after the death of Harun al-Rashid. According to the Byzantine chronicler Theophanes, the Hagarenes "killed, plundered and rampaged in every possible way and indiscriminately against each other and against the Christians," devastating the churches of the Holy City and the desert monasteries. The chronicler tells us of the arrival in Cyprus in 813 of many Christian refugees

> because in Syria, Egypt and Africa there arose total anarchy, murders, robberies, and fornications in the villages and towns. In the Holy City they desecrated the most revered sites of the holy Resurrection. In the desert the famous Lavras of St Chariton and St Sabbas [Mar Saba] and other monasteries and churches were likewise devastated.[68]

It was perhaps during these migrations that the last bearers of the Greek language and Byzantine literary culture left the Middle East.

During almost the same decade, the Coptic community experienced a similar political collapse. Starting in the eighth century, the population growth that was observed in Egypt during the first decades after the Arab conquest stopped. As mentioned, there were repeated uprisings of Coptic peasants against the tax burden, in which Muslims also sometimes took part. The most powerful uprising occurred in the years 829–831 in the Lower Delta. As before, church leaders did not try to lead the revolt and give it the character of a national-religious struggle. Rather, the church preached humility. In 831, the patriarch tried to persuade the rebels to lay down their weapons and avoid a massacre. His peacemaking was not successful. The caliph personally led a punitive expedition, the rebellion was crushed, captured rebels were executed, and their families were sold into slavery. The deserted villages were settled by Muslims and many churches were turned into mosques. After this, the Copts no longer attempted to rebel.[69] According to several scholars, the suppression of the last Coptic peasant uprising "broke the back of mass adherence of Copts to Christianity."[70]

Attempts to explain the decline of Christianity in the Middle East by the fact of the Arab conquest have now been dismissed by scholarship in view of the clear evidence of the dynamic development of Christian communities in the seventh and eighth centuries. Epidemics, earthquakes, and the transfer of the Caliphate's capital to Baghdad, as well as an environmental crisis in the Middle East with desert encroachment and the expansion of nomadic tribes, undoubtedly played a negative role in the fate of Eastern Christians. However, according to scholars, all this is secondary. Something broke within the Christian community, but we are unable to grasp what this something was.[71] There appeared some deep and global laws of historical development, a process of losing vital energy that led to the death of the Classical civilization itself in whose bosom Christianity arose.

The economic system, the culture, and the social relations characteristic of the Late Antique society disintegrated.

This process has been blurred over time, but if one is to choose an approximate date, it would be the civil war between al-Amin and al-Ma'mun in the years 811–813. It seems to have been perceived by contemporaries as a global catastrophe. The political upheavals caused a surge in apocalyptic feelings among Syriac Christians and the circulation of corresponding literature.[72] All this is not without profound symbolism: for them, the end of the world really did come. It was the end of a Middle Eastern society of the "Byzantine character," as we might call it.

The Dark Ages

The Birth of New Ethnic Groups (Ninth to Eleventh Centuries)

Then, out of the darkness of the ninth century emerged a new society of Syro-Palestinian Christians, characterized by increasing Arabization and the loss of contact with Byzantine culture. The language barrier heightened the cultural isolation of the Middle Eastern Melkites from Byzantium. Greek authors of the mid-ninth to eleventh centuries write almost nothing about the Holy Land. Melkite Palestinian sources are few and particular. This vexing lack of sources indicates more eloquently than any texts the drastic drop in the educational level of the general population and the decay of old mechanisms of cultural reproduction. Likewise, almost no archeological sites survive from this era. All this determined the extremely limited availability of information about the Melkite community in the 'Abbasid era.

There is reason to believe that in Middle Eastern Orthodox society the "Byzantine character" lingered in the Holy Land in the seventh and eighth centuries, before disappearing and being replaced by a qualitatively different organism, a different identity. Not only the language changed but also social customs, the economy, and the type of settlement. The Christians' very habitat shrank as they left many parts of Transjordan, Hawran, Upper Mesopotamia, and Southern Palestine. The Melkites of the ninth and tenth centuries, unlike their ancestors, saw themselves as not so much a part of the Byzantine world as of the Arab world.

It is axiomatic that such processes should require a change in attitude and cultural outlook. During this era, Melkite scribes undertook a massive translation of Christian texts into Arabic, trying to create a civilized basis for young people and to restore cultural continuity. The bishop of Harran Theodore Abu Qurra (750–825/830) deserves the title "father of the nation" for Orthodox Arabs.

He was the first to write theological and apologetic treatises in Arabic, formulating a new identity for his community.

It appears that simultaneous to Arabization, the Melkites must have undergone a process of archaization of their social life, the revival of tribal relations in a Christian context. In the context of the Caliphate's growing weakness and the pressure from the nomadic periphery on the fellahin in the countryside, they had to find some means of collective survival. Even in cities where security was greater and the authorities were more capable, the population crept into religiously homogenous quarters. Each represented an ethnocultural reservation, walled with gates. Within them there were markets, baths, institutions of self-governance, and quasi-illicit structures of self-defense. In Baghdad, a system of homogenous quarters formed during a period of political unrest in the tenth century, while in Jerusalem, sources note this as happening during the second half of the eleventh century.[73] In Damascus, a similar transformation occurred between the 'Abbasid revolution and the Burid era (twelfth century).[74] It is not possible to give a more precise date because of the glaring lack of sources.

This is to say, once more, that almost everything changed for the Melkites apart from their religion. Their social degradation was not a unique phenomenon and similar processes took place during those centuries in other lands of the Christian East as well as within the Byzantine Empire itself. The Byzantium of Justinian and the Byzantium of the Macedonian dynasty are two completely different countries bound only by the cultural continuity of the state. Byzantium of the ninth and tenth centuries looks much more primitive than the Eastern Roman Empire of the fourth to sixth centuries, although with no less vitality. A similar deep social degeneration took place in early medieval Armenia. There, during its "Dark Ages" of the seventh to ninth centuries, even the construction of new churches was halted.

The geographically closest example to the Melkites is that of the Copts. We have mentioned the demographic stagnation in Egypt and the permanent "flight from the villages." During the ninth century, between half and two-thirds of agricultural land in the Nile Valley went uncultivated. On the border between the desert and arable land, Bedouin tribes appeared. Although they were few in numbers, as in Palestine, they represented a significant threat to the agricultural population. It was quite symptomatic that it was exactly from the ninth century that Coptic monks in the desert monasteries began to build fortified towers in their monasteries where they could hide supplies and themselves during attacks by nomads.[75]

After a century of instability and rebellions, the church organization, despite its outward conformism and loyalty to the Caliphate, was seriously damaged. According to archaeologists, from the early eighth century to the early ninth century, many small churches in the countryside dedicated to local Coptic saints disappeared or perhaps were destroyed. They were replaced by larger but numerically fewer churches associated with the basic figures of Christian worship, especially St George. The destruction of churches and the decline in the number of priests shows the decay of the old rural communities. The Coptic population was deprived of its roots and lost touch with its "soil," which had been its main source of strength under the Byzantines. The way was cleared for the sacred landscape to be filled anew in the late Middle Ages with the tombs of local Muslim saints.[76]

In Egypt, there was a significant Muslim population in the cities starting in the ninth century. The pace of demographic change was increasing. Muslims went from being a minority to being a majority in Iran in 800 and in the majority in Syria and Egypt in 900.[77]

Arabization

The Arabic language spread among the Christians of the Middle East, displacing Greek and Syriac and necessitating the translation of Holy Scripture, liturgical texts, and the whole literary heritage of Christian civilization into Arabic. This process first began in Palestine, where traditionally worship in Greek and Syriac had coexisted and the translation of the services into a new language did not pose any problem psychologically.

The work of translating Christian literature into Arabic took place primarily in the monasteries of Southern Palestine: Mar Saba and the Lavra of St Chariton, as well as the Sinai Monastery of the Burning Bush. Translations of the Holy Scriptures, as well as of patristic and ascetic literature, were made both from Greek and Syriac. It is believed that the earliest translations date back to the 740s, and by the turn of the ninth century, Arabic Christian literature was already an established phenomenon.[78]

Over the next two and a half centuries, the number of Christian texts in Arabic increased rapidly. About sixty manuscripts have been preserved from the ninth to tenth centuries written in the so-called Old South Palestinian dialect. Ninety percent of them are translations of the books needed for everyday church life: texts of the Holy Scriptures, homilies, hagiography, and patristic literature.[79] Along with this, there are original works that are partly hagiographical in character, partly apologetic, and polemical (five or six items). Their authors sought to prove the orthodoxy of their community in the face of the historical challenge posed by Islam and rival Christian confessions. The cult of Orthodox saints and martyrs, related in one way or another to Jerusalem and to Mar Saba (the Lavra of Saint Sabbas the Sanctified) as the sacred centers of Middle Eastern Christianity, also must have given spiritual support to the Melkite community in a non-Christian environment.

The first Orthodox author to begin writing in Arabic was the aforementioned native of Edessa, Theodore Abu Qurra, a monk of Mar Saba and later bishop of Harran. He left several dozen theological treatises in different languages—his native Syriac, Greek, and Arabic, which was beginning to dominate the Middle East. In his writings, Theodore expounded and defended Orthodox dogmas, including the then-burning issue of the veneration of icons. Many works of Abu Qurra were translated into Greek and Georgian during the Middle Ages. Among Theodore's translators was his brother at Mar Saba, Michael (761–846), syncellus of Patriarch Thomas of Jerusalem. Around 810, Michael composed a manual of Greek grammar and syntax, intended for the Palestinian monks studying Greek as a foreign language. It was part of that same intellectual endeavor of translating the Christian spiritual heritage into Arabic.[80]

In the ninth century, Christian scribes in Baghdad also started to write in Arabic. By the middle of the tenth century, the literary Arabic language was in universal use among the Orthodox of Syria and Egypt. By the late tenth century, Arabic had spread into the Coptic milieu.

Among the earliest classical writers of Arabic Christian literature, apart from Abu Qurra, we can name the scientist and encyclopedist Qusta ibn Luqa from Baalbek (830–912) and the prominent chroniclers Eutychius (Saʿid ibn Batriq), patriarch of Alexandria (876–940), and Agapius of Manbij (d. after 942).[81] The "cultural capital" of Melkites in the Caliphate was Mar Saba (or, more widely, the whole region of southern Palestine), which developed its own school of Arabic Christian theology and even its own distinctive hand among the scribes who wrote so many of the extant Arabic Melkite manuscripts.[82]

The "Orientalization" of the Melkite community is also reflected in its perception of history. Characteristically, the chronicler Eutychius of Alexandria mentions almost nothing about the iconoclast upheavals of the eighth and ninth centuries. The last event in Byzantine church history that is well known to him is the Sixth Ecumenical Council in 681. From the middle of the eighth century, Eutychius stops giving information about the Patriarchs of Constantinople (which by that time was already inaccurate). He wrote,

I have not obtained the names of the patriarchs of Constantinople after the death of Theodore [Eutychius dates him to 773, but such a patriarch is unknown at this time] until the time that I wrote this book, as well as the patriarchs of Rome from the time of Agapius [i.e., the Sixth Ecumenical Council of 681] ... the names of its patriarchs and information about them have not reached me.[83]

In Orthodox chronicles written in the Middle East in the tenth century, Muslim history and Muslim–Christian relations in the Caliphate increasingly displace information about the internal affairs of Byzantium.[84]

Links between the Orthodox of different provinces of the Caliphate were not weakened. In the lives of Palestinian ascetics of the eighth and ninth centuries, there is constant reference to monks of Syrian, Egyptian, and Mesopotamian origin leading an ascetic life in the monasteries by the Jordan. Immigrants from Syria repeatedly became patriarchs of Alexandria. At the same time, Egyptian Melkites sometimes jealously guarded their independence from neighboring patriarchal sees, for example, in 907 making the newly arrived Patriarch of Alexandria Christodoulos (a native of Aleppo), who had been consecrated in Jerusalem, once again undergo the rite of consecration in Alexandria.[85] Patriarch Thomas (807–821) oversaw the reconstruction of the Church of the Holy Sepulchre at the expense of the wealthy Egyptian Christian Macarius, who may have been a Monophysite by confession.[86] Georgian monks continued to live in the monasteries of the Middle East since Byzantine times. Many works of Syriac and Arabic literature from the early Middle Ages are preserved only in Georgian translation.[87] There are some indications suggesting that the greatest authority among the three Middle Eastern Orthodox patriarchs was enjoyed by the patriarch of Antioch, as he had the largest flock and most extensive territory. At the beginning of the ninth century, it was the Antiochian primate who tried to confirm his metropolitan in the capital of the Caliphate.[88]

Despite the Palestinian Christian community's isolation from Byzantium and the West, some ecclesiastical relationships were maintained as pilgrims continued to come to the Holy Land as they previously had. Toward the beginning of the ninth century, the Frankish Emperor Charlemagne's Middle Eastern policy began to intensify. Although medieval chroniclers and Western historians of the nineteenth century exaggerated the scope of Frankish–Arab diplomatic contacts and the degree of Latin influence in the Holy Land, contacts between Aachen and Jerusalem undoubtedly existed. Frankish alms came to the Holy Sepulchre, and in the beginning of the ninth century in Palestine, a community of Latin monks was in continuous residence.[89] The Western pilgrim Bernard, who visited Jerusalem in 867, stayed there in a hostel for pilgrims from Western Europe founded by Charlemagne.[90] In the years 808–809, the dogmatic innovations of the Frankish monks living in Jerusalem, who added the *filioque* to the Creed, drew strong opposition from the monks of Mar Saba. The Latins appealed to the pope, and an embassy to Rome was prepared by Patriarch of Jerusalem Thomas, but it did not take place because of the political turmoil that swept Palestine after the death of Harun al-Rashid.[91]

The second wave of iconoclasm, which began in the Byzantine Empire in 814, provoked sharp condemnation from the Orthodox East. The leader of the Byzantine iconodules, Theodore the Studite, was in correspondence with Patriarch Thomas of Jerusalem who, in turn, appealed to the emperor and patriarch in Constantinople to renounce the iconoclast heresy. In 814, representatives of Patriarch Michael Syncellus and the monks Job, Theodore, and Theophanes went to Byzantium and denounced iconoclast doctrine, for which they underwent years of imprisonment and cruel punishment.[92]

After the final triumph of the veneration of icons in 842, Michael, Theodore, and Theophanes remained in Byzantium, adding to the number of Palestinian monks who settled in Constantinople. This colony of emigrants from the Holy Land, grouped around the Monastery of Chora, played a prominent role in the cultural exchange between Byzantium and the Middle East. In this milieu, supposedly, a number of literary monuments that were well known at that time were composed, such as the apocryphal epistle from the three Eastern patriarchs in defense of icons of 836 or the *Life of Theodore of Edessa* from the middle of the tenth century.[93]

Later, in cases of religious conflict in Constantinople, parties often deemed it necessary to appeal to the opinion of Alexandria, Antioch, and Jerusalem. Thus, members of the Middle Eastern Churches were involved in the debate over the case of Patriarch of Constantinople Photius in the 860s and 870s, but they did not stake out an independent position on the issue.

Persecution

Relations with Muslim authorities, the religious policy of the Caliphate, and the degree of Muslim tolerance for other faiths exerted a decisive influence on the development of the Middle Eastern Christian communities.

The first two centuries of the Muslim Empire, especially the Umayyad era, were distinguished by a fairly high level of tolerance, in which Christians could worship freely, were active in commerce, and held prominent positions in the administration of the state. Harassment of Christians sometimes occurred in the provinces (e.g., Egyptian sources note five waves of persecution from the mid-680s to 717), which was more often motivated by the greed of governors than by religious intolerance.[94]

From what has been said regarding the religious policies of the Umayyads and the early ʿAbbasids, it is clear that real incidents of religious persecution in the eighth and beginning of the ninth centuries were isolated cases. The Christians' misfortunes, so colorfully described in some chronicles, especially those of the Syrian Jacobites, were rather caused by social oppression or civil instability. For example, in the story about the death of the Twenty Sabbaite Fathers killed in the Muslim civil wars in 796, the hagiographer pointedly and at length argued for the legitimacy of regarding the dead to be martyrs, as they could not technically be considered to have suffered for their faith.[95]

In the second ʿAbbasid century, however, the nature of interfaith relations in the Caliphate began to change. In the mid-ninth century, the increasingly obvious crisis of the Caliphate and the weakening of the Islamic world spawned a surge of fundamentalist sentiment among Muslims, which resulted in growing religious intolerance against *dhimmis*.

Periodic bans on the construction and expansion of churches started to be applied. Amid the unrest and anarchy after the death of Harun al-Rashid, Patriarch Thomas of Jerusalem undertook an unauthorized rebuilding of the dome of the Church of the Holy Sepulchre. After stable state power was restored, the patriarch was prosecuted for increasing the height of the dome and was able to exculpate himself only with great difficulty.[96]

The ʿAbbasid Caliph al-Mutawakkil (847–861) waged a systematic persecution of infidels, desiring to strengthen in every way Sunni orthodoxy by suppressing unorthodox sects and movements in Islam as well as the non-Islamic communities. The caliph issued a series of decrees against non-Muslims, placing more stringent constraints and prohibitions on them. *Dhimmis* were ordered to wear special distinctive clothing and were forbidden to ride on horseback or to hold any position in the public service. All churches built after the Muslim conquest were subject to destruction. The abuses of the caliphal administration prompted a revolt by the people of Emesa (Homs) in 855. They were joined by the local Christians, who were pushed to take this step by religious persecution. After the uprising was suppressed, the caliph ordered all churches in the city destroyed and the Christian population driven out. Al-Mutawakkil's persecution led to a massive conversion of *dhimmis* to Islam and the emigration of a significant proportion of the Melkites to Byzantium.[97]

After al-Mutawakkil, Christians managed to recover in part their positions in the state administration, but this caused an ever-growing resentment from ordinary Muslims. At the end of the ninth century and especially in the first third of the tenth century, numerous cases of religious strife and unrest, looting, and the destruction of churches are mentioned. A particularly powerful wave of anti-Christian pogroms swept across the Middle East in the years 923–924, when the Melkite churches in Tinnis, Ashkalon, Ramla, Caesarea, and Damascus were destroyed. In 937, the churches of Jerusalem were attacked and in 940 the church in Ashkelon was once more destroyed and was never rebuilt.[98]

The Byzantine Reconquista

By the 930s, the once mighty Caliphate had fallen into complete decline and broke up into a number of principalities. Egypt, Palestine, and southern Syria were successively ruled by the Turkic Tulunid (869–905) and Ikhshidid (935–969) dynasties. The greater part of northern Syria and Upper Mesopotamia was ruled by the Arab Hamdanid dynasty. Baghdad itself was captured by the Buyids in 945, and the caliphs only retained a shadow of spiritual power. At the same time, the Byzantine Empire launched an offensive against the weakened and feuding Muslim states. In 926, Malatya fell. In 942, the Byzantines, who were at the walls of Edessa, forced the Muslims to hand over to them the city's greatest relic, the image of Christ Not Made by Hands.[99] The greatest success of the Byzantine Reconquista was achieved in the 960s under the leadership of Nicephoras Phocas, who sought to give the Byzantine campaign the character of a holy war against Islam and—as the Arabs believed—saw his mission as being to liberate the Holy Sepulchre and to crush the Kaaba. Nicephoras won a series of brilliant victories over the Muslims and returned Crete, Cyprus, Cilicia, and parts of northern Syria to the empire. The Hamdanids of Aleppo long acknowledged themselves to be vassals of the Byzantine Empire and paid a tribute from which, it was stipulated, local Christians were exempt.[100]

The Muslims' military failures and the influx of refugees from areas conquered by Byzantium greatly exacerbated sectarian tensions in the Middle East. Each triumph by Nicephoras Phocas provoked anti-Christian pogroms in Egypt, Palestine, and Syria. In 960 and 961, Muslim mobs burned and plundered the churches of Fustat, making no distinction between those of the Orthodox and the Monophysites.[101]

In 966, as a result of a conflict with the governor of Jerusalem, Patriarch John of Jerusalem was killed and the Church of the Holy Sepulchre was burned. In 967, Patriarch Christopher of Antioch was killed on charges of having ties with

Byzantium. The true cause of his murder was a longstanding dispute between certain Muslim sheikhs and the patriarch, who was more loyal to the Hamdanid emir Sayf al-Dawla than to the regional elite of Antioch. However, in an atmosphere of inter-religious conflict when five thousand horsemen from Khorasan arrived to take part in jihad, it was very easy to declare the patriarch a Byzantine spy and, after his murder, to organize the looting of the patriarchal residence and the Church of St Cassian. After that, the See of Antioch was vacant until the Byzantines captured the city in the autumn of 969.[102]

Muslim attempts to recapture the city in 971 and 994 were unsuccessful. The new Byzantine Emperor John Tzimiskes devastated Upper Mesopotamia in 972 and then, seeing a serious rival in the Egyptian Fatimids, marched into southern Syria and Palestine in 974 and 975, briefly seizing Damascus and almost reaching Jerusalem. The emperor's sudden death halted Byzantine expansion for a time. After the military campaigns of Basil II the Bulgar-Slayer in Syria in 995 and 999, the political situation on the Byzantine–Muslim frontier stabilized for half a century. There was a bipolar system in the Middle East based on the balance between two great powers: the Byzantine Empire, which controlled a large part of Northern Syria, and the Fatimid Caliphate, whose border ran through Lebanon and Southern Syria. The two empires had a buffer zone centered in Aleppo, which was first a vassal of the Byzantine Empire and then, in 1015, was captured by the Fatimids. The final success of the Byzantine Reconquista was the capture of Edessa in 1031, resulting in nearly half the Patriarchate of Antioch finding itself once again in the Christian empire.[103]

The empire's military expansion was paralleled by the strengthening of Byzantine cultural influence in the Middle East. In 937, the patriarch of Constantinople asked his three Eastern brethren to commemorate him in the liturgy, something that had not been done since the days of the Umayyads.[104] In the middle of the tenth century, a revision of the Typicon of the Church of Jerusalem was undertaken, incorporating liturgical texts of Constantinopolitan origin. In the main churches of Jerusalem, the services themselves were apparently celebrated in Greek.[105]

Christians and the Fatimids

As the Byzantine Empire extended its rule over Northern Syria, the territories of the Patriarchates of Alexandria and Jerusalem and the remaining portion of the Patriarchate of Antioch found itself within the Shiite Fatimid Caliphate, which opposed the ʿAbbasids of Baghdad.

The Fatimid Caliphate represented a typical universal state with claims to possess absolute truth and the desire for world domination. The caliphate's ideologues developed the concept of spheres of imperial space, gravitating toward the caliphal throne in Cairo. The Fatimid *oecumene* consisted of the areas that were under the dynasty's direct administration, the so-called Internal Dawla of Egypt, Palestine, and Syria, and zones of vassal territories, the so-called External Dawla, which included Ifriqiya, Sicily, the Maghreb; the dependent states of Northern Syria and the Jazira; and the Christian countries of Northeast Africa, Nubia, and Ethiopia. The Coptic patriarchal see in Alexandria remained the spiritual center of all the Christians of the Nile Valley. The Monophysite community of Africa remained a significant political force, and the Fatimids actively used the authority of the Coptic Patriarch to build relations with their Christian neighbors to the south.

The imperial character of the Fatimid government necessitated a high degree of tolerance toward Christians. The caliphs considered *dhimmis* to be full citizens and treated them with the same impartiality as the Muslims.[106]

The first Fatimids to rule in Egypt, al-Muʿizz (952–975) and al-ʿAziz (967–996), even permitted open debates between theologians of different religions, something prohibited by *shariʿa*. The caliphs visited monasteries and Christian religious festivals. Christians and Jews everywhere held administrative positions, including the most critical positions of vizier and provincial governors. The dominance of "infidels" at the court provoked a backlash among Muslims and attacks on the caliphs themselves, but an effective apparatus of repression allowed the Fatimids to extinguish any discontent.[107]

Thus, for example, in 993, when the navy that had been constructed for a campaign against Byzantium, burned down in Cairo's naval shipyards, the Cairo mob accused the "infidels" of starting the fire and launched a pogrom against Christians. Dozens of rioters were arrested on the spot and some of them, chosen by lot, were executed. The authorities also announced that anyone appropriating goods stolen from the Christians during the riots would also be punished with death, and so during the night, thieves discarded their loot in the desert.[108]

The Caliph al-ʿAziz was married to an Orthodox Egyptian and strongly patronized the Melkite community. He furnished his brothers-in-law with distinguished ecclesiastical careers—Orestes was enthroned patriarch of Jerusalem and Arsenius became metropolitan of Cairo in 985. Orestes completed the restoration of the Church of the Holy Sepulchre in Jerusalem, which, as mentioned earlier, had been attacked in 966. Arsenius, with the support of the Muslim authorities, seized churches from the Copts that previously had belonged to the Orthodox.

At the end of the tenth century, the Melkites clearly occupied the leading position among all the non-Muslim confessions of the Fatimid state. In the year 1000, Patriarch Orestes of Jerusalem was sent as head of an embassy to negotiate peace. At the same time, according to a Christian chronicle, the young caliph al-Hakim promised in advance to accept any peace terms that the patriarch would be able to negotiate. Orestes remained in Constantinople until his death in 1005. The Patriarchate of Jerusalem de facto came under the leadership of his brother Arsenius, who in 1000 had been installed by orders of the caliph on the patriarchal throne of Alexandria. Thus, Arsenius, the maternal uncle of the ruling caliph, concentrated leadership in his hands over the entire Orthodox community in the Fatimid Caliphate.[109]

The prosperity of the Melkites and other *dhimmis* under the early Fatimids, however, ended abruptly at the beginning of the eleventh century, when the Muslims' accumulated discontent boiled over. This period is closely tied to the personality of the Caliph al-Hakim (996–1021), who launched the most severe persecution of *dhimmis* starting in 1003. The harshness of the caliph's anti-Christian decrees was exacerbated by his mental illness, paranoia, and ruthlessness; al-Hakim seriously sought to eradicate people of other religions, who made up almost half of his subjects.

Each successive year was marked by massive pogroms against churches and Christian quarters and the desecration of Christian cemeteries. With few exceptions, all monasteries and thousands of churches in the Fatimid realm were destroyed, and mosques often were erected over their sites. Crosses were removed from the surviving churches and images of crosses were scratched from their walls. In 1008, the caliph forbade Christians from celebrating the Entry of the Lord into Jerusalem, then Epiphany. There were periodic purges of the state administration, accompanied by the arrest, torture, and execution of Christian officials. In their place, however, other Christians were hired, so lacking was Egypt in qualified Muslim bureaucrats. Starting in 1005, a variety of restrictions were placed on the clothing of *dhimmis*. Christians were ordered to dress in black and wear heavy wooden crosses around their necks, the size of which increased with each subsequent decree.[110]

Al-Hakim's anti-Christian policies reached their apogee in 1009 with the destruction of the Christians' most revered shrine, the Holy Sepulchre, as well as several other Palestinian churches and monasteries. Soon thereafter in 1010, the Egyptian Melkites' main monastery, al-Qusayr on Mount Muqattam near Cairo, was laid waste and the adjacent cemetery was desecrated and destroyed. Patriarch Arsenius ever more clearly understood that his kinship with the half-mad caliph did not guarantee his safety. Tormented by dark forebodings, he spent his time in prayer and fasting, something to which he does not seem to have been inclined during the early, brilliant part of his career. Arsenius could not evade death: in the summer of that year, he was secretly killed on the caliph's orders.[111]

Toward the end of 1010, Palestine and Syria were captured by the Bedouin leader Mufarrij ibn al-Jarrah, who successfully resisted the Fatimids for almost three years. Wishing to keep his borders with Byzantium secure, Mufarrij made a point of favoring the Christians: thus, he organized the elections of the new patriarch of Jerusalem, Theophilus (1012–1020), who was a bishop in Trans-jordan, and supported the beginning of the rebuilding of the Holy Sepulchre. After Mufarrij's death and the restoration of Fatimid power in Syria, Patriarch Theophilus fled, but then returned at the invitation of the authorities.[112]

At the same time in Egypt, the activities of the Orthodox Church were para-lyzed. Empty sees were not replaced and only one Melkite bishop survived the era of al-Hakim. In 1014, the caliph allowed *dhimmis* to migrate out of Egypt and a mass exodus of Christians to Byzantine territory began. Of the remaining non-Muslims in Egypt, a significant proportion accepted Islam, often disingenuously. In the final years of his reign, al-Hakim was fascinated by a new religious quest and halted the persecution of Christians, even turning a blind eye to violations of his own anti-Christian decrees.[113]

The next caliph, al-Zahir (1021–1035) and the regent Sitt al-Mulk, al-Hakim's sister, canceled all the restrictions imposed on non-Muslims. The Orthodox were able to elect a new patriarch and bishops. Christians who had fled Egypt returned and restored their ruined churches. Church holidays were once more observed in all their splendor, and even those who had been forcibly converted to Islam converted back to Christianity without punishment.

Subsequent Fatimid caliphs likewise tolerated Christians and allowed them to hold key government positions.[114] This, however, did not prevent Muslim officials from occasionally solving their own financial problems at the expense of the Christian community. Under pressure from Muslim public opinion, the caliphs sometimes fired Christian officials and levied heavy taxes on the *dhimmis*.

The patriarchs of Jerusalem once more acted as intermediaries in the reestab-lishment of relations between Byzantium and the Fatimids. In 1023, Patriarch Nicephorus was sent by Sitt al-Mulk to Constantinople with a message about the restoration of the rights of Christians in Egypt and a request for the resumption of trade and the conclusion of a peace treaty. Negotiations continued in 1032.

Emperor Romanus III sought for himself the privilege to appoint the patriarch of Jerusalem and to rebuild the Church of the Holy Sepulchre. The final agreement was signed in 1036/1037. Byzantium got the opportunity to rebuild the church in all its glory, which was accomplished in the 1040s. The grandiose building made a strong impression on contemporaries.[115]

Byzantine Antioch

In the late tenth and eleventh centuries the historical destiny of the Melkites of the Byzantine part of Syria (the provinces of Antioch, Cilicia, Malatya, and others) evolved under different circumstances. A significant proportion of the population of these territories was made up of Arabic-speaking Christians, both Orthodox and Jacobite, as well as Muslims.

During the reign of the Emperor Romanus (1028–1034), Byzantine authorities began to persecute the Jacobites. Their patriarch and some bishops were exiled to Thrace, other bishops accepted Orthodoxy, and the rest died in exile. After that, the Syriac Jacobites moved their patriarchal throne to Muslim territory, to Amida (Diyabakir). Characteristically, after the Byzantines captured Edessa in 1031, the local Jacobite Christians left the city for Muslim territory, although a significant proportion of them later returned. The persecution of heretics in the Byzantine border regions was periodically renewed. In the 1060s, the Jacobite bishop of Malatya was sent to Macedonia, where for three years he worked in the fields and vineyards.[116] Monophysite chronicles recount that the Lord was angry with the Chalcedonians for their persecution of the true Christian believers and incinerated by lightening all the Greek churches of Antioch and killed the Byzantine patriarch of Antioch, who, during an earthquake, was swallowed up by the earth with ten thousand of his coreligionists.[117] The origin of this legend is perhaps due to the catastrophic earthquake that destroyed many cities of Western Asia in 1053.

The governors of Antioch were as a rule Greeks coming from the military nobility or state officials. Representatives of the Arab Christian aristocracy also played an important role in the life of the province, such as the magister 'Ubaydallah or the patrician Kulayb, who participated in the confrontation between the rebel Bardas Skleros and the Emperor Basil II in the 970s.[118]

At times, the patriarch of Antioch had great political clout. Among the primates of the Church of Antioch in the late tenth and eleventh centuries are found natives of the central regions of the Byzantine Empire (Greeks and Armenian Chalcedonians) and, during the first decades of Byzantine power, Syro-Palestinian Arabs. A major figure in this series is Patriarch Agapius (978–996), previously metropolitan of Aleppo. After the death of Patriarch Theodore of

Antioch (970–976), Agapius took a list of potential candidates to fill the vacant throne to Constantinople for confirmation by Emperor Basil II. At this time, amid the rebellion of Bardas Skleros, Antioch fell away from the emperor's authority and joined the rebels. Agapius told Basil II, whose military situation at the time was difficult, that he would return Antioch to Constantinople's rule, asking as a reward to be elevated to the patriarchal see of Antioch. Both strong personalities, the emperor and the metropolitan understood that it was expedient for them to become allies. Returning to Syria in secret, Agapius came into contact with the magister ʿUbaydallah, the governor of Antioch, on the emperor's behalf, and convinced the governor to go over to the side of Basil II. Bardas Skleros tried to regain the city several times, but failed. In 977, the emperor suppressed the rebellion, and Skleros fled to Muslim territory. For services rendered to the empire, on January 22, 978, Agapius was elevated to the rank of patriarch of Antioch. In later years, he played a key role in the regional elite of Antioch. The patriarch became friends with the Domestic of the Scholae of the East,[119] Bardas Phocas, and tacitly supported his ambitious plan to seize the imperial throne. As a result, in 987, Phocas's revolt began, with Agapius and the provincial elite standing behind him. Apparently, they hoped to increase his role in the administration of the empire. After the defeat and death of Bardas Phocas in the spring of 989, Agapius, attempting to exonerate himself before Basil II, led a rebellion of the people of Antioch against Phocas's governor, his son Leo. Bardas's secret correspondence fell into the emperor's hands, however, and the patriarch's involvement in the rebellion was revealed. In late 989, he was exiled from his see to Constantinople. Oddly enough, Basil II, famous for his ruthlessness, for some reason did not touch Agapius. The latter spent seven years in the capital under virtual house arrest, while continuing to manage the affairs of his patriarchate. In September 996, after the emperor's persistent coaxing, Agapius agreed to abdicate in exchange for a lifetime pension and the retention of his name in the diptychs. He died a year later in one of the monasteries of Constantinople.[120] According to Nikon of the Black Mountain, a Byzantine canonist of the eleventh century, from this time the custom was established of consecrating the patriarch of Antioch in the empire's capital.[121]

The emperors participated in the election of the patriarchs of Antioch, wanting to see them as reliable servants of the empire. Nevertheless, the patriarchs often behaved quite independently toward Constantinople. The most famous example of this is associated with the figure of Patriarch Peter III of Antioch (1050s), who jealously guarded the independence of his see against the claims of the Patriarch of Constantinople. In particular, Peter took a special, mediating stance in the conflict between Rome and Constantinople in 1054, which led to the final break between Orthodoxy and Catholicism. Antioch's position was determined in particular by disagreement over the See of Constantinople's policy of unifying church rituals. This was unacceptable to the ethnically diverse Patriarchate of Antioch, where the liturgy continued to be celebrated alongside Greek in Syriac and Arabic.[122]

The formation of the Orthodox Arabs' cultural foundation, which had begun with Theodore Abu Qurra and his contemporaries, occurred in a very short time. With Northern Syria returned to the bosom of the empire, Byzantium found that there was an already well-established Arabic-speaking Christian ethnic group there. During four generations of Byzantine rule, it did not show even the slightest inclination to assimilate. The Antioch of the late tenth and eleventh centuries was a major center of Christian culture, both in Greek and in Arabic. Halfway between the city and the sea, on the spur of the rock massif of the Black Mountain, there flourished a constellation of monasteries where monks of Greek, Georgian, Arabic, and Armenian origin labored and an active literary life unfolded. The most notable Byzantine writer from this milieu was Nikon of the Black Mountain, the leading expert in the field of canon law in the second half of the eleventh century. Some of the patriarchs of Antioch, such as Theodore III and Peter III, were also known for their theological works. The aforementioned Patriarch Agapius in the late tenth century was also a gifted writer. The Orthodox Arabs' center of cultural creativity moved from Southern Palestine to Antioch. The historian Yahya of Antioch (d. after 1034), a native of Egypt who moved to Antioch in 1015, continued the chronicle of Eutychius (Saʿid ibn Batriq).[123] The great luminary of medical science of that age, the Baghdad native Ibn Butlan, who authored many treatises of a theoretical and practical character and works on geography, ethnography, and anthropology, was active in Antioch in the 1060s.[124] An Arabic-language hagiographic literature developed. In the late tenth century, the protospatharios[125] Ibrahim ibn Yuhanna wrote the *Life* of Patriarch Christopher who, as mentioned earlier, died at the hands of Muslims shortly before the Byzantines reconquered Antioch.[126] In 1085, the hieromonk Michael wrote the first biography of St John of Damascus, which was immediately translated into several languages.[127] An important milestone in the development of Arabic Christian theology was the work of the deacon ʿAbdallah ibn al-Fadl (d. ca. 1051). In addition to compiling his own interpretations and teachings on the Holy Scriptures, ʿAbdallah collected all the versions of the Arabic Bible that were in use, compared them with the Greek original, edited them, and put into use a complete Arabic version of the Old and New Testament that was used in the Orthodox Church for many centuries.[128]

Although Melkite culture began once more to experience a strong Greek influence starting in the middle of the tenth century, it did not dissolve into a common imperial Greek–Byzantine culture, but rather it maintained its oriental identity and remained in close contact with the rest of the Arab world.

The authority of the patriarch of Antioch extended to the most remote parts of the Muslim world—Marv and Khwarezm.[129] The border between Byzantium and the Muslim states was not an obstacle for lively cultural interactions. The influence of the Arab tradition is so marked that in his chronicle, Yahya of Antioch uses AH dating (as, incidentally, does Eutychius) and both Yahya and Patriarch Agapius begin their works with the phrase "bismillah al-rahman al-rahim" (in the name of God, the munificent, the merciful) instead of the traditional Christian formula "in the name of the Father, Son, and Holy Spirit." Yahya is much more interested in the political history of Egypt and Syria than the wars of his own emperor, Basil the Bulgar-Slayer in the Balkans.[130] The most striking example, however, is the debate among Christians of different countries and denominations over the date of Easter in 1007. On account of differences in calculations and tables, there was vigorous correspondence, consultation, wrangling, and debate in which participated Melkites, Nestorians, and Monophysites from Armenia to Upper Egypt.[131] It is curious that Constantinople remained on the periphery of this dispute, as though the Ecumenical Patriarch meant little to Middle Eastern Christians, even to the Melkites of Byzantine Antioch. Even less did they think of Rome. Even though, according to custom, the pope's name was proclaimed during the liturgy, because of a lack of connections with Rome, no one knew these names. The last pope known to the East, as mentioned earlier, was Agapius, who participated in the Sixth Ecumenical Council in 681. He was commemorated, as a formality, for the next three hundred years.[132]

The relative political stability that was established in Syria was destroyed in the middle of the eleventh century by the arrival of the Seljuk Turks and their devastating raids on the towns of Upper Mesopotamia. The Byzantine Empire's decisive clash with the Seljuks at Manzikert in 1071 ended with the almost complete defeat of the Byzantines and the empire's losing control of almost the whole of Asia Minor.

The situation was aggravated by internal unrest in the Byzantine Empire and the struggle for the throne among various claimants. Antioch was also actively involved in these riots and civil wars of the 1070s. Patriarch Emilian played an active role in the city's affairs and was hostile to the government of Emperor Michael VII Doukas. In 1073, the new governor of Antioch sent from the capital, Isaac Comnenus, managed by cunning to lure the patriarch out of the city and send him to Constantinople and to suppress the brewing revolt of the people of Antioch.[133] Nevertheless, some time later, Northern Syria was lost to the empire.

In the atmosphere of political chaos afflicting Asia Minor after the catastrophe of Manzikert, an Orthodox Armenian, the former Byzantine dignitary Philaretos Brachamios (Varajnuni), managed to create an autonomous principality out of the wreckage of Byzantine provinces including Cilicia, Antioch, Malatya, and Edessa, but it had no real power to resist the Muslim onslaught. In 1084, the sultan of Iconium, Sulayman ibn Kutlumush, invaded the Christian territories of Northern Syria without encountering any serious resistance. In December 1084, the Seljuks seized Antioch with a surprise attack. The city returned to Muslim rule and the Cathedral of St Cassian was converted into a mosque.[134] However, the Turkish emir Yaghi-Siyan, who became ruler of Antioch around 1087, allowed the Orthodox patriarch to return to the city. This patriarch was John the Oxite, who came from the Greek clergy, and was a prominent church writer and an uncompromising lover of truth with a difficult personality. Already as a monk he wrote a treatise against the charisticariate, the practice of members of the Byzantine aristocracy establishing their own monasteries, which, according to John, led to the degradation of the institution of monasticism. In the early 1090s, the patriarch sent the emperor Alexius Comnenus two angry letters in which he sharply criticized his policies, particularly the confiscation of church property, and held the emperor responsible for the state's domestic and foreign problems. In his pamphlets, John also condemned the Byzantine aristocracy and bureaucracy that brutally oppressed the poor. In Antioch, the patriarch polemicized against the Syrian Monotheletes. A treatise on the two wills of Christ was written by the Maronite Bishop Tuma of al-Kfartab in response to the Oxite's attacks.[135]

In itself, the establishment of Seljuk rule in the Middle East in the late eleventh century did not result in a noticeable deterioration of the social status of local Christians.[136] In the eleventh century, the Muslim jurist al-Mawardi formulated another, rather clearly set forth doctrine on the status of *dhimmis* in a Muslim state that would have a great influence on the legal practice of subsequent generations of rulers. Protection was to be granted to non-Muslim subjects when they met six mandatory and six desirable conditions. The first group of conditions included not denouncing the Qur'an, the prophet Muhammad, or the religion of Islam; not marrying a Muslim woman; not inducing a Muslim to renounce his faith; and not aiding enemies of Islam. Failure to comply with any of these conditions placed the infidel outside the law. Desirable conditions included the wearing of distinctive clothing, the prohibition against constructing buildings taller than those of the Muslims, ringing bells, displaying crosses, publicly drinking wine, holding noisy funeral processions, and riding horses. Violation of these statutes did not involve the loss of "protected" status, but was nevertheless punished. The everyday restrictions ("desirable conditions," according to Mawardi), however, were little respected in real life, although from time to time pious rulers attempted to revive them.

For the most part, Christians of that era, like the rest of the population, suffered from the political instability in Syria, the endless wars between miniature emirates, and the violent repartition of territory. Thus, as a result of civil wars between Seljuk rulers and general instability in Palestine, Patriarch Symeon of Jerusalem with his bishops left the Holy Land and moved to Cyprus in the second half of the 1090s (the exact date is unknown). Archbishop John of Tyre, who shortly before had fled to Palestine from Tyre to escape persecution from the Fatimid vizier, came to be the leader of the Palestinian clergy.[137]

The First Crusade

The balance of power in the Eastern Mediterranean changed dramatically in 1097 with the arrival of the European Crusaders who came to liberate the Holy Land from the Muslim yoke. Crossing into Asia, the Crusaders cut through the domain of the Seljuk Sultanate of Iconium and arrived at Antioch. As the bulk of the Crusader army was besieging the city, in the spring of 1098, one of the leaders of the campaign, Baldwin of Flanders, took control of Edessa, where he established a Christian state. A significant proportion of the local Christians, especially the Armenians of Cilicia and the region of the Euphrates, willingly supported the Crusaders. The Orthodox and Syrian Jacobites behaved rather passively. Nevertheless, with the appearance of the Western knights under the walls of Antioch, the ruler of the city, Yaghi-Siyan (a vassal of the Seljuks of Aleppo), found it necessary to take repressive measures against the local Christians. Patriarch John the Oxite was imprisoned, non-Muslims were persecuted, and the Cathedral of St Peter was turned into stables. According to chroniclers, during the siege of Antioch, the Turks hung the patriarch in a cage on the city wall before the eyes of the Crusaders as a way of vilifying the Christian faith. After a seven-month siege, on June 2, 1098, the Crusaders captured Antioch. The Muslim garrison was slaughtered and the city plundered.

The following year, the army of European knights marched into Palestine. With the Crusaders approaching in June 1099, Muslim residents fled Ramla, after destroying the enormous Church of St George that stood among the ruins of neighboring Lydda. Residents of the Christian city of Bethlehem went out to meet the procession of the "Frankish" army, welcoming their liberators. The Muslim governor of Jerusalem (which the Fatimids had managed to regain shortly before) ordered Christians to leave the city to save food in case of a siege. The Crusaders took Jerusalem on July 14, 1099. During the assault, the city's entire remaining population, Muslim and Jewish, was slaughtered.

On the territories conquered from the Muslims, there appeared Christian states: the Kingdom of Jerusalem, the County of Tripoli, the Principality of Antioch, and the County of Edessa.[138]

With the victory of the Franks (Europeans), the situation of Syrian Christians did not improve. The Latins prevented their Eastern coreligionists from having full social standing. There could be no question of admitting them to the ranks of the ruling class. The lands of the Crusader states were divided between European barons, the military orders, and hierarchs of the Latin Church. The local population soon felt the brunt of the Western feudal system and the level of exploitation became higher than it had been previously. Among other things, the Crusaders sought to subjugate Middle Eastern Christians—"schismatics" and "heretics"—to the authority of the Papal See.

Historians identify different trends in the Crusaders' religious policy. Accompanying the First Crusade was the papal legate, Bishop Adhemar of Le Puy, who tried to maintain friendly relations with the Eastern Christians and cooperated with the patriarch of Jerusalem, Symeon, who was then in Cyprus. Adhemar, however, died during the epidemic that followed the capture of Antioch, where they left a mountain of corpses to rot. With his death, the intolerance of the Franks burst out into the open.[139]

The Banishment of the Patriarchs

Immediately upon taking the Holy City, the Crusaders organized an election for the Latin patriarch of Jerusalem. This was followed by the displacement of the hierarchy of the Orthodox Church in the Holy Land and its replacement with Latin clergy, to whom the Eastern Christians were subject. Sites of veneration and the best churches were transferred to the Catholics, who also appropriated the most valuable relics, including particles of the Precious Cross, which were forcibly seized from the Orthodox.[140] Like the previous Muslim rulers of the Holy Land, the Crusaders allowed other religious communities—Muslims, Jews,

Samaritans, and Christians of the non-Chalcedonian churches—to have internal autonomy. At the same time, the Franks did yet not consider the Melkites to be "heterodox" and therefore tried to integrate them into the Catholic Church.

According to later Western chroniclers, the Orthodox Patriarch of Jerusalem Symeon died in the summer of 1099, almost simultaneously with the capture of Jerusalem by the Crusaders.[141] Thus, the Franks had the formal right to fill the vacant patriarchal see. In Orthodox historiography, however, it is widely believed that Patriarch Symeon was still alive in 1106 (his own anti-Latin treatise on azymes references a document dated to 1105).[142] Thus, the election of the Latin patriarch of Jerusalem occurred while there was a living Orthodox primate.

After the death of Symeon, John VIII, formerly the archbishop of Tyre, was chosen as the new Orthodox patriarch. According to some reports, the election was held in Jerusalem; it is unclear what was the attitude of the Latin authorities toward this and what status John had in their eyes.[143] In any case, he already moved to Byzantium by 1107/1108, where he remained until his death. A succession of the Orthodox patriarchs of Jerusalem in exile was formed in Constantinople. The Byzantine emperors attached a great deal of importance to preserving the succession of the Orthodox patriarchs of the Holy Land as a symbol of their claim to be the protectors of Palestinian Orthodoxy. The patriarchs had their residence at the Monastery of St Diomides in Constantinople. Among them were major theologians and church leaders who played a prominent role in Byzantine history in the twelfth century.[144]

Only one of the primates of Jerusalem of this era tried to exercise his pastoral ministry in Palestine. Patriarch Leontius (1176–1185) arrived in the Holy Land but was not allowed by the Latin authorities to serve in the Church of the Holy Sepulchre, which he could visit only as a simple pilgrim. The patriarch settled in Bethlehem, where several attempts were made on his life. The emir of Damascus invited Leontius to move to his territory, but the patriarch declined the invitation. Only at the insistence of Emperor Manuel Comnenus and out of a desire not to provoke sectarian violence in Palestine did Leontius return to Constantinople.[145]

Many Orthodox bishops of the Patriarchate of Jerusalem were forced to leave their sees upon the arrival of the Crusaders. It is known that Savvas, metropolitan of Caesarea, which was captured in 1101 by King Baldwin of Jerusalem, left for the territory of the Fatimids and later is presumed to have become patriarch of Alexandria. The sources also mention a metropolitan of Tiberias who lived in exile in Constantinople in the 1120s.[146]

Relations between the Orthodox and the Latins in the Patriarchate of Antioch were even more dramatic. The Crusaders initially treated John the Oxite, the patriarch of Antioch, with a great deal of reverence. The papal legate Adhemar of Le Puy confirmed him in the dignity of patriarch as head of both the Orthodox and the Latin clergy of Antioch.[147] Soon, however, John's situation was complicated, as Steven Runciman interpreted Adhemar's message to the pope written in the summer of 1098 on behalf of Patriarch Symeon of Jerusalem. In this letter, Symeon was positioned as primate of all the Christians in the Middle East, without any mention of the patriarch of Antioch and his rights. On September 11, the leaders of the Crusader army sent a letter inviting the pope to come to the East and take the See of Antioch as the second see of the Apostle Peter, alongside Rome. Such an invitation, as unrealistic as it was, demonstrates the Crusaders' disdain for the Orthodox patriarch of Antioch.[148]

In October 1098, the Crusaders captured the Muslim city of al-Bara near Apamea. John consecrated a Latin bishop for the city. Although there had not previously been an Orthodox hierarchy in the city, this act was the first step toward the creation of a parallel Latin church structure in the Middle East. After much debate among the leaders of the Crusade over the future of the city of Antioch, the city was retained by Prince Bohemond of Taranto. Many historians consider him to be the central figure in bringing about conflict between Byzantium and the Crusaders, a person who contributed to the irreversibility of the deepening schism between Rome and Constantinople.[149] Of all the Crusaders, he was the most hostile to Byzantium and the Orthodox patriarch of Antioch, whom he considered to be an agent of influence of the Byzantine Empire.

The prince of Antioch maintained close ties with the new papal legate, Dagobert, who became the Latin patriarch of Jerusalem in late 1099. Now Bohemond could completely ignore John. In violation of his rights, Dagobert personally installed Latin bishops in the Antiochian dioceses of Tarsus, Arta, Mamistra, and Edessa. The Crusaders suspected John of plotting to hand Antioch over to the Byzantine emperor. As a result of pressure from them, the patriarch was forced to leave the city sometime before August 1100. In his place, Bohemond installed the bishop of Arta, Bernard of Valence, from whom originated the line of Latin patriarchs of Antioch, subordinate to the pope.[150]

John the Oxite and the Orthodox bishops withdrew to Byzantium. There the elderly John resigned his patriarchal rank and his bishops elected a new patriarch. In this way, in parallel with the Latin patriarchs of Antioch, there continued a succession of Orthodox patriarchs in exile. Almost all of them came from the Greek clergy. Some of them played a prominent role in the life of the Byzantine Church, such as Athanasius I (1157–1171), who took part in theological disputes during the time of Manuel Comnenus, and Theodore Balsamon (1185–1203), the leading canonist in the Orthodox world at the turn of the twelfth to the thirteen century.

The Kingdom of Jerusalem

Despite the best efforts of the Crusaders to get rid of the Orthodox hierarchy, individual Orthodox bishops remained in Palestine. In pilgrimage literature and various documents of the twelfth century, there appear the Melkite bishop Samuel, who was in Jerusalem in the 1130s; Meletius, Archbishop of the Greeks and Syrians of Gaza and Eleutheropolis (1173); and unnamed bishops of Lydda, Acre (Akka), and Scythopolis.[151] It is believed that these bishops performed auxiliary functions under the Latin bishops of Palestine, performing the services in the Byzantine rite and ordaining priests for the local Arab Christian population, but without having any administrative authority.[152]

Against the background of the destruction of the ecclesiastical structures of the Patriarchate of Jerusalem, the flowering of the Palestinian monasteries stands in sharp contrast. By the time of the Crusaders' arrival in the Holy Land, a number of monasteries still existed. In the literature, there are claims that by the end of the eleventh century only two monasteries remained outside the walls of Jerusalem, Mar Saba and Holy Cross.[153] This, however, contradicts the testimony of a Russian pilgrim from 1106–1107, the Abbot Daniel, about the Monasteries of St Theodosius and St Chariton in the Judean wilderness remaining intact and the Monasteries of St John Chrysostom and Kalamon in the Jordan Valley even prospering. Various sources also confirm the presence of three monasteries on Mount Tabor (later authors speak of two monasteries).[154]

The kings of Jerusalem tolerated the Orthodox monasteries and even provided them with protection. In the absence of an Orthodox patriarch in Palestine, the abbot of Mar Saba served as primate of the Orthodox population and clergy, as is evident from Daniel's description of the Easter celebrations in Jerusalem in 1107.[155] The favorable position of the Orthodox monasteries is explained by a certain contradiction in the interests of the papal curia and the kings of Jerusalem regarding maintaining friendly relations with Byzantium and the conclusion of dynastic marriages with Orthodox aristocratic families. The Emperor Manuel Comnenus (1143–1180) sought to be the patron of universal Orthodoxy and took the opportunity to invest heavily in the restoration and decoration of Palestinian churches and monasteries. Moreover, competition did not arise between Latin and Orthodox monasteries for purely geographic reasons. The Catholic monasteries were established either in the vicinity of Jerusalem or in Galilee, in densely populated rural areas, whereas the Orthodox monasteries were located in the Judean desert.[156]

According to several sources, primarily the Byzantine pilgrim John Phocas, a number of monasteries in the Holy Land were restored in the 1180s: in addition to those monasteries mentioned previously, the Monastery of the Prophet Elias between Jerusalem and Bethlehem, the Lavra of St Euthymius in the Judean hills, the Monastery of Koziba (Wadi Qelt), and the Monasteries of St Gerasimus and John the Baptist by the Jordan. The Monastery of the Prophet Elias on Mount Tabor was also renovated, with the nearby Monastery of the Transfiguration having passed into the hands of the Catholics. In the late twelfth century, Orthodox monks from Calabria revived the Monastery of the Prophet Elias on Mount Carmel over Haifa, but later Latin monks settled in the monastery (they had probably lived there for some time together with the Orthodox monks under the same rule), and it went into the jurisdiction of the Latin patriarch of Jerusalem.[157] Archeological surveys have confirmed the renovation of the Monasteries of Koziba and St Gerasimus (Dayr Hajla), which also were decorated with new paintings. In the Monastery of St Gerasimus are preserved Greek inscriptions about the restoration of the monastery during the patriarchate of John (presumably John IX) under the abbot Jacob. Arabic inscriptions from Dayr Hajla and Wadi Qelt contain the names of the artisans who rebuilt the monasteries.[158]

In the Palestinian monasteries, monks gathered from around the Orthodox world. Most visible in the monastic community was the Greek element. At the same time, there was an increased presence of Georgian monks. There is evidence for the establishment of a Georgian women's monastery in Palestine in the 1120s.[159] Natives of the Slavic lands lived in the Palestinian monasteries, as evidenced, for example, by the *Life* of Euphrosyne of Polotsk. Notable is the presence of a community of Frankish monks even in Mar Saba, constituting one of the several autonomous ethnic groups living in the monastery. Historians have noticed traces of influence from the Byzantine monastic tradition on Catholic monasticism in the Kingdom of Jerusalem.[160]

The monasteries received generous contributions from Byzantium, Georgia, and other countries. These funds allowed the monasteries to acquire significant land holdings in various areas of Palestine, especially the Jordan Valley. There are documents conferring villages to Mar Saba by Queen Melisende of Jerusalem (1131–1162) as well as various land transactions of the Palestinian monasteries. According to John Phocas, the Jordan Valley was covered with gardens belonging to the monasteries of the Judean Desert.[161]

The Melkite population of Palestine retained almost as much autonomy under the Crusaders as they had under the Muslims. Rural communities and Orthodox neighborhoods in cities were led by prominent laymen with the title *ra'is* (the Arabic term for head or leader). They decided legal issues within the community and represented their coreligionists before the authorities of the kingdom. Local Christians occupied the lower levels of the state's bureaucracy, such as the posts of scribe and *dragoman* (translator). At the same time, some Melkites managed to reach prominent positions at the court, chiefly as physicians.[162]

Liturgical services in the Melkite communities followed the traditional Byzantine rite. Priests coming from the Arab Melkite milieu were installed by the few Orthodox bishops remaining in Palestine. From liturgical texts of that time, it is clear that during the liturgy the Melkites commemorated the exiled Orthodox patriarchs and ignored the Latin patriarchs of Jerusalem.[163] We may recall the epigraphic inscriptions with the name of the Orthodox patriarch on the walls of monasteries mentioned earlier. Under the conditions of "apartheid," characteristic of the Crusader state, the cultural and everyday alienation between the alien Franks and the indigenous Arab population of the Middle East, the Latins did not seem to be interested in the inner life of their Melkite subjects. Catholic hierarchs were content with a formal expression of submission and payment of tithes by the local Eastern Christian population, while not sufficiently aware of its cultural and religious orientation.[164]

When the Latin patriarchs took over the main shrine of Jerusalem, the Church of the Holy Sepulchre, they nevertheless permitted the Orthodox to worship there to a limited extent, as well as a number of clerics from the non-Chalcedonian churches, an action calculated to induce them to union with Rome. Thus, within the Church of the Holy Sepulchre, there appeared areas belonging to the Armenians, Syrian Jacobites, and Nestorians.

The Principality of Antioch

For almost the entirety of the twelfth century, the Byzantine Empire fought for the return of their former Middle Eastern territories captured by the Crusaders, especially Antioch. Likewise, the emperor considered one of his main objectives to be the restoration of an Orthodox patriarch on the See of Antioch. It was the Latin clergy in particular that formed the core of the anti-Byzantine party in the Principality of Antioch. Several times, Byzantium came close to succeeding. In 1108 Bohemond of Taranto, who had suffered heavy losses from the Greeks at Epirus, pledged to be a vassal of the emperor and promised to return the Orthodox patriarch to Antioch. However, Bohemond's nephew Tancred, who ruled the city, refused to comply with these conditions and, at the time, there were no forces in Byzantium for a military expedition against Antioch. In 1137, the Emperor John Comnenus laid siege to the city and forced the prince of Antioch, Raymond, to recognize the empire's suzerainty, but the pope forbade Catholics from serving in John's army if he attempted to replace the Latin patriarch of Antioch with a Greek. John soon died in 1143, having failed to gain a foothold in Syria. Byzantium's real triumph was Manuel Comnenus' march on Antioch in 1159, when the prince of Antioch, Reynald, realized the complete futility of resistance and went to the imperial camp with an expression of total submission, barefoot and with a rope around his neck. One of the terms of the peace treaty was the prince's obligation to accept an Orthodox patriarch into the city. In 1165, Prince Bohemond III met this condition, and Athanasius I returned to the patriarchal see. The Latin Patriarch Aimery left the city in protest and the pope threatened the prince with excommunication. The conflict resolved itself five years later when Athanasius died in an earthquake, buried under the ruins of his church. After the Byzantine Empire's disastrous defeat in the battle against the Seljuks at Myriokefala in 1176, Constantinople's having any influence in Syria was out of the question, and a quarter of a century later, Byzantium itself fell to the Crusaders.

Nevertheless, it was then that an Orthodox patriarchate was once again restored in Antioch. In the early thirteenth century, the count of Tripoli, Bohemund IV, disputed the claim for the Principality of Antioch from Cilician Armenia, which at the time was in union with the Church of Rome. The pope and the Latin Patriarch of Antioch Peter took the side of the Armenians. Then, in 1206, Bohemond IV deposed the patriarch and invited the Orthodox primate, Simeon II Abu Shayba, to take his place. Despite the excommunication imposed on Antioch by the Latin patriarch, the citizens supported Bohemond's move, which indicates the significant influence of the Orthodox community in Antioch.

The fate of the patriarchs of Antioch evolved even further and they often became the object of bargaining in disputes between Middle Eastern monarchs. Around 1209 Bohemond reconciled with Rome and forced Simeon to leave the city. Subsequently, Simeon was able to return and stay in Antioch in parallel with the Latin patriarch. In the 1230s, Rome realized the impossibility of directly incorporating Eastern Christians into the Catholic Church and moved to create an autonomous Melkite church structure that would be in union with Rome. Simeon rejected this project, but his successor David, who may have owed his election to the prince of Antioch's court, was inclined to negotiate with the pope in the 1240s. Although the Latin Patriarch of Antioch Albert did not welcome the emergence of a parallel hierarch in union with Rome, he nevertheless left David as his deputy when he left for the council of Lyon in 1245. Until 1248, David would be the only patriarch in Antioch. A philo-Catholic sentiment, however, was not generally characteristic of the clergy of Antioch. The following patriarch, Euthymius, refused to recognize the primacy of Rome, for which he was expelled from the city roughly in the late 1250s.[165]

Interregnum (1187–1250)

On July 4, 1187, at the Battle of Hattin, Salah al-Din, the most famous member of the new Ayyubid dynasty that ruled Egypt from 1168 to 1250, destroyed the Crusaders' army and then seized almost the entire territory of the Kingdom of Jerusalem. According to several sources, the Orthodox of the Holy Land welcomed the return of Muslim rule and were even ready to open the gates to Salah al-Din's army. Jerusalem surrendered to the Muslims in the autumn of 1187 and the Frankish population was expelled from the city. After this disaster for the crusading movement, Western European monarchs undertook the Third Crusade to Palestine (1189–1193) but won only a narrow strip along the coast and could not regain the Holy City. The Kingdom of Jerusalem, whose capital moved to Acre, continued to exist for a century, but most of Palestine and Transjordan remained in Muslim hands.

The expulsion of the Latins from Jerusalem gave the Orthodox Church a chance to recover the holy places. The Byzantine Emperor Isaac Angelos negotiated with Salah al-Din for the transfer of the Palestinian shrines into the undivided ownership of the Orthodox Church and for the right of the emperor to appoint the patriarch of Jerusalem. Byzantium's demands were not successful and Salah al-Din retained the prerogative of determining the affiliation of the holy places. In addition to the Orthodox, who regained the Basilica of the Resurrection and a number of other areas of the Holy Sepulchre church complex, the Armenians, Syrian Jacobites, and Nestorians retained possession over their part of the church. Additionally, the Ayyubids set apart areas for their Coptic Egyptian subjects, after which Ethiopians came to Jerusalem. Georgians came to play an increasingly important role within the Orthodox community in Palestine and so they also received their own area in the Church of the Holy Sepulchre. Queen Tamar maintained friendly relations with the Ayyubids and actively funded Georgian monasteries in the Holy Land. In a situation in which the Latins had been expelled from Jerusalem and Byzantium was increasingly weakened, the Georgian Bagratids claimed the role of chief patron of the Orthodox East. Finally, in 1193, after the conclusion of a peace with the Crusaders, the Ayyubids even allowed Latin clergy to worship in the church.[166] In this way, there largely developed the situation that continues to the present day of coexistence and competition in the Holy Sepulchre between Christian denominations whose relations are governed by a non-Christian secular authority.

For unclear reasons, in the late twelfth century, the Orthodox patriarchs were in no hurry to return to the Holy Land and preferred to stay in Constantinople. The first patriarch to reside in the Holy Land was Euthymius III who escaped from the Byzantine capital after the Crusaders seized it in 1204 and presumably was elected to the patriarchal see already in Jerusalem.

In the thirteenth century, the main target of the Crusaders' onslaught was Egypt, where the Fifth (1218–1221) and Seventh (1248–1250) Crusades were sent. On the eve of the Crusaders' invasion of Egypt, the Patriarch of Alexandria, Nicholas I (ca. 1220–1235), sought to obtain the favor of the spiritual leader of the Western world, Pope Innocent III, with whom he exchanged a number of friendly letters. At the pope's invitation, a representative of the patriarch attended the Lateran Council of 1215. After the failure of the Fifth Crusade, Nicholas sent Pope Honorius a letter full of complaints about the miseries of Egyptian Christians and pleas for help.[167]

Perhaps the persecution of Christians in Ayyubid territory during the Fifth Crusade is behind the flight of Patriarch of Jerusalem Euthymius III to the Monastery of Sinai, where he died in 1235. It appears that Euthymius maintained ties with the Crusaders on the eve of their campaign. His appeals to Christians to refrain from pilgrimage to Palestine in order not to enrich the Hagarenes with their gifts clearly resonated with the Lateran Council's prohibition of the sale of weapons and ship timber to Egypt.[168]

Despite all this, the European prelates and knights themselves continued to refer to Eastern Christians as heretics. During the Crusader armies' invasion of Egypt, they plundered and massacred the local population, making no distinction between Muslims and Christians. In 1219, after the capture of Damietta, which previously had been the see of an Orthodox metropolitan and a Coptic bishop, the papal legate established a Latin see in the city and annexed Damietta to the possessions of the Latin patriarch of Jerusalem. The same thing happened after the Crusaders captured the city again in 1249. In the Catholic Church in the thirteenth century, the position of Latin patriarch of Alexandria was introduced, although it remained a purely nominal, honorary title.[169]

The Orthodox position in the Middle East dramatically deteriorated in the twelfth and thirteenth centuries, and not solely because of the various pressures from the Latin Crusaders. On the other side of the front, in the Muslim world, the situation of two centuries of continuous jihad against the infidels spawned the rise of fanaticism and intolerance, and numerous persecutions against Christians. For example, in 1124, almost all churches in Aleppo were taken away from the Christians and converted into mosques.[170]

During military actions, the chief victims were from the local Christian population. For example, during the fierce fighting between the Crusaders and the Muslims for Edessa from 1144 to 1146, the city changed hands several times and eventually was burned to the ground, with almost all its Christian population annihilated. A contemporary of the events, the Jacobite patriarch and historian Michael the Syrian vividly described the final act of this drama:

> The bodies of priests, deacons, monks, nobles and commoners were piled up in a jumble. But if their death was terrible, they did not taste the torment endured by the survivors … The air was poisoned by a putrid stench. Assyria [Mesopotamia] was inundated with prisoners … Around 30,000 died during the first and second siege [of Edessa]. 16,000 were taken off into slavery and one thousand were saved. Not one woman or child survived. They were killed during the massacres or were led off into captivity in various lands. Edessa became like a desert.[171]

At the beginning of his reign, the Sultan Salah al-Din placed especially severe restrictions on infidels. In his edicts, Christians were expelled from government posts and they were required to wear distinctive clothing and not allowed to ride horses. He launched a number of devastating campaigns against Christian Nubia.[172] Another surge of Muslim fanaticism swept the Middle East after Salah al-Din's victory over the Crusaders at Hattin in 1187. "There are no words," wrote Michael the Syrian, "to express how much damage, injury and humiliation at the hands of the Muslims has been suffered by Christians in Damascus, Aleppo, Harran, Edessa, Mardin, Mosul and everywhere under Muslim rule."[173] After defeating the Crusaders, however, Salah al-Din, to strengthen his political position, backed away from a policy of intolerance and returned non-Muslims to the administrative apparatus of Egypt.[174]

New calamities befell the Christians during the Fifth Crusade. The Copts of Cairo were levied with a heavy collection for military expenditures. The Muslim army destroyed all the churches along its path to Damietta. In response to the Crusaders' capture of Damietta, 115 churches were destroyed throughout Egypt.[175]

In 1229, the Emperor Frederick Hohenstaufen was able to negotiate with the Ayyubids for the return to the Crusaders of Jerusalem, Bethlehem, and a corridor connecting them to the coast. At the same time, it was stipulated that the Muslim presence in the Holy City would be preserved, in particular in the religious complex on the Temple Mount and that the construction of fortifications in the city would be forbidden. The Franks' hold on Jerusalem was shaky; the Latin patriarch preferred to stay in Acre. In this situation, the position of the Orthodox Church was not changed.

Patriarch Athanasius II of Jerusalem (before 1229–1244), who presumably came from the Balkans, was in close contact with the entire Orthodox world. He corresponded with the patriarch of Constantinople about ritual differences with the Latins and participated in the approval of the autocephaly of the Bulgarian Church in 1235. In 1229 and 1234–1235, the Holy Land was visited by the Serbian Archbishop Sava Nemanjić who had close ties of friendship with Patriarch Athanasius and the abbot of Mar Saba Nicholas. The *Life* of St Sava of Serbia provides us with detailed information about the state of Middle Eastern Orthodoxy and in particular about the monasteries and monks of the first third of the thirteenth century. Sava made generous contributions to the Palestinian monasteries and places of worship and himself founded several monasteries, including a monastery in Acre that was to serve as a hostel for Orthodox pilgrims. The *Life* repeatedly mentions Athanasius serving the liturgy in the Church of the Resurrection as well as Sava's founding the Monastery of St John the Theologian on Mount Sion, along with the patriarch and the abbot of Mar Saba, indicated the Orthodox Church's strong position in Jerusalem during the second period of Crusader rule.

From the late 1230s, however, the situation in Palestine changed for the worse. Jerusalem became the object of military confrontation between the Crusaders and the Muslims and switched hands several times. Political instability led to the exodus of a large part of the Christian population of the Holy Land. On August 23, 1244, Jerusalem was stormed by an army of Khwarezmians, allies of the Egyptian sultan. Catholics and Orthodox sought refuge in the Church of the Holy Sepulchre but were slaughtered. Among those who perished was Patriarch Athanasius II, who subsequently was canonized as a martyr by the Church of Jerusalem.[176]

Mongols and Mamluks

Having alienated their potential allies, the Eastern Christians, the Crusaders were doomed to defeat in their struggle with the Islamic world with its far superior military and demographic resources. The final chance to change the political situation in favor of the Christians came in the middle of the thirteenth century with the arrival of the Mongols in the Middle East. The Mongols were for the most part shamanists, but were also familiar with the preaching of Nestorianism and Buddhism and were hostilely disposed toward the Muslims. The last united campaign of the Chingizids, which began under Hülegü in 1256, was intended to crush the Muslim states. Moving from Baghdad to Damascus, the Mongols consistently exterminated Muslims but spared the Christian population. Only during the assault on Aleppo in the autumn of 1259 did Orthodox suffer in the heat of the massacre.[177] Georgia, Cilician Armenia, and the Principality of Antioch recognized the suzerainty of Hülegü Khan. At the insistence of Hülegü, who valued his alliance with the Empire of Nicaea, Prince Bohemond VI of Antioch returned the Orthodox Patriarch Euthymius to the city and sent away the Latin patriarch, for which he was excommunicated by the pope.

On March 1, 1260, the vanguard of the Mongol army, led by Hülegü's close associate, the Nestorian Kitbuqa Noyan, arrived in Damascus. Kitbuqa was accompanied by the king of Cilician Armenia, Hetoum, and Prince Bohemund of Antioch. According to the British Byzantinist Steven Runciman, "The citizens of the ancient capital of the Caliphate saw for the first time for six centuries three Christian potentates ride in triumph through their streets."[178] The Christians welcomed the establishment of the new government. It is symptomatic that the victors turned the Umayyad Mosque into a Christian church. By late summer 1260, the Mongols had completed the subjugation of Syria and most of Palestine, but for some reason did not occupy Jerusalem.[179]

At the same time, the Crusaders of the Kingdom of Jerusalem did not perceive the Mongols as allies. There was great prejudice against the invaders among the Europeans. The kingdom was dominated by Venetian merchants who were concerned about the profitable trade with Muslim Egypt. After a local conflict with the Mongols near Sidon, the Christians of Acre entered into an alliance with the Muslims and allowed the army of the Egyptian Mamluks to pass through their territory on their way to the territory of the Mongols.[180]

After the death of the Khagan Möngke, Hülegü returned with most of his army to Tabriz to participate in resolving the question of succession in the state of the descendants of Genghis Khan. The remaining body of Mongols in Syria, headed by the general Kitbuqa Noyan, was defeated on September 3, 1260, in a battle with the Mamluks at ʿAyn Jalut in Galilee. Kitbuqa was captured and executed. At the news of this victory, a pogrom against Christians began in Damascus, the

Cathedral of Mart Maryam was burned, and anyone known to have collaborated with the Mongols was killed.[181] The Mamluks concluded an alliance with Hülegü's Muslim opponents, the Anatolian Seljuks and Khan Berke of the Golden Horde; constricted the Mongols with assaults from different directions; and, in a series of military campaigns, were able to drive them out of Syria. Then came the time of reckoning for Hülegü Khan's Christian allies.

In the 1260s the Egyptian Sultan Baybars waged a number of successful campaigns against the Crusader states and Cilician Armenia. These wars were accompanied by a demonstrative extermination of infidels: mass executions of Christian prisoners of war and civilians. In the summer of 1266, the Muslim army devastated Cilician Armenia, which never recovered from the blow. On May 12, 1268, Baybars' army appeared at the walls of Antioch. At that time Prince Bohemond VI was in Tripoli and his constable Simon Mansel led the defense of the city. The garrison was too small to protect the walls and Mansel was soon captured during a raid. The people of the city were able to repel the first attack, but on May 18, the Mamluks launched a general assault on all sections of the walls and broke through the defenses on one side. The ensuing carnage shocked even Muslim chroniclers. Tens of thousands of the city's inhabitants were killed and the rest were sold into slavery. The city was burned and left completely desolate.[182]

The Orthodox Patriarch Euthymius had once again been exiled by Prince Bohemond of Antioch in 1263 (enraging Hülegü Khan, who continued to be focused on an alliance with the Orthodox world) and at the time of the city's fall was in Byzantium. After the events of 1268, the patriarchs of Antioch never again returned to their former capital.[183]

In those same years, Baybars drew his sword against his former allies in the Crusader Kingdom of Jerusalem in 1260. After the Crusaders' expulsion, however, the Mamluks long anticipated a new landing by European knights. To aggravate the situation, the Muslim authorities destroyed most of the coastal cities and fortifications, such as Ashkelon, Caesarea, and Acre. The Shiites living in Keserwan were subject to extermination or expulsion, because they might, in the opinion of the Mamluks, have supported European invaders.[184] Fears of a threat from overseas were not unjustified; some in the West periodically hatched plans for a new crusade. One such operation was the raid of the king of Cyprus on Alexandria in 1365, which provoked another persecution of Christians in the Mamluk state.

The era of the Crusades was a turning point in the history of Middle Eastern Christianity. Over two hundred years, Christians, who in the eleventh century formed almost half the population in Syria and Palestine, were nearly destroyed to the extent such that by 1082 they were surviving as merely vestigial ethnoreligious groups.

The Century of Persecution

By the end of the thirteenth century, all of Syria had been incorporated into the Mamluk Sultanate. For nearly three centuries, the fate of the Melkites was tied to this state, which became the political and religious center of the Muslim world and the center of Arab culture.

For the first half-century of their reign, the Mamluks were in permanent confrontation with the Mongols over control of Syria. The last attack on Damascus by a descendant of Hülegü, Khan Ghazan, was recorded in 1303. The subsequent disintegration of the state of Hülegü's descendants secured for the Mamluk state a century of peace, interrupted only by conflicts within the ruling elite and coastal raids by European corsairs. The Mamluks waged a number of campaigns of conquest in Eastern Anatolia and Nubia. In 1315, the Mamluk army put Malatya to fire and the sword. In a few blows, Cilician Armenia was finished. The last king of Cilicia, besieged in his capital, surrendered to the Mamluks in 1375. In 1400–1401, Aleppo and Damascus were subject to Timur's invasion, which brought about the complete devastation of Syria. The period of prosperity in the Middle East, however, had ended half a century earlier, after the pandemic of the Black Death in 1347–1348 eliminated between one-third and a half of the region's population. The economic and demographic effects of the plague were not overcome until the Ottoman conquest.

In comparison with previous Muslim dynasties, the religious policy of the Mamluks was distinguished by a much greater intolerance of *dhimmis*. Foremost among the reasons for this intolerance was the psychological effects of the Crusades and the anti-Christian sentiment that they caused, which constantly was stirred up by the sermons of Muslim theologians and found many supporters among the common people who were dissatisfied with the dominance of Christian officials. The long standoff with Hülegü's dynasty, which openly patronized the Christians and relied on allied troops from Georgia and Cilician Armenia, also may have played a role. The loss by Muslim merchants of their standing in Mediterranean trade stimulated the migration of the Muslim middle class into the area of state administration, from which they first needed to push out the Christians. In the period from 1279 to 1447, such public sentiment prompted the Mamluk government eight times to organize large-scale persecution of non-Muslims in Egypt and Syria. This included dismissal of non-Muslim officials from public service, the introduction of distinctive clothing for *dhimmis*, various domestic constraints, and the destruction of newly built churches.[185] In contrast to the era of al-Hakim, when the persecution of *dhimmis* was inspired by the government, in the late Middle Ages, the initiative came from religious circles and the masses—what would now be called "civil society," which sometimes was able to exert effective pressure on the Mamluk military oligarchy.

The Coptic community of Egypt in the early Mamluk era was dynamic and thriving, with a strong sense of identity embodied in an active literary life. At the same time, the relative proportion of Copts in the country's population continued to fall, while the proportion of the Muslim community increased, which, among other factors, took place because of the influx from the outside to the Nile Valley because of the settling of the Bedouin population. The percentage of unmarried clergy among Christians still remained high. In thirteenth-century Egypt, there were about fifty Coptic dioceses and ninety monasteries. Additionally, it is believed that in the Christian milieu, artificial birth control and various methods of contraception were practiced. These phenomena have been well studied on the basis of the example of late-medieval Egypt. But if, after the Black Death, birth control was encouraged by poverty and uncertainty about the future, the motives of the Copts in the thirteenth century were quite different: maintaining a high standard of living within a small, close-knit community. The Copts' wealth and their awareness of a special intracommunal solidarity provoked the hostility of their Muslim environment. Under the Mamluks, the demographic balance swung sharply toward the Muslims, ushering in what historians call "the century of persecutions."[186]

The chronological range of this period is defined in different ways. In our view, it is proper to speak of a time period between the reign of Baybars (1260–1277) and the Alexandrian Crusade in 1365. The Christians of the Mamluk state were subjected to a fierce persecution about once every twenty years, which led to a severe crisis in the Coptic and other Christian communities.

In 1283, riots broke out in Cairo motivated by discontent with the dominance of Christian officials. The sultan ordered the secretaries of the diwans to convert to Islam on pain of death, which they did unquestioningly.[187] The figure of an official of Coptic background who converted to Islam in adulthood for career purposes is typical of the Mamluk bureaucracy. In the first third of the fourteenth century, the former Coptic Christians Karim al-Din al-Kabir and al-Nashw reached the upper levels of the administrative hierarchy. Each successively held the post of *nazir al-khassa*, the manager of the sultan's assets, rising to the second highest position in the state. They were executed in 1323 and 1339, respectively, because of the intrigues of the Mamluk oligarchy.[188]

The most famous anti-Christian campaign in the Mamluk state took place in 1301. Under pressure from public opinion, perturbed by the "audacity" and "dominance" of the Christians, Muslim jurists agreed that

> the Nazarenes [i.e., Christians] should be differentiated by wearing blue turbans … and the Jews by wearing yellow turbans … that they do not go on horseback or carry weapons … and cede the middle of the road to Muslims … that they do not raise their voice above the voices of Muslims, do not build buildings above the buildings of Muslims, do not display their palm branches, do not knock the simandron, and do not buy Muslim slaves.[189]

The enforcement of this decree was accompanied by attacks on churches in Cairo, Alexandria, and Fayyum.

In May 1321, in Egypt, a new wave of pogroms were launched against churches and monasteries. On the same day and hour, from Aswan to Damietta, sixty Christian churches were destroyed. The sultan's authorities were powerless to restore order. In the summer of the same year, catastrophic fires were started in Cairo. A few Christians were arrested on charges of arson and confessed under torture to conspiring to take revenge on the Muslims for the recent pogroms.[190]

The decisive blow to the Christian community is considered to be the persecution of 1354, when, in addition to introducing measures for everyday discrimination and closing churches, the authorities confiscated 25,000 feddans (10,000 hectares) of church property.[191] These funds were to go to the construction of a navy and the ransom of Muslim prisoners.[192] The position of the Egyptian Christians was only occasionally eased by the intercession of Byzantine emperors, the kings of Aragon, who had traditional trade and political ties with the Mamluk state, and the emperors of Ethiopia, who threatened to withhold the waters of the Nile from Egypt.[193]

According to some authors, the persecution by the Mamluks led to the same sharp reduction in the number of Christians in Egypt as had the wars of the Crusaders in Syria and Palestine and the anti-Christian persecutions after the conversion of the Hülegü's descendants to Islam in Iran and Mesopotamia in 1295.[194] With the conversion to Islam of the Coptic cultural elite, there came a sharp cultural decline among the remaining part of the Christian community. Literary creativity and iconography ceased and monasteries went extinct.

The Second Crisis of the Christian East

The social and political discrimination against Christians was exacerbated by a crisis in agriculture in the Middle East brought about by environmental factors as well as the expansion of Bedouin tribes. In the thirteenth century, the invasion of nomads, accompanied by the destruction of the irrigation network in the Jazira (Upper Mesopotamia) converted millions of hectares of fertile land in the Euphrates, Khabur, and Balikh basin into pastureland. Agriculture would only be revived in the region in the 1920s. It was in the thirteenth century that Raqqa (Kallinikos), once the favorite residence of the caliphs, which Arab geographers called one of the best parts of the world, was abandoned by its inhabitants.[195] At this time Sergiopolis (Rusafa), a Christian city surrounded by desert and living off the caravan trade, died out.[196] By the thirteenth century, there is mention of the desolation of the Palmyra oasis, where agriculture was maintained through a complex system of underground channels that since then had been abandoned and dried out.[197] About the time of the destruction of Antioch by Baybars, the largest Syrian monastery, Mar Sam'an on the Black Mountain, came to be uninhabited. Transjordan, whose military and strategic importance increased during the Muslims' wars with the Crusaders, again entered into a period of decline and depopulation after the Crusader states were crushed.[198] In a geographic description from 1300, it is reported that "only ruins remain" of Amman.[199] The exodus of the Christian population from Southern Palestine and Transjordan continued under pressure from the desert. The patriarchs gradually lost contact with Christians living in remote mountain and desert areas, and the territory in which church institutions operated continued shrinking.

A similar process of nomadic expansion took place throughout the Anatolian Plateau after Manzikert. Inner Anatolia is equally suited for agriculture and for cattle. Nomadic Turks simply pushed a significant portion of the agricultural population out of the interior valleys and plateaus, which were now converted into pastures. Christians survived only in coastal areas protected by wooded ridges—in Cilicia, Bithynia, and Pontus—as well as in the rocky canyons of Cappadocia. With the destruction of the agricultural way of life, the cities also fell into decline, as they depended on the receipt of products from the rural districts. The subsequent war finished off the Christian population of the cities, which had no place from which to replenish the demographic losses.

Thus, for example, in 1315 the Mamluks seized Malatya and took its entire population into captivity. After that, the metropolitan's see was moved from the city to a monastery located 90 kilometers southeast of Erzincan (Akilisene) and the metropolitan of Malatya himself was appointed by a decision of the Synod of Constantinople to supervise the dioceses of Neocaesarea, Erzincan, and Kemah. This means first of all that in these areas there were no bishops at that time and, second, that there was no longer any possibility for a church hierarchy to exist in the area of Malatya.[200] In 1317, the inhabitants of Amida (Diyabakir) rebelled against the Artuqid emir who ruled Upper Mesopotamia. A punitive expedition killed many of the Christians of Amida, who were led by the Syrian Jacobite bishop, and the cathedral was burned.[201]

Timur's campaigns at the end of the fourteenth century, with their famous scorched-earth tactics and skull pyramids, were a deadly milestone in the fate of Near Eastern Christianity. After that, the Christian population in Southern and Central Mesopotamia disappeared forever. Churches and monasteries were razed, treasure troves of books perished, and cultural traditions were broken. Muslims suffered no less during these disasters (although some of Timur's actions had an emphatic anti-Christian character), but their greater vitality and dominance in the region allowed the Muslim community to regenerate. Even before then, Mesopotamian Christianity had been in a state of serious decline. Throughout the fourteenth century, the Nestorian community diminished and dioceses disappeared even in large cities, such as Baghdad, Tabriz, and Maragha.[202] The Christians who survived Timur's invasion fled north into the mountains between Lakes Van and Urmia. There, among the warlike Kurdish tribes, the Nestorians forgot their old urban culture, regressed in their development, and reverted to an archaic culture.

The Christians of Eastern Anatolia also suffered serious losses. At Timur's order, all the inhabitants of Amida, including the Christians, were burned in an enormous bonfire. In Tur 'Abdin on the watershed of the Tigris and Euphrates, local Christians were hunted down and those hiding in caves were literally smoked out.[203] The Christians of Sivas were killed when the city was captured in 1400. In 1402, Timur ordered all the churches of Erzincan destroyed.[204] Almost all the sees of Eastern Anatolia disappeared from the *Notitia* of the Church of Constantinople during the fourteenth century. The remnants of the Christian population, cut off from the church hierarchy and literary culture, gradually lost their religious traditions and assimilated to the syncretistic beliefs of the Sufi brotherhoods.

Then, during the second half of the fourteenth century, Turkic tribes settled in the "ecological niche" of Anatolian Orthodoxy. At the same time, it seems, there was a continued demographic expansion of Armenians in Eastern Anatolia, who, for some reason, were less affected by the decline gripping the Christian East.[205] The impression is that between the late fourteenth and sixteenth century ecclesiastical jurisdiction over many areas of Eastern Anatolia passed from the Patriarchate of Constantinople to the Patriarchate of Antioch.

An exception to this general backdrop of decline was the rise of a number of Christian urban centers in Transjordan, especially Kerak and Shawbak. Kerak was one of the most important administrative centers of the Mamluk state. Both cities had large Christian populations. Because of this, in 1301 the governor of Kerak even refused to enforce the sultan's decree on the distinctive clothing of *dhimmis*, in as far as they did not need to be differentiated by them.[206] Many Sinaite monks came from Shawbak, including the monastery's bishop Arsenius al-Shawbaki (ca. 1285–1293), who is mentioned in a number of Arabic and Greek colophons.[207] A famous Greco-Arabic Psalter was copied in 1406 by Metropolitan Joachim of Shawbak, commissioned by Sheikh Yuhanna al-Shawbaki.[208] Scholars have even identified a particular Christian medical school of Kerak in the thirteenth and fourteenth centuries, the best representatives of which were authors of medical treatises and court physicians to the Mamluk elites.[209]

Middle Eastern Monasticism of the Mamluk Period

Many monasteries were destroyed during the war between the Muslims and the Crusaders. In 1183 the Orthodox monastery on Mount Tabor was attacked and the same befell the Monastery of St Euthymius in 1187.[210] As a Muslim spiritual challenge to the monasteries of the Judean Desert, the sultans established in that region the Sufi lodge of Nabi Musa. During its construction, several dozen nearby monastic cells were destroyed. Baybars transferred to its endowment vast lands in the Jordan Valley, which, as it seems, previously belonged to Christian monasteries. Other villages, granted to Mar Saba by the Kingdom of Jerusalem, are also mentioned in documents of the fourteenth century as being Muslim endowments.[211] Thus, many monasteries lost their land holdings in Palestine and were now dependent on alms coming from Christian countries.

The number of monasteries in the Judean Desert steadily decreased. After the twelfth century, there is no mention of the Monastery of St John Chrysostom by Jericho. The latest evidence for the existence of the Lavra of St Chariton is from an Arabic manuscript copied there in 1223. Over the ruins of the Monastery of Kalamon grew, in the twelfth century, the Arab village of Hajla, which was later abandoned under pressure from the Bedouins. It seems that St Sava of Serbia in the 1230s was the last of the pilgrims and writers who visited and endowed the Monasteries of St Theodosius and St Euthymius. In the 1370s the Russian Archimandrite Agrefeny found only ruins on the site of the Lavra of St Theodosius. He is also the last to mention the Monastery of Koziba. The Monastery of St Gerasimus, still active at the time of Ignatius of Smolensk's pilgrimage in 1395, was abandoned by the time the next Russian monk, Zosima, visited Palestine in

1420–1421. Around the same time, if not before, the monastery on the Mountain of Temptation vanished. Zosima was the last to visit the Monastery of St John the Baptist, the largest in the Jordan Valley; later pilgrims in the 1480s describe it as a bandits' lair.[212]

The last monastery remaining in the desert was Mar Saba, which long played an important role in the Patriarchate of Jerusalem. The Lavra had metochia in Jerusalem and other parts of Palestine and even abroad. In some sources, the Lavra's abbot appears as a figure almost equal to the patriarch.[213]

The reduction of the Christian population of Palestine meant that in place of monks of Arab origin there came an increasing number of monks from the Balkans and the Caucasus. As a result, the monasteries lost their Arab character and were "uprooted" from the local soil.[214]

In general, Middle Eastern monasticism of the Mamluk era is distinguished by its exceptional ethnic diversity. Here we can see a certain symbiosis among Greeks, Arabs, Georgians, and Slavs that is best represented in the Monastery of St Catherine on Mount Sinai. The monks of Sinai produced hundreds of manuscripts in whose colophons appear Arabs from Egypt, Palestine, Transjordan, and Syria, as well as Greeks from Asia Minor, the islands, and other regions.[215] The most famous of the monks of St Catherine during the Mamluk era, Gregory the Sinaite (1275–1346), a Greek from Smyrna, was one of the founders of Byzantine hesychasm.[216] Among the brothers of Sinai, there were compact groups of Serbian and Georgian monks.[217]

The monasteries of the Judean Desert had the same international flavor. In this case, the Arab element in the milieu of Palestinian monasticism had grown noticeably weaker. In contrast to the single known Arabic manuscript from Mar Saba during the thirteenth to the fifteenth centuries, copied in 1247, eleven Greek manuscripts have been preserved, copied by monks of Mar Saba, as well as a lengthy colophon written in Greek by the abbot Ioannicius in 1334. Even Greek poet-theologians were living in the monastery at the turn of the thirteenth to the fourteenth century, perhaps including Nilus, author of the poetic diptychs of the Church of Jerusalem. Additionally, in his *Pilgrimage*, St Sava of Serbia mentions groups of Georgian and Russian monks among the brethren of Mar Saba.[218]

On the basis of extant manuscripts of the thirteenth and fourteenth centuries from the Monastery of St John the Theologian, it is possible to draw a conclusion about the mixed Greek and Arab composition of its inhabitants.[219]

Of all the monks of foreign origin in the Holy Land during the Ayyubid and Mamluk periods, the most prominent are the Georgians. The Mamluk elite, which was largely of Caucasian origin, was interested in maintaining friendly relations with Georgia, from which came the main flow of slaves to replenish the Mamluk army. Additionally, in the twelfth and thirteenth centuries, Georgia was a fairly serious force to be reckoned with among the states of Asia Minor. Georgian kings actively patronized Palestinian Orthodoxy and donated large sums to the Georgian monasteries and pilgrimage infrastructure of the Holy Land. According to testimony from the thirteenth century, magnificent caravans of Georgian pilgrims were allowed to pass to Jerusalem free of duty by the Muslim authorities.[220]

Georgia's alliance with the Mongols in the second half of the thirteenth century, however, greatly complicated the situation of Georgians in Palestine. Around 1268 or 1269, the Sultan Baybars turned the Georgian Monastery of the Holy Cross into a Sufi lodge (*zawiya*). The monastery's abbot, Luke, attempted to protest and was killed. It was only after the end of the series of wars between the Mamluks and the Mongols that the Egyptian sultan, yielding to requests from Georgian and Byzantine embassies in 1305–1306 or 1310–1311, returned the monastery to the Georgians and revoked a number of discriminatory measures directed at Christians.[221]

In the fourteenth century, the Georgians founded or restored many monasteries in and around Jerusalem, including the Monasteries of St Thekla, St Catherine, St Basil the Great, St Nicholas, St John the Evangelist on Mount Sion, St Demetrius, and others. The monasteries owned considerable properties, including several villages. The Georgian kings founded the village of Malk and populated it with Georgian colonists who were to support and maintain the monasteries. Later, the villagers were assimilated to their Arab environment and converted to Islam.[222]

Alongside the Georgians, the Serbian monastic community played an increasingly prominent role in Palestine. With his visits to the Middle East, Sava Nemanjić inaugurated an era of close contacts between the South Slavs and the Patriarchate of Jerusalem. Hierarchs of the Serbian Church, some of whom, like Sava, also visited the Holy Land, attempted to transfer the liturgical and monastic tradition of Palestine onto Balkan soil and even imitated the architectural motifs of churches and monasteries of the Holy Land in their church construction. In the early fourteenth century, the Serbian King Stefan Uroš II founded the Monastery of the Archangel Michael in Jerusalem and populated it with Slavic monks. Subsequent rulers of Serbia consistently patronized the Serbian monastic community of Jerusalem. It held one of the most influential places among the Christian communities of the Holy City and, in particular, had its own altar at the Church of the Holy Sepulchre. The destruction of Serbian statehood in the middle of the fourteenth century seems to have had no effect on the Serbian presence in the Holy Land. Although the Monastery of the Archangel was left desolate for some time because of the plague, it was repopulated by Serbs in 1479, and around 1504 Serbs occupied the empty Mar Saba.[223]

The Melkites and Byzantium

Although monasticism in the Holy Land during the Mamluk period was predominantly of non-Arab origin and parish priests were undoubtedly Arab, the ethnic composition of the upper hierarchy of the Church of Jerusalem is less clear. Many historians (Chrysostomos Papadopoulos, Steven Runciman, Joseph Nasrallah) assume a priori that the patriarchs and bishops of Mamluk Palestine were Arabs who bore Greek names only as a matter of tradition.[224] This claim goes back to the historical writings of seventeenth-century Patriarch of Jerusalem Dositheos Notaras and is not supported by sufficient evidence.

The names of the patriarchs of Jerusalem from the thirteenth to the fifteenth centuries are known but, as Richard B. Rose correctly remarks, we do not know whether these people spoke Greek, Arabic, or Syriac and, more generally, whether it would have been of any significance during this era.[225] On the other hand, the Church of Jerusalem had a close relationship with Byzantium, to the point that some patriarchs of the fourteenth century were installed and deposed by the decision of the Synod of Constantinople and the emperors. The patriarchs of Jerusalem often visited Byzantium and lived there for years. It can be argued with a high degree of confidence that a number of patriarchs of Jerusalem were of Greek origin or belonged to Greek-speaking culture and maintained close ties with Byzantium. Additionally, some primates of the Holy City most likely did come from an Arab milieu.

Patriarch Gregory I of Jerusalem (before 1274–1291) was actively involved in the ecclesio-political struggle in Byzantium after the Union of Lyon in 1274. The patriarch acted as a mediator in negotiations between Bulgaria and Egypt for an alliance against Emperor Michael Palaeologus, the union's initiator. Although the planned alliance was never formed, Gregory for his own part denounced Michael's church policy and prompted the Byzantine theologian George Moschobar to compose a treatise against the Latins.[226] Gregory's successor, Patriarch Sophronius (1291–1303), was probably of Egyptian Arab origin.[227]

When Patriarch Athanasius III (1303–1316), during an absence from Palestine around 1308, was deposed through the intrigues of a member of the Palestinian clergy, Gabriel Vroulas, he submitted a complaint to the Byzantine emperor and the Synod of Constantinople. The emperor's envoys who were sent to Palestine to verify the allegations leveled against Athanasius deposed him in absentia and elevated Gabriel to the patriarchate. Athanasius was only able to regain his see by appearing before the emperor in person and convincing him of his cause.[228] This episode provides a vivid illustration of the strength of the ties and the degree of dependence of the clergy of Jerusalem on Byzantium at that time.

However, the next patriarch, Gregory II (ca. 1316–1334), was elected by the local clergy and the patriarch of Constantinople was simply informed of this by his letter. An Arabic note by the patriarch from 1322 appears in an old Greek gospel book.[229] Someone who wrote in Arabic in the margins of a Greek book clearly had to have been an Arab.

The greatest figure in the history of the Church of Jerusalem in the fourteenth century was Patriarch Lazarus. Elected to the patriarchate by the Palestinian clergy around 1334, he went to Constantinople to be confirmed and officially consecrated. Lazarus's rival Gerasimus also went to the capital of the empire and made various accusations against Lazarus, and so an imperial embassy was sent to Jerusalem to investigate. As the trial dragged on, Emperor Andronicus III died in 1341 and a civil war broke out in Byzantium between John Cantacuzenus and John V Palaeologus. Lazarus involved himself in these events on the side of Cantacuzenus, and in May 1346, he crowned him emperor. After that, Patriarch of Constantinople John Kalekas, a supporter of Palaeologus, deposed Lazarus and installed in his place Gerasimus, who departed to Jerusalem. With the triumph of Cantacuzenus in February 1347, the Byzantine government sent an embassy to the Egyptian Sultan Nasir al-Din Hasan requesting Lazarus's reinstatement on the See of Jerusalem. Gerasimus arrived in Cairo in the fall of 1439, hoping to win the Mamluk authorities over to his side, but he died suddenly and so the question of Lazarus's return resolved itself.

During the persecution of Christians in the Mamluk state in 1354, Patriarch Lazarus was taken to Cairo, where he was thrown into prison and subject to beatings. He was arrested once again after the attack on Alexandria by the King of Cyprus in October 1365. By the autumn of 1366 the persecution ceased, partially thanks to the diplomatic intervention of the Byzantine Emperor John V Palaeologus. Lazarus was allowed to go to Constantinople as part of a Mamluk embassy. The signatures of the patriarch of Jerusalem are found on several synodal acts of the Church of Constantinople from 1367 to 1368.[230]

In Lazarus's entourage in the mid-1360s was the Greek adventurer Paul Tagaris, who entered into the patriarch's trust to such a degree that he was appointed *locum tenens* of the See of Jerusalem during Lazarus's absence in Constantinople, and he later laid his claim for the patriarchate.[231]

Patriarch Dorotheus, who headed the Church of Jerusalem for nearly four decades in the late fourteenth and early fifteenth centuries, exemplifies the dual identity of the Middle Eastern Melkites. Several Greek manuscripts copied by the patriarch survive with Greek colophons, one of which is duplicated in Arabic. After Dorotheus, the patriarchate was inherited by his son Theophilus (before 1419–ca. 1424), which indicated the existence of clerical dynasties in the Palestinian Melkite milieu, such as those that existed among the Nestorians, the Maronites, and the Antiochian Orthodox.[232] An Arabic colophon by a certain Jirjis al-Qudsi (i.e., "the Jerusalemite") referred to himself as the nephew of Patriarch Theophilus, which gives reason to believe that Dorotheus and Theophilus were Arabs, albeit deeply integrated into Greek culture.[233]

The Russian pilgrim Zosima, who conversed with Theophilius in 1421, noted that "the priest Akim" who was in the patriarch's entourage, "has a command of both Arabic and Greek, is most beloved by the patriarch, [and] he wants to be one after him."[234] It seems that the dream of the "priest Akim" came true: apparently this is Patriarch Joachim who headed the Church of Jerusalem in the years 1426–1463.[235] There also survives an Arabic-language colophon by Joachim,[236] suggesting that the patriarch was of an Arab background.

In the entourage of the primate of Jerusalem, there were many Greeks as well as Arabs who left their names in manuscript colophons from the thirteenth to the fifteenth centuries.[237] In general, bilingualism and even trilingualism was a common phenomenon among Middle Eastern clergy. More than fifty Greco-Arabic and four Greco-Syriac manuscripts survived from the Mamluk period, and the number of Arabic notes in Greek manuscripts can hardly be counted.[238] Taking into account the characteristic linguistic and cultural pride of the Byzantines, it is appropriate to assume that the majority of bilingual Melkites were Arabs, not Greeks.

In the neighboring Patriarchate of Antioch, Greek influence was not so clearly apparent. For several decades after Baybars's sacking of Antioch, the patriarchs of the city changed their residence and political orientation many times. The patriarchate's territory was divided among rival states—the Mamluk Sultanate, the possessions of the Crusaders, and Cilician Armenia. Byzantium continued to exert a strong influence on the Middle East. Different political patrons (Byzantium, Armenia, the Crusaders) put in place successive first hierarchs of Antioch, and from time to time, schisms occurred on this basis when conflicting candidates for the see were put forward in various parts of the patriarchate.

Euthymius I (before 1258–1277) was admitted into Antioch by Prince Bohemond and then driven out several times. Over the years, the patriarch enjoyed the hospitality of Michael VIII in Constantinople and the Hülegüid Abaqa Khan in Tabriz. After the fall of Antioch, he stayed in Cilicia, one of the few areas of his patriarchate that remained under Christian rule. There, Euthymius was involved in a conspiracy of Orthodox nobility against King Levon of Cilicia, and as a result, was thrown into prison in 1275, although he managed to escape to Constantinople. The patriarch remained in the Byzantine capital until his death. Severely ill, he summoned several Antiochian bishops to Constantinople to elect his successor. Michael Palaeologus, however, preferred for the see a Constantino-politan monk of Frankish noble background, Theodosius de Villehardouin, who seemed more appropriate for his ecclesiastical policy of rapprochement with the West.[239]

After the Union of Lyon was rejected in Byzantium in 1282, Theodosius moved to the Crusaders' Syrian territory. He was succeeded in 1283–1284 by Arsenius, who previously was the bishop of Tripoli. After the death of Arsenius around 1286, on June 29, 1287, the bishops of the Syrian cities belonging to the Crusaders elected Cyril, the bishop of Tyre, as patriarch without the consent of the other bishops of the patriarchate. In turn, the bishops of Cilician Armenia proclaimed Dionysius, bishop of Cilician Pompeiopolis, to be patriarch, but Dio-nysius soon gave up the fight. Cyril arrived in Constantinople in the autumn of 1288, but for many years, he could not obtain official recognition from the Byzantine authorities, as for them he was associated with the Latin Crusaders. He was added to the diptychs of the Church of Constantinople only in 1296. Some authors attribute this change of attitude toward Cyril to the marriage of Emperor Michael IX and Princess Maria of Cilician Armenia. Recognizing Cyril was a friendly gesture by Constantinople toward the Cilician and other Antio-chian bishops. If this conclusion holds true, then it would follow that the bishops of Cilicia, including Dionysius, were loyal to Cyril. In such case, it is a misconcep-tion on the part of Joseph Nasrallah to call Dionysius an "antipatriarch" during the years from 1287 to 1308.[240] The fall of the last Crusader states in Syria appears to have further strengthened the position of the Cilician bishops of the patriarch-ate. After the death of Cyril around 1308, Dionysius renewed his claims to the patriarchate. This time he was recognized by the Byzantine emperor and the ecumenical patriarch. Sometime after 1310, Dionysisus also moved to Constanti-nople, where he died in 1316.[241]

Patriarch Dionysius II, previously bishop of Mopsuestia, similarly to Dio-nysius I, was the protégé of the bishops of Cilician Armenia, where he resided during his patriarchate (late 1310s–1322). Before his death, he chose Sophronius, bishop of Tyre, to be his successor. Sophronius was recognized as patriarch in

Cilicia; however, the bishops of Southern Syria, taking advantage of the weakened ties with Cilician Armenia, elected as their own patriarch the metropolitan of Damascus, Abu al-Najm al-Arshi, and until his death, the Church of Antioch was in a state of schism.[242]

Byzantine influence once again became prominent from the 1340s to the 1370s, during the era of the debates over hesychasm. In 1344 Ignatius, an Armenian by origin—probably of a Chalcedonian Armenian background—was elected patriarch of Antioch. He arrived in Constantinople to receive approval and became involved in the ideological and political struggle around hesychasm and the teaching of Gregory Palamas.[243] Ignatius sided with Patriarch of Constantinople John Kalekas, an opponent of the Palamites. The Hodegon Monastery in Constantinople, where Ignatius and his associate Metropolitan Arsenius of Tyre stayed, became a center of anti-Palamite polemics. Around the end of 1345 or early 1346, Ignatius returned to the East, leaving Arsenius as his representative in Constantinople. With the victory of John Cantacuzenus in the internal conflict within Byzantium in 1347, the position of hesychasm within the empire was greatly strengthened. The church council of 1351 definitively condemned the anti-Palamite views. Arsenius of Tyre attempted to challenge the council's decisions before the emperor, but then he left Constantinople. Patriarch Ignatius at first accepted the decisions of the council but later, apparently under the influence of Arsenius, he once again took an anti-Palamite position.

In the second half of the 1350s, Ignatius was deposed by part of the clergy of Antioch who were oriented toward Constantinople and the Palamites. Pachomius, the metropolitan of Damascus, was proclaimed the new patriarch. Ignatius moved to Cyprus, under the protection of the ruling Lusignan dynasty. On Cyprus, there was a significant community of Melkites from the Syro-Palestinian region. There, under the auspices of the Latin authorities, a circle of Byzantine intellectuals was formed with a pro-Catholic, anti-Palamite orientation. The correspondence of Patriarch Callistus of Constantinople with the Antiochian clergy in the years from 1360 to 1361 indicates that in Byzantium, Pachomius, a supporter of the hesychasts, was considered to be the legitimate patriarch of Antioch. Starting with Pachomius, the residence of the patriarchates of Antioch came to be in Damascus.[244]

An extensive correspondence survives between Patriarch Philotheos Kokkinos of Constantinople (second patriarchate in 1365–1376) with the clergy of Antioch. They discussed a wide range of issues, from attitudes toward hesychasm and the project of reconciliation with the Catholic Church to the canonical offenses of the abbot of Hodegon Monastery, the Antiochian metochion in the capital.[245] After the Mamluk persecution of 1365–1366, which financially ruined the Orthodox Church in the Middle East, Eastern bishops for the first time went to Russia seeking alms. Russian sources mention the arrival in 1371 of a Metropolitan Germanus from Egypt or Palestine, and in 1375–1376, Archimandrite Niphon from the Monastery of the Archangel in Jerusalem and a Metropolitan Mark, who was erroneously associated by them with the Monastery of Sinai. In fact, Mark seems to have come from the Patriarchate of Antioch. It is very likely that he can be identified with Patriarch Mark of Antioch (1376–1378).[246]

After Philotheus Kokkinos, contact between Constantinople and Damascus rapidly diminished. Only occasional evidence of the exchange of letters is preserved. For example, in 1395, Patriarch of Antioch Michael II expressed his support for hesychast doctrine through his ambassador in Constantinople.[247]

The Church of Alexandria occupied a marginal position in the Orthodox East and rarely figures in the sources. Nevertheless, there are sufficient grounds to speak of its mixed Greek–Arabic character and to speculate that its relationship with the Greek world was closer than that of Jerusalem or Damascus.

Because of the small number of Alexandrian clergy, most patriarchs for that see were chosen from among the monks of Sinai, which was another channel of Greek influence. Sometimes, Byzantine church officials purposely sought to bring the liturgical practices and church traditions of the East closer to Greek models. Thus, the greatest Byzantine canonist of the turn of the twelfth to the thirteenth century, Theodore Balsamon, who during the years 1185–1203 nominally occupied the See of Antioch, not only implemented this harmonization in his own Antiochian church but also sought to influence Patriarch Mark II of Alexandria. Mark, who was consecrated in Constantinople, upon arrival in Egypt discovered many customs and rituals common among the Egyptian Melkites that were unusual to him, and so he turned to Balsamon with a number of queries about the permissibility of such traditions.[248]

The Alexandrian primate, Nicholas II, was elected in 1263 under an agreement between the Sultan Baybars and Emperor Michael Palaeologus to fill the See of Alexandria. Soon, however, the patriarch was in Byzantium, where he supported Patriarch Arsenius of Constantinople in his conflict with Michael Palaeologus, motivated by his attitude toward the Union of Lyon. Nicholas's successor Athanasius II (1276–1308/1315), who was elected to the patriarchate from the ranks of the monks of Sinai, also quickly moved to Constantinople, where he lived for more than thirty years. This patriarch was even more involved in the political and ideological confrontation between supporters and opponents of the union; however, with rare skill, he was able to hold an intermediate position on the issue so as to not be persecuted in the event of changes in the political situation. The patriarch's wily resourcefulness allowed him to remain "afloat" for decades, wrote Alexei Lebedev, "the patriarch continued to live in the capital without the troubles that overwhelmed overt supporters and opponents of union."[249]

Athanasius, who was fully absorbed with Byzantine church politics and forgot about his Egyptian flock, is rather an exception among the patriarchs of Alexandria. His successors, as a rule, lived in Egypt and some of them were even Arabs or surrounded themselves with Arab clergy.[250] Thus, Patriarch Gregory II (1315?–before 1335), also a former Sinaite, translated the Typicon of Mar Saba into Arabic.[251] On the territory of Egypt several church manuscripts from the fourteenth and fifteenth centuries were produced, both in Greek and in Arabic.[252] The last Arab patriarch of Alexandria was Gregory V, born in Bostra. In a note in a manuscript on Sinai, his disciple Joachim al-Karaki reports Gregory's death in 1503, after twenty-three years of rule.[253] This, however, is contrary to the dating established in the scholarship for Patriarch Gregory's successor, Joachim I, which is counted from 1486/1487.

The Athenian Joachim Pany ("The Glorious") is a truly epic figure. This man is believed to have lived 116 years and for almost 80 of them led the Church of Alexandria. Even during his own lifetime, legends were told about him and miracles attributed to him. The most famous of these legends recount that the ruler of Egypt, who can be identified with the Mamluk sultans Qaitbay (1468–1496) or Qansuh al-Ghawri (1501–1516), at the instigation of his Jewish advisors planned to exterminate the Christians under his rule. Joachim was invited to debate with the Jews in the presence of the sultan. The patriarch was ordered to prove the truth of his faith by working a miracle: moving a mountain. The patriarch, along with all the Christians, prayed and fasted for three days. The Theotokos appeared to him in a dream and pointed him to a righteous man, a one-eyed shoemaker, whose prayer would be heard in heaven. On the appointed day, the patriarch together with the shoemaker commanded the mountain to move, and it split into three parts. Then the Jewish sage suggested a new test to Joachim: the patriarch had to drink a cup of poison to confirm the words of the Gospel that those with faith can drink deadly poison without harm. The patriarch managed to make the sign of the cross imperceptibly over the cup and drank the poison, which miraculously went out from him from below his ribs. Rinsing the bowl out with water, the patriarch then gave it to the Jewish scribe to drink, who then died a horrible death. The sultan, convinced of Joachim's holiness, gave the Christians all sorts of benefits and favors. He then supposedly converted to Christianity and ended his days in the Sinai desert.[254]

The legend of the one-eyed shoemaker moving the mountain is a wandering literary topos; it is found in Marco Polo and Old Russian Menaia of the thirteenth century.[255] The theme of a Christian bishop harmlessly drinking poison is also found in the literature from the sixth century. Nevertheless, the legend of the miracle performed by Joachim is naturally interspersed with real information reflecting the competition between Christians and Jews to influence the Mamluk authorities in the late fourteenth and early fifteenth centuries, as well as, possibly, an attempted poisoning of the patriarch.

The Shadow of the West

In the first half of the fourteenth century, the Melkites of Syria and Palestine were involved in the attempt to unite the churches, culminating in the Council of Florence in 1439. Middle Eastern bishops did not demonstrate their own initiative in this matter and did not attend the council, instead delegating their powers to members of the Byzantine clergy. The representative of Patriarch Dorotheus of Antioch was Isidore, Metropolitan of Kiev; that of Patriarch Joachim of Jerusalem, Metropolitan Dorotheus of Monembasia; and that of Philotheus of Alexandria, Metropolitan Antonius of Heraclium.[256]

The decisions of the Council of Florence provoked an outcry in Byzantine society, as well as among the Orthodox of the Middle East. In April 1443, on the initiative of Metropolitan Arsenius of Caesarea in Cappadocia who had arrived in the Holy City, the three Eastern patriarchs gathered in Jerusalem and denounced the union and its advocate, Patriarch Metrophanes of Constantinople. The correspondence of Patriarch of Constantinople Gennadius Scholarius with the monks of Sinai in the mid-1450s also indicates the strong anti-Latin sentiment among Middle Eastern monastics.[257]

At the same time, after the fall of Constantinople and the destruction of other Orthodox states of the Balkan and Black Sea region, the Middle Eastern patriarchs were faced with the need to find new political and financial backers. In August 1456, the papal legate Moïse Giblet was sent to the Middle East with the aim of strengthening Rome's position in the region on the eve of a planned crusade by European sovereigns against the Ottomans. Giblet held talks on cooperation with the emir of the Gharb region in Southern Lebanon and met with Patriarch Michael III of Antioch, whom he invited to renew a union with Rome. From Syria, the legate went to Egypt, where he discussed similar issues with Patriarch Mark of Alexandria, and then settled in Cyprus, from which he conducted a correspondence with the Eastern patriarchs. Coming to the throne of Antioch at the end of 1456, Patriarch Mark III yielded to Giblet's urgings and in February 1457 established a commemoration of the pope in the Church of Antioch and began corresponding with Rome. Mark III died around late 1457 or early 1458, and then Joachim III, former bishop of Hama and a longtime supporter of the union, became Patriarch of Antioch. In June 1458, he arrived in Palestine and met with Patriarch Joachim of Jerusalem and Patriarch Mark of Alexandria in the village of Rama or Ramallah. The patriarch of Jerusalem succumbed to the persistent entreaties of his colleagues and joined the union.[258]

Shortly thereafter, in November 1458, the dome of the Church of the Resurrection cracked during an earthquake. At considerable cost, Joachim secured permission from the authorities to restore the dome. However, as the work was nearing completion, Muslim jurists decided to revise their decision and ordered that the restored areas be destroyed. The costs of litigation and the expenses of reconstruction fully depleted the patriarch of Jerusalem's coffers.[259] Obviously hoping for financial support from the Catholic West, in May and June 1459, Joachim signed a letter of the Eastern patriarchs urging the princes of Europe to undertake a crusade, as well as sending a message on his own behalf to the pope.

Having received authority as the representative of the Eastern patriarchs and the emir of Gharb, Moïse Giblet sailed to Italy and on April 21, 1460, signed a pact of union with Rome on behalf of the Eastern patriarchs. In commemoration of this event, the pope ordered translated into Latin the patriarchs' Arabic documents related to their acceptance of the union. These texts were merged into the codex *Liber Rubeus*, which was preserved in the Vatican archives.

Already by the seventeenth century, scholars were questioning the authenticity of the contents of the *Liber Rubeus*. Indeed, false emissaries purporting to be from various Eastern rulers are known to have arrived in Rome in the second half of the fifteenth century with offers of a military alliance against the Turks and even ecclesiastical union. These missions were organized by adventurers from within the papal entourage for propaganda purposes or their own benefit. Arabic sources do not confirm the existence in the 1450s of patriarchs Mark and Joachim of Antioch. The debate about the authenticity of Giblet's embassy and the union of 1458 has continued into modern times and is far from having been resolved.[260]

However, even if we consider the union of the three patriarchs with Rome to have actually taken place, it is clear that the patriarchs, especially Joachim of Jerusalem, soon realized the futility of hoping for aid from the Catholic world. Joachim realized that he needed to look for patrons elsewhere and appealed to the grand prince of Moscow for support. The patriarch personally left to seek alms in Russia, but along the way, in Caffa, he fell ill and died in late 1463 or early 1464. Before his death, he sent a message to Moscow describing the adversity facing the Church of Jerusalem and requesting help. The letter was delivered by his nephew Joseph who, in accordance with the late patriarch's will, was consecrated metropolitan of Caesarea Philippi by the metropolitan of Moscow and was sent home with lavish gifts. The event of a journey to Russia by the patriarch of Jerusalem was extensively utilized by the Muscovite ecclesiastical hierarchy and scribes and it became one of the elements shaping the concept of Russian messianism.[261]

Middle Eastern churches, however, remained willing to accept alms from any benefactor. The monks of the Monastery of Sinai, who were revered far beyond the Orthodox world, were the most broad-minded. According to some accounts, the monastery had chapels for the Syrian Jacobites, the Armenians, and the Copts. The monastery of Sinai received lavish alms from aristocrats and rulers of European countries. Thus, in the late fifteenth century, the monastery was granted annual subsidies from King Louis XI of France, Queen Isabella of Spain, and Emperor Maximilian I. Considerable sums were donated by pilgrims. In the fifteenth century, the monastery designated a special cell and, later, a chapel dedicated to St Catherine, to be used by pilgrims for Latin-rite services. Such friendly relations between the Monastery of Sinai and Catholic Europe were a unique phenomenon in the late medieval world. At the same time, in terms of dogma and ritual, the monks of Sinai remained in the bosom of Orthodox tradition, something emphasized by all Western observers. It is known in particular that the Sinaites sought the views of Patriarch of Constantinople Gennadius Scholarius (1454–1456) as to whether it was permissible to offer prayers for the king of Bosnia who sent the monastery gifts but held a pro-Catholic orientation.[262]

The Flemish chronicler of the late fifteenth century, Theodoric Pauli, wrote that Duke Philip of Burgundy provided annual assistance to the Church of Jerusalem and renovated the Church of the Holy Sepulchre with the sultan's consent.[263] Once again, however, this assistance did not affect the doctrinal views of the patriarchs of Jerusalem.

In 1484, Patriarch Symeon of Constantinople held a church council at which the Orthodox Church definitively rejected the Union of Florence and approved a rite of reception of Catholics into Orthodoxy, designed to maximally facilitate the return of Greeks living in territories conquered by the Ottomans from the Latins, to the faith of their fathers. Although some copies of the council's acts refer to the participation of all the Middle Eastern patriarchs in the work of the council, this assertion seems implausible. It is more correct to assume that the Sees of Alexandria and Jerusalem were represented by exarchs from among the bishops of the Church of Constantinople.[264]

An Intermediate Epilogue

Our understanding of the dynamics of the development of the Palestinian Orthodox community under the Mamluks is extremely scanty. However, through the fragmentary data provided by the sources, a picture emerges of an acutely deepening crisis in Middle Eastern Christianity at the turn of the fifteenth to the sixteenth century.

Under pressure from the Bedouins, the Christian population left Shawbak. The Christian quarter of Hebron disappeared.[265] Monasteries died out, including the Monastery of St John the Evangelist by the Jordan, which was turned into a lair of Bedouin bandits.[266] In the late fourteenth and early fifteenth centuries, pilgrims counted between fifteen and thirty monks at the Monastery of Mar Saba, but by the end of the fifteenth century, something on the order of five or six remained and at the turn of the fifteenth to the sixteenth century, the Lavra had been abandoned by the monks for some time under onslaught from the Bedouins.[267] Pilgrims visiting Sinai in the fourteenth century spoke of hundreds of inhabitants in the Monastery of St Catherine (the most modest figures are between 200 and 240 people), whereas in the first half of the fifteenth century, there were only fifty to sixty and in the second half of the same century, only thirty to fifty. Finally, the traveler Arnold von Harff found only eight people there in 1497. After 1498, any mention of bishops of Sinai disappears for sixty years.[268]

The Sultan Qansuh al-Ghawri, ruling at the sunset of the Mamluk era, was indifferent to religious matters, but public opinion in Egypt was hostile to non-Muslim minorities, who faced severe discrimination. This situation was exacerbated by the state's financial problems, which authorities tried to resolve partially through an extraordinary taxation of *dhimmis*. Portuguese expansion in the Indian Ocean, which undermined Egypt's foreign trade, caused a hardening of attitudes toward Christians, especially those from the West. In a letter to the pope of Rome in 1503, the Mamluk sultan threatened to destroy the Christian holy places of Palestine and Sinai. The Church of the Holy Sepulchre was closed during the years 1511–1512.

Fifteen letters sent by Qansuh al-Ghawri to the Monastery of St Catherine on Mount Sinai have been preserved. Most of these decrees formally confirm the monastery's traditional privileges: the duty-free delivery of goods through Egyptian ports, the free passage of pilgrims and the monastery's alms collectors, and the inviolability of the monastery's endowment properties in various parts of the sultanate. From these documents, however, it can be seen that in times of crisis in the Mamluk state, the authorities were unable to protect from attack remote metochia or even the monastery itself, which was captured and sacked by Bedouins around 1505. The abbot attempted to persuade the Bedouins to return stolen property, but they killed him and, so far as we can determine, the authorities failed to punish those responsible.[269]

The reasons for this decline of the Orthodox East are not entirely clear. A number of explanations could be put forward, from the general environmental crisis in the region of Syria and Palestine to the establishment of Portuguese hegemony over the South Seas. Naturally, not only did the crisis affect the Orthodox but also, by the end of the fifteenth century, only one monk was left in each of the enormous Coptic monasteries, and Nestorian monasteries had disappeared completely. In the last third of the fifteenth and beginning of the sixteenth centuries, the Mamluk state experienced a severe decline and clearly was losing in the conflict with its nomadic periphery.

Another important factor is that around the turn of the century, there was a certain disorganization in the ecclesiastical and social structures of the Arab–Christian world and its acute weakening. As a result, the ecclesio-political vacuum was filled by immigrants from the more viable Orthodox communities of the Balkans. In 1504, Serbs populated the Monastery of Mar Saba. At the turn of the fifteenth to the sixteenth century, with amazing synchronicity, the Greeks gained control of the Patriarchate of Alexandria and of the Monastery of Sinai, and later, the Church of Jerusalem.

The blows suffered by the Middle Eastern Orthodox churches during the first nine hundred years of Muslim rule led to a significant reduction in their flocks, their territory, and the number of their dioceses.

This waning of ecclesiastical structures affected the Patriarchate of Alexandria most of all. For the entire period from the seventh through the fifteenth centuries, we know the names of a few more than a dozen diocesan bishops. The sources from the ninth through the thirteenth centuries mention around six sees. The number of dioceses constantly decreased: in the ninth century, there were about three; in the fourteenth century, no more than two; and by the fifteenth century, all but one had disappeared apart from the patriarchal see. The consecration of the patriarch of Alexandria came to be performed by neighboring Eastern patriarchs outside Egypt. The Orthodox population in Egypt was small and continued to decline. From around three hundred thousand people at the time of the Arab conquest of Egypt (around 5 percent of the total population of Egyptian Christians), the Melkite community decreased to around ninety thousand by the beginning of the thirteenth century and to just a few thousand in the Ottoman period.[270]

Toward the end of the sixth century, the Patriarchate of Alexandria consisted of 151 episcopal sees, including seventeen metropolitans. For the tenth and eleventh centuries, we know the names of the bishops for about a dozen sees. There is relatively complete information on the number of dioceses in the Church of Alexandria starting from the fourteenth and fifteenth centuries. Their number does not exceed fifteen to twenty. Many ancient archdioceses had entirely disappeared, including Hieropolis (Manbij), Anazarbus, Seleucia Isauria, Sergiopolis, Dara, and Samosata.[271] In Byzantine times, there were around sixty sees in the Patriarchate of Jerusalem, whereas at the beginning of the Ottoman era there were no more than three. Many cities that previously had been diocesan centers simply ceased to exist, especially those along the Mediterranean coast, which had been ravaged by the wars between the Mamluks and the Crusaders, and Transjordan, which was most effected by the consequences of the ecological crisis and desertification. In many other areas where urban life still flickered, the Christian population disappeared.

Thus, to sum up the first nine centuries of the life of the Christian East under Muslim rule, it should be noted that the flourishing of Middle Eastern Christians in the first century AH was replaced by a progressive crisis, a worsening in the social situation of Christians, a reduction in their numbers, and cultural decline. These processes reached their peak in the Mamluk Sultanate, which came to be replaced by a new type of state, largely foreign to them—the Ottoman Empire, to which the fate of Middle Eastern Christians became inextricably bound for the next four centuries.

CHAPTER 2

The Political Context: The Ottoman
State and the Orthodox Church

The fate of the nomadic tribe of Caspian shepherds, who amidst the alarm of an invasion of millions of Mongols, appear in the history of the East as the chosen people of the god of war astounds the mind of the observer. Their military exploits at the time when this small tribe was creating its political greatness is worthy of the finest pages from the history of Ancient Rome. . . . After the capture of Constantinople they hastily contracted all the diseases of political frailty, but in the pride of the conqueror renounced civil law and the science of government, foreign to their ancestral instinct.

—Konstantin M. Bazili, 1847

THE OTTOMANS AND THE ORTHODOX: A DIALOGUE BEGINS

The history of Orthodox Christianity in the Middle East in the sixteenth to eighteenth centuries cannot be properly understood without reference to the history of the Ottoman Empire. Of course, this relationship was not as close as the association between ecclesiastical and political history in any of the Christian states. The Ottoman world was characterized by a high degree of segregation between ethnoconfessional groups. In the Muslim chronicles composed in the major cities of the Middle East, it is useless to look for information about the local Christian communities. On the other hand, the Damascene historian of the eighteenth century Mikhail Breik repeatedly made statements in his chronicle such as "in this year the poor Christians of Damascus were struck by a cholera epidemic." Its modern publisher had to add a footnote that, of course, it did not only strike the Christians but also others; however, for Breik, these others practically did not exist.[1]

Nevertheless, despite the isolation of the Christian communities of the Levant, their position could not but be affected by the vicissitudes of political life in the empire and changes in the Ottomans' position toward the Orthodox. Over long centuries of coexistence, relations between the "Rum"[2] and the Ottomans underwent a number of significant changes associated with fundamental changes in the nature of the Ottoman Empire.

The Ottoman state system originated in the ethnically and religiously diverse environment of Asia Minor, in close contact with the surrounding peoples and faiths. The form of Islam common among the Turks of the fourteenth and fifteenth centuries itself had a rather unorthodox character. It was greatly influenced by the Sufism of Asia Minor, which had a syncretistic character and had been influenced to some degree by Christianity.[3] During the time of their conquest of the Balkans, wrote Vasily V. Bartold, the Ottomans "were not religious fanatics. ... Their rulers identified themselves as members of the tolerant dervish orders ... and in their campaigns they used the services of Christians without forcing them to convert to Islam."[4]

It is also known that in their fight against the Byzantine Empire, the Ottomans employed Balkan Bogomils and Jews.[5] Within the ranks of the Orthodox themselves, there were plenty of people who sympathized with the Ottomans. By that point, Byzantium, Bulgaria, and Serbia were so weakened that they could only choose to whom they would submit: to the Islamic East or the Catholic West. A pro-Latin group existed among the Byzantine nobility that sought protection from the Ottoman onslaught with the Western European powers. But they would have to pay for this by entering into religious union with Rome, that is, through the recognition of Latin dogmas and submitting the church to the authority of the pope. Such an agreement at the Council of Florence in 1439 was met with persistent opposition from the bulk of the Byzantine clergy and people. As stated by the Greek Metropolitan Mark of Ephesus at the Council of Florence, "We want ... neither the Latins' help nor their union! It is better for us to be taken by the Turks than by the Latins."[6] The Ottoman elite successfully played on the feelings of hostility toward the Latin West equally felt among Muslims and Orthodox and artfully stimulated Byzantine Turkophilism. For example, after conquring Bulgaria in the late fourteenth century, the Ottomans abolished the Patriarchate of Tarnovo and placed its parishes under the authority of the patriarch of Constantinople, who lived in another country that would be added to the Ottoman Empire only a half-century later.[7] Orthodox metropolitans in Ottoman territories received conditional landholdings, *timars*, just like the ruling class.[8]

During the first two and a half centuries of expansion, Muslims were still a minority of the state's population. The Ottomans did not try to change the traditional way of life in the conquered lands. The local aristocracy retained their landholdings and served the sultans on the same terms as they had their previous

Christian sovereigns. The core Ottoman territories were surrounded by a belt of vassal states ruled by local dynasties, some of which were Christian.[9]

This period of soft hegemony was replaced by a period marked by the absorbing of dependent regions, introducing the military-feudal system of land tenure, and replacing the indigenous aristocracy with governors taken from among the sultan's slaves. The first to conduct such a policy was the Sultan Beyazid I (1389–1402), although he was clearly ahead of his time. The sultan's actions provoked a strong negative reaction not only in the conquered lands but also in Ottoman society, which considered these steps to be a violation of ancient traditions. Beyazid's policies led to a disaster in the battle with Timur at Ankara in 1402, when the sultan was abandoned by many of his vassals.[10]

The defeat at Ankara put the Ottomans and the Balkan world back by a generation. Byzantium received its last respite. Beyazid's successors revived the old principles of indirect rule. The policy of unifying imperial structures was only resumed under Mehmed II the Conqueror (1451–1481) after the capture of Constantinople in 1453.

THE *MILLET* SYSTEM

In building their political system, Ottoman statesmen drew on the experience of previous Muslim empires. This primarily concerned provisions for the non-Muslim population. The Ottomans accepted the norms already developed in Islamic law about the status of *dhimmis*, as well as a system of autonomous ethnic and confessional communities, the *millets*.[11] In a series of decrees from 1454 to 1461, Sultan Mehmed the Conqueror grouped his largest non-Muslim communities into three *millets*, the largest of which numerically was the community of Orthodox peoples, the so-called *millet-i Rum*.

Following the example of the Orthodox *millet*, similar structures uniting Jews (*millet-i Yehud*) and Armenians (*millet-i Ermen*) were formed. The Armenian *millet* was largely an artificial construct of bureaucratic thinking. It included all the Christian and quasi-Christian communities that could not be incorporated into the Orthodox *millet*: Bogomils and Balkan Catholics, as well as, later, the adherents of non-Chalcedonian churches of the Middle East. Elevated to the head of the *millet* was the Armenian patriarch of Istanbul, whose position was extremely ambiguous, as he was far inferior in authority to the heads of traditional centers of the Armenian Church in Ejmiadzin and Cilicia.[12] In the seventeenth century, Jerusalem was established as the fourth patriarchal see of the Armenian Church.

There is an extensive literature on the *millet* system, even in Russian.[13] In one of his works, the nineteenth-century Orientalist I. N. Berezin presents the text of the sultan's *berat* (decree) defining the rights and responsibilities of the Orthodox patriarch at the end of the eighteenth century.[14] Translations of even earlier *berats* are held in Russian archives. One of them was issued in 1669 by Sultan Mehmed IV (1648–1687) to Patriarch Paisius of Alexandria in connection with his restoration on the patriarchal throne.[15] Another was issued at the installment of Patriarch Chrysanthos of Jerusalem in 1707.[16] These documents differ somewhat in scope and content. In particular, the *berat* of Chrysanthos broadly specifies the privileges of the Orthodox Church regarding ownership of various Palestinian holy sites and its relations with other Christian denominations in Jerusalem. However, the basic provisions of the *berats* are the same.

The sultan required that "the election of the Greek [i.e., the Orthodox] patriarch take place impartially and always in favor of a wise man … who is worthy of the trust in the Door of our good fortune, who strives to merit the highest approval, capable of governing, of guarding over and keeping his countrymen in check."[17] The decree ordered that priests and all subjects of the Orthodox confession obey the patriarch "according to the right of his dignity."[18] The patriarchs had total authority over their clergy, installing and deposing bishops. As it said in the charter given to Paisius, "and may they [the Orthodox] hold him [Paisius] in all honor, and … may he have the authority over every clerical rank, and may no one besides him, the patriarch, interfere in these [spiritual] affairs, and whichever priests or other clerical rank will not place themselves under his patriarchal authority as under a shepherd, may they receive punishment in accordance with their ranks."[19] Similar requirements are found in Chrysanthos' *berat*:

> And as to those who are subject to the above mentioned … Patriarch Chrysanthos, let them not dare to depart from or to neglect his orders and his words, but may they be in all duly submissive to his well-reasoned rule … And if he ever punishes or sends into exile whomever from the metropolitans, priests, or monks, let no one dare to resist him.[20]

The patriarchs' rights over the laity were nearly as broad. It was not for nothing that in Greek terminology, the head of the *millet* (*millet başı*) was called the ethnarch, the "leader of the people." The patriarch levied taxes on his flock for the maintenance of the Church. Decisions in cases regarding the property and marriage of Christians were subject to his jurisdiction. At the same time, the patriarch was responsible before the authorities for the political loyalties of their coreligionists.[21]

At the sultan's behest, "Everything related to the general management of the Greek [i.e., Orthodox] people throughout the expanse of the empire, to the ownership of churches and monasteries, their worldly economies, incomes, and expenses ... was subject solely to the judgment of the patriarch and the Synod."[22] The secular authorities did not accept complaints against clergy, leaving them to the consideration of the Synod. The documents stress that the patriarch receives his position for life,

> that neither goodwill, nor any offer of augmenting the annual tax can lead him to be deposed and replaced by someone else. He can be deposed only in the single case of evasion of duty, if he oppresses his subjects, allowing actions contrary ... to the customs of his people, or if he is denounced as complicit in treason against our glorious state.[23]

Ottoman officials could not interfere in the internal affairs of Orthodox monasteries, appeal the judicial decisions of patriarchs and bishops, arbitrarily make searches in churches and monasteries, or prosecute Orthodox clergy for making repairs in them "in accordance with their existing plan within the limits of the existing space and with the special permission of the authorities."[24] Moreover, the patriarchs controlled the property owned by religious institutions, inherited the property of deceased monks and bishops, and had their own service for collecting taxes from clergy and laity. Local authorities were obliged to cooperate fully with these tax collectors.[25] "And whichever gardens and villages and lands by law [belong] to him, the patriarch, in his territory, and to monasteries," said the letter, given to Paisius, "of those gardens, farmland, and villages it is no one's business but the Patriarch's. ... Just like the previous Alexandrian patriarchs owned [property], so now in the same way he, Paisius."[26] The same guarantee was granted in Chysanthos's *berat*: "Vineyards stakes and orchards, and hay, cattle and other similar additional possessions of the Patriarchate of Jerusalem were owned by the previous patriarchs, thus also shall be for Chrysanthos the patriarch."[27]

The Sultan's *berat* confirmed the religious freedom of Christians, requiring that "in no way may anyone use violence with our Greek subjects in order to convert them to Islam."[28] Finally, apart from the specifically designated taxes, the patriarchate was not subject to taxation or imposts.[29]

Of course, in real life, many provisions of the *berats* were not followed. Even aside from this, however, such documents are interesting from a theoretical point of view, as reflections of the image that Ottomans and the Orthodox had of the ideal mechanism for coexistence between the two religions.

The real, rather than ideal, state of affairs in the domain of interfaith relations was, according to witnesses, far from the desired harmony. The patriarchs in Istanbul had "no immunity, no special respect."[30] Some were hanged and many were subjected to various punishments and were thrown in prison.[31] It was rare for a patriarch to manage to stay in power for more than two or three years. Often they were deposed by the Synod at the behest of the Sublime Porte, although it was often through the intrigues of their own entourage, which bought the support of the Ottoman administration. Between 1454 and 1895, the patriarch of Constantinople changed 157 times. Many patriarchs held the throne repeatedly, however, so the total number of patriarchs during this period was 105.[32] From time to time, other bishops, priests, and laity were subject to various types of persecution. The churches of the Eastern Mediterranean have canonized 108 martyrs who suffered for their faith under Ottoman rule up to the beginning of the nineteenth century.[33]

Sources describe in detail the arbitrariness of government officials toward the *dhimmis* and the abuses that prevailed in the collection of taxes.[34] A Venetian diplomat of the sixteenth century states, "Even in that case, when [the Christians'] land is fertile, they care only about acquiring as much as is needed to pay the *kharaj*[35] and to sustain life, because if they had anything extra, the Turks would take it away from them."[36]

The ecclesiastical organization of the Christians also constantly suffered from the greed of the Ottoman pashas. The costs for the construction and repair of churches were particularly expensive, because for any improvements, it was necessary to get permission from Istanbul, which entailed the payment of bribes to local and central authorities and to chancellery officials. At times, receiving the appropriate *firman* (a decree from the sultan) was more expensive than the repairs themselves.[37]

Constantine Bazili, the Russian consul in Beirut from 1839 to 1854, gave a vivid description of the position of the Orthodox Christians of Palestine at the beginning of the nineteenth century:

The normal annual fee to the Pasha of Damascus from the Greek Monastery [i.e., the Patriarchate of Jerusalem] was one thousand purses.[38] Moreover, up to five hundred purses were spent on the pasha's retinue and gifts and for provisions when the pasha went to Jerusalem. They paid two hundred purses to the Mullah of Jerusalem during his visit and it was rare that the mullah did not find occasion in the ordinary one-year term of stay in Jerusalem to take as much or even twice as much. As much was spent on his *katibs* [secretaries] and members of *mehkeme* [shari'a court], and also for the *muselim* [*mutasallim*, the mayor] and his retinue. It was necessary that about 500 purses a year were given to different Muslim families for the sole end that they would not persecute the Orthodox monastery. To these constant, almost legal fees—for a long abuse wielded the force of law—one can attribute the amount of the *kaffar* [i.e., duties levied on pilgrims at holy places] which, if a round number is used, amounted to 500 piasters per each pilgrim. There was still an important and devastating article— *cereme*, or fines, arbitrarily imposed by Pashas, mullahs, and *muselim*s in their own favor at every opportunity: if two pilgrims would scuffle and from this a turmoil between the two confessions took place, if the tiles of a monastic building were shifted in order to fix the leaks in the roof, if a window, broken by the wind, was fixed. All such cases demanded from the monastery 10, 50, or 100 thousand piasters on the grounds that the repair of the churches in the Ottoman empire were subject to the authority and approval of the local courts.[39]

To this we can add the many domestic constraints on Christians and the humili- ating regulations for *dhimmis* regarding behavior, communication with Muslims, the wearing of distinctive clothing, and so on.[40] Christian churches were not to have crosses or bells or look prettier than the most wretched mosque. Religious processions passed through Muslim neighborhoods quickly, the priest placed a veil over the cross, and images of saints were not taken out. Christians were not allowed to ride horses or to serve in the army.[41]

However, when familiarizing oneself with these sorts of observations and statements, it should be remembered that they cannot be trusted uncritically. The intentional or unwitting demonization of the Ottoman Empire was a character- istic feature of European and Russian Orientalism of the nineteenth century.

In general, the Ottomans were relatively tolerant of the Orthodox Church, at least in the empire's early centuries. It we speak of violations of human rights, interference in church affairs and the overthrow of patriarchs, we must admit that all this was possible only under the condition of the Greek clergy's moral degradation and the internecine intrigues among the hierarchs, into which they tried to draw the Ottoman authorities.[42]

The way of life of the *raya* (the taxpaying population) under Ottoman rule did not change, especially in those provinces where the Orthodox were the majority.[43] For the most part, legal restrictions on Christians were not implemented even in predominantly Muslim areas, which occasionally forced authorities to reissue decrees regarding the need for strict enforcement of the domestic restrictions imposed on the infidels by the *shari'a*, but each time without success.

Paradoxically, the Muslim conquest led to an unprecedented consolidation of Orthodox ecclesiastical structures. Almost the entire territory of the Patriarchate of Constantinople was once again united under one government. As the British Byzantinist Steven Runciman wrote,

> The Byzantine thinkers who had rejected Western help, which at best could only have rescued a small proportion of Orthodox territory and which involved the union of the Church with Rome and a consequent deepening of the divisions within the Church, were justified. The integrity of the Church had been preserved, and with it the integrity of the Greek people.[44]

Ottoman military expansion in the Eastern Mediterranean automatically signified an Orthodox spiritual reconquista. The ecclesiastical structures were restored in all areas where Orthodoxy had given way to the West during the years of Byzantine decline: in the Peloponnese, the islands of the Archipelago, and Cyprus.[45] The presence of the Catholic Church in the empire was suppressed in every way. The *millet* system cemented the various peoples of the Ottoman ecumene in the face of a common enemy—Western civilization.[46]

In view of what was said previously, the Church was completely loyal to the Ottomans. Historians have noted that at the end of the eighteenth century, many Greek authors were more attuned to the Ottoman Empire than to current Greek historiography.[47] The relationship between the Ottomans and the Greeks was not simply coexistence between conquerors and the conquered. Within the state, a symbiosis formed between the Ottoman government and the elite Constantinopolitan Greeks, who would later be called Phanariots, after the Phanar quarter of Istanbul where the patriarch of Constantinople resided. They formed a sort of "aristocracy of intellect and talent … work and resourcefulness"[48] that held a strong position in trade and finance and played an enormous role in the life of the state until the Greek Revolt of 1821. The Greeks were the Ottomans' junior partners in the management of the empire, occupying key positions in the Orthodox *millet*.

From among them came all the higher clergy of the Patriarchate of Constantinople who possessed, as noted earlier, the prerogatives of secular power alongside their religious functions. Greek laypeople played an ever-increasing role in the administrative apparatus of the Patriarchal Synod. They often held the positions of *chartophylax* (secretary), *skevophylax* (keeper of liturgical vestments, icons, and relics), *logothete* (who was in charge of the Church's economy), and the jurists who worked in the patriarchate's courts.[49]

As the prerevolutionary church historian Alexei Lebedev wrote, "despite the Turkish yoke, or rather, because of this yoke, the Greek bishops lived at ease."[50] This idea is shared by the modern Western scholars Benjamin Braude and Bernard Lewis, who emphasized how often the imperial ambitions of the Patriarchate of Constantinople, which claimed universal spiritual authority, coincided with those of the Ottoman authorities, the heirs of the tradition of Byzantine sovereignty. To regard the Slavic, Romance-speaking, Anatolian, and Middle Eastern Christians as "Rum" and to incorporate them in the "Millet-i Rum," to some degree, was not their own choice, but rather it was the result of the Ottomans' Islamic worldview and the aspirations of the Ecumenical Patriarchate.[51] In the eyes of the Ottomans, the patriarch of Constantinople, the *millet başı*, was the sole primate of the empire's Orthodox population. To manage their Christian subjects easily, the Ottoman authorities subjected all Orthodox churches in the territories that they controlled, including the Middle Eastern patriarchates, to the authority of the Phanar, even though this was contrary to the canons of the Church. The incorporation of the Arab East into the empire encouraged an influx of Greek monks into the Patriarchates of Jerusalem and Alexandria, which led to the complete Hellenization of the upper hierarchies of both churches. In the eighteenth century, the Greeks asserted their hold over the Patriarchate of Antioch. However, this process of Hellenization began long before the Ottomans' arrival in the Middle East. On the other hand, the Phanar's control over the Middle Eastern patriarchates in the sixteenth and seventeenth centuries was purely symbolic.

In addition to religious positions, the positions of dragomans (translators) and the secretaries of the pashas were also in the hands of Phanariots. The position of the grand dragoman of the Porte held special influence and sometimes had a major influence on the foreign policy of the empire. This post was the monopoly of Phanariot clans until 1821.[52] The Ottomans periodically granted Phanariots autonomous control over the Danubian principalities of Moldavia and Wallachia, where the Greek rulers donated vast lands, estates, and monasteries to the Brotherhood of the Holy Sepulchre (i.e., to the patriarch of Jerusalem). These so-called dependent properties were one of the chief sources of the patriarchate's income.[53] The administration run by the Phanariots, both bishops and laypeople, was characterized by the ruthless plundering of the Christian population. Abuse, corruption, and an arrogant attitude toward Orthodox of a non-Greek background, including their culture and their traditions, significantly diminishes (in the eyes of most historians) the Phanariots' undoubted merits in preserving Orthodoxy under non-Christian rule.

THE GOLDEN AGE OF THE EMPIRE

During the 1520s, the Ottoman Empire made its major breakthrough toward being a world power. In just a few years, the empire doubled in size spreading over Asia Minor and North Africa. The Mamluk Sultanate, a claimant to hegemony in the Muslim world, was defeated. Istanbul inherited its leadership, which stimulated the drift (which had begun much earlier) of Ottoman society from the folk Islam of the dervishes to Sunni orthodoxy. The sultans accepted the title of Khadim al-Haramayn ("servant of the two shrines," i.e., Mecca and Medina) along with the mission of supporting the livelihood of the holy cities of the Hijaz. In the Ottoman Empire's confrontation with Shiite Iran, many Anatolian Sufi brotherhoods sided with the Iranian Shah Ismail, who was ideologically close to them and a native of the dervish milieu. This worsened the gap between the Sufis and the Ottoman authorities.[54]

Important changes occurred in the ethnic and religious makeup of the state. If in the fifteenth century up to a half of the *timariots*[55] in Serbia, Macedonia, Albania, and Bulgaria were Christians, in the following century, there was a mass conversion of the Balkan servile nobility to Islam. The *timariots* consolidated into an empire-wide caste.[56]

During the reign of Suleiman the Magnificent (1520–1566), the empire reached the apogee of its greatness. The state's sphere of political interests extended from the Western Mediterranean to Indonesia. A well-known prayer in Europe at that time was for deliverance from the plague, the comet, and the Turk. An area of free trade from the Middle Nile to Central Europe contributed to the rapid development of an Ottoman world economy. The gigantic bureaucratic machine worked flawlessly. Order and security combined with economic prosperity stimulated a population explosion, doubling the populations of the Balkans and the Levant. In all corners of the empire, roads, bridges, caravanserais, fortresses, markets, and hospitals were built. It was during this span of two or three happy generations that Sinan's architectural masterpieces were erected, the unique style of Ottoman miniatures was developed, and blue Iznik tiles appeared.

At the very beginning of this golden age, extensive territories inhabited by Arab Christians were incorporated into the empire. How did the Melkites react to the arrival of the Ottomans? According to modern researchers, the "prolonged time of troubles could only intensify the Christians' self-view as being isolated communities of believers, punished by God for some unidentified sins."[57] The *dhimmis* had long been turned into a passive object of history and would have perceived the change of ruling dynasties with complete indifference.[58] Without being participants in the historical process, Christians still exhibited some interest in it: the colophon of a Melkite manuscript mentions the defeat of the Mamluks at Marj Dabiq in Autumn 1516 and the Ottomans' entry into Aleppo.[59]

After the Ottoman conquest of the territory, Bilad al-Sham was divided into a few *elayet* (provinces): Aleppo, Damascus, Tripoli (Tarabulus al-Sham, from 1578), and Sidon (from 1643). The provinces were subdivided into smaller administrative units (*sanjak, qada, nahiya, liwa*). The boundaries of the *elayets* were not stable, such that, for example, in the eighteenth century the district of Jerusalem was for some time removed from the province of Damascus and put under the direct authority of the Sublime Porte.

At the head of each province was the *beylerbey* (governor, Arabic *wali*) with the title of pasha. To prevent separatist tendencies, pashas were changed quite often, so they were in a hurry to squeeze as much money as they could out of their province as soon as possible. The pasha had broad military and administrative powers, having under his command the local administrative apparatus and armed forces. The rulers of *sanjaks, sanjak-beys*, enjoyed much the same absolute authority over their own territories.

In parallel to the military and administrative authorities, and independent of them, there existed judicial institutions represented by *qadis* (judges) of various ranks. Another independent structure, designed to balance the independence of the governors, was the province's financial system with its own hierarchy of officials, led by a *defterdar*. Regional notables and local military leaders of different levels could play an important role in the province's affairs.[60]

Even in the sixteenth century, a number of Middle Eastern territories were controlled only nominally by the Ottomans. These were primarily Mount Lebanon and the Transjordanian Plateau, which were in practice ruled by local tribes and clans that received Ottoman administrative ranks.

At the heart of the Ottoman political system lay the institution of conditional landholdings. Allotments of land—*timars* and *ziamets*—were distributed to representatives of the military caste, the *sipahi* cavalry, who for their service received part of the tax revenues from the taxpaying population, the *raya*.[61] Dependent peasants had certain rights in the possession, transfer, and inheritance of their land. The Islamic East did not know serfdom and farmers could move freely. Thus, in the sixteenth century, rural overpopulation in the Ottoman Empire led to a mass exodus of people from villages to the cities.[62]

Along with the hereditary military nobility, the *sipahi*, who were Muslims by birth, a significant role in the government was played by the "state servants," *kapıkulu*, who formed the elite military Janissary units. Migrants from this background were placed in the most important government posts.[63]

The Jelali Revolts: The Saga of Fakhr al-Din Ma'an

By the end of the sixteenth century, there was a growing crisis in Ottoman society. The economy was unable to absorb the surplus population. All land that was suitable for the farming practices of that time was already under cultivation. The end of successful wars (Ottoman expansion ended with the conquest of Tunis in 1574) meant the end of spoils of war and, more broadly, the exhaustion of extensive sources of growth. The center of world trade shifted from the Mediterranean to the Atlantic. The influx of cheap American silver into the Levant and the subsequent "price revolution" led to a complete breakdown of Ottoman finances and the system of military-feudal land tenure. The crisis of the *sipahi* land management led to a decline in the military's fighting capacity. The authorities tried to cover the cost of maintaining the troops and the bureaucracy by dramatically increasing taxes and introducing the practice of tax farming. Sources from the late sixteenth century speak of the massive devastation of the peasantry, hunger, and flight from the villages.[64]

All this led to a series of uprisings involving Anatolian peasants, the urban plebs, and predatory bands of former soldiers. Throughout the 1590s and 1600s, the rebel movement known as the Jelali Revolts completely devastated Anatolia. During the same period, uprisings stretching from the Danube to the Morea and statements against the Ottomans by the Wallachian ruler Mihai seriously shook Ottoman authority in the Balkans.[65]

Simultaneous to these rebellions was an uprising of the Kurdish leader 'Ali Jumblat, who captured Aleppo and Damascus in 1606. Taking the rebels' side were the Druze emirs of Mount Lebanon, led by Fakhreddin Ma'an, ruler of the Chouf region. The following year, 'Ali Jumblat was defeated and surrendered to the Ottomans, but the Ma'an clan's position in the Lebanese mountains remained intact.[66]

Although this territory was considered *de jure* to be under direct Ottoman rule, in actuality, dynasties of Druze emirs and other regional leaders, including Maronite Christians, ruled in the Lebanese mountains. They only nominally recognized the Ottoman authorities and paid taxes irregularly. The mountain leaders had their own armies, which in terms of their level of being equipped with the latest firearms, outnumbered the detachments of Janissaries in Damascus. Periodically, the Sublime Porte found it necessary to undertake large-scale punitive expeditions to disarm tribes and bring the Lebanese rulers into obedience (in 1574, 1576, and especially in 1585).[67]

The rise of Fakhr al-Din Ma'an began in the 1590s when he was received into the administration of the sanjak of Sidon. Initially Ma'an enjoyed the support of the Ottomans, who wanted to maintain the obedience of the rest of the Lebanese leaders through him. The emir, however, gradually became a semi-independent ruler who controlled large areas of Lebanon with a large army and a network of fortresses. Ma'an pursued an independent foreign policy to the point at which he concluded an alliance with the Duchy of Tuscany. This situation became intolerable for the Porte. To suppress the internal unrest and make peace with various external enemies, the Ottomans set things in the Syrian provinces. In 1613, two thousand Janissaries from the capital and units from fourteen *beylerbeys* and fifty *sanjak-bey* were directed against Ma'an. Most of Ma'an's fortresses surrendered to the Ottomans and he fled by sea to Tuscany.[68]

Over the next few years, however, Ma'an was gradually able to regain lost territory, in particular returning the sanjak of Sidon-Beirut to his control. In 1617, Ma'an was pardoned by the Ottomans and returned to Lebanon. Ma'an's main rival in the region was the Sayf clan, which was more loyal to Istanbul and controlled the region of 'Akkar in the far north of Lebanon, periodically being granted governorship of the Eyalet of Tripoli. As a result of a long struggle that proceeded with varying degrees of success, during the internecine wars between the Lebanese emirs, interspersed with intrigues at the Sublime Porte and bribes offered to the grand vizier, in 1627, Ma'an succeeded in defeating the Sayf clan and seized the Pashalik of Tripoli.[69]

Despite his Druze background, Ma'an actively protected the Christians. He encouraged Maronite peasants to colonize the southern Lebanese mountains, where they developed commercial sericulture. The silk trade with European merchants was one of the foundations of Ma'an's prosperity. Under Ma'an, Sidon became the chief port of the Eastern Mediterranean.

Ma'an's strength increasingly frightened Istanbul. Ma'an controlled a significant part of Syria and could capture Damascus at any moment. Having achieved a breakthrough in the war with Iran, Sultan Murad IV moved a portion of his newly freed troops against his unruly Lebanese vassal. Just as had happened twenty years earlier, the Ottomans overcame Ma'an's resistance relatively quickly. He hid in the mountains but was smoked out and taken to Istanbul, where he was executed in 1635.[70]

In the memory of later generations, Ma'an became a legendary figure, one of the heroes of the Lebanese national myth. A considerable contribution to this was made by Christian chroniclers, especially Maronite Patriarch Istephan al-Duwayhi (1629–1704). The patriarch's positive attitude toward the emir is amply illustrated by the following words from his chronicle,

Under the rule of Fakhreddin, the Christians could hold their heads high. They built churches, rode horses with saddles, wore turbans of muslin, ...

inlaid belts, … and muskets decorated with precious stones. Missionaries from the lands of the Franks came and settled in Mount Lebanon because most of his troops were Christians and his governors and servants were Maronites.[71]

For some time, the Ottomans failed to extinguish regional separatism, at least in the European and Asian provinces. In the history of the Ottoman Empire, the century from the conquest of Tunisia to the siege of Vienna in 1683 was a period of political and military balance, when the empire had ceased its triumphant expansion but still inspired awe in its neighbors. The grand viziers from the Köprülü family, who stood at the helm of the state in the second half of the seventeenth century, tried to restore the Ottomans' former glory, revive the *sipahi* system, and resume an offensive policy. The bloody Candian War with a coalition of European powers for possession of Crete continued over the quarter-century from 1654 to 1669. The devastated island went to the Ottomans, but at the cost of enormous losses.[72]

In the seventeenth century, the military and administrative structure of the Syrian provinces had changed significantly in comparison with the Ottoman golden age. Conventional *timar*-holdings were replaced with the tax farming system of *iltizamat*. *Multazims* (tax farmers) sought to make their status and tenure lifelong and hereditary. Janissary detachments (*ocaks*) stationed in Damascus, Aleppo, and other cities played a major role in ensuring security in the provinces. Despite the efforts of the central government, there was a process of Janissary *ocaks* merging with commercial and industrial corporations, which naturally led to a drop in the fighting qualities of the military units. Various factions of the Janissaries were in constant conflict with each other and with the Ottoman governors. The political chronicles of Syrian cities abounded in rebellion and sedition.[73]

SEPARATISTS OF THE EIGHTEENTH CENTURY

The defeat of the Ottomans at Vienna in 1683 and their subsequent total defeat in the war with the Holy League (1683–1699) marked the beginning of a new stage in the history of the empire. The Ottoman state weakened, losing wars and territories. The Sublime Porte was losing real control over remote provinces where local elites (*a'yan*) were strengthening and claiming their share of power. In the Middle East, this image of imperial crisis was aggravated by pressure from the nomadic periphery, incursions by Bedouin tribes into agricultural areas, and a new wave of peasants leaving areas adjacent to the desert.[74]

The al-'Azm clan came to the fore of the Syrian regional aristocracy of the eighteenth century, with a number of its members ruling various Middle Eastern provinces for decades. As'ad Pasha al-'Azm, who governed the Elayet of Damascus for fourteen years (1743–1757), attracted the most attention from his contemporaries and descendants. For all their prestige and power, the al-'Azm were loyal to the Sublime Porte, which easily shifted them from their posts when necessary.[75]

The Ottoman authorities developed much more complicated relations with the ruler of Safad, Sheikh Dahir al-'Umar. In 1740, the sheikh of Galilee extended his rule over the northern part of the Palestinian coast. Under his rule, the city of Acre became the largest port of the Levant and a powerful fortress. Dahir's dominion became a quasi-state with its own economy, administration, and army, and the sheikh conducted a completely independent foreign policy for years while remaining in open rebellion. In the early 1770s, Dahir maintained an alliance with the ruler of Egypt, 'Ali Bey, who had fallen away from the empire and the command of the Russian fleet operating in the Mediterranean during the Russo–Turkish War of 1768–1774. Not once did the allied forces defeat the Ottoman pashas, and in 1772, 'Ali Bey's army captured Damascus. In 1773 and 1774, Russian troops occupied Beirut. On the second occasion, they held it for an extended period.[76] After the war, the Ottoman governor in Beirut began to persecute local Christian merchants. "Among them were some," the chronicler wrote, "that he executed by impaling, hanging by the ribs and by the neck. He treated them so severely on account of denunciations by slanderers alleging that they committed crimes during the war with the Russians."[77]

Eventually, 'Ali Bey was overthrown and killed in 1773, the Russian fleet departed, and the Ottomans were able to do away with Sheikh Dahir, who had caused so many problems for them. An expedition led by the commander of the fleet, the Kapudan Pasha, captured Acre in 1776. Dahir was killed and his territories were returned to Ottoman control.[78]

Christian chronicles describe the 1770s as the most difficult period in the memory of the generations then alive. The Russo–Turkish War, internecine conflict between Janissary *ocaks*, the atrocities of Bedouin bandits, the campaigns of the rebellious Egyptian Mamluk 'Ali Bey and his ally Dahir al-'Umar, and the Ottomans' suppression of Dahir's uprising all primarily affected the civilian population, including, of course, the Christians. The records for those years in the Damascus chronicle of Mikhail Breik is a continuous lamentation about the disasters of the Christians, prayers to God for mercy, and curses upon rulers, including Dahir,[79] whom the author had praised thirty years earlier.[80] The most tragic events of that time are associated with the campaign in 1775 against Dahir and the Egyptian Mamluks led by Muhammad Bey Abu al-Dhahabi, when the Mamluks captured Jaffa after a stubborn siege, plundered it, and massacred the entire population, according to the well-known Egyptian chronicler al-Jabarti, "making no distinction between *sharif*,[81] Christian, Jew, wise, foolish, free, slave, oppressor or oppressed … they erected several towers from the severed heads."[82] It is curious that while Mikhail Breik describes these events in exactly the same way,[83] the anonymous author of the Beirut Ecclesiastical Chronicle only mentions the extermination of Christians without any interest in the other categories of victims.[84] This is how legends of Ottoman fanaticism developed in the nineteenth century.

The next quarter-century of Middle Eastern history, from 1776 to 1804, took place in the shadow of the epochal figure of Ahmad al-Jazzar, the new ruler of Acre and Sidon. The Bosnian-born former Egyptian Mamluk who proudly bore the name Jazzar, meaning "butcher," became just as much of an epic hero of his century as Ma'an had been for the previous century. It would be more suitable, however, to call Jazzar an antihero: contemporary chroniclers recount his extreme cruelty and tyrannical rule with horror. In the words of the Beirut Orthodox chronicler, "the horror, carnage and destruction that took place in [Ahmad Pasha's] time defy description. One thing must be admitted: he did not cause harm to the faith and did not revolt against the religious convictions of anyone."[85]

Ahmad al-Jazzar presented himself as faithful servant of the sultan's throne, but at the same time, he ruled in an entirely arbitrary manner in his own domain. It seems that Istanbul was resigned to this state of affairs, as al-Jazzar at least kept order and paid taxes regularly. The ferocious pasha kept the Lebanese mountaineers and Bedouin tribes at bay. He was appointed *wali* of Damascus and leader of the *hajj* caravan four times.

Mount Lebanon, which was also in al-Jazzar's sphere of influence, as before, had a considerable degree of autonomy. After the suppression of the Ma'an dynasty in 1697, it went under the political hegemony of the Druze Shihab clan. The new dynasty still patronized the Maronites, who constituted a significant portion of the army and administration. The emirs relied on this force in confrontations with the Druze nobles. In the middle part of the eighteenth century, one branch of the ruling family even converted to Maronite Christianity.

During the years 1763–1790, the emir of Lebanon was Yusuf Shihab, who for many years maintained a balance between the Sublime Porte; Sheikh Dahir; Russia (during the Russo–Turkish War, he repeatedly requested Russian citizenship); and, finally, al-Jazzar. The complex relationship between the emir of Lebanon and the pasha of Sidon ranged from hostility to alliance and ended with Ahmad al-Jazzar strangling Yusuf after another of his rebellions. Exploiting the discord within the Shihab clan, al-Jazzar made Bashir, Yusuf's young nephew, the new emir, who managed, with brief interruptions, to remain in power until 1840.[86]

Starting with Napoleon Bonaparte's Egyptian expedition of 1789, the Middle East once again found itself in the midst of hostilities. In February 1789, the French army invaded Syria and blockaded al-Jazzar in Acre. Those being besieged were effectively supported by the British fleet. An epidemic broke out in the French camp. In May, Napoleon lifted the siege and retreated to Egypt, where the French forces eventually surrendered in 1801.[87]

After the French landing in Egypt, in July 1798, the authorities in Jerusalem held hostage several dozen Christian bishops of all denominations, including thirty Orthodox bishops headed by the patriarchal vicar Metropolitan Arsenius, in the Church of the Holy Sepulchre. The hostages were detained for 108 days, all the while awaiting execution, then they were released at the command of the sultan with the assistance of Ahmad Pasha al-Jazzar. When Napoleon marched into Syria, the Ottomans once again imprisoned around a thousand Christians—a few hundred from each denomination—in the church, only releasing them after the French retreated.[88] During the war, the situation in Syria was tense and restless. The Christians suffered violence from the Muslims, especially in Damascus, where the inhabitants had expelled the pasha and chaos and anarchy reigned.[89]

THE GREEK UPRISING: THE EMPIRE ON THE VERGE OF REFORMS

After the death of Ahmad al-Jazzar, one of his Mamluks, Sulayman (1804–1819) gained control over the pashaliks of Sidon and Tripoli, and later, the young and ambitious Pasha ʿAbdallah (1819–1831) repeatedly raised rebellions against the Sublime Porte and led Syria and Palestine into a spiral of unrest.

In the same period, there was a radical shift in Ottoman–Orthodox relations. The centuries-old symbiosis cracked. With the turn of the eighteenth and nineteenth centuries, the ideas of the French Revolution began to arise in the Greek environment, including nationalist sentiments in their modern form. Greek nationalists considered their enemies to be not only the Ottomans but also the upper church hierarchy of the Orthodox *millet*, the old Phanariot elite, who were rather content with the existing state of things.[90] At the beginning of the nineteenth century, the political situation in the Balkans somewhat resembled the situation in Syria and Palestine. There had been semiautonomous principalities headed by Muslim *aʿyans*. These rulers surrounded themselves with Greek advisors and even troops recruited from the Greeks. The centralist policy of Sultan Mahmud II (1808–1839) put an end to the prosperity of the regional Greek elites and became the immediate impetus for the Greek uprising of 1821.

After that, throughout the Empire including in the Middle East, began a reign of terror against the Orthodox. The cities of Palestine were occupied by Turkish troops, Christians were forced to renovate fortifications, clear out ditches, and so on. Their homes and monasteries were searched, weapons were seized, and the authorities imposed all new extortions from the Orthodox. After news of the mass executions of the Greek clergy in Istanbul, the Jerusalem "mob" and "lovers of chaos" began to openly prepare for a pogrom against the Greeks. The tension reached a critical point on July 8, 1821, but the pasha of Damascus, Darwish, intervened, prohibiting the murder of the *raya* without his permission and the Jerusalem mufti was able to restrain the Muslims from a pogrom. The very same Pasha Darwish saved Antiochian Patriarch Seraphim from imminent execution. But if in the Vilayet of Damascus, the Orthodox were saved by the intersession of the pasha, the pasha of Sidon was himself the initiator of persecution in his lands. "There was no evil that was not done to us; defamation, theft of property, grievances, imprisonment, … lashes, all this was used against us and ours," lamented the chroniclers.[91] The affliction of the Christians only began to decline in the late 1820s, after the beginning of the Russo–Turkish war and the turn to tolerance in the policy of Mahmud II.

This sultan, who sought to centralize and westernize the empire, is considered to be one of the most capable Ottoman reformers of the nineteenth century. His contemporary and rival was the powerful pasha of Egypt, Muhammad ʿAli (1805–1848), who in those same years led by his command the modernization of military-administrative structures and the economy. Muhammad ʿAli dreamed of independence from Istanbul and the transformation of Egypt into a regional superpower. Although he feigned being a loyal vassal of the sultan, in 1831, the mask was dropped and the Egyptian army invaded Palestine. Only the intervention of Russia spared Mahmud II from ultimate defeat. According to the peace agreement, the entire territory of Greater Syria was transferred under the control of Muhammad ʿAli. According to the unanimous opinion of scholars, the Egyptian occupation of the Middle East, accompanied by a radical modernization of traditional Syrian society, opened a qualitatively new epoch in the history of the region. The year 1831 became the true boundary between the Middle Ages and modernity for Syria and Palestine.

CHAPTER 3

Geography and Demographics

[In] the neighborhood of the mountain of Harran all of the many cities and villages are empty ... in many abide a small number of Arab inhabitants, some have fifty houses, others thirty, others less, some ten and five, and in some places only one house is inhabited.

—Vasily Grigorovich-Barsky, 1728

Many researchers are inclined to regard the Christian East mainly from the perspective of philology and theology, through the prism of literary texts. Scholars rarely ask questions about the material life of Middle Eastern Christians such as how many years these people lived, what illnesses they had, and how they treated them. How many times a day did they eat and what did they eat? How many children were in their families? Did they have love in the usual sense of the word? How did they dress? Did they have furniture in their homes or were they accustomed to sitting on mats and, if so, starting in what century?

It is still difficult for us to understand that the Christian East is nearly as much a full-fledged civilization as those of the Byzantines and Muslims. For this reason, it deserves to be examined from the same angles as other cultural and historical worlds, including material culture, interaction with the natural environment, the economy, the dynamics of social networks, and demographic trends. We cannot adequately treat the Orthodox East without taking into account its natural and geographic background and its demographic variables and, in particular, without answering the question, how many Christians were there in Ottoman Syria and what percentage of the population did they represent?

Climate and Nature

The zone of settlement of the Orthodox Arabs was generally limited to the region of Greater Syria (*bilad al-sham*)—the western half of the Fertile Crescent, the territory of modern Syria, Lebanon, Palestine, and Jordan.[1] Geographers divide this space into five climactic zones, stretching meridionally from north to south.

The first zone is the narrow strip of fertile coastal plain, stretching for 800 kilometers from the Gulf of Alexandretta to the Sinai. In the north (the plains of Alexandretta and Lattakia), it is 10–20 kilometers wide. In the center, along the coast of Lebanon, it narrows to just a few kilometers and in the south, in Palestine, it again expands to a width of 30–50 kilometers. From the east coast, it is abruptly bordered by towering mountain ranges, and in several places, the mountains nearly abut the sea. The strip of mountains facing the sea is a plateau constituting the second geographic zone of Syria. The wall of cliffs is broken only in a few places—in the north, by the Orontes (Nahr al-'Asi) and further south by the Nahr al-Kabir between Tartus and Tripoli and the Jezreel Valley by Acre. To the north, the high Amanus Mountains (Gavur Dağı) bend around Alexandretta, separating Syria from Asia Minor. Bounded to the south by the Orontes, it transforms into the Jabal al-Nusayr, the shelter of Shiite sects stretching down to the Nahr al-Kabir River, beyond which begins the Lebanon Mountains (Jabal Lubnan), the highest of these mountain ranges. From north to south, it stretches for 200 kilometers, with a width of 30 to 40 kilometers. Many of its peaks are covered with snow for six months of the year. The highest of them, Qurnat al-Sawda, is more than 3,000 meters high. To the south, after the Jezreel Valley, there is a band of low plateaus and mountains of Palestine, which merges with the Sinai Massif (as high as 2,600 meters).

To the east of these ridges, the relief is sharply reduced and there is a strip of lowlands and valleys that make up the third geographic region. It begins with the Karasu River Valley and the marshy lowlands near Lake Amik and continues into the Orontes River Valley, which diverts to the east at the midpoint of its course, toward Homs and Hama. To the east of the Lebanon Mountains lies the Bekaa Valley, with a width of 8–14 kilometers. This is where the Orontes originates, flowing south to north. Just to the south is the source of the Litani River, which flows to the south and forms the southern border of Jabal Lubnan. The descent in terrain proceeds further to the valley of the river Jordan, which lies in the intermountain basin of Lake Tiberias, to the lower reaches of the Jordan, to the depression of the Dead Sea and further to the lunar landscapes of Wadi Arava, which leads out to the rift of the Gulf of 'Araba.

The fourth natural zone is a strip of mountains with a width of 100–150 kilometers bordering the lowlands to the east. It is not as high as the western slope—in the north Kurd Dagh reaches 1,200 meters and to the south the al-Zawiya mountains reach 900 meters—but farther south, it turns into the massive Anti-Lebanon mountain chain with peaks as high as 2,500 meters and Mount Hermon (2,814 m).

Even farther south are the lower ridges of the chain, which turn into the Trans-jordanian Plateau.

Finally, to the east of this system of mountain ranges lies an arid plateau. In the north, a zone of steppes, stretching to the Euphrates, passes from the south to the rocky wasteland of the Syrian Desert. East of the Anti-Lebanon range is a significant elevation with the mountain ranges of Maaloula and al-Nabak. Not far from the southern spurs, in the Ghouta oasis, in the valley of the Barada River, is Damascus, surrounded by arid steppes and deserts. To the southeast of Damascus stretches lava fields and the fertile Hawran Plateau, protected from the desert winds by the Jabal Druze range.[2]

The climate of Syria varies sharply from the coast to the east, changing within 50–100 kilometers from maritime to continental. The western slopes of the mountains take on the bulk of the precipitation, and the interior climate of Syria is more dry. As Constantin-François Volney wrote, the coast "presents itself as a hot, humid, and not very healthy valley which, however, is quite fertile; the other [region] bordering it has harsh and mountainous land, the air is drier and healthier."[3] The coastal plain—wet subtropics—was densely populated and covered in orchards and vineyards. In the foothills, they cultivated olives and mulberry trees (silk was a basic Lebanese export crop since the seventeenth century). On Mount Lebanon, they developed terraced farming. To the north, in the Jabal ʿAlawi massif, deforestation has led to catastrophic soil erosion and the desertification of mountain slopes. The eastern mountain range is composed of permeable rock, so the rock face is exposed in many places. Agriculture is only possible in the basins; sparse settlements huddled around water sources. The intermountain basin—the Bekaa Valley and the regions to the north and south of it—is characterized by an arid climate that requires irrigation. The Bekaa was the breadbasket of Lebanon; there they had two yearly harvests—wheat and cotton. In interior Syria, dryland farming was possible only on the narrow strip of foothill plains. The border of this extended theoretically east of Aleppo, Hama, and Homs and west of Damascus, bending from the east around Hawran and around the Dead Sea from the west. In reality, however, the border lies much more to the west, since the closer they were to the desert, the worse were the crops and the more vulnerable to pressure from the Bedouins.

In the Middle Ages and into modern times, the Middle East became a zone for one of the biggest ecological crises in history. Millennia of extensive farming, started at some point as slash-and-burn farming, resulted in nearly complete deforestation. The degradation of vegetation was followed by catastrophic erosion of the soil: winter rains washed away a meter-deep layer of fertile soil over the course of two thousand years. The Syrian Desert likewise was depleted by millennia of unsustainable grazing; the ground cover was degraded, the soil was blown off by winds. Moreover, one of the peak periods of desiccation in Asia occurred around the seventeenth and eighteenth centuries. All of this caused the migration of nomadic tribes into the agricultural regions and then caused the displacement of the peasant population. The status of agriculture in the Middle East depended directly on the strength of state structures and their ability to protect the sedentary population from the pressure of the nomadic world. After the Roman Empire, rare was the government that controlled the Syro-Palestinian region and was able to successfully counter nomadic expansion.[4]

In general, the worsening of the ecological situation in the Middle East was caused by the drying of the climate as well as by human factors, leading to a severe demographic crisis in the Middle Ages. If in the Roman era, the population of Syria was around six to seven million people, by the early medieval period, it was closer to three million and would continue to decline because of various disasters, such as the Crusades, the invasion of Timur, and periodic outbreaks of the plague (including the famous Black Death of 1347–1348). In the end, according to various estimates, by the beginning of the sixteenth century, the Syrian population was two or—even more likely—one million people.[5]

HISTORICAL DEMOGRAPHICS: CRITIQUE OF THE SOURCES

It is difficult to determine the proportion of Christians in the population of Syria. The sources, which cover the population numbers and the settlement distribution of Christians in Ottoman Syria, vary greatly in quality and scope depending on the century.

The most detailed of these sources, the Ottoman tax registers (*tapu defteri*) of the sixteenth century, contain the results of periodically conducted censuses and taxable assets. The Ottoman bureaucratic machine was notable for its maniacal thoroughness, capturing not only the number of the tax-paying population (often by name) but also the blind, the insane, and other invalids, as well as—what is of particular value for us—the number of monks of various monasteries, who by law were not subject to the poll tax. Unfortunately for historians, since the beginning of the seventeenth century, such regular and comprehensive censuses of the population stopped because of the weakening of the Ottoman government apparatus and central control over the provinces, which resumed only in the second half of the nineteenth century, falling beyond the chronological scope of this study. Data on the demographics of the seventeenth century through the early nineteenth century are provided largely by accounts of foreign travelers visiting Syria during this period. Their estimates are hardly exact; however, it is not worth exaggerating the accuracy of the censuses that were conducted by the corrupt Ottoman bureaucracy.

In the 1950s, Ottoman demographic statistics were introduced into scholarly circulation, and almost immediately after this, a wave of criticism was raised against these sources, critisizing them as unreliable. The count of the non-Muslim population appeared to be clearly underestimated. Censuses contradict each other, occasionally reporting phenomenal demographic jumps over a short period of time. The ratio of Christians and Jews in some provinces strikingly contradicts the observations of travelers. Finally, the percentage of the Christian population recorded in the censuses of the nineteenth century appears to be several times higher than that of the sixteenth century. In addition to all this, no data indicate whether the rates of fertility and mortality among Christians and Muslims differed markedly.[6]

It is worth noting that the very quality of the compilation of the registers changed over time. The tax censuses from the time of Suleiman the Magnificent, when the empire was on the rise and the bureaucratic machine was the least corrupt, evoke more trust than the documents from the end of the sixteenth century, a time of trouble and anarchy when it became technically impossible for scribes to work outside the boundaries of the cities. This is quite evident in the last Syrian census of 1596/1597, which is clearly flawed and full of gaps and inconsistencies.

The writings of Paul of Aleppo give a vivid picture of the process of drawing up the tax registries, describing one of the local censuses of the tax-paying population in Damascus in 1659. This whole enterprise appeared tragi-comic: several Christian bishops attempted to appease the Ottoman officials with bribes to understate by several times the number of Christian taxpayers. The Turks, graciously having "not noticed" one hundred people sheltered from the census, uncompromisingly caught the one hundred and first and fined him mercilessly. "Satisfied," the official set the list under the dictation of the patriarchal clerics, "and it was the grace of God," says Paul, "because otherwise, if he had counted the priests, the deacons, the children and the infants, as ordered by the *buyuruldu* [decree] ... it would have been bad."[7] "The agha set up camp at the entrance to the quarter," continued Paul,

> and gave reminders, warnings and threats to the important people ... lest they hide anyone. Therefore, whoever was a brave soul and was not registered on the list, being known only to us, passed by unnoticed, but the timid were caught, giving themselves up ... The inhabitants of Baalbek were many, but the majority of them we have expunged [from the registry] and of them we recorded, with the consent of the *agha*, no more than 43 names; although there were more than one hundred and fifty, but they are extremely poor.[8]

The same thing happened in other cities and villages. For a reasonable bribe, young men were recorded as minors, and the mentally retarded were concealed. With the completion of the census ensued the apotheosis of administrative zeal: "The *agha* with his ministers resorted to a investigation and, having caught the first one he chanced upon, imposed fines on his family and the inhabitants of the quarter for not having declared his name."[9] Of course, in this instance, the census takers were interested in personal gain and not in the accuracy of the statistical data.

It is perfectly clear that the number of Christians in the Ottoman censuses was understated, but to answer to what degree it was understated is highly problematic. The low bar—the data of the *tapu defteri*—shows that in the middle of the sixteenth century the proportion of Christians in the population in the three Syrian *eyalets* was about 10 percent (7–8 percent in Damascus, less than 4 percent in Aleppo, and around 20 percent in Tripoli).[10] In reality, they could have been 15–20 percent,[11] and some authors speak of 25–30 percent.[12]

Nevertheless, in reconstructing the demographics of the Syrian Christians, it seems legitimate to rely on the data from the Ottoman censuses. We bear in mind, first, that these figures are underestated and, second, that absolute figures are not important for use but rather are relative indicators: the Christian presence in one area or another, its specific influence, and the fluctuation of its influence.

The most general overview of the demographic data shows that the Christians lived in different proportions throughout all the regions of Syria and Palestine wherever there was a settled, agricultural population—on the coast, in the mountains, and along the western edge of the Syrian Desert. The eastern border of the Orthodox settlements (with the exception of isolated islands) extended in a line: Kerak-Hawran-Damascus-al-Nabak-Homs-Hama-Aleppo. Farther to the northeast, Christian communities were found in Upper Mesopotamia, following along the curve of the Fertile Crescent up to Bagdad. They also rather densely settled the mountains of Kurdistan and the Armenian highlands, but the Orthodox among them until the sixteenth century virtually disappeared, with the exception of a few villages around Amida (Diyabakir) and Erzurum.

The Orthodox settled in both rural and urban areas; the majority of sources are related to the urban communities—to those centers where the church hierarchy and intellectual elite were located. The reality of medieval Syria, however, is such that it is not always simple to make a clear distinction between city and country; many cities fell apart, were deserted, and grew dilapidated. Nevertheless, the general background is one of a number of major urban centers with a large proportion of Christians. The history of Middle Eastern Orthodoxy, as described in the chronicles, is 90 percent the history of a few cities.

Two Major Cities: The Christian Population Boom

The first of the urban centers in the region is Damascus: the capital of the vast pashalik and the residence of the patriarch of Antioch. Tax registers from 1543 to 1569 mark a doubling of the Christian population in Damascus (this number includes migration from surrounding areas). In 1569, there were 1,021 Christian households for every 7,054 Muslim households and 546 Jewish households in the city. In terms of the number of inhabitants, the Christian population is estimated at 6,290 people—12 percent of the overall population of around 52,000.[13]

This same proportion was maintained half a century later: in 1700, the Christians made up 11 percent of the sixty to sixty-five thousand inhabitants of the city.[14] Against this background, the data cited by Thomas Philipp, proposing twenty-five thousand Christians in Damascus in 1730, appear undoubtedly exaggerated.[15] For ages, Christians had settled compactly in the northeastern neighborhoods at the gates of Bab Sharqi and Bab Touma. In Ottoman times, pockets of Christian settlements in the new suburb of Maydan stretched out in a long ribbon from the southwest edge of the city along the road to Mecca.

The Christians of Damascus were made up of five communities (*jama'at*): the Orthodox, the Syrian Jacobites (150 families in 1719), the Maronites (50 families in 1710), the Armenians (according to various data, between 13 and 30 households in the sixteenth century), and the Franks (colonies of European merchants).[16]

The Orthodox were the most prominent community in the city. They had three churches—the Cathedral of the Theotokos with many chapels, the Church of St Nicholas, and the Church St Cyprian and St Justina—all ancient buildings that were periodically renovated.[17] Grigorovich-Barsky left a description of the patriarchal church in 1728, noting that it was great in length and width "and on the outside and from above it is not beautiful, inasmuch as it has no cupolas, no sort of decoration … the inside though is decorated with icons, pillars, polyeleoi, and chandeliers."[18] Amid the many altars of the church stood two main ones: the winter chapel of the Holy Entrance of the Virgin, with two columns, rather gloomy "for the chapel is situated between other buildings … and thanks to this it grows dark,"[19] and the summer chapel of Holy Apostle Ananias.

At the beginning of the Ottoman era there was one more church that belonged to the Christians in Damascus—St Ananias—whose underground vault it appears was united to the same building as a Muslim mosque—a rare but not entirely unique event in the Middle East. Later, the Christians lost the church sometime between the middle of the sixteenth century and the middle of the seventeenth century.[20] Of the later writers who remembered it, it was in particular Vasily Grigorovich-Barsky who described the then already abandoned building: "That church has entirely grown into the ground from old age and became desolate, and is found in one Hagarene courtyard."[21]

The ancient residence of the patriarch, which stood next to the cathedral, was completely rebuilt in the late 1650s, upon Patriarch Macarius's return from Moscow with rich gifts from the tsar. Part of the funds went toward the reconstruction of the patriarchal court, which became one of the most luxurious buildings in Damascus.[22] The most detailed description of the patriarchal palace and its gardens and fountains belongs to Paul of Aleppo, who himself oversaw their construction.[23] Many decades later, pilgrims passing through Damascus spoke of the patriarch's court in the most glowing of terms:

> The most holy [patriarch] has six cells, which are very beautiful, and in every cell, a marble fountain is installed, [where there is] always living water— taking out the plug, you can draw fresh water, as much as you need … Green oranges, lemons—some are ripe, and some are still growing, good grapes, many birds, doves sit on shoulders and on the table the doves pick up crumbs,

as wrote Ippolit Vishenski at the beginning of the eighteenth century.[24] Twenty years later Grigorovich-Barsky left his description,

> Inside the palace the covering is decorated with various flowers, and by crushed marble pieces, so also the floor is laid out with black, scarlet, and white marble boards, and so polished that it glistens like a mirror … there is also a bathhouse for the patriarch, which is well set up with cold and hot running water. And there is running water passing through all the buildings by the kitchen.[25]

In 1648, there were thirty priests counted in the Orthodox community of the city, but this number would fluctuate greatly.[26] Ippolit Vishenski, having visited Damascus in 1708, wrote that the patriarch had ten monks and, in the church, forty priests and fifty deacons served in turn.[27] Among the names of those who elected Uniate Patriarch Cyril Tanas in Damascus in 1724, there were signatures from twenty-nine priests and three deacons,[28] but it is not certain that they were all inhabitants of Damascus. Grigorovich-Barsky recalls how in Damascus in 1728 there were fifteen priests, but the Orthodox community at that time was greatly reduced because of massive conversions to the Unia.[29] In 1754, Patriarch

Sylvester prepared holy chrism in the presence of two bishops, seventeen priests, and nine deacons, evidently all from Damascus.[30]

Even more than in Damascus, economic factors impacted Aleppo, also the capital of an *eyalet* and the third largest city in the empire. The demographics of Aleppo in the sixteenth to nineteenth centuries have been examined in some detail. The Ottoman registries in 1585 recorded 309 Christian houses, constituting less than 4 percent of the overall buildings of the city. In the next century and a half, however, there was an abrupt increase in the number of Christians, mainly because of migration from the neighboring areas in northern and central Syria and south-eastern Anatolia. In Ottoman lists of *jizya* payers (i.e., able-bodied adult men), in 1640 there were 2,500 Aleppo Christians, in 1695 there were 5,391, and in 1740 there were 8,120. At the same time, the general urban population reached one hundred thousand by the middle of the seventeenth century and did not increase any further, and by the end of the eighteenth century, it began to dwindle in connection with the progressive economic decline of the city. With this in mind, the percentage of Christians in 1800 was 20 percent of the general population of Aleppo.[31]

In the fifteenth century, the Aleppo Christians, for reasons that remain unclear, moved out of the central part of the city, surrounded by the medieval walls, and into the northwest outskirts of Saliba-Judayda and, in the following century, they filled all the northern suburbs of Aleppo. Sources from the 1660s count Christians in seventeen neighborhoods; data from the 1670s count twenty-six. The neighborhood of Judayda, where there were churches of all denominations, was entirely Christian. Farther east, the percentage of Christians in the population fell to 50 percent in the areas adjacent to the northeast gate of Bab al-Hadid.[32]

The main Christian communities of the city in the sixteenth and seventeenth centuries were the Orthodox, the Armenians, the Syrian Jacobites, the Maronites (three thousand people in 1665), and a small group of Chaldeans. Nearly all of them had their own bishops and churches. The Orthodox, according to the data of Bernard Heyberger, had two churches—one of the Theotokos and another of St George—and in 1668 twelve priests were counted.[33] Grigorovich-Barsky left a brief description of the Melkite church of Aleppo: "it is a little one built from stone and very beautiful from the outside, inside it is prettily decorated with an iconostasis and silver chandeliers."[34]

Since the end of the fifteenth century, Aleppo had been on the rise as the center of transcontinental trade, particularly for Iranian silk, and in the city, there were colonies of French, English, Venetian, and Dutch merchants, acting as the consulates of European powers. The prosperity of Aleppo lasted until the second half of the eighteenth century when, for various reasons, the centers of economic activity shifted to the cities along the Lebanese–Palestinian coast, and Lebanon and southern Syria experienced a boom in commercial silk and cotton growth, affected by the needs of the French industry.

MOUNT LEBANON: A CHRISTIAN RESERVATION

Active trade in the ports of the Levant continued in the sixteenth and seventeenth centuries. The largest of them in the sixteenth century was Tripoli (Tarabulus al-Sham), the capital of the third Syrian pashalik, alongside Damascus and Aleppo. According to a traveler in 1623, one could count 2,600 Christians in a city of 9,000 inhabitants—30 percent of the population (Maronites, Orthodox Arabs, and visiting Greek and Frankish merchants). The sources begin in the eighteenth century to mention the presence of Latins, Maronites, and Orthodox (St George) churches in the city, noting that the latter "building was decrepit and hardly beautiful."[35] Grigorovich-Barsky wrote in 1728 that the Orthodox in Tripoli were nearly two hundred souls,[36] but this insignificant figure is not entirely in harmony with the visible role that the Orthodox community of Tripoli played in the life of the Patriarchate of Antioch.

The district adjacent to Tripoli—the triangle between Jubayl, Tartus, and Homs from the valley of Nahr al-Kabir in the middle—was one of the centers of the densely packed Christian settlements. The mountain range in the area of Jubayl-Batroun-Jubbat Bsharri is known as the historical homeland of the Maronites, where they stayed during the darkest period of their history between the defeat in the Crusades and the Ottoman conquest of Syria. It is here that the mountain monastery Qannubin was settled, where the Maronite patriarch moved his residence in the fifteenth century, escaping the Mamluk persecutions.[37] Here, on the Koura Plateau, is situated the only region in Lebanon that is still densely populated by the Orthodox. Sources from the sixteenth and seventeenth centuries recorded that here, as in the north on the ʿAkkar Plateau and in Jabal ʿAlawi, the majority of villages were fully Christian, including the Orthodox ones: Sisniya (the homeland of Patriarch Joachim ibn Ziyada of Antioch), Bubayda, Safita (the homeland of Patriarch Joachim Daw), Tannurin, Marmarita (from here came the prominent late-sixteenth-century writer Metropolitan Anastasius), Hisn, Anas, and others.[38] In this area, there were a number of episcopal sees, including Safita, Bsira, and Marmarita (al-Husn), of which Patriarch Macarius al-Zaʿim wrote in the middle of the seventeenth century,

The *khuri* [i.e., priest] Masʿad al-Husni told me that in the country of al-Husn and in Safita and in Marmarita there were more than five thousand homes of our community; in Marmarita there were three churches and twenty-four priests and deacons served in the first one, and in the second one, twelve priests and deacons, and in the third, eight priests and deacons. However because of sins and due to oppression the number of people has decreased.[39]

In the sixteenth century began the migration of Christians, especially the Maronites, from the overpopulated mountains of Northern Lebanon southwards, to the region of Keserwan, between Tripoli and Beirut. This area, formerly settled by Druze and Alawites, was devastated by the Mamluk armies in the beginning of the sixteenth century and was depopulated. The resettlement of Christians contributed to the close cooperation between the "aristocratic" Maronite Hubaysh and Khazin clans and leaders of these lands, the emirs of the 'Assaf (in the sixteenth century) and Ma'an (end of the sixteenth century) families. In the sixteenth century, the rapid increase in the number of Christians is notable in sixteen villages of Keserwan; toward the beginning of the seventeenth century, they were already the majority population of the province. In the beginning of the seventeenth century, during the epoch of the hegemony of Emir Fakhr al-Din Ma'an in Lebanon, a protector of the Christians, the Maronites began to resettle farther to the south, in the Shuf region, between Beirut and Sidon. The Ottoman registers from the 1520s to the 1560s almost never mention the Christian presence in south Lebanon, and in the middle of the seventeenth century, Paul of Aleppo already counted ten Christian villages around Beirut and to the south, along the Lebanese ridge and the coast.[40]

The same processes were at work in the coastal towns. The Christian population of Beirut from 1523 to 1569 grew from 66 to 110 families, whereas in total the population count was not more than 10–12 percent. During the reign of Ma'an, the influx of Christian into the city grew, although we do not have exact figures.[41]

The chronicles mention two Maronite churches in the city, which later were captured by Muslims and converted into a caravanserai and a mosque (in 1570 and 1661, respectively). Around the end of the sixteenth century, the Maronites and the Orthodox signed an agreement on the joint use of the local Orthodox church—an infrequent event in the history of the Syrian church. In exchange, the Orthodox were allowed to use the Maronite church outside the city.[42] According to testimony from the eighteenth century, there were three churches in the city—the Maronite, the Latin (at the French consulate), and the Orthodox of the Great Martyr George—the patron saint of Beirut, which was "bigger and more beautiful than the others. ... an ancient structure," according to the description of Grigorovich-Barsky.[43] The church had a number of chapels. When in the eighteenth century the Uniates broke from the Orthodox community, they laid claim to the north side-chapel of St Elias for a long time. In 1764, the Orthodox of Beirut rebuilt and expanded the ancient church, but during the construction mistakes in measurement were committed, the pillars of the church appeared "thin and disproportionate," and in March 1767, the church collapsed, burying in the ruins eighty-seven people. By March 1772, it was rebuilt anew; the chroniclers called it the best in Syria.[44]

In Sidon (Sayda), by the beginning of the Ottoman epoch, the Christian presence nearly disappeared. Tax documents mention three Christian households at the end of the sixteenth century. In the epoch of Fakhr al-Din and the revitalization of trade with Europe, however, Christians again began to migrate to the city and from the beginning of the seventeenth century on, the names of Orthodox and Maronite bishops of Sidon frequently appear in the sources. Grigorovich-Barsky recalls the Melkite Church of St Nicholas in the city and the Catholic church at one of the European consulates.[45]

THE QALAMUN PLATEAU: THE DISAPPEARING RESERVATION

The second area of densely populated Christian residences was in a rural area north of Damascus—the Qalamun Plateau, which lies between the eastern slope of the Anti-Lebanon range and the parallel range that separates the plateau from the desert. The sources of the sixteenth century note that fourteen Christian villages were located there adjacent to each other. Thirty kilometers to the north of Damascus, prevalent on the local summit, stood the most famous monastery in Syria—Saydnaya. At the foot of the mountain lies the Christian village of Saydnaya, which counted, according to the 1569 registry, more than 1,380 residents. This figure did not change and, after one and a half centuries, the pilgrim Ippolit Vishenski wrote in 1708, "Near the monastery, there is a village, [where live] Christians, all Arabs, there are about three hundred houses, only one Turk who is the chief."[46] Approximately the same number lived in the neighboring town of Ma'arrat Saydnaya, 170 houses were noted in the settlement of 'Ayn al-Tina, 1,270 inhabitants in Maaloula, which was known until now as one of the last surviving centers of the Aramaic language. From the documents of the sixteenth century, it is clear that in all of these villages the Christian population increased by more than 50 percent within twenty-five years. The sources mention numerous churches and priests in the Christian villages of this area (Jubbat al-'Assal). In Maaloula, Grigorovich-Barsky counted five priests and three churches.[47]

Farther to the northeast lies the area of Qara, which also has a significant proportion of Christians, although in contrast to the previous region, the population there was mixed: Christians made up one half of the inhabitants of the village. In Qara at the end of the sixteenth century, they counted 1,658 people (Patriarch Macarius pointed out the prosperity of Christians in the area), in Yabrud there were around 1,500, in Dayr ʿAtiya there were 135 households, in Nabak there were 142, and in other villages there were 30 to 70 households. In addition to the Orthodox, many Syrian Jacobites lived in this area; in particular, they constituted the entire Christian population of Nabak.[48] The number of residents and the confessional proportions in these settlements fluctuated widely, as is clear from a comparison of the Ottoman *defters* of the sixteenth century and the observations of Grigorovich-Barsky in the beginning of the eighteenth century, who specifically noted the low number of Christians in Qara. The sharp decline in the Christian population took place in the first half of the seventeenth century, in connection with the abolishment in 1645 of the local bishop's seat.[49] Grigorovich-Barsky did not find an active church in the village and everything was lying in ruins. The best preserved church, St Nicholas, had been turned into a mosque, "and there the church was beautifully built on the outside and inside, and other beautiful churches exist for a time, now they were ruined and empty, only the walls remain and foundations survive."[50] Grigorovich-Barsky encountered the ruins of churches all throughout this area, especially in Yabrud. The only active church in Yabrud he described as such, "small, poor and inclined to fall, not having any sort of decoration: the Arabs do not allow any renovations, nor for anything else to be built."[51] Within ninety years, Paul of Aleppo, recalling these churches, said nothing about their poor conditions.[52]

THE BEKAA AND CENTRAL SYRIA

Outside of these areas of Christian settlement one finds separate islands of Christians. For example, in the Bekaa Valley in the sixteenth century, Christians are recorded only in 15 of more than 160 villages; the largest of them are Furzul, ʿAqura, and Hamara (293, around 200, and 159 Christian households, respectively). Christians migrated from the somewhat-dangerous towns in Baalbek; under the stable rule of the Harfush Shiite dynasty, the number of Christians in this city grew almost threefold between 1523 and 1596, reaching 312 households for around 1,000 Muslim families.[53] Fifty years later, during the time of Macarius and Paul of Aleppo, around 150 Orthodox families were counted.[54] The Maronite patriarch and historian Istifan al-Duwayhi recalls there being two churches in the city—one Maronite, one Orthodox—which suffered in 1623 when the city was taken by Fakhr al-Din's troops. Grigorovich-Barsky found only one church in Baalbek, apparently Orthodox, and three hundred Christian households. In the southern spurs of the Anti-Lebanon mountains, the Christians lived in seven villages in the al-Zabadani area, and in 1569, the most evident groups were in the villages of Kafr Amir (seventy-one households) and Bludan (sixty-five households, but the Muslims are not recorded).[55] In the eighteenth century in the southern part of the Bekaa Valley, new Christian villages began to develop, above all Zahle, to which the metropolitans of Baalbek periodically transferred their residences, and likewise Hasbaya and Rahaya.

Fewer data survive on the Christians of central Syria. It is known that Homs, which became half empty, had been an important center for the Syrian Jacobite settlement, which had three churches. The Orthodox, however, dominated among the Christians. Grigorovich-Barsky mentions two Orthodox churches, built, according to legend, by St Helen: the Church of the Forty Martyrs, with its beautiful marble columns, and the Church of the Holy Martyr Julian, later ruined by incompetent restoration. The first of these churches, according to Grigorovich-Barsky,

> While it may not be exceedingly large, it is big enough ... and from the outside little beauty shows, on the inside it is very beautiful. Mostly thanks to the five handsome marble columns ... and the church is of the same diocese where they have acquired small pieces of the relics of the Forty Martyrs.[56]

Fr Louis Cheikho reported having seen a wooden iconostasis and cathedra, which were made in the middle of the eighteenth century by the residents of Homs for their cathedral.[57]

The city walls of Homs collapsed and in the decay, the Christians, whose population had reached twelve thousand people in the sixteenth century, became a minority. Data from the turn of the nineteenth to the twentieth century speak of a third of the population, but for the early Ottoman period, this proportion must have been even less. The city's ancient churches were destroyed or converted into mosques, and the Christians were left with one church, of Byzantine construction. One of its altars was allotted to the small Syrian Jacobite community. Grigorovich-Barsky mentions in relation to this, "I do not know, due to what fault the Orthodox do not prohibit them [from using the church], they have power and numbers."[58] To the southwest of Hama is the village of Kafr Buhum, the birthplace of Patriarch Ignatius 'Atiya, where, according to the memoirs of Macarius al-Za'im, only the tax-paying (*jizya*) men were counted and were numbered at 1,025 men.[59]

Between Homs and Hama in the sixteenth century lay the Diocese of Euchaita with many Christian villages: Hanak, Mharadeh, Maʿalta, Afyun, Albaya, and Bsarin.[60] As Patriarch Macarius wrote,

> The *khuri* Jurjis al-Hamawi told me, that when he was a child, it was known that in a certain Mharadeh [20 kilometers northeast of Hama] there were around four thousand people. And the metropolitan of Euchaita resided there and cared for his people … and he [i.e., Patriarch Michael, 1576–1581] ordained Gregorius al-Hamawi as metropolitan for that city … And that Gregorius, having come from Mharadeh, ordained 35 priests and 14 deacons.[61]

After the death of the next metropolitan of Euchaita, Malachi, in 1596/1597, according to Macarius,

> the late patriarch Ibn Ziyada came to the land of Hama and Homs … and he did not want to ordain a bishop there, but divided the diocese between the metropolitans of Hama and Homs and gave Mharadeh, Hanak, and Maʿalta to the metropolitan of Hama, and to the metropolitan of Homs he gave the villages of Albaya, Afyun, and Bsarin. And the Diocese of Euchaita has vanished, from that time until today.[62]

In the same way, during the reign of Patriarch Euthymius III (1635–1647), the see of Apamea came to an end.[63] It had been one of the largest cities in Roman Syria and by the late Middle Ages, it was almost completely deserted because of the spread of malarial marshes around the city.[64]

In the east, in the direction of the Syrian Desert, the *liwa* of Tadmur (Palmyra) is located, which has three villages with Christian populations in the sixteenth century (largely Syrian Jacobite), including the village of Sadad with more than a hundred and fifty houses, and the village of Hadaf with sixty-two.[65] Between Hama and Aleppo, Christian communities are recorded in Idlib (in the beginning of the eighteenth century, there were around one hundred Orthodox men, four to five priests, and a dilapidated church) and Shughur (sixty Orthodox people, one priest, and "they have an exceedingly small and poor church").[66]

THE NORTHWEST COAST

Along the coast, to the north of Tartus, the Christians lived in Banyas, Jibla, and Lattakia (Laodicea). Grigorovich-Barsky recalls there being in Lattakia four churches, relative new and built under the Ottomans.[67] According to some data, the Diocese of Lattakia included Antioch (Antakya), the former seat of the patriarchate. The local Christians prayed in an ancient cave church, not having the opportunity to build a new church. The Muslim authorities prohibited them from building, according to Grigorovich-Barksy, having made a scene of rare intolerance, "they want the unbelievers, that is the Christian people from all over to be eradicated, however by the will of God they are not worn down and will not be diminished, but still more abound."[68]

Farther north a large Orthodox community was recorded in Iskanderun, Aleppo's gateway to the sea. The Christians lived in different areas around the perimeter of the Bay of Iskanderun and in Cilicia, in the cities Bayas (Payas), Adana, Tarsus, and others. Payas became a diocesan seat in 1613/1614 in connection with the economic importance of the region bordering Iskanderun.[69] In Cilicia and Iskandarun, a dense Greek population (colonies of Cypriots) was preserved alongside Orthodox Arabs.[70]

The Ottoman census of the sixteenth century mentions a significant Christian population in the rural areas around Aleppo—3,386 households in 1584/1585. In the following century and a half nearly all of these Christians resettled to Aleppo.[71] There are also well-known Orthodox communities in the smaller cities of the region. Sophronius was a native of Kiliza (60 kilometers north of Aleppo), who in the 1770s successfully took the patriarchal thrones of Jerusalem and Constantinople.

THE EDGES OF THE ANTIOCHIAN PATRIARCHATE: NORTH AND SOUTH

The real *terra incognita* of the Antiochian Patriarchate is the vast territories of eastern Anatolia. Only fragmentary information is preserved about the local Orthodox communities, not giving a coherent picture, but it nevertheless leads us to the conclusion that there was a significant Christian presence in the region at the time of the Ottoman conquest. During the course of the sixteenth century, the Orthodox presence would be reduced dramatically. The episcopal sees of Edessa, Nisibis, and Mayyafariqin (Silvan) ceased to exist. The only bishop left in Upper Mesopotamia was the metropolitan of Amida (Diyabakir).[72] The colophon of one Melkite manuscript tells of the journey in 1593 of Patriarch Joachim ibn Ziyada to Amid to settle problems with the governor, Ispir Pasha, who was persecuting local Christians.[73] From various sources we know some of the names of metropolitans of Amid from the seventeenth century.[74]

Farther to the north is the diocese of Theodosiopolis (Erzerum) belonging to the Antiochian Patriarchate. According to Arseny Sukhanov in regard to 1653, the congregation spoke Armenian and Turkish and used Armenian books for the services.[75] According to some sources, the actual residence of the Erzerum metropolitan was located in the village of Çemişgezek at the upper reaches of the Euphrates.[76] Despite the considerable number of bishops in Erzerum in the sixteenth and seventeenth centuries noted in the sources,[77] the impression forms that the Anatolian Christians of the remote mountain villages went years without seeing a priest or a service, as a result of which the religious expression of the population deteriorated. In the 1590s, a monk from Allepo, fraudulently posing as a bishop, toured the area of Diyabakir, Çemişgezek, and Kemah, ordaining priests and collecting tithes. The local Christians, never having seen a bishop, welcomed him with honor. By action of the patriarch of Antioch, the imposter was arrested by the Ottoman authorities and taken to Istanbul, where he escaped punishment by converting to Islam. Many ordained priests and various Christians of the northeast edge of the patriarchate followed his example, where, according to Macarius, there had been as many Christians in that time as there were then (i.e., in the middle of the seventeenth century) in the entire patriarchate. In the course of his travels, Macarius came across these formerly Christian villages, "having seen many of them here, worthy of mourning."[78] It is worth bringing up a corresponding fragment from an unpublished description of the dioceses of the Patriarchate of Antioch by Macarius,

> And I tell you also, that when we were walking in the land of al-Kurj in the year 7174 (1665/1666) from the creation of the world, and we arrived during our travels at the city of Malatya and from there were went to visit our community in Çemişgezek, not sure of its environs and we looked around it and in that country there were only 12 [Orthodox] families remaining of them. And we took with us our priest, and he was an old enough man that he made the rounds with us of all the houses in that land. And he submitted to our word and remained with us for a long time and told us how in his day [his youth] there was, only in terms of Çemişgezek and its surroundings, 48 priests in addition to the priests of other local lands, whose extent—[was a] 20 days [journey], because he went with us from one place to another and showed us along the way the towns on our right and on our left, which were not counted and told us how the majority [of inhabitants] were from our community. And because the patriarch and bishops and adequate priests rarely visited, they left our faith for another. And … there remained of them only 700 households, scattered in many places.[79]

In the southeastern periphery of the patriarchate, the Christian population also declined. On the Hawran Plateau a small group of Christians survived, constituting, as a rule, an insignificant minority in Muslim villages. In Bosra, the ancient center of the metropolitan of Hawran, there were twenty-three Christian households counted in 1569 out of more than a hundred Muslim households.[80] Under pressure from the Bedouins, *fellahin* left their lands and went to the cities or to the coast. By the estimates of historians, the border of the desert in Hawran advanced 25–30 kilometers over the course of two hundred years, "having absorbed" some tens of villages. The fortress of Bosra and Salkhad, fortified in the sixteenth century for protection against Bedouin onslaught, by the beginning of the nineteenth century, lay in ruins and had no more garrisons. Salkhad was abandoned by the population in 1795, the remaining population of Bosra paid tribute to the Bedouins,[81] and the Christian population of this city moved at the end of the eighteenth century to a less dangerous area, which caused the temporary dissolution of the metropolitan see of Bosra and the Antiochian church.

ADMINISTRATIVE STRUCTURES OF THE CHURCH OF ANTIOCH

The diocesan centers of the Antiochian See were grouped into two chains of cities stretched out along a meridional direction: one was along the coast, and the other was parallel to it in the depths of the country, between the eastern slopes of the mountains and the Syrian Desert. The most significant were the sees of Damascus (the residence of the patriarch) and Aleppo. In Damascus, along with the patriarch, there existed for a while the post of "bishop (metropolitan) of the patriarch's cell," that is, a deputy to the patriarch in the capital diocese.[82] The diocesan bishops in the sixteenth century were ordained as metropolitans or bishops and toward the first third of the seventeenth century, tentatively under Patriarch Euthymius III, the heads of the episcopal sees could also be called "metropolitan."

Throughout the Ottoman period, the episcopal sees were kept in major cities—between Damascus and Aleppo were Hama (Epiphania) and Homs (Emesa), and on the coast were Beirut, Tripoli, ʿAkkar, Lattakia (Laodicea), and Bayas. To the south of Beirut, lay the Diocese of Tyre and Sidon, sometimes divided into two, according to its major cities. Even farther south the See of Acre (Ptolemais), traditionally counted in the Antiochian Patriarchate, was transferred to the Jerusalem Patriarchate around 1620.[83] To the south, west, and north of Damascus there was an entire row of metropolitan sees in the smaller, semiagrarian cities: Saydnaya, Qara, Yabrud (Pamphilia), Maaloula (Syrian Selecuia), al-Zabadani (Abida), and Bosra (the Diocese of Hawran). Fluctuations in the number of Christians in these places determined the fate of the sees: they were abolished or were combined. In the 1640s, the Diocese of Qara ceased to exist, and the Diocese of al-Zabadani stopped being mentioned at the turn of the seventeenth to the eighteenth century. Yabrud was added to the diocese of Maaloula in the seventeenth century; in the 1720s, Maaloula was joined to the diocese of Saydnaya; and the episcopal sees of Saydnaya and Hawran existed with interruptions in the second half of the eighteenth century. Between these major cities, in the Bekaa Valley, was the metropolitan of Baalbek (Heliopolis). In the eighteenth century to the south of Baalbek, the new Christian center of Zahle began to grow. The diocesan seat subsequently was moved to one city and then to another of these cities. At the end of the sixteenth century and the first half of the seventeenth century, the episcopal sees disappeared in Jabal ʿAlawi and northern Lebanon, as well as in Marmarita (al-Husn), Batroun, and Safita, as did the episcopal dioceses of Apamea and Euchaita in central Syria. To the north of Aleppo, after the dissolution of the sees of Upper Mesopotamia (Edessa, Nisibin, and Mayyafariqin), Amida (Diyabakir), and Theodosiopolis (Erzerum) remained and were periodically combined with one another. Georgian parishes that fell within the boundaries of the Ottoman Empire (the Pashalik of Akhaltsikhe) were formally counted as part of the Antiochian Patriarchate; however, it is unlikely that the patriarch governed these lands in actuality.[84] Sometimes, titular sees—Palmyra and others—appear in the sources.[85]

The Holy City

In the territory of the Jerusalem Patriarchate, the Christians made up a smaller proportion of the population than on the Syro-Lebanese coast. The main concentration of Christians appears only in a few urban centers, above all in Jerusalem with its holy places and the many monasteries of different confessions. The dynamic of the changing size of the various communities of Jerusalem in the sixteenth century was sufficiently and minutely recorded in Ottoman documents. Let us cite some figures from those documents:[86]

	1525*	1533*	1538/9	1553/4	1562	1566*
Muslims	635	937			1627	1985
Jews	199	224			270	321
Total Christians	129	164			387	388
• Melkites	96	85	85	135	181	184
• Nestorians	8	?	13	22	19	22
• Armenians	15	13	?	54	31	54
• Copts	?	26	32	43	53	43

For the later period there is a relatively reliable source—the register of those who paid the *jizya*, made in 1690/1691. The register determines the number of tax-paying Christians in Jerusalem (i.e., the heads of families) to have been 622.[87] The conversion of this number of heads of households into the number of people in the population can be carried out by a few methods. Different coefficients (from 4.5 to 6) can be used to multiply by the number of households and then add onto that figure the number of single men. The Israeli researcher Oded Peri studied the historical demographics of Christians of Jerusalem and derived the figures of 1,720 people in 1562/1563 and 2,800 people in 1690/1691.[88]

The growth of the Orthodox population provided to a large extent for the migration of Melkites to the city from Bethlehem, Beit Jala, and Hebron and from the surrounding villages (these migrants were recorded in the Ottoman registers and, as *dhimmis*, were required to pay the *jizya* to the place of their birth).

The Christians of Jerusalem present a diverse picture in terms of ethnicity and confession. Nearly every confession had its own monastery in the holy city. In addition to the Orthodox majority (58.5 percent of the Christians in 1690/1691), there were Armenians in Jerusalem who had settled in one of the four quarters of the old city, in the center with the monastery of Mar Yaʿqub (St Hagop, in the Orthodox tradition the Holy Apostle James), the residence of the Armenian patriarch in Jerusalem. The Ottoman sources mention a tripling in the number of Armenians in Jerusalem between 1563 and 1691, from 189 to 640 people (23 percent of all Christians in Jerusalem). Part of this increase was due to the relocation of Bethlehem's Armenian community to Jerusalem. In Bethlehem, the community completely disappeared in the first half of the seventeenth century.[89]

The number of Copts, who in 1562/1563 formed the second largest Christian community after the Orthodox at 326 people, would decline in the course of 130 years to 113 people. The Syrian Jacobite community grew during that same time period from 119 to 180 people. The Nestorians gradually disappeared over the course of the seventeenth century. The Ethiopian colony also fell into decline.[90]

Catholics (Franciscan monks) had a monastery on Mount Sion outside the city walls. Around 1562 (according to other sources, in 1551/1552), the Franks were expelled from the city by order of the sultan. The monastery and its surroundings were transferred into the ownership of a Sufi sheikh. The Latins bought one of the Georgian monasteries outside the city and moved there.[91] The Ottoman sources of the end of the seventeenth century count twelve Catholic families (fifty-four people) in Jerusalem, who were migrants from Bethlehem and largely of Arab descent. In addition to the Latin-rite Catholics, there was another Catholic community in the holy city—the Maronites (166 people at the end of the seventeenth century).[92]

Among the Orthodox sufficiently distinct groups stood out, including the Georgian and Serbian monks who had their own monasteries in and around Jerusalem. (On the Serbian and Georgian presence in the Holy Land, see Chapters 4 and 5.) The Muslim author al-'Ulaymi (died 1520) counted around twenty churches and monasteries in Jerusalem. The pilgrims of the sixteenth and seventeenth centuries mention about seventeen to eighteen Orthodox monasteries.[93]

Inside the main Christian holy place—the Church of the Holy Sepulchre—almost all known ethnoconfessional groups had their own altars and chapels, and they waged a bitter struggle for the possession of one or another holy place.[94] The monks of different confessions forever took turns living in their sections of the church, where, according to Russian witnesses in the middle of the seventeenth century, there were five to eight Orthodox, twelve Franks, six Armenians, two Copts, two Ethiopians, and two Nestorians.[95]

The total number of Orthodox clergy in Jerusalem is quite difficult to determine. Monasticism will be discussed separately later in this text and different figures exist for the secular clergy. Arseny Sukhanov noted that at one service in the fall of 1651, there were seven priests and deacons, whereas Grigorovich-Barsky counted between thirty and fifty priests and ten deacons at a hierarchical service for Great Lent in 1727, although that number included priests on pilgrimage, hieromonks from surrounding monasteries, and priests from the villages.[96]

The Palestinian holy places attracted pilgrims from all ends of the Christian world. Closer to Easter, the Christian population of Jerusalem significantly increased thanks to the influx of pilgrims.

BETHLEHEM AND ITS SURROUNDINGS: THE MAIN CHRISTIAN ENCLAVE OF PALESTINE

Around Jerusalem the sources note a relatively large concentration of Christian settlements. Above all was the place of Christ's birth in Bethlehem (10 kilometers from Jerusalem), where the Christian population from 1525 to 1596 grew from 61 households to 287 (the Muslims in the city were at first a third less, and by 1566, they caught up with the number of Christians; the census data from 1596 do not include figures for Muslims).[97] Travelers in the middle of the seventeenth century mentioned the decline of Bethlehem's population: three hundred households remained—half Muslim, half Christian (according to Arseny Sukhanov). Jonah the Little gives smaller figures: 130 homes of Turks, 100 of Greeks (i.e., Orthodox), and 30 of Franks (Catholics).[98] According to the calculations of Oded Peri, the Christian population of Bethlehem between 1563 and 1691 declined from 870 to 650 people because of mass migration to Jerusalem.[99]

Bethlehem in the sixteenth and seventeenth centuries was practically the only place in the holy lands with a large Arab Catholic population. The Latinization of the local inhabitants happened under the influence of Franciscan monks who lived permanently in the city at the Church of the Nativity. As Grigorovich-Barsky wrote of it, "so now, when the Roman monks had settled there, they attracted everyone to their rule and custom, since they did not give alms with sermons (as I heard), but with gold … and this poor folk is quite deceived by it."[100] The ancient church of Palestine—Bethlehem's Basilica of the Nativity—was surrounded by monasteries of the Christian confessions (Catholics, Orthodox, and Armenian), vying for power in the holy place. From the southeast, a tower with cells rose over the church—the residence of the metropolitan of Bethlehem, where, according to Arseny Sukhanov, fifteen monks lived.[101]

Between Jerusalem and Bethlehem lay the entirely Christian village of Beit Jala, whose population sometimes exceeded that of Bethlehem. Turkish statistics from the sixteenth century noted the increase in the number of households in Beit Jala from 129 in 1525 to 292 in 1566. By 1596, this figure dropped to 239. In 1652, Arseny Sukhanov and Jonah counted three hundred households and mentioned the church of St Nicholas, writing "priests serve in it by the Arabic books"; Grigorovich-Barsky wrote that twelve priests and deacons lived at the church.[102] According to the Ottoman data from 1690/1691, there were 143 Christian homes in Beit Jala; that is, for the period 1563–1691, its population declined from 1,075 to 645 people. The reason was the same as in Bethlehem, namely, migration to Jerusalem.[103]

The largest city south of Jerusalem was Hebron (al-Khalil); however, its Christian population was already quickly disappearing by the beginning of the Ottoman era: the census of 1533 mentions a few Christian families, but already in the beginning of the 1540s, they had left the city and moved to Gaza.[104] The sources from the seventeenth and nineteenth centuries do not show any Christians in Hebron, although there were Christian villages in the surrounding areas.[105]

In the greater area of Jerusalem in the sixteenth century, there was a large number of Christians in Ramallah (seventy-one Christian households and seven Muslim households in 1596). The sources also note four purely Christian villages, including large villages, up to one hundred households, and nine villages with an insignificant Christian minority.[106]

TRANSJORDAN: THE ONSLAUGHT OF THE DESERT

In the majority of the different areas of Palestine the Christian population was sparse and scattered throughout in small groups. Hence, in Transjordan (the Liwa of ʿAjlun) the Orthodox were noted in a little more than twenty villages, and in only five of those did they outnumber their Muslim neighbors. In the same city of ʿAjlun in 1596, 23 Christian households were counted and 330 Muslim ones. In the city of Salt, 25 were counted to 39, respectively, and in Kerak, 103 were counted to 78. The city of Shawbak in the neighborhood of Kerak had been predominantly Christian during the time of the Mamluks, but in the sixteenth century, the Christian population quickly declined (by the end of the century, only five families remained). At that time, the majority of those who left Shawbak were recorded in the tax registers of Gaza, where many of the people migrated to escape the Bedouin attacks.

Under pressure from the Bedouins, the settled peoples of Transjordan retreated to the northern part of the region, to the relatively fertile and hilly lands between the rivers Zarqa and Yarmouk. Here, in a stretch of land no wider than 30 kilometers, there were up to eighty families from the Liwa of ʿAjlun. In the south, between wadi Zarqa and Kerak, settled farmers held only the enclave of the city of Salt.[107]

Despite the general decline of Transjordan, settled groups of Christians remained there even longer, sometimes becoming completely uncivilized and nearly forgetting their faith. Arseny Sukhanov encountered some such *fellahin* in the middle of the seventeenth century in Jerusalem,

> and everyone is from different places and from faraway villages, where they live together with Turks, and under Turks, and they have neither a church nor a priest; only on Pascha do they come to Jerusalem and take communion here, but no one knows them, they simply call themselves Christian and some are from the Transjordan desert.[108]

GALILEE

Even rarer were Orthodox settlements in Galilee (the Liwa of Safad): 282 villages were counted there, and Christians lived in only six of them. Even Nazareth, greatly fallen into decline "because of the malice of the Turkish rulers," as expressed by a contemporary,[109] had only seventeen Christian families for two hundred Muslim families in the middle of the sixteenth century. The local Christian community had been subjected to severe persecution by the Mamluk Sultan Baybars in the thirteenth century and, since that time, it apparently never recovered.[110] At the site of the Annunciation, on the foundations of a Byzantine church, the Franciscan monks built their own monastery in 1620. The Orthodox metropolitan of Nazareth, Gabriel, wrote about this with grief in 1651:

> And at about half a day from the city [of Nazareth], there is a very beautiful monastery, but it was bought by the Papists from the Turks for gold, and Papist monks dwell there, because of our sins and our poverty, for we do not have so much gold. If we had gold, we would have driven them out of our monastery.[111]

As for the Christian presence in Nazareth in the seventeenth century, the data are vague. The pilgrim Vasily Gagara wrote in 1635–1636, "Arabs live there [Nazareth], there are no Christians, and foreigners live in the monastery."[112] Gabriel, the metropolitan of Nazareth, does not directly speak about the Christian population of Nazareth in his description of the Holy Land. He only mentions that "in the midst of Nazareth is the house of St Joseph the Betrothed, and there lives the metropolitan with his monks."[113] What is known is that the Catholic rotunda of the Annunciation and the house of Joseph are now located on the boundary of one of the church complexes. If Gabriel of Nazareth was not mistaken about his stay in the house of Joseph, that means that the Catholics seized these territories in several stages. Grigorovich-Barsky and Sergei Pleshcheev discuss the Catholic church on the site of the house of St Joseph.[114]

Over the course of the eighteenth century, there was apparently a significant migration of Christians to the city and its surroundings. Sergei Pleshcheev noted that in 1772, in Nazareth and the villages in the vicinity there were few Muslims, "but almost everyone is of Catholic or Greek law."[115] At that time in the same city, in addition to the Catholic monastery, there were also Greek-Catholic, Maronite, and Orthodox churches. The present-day Orthodox church of the Archangel Gabriel, built in the 1760s, was the very one whose service was visited by Russian Naval Lieutenant Pleshcheev, who had come to Palestine to negotiate with Sheikh Dahir al-ʿUmar: the liturgy "was performed by the priest and deacon in Arabic, but because of me, the deacon read the Gospel in Greek having gone up to the pulpit, and the priest read it also in Arabic for the general assembly and in the litanies they mentioned my name."[116] Avraam Norov noted in 1835 that the Christians made up a third of Nazareth's population of four thousand.[117] In Judea, small groups of Christians lived in a few villages around Nazareth, and there was also a very small Christian population in Nablus.[118]

CHRISTIAN COMMUNITIES ON THE COAST: THEIR RISE AND FALL

To the west of Jerusalem, the Christian presence was noticeable in five villages of the Gaza liwa. In the town of Dayr al-Darum, at the end of the sixteenth century, there were 125 Christian families, just a little less than there were Muslim. In Lydda, the Christian population almost doubled between 1525 and 1555, reaching 245 families, equal to the Muslim families.[119] Subsequently, the village fell into decay; Ivan Lukyanov wrote in 1701, "Now the entire place is ruined, and the church of the martyr [St George] is entirely ruined; it was entirely finely decorated and now only the altar walls are standing."[120] By 1838, in Lydda, there were one hundred Orthodox families.[121]

In 1596, in Ramla, there were 40 Christian households and 216 Muslim households.[122] Ramla lies along the path of pilgrim caravans heading toward Jerusalem, so it is quite frequently described by travelers in the sixteenth through nineteenth centuries. In 1593, Trifon Korobeynikov gave alms to a priest Genna in this town at the church of George the Wonderworker.[123] Arseny Sukhanov (1652) noted, "the village of Ramla is large, the yards and houses and all the buildings are stone, new and strong," the Church of St George is "very big, high, on top is an arch in the middle … there are four pillars made entirely of marble, white, on the top of them in the church … even there on the pillars was put an icon of the martyr George."[124] Grigorovich-Barsky wrote about the decay of the church seventy-five years later and noted how "the decoration of the images is partially splendid."[125] To serve the pilgrims who would stay in Ramla for the night on the way from Jaffa to Jerusalem, hotels were built in the city, owned by several different Christian confessions. Lukyanov noted how the Catholic mission, just like the Armenian one, "was exceedingly finely decorated … and the Greek one is not so; indeed, everything that the Greeks have is worse than what heretics have; those are rich scoundrels who bought up the best places from the Turks, and everything bad is given to the Greeks because the Greeks are paltry in faith and in name."[126] In the beginning of the nineteenth century, the Christians in the city constituted about one-third of the three thousand inhabitants.[127]

On the coast of Palestine a very large Orthodox community lived in Gaza (25 percent of all inhabitants). During some decades of the sixteenth century, Gaza even exceeded Jerusalem in terms of the size of its Christian population: 233 families in 1525, 331 in 1555, and 272 in 1596. Over the years, they also counted in the city from five hundred to one thousand five hundred Muslim households, around one hundred Jewish families, and a small group of Samaritans.[128] The rapid increase in the Christian population is explained by a significant migration of Orthodox families to Gaza from Transjordan, Hebron, Bethlehem, and greater Jerusalem, indicating the political stability in the city, which had not been exposed to Bedouin raids.[129] The Orthodox community in Gaza, however, subsequently would decline just as rapidly because of the migration of Christians and conversions to Islam. At the turn of the 1740s to 1750s, Macarius, the patriarch of Antioch, at the request of the remaining Christians of Gaza, sought 2,000 piasters from the Ottoman authorities to delete 141 names from the list of those paying the *jizya*. After this, around forty names remained.[130] It is possible that, in reality, the number of Christians in Gaza in the middle of the seventeenth century exceeded 40 families, but it was certainly fewer than 180. In the 1660s, the See of Gaza was nominally occupied by the famous Greek ecclesiastical figure, Paisios Ligarides. He never spent a single day in Gaza, although during his stay in Moscow, he repeatedly complained about the poverty and debt of his see. The heavy debts certainly did exist, but not one kopeck of the alms from Moscow ever reached the See of Gaza because Paisios used these funds for his own purposes.[131] In 1838, 150 Orthodox families were counted in the Diocese of Gaza.[132]

Farther north along the coast lies Jaffa, which was, according to the opinions of travelers in the middle of the seventeenth century, abandoned and dilapidated.[133] Only from the late seventeenth century did the city begin its rise, becoming the export center for Palestinian soap and soap manufacturing. In the early eighteenth century, the Ottomans restored the fortress of Jaffa and established a Janissary garrison there.[134]

The city, however was an important point on the pilgrimage path to Jerusalem: a significant number of pilgrims arrived in Palestine by sea, namely, at the port of Jaffa. For a long time, there was a Greek mission for pilgrims; in 1723, it was rebuilt "beautifully and wisely," according to Grigorovich-Barsky. At that time, the Orthodox Church in the city was distinguished, even by eastern standards, by its uncommon poverty.[135] In 1774, in the course of the Ottoman's suppression of the uprising of the Palestinian sheikh Dahir al-'Umar, Jaffa was captured by the Egyptian Mamluks, and its population, including Christians, was massacred. The Mamluks made a huge pile of severed heads.[136] According to authors from the first third of the nineteenth century, the city had around six hundred Christians and four thousand Muslims.[137]

The information on the Christian community in Haifa is contradictory. European observers in 1815 estimated the city's population at one thousand families, of which half were Melkites. Avraam Norov estimates twenty years later three thousand inhabitants in Haifa, of which three to four hundred were Christian.[138]

To the north of Haifa was another port, Acre, which for a long time lay in ruins but began to grow rapidly from the eighteenth century on, undermining the commercial importance of its competing neighbor, Sidon. Acre gained an even greater political and economic role in the second half of the eighteenth century when Sheikh Dahir al-'Umar, the powerful leader of Galilee, moved his capital there. As a consequence, when the city returned to being under direct Ottoman rule, the center of the Pashalik of Sidon moved there. The ramparts of Acre repelled the siege of Napoleon in 1799, but they could not stand against the forces of Egyptian Muhammad 'Ali Pasha in 1831. In the nineteenth century, the city began to decline again. In its best years, during the 1760s and 1770s, Acre could claim fifteen to sixteen thousand inhabitants; in 1815, there were seven thousand five hundred inhabitants, of which many were Christians, and of those, some two thousand were Uniates (Greek Catholics).[139]

THE CHURCHES OF THE JERUSALEM DIOCESE

The number of churches in the Diocese of Jerusalem at the beginning of the Ottoman era was extremely low, only a little more than in the nearby neighboring Patriarchate of Alexandria, where there were practically no bishops apart from the patriarch. In the Palestinian church of the sixteenth century, if one does not count the bishop of Sinai (later, archbishop), who was always separate, there were only ever two diocesan bishops—the metropolitan of Bethlehem and the metropolitan of Gaza,[140] which, we recall, was the city with the largest population of Christians.

Trifon Korobeynikov came upon a situation in 1593, when, after the death of the metropolitan of Gaza in Palestine, there remained only one diocesan bishop.[141] In the late sixteenth century, the metropolitan of Caesarea of Palestine arrived in Moscow with a message from the patriarch of Jerusalem.[142] It is possible that in this case, we are dealing with a nominal title, assigned to the head of an embassy to increase its prestige, because until the 1660s one does not find the title of metropolitan of Caesarea in the available sources (the city of Caesarea itself lay in ruins after the thirteenth century and was uninhabited). According to testimony given at the Posolsky Prikaz (Foreign Affairs Office) in 1619 by the cellarer of the Novospassky monastery, a Greek Ioannicius, who was a former attendant of the patriarch of Jerusalem, in the 1610s in Palestine (without Sinai) in addition to two aforementioned bishops, they also had a bishop of Lydda.[143] In the period of 1646–1648, the see of the metropolitan of Nazareth appears in the Patriarchate of Jerusalem.[144] In 1661, the metropolitan of Petra in Arabia is first mentioned, in 1666 the metropolitan of Caesarea in Palestine is first mentioned, and in 1670 the metropolitan of Ptolemais (Acre) is first mentioned.[145]

The appearance of these sees could be connected with the growth of some urban centers in particular Acre. Others could have a titular character, created for a particular candidate—like the see of the bishop of Caesarea, which had become one of the steps along the way in the dizzying career of Patriarch Dositheus Notaras.

The pilgrim Lukyanov in 1701 in Jerusalem found five metropolitans—of Caesarea, of Lydda, of Ptolemais, of Nazareth, and also of Jordan,[146] who was the primate of the short-lived see of ʿAjlun.[147]

In 1709, Patriarch Chrysanthos drew up an inventory with a general series of the historiogeographic works of the dioceses of the Church of Jerusalem. This list appeared as follows: (1) metropolitan of Caesarea of Palestine and the exarch of Palaestina Prima (in this title the early Byzantine tradition is replicated); (2) metropolitan of Scythopolis and exarch of Palaestina Secunda; (3) metropolitan of Petra, exarch of Palaestina Tertia and Arabia Petraea; (4) metropolitan of Ptolemais and exarch of all Phoenicia; (5) metropolitan of Bethlehem and exarch of all Judea; (6) metropolitan of Nazareth and exarch of all Galilee; (7) the archbishops of Lydda, Gaza, Siani, Jaffa, Nablus and Samaria, Sebaste, and Mount Tabor; and (8) the bishop of Philadelphia, subordinate to the metropolitan of Petra.[148] A considerable portion of these sees were purely titular: in addition, it is doubtful that all of them were filled in the time of Chrysanthos. It is more likely that in his list, this pedantic scholar did not reflect the actual state of affairs, but rather some ideal order. The first actual metropolitan of Scythopolis, as far as we know from the sources available, was mentioned only in 1774; the first archbishop of Sebaste known by name died in 1799; and the titular bishops of Philadelphia and Tabor appear only in documents from the 1830s.[149]

With this in mind, in the sixteenth century in Palestine (not counting Sinai), there were two diocesan bishops. At the end of the seventeenth century, the number had grown to seven, and by the end of the eighteenth century, the number had reached nine. At the same time, many of these bishops were titular and resided, as a rule, in Jerusalem at the patriarchate.

DEMOGRAPHIC DYNAMICS AND INTERNAL MIGRATION

Bringing all this into a review of the state of the Christian population in Syria and Palestine, one should mention that the dynamics of change in numbers generally correspond to the scholarly assessment of demographic patterns for the sixteenth and eighteenth centuries. In particular, Fernand Braudel described "the Mediterranean demographic explosion of the sixteenth century," when with a rapid pace (0.7 percent per year) the populations of Spain, France, and Italy grew, and the European and Asian provinces of the Ottoman Empire grew at an even greater rate (1 percent).[150]

The population of the Ottoman Empire during the sixteenth century increased from twelve to thirteen million to twenty-five or even thirty-five million people, including in Syria, where, by some estimates, it went from one to one and a half million people.[151] Damascus and Aleppo demonstrate, as well as the cities of Palestine, some deviations from the demographic trends: their number of inhabitants peaked in the 1550s and, by the end of the sixteenth century, already had markedly declined.[152]

In the late sixteenth century, Mediterranean countries experienced a period of social and economic crises that led to demographic decline. In the Ottoman Empire, this period was marked by the end of victorious expansion, a crisis of the *sipahi* system, and the inability of the economy to absorb the surplus population, which resulted in a period of rebellions, wars, and punitive campaigns in the late sixteenth and early seventeenth centuries ("the Jelali revolts") and led to a sharp drop in the population—in some places, to the levels of the early sixteenth century. After a protracted stagnation of growth, exacerbated by the deterioration of the climate and outbreaks of the plague, the second half of the seventeenth century began, although not everywhere, with slow population growth (0.2 percent per year), reaching 2 two million people in Syria in 1800.[153]

Turning to the specifics of the Christian settlements in the region, we notice that almost nowhere was there a continuous Christian population (an exception, perhaps, is the northern part of the Lebanon mountains), even in those areas where there was a very high number of Christians. So, for example, in the north of Damascus, where there were many densely populated Christian and mixed villages, the number of Muslim villages was always still much higher: in the area of Qara, the Christians lived in seven of seventeen villages; in the area of Jubbat al-'Assal, they lived in five out of thirty-seven; in the area of al-Zabadani, they lived in six out of twenty-three; and even in northern Lebanon in Keserwan, they lived in only sixteen of the thirty-six villages.[154]

Christians seem to have preferred to settle separately from Muslims. Most of the villages inhabited by Christians were entirely Christian or had only an insignificant Muslim presence. Even more symptomatic, despite the active migrations of the rural population, is that none of the Christians attempted to establish themselves in Muslim villages or vice-versa. Even in the course of the Christian colonization of Keserwan in the sixteenth century, the migrants settled in one of those sixteen villages where there had already been a Christian population, not trying to encroach upon any of the remaining twenty Muslim villages. Large cities, of course, had a diverse confessional character but even in this case Christians often (although not always) aimed to settle close together in their own quarters.

There were mixed villages, however, where Christians made up a small minority, many of which were villages in Hawran, Transjordan, and Judea. It seems that the population there was the remnant of indigenous Christians, rather than being recent migrants.

Great geographic mobility and active migration within the country was common to the inhabitants of Ottoman Syria, especially to Christians. Modern study firmly supports the notion that increased urbanization was a leading demographic tendency of the Christian, in particular the Orthodox, population of greater Syria (with the exception of Mount Lebanon) from the sixteenth to eighteenth century. The first scholar to write about this seems to be Robert Haddad, who paid particular attention to the seventeenth-century abolishment of the episcopal sees in the agrarian hinterlands north of Damascus.[155] Bruce Masters explored the processes of urbanization using Aleppo as an example. He found the ratio of the urban Christian population to the rural population to be 1:11 in 1585 and 2:1 in 1695.[156] Oded Peri looked at the same processes in Palestine using Jerusalem and the surrounding semi-agrarian Bethlehem and Beit-Jala as examples. In 1563, 46.9 percent of the Christians from these three areas lived in Jerusalem, and by 1691, 68.4 percent of the Christians were in Jerusalem.[157]

As mentioned, these groups of migrants were singled out in the Ottoman tax registers because their presence was so noticeable. They were, for example, migrants from the towns around Tadmur (Palmyra) in Hama, farmers from the entire Bekaa Valley in Baalbek, migrants from the rural backwaters of Palestine and Transjordan in Jerusalem and especially in Gaza, and a disproportionate number of young unmarried people in Maaloula.[158]

The data presented in this chapter evidence the depopulation of the Christian villages around Aleppo, in Central Syria, in the region to the north of Damascus, and in Transjordan. The only area where a dense rural Orthodox population survived was in the Koura Plateau in northern Lebanon. At the same time, the Christian communities of Aleppo and Damascus grew, and in the eighteenth century, those of the coastal cities grew. According to Bruce Masters, during the Ottoman era, "the transformation of the Christian population of the region from predominantly rural to increasingly urban"[159] took place, in contrast with a Muslim population that was, despite similar processes of urbanization, still predominantly rural.

Among the reasons for this urbanization was agrarian overpopulation. A shortage of land pushed young peasants into the city, especially during the population boom of the sixteenth century, as well as during later periods.[160] Another reason for the migrations was the political instability of the many regions of Syria and their lack of protection against the expansion of nomadic tribes. The progressive desiccation of the Syrian Desert led to new Bedouin encroachments in agricultural areas and pushed out the sedentary peasant populations.[161] In addition, in situations in which the nomadic economy could not provide enough to live on, the traditional Bedouin occupation was robbery.

The Ottoman administration had little power to oppose this locally. Messages from foreign travelers in the Middle East are full of references to the "Bedouin threat." According to Mikołaj Nicholas Radziwiłł (1583),

> they [the Bedouins] are so terrible to the Turks that if ten of their men are sitting on horses with long lances and wear only shirts … then there are thirty Turks with guns who can barely approach them by reason of their immense courage and audacity.[162]

Attempts by the Turkish authorities to pay off the Bedouin sheikhs turned into military confrontations, but these confrontations did not bring stability. The villages of Transjordan were deserted, untilled fields lay fallow in Galilee, and Christian monasteries stood abandoned on the edge of the desert. Caravans of pilgrims could travel from Jaffa to Jerusalem or from Jerusalem to Jordan only with the protection of hundreds of soldiers. Radziwiłł told how once a *sanjak-bey* from Jerusalem with an entourage of fifty horsemen barely escaped from Bedouins on the way to Bethlehem, which is only a few kilometers from the walls of Jerusalem. Grigorovich-Barsky recalls the threat of Bedouins on the way from Qara to Homs. In the late 1780s, the Uniate Metropolitan Germanus Adam along with a hundred attendants was robbed clean by Bedouins on the way from Lebanon to Aleppo, that is, in the midst of farmed land with a settled population.[163] Grigorovich-Barsky expresses in his tirade all the hatred of settled people for nomads after their last close contact with the Bedouins,

> Oh unbelieving and depraved race! … Not only is no sort of virtue, they also have no human character or customs … Who can articulate their savage anger and bestial customs? For whoever would want to show the legacy of their cruel existence and customs, it would be loathsome not only in the writing but also in reading.[164]

Under pressure from the Bedouins the population of the inland area of Syria moved to safer areas toward the coast. Significant migrations of Christians to the coast took place in the eighteenth century on account of the economic renewal in these territories, which had been drawn into the growing greater

Mediterranean trade. The Christian migrations at that time to the coastal towns and farther into Egypt were connected with the development of the Melkite Uniate community, which is discussed in detail in Chapter 9.

More than their Muslim neighbors, the Christian *fellahin* struggled from all these economic and political problems, as well as from the additional burden of the poll tax, which, in reality, was paid collectively by the entire community. The exodus of part of the Christian population increased the burden on those who remained and could have triggered a chain reaction of resettlement to cities.[165] In general, it follows from this to note the great mobility of Syria's Christians, which psychologically predetermined the mass emigration of Middle Eastern Christians beginning in the late nineteenth century, and which now calls into question the very preservation of their historical homeland.

CHAPTER 4

Shepherds and Flock

The Social Structure of Middle Eastern Orthodoxy

Christian societies in the Afro-Asian world, both in the Middle Ages and in the modern period, had an extremely heterogeneous social nature. There were stable states, such as Ethiopia and Georgia or the late Himyarite and Nubian kingdoms. Nomadic Christian societies sometimes established their own protostates—for example, the Ghassanids and, to some extent, the Lakhmids in pre-Islamic Arabia; the Berbers of the Sahara; and some Turkic tribes of Central Asia (the "Steppe Nestorian Super-Ethnos," in the words of Lev Gumilyov). Christianity among the nomads was unstable and short lived because of the weakness of its "civilizational foundation," easily destroyed by political cataclysms. Not much more viable were the urban merchant and artisan diasporas of Christians in Marv, Samarkand, and Khwarazm and the oases along the Silk Road. These enclaves were liable to wither, not only as a result of political turmoil but also because of changes in the economic situation. The same fate befell the Carthaginian Church, with its Latinized townspeople cut off from the indigenous rural world. Only those Eastern Christian communities that maintained contact with the "soil" and had a significant stratum of peasantry, the conservative keepers of tradition, were able to survive and exist into the present day. Nevertheless, not all "peasant" societies managed to remain. Some of them could not withstand the pressure of the nomadic world, including the Mongols and Turks, who destroyed the irrigation system of Mesopotamia and over six to seven hundred years turned many fertile lands in the region into pastures. This resulted in the catastrophic decline of Christian farmers and the disappearance of the local Christian community as a whole. In itself, however, a numerous peasantry was not sufficient for the survival of a people. The true guardians of identity were the other social groups representing the intellectual elite. In the case of the Christian communities of the East, this role was usually played by monastics. In isolation from monks and monasteries, the peasantry under non-Christian rule quickly lost the foundations of their religious beliefs and turned into what historians of the nineteenth century called "ethnographic material."

Among the Orthodox of the Middle East, there were representatives of various social groups. The core of their community was made up of peasants, gathered together into rural communities cultivating the land, which for the most part belonged to the state or was transferred to the conditional holding of the *sipahi* class. There were various gradations of the status of peasants, their rights to farmland and, accordingly, the share of the harvest paid in taxes to the state or to the landowner. The most prosperous region of Bilad al-Sham was Mount Lebanon whose economy starting in the seventeenth century focused on the commodity production of silk and other industrial crops.[1] Christians were also a significant part of the urban merchant and artisan classes. According to the observations of historians, there were no particular trades in Ottoman Syria that were designated solely for ethnoreligious minorities,[2] but there was some specialization of occupations. The most common professions among Christians were blacksmiths, masons, carpenters, bakers, butchers, jewelers, doctors, and money lenders.[3] Of particular note was weaving, the manufacturing of cotton and silk fabrics. This was the main craft of the inhabitants of Damascus, Aleppo, Beirut, and other cities of Syria. In the early nineteenth century, half the population of Aleppo and Damascus lived off of income from textile manufacturing.[4] It is no wonder that during his stays in Georgia and Ukraine, Patriarch Macarius advised that they develop sericulture and the production of industrial crops.[5] Sericulture, along with the cultivation of citrus fruits and grapes and income from watermills, was the basis for the existence of the Lebanese monasteries.[6] Silk was also one of Syria's most important exports. The Christian merchants of Aleppo, Beirut, and Sidon played an important role in international trade.

The Melkites of Ottoman Syria, like most other non-Muslim social groups, constituted a society with an incomplete social structure. They did not have their own feudal aristocracy or military nobility. Among Middle Eastern Christians, the role of the elite was played by the clergy who possessed a theocratic authority going beyond purely ecclesiastical affairs. Additionally, there was a stratum of secular quasi-aristocracy—"sheikhs," "*a'yan*," and "archons." This stratum was made up of the upper echelon of merchants, including the heads of corporations of artisans, wealthy money lenders, and tax farmers (*multazim/-in*), who interacted closely with the Ottoman administration and sometimes directly intervened in the affairs of the state. Of great importance were Christian scribes (*katib/ kuttab*) in the Ottoman bureaucracy, who had the opportunity to influence the religious policies of pashas and *qadis*.

The Strength of the Weak: Kinship Ties

Weak legal protection for the tax-paying classes in the Ottoman Empire contributed to the preservation of strong community bonds and collectivist principles in the lives of Christians. The sources do not permit us to fully reconstruct a picture of these relations, but we can state with confidence that family and clan groups in villages collectively paid taxes and defended their members in the event of any conflict.

Clan ties were weaker in cities, but different forms of self-organization of residents existed, including Christians, by lines of ancestry, profession, territory, and religion. The basic unit of registration in the Ottoman registers was the household (*khan*), a small family of two or three generations. Around this, there was a large community of kinship. For example, among the Christian groups of Gaza in the 1538/1539 census figures, the community of Rizqallah (thirty "houses," that is, families, and five unmarried people). The first on the list of its members is Rizqallah *walad* (son of) Tuma; at least ten householders and two unmarried men were sons and grandsons of Tuma.[7] In documents about the election of metropolitans and patriarchs, the electors' signatures often are grouped by family, as illustrated by the election of Uniate Patriarch Cyril Tanas in 1724.[8] The electors of the Uniate metropolitan of Beirut in 1812 also signed on behalf of their clans (*bayt/buyut*, meaning "house")—"Bayt al-Jundi Niqula," "Bayt Yared," and "the children (*awlad*) of Gabriel Sabbagh and all Bayt Sabbagh."[9]

Many Christians had a fairly strong family consciousness, keeping the memory of their ancestors at least back three or four generations. Paul of Aleppo called himself the son of Macarius, son of the priest Paul, son of the priest 'Abd al-Masih al-Proks surnamed Bayt al-Za'im.[10] Thanks to interesting notes in the manuscript of Macarius's translations, we can trace the descendants of Paul though his son Hanania. In 1734, the manuscript was acquired by Nicholas, son of the then-famous church leader Elias Fakhr, from Paul, son of Farah, son of Hanania, son of the deacon Paul, son of Patriarch Macarius al-Za'im.[11] As a further example, the copyist of an old manuscript who was working in Damascus in 1561 was called "Deacon Mikhail, son of al-Ibrutus [the archpriest] Sulayman, son of the *khuri* Yuhanna, son of al-Ibrutus Dawud, son of the *qassis* Yuhanna [from] Kafr Buhum in the district of Hama."[12] Copyists of manuscripts, donators of endowments, and those participating in litigation often named themselves by attaching a lengthy genealogy of their ancestors.

For many groups of Eastern Christians, the late medieval and early modern period is characterized by distinct processes of social archaization and the revival of tribal relations. This was most clearly manifest in remote and isolated areas, particularly in the mountains where there were no cities, roads, or effective Ottoman authorities. A classic example of the archaization of Eastern Christian communities was the Nestorian Assyrians, who after Tamerlane's invasion huddled in the mountains of Hakkari in Kurdistan and lost all their cultural traditions. Tribal organization and a fighting spirit were revived among them and institutions of tribal leaders and their retinues were established. The characteristic feature of the Assyrians' everyday life in the Ottoman era was the decline of religious life, monasteries, and education and, finally, the degeneration of the church organization into a feudal aristocracy with the transfer of the position of patriarch by inheritance within one ruling clan.

At the same time, the degree of archaization could differ significantly among different Christian communities. Thus, in Syria most of the factors leading to archaization were only weakly present. The gravitational pull of two cities, Damascus and Aleppo, exerted a dominant influence on the social structure of the Orthodox, absorbing a significant proportion of the surrounding rural population. These cities were linked by the busy Hajj Road, which stretched along the fertile plains, more or less controlled by imperial authority. The cities had thriving groups of Christian artisans, merchants, and officials. The clergy were relatively numerous and educated and had considerable creative potential. The *fellahin* of the plains did not have the skills for self-organization and self-defense.

As for the Patriarchate of Jerusalem, there the Ottoman pasha effectively controlled only a coastal strip around 10–20 kilometers wide, up to the slopes of the Judean Hills. In the country, Jerusalem and perhaps Nazareth remained under the firm control of the state. Consequently, observers noted the contrast between the urban Christians and the population of the "wild" countryside: "Devout Christians of the Holy City," wrote the pilgrim Melety in 1794, "in customs and in outward appearance they supersede the other tribes of Arabs; [they are] gracious, intelligent and comely."[13]

One kilometer outside the walls of Jerusalem, the Ottoman Empire "ended" and there began a zone where people lived according to laws having nothing to do with the *shari'a* and the Ottoman *kanun-name*. The Palestinian hinterland was controlled by a number of sovereign feudal clans, a classic example of which was the Abu Ghosh clan, who controlled the ravines of the Judean Hills on the road from Jaffa to Jerusalem. Dependent villages paid rent to the sheikhs; went to their courts to resolve their conflicts; and, in the case of civil wars, provided auxiliary militias. It was claimed that the sheikh of Abu Ghosh could muster an army of ten thousand soldiers, although this may be an exaggeration, given the depopulation of Palestine. The Orthodox villages aligned with this or that sheikh and were actively involved in such conflicts, and the Christians were often quite warlike and prone to violence.

A characteristic feature of the Christians' tribal system was the custom of blood vengeance. Porphyry Uspensky describes such an armed clash that took place in 1843 between the inhabitants of the Orthodox village of Beit Jala and the people of Bethlehem in which the Christians of Bethlehem were supported by their Muslim neighbors.[14] This fact once again demonstrates how unimportant religious differences were on the periphery of the Ottoman world. In this case, the clergy were not able to influence the people in terms of the refinement of manners. When the metropolitan of Bethlehem intervened in the conflict, he was nearly killed by the excited residents of Beit Jala. In the words of Porphyry, one of the hierarchs from the Brotherhood of the Holy Sepulchre, "Blood vengeance is a hereditary defect of Arabs. It's impossible to wipe it out ... We do not have the power."[15]

From the many accounts, it is clear that Christian men in rural areas almost without exception carried weapons. In many villages, there were various sorts of watchtowers and fortifications for defense from Bedouins or neighboring *fellahin*. In most remote areas, people sometimes, on the contrary, joined with the Bedouins against the Janissaries of the pasha of Damascus who were sent to collect taxes. According to Constantin Volney, "ignorant people ... sometimes pay them tribute for their rifle shots; the inhabitants of Nablus, Bethlehem and Gabrun [Hawran] are especially disposed to do this, and through these things they have earned themselves several special liberties."[16]

We note that the majority of the population of Bethlehem was Christians of the Orthodox or Catholic confessions. The bellicosity of the people of Bethlehem is described in vivid terms in the sources. The Russian pilgrim Melety, who visited Palestine in 1794, noted that "[t]he spirit of the inhabitants of Bethlehem is perfectly heroic compared to other Arabs, although they are equally inclined towards robbery. And although they ... differentiate themselves from others by faith, they are strongly connected together by bonds of the same tribal nature and general interests."[17] The people of Bethlehem did not allow the Ottoman administration into the city and, in league with the inhabitants of Kerak (also Christians) and Bedouins, went out to engage in brigandage along the Hejaz Road. In the market of Bethlehem were sold goods robbed from caravans that did not survive the journey between Mecca and Egypt.[18]

The strongest tribal relations were among the Christians of Transjordan. Given the powerlessness of the Ottoman authorities, deurbanization, and the influx of Bedouin tribes, the only path available for the remnants of the settled

Christian population to survive was "barbarization," that is, the reconstruction of an archaic tribal structure, which was the same type of social organization as their nomadic Muslim neighbors. In this region that was marginal in all respects, scholars note that *sharia* law defining the status of *dhimmis* was not in force: the relationship between the Christian and Muslim tribes was on an equal basis, based on the actual balance of power, including armed men and guns, and tribal confederations included both Christian and Muslim clans.[19]

It seems as though if the Patriarchate of Jerusalem had existed in complete isolation, they would have reached the same degree of social degradation as the Nestorians of Kurdistan, including the loss of cultural traditions and the degeneration of the clergy into a hereditary feudal aristocracy. In fact, the Palestinian *fellahin* may well be likened to the Assyrians of Hakkari. The holy places of Palestine, however, attracted pilgrims and monks from more "cultured" countries of the Orthodox world—Greeks, Georgians, and Serbs, who supported the monasteries and literacy in the Holy Land. There came to be a contrasting picture: a developed church organization, monasticism, and intellectual activity represented by foreigners existed against the background of the archaic tribal life of the local Christians.

THE CHRISTIAN RELIGIOUS ELITE

Alongside the tribal groupings, Christians in the cities came together according to residential quarters, led by an elder referred to as *sheikh al-hara*. In areas with a mixed population, such as Jerusalem, this position would be held by a Muslim. Similarly, only Muslims headed the craft corporations (*asnaf*), which included both Muslim and Christian artisans.[20] In general, these Muslim leaders tried to defend before the authorities the common interest of both the Muslims and Christians counted among their group, but the status of the Christians remained second class and, in particular, they accounted for a disproportionate share of tax payments.[21] Apparently, in places where Christians lived in a compact quarter, the sheikh of the quarter would be Christian. Paul of Aleppo wrote that "ordinarily, the sheikh ... of Christian districts was a Christian and was appointed with the consent of the patriarch and his fellow Christians," although such a procedure was not always followed.[22] The elders of Christian quarters are constantly mentioned in descriptions of the census of the taxpaying population of Syria in the late 1650s as intermediaries between the Ottoman authorities and Christian residents.[23] The position of the sheikh of the Christian quarter of Damascus was still in existence more than a century later, in the 1760s.[24]

Such sheikhs also headed the Christian villages. Of course, in terms of wealth and power, none of them could compare to the Abu Ghosh. Nevertheless, the sheikhs of Christian villages are sometimes described in impressive terms. In his diary, Porphyry Uspensky relates the following episode (1844):

> He … bowed to me, with all the courtesy of a noble Arab, and set off ahead on his good chestnut horse. He was dressed in a simple but clean checkered robe; he had no weapons on him; a single shank with a pipe was stuck in his belt; this meant that he is *noli me tangere*, that he was not afraid of any-one, because everyone was afraid of him. Apostoli [the cleric of the Holy Sepulchre] told me on the way that this sheikh can read and write Arabic, he knows all the roads very well … apparently, he is not yet old. Yet he is already 80 years old; he outlived two wives, brought 17 children into the world, and his current wife is expecting now. This story made me look at him more attentively; he was lean, thin … with a black beard and barely noticeable streaks of gray; he carries himself properly on a horse and gal-lops briskly like a young man. All the Arabs who met him along the road … greeted him, and he spoke with them authoritatively.[25]

Sometimes the urban sheikhs were part of the patriarch's inner circle and man-aged the community together with the ecclesial hierarchy. In Jerusalem in the sixteenth century, there existed the position of assistant to the patriarch (who could be a layman) with the title *ra'is* (head) or sheikh, who was in charge of the daily affairs of the Christians. The dragoman of the patriarchate also had an important role, acting as interpreter and mediator between the bishops and the Ottoman authorities and holding the responsibility for organizing pilgrimage.[26]

Christian financiers and bureaucrats could be found in the entourage of almost every significant Ottoman administrator or Lebanese emir. Various groups of Orthodox, Maronites, Melkite Uniates, and Jews fought among them-selves to influence rulers. The Orthodox managed to achieve a leading position in the court of the Sayf dynasty of emirs who ruled Tripoli in the late sixteenth and early seventeenth centuries.[27] There were many Orthodox in the circle of Ahmad al-Jazzar. These included the Sakruj brothers, his closest advisors in Acre, and the sheikh Yunus Niqula, who headed the customs office of Beirut as well as the finances and management of public property. Al-Jazzar, who began his letters to Yunus with such phrases as "O you, glory to those such as you who are true to their words, our honorable sheikh," even appointed the *mutasallim* of Beirut on Yunus's recommendation, at least according to the Orthodox chronicle, whose author had the deepest respect for this *a'yan*. The basis for this was such: Yunus, who was closely associated with both al-Jazzar and Yusuf Shihab, was involved in the bloody civil wars in Lebanon, in big politics, and in big business dealings, and yet managed to die a natural death—and not even as a pauper— something which almost none of the companions of the famous pasha of Acre managed to achieve.[28]

Senior Christian officials at times behaved with the dignity and arrogance more peculiar to well-born aristocrats than disenfranchised *dhimmis*. In 1750, the *wakil* of Homs, 'Abdallah Yaziji, who was in the service of the pasha of Damascus, was dismissed for his arrogance and insubordination.[29] Ahmad al-Jazzar once placed the sheikh Yunus Niqula under arrest and fined him one hundred purses. The Sakruj brothers advised Yunus to plead poverty and not rush to pay and thus wait until the irascible pasha cooled down and reduced the required amount. According to the Beirut chronicle, "the sheikh, out of pride and being unaccustomed to such things, told the teachers [that is, the Sakruj brothers had the honorary title *mu'allim*, i.e., teacher] 'Fine then! Let him receive one hundred purses, just let him release me today!'"[30]

THE STANDARD OF LIVING

The question of the standard of living and property ownership among the Orthodox of the sixteenth to eighteenth centuries is rather complicated. This issue requires specialized research and the data are scattered and not representative. It is probably not wrong to state that the Melkites' standard of living was comparable to that of the Muslim tax-paying classes, although the degree of exploitation of Christians was certainly greater because of the poll tax. Economic differences among the Orthodox were determined, among other things, by geographic factors. Some regions, such as Aleppo until the end of the eighteenth century, Mount Lebanon, and the Mediterranean coast, had dynamic economies, whereas other regions such as inner Syria, Transjordan, and much of Palestine were stagnant. Christian chronicles speak of the wealth and poverty of the residents of certain localities,[31] but all of this amounts to subjective judgments and it is difficult to say exactly what the authors mean by "poverty" and "wealth." There are interesting figures about payers of the *jizya* (who are divided into three categories) in the areas of Jerusalem and Sidon. In the 1720s and 1730s, 80 percent of non-Muslims paid the average tax rate, whereas 10 percent paid the highest and lowest rates, respectively. By 1804, there was an erosion of the middle class, whose proportion fell to approximately 60 percent, a slight reduction in the proportion of the rich to 7–8 percent and an increase in the proportion of the poor to 32–34 percent.[32]

In the second quarter of the sixteenth century, the patriarch of Antioch established fixed amounts for bride prices, which were divided into four categories from 12 to 48 piasters,[33] which may indicate a fourfold disparity in income of the Christians of Damascus. It seems that in reality the gap was wider. If the cost of a wedding ceremony is a one-time act that is more or less feasible even for the poor, the highest and lowest rate paid to the bishop, according to Konstantin M. Bazili in 1840, differed twenty-five-fold.[34] The Beirut chronicle from the late eighteenth century mentions that the local Christians (who were some of the most prosperous in Syria) went out in brocade robes and embroidered cashmere. When the Druze plundered the houses and shops of the Christians of Beirut in 1772, they smashed the expensive porcelain and glass that they could not carry away.[35] Ivan Lukyanov recounted how an "Arab clerk of the Greek faith" living in Ramla regaled all the Orthodox pilgrims making their way to Jerusalem by caravan, "and we were about two hundred guests."[36]

On the other hand, Vasily Grigorovich-Barsky constantly noted the poverty of the population of Palestine, because of the bad climate and the fact that "the people are ill-tempered and lazy about all work."[37] Describing the inhabitants of Beit Jala, he says,

> In this village we saw only two superiors wearing clothes hardly better, the others are all naked, some only in a single coat, others covered in a sort of sackcloth; others still all in the same clothing, even if it was wintertime. Their clothing is a common one … it is thick, sown together badly from sackcloth, that is, woven from camel hair, white and black, some wear sandals of leather, others of wood, others only have leather tied under their feet … many of the rest go barefoot, especially the women.[38]

THE ECCLESIASTICAL ECONOMY

The Orthodox Church in the Ottoman Empire had to mainly rely on its parishioners to maintain its existence. In 1679, Patriarch Dositheus of Jerusalem described this in picturesque terms, "We have no other help than wretched help from the poor."[39] If in Christian countries the Church often had extensive landholdings, such opportunities were severely limited in the Ottoman Empire. Although Christians could establish endowments for the benefit of religious institutions, the size of such donations seems insignificant. Under Ottoman law, the free sale and purchase of agricultural land was virtually impossible. It was easier to alienate houses, gardens, and vineyards[40] and these constituted the basis of ecclesiastical—primarily monastic—holdings.[41]

In cities, the church hierarchy owned houses and shops that could be rented. A particularly large number of buildings belonged to the Orthodox Church in Jerusalem.[42] The patriarch of Jerusalem, who was residing in Constantinople in the 1680s, warned his representative in Palestine that he could not sell, exchange, or donate any house, workshop, garden, tree, or field without the patriarch's approval.[43] Paul of Aleppo mentions that the patriarchate in Damascus owned a multistory inn, left by a bequest. Its rooms were rented to the poor and then there settled in it "immoral women" "and there were many attempts to evict them for their hypocrisy, vice and ill repute … with no success."[44] "But I drove them out immediately," Paul proudly announced, after which the building was razed, rebuilt as a workshop, and rented out. The annual income it provided grew from 25 to 120 piasters.[45] The church's business activity, however, did not always meet with approval from the public. The chronicles mention that the primate of Antioch in the 1770s, Daniel, was fond of lending and financial activity, and the Christians reproachfully called him "the usurer patriarch."[46]

In addition to the real estate belonging to the Church in Syria and Palestine, the Middle Eastern patriarchates also owned vast estates located hundreds of kilometers from the Holy Land—in Wallachia, Moldavia, and Georgia. At various times, the local aristocracies complained about the demands of the Palestinian church's multiple estates, vineyards, monasteries, and other landholdings, which produced considerable income.[47]

The See of Antioch received such donations on an incomparably smaller scale and had to rely on internal resources, especially the collection of tithes from the Syrian Christian population. This tax was called the *nuriya*. There is no record of its size, whether or not it was one-tenth of the Christians' income. Konstantin M. Bazili, however, cited the amount of the annual *nuriya* to the bishop in the mid-nineteenth century as being, in the Russian currency of his time, between 10 kopecks and 2.5 rubles per family.[48] It most often was paid with money.[49] Parallel to this, there were various additional fees for the Church that often were paid in kind. Thus, the sources mention the imposition of a tax on the Christians of Aleppo for the benefit of the poor, which was paid in raw silk.[50] By unwritten tradition, two batches of wine were sent from Saydnaya to the patriarchal table. During Macarius's long absence from Syria during the 1650s, the custom was forgotten and upon his return he had to work hard for its renewal.[51] In the 1760s, the vicar of the patriarch of Antioch, contrary to custom, instituted fees for weddings, as well as for burials of rich people, which increased the hostility of the Christians of Damascus.[52]

In Damascus, the *nuriya* was personally collected by the patriarch once a year during his visitation to Christian homes for the blessing of water before Easter. According to rumors, in 1672, Patriarch Macarius was poisoned by ill wishers in the Maydan quarter of Damascus during this ceremony.[53] Sometimes, the patriarch personally went to collect tithes in his dioceses. Paul of Aleppo mentions visits to Aleppo every three years in the 1630s by Patriarch Euthymius III to collect fixed payments. The patriarch would spend more than three months in Aleppo and then the metropolitan solemnly escorted him to the boundary of the diocese.[54] It appears that, formally, a tithe was supposed to be paid once a year. In one place, Paul of Aleppo calls it the "annual fee."[55] In some cases, the patriarchs sent metropolitans or similar figures to collect the tithe.[56] There is a record from Deacon Hanania, grandson of Patriarch Macarius, which he left in a book at Balamand Monastery near Tripoli, where "his aforementioned master and father [i.e., Macarius] sent him to collect his *nuriya* due from the Christians living on the coast."[57] Additionally, there was a procedure for collecting tithes when it was carried out by bishops in their own dioceses who then sent the amounts collected to the patriarch.[58] No doubt, in remote areas of the patriarchate, taxes were paid extremely irregularly. Moreover, not every patriarch had the power to force even metropolitans of nearby dioceses to pay tithes. We know that in the mid-1620s, the patriarch of Antioch, with the support of an Ottoman pasha, sought payment from the metropolitan of Aleppo, who was twelve years in arrears.[59] In 1767, the Christians of Maaloula, who supported the Unia but were formally under the jurisdiction of the Orthodox patriarch, refused to pay taxes to the patriarchal vicar, driving him out of the city and even trying to kill him.[60]

It may be surmised that the tithe did not apply to the poor population, so far as the church authorities even had to pay more for their arrears on the poll tax (*jizya*).[61] Almost all of this also applies to the Orthodox population of Palestine.[62] The main source of income for the Patriarchate of Jerusalem was not collections from local Christians but from pilgrims' donations and landholdings in the Danubian principalities.

Specific figures about the Patriarchate of Jerusalem's financial situation are available only for the nineteenth century, with the earliest data having been collected by Konstantin M. Bazili (from 1846–1847), although their authenticity cannot be verified. Noting that almost no income came from the dioceses (apart from Ptolomais, i.e., Acre) because of the poverty of the Arab population, Bazili names endowments assigned to the Holy Sepulchre as the main source of income. Possessions in the Danubian principalities and Georgia brought in 1.5 million piasters a year or 90,000 rubles at the exchange rate of the time. Pilgrimage (on average eight hundred people per year) brought in 150,000 piasters, and donations, fees and alms collections brought in 340,000 piasters, for a total of 2.04 million piasters or 120,000 rubles.[63] The patriarchate's monthly financial needs—the maintenance of monasteries and places of worship, alms for poor parishioners, operating schools, the struggle with other churches over claims to possession of the holy places—far exceeded its income.[64] Along with cash receipts from pilgrims coming to Palestine, the See of Jerusalem (and, to a lesser extent, Antioch) also received large amounts of financial assistance from the Christian princes and aristocracy of Wallachia, Moldavia, Georgia, Muscovy, and Ukraine. Eastern patriarchs often went to collect alms in the Danubian principalities and other Christian lands.[65]

PALESTINE: GREEKS VERSUS ARABS

The Orthodox communities of the patriarchates of Jerusalem and Antioch were different from each other and this left an imprint on their inner life, relations with the Ottomans, and other aspects of their existence. The chief difference is the relative proportion of the Greek community and its role in the management of the church and community. Inversely proportionate to Greek influence was the degree of self-organization of the Arab laity and the significance of their local structures of governance.

The deep crisis of Palestinian Orthodoxy during the Mamluk era and the contribution to Middle Eastern Orthodoxy by Greek, Georgian, and Slavic monasticism has already been mentioned. The Serbs inhabited Mar Saba and its metochion in Jerusalem, the Monastery of the Archangel Michael. Several monasteries near Jerusalem belonged to the Georgians, as well as a part of the Church of the Holy Sepulchre at Golgotha. The Greeks dominated the Monastery of Sinai and many of the monastic houses of Palestine and were well represented among the higher clergy and the patriarch of Jerusalem's entourage. In the late fifteenth century, the Patriarchate of Alexandria and the Monastery of St Catherine on Sinai passed under the control of Greeks, and in the early sixteenth century, they occupied key positions in the Church of Jerusalem.

In the local historiography,[66] Greco-Arab relations in the Patriarchate of Jerusalem during the twelfth to sixteenth centuries usually are described using the words of Patriarch Dositheus, who wrote at the beginning of the seventeenth century. His narrative is simple: during the Mamluk era, the Church of Jerusalem was completely Arabized and fell into disrepair. "The Greeks and Arabs were at odds with each other because the former had lost the places of worship and the Arabs had usurped the places of worship and feared losing them, because for the most part they did not allow the Greeks to come worship in Jerusalem."[67] After the Ottoman conquest, Greeks had the opportunity to come to the holy places of Palestine, settle there and hold positions in the local Orthodox hierarchy.

Unfortunately, little of Dositheus's chronicle is accurate when it comes to events more than a hundred years removed from the time of its writing. The author's political bias and fundamental lack of information led to gross distortions. This applies, in particular, to the extent of the Greek presence in the Church of Jerusalem in the pre-Ottoman period. Little is known about the state of the patriarchate when it was still led by Arabs. Later Greek chroniclers tended to portray the situation in a gloomy light, emphasizing the patriarchate's poverty and the merging of a corrupt clergy with the secular Christian elites. Dositheus Notaras explained the ousting of local Christians from the highest positions in the hierarchy by the fact that "the Arabs behaved extremely poorly, and they were always favored excessively.... The patriarchs of the Arabs began to divide power indiscriminately with their kinsmen and the natives," pandering to extended family networks to the detriment of the Church.[68] Undoubtedly, influential Christian clans were closely intertwined with the church hierarchy. Such cases also could be observed in the neighboring Patriarchate of Antioch, as well as among the Maronites and the non-Chalcedonian churches. How did it come about that the Palestinian Arabs, who undoubtedly had some measure of self-organization, failed to keep control of the patriarchate in their hands?

The process of Hellenization in the Palestinian Church is associated with the name of Germanus, a Peloponnesian Greek who came to be the abbot of Mar Saba and then, in 1534, patriarch of Jerusalem. Later Greek tradition claims that, finding himself in the Holy Land in his youth, he mastered the Arabic language to such an extent that he was considered an Arab when he was elected patriarch. During his long reign (1534–1579), Germanus, who survived all the Arab bishops of Palestine and replaced them with Greeks, initiating the Hellenic xenocracy (foreigners' rule) in the Church of Jerusalem.[69] Historians of the second half of the nineteenth century doubted the authenticity of this legend, treating the incident in an "anti-Phanariot" spirit. Thus, Alexei Lebedev wrote,

> The patriarchate of Constantinople, taking advantage of the confusion
> of the Palestinian Arabs, which occurred as a result of the swift change
> from the previous government to the new one, and supporting the latter ...
> well appreciated the advantages of their position and with a swift blow
> assumed the end of Arab patriarchal power.[70]

It is hard to believe that the Arabs, with their developed group consciousness, were unaware of Germanus's origins. More likely, he could have been brought to the patriarchal throne during infighting between various Arab clans as a neutral party acceptable to all candidates, not bound by close ties with any of the factions. Moreover, Germanus may indeed have relied on the support of the Ottoman authorities. Greek chroniclers of the seventeenth and nineteenth centuries directly link the Ottoman conquest of the Arab East with the inroads of the Greeks into the leadership of the Church of Jerusalem.[71] There are, however, examples of Patriarch Germanus being persecuted by the Ottoman authorities: in the 1530s, he was accused of illegally renovating churches in Jerusalem. He was brought in chains to the *sanjak-bey*, whom he was barely able to pay off.[72] These two scenarios do not contradict each other, however. The government could punish the patriarch for offenses while at the same time upholding his authority in the community. It is possible to find in Jerusalem court records from the sixteenth century decisions to punish Christians for disobedience to their spiritual authority. There are also, however, cases of the leader of a community being deposed under pressure from coreligionists, as happened with the Ethiopians in 1535.[73] That is, Germanus had to avoid major conflicts with his Arab parishioners. Contrary to Dositheus's assertion, not even all the episcopal sees were in the hands of Greeks. And this was the case despite the fact that there were only two metropolitan sees in the patriarchate at the time, Bethlehem and Gaza, excluding the semi-independent see of the bishop of Mount Sinai, instituted by Germanus in 1540 and immediately occupied by Greeks. The metropolitan of Bethlehem in the 1570s was the Arab Joachim, a native of North Lebanon and a former monk of Mar Saba.

During the era of Germanus, the Arabs were unlikely to have perceived the establishment of the Greek xenocracy. They continued to control the finances and economy of the church, "having, however, in mind only their own benefit" according to a caustic remark of Dorotheus.[74] The patriarch was surrounded by Arab sheikhs, who together with him ruled the Orthodox community. We have mentioned that the positions of *ra'is* (sheikh) and dragoman were filled by native-born Christians. Enjoying a particularly high status was the lamplighter of the Church of the Holy Sepulchre, called *al-qandaloft*. In April 1539, when there was a discrepancy between the dates of the Orthodox and Armenian Easters, the Holy Fire, to everyone's surprise, came twice, on both Easters. Among the Orthodox, there was a tendency to blame the lamplighter of the Holy Sepulchre, who was supposed to have received from the "heretics" a bribe of one thousand dinars and to have lit the lamp for them at the necessary moment.

This person bore the typical Arab nickname *al-naqqash* (dyer) and so was not only an Arab but also, it seems, a layman.[75] Describing the Church of the Holy Sepulchre in 1560, Vasily Poznyakov said, "[a]nd inside the Holy Sepulchre itself burn 43 chandeliers day and night; and the oil is poured into these censers by the treasurer of the Holy Sepulchre, his name is Galel [variant: Galeil]."[76] No doubt, he had in mind the Arabic name Khalil. Thus, this man was not only the lamplighter but also the treasurer—that is, he controlled the patriarchate's budget.

In an environment in which the impact of the Arab elite on the affairs of the patriarchate remained high, securing the continuity of Greek authority through the transfer of the patriarchate from Germanus to his nephew Sophronius, who would go on to occupy the see for the next thirty years, was a complex operation. Germanus ceded power to Sophronius during his own lifetime, but this required the consent of the Orthodox community. In the highest circles of the church, difficult negotiations turned into conflicts. In the colophon of an Arabic manuscript, the metropolitan of Tripoli, Dorotheus Daw, reports about his stay in Jerusalem during the winter of 1578/1579 as an arbitrator designated by the patriarch of Constantinople to resolve a conflict between Patriarch Germanus on the one side and the metropolitan of Bethlehem and the monks of Mar Saba on the other. Simultaneous to Dorotheus, the metropolitan of Saydnaya, Simeon, was sent to Jerusalem as exarch of the patriarch of Antioch.[77] It is more than likely that Joachim challenged the hereditary transfer of power to Germanus's nephew and himself laid claim to the patriarchate. This was the last attempt to save the Arab presence among the higher clergy of Jerusalem, although the parties to the conflict did not, of course, think in these nationalistically colored categories. The Serbian monastic community that predominated in Mar Saba was more concerned with the struggle for the patriarchal see than with establishing its own autonomy from the Patriarchate of Jerusalem, although its voice also had weight in the election of the new head of Palestinian Christians. Undoubtedly, there was a preliminary agreement between the Sabaites and their former confrere Joachim, and they presented their claim to the patriarch at the same time. In Dositheus's chronicles, it is also mentioned that the Serbian monks took their conflict with the patriarch to the rest of the patriarchal sees, inviting representatives of the churches of Alexandria and Antioch to Jerusalem as intermediaries. The intermediaries supported the Serbian community's demands for independence from the See of Jerusalem "either by bribes or for want of common sense, but all to their shame," as Dositheus said.[78] Germanus lost in the dispute with the Sabaites but it seems that as a concession, the Serbian monks agreed to support the transfer of patriarchal authority to Sophronius. Now Metropolitan Joachim had lost. Left without allies, he was forced to abandon his struggle.

In the end, on May 3, 1579, the *qadi* of Jerusalem received the petition to install Sophronius on the patriarchal throne. The list of people petitioning for the approval of the new patriarch appears more than impressive: Patriarch Sylvester of Alexandria, who had come to Jerusalem for the occasion; Bishop Eugenius of Mount Sinai; Metropolitan Nectarius of Gaza; Athanasius, head of the Serbian Monastery of the Archangel; and the Priest Jacob, head of the Georgian community. We note that Metropolitan Joachim of Bethlehem was not among the signatories, which allows us to understand the reason for the conflict that Dorotheus Daw had come to resolve. Next come the names of eight *a'yans* of the Arab Orthodox community. The first to be named is already known to us, the *mu'allim* (teacher) Khalil ibn Ibrahim al-Qandaloft, about whom Vasily Poznyakov wrote. Following him are Mikhail ibn Musa al-Sabban ("soapmaker"), Ya'qub ibn 'Isa ibn Zurur (?), 'Isa ibn Sulayman al-Khalili (i.e., a native of Hebron), and others. Unfortunately, not all the names can be deciphered with confidence. Sophronius's consecration was accompanied by a written commitment by the Arab clergy of Jerusalem not to challenge this decision, under penalty of a substantial fine. For his part, Sophronius pledged to give twenty pieces of silver each year to the Orthodox in Jerusalem as a subsidy for their payment of the *jizya*.[79]

Like Germanus, Sophronius designated his successor during his own lifetime, in this case his cousin Theophanes, who held the patriarchal throne from 1608 to 1644. The Greeks did not feel confident at the head of the Patriarchate of Jerusalem, and so they tried to arrange the transfer of power to their next compatriot while the patriarch was still in good health to avoid any possible complications. Theophanes's position was stronger than that of his predecessors, however, and he managed to push the Arabs out of the management of the church economy. (As Dositheus put it, "He put a stop ... to the former pride of the natives.")[80] Perhaps one of Theophanes's last Arab officials appears in documents of the Muscovite Posolsky Prikaz (Foreign Affairs Office) among the petitions for alms coming to Russia from the East in 1636. This man, Avraam, is designated in Theophanes's letter as "a son of good people and of the patriarchate ... a boyar's son,"[81] that is, he was likened to the Muscovite rank of so-called patriarchal boyar servants (i.e., lay officials in charge of the administrative apparatus of bishops).

After the death of Theophanes, on March 23, 1645, the Greeks held the election of the new Patriarch Paisius, already without the participation of Arabs and even outside of Palestine, in Moldavia, where the Church of Jerusalem held vast estates and a significant proportion of the clergy of Palestine spent their time. The Arabs' dissatisfaction broke out when Paisius entered Jerusalem in the winter of 1646.[82] The patriarch was greeted with a peculiar form of protest: the Arab priests stacked a pile of stones before the gates of the city as a sign of rebellion.[83] Paisius, however, called to his support the Ottoman authorities,[84] who forced the "rebels" to obey their lawful first hierarch. As the Greek chronicler Maximus Simais wrote half a century later, Paisius "eliminated the intrigues of the Christians and taught them enough that they turned to the greatest obedience, order and lasting peace and now they show the patriarchs respect."[85]

Over time, the Arabs were also almost entirely supplanted from the Palestinian monasticism, the so-called Brotherhood of the Holy Sepulchre, a kind of monastic order uniting the monastic clergy of the Church of Jerusalem. Authors of the late nineteenth century emphasized that the statutes of the Brotherhood forbade the tonsuring of Arabs as monks and even hiring them to perform any services. Only the lower level of the clerical hierarchy remained for the Arabs— positions as parish priests in the cities and villages of Palestine. In the eighteenth century, however, two Arabs rose to the patriarchal throne of Jerusalem, but both of them—Sophronius (1771–1774) and Anthimus (1788–1808)—came from Syria and were not connected to the local Palestinian population. The 1765 charter of the Brotherhood of the Holy Sepulchre even forbade the Greek monks from having any financial relationship with Arabs or any further collaboration with them to the detriment of any member of the Brotherhood of the Holy Sepulchre.[86]

An in-depth familiarity with the sources, however, prompts a certain degree of adjustment of the image of total Greek dominance in the Church of Jerusalem. First, for many Anatolian "Greeks" attached to the Holy Sepulchre, their native language was Turkish and not all of them understood the texts of the Greek liturgical books.[87] Additionally, in pilgrims' descriptions from the reigns of Paisius and Dorotheus and the late eighteenth century, Arabs repeatedly appear as members of the Brotherhood of the Holy Sepulchre.[88] There were also Slavs, Romanians, Georgians, Albanians, Orthodox Armenians, and even one Ethiopian.[89] In the women's monasteries of Jerusalem, there were no less Arab and Slavic nuns than there were Greeks.

The Greek chauvinism of members of the Brotherhood of the Holy Sepulchre had a cultural-linguistic rather than ethnic character. They were ready to accept as one of their own any person who was integrated into Greek culture. Moreover, Arabs sometimes could have a successful career in the Church of Jerusalem and reach episcopal rank. There is a colophon to an Arabic manuscript left

in November 1687 by the Jerusalem native 'Isa ibn Shahin, who refers to himself
as a disciple of one Kyr Photius, metropolitan of Jabal 'Ajlun (in northern Transjordan).[90] This same Photius copied the Triodion in November 1689, where he
wrote his name in his native language as "'Abd al-Nur ibn Yusuf al-Sallal, from
the village of Anfah."[91] Photius (in Arabic, 'Abd al-Nur) is clearly the "metropolitan of Jordan" whom Ivan Lukyanov met fourteen years later in the Monastery
of St Nicholas in Jerusalem and wrote, "And the metropolitan of Jordan, who is
an Arab, served the liturgy, and he said the spoken parts in Arabic; the Arabic
language is very coarse."[92] Evidence from another pilgrim allows us to identify
this "metropolitan of Jordan" with Photius. Andrei Ignatiev mentions the participation of the "bishop of Transjordan," "the Arab Photius" in the consecration
of the archbishop of Sinai on Epiphany 1708.[93] There is no doubt that all three
of these sources are discussing the same person. 'Isa ibn Shahin was not the only
one to refer to himself as a disciple of Photius, metropolitan of 'Ajlun. There is
a similar colophon from 1722 by the priest Jabir ibn Mash'al from Ramallah.[94]

In the eighteenth century, a new major urban center developed in the patriarchate, Acre, which had a significant Christian population. The local Christians,
who were active, enterprising, and literate, were distinct from their coreligionists
in the patriarchate's hinterland. Catholic propaganda was active in Acre, and the
city became one of the centers of the Melkite Uniate Church. It must be credited
to the Brotherhood of the Holy Sepulchre that they realized that the metropolitan of Acre should only be an Arab and, in 1713, they put on the throne the same
Photius/'Abd al-Nur (d. 1721).[95]

In 1740, an even better choice was made in the patriarchate. Sophronius al-
Kilizi, born in northern Syria, was the greatest Arab theologian of his century
and the author of several polemical and educational works. Although he largely
appears as a man of Greek culture, recognized by the Phanariots as one of their
own, Sophronius nevertheless did not break from the Arab environment and
acted as an intermediary between the two variants of the Orthodox culture of
the Levant: Greek and Arab. After a series of dramatic turns in his biography, in
1770, he was elected patriarch of Jerusalem and four years later he moved to the
See of Constantinople—a unique event in the Ottoman Empire.

No less colorful a figure was the other Arab, Patriarch Anthimus, who led the
Church of Jerusalem from 1788 to 1808. He came from a Mesopotamian Nestorian background. As a child, he was captured by Bedouins, bought by members
of the Brotherhood of the Holy Sepulchre, converted to Orthodoxy, and received
a Greek education. Anthimus seems to have fully assimilated to his Greek environment. He was secretary of the Brotherhood of the Holy Sepulchre, headed the

seminary in Jerusalem, and wrote theological treatises in Greek. He translated these same treatises into Arabic, however, and it was in Arabic that he published in Vienna his theological and educational works, which had a wide circulation among Orthodox Arabs.

On occasion, Palestinian Arabs made a career in the neighboring Patriarchate of Antioch. Porphyry Uspensky wrote describing one of them in 1843, "The Metropolitan Jacob of Selucia of the native Arabs ... a perfect ignoramus, a Bedouin; he smelled like a dog; his hands were unusually black."[96]

Discussion of interethnic relations in the patriarchate should not exaggerate the conflict between the Greeks and the Orthodox Arabs, as typically was done by observers of the nineteenth century. Before the arrival of nationalist ideologies to the Middle East, such ethnophobia was largely drowned out by a feeling of religious unity. In the sixteenth and eighteenth centuries, Greeks and Arab Christians perceived each other as "their own," albeit with some reservations. A significant proportion of members of the Brotherhood of the Holy Sepulchre, not excluding patriarchs, knew Arabic and focused on the needs of their flock, despite the fact that they, of course, looked down on them. Patriarch Dositheus specifically enjoined that a proportion of the young monks study Arabic. He even admonished members of the Brotherhood of the Holy Sepulchre, "Love the Christians. Make sure to care for their multiplication and salvation.... Visit the widows and orphans, honor the priests and do not despise the very small."[97] Priestly vestments were issued to rural churches at the Brotherhood's expense. Dositheus, however, recommended that strong linen robes be prepared and that satin vestments should not be given. He also ordered that a distribution of Arabic liturgical books be organized and that they be sent to rural perishes where they were needed, although this was at the parishes' expense.[98]

The Brotherhood of the Holy Sepulchre served as an organ of social support for the Orthodox community, paying taxes for the poor, ransoming Christians during times of war in Palestine, and materially supporting the orphaned and needy. It is interesting that the Arabs perceived such charity as the patriarchate's direct responsibility. In 1852, Porphyry Uspensky was a witness to the rebellion of the Arabs of Bethlehem against the local metropolitan who had refused to make increased payments to his parishioners.[99]

For their part, the Orthodox Arabs always supported the Greeks in their struggle with the Catholics and Armenians for possession of the holy places to the point that bishops sometimes had to restrain the ardor of their flocks, fearing bloodshed. During the persecutions against the Brotherhood of the Holy Sepulchre in the 1820s, when it was completely bankrupted by Ottoman extortion, *fellahin* brought free bread to the monks.[100] In general, Arabs should not be perceived as a sort of downtrodden "herd," kicked around uncontrollably by the Phanariots. Earlier, we discussed the warlike and ferocious manners of the Palestinian Christians. At the same time, the Christian Arabs were completely uneducated and, so to speak, apolitical. They took the domination of the Greeks in the patriarchate for granted.

Grigorovich-Barsky paints a downright touching picture of the meeting of a Greek bishop in the Arab village of Beit Jala in December 1726:

> There, when the bishop was entering in, all the people from the village came out with wives and children to meet him and accompanied him with much festivity, and shouting, and crying out, singing and chanting some words in the Arabic speech, and they did all in accordance with their custom out of their simplicity and humility—some, running up to his horse, kissed his hand, some crawled up to the rooftops of the houses, stood there and greeted him, shouting with the loud voice, and some went ahead of him, and some followed him, crying: "Blessed is he that comes!"[101]

When the bishop and his companions served the liturgy and then returned to the inn, "then the poor Ethiopian people, each proportionate to the ability of his own house … brought to the inn and presented to us a satisfying meal … and many people served us out of zeal and out of their simplicity of heart, and others stood by."[102] The villagers' joy could largely be attributed to the fact that they had not seen their bishop for four years,[103] however, even though Beit Jala is just a few kilometers from Jerusalem. Greek bishops no longer bothered to visit remote corners of the patriarchate.

To summarize, we note that the most important condition for the establishment of the Greek xenocracy was a general decline of the Christian Middle East during the Mamluk era. The Orthodox communities of the Balkans were more resilient and capable of expansion. The preservation of Greek hegemony in church structures promoted the "archaization" of a significant proportion of the Arab Christian population of the patriarchate. Rural communities were locked into their tribal framework, losing a connection to the clergy of Jerusalem and making no claim to participate in the management of the church. The ethnic consciousness of the Arab was drowned out by a religious worldview on the one hand and clan solidarity on the other hand. An educationally and economically independent Arab urban elite would have been capable of real competition with the Greeks, but elite groups were in their infancy among the Orthodox Arabs.

It was only in the nineteenth century that their level of self-awareness and self-organization came to be sufficient to challenge the authority of the Brotherhood of the Holy Sepulchre.

Serbian Monks in Palestine

By the late seventeenth century, the Greeks and Arabs were the only representatives of Orthodox peoples in Palestine. The Serbian and Georgian communities, which had flourished in the Holy Land for many centuries, slowly faded away.

The Serbian presence in Palestine dates back to the thirteenth century. Active pilgrimage to the holy places, which was initiated in 1229 by St Sava Nemanjić, the first archbishop of Serbia, led around 1313–1315 to the founding in Jerusalem of the Monastery of St Michael the Archangel (Dayr al-Sirb, in the Arabic sources), the patron saint of the Serbian state. The kings of Serbia provided generous patronage to the monastery and organized the relocation of monks there from the Balkans. The Serbian colony in the Holy Land flourished in the second half of the fourteenth century together with its patron, along with which it entered into a period of decline in the fifteenth century. The Slavic monastic community in Palestine was nevertheless quite resilient, surviving the end of the Serbian state by almost two centuries. Moreover, in 1504, the Serbs even expanded their holdings, taking the Monastery of Mar Saba, which had been abandoned by monks on account of the Bedouin threat.[104]

The Greeks, who dominated the leading positions in the Patriarchate of Jerusalem after 1534, found a rival in a Serbian community that was in many ways similar to them. It appears that no historians have written that in the brotherhood of the Sabaites we witness another monastic republic, like Athos, Sinai, or the Brotherhood of the Holy Sepulchre. It was a sort of order with a strong esprit de corps, a network of landholdings, a self-sufficient economy, and, of course, a specific subculture determined by the Slavic origin of most of the monks. The core of the brotherhood was made up of Mar Saba and the Monastery of the Archangel in Jerusalem. They constituted a single body with common management and treasury.[105] Monks moved freely from one monastery to the other particularly in times of increased Bedouin attacks on the Lavra, when the majority of its inhabitants moved to the Monastery of the Archangel Michael within the walls of the city. The Lavra also had a number of metochia that collected alms and supported pilgrimage. The first such metochia were founded by Sava Nemanjić on Mount Sion and in Acre.[106] These monasteries were destroyed with the expulsion of the Crusaders. In the thirteenth and sixteenth centuries, the Lavra possessed a monastery in Paphos on Cyprus.[107] In the 1580s, the ruler of Moldavia gave Mar

Saba a metochion in Iasi.[108] No doubt there were more metochia, but the sources do not contain sufficient information about them.

At the same time, the Serbs did not aspire to leadership in the Palestinian Church, even as they jealously defended their autonomy within the patriarchate. The Serbs "diverted" to their monasteries a proportion of the flow of pilgrims, who appear to have primarily been Slavs, thereby depriving the patriarchate of income. Using the proceeds from pilgrimage and the scant stream of alms from the Slavic lands, the Serbian monks maintained financial independence from the Patriarchate of Jerusalem and paid their own taxes for themselves. According to Dositheus, the Serbs demanded that they be specially allocated a section of the Holy Sepulchre and their abbot defiantly approached the patriarch of Jerusalem with his staff, in violation of his canonical subordination.[109] Dositheus either concealed from his readers or did not know that the Serbs did not "demand" a section of the church, but rather already possessed it. This had been reported by pilgrims in the fifteenth century.[110] A "Serbian throne" near the Holy Edicule is mentioned in a Greek *proskynetarion* from the 1580s.[111] The conflict between the Sabaites and the patriarch of Jerusalem in 1578–1579 and the efforts of the other Eastern patriarchs to reconcile the two parties has been discussed. The hostility of the Greeks toward the Serbian monks of Mar Saba is clearly visible even a century later, when Dositheus declared in exasperation, "And if only the Serbian monks knew how to read the life of St Savva we would be so proud!"[112]

Although it strove for independence, the Serbian community nevertheless did not cultivate isolationism, but rather maintained contacts with the entire Orthodox East. It appears that Mar Saba enjoyed special authority in Syria and three patriarchs of Antioch came from the Lavra in the seventeenth century. In a letter to Ivan the Terrible, thanking him for sending alms, Patriarch of Antioch Joachim Jum'a asked, "Again never forget the holy monastery of St Savva the Sanctified, it remains there with great intersessions for you, the tsar"[113]—a rare case of a patriarch asking for assistance that is not for one of his own monasteries. Petitioning the Russian tsar for alms in 1594, the patriarch of Antioch suggested that they be sent to the Monastery of the Archangel and the Lavra for the monks who had been sent to Moscow, and whom he named as authorized representatives of the patriarchate.[114]

The Serbian community played a prominent role in the life of the Palestinian Church. One may recall the circumstances of the election of Patriarch Sophronius in 1579 when the Serbs, in the person of Athanasius, abbot of the monastery Dayr al-Sirb,[115] made up one of the elements of the Orthodox community in its petition to the Ottoman authorities to recognize the new patriarch.

Number	Year	Historian	Lavra	Dayr al-Sirb (Archangel Monastery)	In Both	Total, including those who left for obediences	Footnotes
1	1547	Monk Sophronius	50				A. Cohen, p. 87
2	1553/1554	Ottoman tax registry	20	15			A. Cohen, p. 87
3	1562/1563	Ottoman tax registry	31				A. Cohen, p. 90
4	1584	Mikołaj (Nicholas) Radziwiłł	Approximately 30				Mikołaj (Nicholas) Radziwiłł, p. 138
5	1593	Trifon Korobeynikov			80	250	T. Korobeynikov, p. 99
6	Between 1608 and 1634	Proskynetarion 1608–1634	"The lavra was rich with monks"				Proskynetarion 1608–1634, p. 69 p. 69
7	1619	Ioanniky the cellarer	50	60			RGADA F. 52/1. 1629 No. 22. L. 6
8	1636	Vasily Gagara	90 or 110 (in different redactions)				V. Gagara, p. 13, 59

The size of the Serbian community in the Holy Land can be determined on the basis of Ottoman tax registries and the reports of travelers who visited the Palestinian monasteries. At the same time, however, it should be taken into account that not all the monks of Mar Saba were Serbs. Among them were Greeks (some of whom rose to high positions, as evidenced by the report that Patriarch Germanus had been abbot of the Lavra before his election as patriarch) and Arabs (a native of the city of Hama, 'Abd al-Karim Karma, the future patriarch of Antioch, took his vows in the monastery in the 1590s). Archimandrite Leonid wrote about the growing importance of Greeks in the monastery starting in the early seventeenth century, although even then the main figures in the monastery were chosen from among the Serbs.[116]

On the basis of this table, it appears that the total number of inhabitants of the Serbian monasteries was roughly a few dozen people, out of a total monastic population in Palestine that numbered, according to Trifon Korobeynikov in 1593, around two to three hundred people.

Pressure from the Bedouins, the dilapidation of ancient monasteries, and the end of financial support from the Balkans were the main problems facing the Serbian community. Starting in the second half of the sixteenth century, the Palestinian Serbs, following the example of the Balkan compatriots, started to seek the protection of the Russian tsars, and for a time, Muscovy rather than Serbia was the major donor to Mar Saba. Some writers of the nineteenth century suggested that Moscow hoped to make the Serbian community into a pillar of support for Russian ecclesiastical interests in the Holy Land.[117] This account is far too colored by pan-Slavism to account for the realities of the sixteenth century. However, the Serbian monks repeatedly and deliberately received substantial financial assistance from Russia.

The first example of such assistance goes back to 1552 and has a somewhat-legendary character: information about it is not found in the Russian archives, but rather in accounts from later pilgrims. According to this story, two elders of the Monastery of the Archangel, Moses and Methodius, received a generous gift for the restoration of the monastery's refectory from Ivan IV and Metropolitan Macarius of Moscow. Out of gratitude, the Serbs set up a chapel in the monastery church dedicated to St John the Baptist, the tsar's patron. These events became the subject of pious legends about how the *sanjak-bey* of Jerusalem once again determined to destroy the restored refectory, but through the monks' prayers to the Archangel Michael, the bey was found dead at the gate to his house, stabbed with a scimitar, and the Turks never again infringed upon the monastery.[118]

The first documented evidence of contact between Mar Saba and Russia (archival documents of this type are, incidentally, the main source of history for the Serbian community of Palestine from the second half of the sixteenth century to the early seventeenth century) is a message from Abbot Joasaph of the Lavra to Ivan IV, dating from the late 1550s. The text itself of the letter has not been preserved, but its contents are summarized in the response to it:

> You wrote to us, that you had no one to build churches or cells in the Lavra. And you are greatly insulted by the Arabs, because of how the monastery fence has decayed, and we would grant to you to send you alms for the building of the church and the monastery.[119]

Alms in the amount of 200 rubles were sent to the Lavra with the embassy of Vasily Poznyakov.

Starting in the 1580s, contacts between the Serbian monasteries and Russia became more frequent and embassies were sent to Moscow one after another. During this period, living in the Serbian monastic community was the cellarer Damaskin, a native of Macedonia and a "great elder," as he is referred to in the Russian sources. In addition to the Moscow archives, he is mentioned by the Polish pilgrim Mikołaj Radziwiłł, who met Damaskin at the Lavra in 1583 and rather productively communicated with him, as Damaskin knew Polish, thanks to a long journey through the Polish Commonwealth to Moscow. Repeatedly visiting Russia (before 1583, in 1586–1588, 1590–1591, and on other occasions), Damaskin entered into the special confidence of Boris Godunov and received generous gifts from him, not only for the Lavra but also for himself. Many historians have described the episode in 1591 when Godunov gave Damaskin a great deal of alms for the Serbian monasteries of Palestine unbeknownst to the Greek bishops with whom Damaskin was returning from Moscow. Andrei N. Muraviev promoted a romantic version of this story, in which these funds were intended for a tacit commemoration of the soul of the murdered Tsarevich Dmitri. Later authors interpreted the situation more realistically: Boris Gudonov, who knew about the tensions in Palestine between the Serbs and the Greeks through Damaskin and other informants, provided special protection to the Serbs, but in secret, so as not to displease the Greeks.[120]

In 1592, 150 rubles were sent to the abbot of Mar Saba, Christopher, via Damaskin and another 90 rubles were sent to the abbot of the Monastery of the Archangel, Cyril. The elders of the monastery were issued charters permitting them free passage to Moscow for alms-seeking.[121] We know of another journey to the court of the Russian tsar by Damaskin in the spring of 1594.[122] After that, however, Damaskin decided for some reason to settle permanently in Moscow, and the alms he was given did not reach Palestine.

In the Russian archives, there is also information about awards sent to Mar Saba in 1597 and 1599, but an embassy arriving there in 1603 headed by Archimandrite Gregory conveyed the desperate message that aid had not been received from Russia in fourteen years and that the situation in the monastery had become catastrophic. In a letter dated September 1602, the abbot of the monastery, Gabriel, wrote,

> Here, in the holy places, there is much grief, needs, and hunger, of the sort which did not happen in our days, and the violence of the Arabs has multiplied, such that we barely survived in these holy and divine places here. But we stood fast in the waterless land ... fiercely enclosed ... by the Arab peoples, which have multiplied due to our sins. We then, humble, incapable of enduring such necessities, departed for a short time, until the wrath of God, the great hunger and need, would pass by, so that we also may take a little respite from our labors. And may the Lavra stand closed for some time, until the Arab race become peaceful; and now not many elders abide there, enclosed in the monastery for fear of the Ishmaelites. Thus we, on the advice of our most holy patriarch, Sophronius, having taken all of the church vessels, came to the holy city Jerusalem, to our other monastery of the Archangel, where we unceasingly pray for your crown.[123]

Incidentally, a manuscript exists that was copied by the most famous monk of the Lavra of that time, 'Abd al-Karim Karma, which was made in February 1604 at the Monastery of the Archangel, where the future patriarch and the other brothers holed up, waiting for troubled times to pass.[124] Archimandrite Gregory also wrote about this in his letter to the head of the embassy,

> Because of their sins [i.e., of Mar Saba brotherhood], great poverty came to be in the monastery, as well as the impoverishment of the alms, because a great war began between the Turkish tsar with the Caesar [i.e., the Holy Roman emperor] and the Moldavian voivode, and the alms from everywhere to the monastery has stopped, and the poor ones who pray for the tsar [i.e., the Lavra's inhabitants] came to be in great need, naked and barefoot, from the top of their head to their feet they perish, everything in the monastery has become dilapidated, no one to repair anything because of great poverty.[125]

The embassy was solemnly received by the tsar and the patriarch, receiving generous gifts. It was sent back in 1604 along with the cellarer Damaskin, who had spent all those years in Moscow. The monks of the Lavra were given a charter in the name of Tsar Boris, modeled on the one they had received from Fyodor Ivanovich in 1592. Special cells in the Greek hostel near the Monastery of the Theophany were reserved for the monks, becoming a sort of metochion for the Lavra.[126] The following decade and a half, when, because of the Times of Troubles in Muscovy, the Palestinian monasteries did not receive any Russian alms, would prove fatal for the Serbian monastic community. Monks, however, returned to the monastery, if one is to believe the testimony of the Greek cellarer of the Novo-spassky Monastery, Ioannichius, that before 1619, the number of monks in the Lavra reached fifty under the patriarch of Jerusalem, although the abbot remained in the Monastery of the Archangel in Jerusalem.[127] The problems of the Sabaites are even reflected in documents of the Sublime Porte. A *firman* mentioned that because of the destruction of the monastery walls, "Arab bandits" (i.e., Bedouins) robbed the monastery, striking the monks with arrows and stones. Around 1603–1605, the Sabaites received permission from the Ottoman authorities for a partial reconstruction of the monastery fortifications. The approval of documents and construction dragged on for many years.[128]

By 1612, the Serbs finished construction of a tower on the south side of the Lavra, named after St Simeon of Serbia (then when the Greeks took the monastery, they renamed it for St Simeon the Stylite). The tower was meant for protection against the Bedouins. Archimandrite Leonid, however, assumed that by doing so the Serbs were attempting to separate themselves from the Greek monks without leaving the monastery and to consolidate control over buildings in the monastery complex that would belong exclusively to them.[129] In an Ottoman document from July 1613, they vaguely referred to some "wicked ones," who caused resentment and violence to the Sabaites monks with the license of the Jerusalem *qadi*. According to Serbian scholars, it is then a question of their Greek competitors seeking to gain mastery over the monastery.[130] Construction work at the monastery plunged the Serbs into heavy debt from which they could not get out.

In the 1620s, however, contacts between Russia and Palestine were renewed. Emissaries from Moscow arriving in Istanbul sent alms for the Lavra, and Sabaite archimandrites came to Russia either as part of an embassy from the Patriarchate of Jerusalem or separately in 1625, 1629, and 1636. In letters from Palestine, the situation of the monks of the Lavra is described in increasingly gloomy colors. As Patriarch Theophanes of Jerusalem wrote in 1625,

They are in great need in their holy monastery, because the Arabs harass them day and night. And it is wonderful in these days how they abide in the desert and maintain the holy lavra because before this there was ... in the Jordan desert 300 monasteries and now they are the only one remaining ... and the holy Lavra of St Sabas barely holds on.[131]

He was echoed in 1636 by Abbot Athanasius, who said when writing to Tsar Mikhail Romanov,

> We suffer constantly in great debt because of the Hagarites and Arabs, who abide there, and we bear great offense from them. Help us to repair the holy monastery because it has become ruined by its old age, the walls and the cells are broken and the holy images are damaged. By the grace of God we ... have established a few cells as before for the peace of the brothers, but we are in debt because of this and we do not have any way to pay the debt.[132]

The embassy sent by Abbot Athanasius in 1636 was the last one to be sent from the Lavra. Deprived of a regular source of income and in a difficult relationship with the Greek patriarch, the Serbs could not keep their monasteries and soon after 1636 they were forced to leave them. Between 1636 and 1640, Patriarch Theophanes of Jerusalem paid off the Serbian debt of 54,000 piasters and gained control over both monasteries.[133]

The Georgian Presence in the Holy Land

The fate of the Georgian monastic community in Palestine was somewhat similar to that of the Serbian one. Georgians had appeared in the Holy Land in the Byzantine period and their presence continued in the early Arab period. In 1038, they founded the Monastery of the Holy Cross a few kilometers from Jerusalem, which later would become the core of the Iberian colonies. Georgian influence in Palestine reached its peak during the Mamluk period. The Georgians possessed the site of Calvary in the Church of the Holy Sepulchre, dozens of monasteries, and large landholdings. They received generous alms from Georgia and were virtually independent of the patriarchs of Jerusalem.[134] The crisis in the Georgian state starting in the fifteenth century, which reduced the amount of financial support from the mother country and the influx of new monks, and the collapse of the Mamluk sultanate that patronized the Georgians, led to a growing decline in the Iberian community in Palestine.

Unable to maintain their monasteries, the Georgians sold or leased them to other confessions. Originally belonging to the Georgians was the Monastery of St John, which was loaned to Franciscan monks after their expulsion from Mount Sion by the Turks in 1551/1552.[135] Under Patriarch Theophanes, the Georgians gave the monasteries of St Thekla and St John the Baptist to the Greeks. After that, there remained in their hands another five monasteries in addition to the Monastery of the Holy Cross.[136]

The literature suggests that most of these monasteries were abandoned in the sixteenth century and the remnants of the Georgian colonies were concentrated in the Monastery of the Holy Cross where the Ottoman tax registries for the years 1553/1554 and 1562/1563 note fifteen Georgian monks.[137] However, when Trifon Korobeynikov distributed alms to the monasteries in Palestine in 1593, he noted the presence of monks in the Iberian monasteries of St George, St Theodore Stratelates, and St Nicholas the Wonderworker in Jerusalem. While there were bishops who had come on a pilgrimage from the Georgian lands and spent a long time in the monasteries of Palestine,[138] the local Iberian community was headed by the abbots of the Monastery of the Holy Cross, who held the rank of simple priests. The aforementioned transfer of patriarchal power from Germanus to Sophronius in 1579 was confirmed by, among others, the priest Jacob, head of the Georgian community.[139] The elder Joseph (the "builder," i.e., the rector) represented the Palestinian Georgians to Trifon Korobeynikov, obtaining from him 100 gold pieces for the maintenance of the Church of the Crucifixion (Calvary). Another elder Joseph (most likely the same person) was issued 40 gold pieces for the Monastery of the Holy Cross.[140] In sources from the early 1650s, there are references to Georgian monks in the Monastery of St Nicholas, which apparently acted as a metochion of the Monastery of the Holy Cross. The other Iberian monasteries seem to have been abandoned or rented out to laypeople.[141] By that time, the Georgians had lost their sections in the Church of the Holy Sepulchre. According to one traveler, they had been utterly impoverished by extortion and were forced to sell their right to half of Golgotha for 14,000 piasters.[142]

In the late sixteenth century and the first half of the seventeenth century, the patriarchs of Jerusalem, Sophronius and Theophanes, undertook efforts to secure a stable flow of financial assistance from Georgia to the Holy Land. First, starting in 1588, the kings of Kartli and then the rulers of the other Georgian lands donated significant amounts of money and property (churches and villages, as well as rent from certain groups of serfs) to the Holy Sepulchre and the Georgian monasteries in Palestine. Most donations took place in the second decade of the seventeenth century and are associated with the visit of Theophanes to Georgia around 1613. The cash income generated by these assets was distributed in a certain proportion between the Georgian monastic community and the patriarchate, but these revenues were irregular, and for the most part, they ended up in the possession of the stewards of the Brotherhood of the Holy Sepulchre's holdings in Georgia.[143]

The fact that the Patriarchate of Jerusalem depended on these donations meant that relations between the Greeks and the Georgian colony in Jerusalem were not as strained as the relations of the former with the Serbs. In his letters to the Georgian rulers, Patriarch Dositheus compared them with St Constantine and commemorated the Georgian kings' patronage of the holy sites of Palestine under the Mamluks, saying that "inasmuch as the Iberians helped the Greeks during their time of need, we shall now serve the Iberians in their time of need" and, citing the saying from the New Testament that "there is neither Greek nor Jew," he stated that "therefore in Jerusalem let him be anathema who says that there is a difference between Iberians and Greeks."[144]

Another factor that made the situation of the Georgians easier than that of the Serbs was that there was a lesser degree of threat from the Bedouins to the Georgian monasteries. If Mar Saba was deep in the Judean Desert, the Monastery of the Holy Cross was at least to a certain extent protected by Jerusalem from attacks by the nomads. Nevertheless, even the Monastery of the Holy Cross had to pay off the Bedouins, something that worsened its already difficult financial situation.[145] Another heavy burden for the monastery was the cost of maintaining the Georgian pilgrims who came to Palestine. This one obligation created a debt of 94,000 piasters for the Monastery of the Holy Cross.[146]

The monastery, however, knew periods of temporary recovery, especially in the 1740s when its abbot was Nicholas (in the world, Nicephorus Cholokashvili, d. 1658), a member of the Georgian aristocracy who was close with King Teimuraz of Kartli. During this time, Cholokashvili went at the king's request on embassies to various sovereigns of Europe and Asia, including three to Russia. He spent time in Italy, France, and Spain, knew seven languages, and was regarded as a "philosopher" and "orator." In Jerusalem, the Georgian archimandrite became friends with Patriarch Theophanes who, according to Dositheus, before dying appointed Nicephorus as his successor. The Brotherhood of the Holy Sepulchre, of course, did not allow the patriarchal throne to depart from Greek hands and, it seems, did not forgive Nicephorus his ambitions. This is how A. Tsagareli explained Dositheus Notaras's sharply worded comments about Cholokashvili, that the Georgian archimandrite "traveled among the Franks and various peoples. Outwardly he was a monk, but in his heart he was a proud and alluring man."[147] Nicholas organized large-scale reconstruction works at the Monastery of the Holy Cross,[148] which were praised by Arseny Sukhanov when he visited there in the early 1650s:

The church is large and more beautiful, everything is newly executed, the bridge is paved with a pattern of small multi-colored marble, there are countless cells, the wall is as high as a city, everything is new; in all of Jerusalem there is no other monastery like it, [none] of which are built so entirely, and Iberians live in it ... and the patriarch does not own them.[149]

The restoration of the Monastery of the Holy Cross, one of the brightest architectural projects undertaken by Palestinian Christians in the early Ottoman era, was ultimately the swan song of the Georgian colony in the Holy Land. Nicholas's ambitious undertaking ultimately undid the monastery's finances. Cholokashvili left Jerusalem around 1648 and, according to Dositheus, "since then.... bad abbots have come to the Monastery of the Holy Cross, bringing it into debt. The monastery received nothing from Iberia on account of the alms collectors' greed."[150] After some time, the Georgians were finally forced to leave their monasteries because of the unbearable debts. According to Dositheus,

A monk or layman from among the Iberians came to Jerusalem. The Turks threw him in a tower and demanded money from him. They seized the property of the Monastery of the Holy Cross and added it to their own property. Of the abbots of the Holy Cross, they killed Gabriel, Joseph fled from Jerusalem during the night, and Meletius was kept in prison for many years.[151]

The date when the Georgian monasteries were abandoned is not entirely clear. In a letter from 1706, Patriarch Dositheus wrote that the monasteries had been in ruins for around forty years.[152] It is unlikely that he had in mind forty years before 1706, since by 1685, Dositheus was able to pay off the Georgians' debts and reopen the monasteries. An assumption of forty years before 1685 is also not consistent with the sources, which in the early 1650s mention a Georgian monastery existing two *versts* to the west of Jerusalem "and pious Georgian monks tend the corn with their own hands, sow, plow and reap, and dig the grapevines, and ... fed and gave water to visitors."[153]

Starting in 1659 and several times in the 1660s, Georgian hierarchs attempted to raise money to release the Palestinian monasteries from their debts, but for various reasons, these efforts did not find success. The Muslim authorities sealed off the monasteries and they were dilapidated and abandoned, whereas the Latins and Armenians offered to pay off the debts to gain possession of them. Finally, in 1681–1682, Patriarch Dositheus traveled to Georgia and was able to negotiate with the Georgian king to pay off the debts of the Iberian monasteries.

Having collected the necessary money in the Georgian lands, to which he added some of his own funds, in 1682, Dositheus paid off the Iberian monasteries' debts with interest; regained their landholdings in Palestine; built new walls and cells; and, by 1685, divine services resumed in them.[154] Now, however, the monasteries were owned by the Greeks, although by inertia. For some time, Dositheus considered his spending on the maintenance of these monasteries to be grants to the Georgians[155] and was prepared at any time to transfer them into the control of an abbot sent from Georgia. "If he does not have an income for the maintenance of the monasteries," stipulated the patriarch in 1706, "in this case let the Greek fathers manage the Christians' debt, which one church possesses in respect to another church, above all the Holy Sepulchre, which is the common church ... of all Orthodox."[156]

Thus, the Iberian monasteries came under the control of the Greeks, the Georgian colony in Palestine disappeared, and the properties in Georgia that had been donated to the Palestinian monasteries came under the control of the Greek Brotherhood of the Holy Sepulchre. Pilgrims continued to come to Palestine from Georgia in the eighteenth century and the rulers of the Georgian principalities corresponded with the patriarchs of Jerusalem and sent them gifts, while the Brotherhood of the Holy Sepulchre received income from Georgian estates.[157] A stable Georgian monastic community was not established, however, and the occasional pilgrims left melancholy records in the margins of unused Georgian manuscripts that there were no more Georgians in the Monastery of the Holy Cross.[158]

The Brotherhood of the Holy Sepulchre had become the sole representative of the Orthodox Church in Palestine.

THE BROTHERHOOD OF THE HOLY SEPULCHRE: AN INSIDE VIEW
The Brotherhood of the Holy Sepulchre was intrinsically not homogeneous. Within it, a number of smaller groups unofficially existed on the basis of clans or common homeland. The first four Greek patriarchs were related to each other, forming a veritable "Peloponnesian dynasty" at the head of the Church of Jerusalem from 1534 to 1660. Dositheus and his nephew Chrysanthos constituted a second Peloponnesian dynasty from 1669 to 1731. Ruling in the interval between these two clans was Patriarch Nectarius, a Cretan who was soon forced to abdicate, perhaps because he was a "foreigner" and did not figure into the balance of forces within the Brotherhood of the Holy Sepulchre.

Incidentally, other ecclesiastical structures within the Orthodox *millet* were built on the same principle of clannishness. From the late sixteenth century through the first half of the seventeenth century, the Patriarchate of Alexandria was for the most part headed by Cretans who also dominated the Monastery of Sinai. The Greek bishops active in the Patriarchate of Antioch in the seventeenth century were natives of Chios and in the eighteenth century were Cypriots.

Within a patriarch's entourage there almost always numbered some of his relatives, fellow countrymen, and people who were close to him for other reasons. Thus, Patriarch Paisius, who had been an abbot in Iasi, and Patriarch Chrysanthos, who had spent long years in Moldavia, sought to promote the Greek abbots of Moldavian monasteries as hierarchs, and in this, Chrysanthus was met with resistance from members of the Brotherhood of the Holy Sepulchre in Palestine.[159] In 1630, Patriarch Theophanes had to justify himself to the Russian government for "consecrating his own as metropolitans."[160] In fact, the accusations were well grounded. The patriarch's right hand, the metropolitan of Bethlehem, was his first cousin, and he granted an entire brood of nephews, including the future Patriarch Paisius, the rank of archimandrite, assigning them to manage the Moldavian properties of the Holy Sepulchre and sending them on diplomatic missions to Moscow.[161] An interesting point is found in a statute of the Monastery of Sinai from 1671:

> Inasmuch as a monk has no ... family since he has renounced all of this in his vow, it is therefore unjust for anyone to abusively designate another brother as family, to name Cretans, Rumeliots, or Cypriots ... or to help biasedly, such as their countrymen, inasmuch as we are all brothers in the sight of angels and we all have one homeland on earth—the holy monastery and the heavenly homeland—Jerusalem on high.[162]

In general, the feuds within the Brotherhood of the Holy Sepulchre were in no way comparable to the scandalous intrigues of the Phanariots in the capital. The higher clergy in Jerusalem was much more united than that in Constantinople. Perhaps this is because of the constant conflicts with the Catholics and Armenians as well as the opposition—albeit still implicit—between a few hundred Greeks at the top of the Church of Jerusalem and the tens of thousands of Arab Orthodox of Palestine. Of course, there were internal quarrels within the Brotherhood of the Holy Sepulchre. An idea of this can be gleaned from the rare chroniclers of the Brotherhood. Thus, Dositheus says of the financial losses of the Holy Sepulchre, which occurred "from the carelessness of our own people, from their disagreement and the jealousy and strife among them."[163] The abdication of Patriarch Nectarius in 1669 was largely due to the enmity "of monks who were proud and dissatisfied with their own state."[164] In the disciplinary regulations of the Brotherhood of the Holy Sepulchre from the sixteenth and eighteenth centuries, one constantly encounters threats of punishment for mutual strife.[165] Be that as it may, the Brotherhood of the Holy Sepulchre managed not to wash its dirty linens in public and, with rare exceptions, their infighting did not draw in the Ottoman authorities.

In contrast to the leapfrogging of patriarchs in the capital, who were installed and overthrown almost every year on account of the intrigues of their own clergy and Ottoman dignitaries, over a period of 350 years the See of Jerusalem changed hands only seventeen times. Palestinian chronicles and the writings of later historians[166] provide an understanding of the basic rules for the replacement of a vacant patriarchal throne. Until the middle of the seventeenth century, the bishops and monks in Jerusalem elected the patriarchs; then, after Paisius (1645), the elections themselves started to take place under the control of the Ecumenical Patriarchate, as a rule in Istanbul. The ceremony was attended by the patriarch of Constantinople and his synod (the relevant documents always stress his right to patronize the other Eastern Churches) and influential lay Phanariots, including the grand dragoman and the rulers of Moldavia and Wallachia, as well as any clergy of the Brotherhood of the Holy Sepulchre who happened to be in the capital. The final decision was sometimes approved by the clergy in Palestine. Conflicts did not arise between Jerusalem and Constantinople because almost every patriarch chose his successor ahead of time and the patriarch's will was always respected. There is no evidence for Ottoman intervention in filling the See of Jerusalem during the sixteenth and first half of the seventeenth centuries. Each patriarchal election was confirmed with the relevant *berat* from the sultan, but for the most part, this was merely a formality enshrining a decision that already had been made.[167]

The overthrow of hierarchs, a frequent occurrence in the capital, did not occur in Palestine. Out of seventeen primates of Jerusalem, nine ruled for life, one (Sophronius, 1770–1774) was transferred to the See of Constantinople, and seven abdicated. For the most part, we know that these abdications were done voluntarily on account of old age.[168]

THE ANTIOCHIAN CLERGY

The Metropolitan of Seleucia served in the monastery church with four priests, without a deacon, without a miter, in an ordinary kamelavkion, in which he goes to the bathroom. A peasant in a sakkos! Barefoot, half-naked boys were his acolytes …

Porphyry Uspensky, 1843

In the Patriarchate of Antioch, which was almost entirely Arab in its composition, relationships among the patriarchs, clergy, and laity developed differently than in Palestine. At the same time, the institution of the church played the same role in Syria as it did throughout the empire, taking the role of leadership in the Orthodox community not only as the intermediary between the people and God but also between the flock and the Ottoman authorities. The clergy was in charge of the allotment of taxes among Christians and defended the interests of the community before the Muslim administration. Although, as a rule the *jizya* was paid by the Christian communities themselves, the church hierarchy negotiated in advance about the list of Christians recorded in the tax registers and, under various pretexts, sought to strike more names off of it.[169] No less important were the internal functions of the church, most importantly social support for the lower strata of the population. The bishops and monasteries provided assistance to the poor and wayfarers. This support, however, was not always voluntary: The patriarchal vicar, Paul of Aleppo, describes how, during a famine year, the poor broke into the patriarchal residence where he kept food stocks, "and I," says Paul, "had no power to block their entrance."[170]

Church authorities tried to resolve conflicts within the community. As mentioned, bishops were given judicial authority. The range of issues for which the higher clergy were responsible was quite extensive: from allocating the powers of priests to regulating the shape of women's hats, from determining the age of brides and the size of bride prices to performing exorcism on the possessed.[171] Particularly noteworthy in this respect was the activity of Metropolitan Meletius Karma, who headed the Diocese of Aleppo from 1612 to 1634. A man of fanatical faith, a "religious fundamentalist" in modern terms, Meletius attempted to guide the life of his flock according to the rules of the church, fighting against secular "excesses"—"expensive luxuries" and "indecent singing and dancing." According to Mikhail Breik, he "forbade women from dressing in indecent foreign clothing and painting their faces because all this destroys souls."[172] The metropolitan sought to maintain social justice within the community, limiting the spending of wealthy members of his congregation and requiring them "to save some money for the poor every day."[173] Meletius spent the funds of his see for the benefit of the poor, on decorating the church, and on an impressive metropolitan's residence. Of particular importance because of his "clericalist" inclination, he paid for the education of the lower clergy in his own image and likeness "because [priests] must be a light to the world."[174]

The priests of the Church of Antioch were divided into two categories with slightly different prerogatives and vestments—*qassis* (monks or priests without parishes) and *khuri* (parish priests).[175] The state of the secular clergy in Syria can be ascertained primarily from relatively recent ethnographic observations made in the nineteenth century. It is not likely a mistake to project this information, with some modification, back onto previous centuries.

The Orthodox inhabitants of towns and villages chose candidates for the priesthood from among themselves—literate older men respected by their neighbors. During elections, however, disagreements and conflicts often broke out and residents were divided into warring factions, with each nominating their own candidates. The bishops ordained the chosen candidates and on rare occasion metropolitans themselves selected the priests.[176] The income from performing ecclesiastical duties was not enough for a livelihood, and priests continued to engage in trades or agriculture or received support from their adult children. Information that urban priests received a salary applies to the nineteenth century. As a whole, parish clergy were no wealthier than their flock.[177]

Inheritance of priestly dignity within a family occurred frequently, but was not an obligatory rule. Copyists of manuscripts listed their ancestries in colophons, providing many examples of priestly dynasties, as well as mixed genealogies, in which generations of priests and laymen alternated. Later observers tended to emphasize the clergy's low level of education. In the mid-nineteenth century, I. N. Berezin wrote that, for lack of schools, the clergy did not even have proper knowledge of religious dogmas.[178] An early-twentieth-century author noted that most of the priests "have only an elementary education … and still devote their leisure time to agricultural work."[179] At the same time, there could be found among the clergy, particularly those in the cities, people who were well-educated by the standards of the time.

Foreign observers were most struck by the proximity of life and customs between the parish clergy and the laity, and all this had a bright oriental coloring: carpets and mats instead of furniture, coffee and nargileh, and strictly separated women's quarters. Priests only differed from their parishioners by their black cloths and the black turban on their head. This similarity is especially apparent in semiremote regions: "Just like the laypeople, the priests in Hawran prance upon their thoroughbred Arab horses armed with long spears and swords and regularly join their parishioners in practicing farming and animal husbandry."[180] Such a sharply critical writer as Porphyry Uspensky, generally spoke positively about the lower clergy: "They [the clergy] soberly, honestly, humbly, and strictly, with understanding to the full extent, fulfill the rites and ordinances of the church and engage in teaching some of the village boys to read church texts."[181] Some observers repeated these assessments ("In terms of morality, the parish clergy in Syria are unimpeachable. The parish strictly monitors this"),[182] whereas others dispute them (the priests "sink to the level of the congregation in different ways, they do not stand up to their hierarchical calling").[183] Both assessments seem fair in their own way.

Priests had a prominent role in administrating the patriarchate's affairs. Representatives of the secular clergy were directly or indirectly involved in the election of patriarchs, attended their enthronements, and sealed with their signatures the corresponding conciliar acts. Macarius al-Za'im lists twenty-five priests who were present at his enthronement in 1647. Patriarch Cyril, speaking about his election as patriarch in 1672, gives a list of twenty-four *khuris*, four *qassis*, and five deacons who took part.[184] It seems that these were the priests of Damascus, neighboring villages (some of them have the *nisba*[185] al-Saydnawi, indicating that they were from Saydnaya), and people accompanying the metropolitans of neighboring dioceses. When corresponding with French diplomats regarding theological matters, Patriarch Macarius confirmed his "Confession of Faith" with the signatures of not only two metropolitans but also nine priests.[186]

When leading the community, if the ecclesiastical hierarchy encouraged its cohesion and religious solidarity, it benefited both morally and materially. Thus, for example, during the construction of the patriarchal residence in Damascus in the 1650s, the Christian masons worked with unprecedented enthusiasm, according to Mikhail Breik, who reported, perhaps with some exaggeration, that they performed such work in eighty days as they would have in two years for a Muslim customer.[187]

The administrative roles of bishops and patriarchs were performed by *wakils* (representatives) who were in charge of finances and church properties, taking the hierarch's place in his absence. The post of patriarchal *wakil* could be taken by a metropolitan or a simple priest—it did not depend on his place in the church hierarchy but rather on informal networks and personal influence. For many years, Paul of Aleppo had autocratic control over the affairs of the community in Damascus while only a deacon. The *wakil* could be a layman as, for example, was Michael Tuma from Amioun (d. 1763), who was Patriarch Sylvester's closest aid for more than thirty years.[188] Concentrating considerable funds in their own hands and almost exclusively managing the church's economy, especially during the patriarchs' frequent absences, the *wakils* sometimes became an independent power, an intermediate authority between the community, the patriarch, and the Ottoman government. This situation opened the way for various types of abuse. Especially notorious for his tyranny was the *wakil* Jiris al-Halabi (d. 1767), who relied on the support of the Turkish administration and burdened the community with exorbitant taxes. During services in the cathedral, he occupied a higher place than the metropolitans. According to Breik, the Christians suffering from Jiris's omnipotence could hope only in God.[189]

Whenever possible, the bishops tried to put a stop to their deputies' corruption. A church council of 1628 condemned the practice of obtaining the post of *wakil* through bribes. "It was a great misfortune," say the acts of the council,

> [when] the *wakil* was a simple layman but entered into the affairs of priests and objected to bishops in matters of faith. And it is no longer allowed as it had been according to former customs. And may the patriarchal *wakil* not enter into the territory where there already is a bishop.[190]

While he was bishop of Aleppo, Patriarch Macarius appointed forty *wakils* so that they could act as managers in pairs, to be replaced by the next pair the following year. "And the church's revenue began to thrive, with God's blessing," recounts Macarius's son Paul, never missing the opportunity to praise himself or his father. "Its cellars were filled with oil from year to year, its stores were filled with wax candles, and its treasury was provided with every need."[191]

The *wakil* usually was appointed by the patriarch, but sometimes (and this option was, of course, worse for the Christians) the Ottoman authorities interfered in the process. Such was the case in Aleppo in the 1650s, when the *wakils*, according to Paul,

> were appointed by means of those people who had power, according to the command of the pasha, by virtue of an advantage in the struggle and feuds, thanks to the weight of purses of money and to patronage, burdening of the Church with thousands in debt—yes the Lord will repay them just as they deserve![192]

Diocesan Bishops and Regional Centers of Power

The life of the Arab Orthodox of Syria was defined not only by the ecclesiastical hierarchy and the institution of the vicar acting in its name but also by a solid latticework of horizontal connections and organs of local self-rule. The urban Orthodox community had an organizational structure led by priests and a secular nobility, including a'yans, archons, and sheikhs. The communities acted as an independent force in contacts with metropolitans and patriarchs. There are cases in which townsfolk brought their bishops to trial before the Ottoman *qadi* and even banished unwanted metropolitans. More often, however, there was agreement between the bishop and his flock, as the community usually put forward a local candidate for the episcopacy, and the patriarch only consecrated the cleric sent to him. An analysis of the origins of the known metropolitans of Beirut and Aleppo from the sixteenth to the eighteenth centuries shows that most of them were locals, and sometimes they were members of prominent families of the cities. Fewer metropolitans were from other cities, but in such cases, they were closely associated with the local elites. There are few examples of a patriarch installing a bishop without the prior consent of his future flock.[193]

Taken as a whole, the geographic origins of Antiochian bishops reflect interesting demographic trends. Among the senior clergy of the second half of the sixteenth and first half of the seventeenth centuries, very many (as much as half) are natives of remote rural areas, especially the villages of Koura and 'Akkar. It is also evidence of the high social mobility of Christians that six of the eleven patriarchs from this period came from villages and small towns. Starting in the early seventeenth century, a growing number of men from the major cities of Damascus and Aleppo are found among the higher clergy. After the 1650s, with the increasing urbanization discussed in the previous chapter, "rural" bishops almost entirely disappear, and for the most part, city people stand at the head of the church, especially from the two main cities.[194]

A characteristic of the Antiochian bishops was that not all of them came from a monastic environment. In Ottoman Syria, the monastic clergy did not have a monopoly over posts at the top of the ecclesiastical hierarchy. Many bishops came from the secular clergy and even the laity and were only tonsured just before ordination. Other metropolitans engaged in worldly trades before their election—bookbinding, medicine, and weaving. Early in his career, Patriarch Ignatius 'Atiya was the secretary of Lebanese Emir Fakhr al-Din Ma'an.[195] One might recall the names of the early-sixteenth-century Patriarchs Dorotheus and Michael—ibn al-Sabbuni ("son of the soapmaker") and Ibn al-Mawardi ("son of the rosewater-seller"),[196] although these names do not necessarily reflect the trades of the patriarchs themselves before their election. According to Carsten Walbiner,[197] in the seventeenth century, only about half of the metropolitans whose origins are known can safely be said to have been monks before their consecration. Identifying the others is often complicated by the fact that upon elevation to the episcopate, all—both monks and nonmonastics—changed their name (i.e., a change of name does not indicate adopting monasticism), as well as the fact that the terms for "priest"—*khuri* and *qassis*—are widely used for both secular clergy and hieromonks.[198] The most reliable evidence for the nonmonastic origins of some bishops is the fact that they had children. In addition to the well-known Paul of Aleppo, Patriarch Michael ibn al-Mawardi (1523/1524–1540) and

Dorotheus IV (1604–1611) had their sons as deacons. In 1646, Patriarch Michael's son 'Isa donated an ancient book of ecclesiastical laws, the *Nomocanon*, to the Church of Sts Cyprian and Justina in Damascus, apparently in remembrance of the soul of his father. The registration of this gift was personally witnessed by the patriarch at the time, Joachim ibn Jum'a.[199] Some bishops have the element "abu" ("father of") in their names, such as Gregorius al-Hamawi Abu Constantine, metropolitan of Euchaita in the 1570s.[200] In total, we count nine bishops whose sons are mentioned in various sources.[201]

The urban communities entered into a complicated relationship with the Ottoman pashas. They corresponded with each other, with the patriarchs of neighboring sees, and with the Sublime Porte. That is to say, they were full-fledged political actors. When sending letters to Syria, patriarchs of Constantinople addressed their "hierarchs, clergy, archons, elders and all Christians of the See of Antioch."[202]

The leaders of urban communities, drawing on their resources, the support of their compatriots, and ties with the Ottoman administration, could sometimes play a greater role in the lives of Christians than the church hierarchy. Discussing the dethronement of one patriarch and the elevation of another in the early seventeenth century, a chronicle states that this happened "in the days of Sheikh George son of Samur."[203] It would not have been surprising if the lifetime of the sheikh had been dated according to the patriarchs contemporary to him. The chronicler, however, recorded it in the opposite manner, such that the sheikh seems to be the more important figure. Moreover, the fact that readers of the chronicle living more than half a century later understood who this George was without comment means that he left a very long memory of himself.

Given the power of local elites, we can say that the authority of the patriarchs of Antioch over their flock was not absolute. The patriarchs did not have a coercive mechanism. To maintain their authority, if necessary, they had to rely on the Ottoman administration. Thus, the powers of the patriarch depended first of all on his relations with the Ottoman pashas (i.e., whether or not the patriarch was solvent, as any interaction with the authorities required making payments) and, second, on the degree to which the pashas controlled their own territory. Diocesan bishops and regional secular notables, in turn, could directly negotiate with the local Ottoman authorities and buy their support and thus feel quite independent from the patriarch sitting in Damascus. From the sources, we know many examples of fierce infighting between bishops, violations of the canons, and other offences to which the patriarch had to turn a blind eye for fear that the bishops otherwise would cause "many trials and tribulations."[204] Thus, during the time of

Macarius's absence from Syria in the 1650s, many "lawless and shameful acts" were left uncontrolled by the metropolitans of Aleppo and Homs. With the support of the secular authorities, they severely oppressed the Christians and exceeded their canonical authority. The metropolitan of Homs even attempted to seize the patriarchal throne. Nevertheless, when Macarius returned to Syria, for some reason, he did not reveal his anger and treated the metropolitan of Emesa with feigned friendliness, exactly as the Sublime Porte might do in dealing with a powerful pasha who should be strangled when an opportune moment has not yet arrived. Even later, when Macarius convened a council and deposed the metropolitan, he fled to Aleppo and stayed there "persisting in his hypocrisy" until his death.[205]

Carsten Walbiner has drawn attention to a characteristic detail: at times of unrest in the Patriarchate of Antioch, various pretenders to the see declare themselves patriarch and erect bishops over the territories they control. Eventually, one of the two rivals would win, but he would never change the bishops appointed by his opponent.[206] Otherwise, it would have been necessary for the patriarch to enter into the entire diocese supporting its bishop.

LOCAL COUNCILS

The activity of regional elites and the influence of diocesan bishops contributed to the preservation of the institution of the church council that addressed important issues of religious and social life. As noted, however, alongside the metropolitans, dozens of priests and sometimes lay elites attended the councils. First, the elections of many patriarchs of the sixteenth and seventeenth centuries took place at councils. Second, when they did not have sufficient authority to punish recalcitrant metropolitans, patriarchs sought conciliar authorization to resolve internal church conflicts. Thus, in 1624 and 1626, Cyril Dabbas convened councils of the metropolitans who supported him to denounce the metropolitan of Aleppo, Meletius Karma, who stubbornly refused to obey the patriarch and pay him tribute.[207]

The prolonged struggle for the See of Antioch between Patriarchs Cyril Dabbas and Ignatius ʿAtiya was resolved in 1628 at a council of Syrian bishops in the town of Raʾs Baalbek, where Dabbas was deposed and condemned. The council's participants also drafted twenty canonical decrees, many of which dealt with the election of patriarchs and were intended to prevent a recurrence of the recent ruinous turmoil. "It was the custom of the Christians," reads the first of the council's decisions,

> that if the patriarch dies, there should come two or three bishops [to consecrate the patriarch] and pray over him in the absence of the others.

However, it is no longer permitted to become patriarch except in the presence of the bishops of all the dioceses. If someone violates this conciliar decree, let him be excommunicated.[208]

To avoid conflicts, it was instructed that candidates for the patriarchate be selected in consultation with the people and that the choice itself be made by lots. A direct indication of how the hegemony of the previous elites appeared can be found in the phrase "It was ... the custom that ordinary Christians (*a'wam al-masihiyin*) and some priests would interfere in the affairs of the patriarchate and the patriarch acted at their request." All of this, again, was strictly forbidden.[209]

As mentioned, the council of August 28, 1659, was organized by Patriarch Macarius to condemn Metropolitan Athanasius of Homs. This event was attended by seven metropolitans, all the priests of Damascus, and "honorable persons." Athanasius was accused of usurping the authority of the patriarch, numerous violations of the canons, bribery, and other irregularities. The council decided to defrock him and excommunicate him until he repented. The relevant decrees were sent to the diocese, which began with the formulation "I, Macarius, Patriarch of Antioch, in accordance with the provisions of Christian law, by the command of the Almighty and the sultan, have judged ... "[210] According to Paul, the bishops were delighted with the condemnation of the metropolitan of Homs because "he and his tongue were a knife to them."[211]

Thus, no special group solidarity was observed among the metropolitans, and they were often at odds with each other. In the history of the Patriarchate of Antioch, however, there is known to have been one council, conducted in early 1767 in Damascus under Patriarch Philemon, where the bishops' party demonstrated solidarity in favor of strengthening the role of the synod and limiting the autocracy of the patriarch and his influence on the ecclesiastical affairs of the laity. According to the decisions of the council, the appointment of bishops, judgment against them, and the appointment of a locum tenens during the absence of the patriarch, not to mention the abdication or election of the patriarch, had to take place with the synod's participation: "Let everything be accomplished with the knowledge of the synod," read one of the decisions, "and not according to the opinion of any one person"; "the income and expenses of the See of Antioch should be written in a book with the fear of God and without concealment."[212] Most of these decisions, however, remained on paper.

At the councils, the church hierarchy also by virtue of its theocratic authority regulated the social life of the flock and family and marital relationships. The famous council of 1573 conducted by Patriarch Joachim ibn Jum'a decided about the size of a bride price: it was divided into several categories, depending on the property status of those entering into marriage and rigidly fixed—the bride's parents were forbidden to require more. The resolution was engraved on the threshold of the gate to the Church of Sts Cyprian and Justina. Joachim secured letters from the other three Eastern patriarchs threatening with excommunication anyone who did not obey the established order.²¹³

Similar attempts to regulate the life of the clergy and laity took place at the Council of Ra's Baalbek in 1628. The canons of the council are interesting in terms of the ideas of the Arab Orthodox, or more precisely the most radically inclined circles of the clergy, regarding the social evils that needed to be eradicated. The "worst sin" was declared to by simony, the levying of fees by bishops for ordination to the priesthood. It also recommended that no person become a priest without a prior inquiry about his way of life. Priests were forbidden to take money from their congregations for the remission of sins. Such levies were hypocritically called "alms for the poor." It also sought to regularize the collection of alms for churches and monasteries because many unaccountable wandering monks practiced these collections. There were even clashes between competing alms collectors.²¹⁴ The council also repeated the earlier establishment of a fixed bride price because, as was stated in the relevant conciliar acts, some were demanding exorbitant amounts of money, "such that girls have reached the age of women without being betrothed and men have grown old unmarried."²¹⁵ At the suggestion of the puritanically minded Metropolitan Meletius Karma, a variety of ethical regulations were introduced. Thus, for example, luxuriant weddings with music, dancing, gluttony, and drunkenness were condemned. For the same reason, the council attempted to forbid holding celebrations for baptisms, which, according to Karma, amounted to the same drunkenness and gluttony, causing unnecessary costs for Christians. The canons especially forbade the drunkenness of priests at weddings, with an admonition that winebibbers would not enter the kingdom of heaven. The participants of the council also condemned various superstitions that existed among the people, such as wearing amulets, belief in charms, spells, and astrology.²¹⁶ Unsurprisingly, there was an attempt to implement the decisions of the council: a text from 1629 was signed by all the priests and *wakils* of Saydnaya, who committed to curb extreme displays of joy and sorrow (meaning boisterous feasting an funeral laments) on the part of the villagers.²¹⁷

The councils also dealt with complex religious issues, such as calculating the date of Easter in 1539, on account of which a tough debate erupted between the Orthodox and "heretical" confessions. In the end, Patriarch Michael called a council in the city of Qara, which was attended by the bishops of Yabrud,

Saydnaya, Baalbek, and al-Zabadani, as well as *"khuris, qassis*, and deacons from all the lands of Antioch." After lengthy proceedings involving the participation of authoritative scholars, it approved a precise calculation for Easter and paschal tables for two hundred years into the future.[218]

The Church of Antioch's relationship with the Western Christian world represents a particular problem to historians. According to Catholic authors, in either 1617 or 1618, Patriarch Athanasius II gathered the bishops in Damascus and discussed with them the prospects of reunion with the Church of Rome.[219] There is also mention in the literature of a council held in Tripoli in 1680 by Patriarch Cyril to affirm the dogmatic formulations in use in the Church of Antioch.[220] If this council did indeed take place, it could be connected to the spread at that time in the East of disputes over Protestant doctrine and its refutation.

THE STRUGGLE OF REGIONAL ELITES FOR LEADERSHIP

The inner life of the Patriarchate of Antioch evolved much more dramatically than that of Jerusalem. The history of Orthodox Syria is full of ambitious metropolitans competing for the patriarchal throne, with regional groupings of *a'yans* backing them. Every patriarch attempted to put his fellow countrymen or even relatives into key positions in the church administration and vacated bishoprics. Accordingly, one or another regional elite gained a dominant influence in the affairs of the church. In the sixteenth to eighteenth centuries, fights over the patriarchate repeatedly led to major conflicts in the Orthodox community in Syria. In this struggle, there were three or four main centers of power—Damascus, Aleppo, Tripoli, and, to a lesser extent, Hama. The Damascus community had the greatest direct influence on the choice of patriarchs because of the weight given to Damascus by its role as the residence of the patriarch and, more generally, the political center of Bilad al-Sham. Aleppo was the economic capital of Syria. The local Christians had significant financial opportunities and numerically accounted for a significant proportion of the flock of the Church of Antioch. Tripoli was, along with Damascus and Aleppo, the third capital of a Syrian pashalik and, in the sixteenth century, was the largest port on the Eastern coast of the Mediterranean. Its surrounding region had the highest concentration of Christians in Syria. In the early seventeenth century, however, Tripoli's economic position worsened, and this had an immediate effect on the political weight of its Orthodox elite.

The first patriarch of the Ottoman era about whom more is known than a name and the approximate dates of his reign is Joachim IV ibn Jum'a (1543–1576) who before his election as patriarch spent eleven years as metropolitan of Beirut.

The first seven years of his patriarchate were overshadowed by a conflict with the metropolitan of Qara and ʿAkkar, Macarius ibn Hilal, a native of Damascus who also claimed the patriarchal throne. It is noteworthy that the Damascus community was divided in its sympathies: Joachim and his supporters prayed in the Church of Sts Cyprian and Justina and Macarius's supporters took the little Church of St Ananias. It is possible that Macarius's claims also were supported by the influential Christian elites of the region of Tripoli and ʿAkkar. In the colophon to one manuscript (Macarius was a prolific copyist who is known to have copied several books), he refers to himself as "metropolitan of Qara, ʿArqa, ʿAkkar, Tripoli, Beirut, Tyre, Sidon and Acre."[221] Does this resounding title reflect his ambitions or his real sphere of influence? The entry unfortunately is not dated so we cannot say whether it is from the time of Macarius's competition with Joachim or from an earlier period. Before his death in around 1550, Macarius reconciled with Joachim.[222]

After Joachim's death, the bishops chose three candidates for the patriarchate: Metropolitan Gregorius of Aleppo, Metropolitan Dorotheus Daw of Tripoli, and Metropolitan Macarius al-Hamawi of Euchaita, offering them to agree on who should become patriarch. Gregorius, who did not want to leave a city where he had a strong position and build a relationship from zero with the willful and strong Christian community of Damascus, refused the patriarchate and voted for the elderly Macarius. Dorotheus, left in the minority, had to do the same and Macarius was elevated to the patriarchate under the name Michael[223] (in the sixteenth and seventeenth centuries, most patriarchates of Antioch traditionally changed their names upon reaching the throne).

Michael, however, did not have any relationship with the people of Damascus, and in 1581, they forced him to abdicate and leave the city. Michael went to his home city of Hama where he was visited by Metropolitan Gregorius of Aleppo, who was troubled by the excessive strength of the laity of Damascus and persuaded him to withdraw his resignation and anathematize the leaders of the community in Damascus. Meanwhile, the residents of Damascus invited Dorotheus Daw and installed him as patriarch under the name Joachim. Along with the bishops and priests who joined him, Joachim excommunicated Michael and his supporters. "Thus the See of Antioch was divided in half," wrote a chronicler, "and there was a great and unspeakable schism. Countless money was spent to the point that some, due to the great distress, renounced the Christian faith and some have been killed unjustly, among other trials."[224] Michael twice traveled to Constantinople to assert his rights before the Synod of Constantinople and the Sublime Porte. Before leaving Syria, he appointed Gregorius as his representative in all the dioceses obedient to him, granting him the right to wear the sakkos, which enhanced the metropolitan see of Aleppo. Michael received a *firman* from the sultan recognizing him as the only legitimate patriarch, but his opponents from among the Christian notables of Damascus and Tripoli were able to buy off the pasha of Damascus, who agreed to ignore the sultan's order. In the end, Michael was unable to regain his authority and died having been forgotten.[225]

After having won, however, Joachim found himself in an extremely difficult financial situation. He clearly offered more than he could pay for the support of the pashas of Damascus and Tripoli. The Ottoman authorities did not stand on ceremony with insolvent bishops, and Joachim went into hiding from the pashas' wrath in the Lebanese mountains, in the territory of the Shiite Harfush dynasty, who in practice did not obey the Ottomans. In 1584, the patriarch fled Syria for Istanbul, hoping to obtain financial assistance from the Greeks of the capital. When he became sure that this was impossible, he went to seek alms in Russia in 1585.[226]

Returning to Syria in 1587 with generous gifts from Moscow, Joachim managed to pay off his debts and assert his authority thought the patriarchate. This was the time of greatest influence for the regional elite of Tripoli, from which the patriarchate came. His right-hand man was a prominent church leader and writer, Metropolitan Anastasius al-Marmariti ibn al-Mujalla who, exceptionally, headed four dioceses: Tripoli, Beirut, Tyre, and Sidon.[227] In October 1592, Joachim died under unclear circumstances in Hawran. After a one-year interregnum accompanied by a struggle for the throne between various regional centers, the metropolitan of Homs, Joachim VI ibn Ziyada, was chosen as patriarch. He was a native of the village of Sisniya, near the 'Akkar Plateau, the region of origin for most of the leaders of the Orthodox elite of Tripoli.

As mentioned, Joachim VI could barely control his bishops, who became independent, semifeudal rulers. The patriarch of Alexandria, Meletius Pegas, addressed angry accusations at him:

> I hear that there [in Syria] the bishops hijack thrones and in place of one canon they follow two or three illegitimate ones … and for the sake of what? Because of covetousness, which is the love of money … and you, most holy leader, how are you are silent about the law of God? Don't you know how David fearlessly says, "I stand before kings and am not ashamed."[228]

In the last quarter of the sixteenth century, there predominated in the Patriarchate of Antioch a duopoly of Tripoli and Damascus elites and from the early seventeenth century, Damascus found itself holding complete power. It was there during those years that the head of the local Christian community, Sheikh Jirjis ibn Samur came to prominence and, together with his supporters, wielded despotic control over the patriarchal see. In 1604, Jirjis forced the enfeebled and increasingly blind Joachim VI to relinquish power. In his place was installed the Damascus *a'yan* 'Abd al-'Aziz ibn al-Ahmar, who upon becoming patriarch took the name Dorotheus (1604–1611).[229]

After the death of Dorotheus, there was another round of struggles over the patriarchal throne, the winner of which was the metropolitan of Hawran and native of Damascus Athanasius Dabbas, who made a written promise that he would annually pay the backtaxes of his parishioners. He proved, however, unable to do this, and the Christians brought him to the court of the *qadi* of Damascus. As a result, Athanasius was imprisoned around 1618.[230]

The people of Damascus deposed him by common consensus and elected to the patriarchate the metropolitan of Tyre and Sidon, Ignatius 'Atiya, who had once been the secretary to the powerful Lebanese Emir Fakhr al-Din Ma'an. Accompanied by members of the Damascus Christian elite, Ignatius left to be consecrated in Constantinople. In the meantime, Athanasius apparently paid a ransom and was released from prison and moved to Tripoli, where he was still recognized as patriarch. The people of Tripoli fought to regain their previous influence, and therefore they opposed Damascus by supporting Athanasius and then, after his death in the early spring of 1618, they organized the election of his brother, Cyril Dabbas. Ironically, Cyril and Ignatius were consecrated on the same day, May 3, 1618. This was followed by further turmoil in the Patriarch-ate of Antioch. "Then between the Christians of the See of Antioch there were battles, temptations and countless losses," says the chronicle.[231]

The rivalry between the two patriarchs was superimposed over the confron-tation between the Lebanese feudal dynasties of Ma'an, who controlled South and Central Lebanon, and Sayf, who controlled the region around Tripoli. The people of Damascus, however, were able to pay off the sultan's officials and pre-vent Cyril's entry into Damascus, and although the military and political position of the Sayf was growing weaker, it would not be until 1625 that the dynasty was completely crushed by Ma'an. It seems that even earlier, in 1624, Cyril felt the shakiness of his position in Tripoli and moved to Aleppo, away from the Ma'an. There, however, he encountered stiff opposition from the local Christians and Metropolitan Meletius Karma. The rich and powerful community of Aleppo did not want to obey a patriarch who was an outsider to them. For a few years, Mele-tius and the local Christian *a'yans* boycotted Cyril and refused to pay him tribute. He, in turn, summoned councils of bishops against Meletius, went to Istanbul to have his legal rights confirmed, and entered into legal proceedings against Meletius before the local authorities. As a result of these proceedings, the metropolitan was beaten with rods and twice imprisoned, the second along time with twenty-seven Christian sheikhs of the city.

Ultimately, the Orthodox inhabitants of Damascus, devastated by years of turmoil, were "reduced to the most miserable condition" and capitulated to Cyril. He suggested to Fakhr al-Din to convene a council of Syrian bishops to give a final resolution to the conflict between the two patriarchs. Apparently, Cyril was counting on his own victory, but something radically changed in the political situation, because when the bishops came together in 1628 for the council in the village of Ra's Baalbek, Cyril refused to attend. Perhaps this this was because the Ottomans transferred Fakhr al-Din to the Pashalik of Tripoli in 1627. Thus, the Lebanese emir had the opportunity to put pressure on the metropolitans who supported Cyril. Other bishops were associated with the Ma'an dynasty or with the communities of Damascus and Aleppo and so would have been hostile to Cyril. Fakhr al-Din had sufficient influence in Damascus to get the local authorities to extradite Cyril, who was brought to the council in chains and condemned "on account of violations of the sacred canons. Moreover, he became patriarch without the consent of his flock and caused great damage and losses to all Christians."[232] The deposed patriarch was sent to prison or, according to other sources, was beheaded by Fakhr al-Din's men.[233]

Following these events, the community of Tripoli no longer attempted to compete for predominance in the patriarchate. Ignatius received full patriarchal authority, having preferred, however, not to give up the possessions of the Ma'ans. He died during the Ottoman suppression of Fakhr al-Din's rebellion in 1634 and the metropolitan of Aleppo, Meletius Karma, was chosen as patriarch, taking the name Euthymius (1634–1635).

Starting from that time, there was almost forty years of hegemony of the community of Aleppo over the Church of Antioch. The Damascus faction, severely weakened by recent internal strife and most of all fearing its recurrence, meekly agreed to the patriarchate being inherited by representatives of the Aleppo party. Karma bequeathed the throne to his disciple, the Greek Euthymius al-Saqizi (of Chios) and the episcopal see of Aleppo to his other associate Meletius (the future patriarch Macarius), from a priestly family of Aleppo. The new patriarch elevated him to the metropolitanate "and," wrote Paul of Aleppo,

through his great sympathy for Meletius and out of respect for the will ...
of his late teacher ... made Meletius catholicos, having distinguished

him before the rest of the bishops of his throne and gave him the title of exarch, that is, the authorized guardian over the cities around Amida (Diyabakir) and its provinces, as well as over the city of Antioch, the patriarchal throne.[234]

Thus, the metropolitan of Aleppo came to be second after the patriarch in the Church of Antioch.[235]

In 1647, before his death, Euthymius al-Saqizi handed the patriarchal throne over to Meletius, but with the consent of the *a'yans* and priests of Damascus who "implored the metropolitan [i.e., Meletius] to come without delay … so that no strife, temptation or fraud occur on account of his tardiness."[236] In December 1647, he was consecrated patriarch with the name Macarius. In the following decades, the influence of the people of Aleppo in the affairs of the Syrian church would reach its peak. The patriarch's alter ego was his son, Archdeacon Paul of Aleppo. Both Euthymius and Macarius readily appointed natives of Aleppo as bishops, patriarchal exarchs, and other positions. An interesting statistical inference can be made from Macarius's personnel policies in the period 1647–1652, which are well reflected in the sources. During these years, he consecrated eleven metropolitans: five were born in Aleppo, three came from the dioceses to which they were appointed, and not a one was from Damascus.[237]

Macarius, like many other patriarchs, was faced with the problem of his relationship with his base, his former metropolitan see from which he moved to the patriarchal see. In consecrating a new bishop of Aleppo, Macarius unwittingly created an intermediary divide between himself and the city's influential community. We have already discussed the patriarch's conflict in the late 1650s with Metropolitan Athanasius of Aleppo. After Athanasius's death, Macarius was clearly in no hurry to fill the vacant see. Instead, he appointed his vicar in the city, the simple priest Neophytus, who also led the local Christian community in the 1560s, during Macarius's long journey to Georgia and Russia.[238]

The authority of Macarius and Paul of Aleppo was so great that upon Macarius's death the patriarchal throne was given to a representative of the younger generation of the al-Za'im clan—Paul's twenty-year-old son (in monasticism, Cyril) who, of course, did not have any personal merit for the position. Cyril was, in many respects, the protégé of the Damascus community. Although its roots were in Aleppo, over the previous decades, the al-Za'im clan had merged with Damascus and was seen as being one of their own.[239] Cyril, however, did not have 100 percent support from the Orthodox community, which forced some of the *a'yans*, his supporters, to resort to the help of the local Turkish authorities. Once bribed, the pasha put strong pressure on the Christians, urging them to agree to install Cyril as patriarch. This Turkish intervention provoked the resistance of a number of bishops and part of the communities of Damascus and Beirut, although they did not have decisive influence. Opponents of the new patriarch wrote to the Synod of Constantinople, "By fault of the kin of the deceased Macarius we have become powerless."[240] Opposition to Cyril coalesced around Metropolitan Neophytus of Epiphania, a Greek from Chios and nephew of Patriarch Euthymius al-Saqizi and sought the support of the Ecumenical Patriarch, asking him to depose Cyril and give them a new primate by his authority. In the autumn of 1672 a council was called in Istanbul that excommunicated "the vicious Cyril" and elected Neophytus patriarch. Cyril did not recognize this decision and the church split. "Inflamed by evil passions, losses and damages accumulated," wrote Mikhail Breik, "[d]ue to avariciousness and equal vehemence on both sides, deeds wretched and worthy of mourning were committed: bishops ran into debt, and people thought nothing of Christian integrity."[241]

Cyril's initial position in this struggle was better than that of many of his predecessors. Both main centers of power were for Cyril and the al-Zaʿim clan: Damascus, which nominated him for the patriarchate, and Aleppo, where relatives of Macarius continued to live, in particular his grandson Hanania, who at the time was a major silk merchant. In September 1678, a large delegation of Aleppo Christians appealed to the *qadi* of the city with complaints about Patriarch Neophytus, accusing him of illegal levies, ignorance of the canons, and not knowing Arabic. According to Bruce Masters, this last accusation was a propagandistic exaggeration. The people of Aleppo pointed to Cyril as their true patriarch, a man of high moral character, a connoisseur of ecclesiastical rules, and an expert in Arabic. Masters is correct in pointing out that Cyril's piety and mother tongue played a much less important role here than his place of birth and business ties with Aleppo's merchant elite.[242]

The struggle between the two patriarchs ended in 1681 with the defeat of Neophytus, who recognized the primacy of Cyril and in return received the Diocese of Lattakia, where he died in 1685.[243] However, a year later, Cyril recklessly quarreled with one of the main powers in the patriarchate, the community of Aleppo. "Reasonable and honorable Christians" of Aleppo asked Cyril to appoint as their metropolitan Procopius Dabbas, a native of Damascus and a monk of Mar Saba, famous "for his learning and the virtuousness of the life."[244] For this, Cyril demanded from them 2,500 qurush to cover the debts of his see. The privileged Aleppo community took this as a direct attack on its position in the patriarchate. The response was immediate: Procopius was sent to Constantinople with a complaint about Cyril's lawlessness and oppression. He returned with a *berat* appointing him to the patriarchate and, on June 25, 1686, was enthroned in Damascus with the name Athanasius III. Cyril refused to abide by the decision of the synod of the capital and attempted to win it over to his side. Orthodox society in Syria was once again split. Cyril entrenched himself in the patriarchal residence "as though in the property of his grandfather and father,"[245] whereas Athanasius, feeling the fragility of his position in Damascus, moved to Aleppo.

It is quite difficult to trace the vicissitudes of the struggle between the two patriarchs. Even chroniclers of the eighteenth century were confused about it. It can only be noted that in October 1694, Athanasius, seeing that the Syrian Christians had grown weary of unrest in the church, went to reconcile with Cyril and renounced all claims to the patriarchal throne. In 1705, the Synod of Constantinople made him archbishop of Cyprus. Around 1712, according to Breik's inconsistent dating, Cyril and Athanasius finally settled their dispute under the terms of partitioning the Patriarchate of Antioch (with Athanasius receiving control of Aleppo) and deciding that when one of them died, the other would inherit authority over all Syria.[246]

The first to die was Patriarch Cyril, in 1720. Under Athanasius, who occupied the see from 1720 to 1724, the Aleppo community once again began to dominate the Syrian church. Athanasius eagerly appointed new bishops from among Aleppo's residents, and in the 1720s, the city itself became the patriarch's residence.[247] It is entirely possible that in this way the seat of the Patriarchate of Antioch might have moved from Damascus to Aleppo, but the dramatic events associated with the formation of the Catholic Unia completely undid the balance of relations between the regional centers of the Orthodox Church in Syria.

In the eighteenth century, the struggle between local groups for predominance in the Patriarchate of Antioch was complicated by the confrontation between Orthodoxy and the Unia, splitting the Christian communities of each city. These processes sometimes overlapped and sometimes were in parallel, with inter-regional rivalry particularly noticeable in the Uniate communities. After the victory of support of the Unia in Aleppo, the city dropped out of the circle of Orthodox cultural and political centers of influence, and its former role largely shifted to Beirut. In the eighteenth century, another motif is woven into the life of the Church of Antioch—relations between the Arab Orthodox Syrians and the Phanariot Greeks who controlled the patriarchal throne.

These Orthodox-Catholic and Arab-Greek conflicts will be discussed in the following chapters. Here we will note that the Orthodox of the Ottoman East in the sixteenth through eighteenth centuries demonstrated an unquestionable vitality and demonstrated a variety of ways of adapting to their social and political environment. These social models ranged from the warlike tribal groups of the Palestinian and Jordanian hinterland to the dynamic and highly intellectual communities in the major Syrian cities. Neither one nor the other resembles the voiceless and downtrodden "herd" that Middle Eastern Christians are perceived to be by many modern outside observers.

CHAPTER 5

Monasteries and Monasticism

The readings are not done at meals, except when guests are present, since they are all simple and do not comprehend literary writing, but many are those who do not even know common Greek, but rather only Turkish; they are from Anatolia, they all speak in Turkish, and if they read the Greek books in church, they do not understand (what they read), for they have only learned to read in order to read in church, so that the Christian faith does not disappear. As for the others, even if they know Greek ... they are either deaf or blind or very old, these the patriarch has left to live there, where there is not much speaking and they remain in silence.

—Grigorovich-Barsky, 1726

The Ages of Middle Eastern Monasticism

Monasticism has played an outstanding role in the history of Christian civilization and so we shall not attempt to give an analysis of all of its aspects. The monastic movement was an outlet for religious energy, pouring out into various sectors of the Christian world. It was a refuge from the cruel world for sensitive souls, because in monastic asceticism, the mystical path of the knowledge of God was put into practice. We must put aside all of these concerns, which are inaccessible to the methods of positivist scholarship, but nevertheless monasteries played, along with other factors, an important social, economic, and cultural role. They were centers of production and economic development, especially in border regions and on marginal land. The monasteries' economic resources and moral authority sometimes allowed them to participate actively in politics and to play the role of patron or mediator in relation to various social groups. In periods of unrest or in regions where state authority was weak, the monasteries took over many of the roles of government. During the Middle Ages, cultural creativity was largely concentrated within monastery walls, especially during periods of decline in cities, the other centers of cultural development.

All of these phenomena, which can be observed in one form or another in the Byzantine Empire, the Christian West, or Russia, took place in the Christian East, particularly among the Melkites.

The ascetics of the fifth to seventh centuries, who left the world for the valleys of the Judean desert, entered into the most glorious pages of the annals of Byzantine monasticism. The images of Euthymius the Great, Abba Gerasimus, and Sabas became the unattainable role models for countless monks throughout the Christian world. Archaeologists have discovered thousands of monasteries on the territory of Byzantine Palestine. In the Judean Desert alone, tens of thousands of monks practiced asceticism. Syrian monasticism, which generally has been less studied, also provided examples of otherworldly asceticism, most perfectly embodied in Simeon the Stylite. The scene of his spiritual exploits became a center of pilgrimage and, along the paths leading to it, a network of monasteries emerged.

The Persian invasion of 614 was a catastrophe for Palestinian monasticism. This was the case not solely because of the thousands of slaughtered monks whose bones, laid up in caves, came eventually to be venerated by generations of pilgrims. Its most serious consequences were the undermining of the economy and social structure of Syro-Palestinian society, which led to an acute weakening of Greek culture and the Orthodox Church. The Arab onslaught arrived in an already ailing Byzantine East. According to archaeological findings, many monasteries had already been abandoned by the first half of the seventh century. However, the wounded tree that was Eastern monasticism in the early Muslim era still had enough vital sap for another couple centuries of flourishing and growth, reflected in the lives of John of Damascus, Stephen the Wonderworker, and the writings of Stephen the Younger of Mar Saba. These sources for the history of monasticism in the Middle East dry up around the beginning of the ninth century. Despite some manuscripts from the scriptoria of Mar Saba, the Monastery of St Catherine on Mount Sinai, and frequent references in the chronicles of the Monastery of St Simeon, which evince particular monastic cultural activity, the overall impression is one of decline in the tenth and eleventh centuries, with the exception, of course, of the region of Byzantine Antioch.

Considerable growth of Palestinian monasteries occurred during the Crusades. The famous, ancient monasteries received abundant alms from Christian princes and owned vast lands across Palestine. Both of these sources of income were lost after the Muslim Reconquista. Middle Eastern monasteries during the Mamluk period decayed along with the simultaneous decline and extinction of the surrounding Christian communities. New avenues for the replenishment of monastic brotherhoods came from the Balkans and the Caucasus. Georgian, Greek, and Serbian monks dominated the monasteries of Palestine and Sinai from the thirteenth to the fifteenth centuries. After the political demise of Serbia and Georgia in the fifteenth century, however, their monastic presence in the Holy Land weakened. The evolution of Syrian monasteries is more difficult to trace, but after the conquest of Antioch by the Mamluk Sultan Baybars, it is believed that monasteries only persevered in regions densely populated by Christians in Southern Syria and Northern Lebanon.

Monasticism and the monastic life in the Patriarchates of Jerusalem and Antioch were sharply different, just like the differences in ethnic composition and social organization described in Chapter 4. In this light, the monasteries of Syria and Palestine should be considered separately.

The Monasteries of Jerusalem: Decline?

The monasteries of the Patriarchate of Jerusalem are divided into three groups: those located in Jerusalem, those monasteries located outside the city walls in different areas of Palestine, and the complex of monasteries in the Sinai. The monastic communities of Sinai deserve a separate story, and in this monograph, we will set aside this subject.[1] The monastic communities of Jerusalem are described in detail in the pilgrimage literature and other sources, such as Ottoman decrees and the documents of the Foreign Ministry in Moscow. Through these, we can trace the details of transformations in the condition of monasteries in the sixteenth through eighteenth centuries. There are divergences, however, between sources about the number of monks in Palestinian monasteries. We tend to most trust the information from Russian pilgrims, among whose descriptions were most precise were those from Trifon Korobeynikov (1593), Arseny Sukhanov (1652), and Vasily Grigorovich-Barsky (1726). Statistics from Ottoman censuses may be too low and the numbers from Greek informants preserved by the Moscow Ambassadorial Service are certainly overstated.[2] The Greeks were concerned with securing more alms from Russia for their monasteries, so they severely exaggerated the number of monks in them. In the Ambassadorial Service, there is a picture of how much was donated to each monastery according to the number of monks. Upon examination of Trifon Korobeynikov's data, we can note that because he was burdened with financial responsibility, and thus scrupulously recorded the actual numbers of monks in the Palestinian monasteries, we can see that the figures in that depiction were inflated about threefold.[3]

The earliest testimony of the Ottoman era regarding the numbers of monasteries in Jerusalem belongs to Vasily Poznyakov (1560),[4] who wrote of seventeen monasteries, many of which, however, were "empty because of the pagan Turks."[5] In the sources of the sixteenth through eighteenth centuries, a total of more than eighteen monasteries are recorded, but some are mentioned by only one or two authors and their existence is doubtful. In "The Journeys" and embassy documents, there quite often figure fifteen monasteries in the holy city.

Chief among them was what was referred to as their patriarch, the Monastery of Sts Constantine and Helen which served as the residence of the patriarch or his deputy. The monastery is directly adjacent to the southern wall of the temple of the Holy Sepulchre and includes its three Orthodox chapels: the Churches of the Resurrection, St Jacob, and the Forty Martyrs, where the patriarchs were buried.[6] From these churches leading up to the patriarchate is a staircase with thirty-eight steps. In the patriarch's cell there was a window looking out on the Church of St Jacob. According to one of the descriptions, "When the patriarch did not go down into the church, he would speak with the people from there."[7] In the monastery, there were the patriarch's chambers, the refectory, four floors of hostels for monks and pilgrims, and cisterns to collect rainwater. "Numerous cells of the patriarchate are improperly arranged and divided up by galleries and terraces," wrote Andrei N. Muraviev in 1830.

> There are the reception hall, synodikon room, and library, which still pre-serves a quite extensive collection of ancient books and manuscripts … The gloomy Church of Constantine and Helen, decorated with old Greek painting, is adjacent to the southwestern part of the temple and from its inner window the Holy Sepulchre is visible.[8]

"The [monastery] is quite massive and the cells in it are decorated in an exceed-ingly splendid manner," wrote the Russian pilgrim monk Serapion in the middle of the eighteenth century. He also noted that all six bishops of the Church of Jeru-salem live there, "who govern all sorts of affairs" and conduct worship services in the absence of the patriarch.[9] According to the cellarer Ioannikii, the "cathedral elders" under the patriarch numbered as many as sixty people.[10] One hundred years later, Ippolit Vishenski gave the similar figure of seventy monks. One hun-dred years later, the pilgrim Melety spoke of about one hundred monks and nov-ices. "And there are more than a few brothers in it," confirmed Serapion.[11]

Located opposite the patriarchal residence on the other side of the square in front of the temple of the Holy Sepulchre is the Monastery of Abraham, reputed to be the site of the sacrifice of Isaac. Because the monastery was small (Ippolit Vishenski lived there with the abbot and two monks) and because it was directly adjacent to Calvary, many pilgrims apparently perceived it as part of the complex of the temple of the Holy Sepulchre and did not mention it among the monasteries of Jerusalem. More often than not, it appears only in descriptions from the eighteenth century and later.[12] Adjacent to the Courtyard of the Patriarchs was the largest women's monastery in the city, the Monastery of the Dormition of the Virgin, also called the Entry, the Hodegetria, and the Great Panagia. From Greek *proskinitaria* of the sixteenth century, it appears that the monastery was at one time lost to Christians. As reported by the anonymous author of a poetic description of the Holy Land in the 1580s, "The monastery was recently destroyed by the Arabs. I pray to God that none of them remain. Part of it they destroyed and they live in part of it. They trample on the holy places."[13] It is not entirely clear how to interpret the word "recently." On a *proskinitarion* from the first half of the sixteenth century is written, "To the west of the Holy Sepulchre at a distance of one stadion is the Monastery of the Hodegetria where Greek nuns lived."[14] The word "lived" is used in the past tense. If this turn of phrase is not by chance, it would mean that the monastery was seized by a local Muslim community shortly before 1550. However, by the turn of the sixteenth to the seventeenth century, the patriarch somehow managed to regain the monastery and revive monastic life there. Receipts from the Posolsky Prikaz (Foreign Affairs Office) from the end of the sixteenth century through the first third of the seventeenth century talk about from thirty to fifty residents. Trifon Korobeynikov found twenty nuns led by the Abbess Christina. Jonah Malenki found around thirty and Ippolit Vishenski around forty. He called it, "having started under the nuns' [women's] monasteries."[15]

In addition to these monasteries, another Jerusalem monastery also figures in the sources, the Monastery of the Most-holy Theotokos, which is called the Monastery of the Nativity of the Most-pure Theotokos, the Monastery of the Presentation, the Small Panagia, or Saydnaya. The final name, identical to the famous monastery outside Damascus, comes from an ancient icon of the Theotokos located in the monastery, which Porphyry Uspenski believed to be a copy of the miraculous Saydnaya icon. Trifon Korobeynikov gave alms at the monastery to its Abbess Martha and six nuns, a depiction of 1628 gives a figure of ten nuns and, in 1651, Arseny Sukhanov says that there were no longer any religious and that "lay people" were living there.[16] It is apparently for this reason that subsequent pilgrims rarely mention the monastery; only Vishenski (1708) and Melety (1794) speak of it. However, in the days of Porphyry Uspenski, the monastery was quite large and had thirty nuns.[17]

Next to the patriarchate was the women's monastery of the Holy Martyr Thekla that originally belonged to the Georgians who ceded it to Patriarch

Theophanes. It was rebuilt under Patriarch Paisios. Trifon found two people there, while dubious descriptions from the 1620s report fifteen to twenty nuns, and sources from the 1650s call the monastery a guesthouse for pilgrims where one hieromonk celebrates services and "the church is good, lots of bunks and lots of water."[18] Starting at the beginning of the eighteenth century, the monastery disappears from pilgrims' reports. It may have been lost to the patriarchate or rented to Arabs.

Near the temple of the Holy Sepulchre, "40 fathoms from the patriarch's court" by Sukhanov's reckoning, stood the Monastery of St John the Baptist. Contrary to the optimistic picture of twelve to fifteen inhabitants, Trifon met there only the abbot Parthenios and two monks. He paints a very bleak picture: "It is all empty: the church still stands, but all the cells have fallen in and overgrown with earth, and there are very few which are still standing." They lodged pilgrims there, but after Easter "it stands empty, one or two [monks] live [there], they come from the patriarchal court."[19] To the north of the patriarchate was the Monastery of St Nicholas, the Georgian metochion that was discussed in a previous chapter. Trifon Korobeinikov transmitted alms to the "builder" Joseph and seven monks. Data for the middle of the seventeenth century are contradictory: some observers say that there were "Iberian monks" living there, whereas others say that the Georgians rented cells to laypeople. After its transfer into the hands of the Greeks it was for some time a women's monastery, as attested to by the early eighteenth century authors Ippolit Vishenski and Varlaam.[20] Half a century later, Spiridon noted "there are monks living there."[21] It is possible that the monastery was already a hostel for male pilgrims under the direction of some monks from the patriarchate. Melety describes it as such in 1794 and Porphyry Uspenski in 1844.[22]

For a long time, the second most important monastery after the patriarchal one was the Serbian Monastery of the Archangel Michael, a metochion of Mar Saba. After the extinction of the Serbian colony in Palestine, the monastery was deserted. "There live two or three beggarly and crippled elders," wrote Sukhanov. "That monastery is better than all, the church and refectory beautiful, many chambers, and cells, and a lot of water, and a great garden.... The patriarch has possession of the entire estate and gives nothing to the monastery."[23] Grigorovich-Barsky also wrote about the small number of inhabitants in the monastery.[24] In the eighteenth and nineteenth centuries, the monastery, like many others, served as a hostel. Even in the middle of the nineteenth century, Porphyry Uspenski saw icons with Serbian letters in the monastery.[25]

Next to the Monastery of the Archangel was the women's monastery of St George, where there lived according to Trifon ten nuns and according to Iona thirty, and according to the testimony of Grigorovich-Barsky, "a small number of nuns." As he describes the monastery, "There is a small church with a simple structure, not having above even a single cupola, but beautiful inside, and many silver lampadas, and that time decorated. That monastery is dilapidated and narrow."[26] It seems that it finally fell into decay in the eighteenth century and was converted into a hospital for pilgrims at the expense of Greek benefactors from Venice. Melety already calls it a "hospital" in 1794 and a half-century later Uspenski wrote in his diary, "Visited the monastery of St George. It is not so much a monastery as an outhouse."[27] Elsewhere in his notes he remarked skeptically, "Perhaps early on patients were put in it but now it is extremely neglected. It is possible to lose health more than recover it there."[28]

There was another Monastery of St George in Jerusalem, in the Jewish Quarter on Sion. In the time of Trifon Korobeinikov, an abbot and seven monks lived there, whereas according to receipts of the 1620s, there were ten monks and in Sukhanov's time laypeople paid rent to Georgian monks. "The monastery is squalid and sparsely decorated," noted Grigorovich-Barksy.[29] Later authors mention it as a hostel for pilgrims.[30]

Among the other monasteries of Jerusalem should be mentioned the women's monastery of the Great-Martyr Catherine, which according to Trifon Korobeinikov had ten nuns. According to the "receipts," it had twenty-five to forty, which is similar to the figures given by Iona and Gabriel of Nazareth.[31]

The Georgian Monastery of Theodore Stratilates and Theodore the Tyro had two inhabitants at the end of the sixteenth century and by the middle of the seventeenth century was empty and rented to laypeople.[32] In 1708, Ippolit Vishenski called it a women's monastery, perhaps erroneously, but Serapion (1754) and Melety (1794) described it as a hostel for pilgrims.[33]

The Monasteries of St Basil of Caesarea and St Euphemia underwent a similar evolution. Trifon Kolobeinikov mentions one old man there, in a manner resembling a hospice. Inaccurate receipts from 1628 call them women's monasteries, each with an abbess and six to ten nuns. Arseny Sukhanov reported that "laypeople" were living there and paying rent to the Georgians.[34] As we have seen, this is a situation similar to the monasteries of Theodore Stratelates, Basil of Caesarea, St George, and the Wonderworker Nicholas. Who the tenants of the Monastery of St Euphemia paid is not clear; perhaps it was the patriarch. In these reports from Sukhanov, the following details of the travails of the Georgian Palestinian community appear: unable to maintain ruined monasteries, they rented them out to residents of Jerusalem. Subsequently, when the Greeks purchased the Georgian properties, they tried to revive monastic life in the houses of St Basil and St Euphemia, and authors of the eighteenth to mid-nineteenth centuries refer to them as women's monasteries.[35]

Porphyry Uspenski describes the Monastery of St Demetrius of Thessalonica as being put together "from different purchased houses and thus the cells are here and there, haphazard."[36] The monastery consisted of six monks at the end of the sixteenth century. According to the contradictory receipts of the 1620s (some call it a men's monastery, some a women's monastery), it had thirty and appeared to have been almost empty at the time of Arsenii Sukhanov's visit to Jerusalem. Grigorovich-Barsky wrote, "If the church there is not large, but entirely well built of hewn stone ... The monastery is a dilapidated structure, the building and cells in it are many, but there are few monks, they only reside for the sake of the church's needs," and the rest of the cells were occupied by pilgrims.[37] It is in this way, as a monastery for three hundred pilgrims, that the monastery is mentioned by other eighteenth-century observers.[38]

In addition to those mentioned, the sources occasionally mention monasteries in Jerusalem dedicated to St Onuphrius the Great, the Holy Martyr Pelagia, and the Conception of St Anne. The first two only appear in the testimony of the cellarer of Novospaski, Ioannikii.[39] All other sources are silent about them and we already know the worth of Ioannikii's data.[40] The Monastery of St Pelagia can be identified with a church of the same name that stood on the Mount of Olives and was described in detail by all pilgrims of the Mamluk era. In the Ottoman era, however, according to V. Poznyakov, the dilapidated church was closed by the Turks and worship was not conducted in it.[41] That is to say, the cellarer Ioannikii, for the reasons mentioned, portrayed long-abandoned churches and monasteries as still existing.

The Monastery of St Anne is briefly mentioned in a Greek *proskynitarion* from the beginning of the seventeenth century as well as by I. Lukyanov (1701). Macarius (1704) reported that "the Franks conduct services" at that monastery.[42] That is, the monastery was lost to the Patriarchate of Jerusalem and somehow fell into the hands of the Catholics.

The Monasteries of Jerusalem: How Many Were There?

And so, to summarize the information that has been presented, we can once more call into question the reliability of the figures from the "receipts" of the Posolsky Prikaz (Foreign Affairs Office). Otherwise, we would be forced to conclude that there was a sharp, cataclysmic depopulation of the monasteries of Jerusalem in the 1630s and 1640s of the seventeenth century. If we compare the data from the end of the sixteenth century reported by Trifon Kolobeinikov with data from the middle of the seventeenth century reported by Arseny Sukhanov and Iona, we will not see so sharp a contrast. Trifon gave alms to fourteen monasteries, including the patriarch whom he does not mention separately. Of these, only five monasteries had more than ten monks, and in four monasteries, there were one or two inhabitants. That is, they had by then already virtually ceased to exist. Sixty years later, of those fourteen monasteries (again, including that of the patriarch) referred to by Arsenii and Iona, only four had more than ten inhabitants, seven (mainly Georgian) were leased to laypeople, and the rest were turned into hostels for pilgrims, containing one to three monks.

The authors of the early eighteenth century (Lukyanov, Macarius, Seliverst, and Varlaam) are not careful about their lists of monasteries: the numbers fluctuate, many undoubtedly extant monasteries are not mentioned, others are listed twice, and some phantom monasteries of St Chariton and St Barbara appear. The most satisfactory description is that of Ippolit Vishenski who gives a list of fourteen monasteries, albeit with a slightly different composition. In the pilgrim writers of the eighteenth century, the Monasteries of St Thekla and St Anne disappear, but the Monastery of Abraham, unknown to travelers of the seventeenth century, emerges. Writers from the beginning of the eighteenth century rarely report the number of monks in Jerusalem, although they do include information in the description of each active monastery: "the monasteries have many empty cells and few monks."[43] In 1745, Serapion lists thirteen monasteries in Jerusalem, of which, according to him, five housed pilgrims and six housed monastics (in this case, he combines men's and women's monasteries) and of the remaining two he says nothing.[44] Melety (1794) indicated that out of nine men's monasteries, all but the patriarchal monastery were occupied by pilgrims. "For each of the men's monasteries, the patriarchate appoints the abbot, a serving hieromonk, a deacon, and the necessary number of servers, selected from novices and hired Arabs. In the convents, the number of nuns is rather modest, and these are of Greek or Arab origin. The old Arab priests celebrate the divine services at their places.[45]

Melety counted five women's monasteries in Jerusalem, so the total number of monasteries is again fourteen.

A. N. Muraviev visited Jerusalem in 1830, at the time of greatest decline for the Brotherhood of the Holy Sepulchre, which had been devastated by ten years of Ottoman persecution. This author's description is pessimistic,

> Twelve monasteries, in addition to the temple of the Resurrection and the
> Patriarchate, today bear witness in their misery to the former wellbeing
> of Orthodoxy in Palestine. They almost all serve as metochia for pilgrims …

There are almost no brothers in them, apart from two or three houses. Monks hold out in the patriarchate near the chief holy place, as if in a last stronghold, but even thence their hunger persists. Only the abbots, as the solitary guards, remained within the empty walls, surrounded for the most part by fertile gardens.[46]

In 1844, Porphyry Uspenski described the thirteen monasteries of Jerusalem. From the standard list only the Monastery of St Theodore Stratilates disappears, possibly because Uspenski was unable to visit it. All male monasteries apart from the patriarchate remained hostels, as before, while five women's monasteries housed at least sixty nuns.[47] His contemporary, K. M. Bazili, gives the same figure: fifty to sixty nuns of Greek, Bulgarian, and Serbian origin.[48]

Let us turn now once again to the reports of Trifon Korobeinikov. When we add up the data from 1594 for all the women's monasteries of the holy city, we arrive at the same numbers as the authors of the first half of the nineteenth century: about fifty nuns. That is, their numbers remained stable over two and a half centuries.

As regards men's monasteries, according to Trifon, in all the Georgian monasteries within the walls of Jerusalem, there were about twenty monks (and within sixty years, there would be none). According to Trifon and the cellarer Ioannikii, apart from the patriarchal monastery, only the Monastery of the Archangel, belonging to the Serbian colony, housed a large monastic community. The remaining men's monasteries had only a few inhabitants. With the collapse of the Georgian and Serbian monastic communities, their monasteries became empty. Even though the Greeks were able to keep them under the control of the Orthodox Church, they were unable to repopulate these monasteries. They turned them into hostels for pilgrims and so they were no longer monasteries in the fullest sense of the word. Thus, the real decline in numbers for Palestinian monasticism is associated only with the departure from the Holy Land of Serbs in the 1630s and Georgians in the 1650s. The number of Greeks remained stable, as did the structure of the Greek monastic community, which consisted of a dominant patriarchal monastery and numerous hostels for pilgrims, which were called monasteries.

Mar Saba (The Lavra of St Sabas the Sanctified)

Similar processes of decline can be observed in the monasteries outside Jerusalem. Of these, the largest and most famous was the Lavra of St Sabas the Sanctified (Mar Saba). The role of that monastery in the history of Eastern Christian civilization is comparable to that of Sinai and Mount Athos. The Lavra is located on a desolate mountain range 15 kilometers to the north of Jerusalem, not far from the Dead Sea, which can be seen from the monastery's high tower. The way from Jerusalem to the monastery leads through the Wadi al-Nar (the Vale of Tears) where, according to legend, a river of fire will flow on Judgment Day. Closer to the monastery, many caves and cells were carved out of the high cliffs on both sides of the gorge by hermits who labored there in early Byzantine times. "And these cells hang throughout under the mountain, like swallows' nests, if you look at them, and from the very gaze terror strikes a man: it is impossible to walk or climb up to many of these cells," wrote the eighteenth-century pilgrim Serapion.[49] He was echoed by the nineteenth-century traveler Andrei Muraviev, a person of a different culture who expressed the same feeling: "Their mountain shelters, like birds' nests, still are seen at the height of the cliffs, amazing the traveler with such memory of wondrous people who could by such measures defy everything earthly, that remained a strange riddle to us, alien to the flame of their times."[50]

The monastery itself resembles a fortress, also cleaving to the mountain over a deep chasm. "And as you look into the abyss," wrote the hieromonk Makary in 1705, "both the soul and the body are mortified by the great and terrible depths."[51] In old drawings and photographs, the Lavra appears as a jumble of buildings on ledges going up the steep mountain slope. Because of the high towers and buttressed walls, the dome of the church and the windows and roofs of the two- and three-story cells appear to be clinging to each other. The mountain is folded into horizontal plates whose lower levels are covered with piles of rubble and debris, while the top is flat. At the very edge of the peak stands a massive rectangular tower. There is another tall, square-shaped tower located a little ways from the walls of the enclosure. Apparently this is a watchtower built by the Serbs in the early seventeenth century.[52]

Within in the monastery there seven or eight churches, including the Cathedral of the Annunciation of the Theotokos, which was rebuilt in the fourteenth century at the expense of Ioannes Kantakouzenos, who is portrayed in one of its frescoes. It was one of the few churches in the Middle East that had a cross on its dome and bell tower. Pilgrims who came to the monastery were shown the cells of St Savva and St John of Damascus and the monks' tombs. "The many cells were countless," wrote Sukhanov, "others were collapsed, and many whole."[53] From the testimonies of pilgrims, it can be concluded that after the Serbs left the Lavra around 1636, it was for some time occupied by Bedouins, but soon, under Patriarch Paisios, a group of around ten to fifteen monks returned there.

In January 1649 the archimandrite Neophytos of Mar Saba came to Moscow in Paisios's entourage, seeking alms for the monastery and carrying charters given to the Lavra by earlier Russian tsars.[54] The monastery's position remained extremely difficult in the second half of the seventeenth century. The monks lived as in a besieged fortress surrounded by hostile Bedouins. Provisions were delivered to the monastery from Jerusalem and rainwater was collected in cisterns, where it was heated unbearably hot from the sun. The well that had once been dug by the prayer of Mar Saba in the gorge beneath the monastery walls was now unreachable "on account of the Arabs."[55] It is possible that in the 1660s or 1670s the monastery was once more abandoned by monks to the Bedouins' wandering livestock. It was only in 1688 that Patriarch Dositheos restored the monastery at the expense of 12,000 piasters.[56] At the beginning of the eighteenth century, another step was taken to restore the crumbling Lavra at the expense of the ruler of Wallachia.[57]

It seems that the monastery had become something of an almshouse, where elderly monks lived out their years. "And in that monastery there are a few monks, all of them old," wrote the pilgrim Macarius in 1705.[58] Ippolit Vishenski (1709) puts the number of monks and novices at fifteen and Varlaam (1712) puts it at five or six.[59] Authors of the second half of the eighteenth century give somewhat-larger figures: thirty monks according to Ignatii Denshin (1770s); twenty-five according to Volney (1784); and twenty, including in addition to Greeks some Ukrainians, Bulgarians, and Arabs, according to Melety (1794).[60] Even though monastic order was strictly observed ("The church rule is perfect and deemed good, with the fear of God … without whispers or indecent conversation"),[61] the monks' level of education was low. We refer the reader to this chapter's epigraph, which refers specifically to the inhabitants of the Lavra of Mar Saba.[62]

The Lavra had no source of income apart from pilgrims' offerings. As before, provisions had to be brought in from Jerusalem. The monastery also continued to be threatened by attacks from nomads. The monks, fearing the "Ethiopians," rarely left the monastery. A monk constantly monitored all movements in the area from a high tower and rang the bell when the Bedouins appeared.[63] As Grigorovich-Barsky noted with regret, "That monastery in all things is splendid and silent for the life of a monk, only they have not a little poverty and bitterness from the Arabs."[64] The vicinity of the monastery was controlled by the al-ʿUbayd tribe who, according to legend, were descended from slaves donated to the monastery by the Emperor Justinian and settled in its surroundings. Although the Bedouin of al-ʿUbayd had long ago been Islamized, they regarded themselves as living under the monastery's patronage and demanded that it pay all their taxes and fines imposed by the pashas.[65] Every day between five and thirty nomads would appear under the monastery's walls and "cry out under the monastery, pounding on the stone walls and calling out in loud voices, and to take away food-stuffs."[66] They lowered food down to them on a rope from the tower. Naturally, they did not open the gate. Ivan Lukyanov gives an even more colorful description of the Bedouins standing before the monastery walls and demanding bread:

> and the elders ... throw to them from the fence, like to dogs with so little bread; another which will pick up ahead and plod along ... and others screech like wild birds, looking up, waiting for [something] to be thrown; so they throw to another and so plod along; and so the elders are plagued with them; and it's impossible to exit the monastery, they plunder. But from above the elders order them not to look at the dogs."[67]

The monastery saved itself from the worst problems by paying an annual tribute to the sheikh of al-ʿUbayd. The Bedouins believed it their right to collect payments from the monastery and did not feel any special gratitude for this "charity." When they met a familiar monk along the road, they were liable to strip and rob him.[68] The tribute did not, however, always save the monastery from the nomads, whether from small tribal groups under no one's control or from nomads who were driven from their traditional territories by drought and forced to migrate in search of water and pasturage. In March 1800, the Bedouin tribe of Hijja burned the monastery's gate, forced their way in and plundered it. Greek chroniclers did not fail to note that within six months God's justice punished the robbers, who lost sixty men in a skirmish with a neighboring tribe.[69] Over centuries in a dangerous neighborhood, the monks clearly came to understand Bedouin genealogy and tribes and knew all their elites personally.

Did the monks try to resist their oppressors? In the first half of the nineteenth century, one often encounters among the monastic brethren retired Russian soldiers who had not forgotten how to handle weapons. In the monastery, there was an arsenal of fifteen old and defective rifles (we might add, by the way, that the Monastery of Sinai also kept a few guns in case of siege). Porphyry Uspensky leaves a comical description of how a schemamonk keeping watch loaded a gun with a broken lock, then took a piece of coal with tongs from the oven and placed it in the barrel-hole. The rumble of the shot, echoing in the mountains, must have made a strong impression on the Bedouins.[70] It appears that nothing further was required. Mindful of the Bedouin custom of seeking blood revenge, the monks were unable to shoot to kill their oppressors.

After the start of the Greek uprising of 1821, the Patriarchate of Jerusalem, ravaged by Turkish extortion and harassment, was no longer able to support the monastery and pay off the Bedouin. Around 1823, the Lavra renounced patronage of al-ʿUbayd and the *mutasallim* of Jerusalem threw a few members of that tribe in prison for tax evasion. Then al-ʿUbayd seized the monastery, beat its monks, looted its stores, and held it until the Greeks bought out those who had been arrested. In lean years, the monastery had to feed the entire tribe, which numbered 185 men at the beginning of the 1830s. Resistance to these exactions on the part of the monks ended badly. Once the abbot Neophytos was struck with a sword. More than once (e.g., in 1828 and 1832), the monks had to abandon the Lavra and go up to Jerusalem. Only the Egyptian occupation of Syria put an end to the tyranny of the Bedouins.[71]

The Monastery of the Cross

Second in importance to the Lavra was the Monastery of the Precious Cross, which as mentioned, had much earlier belonged to the Georgians. It stood 5 kilometers to the west of Jerusalem, surrounded by groves of fig, olive, and cypress trees, which disappeared, however, in the nineteenth century, when only the monastery's vineyards on the surrounding hills remained. In contrast to the Lavra, which was located in a barren desert, the Monastery of the Cross was the breadbasket of the patriarchate. Its monks grew wheat and produced wine and oil.

A. Tsagareli, who visited the monastery in 1883, wrote, "Then, as now, it more resembled a fortress than a monastery."[72] The walls formed an irregular quadrangle with only a small door. The space inside was divided into several courtyards surrounded by monastic cells that, at the end of the seventeenth century, numbered almost four hundred. The cathedral church with a small dome and surrounded by a series of windows was built in the eleventh century and restored and repainted in the 1640s.[73] Vasili Grigorovich-Barsky wrote that the church, "if on the outside it had little grandeur, the inside is exceedingly beautiful, the iconostasis is great … from above down to the ground … at her base in former times was marble, now it is simple white stones that look like marble … in a manner that is beautiful and worthy of amazement."[74] In its frescoes were painted universal and Georgian saints, Georgian kings, dignitaries, and other benefactors of the monastery and the monastery's monks, all of which the artist painted naturalistically with Caucasian characteristics.[75] Visiting the monastery a hundred years after its restoration, the monk Serapion said, "Everything in it, the icons and the writing on the icons and books, a great multitude, is still to this day Georgian, though now this monastery is held by the Greeks."[76]

Abandoned in the middle of the seventeenth century, the Monastery of the Cross was revived in 1685 by Patriarch Dositheos who was able to regain the monastery's lands and restore its economic activity. However, the patriarchate was unable to repopulate the monastery. The Greeks kept only a small number of monks there for farming and to serve incoming pilgrims. "An amazing monastery, but wholly empty," wrote Lukyanov in 1701, "only two or three elders live there for the sake of the service and the worshipers: they run the holy places and gather money."[77] The monastery's history evolved rapidly. It was attacked by Bedouins and other bandits and monastic traditions preserve the memory of monk-martyrs who fell at the hands of the Muslims.[78] Serapion, who visited the monastery in 1750, wrote about a huge blood stain in the middle of the church. In his words,

> a few years before this, robbers or barbarians, beat up all the brothers in the church, and now it is well known where the barbarians spilled their blood like it was water, now there are few brothers in it [the Monastery of the Cross], except only five, and in the monastery they have rather empty cells.[79]

Later, Palestinian Greek chronicles also mention the monastery's conflicts with the Muslim inhabitants of the nearby village of 'Ayn Karem. In April 1794, they broke into the monastery, killed the abbot Ieremias, and seized 8,000 piasters. In July 1802, after a quarrel with the Greeks, the inhabitants of the mountain cut down forty-three olive trees belonging to the monastery.[80]

Visiting the Monastery of the Cross in 1830, A. N. Muraviev wrote, "The cells and the refectory are pretty, but now everything is empty. Only two monks live there. The monastery is occasionally enlivened by admirers, chiefly Armenians and Georgians.... This monastery would be one of the most magnificent in Palestine if the Greeks who now own it could maintain it."[81] Gradually, the monastery began to fall into decay. In the 1840s, K. M. Bazili found a Georgian abbot there.[82] However, in the second half of the nineteenth century, the Monastery of the Cross again played a prominent role in the Church of Jerusalem, as within its walls there was an active printing press and theological school.

The Other Palestinian Monasteries: A Chronicle of Agony

The Monastery of the Prophet Elijah, located halfway between Jerusalem and Bethlehem, did not present itself in the best light. This was not the first desolation in its history. At the end of the fifteenth century, Daniel of Ephesus wrote that the monastery was devoid of monks but still remained in Orthodox possession.[83] It was subsequently resettled and in the Ottoman census of 1553/1554 a

Dayr Mar Elias is mentioned that appears to be the same monastery. It mentions the presence of one monk as the scribe who apparently received a bribe to understate the real number of its inhabitants.[84] In 1593, Trifon Korobeinikov gave alms in the monastery to its abbot Dorotheos and seven monks.[85] In 1635, Vasilii Gagara found a rather large brotherhood of thirty monks there.[86] Then, apparently, it fell into disrepair, but under Paisios, it was surrounded by a new wall and became one of the economic centers of the patriarchate. As Iona described it in 1651, "built like a high city, in it a great church, and the patriarch's elders plow the land for the patriarch and monastery and there are great vineyards of the patriarch there and many olive trees."[87] Arseny Sukhanov compared the dimensions of the monastery church with the Arkhangelski Cathedral in Moscow.[88] The most detailed description of the monastery was left by Grigorovich-Barsky in 1726:

> [I]f there is little to be seen from the outside, on the inside it contains many buildings ... and it is narrow inside. They even have a most excellent church, large and high, with one cupola, which you can see from far outside the monastery, supported by six columns ... one church was once exceedingly beautifully painted with icons, but since it had decayed, thanks to this it was renovated with tar ... In this way the connection between the cells was so narrow as if from nowhere below could there be a path to the gates, but the monks, for the sake of the rule, descended the stone walls from above down to the door ... the refectory building was small and there were as such few cells, since the church filled the whole monastery with its majesty.[89]

Pilgrims staying in the monastery in the early eighteenth century on their way to Bethlehem did not mention any obvious signs of decline. Vasilii Grigorovich-Barsky, however, wrote that the monks at the monastery were few and that, despite it being suitable for monastic seclusion, "because of the Arabs [the monastery has] not a few needs, inasmuch as all their days and nights they supply the Arabs food through a small window, in a lowered basket."[90] Serapion complained about the same "annoying requests" from the Bedouins in 1750.[91]

The monastery is mentioned from time to time in Palestinian Greek chronicles from the beginning of the nineteenth century. During the uprising of the inhabitants of Southern Palestine against the Pasha of Damascus in February 1825, the rebels used the Greek monasteries as defensive positions and also hid their property there: the people of Bethlehem in the Monastery of the Venerable Cross, the Bedouins of al-'Ubayd in the Lavra, and the inhabitants of Beit Jala and several surrounding villages in the Monastery of the Prophet Elijah.

The Turks ransacked the monasteries and took everything found in them—property, provisions, and money—without first determining to whom it belonged. When he seized Flavian, the abbot of the Monastery of the Prophet Elijah, the pasha interrogated him about where he hid the peasants' money. The abbot divulged nothing and so he was brutally beaten and chained in the open air, in the cold and rain. The pasha ordered Flavian hanged, and it was only the intercession of a high official that saved his life.[92]

The subsequent history of the Monastery of the Prophet Elijah is poorly known. In 1830, A. N. Muraviev found nothing there worthy of his attention.[93] In the 1840s, K. M. Bazili wrote of the monastery's utter desolation.[94]

Even earlier, the same fate befell the fourth monastery of Palestine, the Monastery of St George located one kilometer to the west of Beit Jala. The monastery was famous for a miraculous relic, the chains of St George, which gave healing to demoniacs. Even Muslims brought gifts to the monastery because it was believed that its patron helped everyone, regardless of creed. Gabriel of Nazareth claimed that the monastery's cattle, oxen, horses, and sheep did not need herders, "because they themselves honor in many ways the miraculous St George all the days."[95] The "receipts" of the 1620s report that around ten monks were in the monastery. The monastery itself, it seems, was subordinate to the metropolitan of Bethlehem. As Iona wrote, "The monks of Bethlehem live in the monastery and plow its fields."[96]

This note from Iona in 1651 is the last mention of the monastery as still functioning. When Patriarch Dositheos lists the Palestinian monasteries in the 1689 charter of the Brotherhood of the Holy Sepulchre,[97] he makes no mention of it. In 1708, Ippolit Vishenski wrote of the monastery, "While the monastery is good stone, it is empty, it's impossible to live because of the Turks."[98] The monastery's church and the chains of St George were transferred to Jerusalem, where they continued to be venerated by the surrounding population. I. Lukyanov recounts how during the pasha of Jerusalem's war with the Bedouins, a monk sent with letters from Jerusalem to Ramla wore the chains of St George under his clothing for safety along the way. "The Arabs so fear George that they did not touch that man, but rather kissed the chains and gave him bread and vegetables."[99] The monastery was only restored from ruins in the 1850s.[100]

The rest of the monasteries of Palestine were already in ruins at the beginning of the Ottoman era. The monasteries of St John the Baptist, St Gerasimus, St Theodosius the Cenobiarch, Euphemia the Great, and the Lavra of St Chariton, all of which are located to the east of Jerusalem and Bethlehem on the mountain range between Jerusalem and the Jordan or in the Jordan Valley, a few miles to the south of Mar Saba, are meticulously listed in pilgrims' descriptions. For each one of these, the authors add, "empty and dispersed," "and there empty," and "everything there empty, only know the space."[101]

The Monastery of St John the Baptist resisted the desert's onslaught the longest. In the literature it is widely believed that the last strong evidence for the monastery being in operation is due to the pilgrim Zosima in 1421, while Western travelers of the 1480s and 1490s wrote that the monastery had become a haven for bandits.[102] Describing the monastery in the same period, Daniel of Ephesus did not say anything in specific, although he mentioned the desolation of the neighboring monasteries.[103] Likewise *proskynitaria* of the 1580s mentioned the monastery in the abstract, although from the text, it is clear that the monastery's buildings were still intact.[104] Against the backdrop of the general opinion on the extinction of the West Bank monasteries, the description of the Monastery of the Forerunner by Vasily Pozdnyakov (1561) stands in sharp contrast,

> In that monastery was an abbot and brothers. And on the evening of the feast of Holy Theophany the abbot came along with a priest from that monastery to the church of Holy Epiphany [on the shores of the Jordan] and served the holy service … and again they left for their monastery.[105]

How do we reconcile this contradiction? It does not work to attribute it to Poznyakov having dishonest informants, non Vasili himself—"we drank that holy water of the Jordan"—that is, he has seen the area with his own eyes.[106] It can be assumed that at some point there was an attempt to revive the Monastery of St John the Baptist. But already in the early 1590s (the time of Trifon Korobeinikov's mission), the monastery was definitively abandoned. Its structure, however, remained for quite some time, like the Monastery of St Germanus, of which Arseny Sukhanov wrote, "the building is great, it stands complete: the church, the chambers, the fence are only a little spoiled."[107] Seventy-five years later, Grigorovich-Barsky visited that site and his description is quite different from the evidence from previous pilgrims. "We have seen nothing that is intact, only the remains of monasteries and a church," tells a traveler,

> part of the altar stands painted with icons of the saints, the holy table, on which the Divine Liturgy was celebrated lies broken on the ground, which we kissed in veneration. … Perceived even this, as the monastery was surrounded by a high wall … however it was built from stone that was soft, sandy and weak, and for this reason, after being deserted for many years it has collapsed.[108]

Thus, at the beginning of the Ottoman era, there were only four Orthodox monasteries in Palestine outside of Jerusalem, five if the Monastery of St John the Baptist is included. Their history in the sixteenth to eighteenth centuries had a fluctuating character, with periods of neglect and disrepair alternating with reconstruction and resettlement. If the sixteenth century is characterized by a revival of monastic activity (the resettlement of the Monasteries of Mar Saba, the Prophet Elijah, and even John the Baptist), in the second third of the seventeenth century, almost all of them fade away (the Serbs leaving Mar Saba, the Georgians leaving the Monastery of the Cross, and the abandonment of the Monastery of St George). The Greeks were able to keep these monasteries for themselves, but in fact they only held them as caretakers, with the exception of the Lavra of Mar Saba. According to the available information, the extinction of monastic life in the Holy Land in the seventeenth and eighteenth centuries can be explained by the economic and demographic problems of the Orthodox community, which were exacerbated by pressure from the Bedouins.[109]

The Brotherhood of the Holy Sepulchre: Structure and Composition

Despite the decline of the monasteries, monastics as a social group played a key role in the Church of Jerusalem, subordinating to their leadership the Arab secular clergy and the lay elites of the Orthodox community. The Greek monks of Palestine were merged into a kind of monastic order, the so-called Brotherhood of the Holy Sepulchre. The time of its occurrence and the circumstances of its early history are portrayed in the literature in a contradictory manner. According to one version, the Brotherhood was originally a monastic community that lived in the monastery in the patriarchal church of the Holy Sepulchre and was headed by the patriarch. The Palestinian bishops and the abbots of other monasteries primarily came out of this milieu, and they all continued to be members of the Brotherhood.[110]

It is clear that the Georgian and Serbian monastic colonies were not subordinate to the patriarch of Jerusalem and were not included in the Brotherhood of the Holy Sepulchre. They were its counterparts with their own hierarchical structure and autonomous economy, and they were clearly aware of their collective interests and ethnic solidarity. With the end of the Serbian and Georgian presence in Palestine, the passing of the monasteries of these communities into the hands of the Greeks, and the decline of Palestinian monasticism—which all depended on the Patriarchate—in the final assessment of the Greek xenocracy in Jerusalem, the concepts of the "Greek Brotherhood of the Holy Sepulchre" and "Palestinian monastic clergy" came to be one and the same.

It is possible to adequately reconstruct the internal structure of the Brother-hood from its statutes of the seventeenth and eighteenth centuries.[111] The earliest of them, attributed to Patriarch Theophanes, was introduced before 1624, but it has not survived. It is only known that the Brotherhood was approved as a ceno-bitic monastery, with a general treasury and other relevant attributes.[112] Because of the prolonged absences of the patriarchs from Palestine, the role of the *epitro-pos*, the patriarchal vicar who led the Brotherhood in the patriarch's absence, was great. The *epitropos* could be a bishop, an archimandrite, or even a simple monk. Here, informal authority counted for more than high rank. In the early sixteenth century, despite the presence of several metropolitans in Jerusalem, the position of the *epitropos* of the Holy Sepulchre was held by the monk Neophytos. It should be added, however, that he was the older brother of the then-patriarch Chrysanthos.[113]

The *epitropoi* were often unable to keep the warring monastic factions under control, and so under Patriarch Dositheos in the 1680s, there developed a form of collective management for the Brotherhood—the "synaxis of chosen men," which was made up of four influential monks led by the *epitropos*. Among the members of the synaxis, the secretary stood out. In the 1840s, Porphyry Uspenski called the most influential member of the Holy Synod of Jerusalem, the secretary of the Brotherhood, the monk Anthimos, whose heavy walking stick was feared not only by ordinary monks but also by metropolitans.[114] An important role was also played by the *skevophylax*, who was responsible for finances but apparently was not a member of the synaxis. Dositheos attempted to avoid concentrating power within a single administrative authority. This was the intended purpose of designating a number of inviolable positions—such as the secretary (who kept the large printing press), the *skevophylax*, and the keeper of the patriarchal cells—whom no one but the patriarch could remove. In the case of the death of any member of the Brotherhood's senior leadership, the *epitropos* was able to put another ("whom the synaxis recognizes as worthy") in the vacant position, although only with the patriarch's consent. At the same time, the synaxis could of its own authority dismiss "unworthy" abbots.[115] The monasteries of the Arch-angel, St Thekla, St Demetri, Bethlehem, the Lavra of Mar Saba, the Prophet Elijah, and the Cross had to submit financial reports to the patriarchate annually after Easter. Surplus funds were collected in the treasury of the Holy Sepulchre, while at the same time, the statutes read, "No one shall be a mediator and inter-cessor for another." Surplus figs, olives, lentils, and barley from rural monaster-ies also were handed over to Jerusalem and the abbot could not "in any way be contrary to this," which apparently was in reality often the case.[116] Any financial transactions or real estate deals on the part of the *epitropa* and synaxis were considered invalid without the sanction of the patriarch. The *skevophylax* had to keep careful accounting records and report his expenditures. The distribution of alms and the presentation of gifts to important people, including Ottoman officials, were not to be made on behalf of the *skevophylax*, but rather through the patriarch or *epitropos*. Gifts passed by pilgrims "under the guise of charity" personally to the *skevophylax* should be put "with a clear conscience" into the treasury of the Brotherhood.[117]

The statutes of the Brotherhood always call for conciliarity and unanimity: "Let no one seek his own will, but rather he should be committed to ensuring that which is approved by the Brotherhood."[118] Internal conflicts were a serious problem for members of the Brotherhood. For mutual strife, the patriarchs threatened banishment to other monasteries for various periods. The chief place of exile was Mar Saba, which Porphyry Uspensky once called "Jerusalem's Siberia."[119] The Brotherhood was divided into clans cemented by patron–client ties and ties with fellow countrymen. Influential monks defended their countrymen from punishment for offenses and promoted them to prestigious positions, something strongly condemned by the statutes.[120] The guidebook of the Brotherhood sought to maintain group solidarity within its "orders": as the regulations prescribed, "Let none of the brothers dare to inform pilgrims of the secrets of the monastery, nor to disclose the brothers' defects." They threatened with a curse anyone who provoked the Arabs against any of the monks "or even gives them an excuse to inflict … harm on the holy monastery."[121]

Dositheos insisted on secrecy in the domain of financial affairs and the ecclesiastical policy of the Brotherhood. "Let no one know your secrets," he advised, "that is, income, expenses or our [patriarchal] decrees."[122] Internal problems of the monastery were not to be discussed openly.

Judging by the statutes, the patriarchs cared a great deal about matters of discipline, maintaining a pious way of life and *esprit de corps* among the monks. The communistic principles of cenobitic houses often came into conflict with weak human nature. Those who did not attend church services were to be denied wine and vegetables on that day and so could have only bread and water. Healthy monks were not permitted to eat meat, while the ailing could, with the permission of their confessor, although not in the presence of laypeople. Likewise, they were not permitted to smoke tobacco in front of strangers. Meals were common in the Brotherhood and not attending them was condemned, because monks clearly ate more satisfying food somewhere else. In the patriarchate, the rules for food rations were limited. Thus, in particular, it is noted that "no one except for the ailing shall be issued sugar out of term, so that there will not be luxury and temptation."[123] "Prepare as much wine as is needed," Patriarch Dositheos instructed the brethren, "but do not try to fill, as someone said, forty kegs. Fear God!"[124] Likewise, the issuance of soap, candles, and unfrayed clothing, to be worn before pilgrims and on feast days, was regulated.[125] The statutes also sought to regulate the monks' daily life. The gates of the patriarchate were ordered locked after dark. "The lazy should not walk in the streets and bazaars or indulge in idle talk, especially at night," read the statutes, "But all should to their best ability carry out necessary business or practice reading the divine books. Those who cannot read should listen to others' reading and let them not seek authority, but rather seek the kingdom of heaven."[126]

Members of the Brotherhood were allowed to have personal property and so within the Brotherhood there was stratification, with some members at the top owning significant amounts of money and valuables. The aforementioned secretary Anthimos is said to have amassed 4 million piasters.[127] Constantin-François Volney complained of the Greek monks' "putting to evil use" income from pilgrimage. He wrote, "They [i.e., presumably, their Franciscan neighbors] are annoyed at their luxury, which provides them with china, carpets and even sabers, daggers and staffs with which they decorate their cells."[128] After a monk's death, however his property went to the Brotherhood. This involved a complicated procedure of taking hold of valuables, making an inventory of them, and transferring them to the *skevophylax*, while the rest was distributed to the poor monks. In this connection, Patriarch Meletios and other bishops forbade members of the brotherhood from keeping their property in private homes, with relatives, and so on.[129]

The Moral Character of Members of the Brotherhood of
the Holy Sepulchre

But truth forces me to detect all the abominations of this place. I am an axe and
I lie at the roots of a rotten tree.

—Porphyry Uspenski, 1844

The leaders of the Brotherhood paid particular attention to the moral climate in its monasteries. Statutes prescribe lodging female pilgrims, nuns, and the families of pilgrims in the Monastery of St Thekla, separate from the main mass of male pilgrims. It was stipulated to pilgrims visiting the Monastery of the Cross that women and girls should not go there at night. A variety of prohibitions and restrictions prevented members of the Brotherhood from communicating with nuns and prevented nuns from communicating with the outside world.

Those caught committing debauchery were subject to unconditional expulsion from the Brotherhood, even though Dositheos treated other offenders in a more lenient manner, excluding the guilty from the Brotherhood's synodical decision making only after a first and second warning. Dositheos also prohibited "beardless" novices from staying at the patriarchate, as "they are a cause of great dishonor and spiritual harm."[130] He sent all of them to Mar Saba to learn monastic discipline. All new monks entering into the Brotherhood had to spend a similar trial period of a year or more in the monastery.[131]

We should not forget, however, that what we have before us are merely legal documents unlikely to be effective in real life. The moral character of the Brotherhood's monks was far from the model drawn by Dositheos. Porphyry Uspenski left grotesque descriptions of the corruption that prevailed among the clergy of Jerusalem. Monks of the Brotherhood openly cohabitated with nuns, the so-called *gerondissas* (eldresses). The abbot of almost every monastery had a concubine, not excluding the hideous abbot of the Monastery of St George, although, as Porphyry sarcastically noted, "They were made for each other. She [the *gerondissa*] was as pockmarked and ugly as he himself."[132]

Simple monks contented themselves with random encounters, sometimes even with Muslim women, which exposed them to the risk of death. Directly adjacent to the Church of the Holy Sepulchre was the former building of the Latin Patriarchate, built by the Crusaders. In Ottoman times, it belonged to the noble Muslim Alemi family. The windows of the Alemis' harem overlooked the rotunda of the Holy Sepulchre (it happened that hermits threw orange peels into the opening of the rotunda) and the door of the women's quarters led to the roof of the temple, the south part of which belonged to the Greek Patriarchal Monastery. Sometimes inhabitants of the harem made their way onto the monastery's roof or brought monks there. When Muslim husbands suspected something was wrong and complained to the court against the patriarch, he cynically replied, "You have mares and I have stallions. Lock yours up and mine won't be jumping on them."[133] They walled up the door. In this respect, the patriarch's perception of his monastic brethren as "stallions" is characteristic. Unfortunately, Porphyry's informants could not date this tradition, only saying that it all happened "in the old days."

Some of the bishops, in accordance with their high status, kept entire harems. In Porphyry's days, the *gerondissas* of the Brotherhood's high dignitaries were placed in the Monastery of the Dormition (the Great Panagia), obviously because of its convenient location in proximity to the patriarchate. Most famous for his sensuality was Metropolitan Kyrillos of Lydda (later Patriarch of Jerusalem from 1845 to 1872), who arranged a convent for his three concubines. "Two of them are natives of the Island of Mytilene," wrote Porphyry, "while the third is Constantinopolitan. The oldest is thirty years old, her niece is twenty, and the Constantinopolitan, daughter of the concubine of the abbot of the Monastery of St Elias, is fifteen. The latter recently gave birth. I do not remember if it is the son or daughter of His Eminence Kyrillos."[134] Although the bishops and archimandrites could not officially recognize these children as their own, they continued to take care of them and gave their daughters in marriage with good dowries. Characteristically, the Brotherhood's metropolitans attempted to bring forward some canonical arguments in defense of these "womanizers." The final and strongest arguments were those such as "We were not the first to have *gerondissas*. This has been done here already since olden times."[135]

Accordingly, the question arises: how long is "olden times"? Does Porphyry's evidence reflect moral decay that was characteristic of the Brotherhood of the Holy Sepulchre in the first half of the nineteenth century, or was it a strong tradition that went unnoticed by the exalted pilgrims of earlier times? Of course, not all pilgrims had tunnel vision. Suffice it to recall Arseny Sukhanov, who by and large was not on pilgrimage but rather fulfilling an official duty. This precursor of the "Eastern Spy" Uspenski was hypercritical of Levantine Christians, even of such situations "where the eye that loves its neighbor sees nothing corrupt," as Sukhanov's main opponent in Russian literature, Hieromonk Melety put it.[136] And yet neither Sukhanov nor the equally Grecophobic Ivan Lukyanov reproached members of the Brotherhood for the sin of voluptuousness. It cannot be excluded, however, that these medieval people maintained some moral taboos in their literary works regarding subjects about which it was not thought possible to write. For Porphyry, there were no taboo subjects. If not for his furious temper and ruthless pen, we would not have learned about the harems of the metropolitans of Jerusalem, as neither A. N. Muraviev nor Konstantin M. Bazili, nor any of their contemporaries touched on such delicate topics.[137] Historians have long noted that a spiritual career was one of the few channels for social mobility and outlets for energy and ambition open to Ottoman Christians. Examples of ecclesiastical clans and factions[138] group together several close relatives, and here it is obvious that we are not dealing with devout ascetics but with people who are concerned purely with worldly interests and ambitions, that is, ordinary people with human passions and an excitable temperament.

It should be remembered that the provisions of the statutes of the Brotherhood of the Holy Sepulchre obviously did not come out of nowhere. One can also look at the ledger of Trifon Kolobeinikov, which records exceedingly strange pairings in some of the monasteries of Jerusalem, such as the builder elder Ioseph and the eldress Thekla at the Monastery of Theodore Stratilates and the elder Ioseph and eldress Varvara at the Monastery of St Thekla.[139] All of this is similar to the monastery-hostels and titular abbots with their concubines described in the nineteenth century by Porphyry Uspenski. Perhaps "the pleasure of women" did not flourish in Palestinian monasticism in the sixteenth and seventeenth centuries as much as it did in the mid-nineteenth century, but it seems that on some level it was always present.

Recruitment and Centers of Influence of the Brotherhood

The sources make it possible to identify two main channels for replenishing the Brotherhood with new recruits. First of all some pilgrims settled in Jerusalem, taking monastic vows if they had not done so before, and joined the ranks of the Brotherhood. This is how a small number of Arabs and other non-Greeks came into the Brotherhood. Patriarch Parthenios's statutes even stipulate the size of the entrance contribution that was to be paid to the Synod and to the Brotherhood's treasury by a nun who wished to remain in Jerusalem. This did not give the right, as Parthenios noted, for women "of a bad life," based on homelessness or a relationship with the monks, to enter freely into the monasteries.[140] Here we see a reference to the second and chief way of recruiting members into the Brotherhood: recruitment from the Balkans and Greek islands of relatives and friends of members of the Brotherhood who were already in Jerusalem. In most biographies of Palestinian bishops that are known to us, these are the circumstances that are mentioned for their arriving in the Holy Land.

Because of the patriarchs' long stays in the Balkans, two centers of power in the Brotherhood gradually emerged: one in Jerusalem headed by the vicar-*epitropos* and another in Constantinople or the Danube principalities, in the person of the patriarch. The privileged Balkan branch sought to play a leading role in the Brotherhood, which was met with resistance from the Palestinian branch, which bore the burden of maintaining the holy places. According to Arseny Sukhanov, in the early 1650s, Patriarch Paisios and his "pitrop" [*epitropos*] so actively sought to "change" each other that even the Pasha of Jerusalem tried to make peace between them.[141] Patriarch Dositheos's relations with his Palestinian vicars were uneasy in the 1680s, when they wrote, "if the patriarch will stay living in his house and rule with violence, let him be anathema." Dositheos raged indignantly,

Fathers, what evil have we done you? The brothers of the Holy Sepulchre are endangered in the world and live in poverty and we have made your sanctity as caretakers of your house and your cells … what evil have we done you? Because when a letter arrives from you, you cause us suffering and we fall into sickness.[142]

Seeing that the strife within the Brotherhood threatened to plunge it into heavy debts, Dositheos defiantly threatened to abdicate.

A century and a half later, Porphyry Uspenski captured the voice of the other side, when he spoke with the secretary of the Brotherhood, Anthimos, about the then-patriarch Kyrillos. Anthimos, who had no love for Kyrillos, reproached him for his uncontrolled waste of the Brotherhood's treasury and immoral life. "Between us has reigned division," the secretary complained. "Those around the patriarch proudly tell us, 'We are patriarchal while you are monastic!'"[143] In 1714, the Palestinian metropolitans and monks strongly opposed Patriarch Chrysanthos's intention to elevate bishops and abbots for the Brotherhood's monasteries in Moldavia and Wallachia.[144] The protest was a success, but in general, at the top of the Brotherhood (around thirty monks), it was difficult to settle on any single course of action and so the patriarchs of Jerusalem usually dominated the Brotherhood.

THE SYRIAN MONASTERIES: SOURCES

Information about the monasteries of the Patriarchate of Antioch is much scarcer than information about the Palestinian monasteries. Writers on their way to the holy places, the main source of information about Middle Eastern monasteries, rarely wandered into Syria. One of the few exceptions, Vasili Grigorovich-Barsky, left a description that is unsurpassed in its completeness and detail. Grigorovich-Barsky's records, however, represent only a single moment in time, establishing the state of Syrian monasticism in 1728. It is difficult to grasp the evolution of monasteries during the Ottoman era. Grigorovich-Barsky, of course, provides some historical information, such as that a particular monastery was founded "during the Greeks' captivity," but how should this be understood? The entire post-Byzantine era or specifically the Ottoman period? There are even more uncertain dates reported by that traveler, and the dates that are verifiable indicate that, as a rule, Barsky was seriously erroneous in his dating. Monasteries' manuscript collections partially help to compensate for these shortcomings. Manuscript colophons sometimes contain references to various events in the life of the monastery, out of which a more or less coherent picture can be put together. It should also be noted that Barsky did not visit all the monasteries of Syria, and we have almost no information about what was left out of the author's field of vision.

Grigorovich-Barsky described eleven active monasteries in the See of Antioch. The next detailed description of Syrian monasteries belongs to Porphyry Uspenski, in the 1840s, and he lists eighteen monastic houses.[145] Two of them, according to Porphyry, had emerged in recent times that are after Grigorovich-Barsky's travels. Another clearly existed before 1728. A difference of four monasteries remains, and we are unable to say whether they were founded in the interval between Grigorovich-Barsky and Porphyry or that Grigorovich-Barsky simply missed them. At first glance, it is noteworthy that the monasteries are divided into two regional groups. The monasteries of Inner Syria along the line from Damascus to Aleppo are ancient, even Byzantine constructions that for the most part lay in ruins, with only a few of them supporting life. The monasteries of the coast, mainly in Tripoli and 'Akkar, were more numerous and their founding in most cases already belonged to the Ottoman era.

The Monastery of Saydnaya

The largest and most famous monastery in Syria was the Monastery of the Nativity of the Most Blessed Theotokos in Saydnaya, 30 kilometers north of Damascus.[146] Standing at the top of a mountain, during periods of unrest it was often the refuge of Christians and the place for saving the treasures of the patriarchate. The founding of the monastery goes back to the era of Justinian. Little remains there from Byzantine times, however, and the monastery has been rebuilt several times. In the period under review, this was done in particular in 1762, three years after the major earthquake that toppled many of the mosques and minarets of Damascus. Although the monastery's church withstood the earthquake, it too was in need of reconstruction. This was done, according to a pointed remark by Mikhail Breik, not by the patriarch and his vicar, but "first of all, by Our Lady the Virgin Mary … who led some pious and charitable Christians to attend to the construction and, secondly, by the mufti Sheikh 'Ali al-Murad, whom she inspired to say 'Go build that monastery.'"[147] The monastery is surrounded by thick walls with several gates of wrought iron in the shape of a triangle stretching east to west. "The wall is essentially of cross-sections of smooth stones," wrote Grigorovich-Barsky, "and the buildings are strong affairs, and if because of many years and disrepair much has fallen from above, still it was restored again."[148] In the monastery there were eighty cells for monks and pilgrims, "not at all grandiose, but simply built," noted Grigorovich-Barsky.[149] He also praised the monastery's Church of the Nativity of the Theotokos, which is somewhat similar to the church in the Monastery of Sinai, also built by Justinian, though surpassing it in all respects,

Above it has no cupola, but an extended covering, sharply brought together and bolted with plinths, inside even the footing is smoothly fitted with stone tablets, it has entirely stone pillars standing in four rows. ... Inside it also has a stone iconostasis with decorations, candelas and chandeliers, and the base of the altar is laid with separated marble.[150]

The church had four chapels. In one of them services were held by the Syrian Jacobites who came to venerate the miraculous icon of the Virgin, the monastery's chief relic. The icon, according to legend painted by St Luke the Evangelist, had been brought to the monastery at some point by a pilgrim monk and was encased in a marble case and decked with gold and a pavement of stones. It was believed that the shrine gives healing from diseases not only to Christians "but also to [people of] other faiths, if they come with faith."[151] Literature about the miracles of the icon of Saydnaya goes back to the Middle Ages. Pilgrims and writers of the Ottoman era contributed many new traditions.[152] In 1767, Patriarch Philemon seized the monastery's treasures to cover its costs, which left a depressing impression on his contemporaries. The patriarch's demise was considered God's punishment for his insulting the monastery.[153]

Grigorovich-Barsky wrote that in former times monks had lived in the Monastery of Saydnaya, then "left because of the many taxes" and the monastery "is now populated by maidens and nuns."[154] It is not clear when this change occurred. There is, however, the well-known message sent in 1560 by Patriarch Joachim Jum'a to the tsar of Muscovy, in which the patriarch wrote,

Here in our lands there is found the monastery of the Most Pure [Theotokos] near the city of Damascus... and more than forty brothers are found in it... who are deprived of any good thing. And for the sake of your eternal commemoration, send them alms... as God shall instruct you.[155]

At first, the current author believed that "forty brothers" was a translator's mistake,[156] and then I became inclined to believe that Patriarch Joachim's letter reflects the situation mentioned by Grigorovich-Barsky. That is, it is the latest evidence for male inhabitants of the monastery.[157] However, it seems that that assumption is unlikely. Already by 1576, a half-dozen years after Joachim's letter, the priest Musa donated a book "to the Church of Our Lady the Theotokos in Saydnaya and to the nuns who abide there,"[158] and in 1593, Trifon Korobeinikov donated 120 gold pieces of royal alms to the "girls' monastery" of the Most-pure Theotokos with sixty nuns.[159] Even more convincing evidence comes from the

Florentine pilgrim N. Frescobaldi in 1384, who refers several times to Saydnaya as a women's monastery.[160]

Some sources contain information about people who headed the monastery at the end of the sixteenth and seventeenth centuries. The archives of G. A. Murkos contain photocopies of some documents from the Monastery of Saydnaya for the period from 1591 to 1630.[161] Recorded in these texts are real estate transactions made on behalf of or in the presence of *al-ra'isa* (Abbess) Martha, daughter of Hajji Sa'ada from the village of Balat in the district of al-Hisn. Her name appears in documents of 1592, 1608, and even 1628, although in the latter case it is without a *nisba*, so we cannot be fully sure that it is the same Martha. If this is nevertheless the case, then it turns out that this woman led the largest Syrian monastery for nearly forty years.

The priests who served in the monastery church also took part in the management of the monastery. One of them, "the Arab priest Moses of the city of Damascus of the church of the Assumption of the Most-pure Mother of God [meaning the Saydnaya Monastery]," came to Moscow in the autumn of 1644 to request alms.[162] At the Posolsky Prikaz, Moses said that, around 1636,[163] "[i]n that church two pillars collapsed and I … built that church, and the Turks saw how my church was built and in hate unjustly pinned on me penalties of 750 rubles."[164] Moses apparently tried to do the repairs in secret, without the *qadi's* expensive authorization, but he was exposed:

> those penalties for the debt plagued me for a long time, and I, not wearing down their great debt, pledged to the infidels for that debt my wife and children, and what happened … the Turks plundered all parts of the church structure, books and vestments, and everything.[165]

Before his departure from Moscow in the spring of 1656, Patriarch Macarius ibn al-Za'im addressed the tsar with a petition for him to grant charters to three Syrian monasteries—Saydnaya, Balamand, and St George Humayra—for the right to receive alms from Russia in the future. These charters were granted, including for the Monastery of the Nativity of the Most-holy Theotokos of Saydnaya, to the Abbess Mary and the sisters.[166]

In the second half of the seventeenth century, there were some dramatic changes to the status of the Monastery of Saydnaya. The position of abbess was abolished and, by the authority of the patriarch, the rector of the priests of Saydnaya was put at the head of the monastery. Ippolit Vishenski describes the situation in 1708: "in that monastery there are forty nuns, all of them old and infirm. There is an abbot there and with him fifteen monks."[167] During the day, the monks, pilgrims, and also the metropolitan of Saydnaya stayed in the monastery, while at night they went down to the village, "so there will be no temptation for the people," as Grigorovich-Barsky explained.[168] The village priests alternated serving in the monastery church, "the others going about their work in the church and monastery as monks."[169] It seems that this "temptation" of which Grigorivich-Barsky wrote befell an English traveler, Henry Maundrell, who reports in 1697 that "Now [the monastery] is in the possession of twenty Greek monks and forty nuns, who, as it seems, live together without any order or separation."[170] Maundrell spent less than a day at Saydnaya and returned to Damascus to spend the night, so he was not able to make a fair depiction of the monastic arrangement. It is worth noting, however, that among the Maronites, the phenomenon of "double" monasteries where men and women labored together had long been known, before the Vatican put an end to it.[171]

Among the abbots of Saydnaya was the famous chronicler, the priest Mikhail Breik, who was appointed in 1768 as the monastery's *ra'is* and *wakil*. He lasted only a year in this service and then left "due to great fatigue and the lack of order."[172]

In the 1840s, Porphyry Uspenski found thirty-eight nuns in the monastery. "Their clothing," he wrote, "consists of a long black robe and their head is covered with a long black scarf, so their faces cannot be seen apart from the eyes."[173] The nuns led a strict life of fasting; they only left the monastery for the cemetery. As earlier, management was headed by male trustees, a priest and a layman who changed every year and reported income and expenses to the patriarchate.[174] The monastery supported pilgrims seeking alms, especially women. In the time of Porphyry, each diocese of Antioch had special alms-collectors for the monastery. Sometimes the patriarchate also supported the monastery. Ippolit Vishenski wrote that the patriarch "sends them their necessities from Damascus."[175] Additionally, the monastery possessed its own significant economy: according to the same author, "much of every vegetable, and many cows and sheep."[176] In the time of Porphyry Uspenski, property in Damascus registered to the monastery included 400 olive trees, 150 goats, oxen, and farm implements.[177] As mentioned, we have access to copies of parts of the Monastery of Saydnaya's record books, which allow us to draw some conclusions about the monastic economy in Syria at the end of the sixteenth and first third of the seventeenth centuries. We have four passages at our disposal from 1591–1592 and the autumns of 1608, 1628, and 1630, with a total of fourteen entries. These are primarily acts of donating various kinds of property to the monastery and, less commonly, the exchange of plots of land or the sale by the monastery of buildings that belonged to it. The frequency of transactions ranges from one a year in the period from October 1591 to September 1592 to about six in the period from September to December 1608. Plots of uncultivated land, vineyards, mulberry groves, and buildings ("cells") were donated to the monastery. Sometimes, it was stipulated that revenues from a given endowment were intended for wayfarers, pilgrims, monastics, and so forth. Usually, when the boundaries of an endowment plot are described, adjacent lands are also listed: private property, communal lands, and beaten track. Quite often, among these lands appear "private property of the church" and "endowment of the cathedral church." It is not clear there whether it is a question of the possessions of the Monastery of Saydnaya or of some other church. It seems likely to us that they are the monastery's lands.

The donors themselves can be divided into several categories. First of all is the higher clergy: in 1608, Simeon, metropolitan of Hama, gave in endowment to the monastery a vineyard he had bought; the aforementioned Abbess Martha al-Balatiyya acquired land and donated it in endowment to her own monastery. Second is the lay elite: for that period we know the Damascene Sheikh Jurjis ibn Samur (it is known that in addition to real estate, he donated to the monastery the silver frame for the miraculous icon of the Theotokos),[178] Ibrahim ibn Rizqallah ibn Najib (a notable), Zakariya ibn al-Kubri from al-Zabadani, a certain Hajj Mikhail, and others. It is clear that a pilgrimage to the holy places was a fairly expensive undertaking and so the latter donor belonged to the Christian elite. Of course, among the pilgrims there were also poor vagabonds, but such people are not in a position to establish an endowment. Among the donors in 1608 was the monk Sulayman ibn al-Ahmar, perhaps a relative of Patriarch Dorotheus ibn al-Ahmar (r. 1604–1611). The third group of donors is other laypeople, some with the honorary title *mu'allim* ("teacher") and priests who established endowments or had other financial business with the monastery and who logically belonged to middle and upper strata of the Christian community. The geographic area from which the donors came is quite extensive, from Damascus and al-Zabadani to Hama (190 kilometers as the crow flies). Many, however, did not indicate their place of residence or they came from a village that cannot be identified. It is also difficult to locate the endowment lands. On a purely speculative basis, one can assume that they are unlikely to have been more than a day's journey from the monastery, although other monasteries of the Christian East held real estate as much as 2,000 or more kilometers away.

In the case of the Monastery of Saydnaya, it can be said with a high degree of probability that the endowed orchards and vineyards were not cultivated by the ("old, infirm") nuns. These lands were undoubtedly leased to neighboring peasants who paid the monastery some share of the harvest. On the analogy of the orchards of the Monastery of St Catherine on Sinai[179] and the Greek Catholic monasteries of Lebanon in the eighteenth century,[180] it can be assumed that rent was one half of the harvest. As regards the monasteries in Lebanon, however, part of the land was worked by the monks.

As it received considerable income from its properties, the monastery also bore substantial expenses to feed pilgrims and travelers, as well as, it seems, Muslim pilgrims passing by in the direction of Damascus or Aleppo; it is namely for this, that one must apparently remember the words of V. Grigorovich-Barksy, that the monastery, "has resentment for the Arabs, inasmuch as it is positioned along the great road and many of the passersby eat their bread."[181]

In and around the village of Saydnaya in the Byzantine period there had been forty churches and monasteries. By the Ottoman period, only the foundations of many of them remained. At the end of the seventeenth century, Henry Maundrell lists sixteen churches nearby: "I visited many of these churches, but found them so ruined and desolate that I decided not to examine the rest."[182] There exist documents from the end of the sixteenth century signed by the hand of Patriarch Joachim Daw (r. 1581–1592) regarding real estate transactions between the Monastery of St Barbara and the kellion of St George in the area of Saydnaya, which both had disappeared a century later.[183] In these monasteries, which were not very much frequented, priests served the liturgy on certain days. The best preserved of all were the Monasteries of St George and the Holy Apostle Thomas. As Vasili Grigorovich-Barsky wrote of the former, "the church is still small, and strongly done of great cross sections of stones, and it has been desolate for years; there are few cells around it." There were no monks there, but there did live a priest, "so that the monastery would not become desolate."[184] Sometimes they even restored the monastery, as in 1781 when, under the leadership of the *khuri* Christopher ibn al-Musabani, they restored its arch and decorated it "and it became," in the words of Breik, "a joy to those who see it, may the Lord fortify it."[185]

The second monastery, of St Thomas, was, according to Grigorovich-Barsky,

> empty and ruined, nothing was left there of the cells, only the base and parts of the walls, the church was still whole and still abiding till now … and the gates are shut, and no Christians go there by their will or celebrate the Liturgy.[186]

In 1843, Porphyry Uspenski examined the half-dozen abandoned monasteries around Saydnaya. Half of them only remained as barely distinguishable piles of stones.[187]

Other Monasteries in Inner Syria

Farther north were the monasteries of Maaloula, the Monasteries of St Thekla, and St Sergius and St Bacchus. The still-extant Monastery of St Sergius and St Bacchus was, according to Grigorovich-Barsky's description, on the hill over-looking the village,

> in dimension it is not great, but it stands in a beautiful space, and the Church has a stone cupola ... and desirably built with pillars and shop-stalls, and painted with icons along the walls.... There are few cells built, as the whole monastery is not very big, and has grown empty and is on the verge of decline, inasmuch as not one lives inside, thanks to the discomfort and temptation of the infidels, who became used to getting their food and drink from the monasteries.[188]

Like some of the churches of Saydnaya, the monastery was "mothballed." Presbyters from the village would occasionally unlock it and hold services there for arriving pilgrims.

Regular services were conducted in two of the village's other churches, including in the cave Church of the Holy Martyr Thekla, where the saint's wonderworking relics were kept in a side niche. They were an object of veneration even by local Muslims, as "no small number of them have received healing and for this reason they hold the saint's name in reverence."[189]

It is worth mentioning that Paul of Aleppo in 1642 and Grigorovich-Barsky in 1728 speak only of the Monastery of St Sergius and the church—not monastery—of St Thekla.[190] Subsequently, the Monastery of St Sergius and St Bacchus fell into the hands of the Uniates (the exact date is not known), while the Orthodox retained the Monastery of St Thekla along with the Church of John the Baptist. According to Breik, the church was rebuilt in 1756, but it was in a wretched state when Porphyry Uspenski found a Greek abbot with a deacon and two novices there.[191]

According to the description of Grigorovich-Barsky, the next major Christian center in the region, Yabrud, did not have any functioning monasteries, although it was filled with ruins of early medieval churches. Eighty-five years earlier, Paul of Aleppo visited the cells of Mar Konon, a Byzantine cave monastery carved high into the rock that was apparently abandoned at the time.[192]

Finally, in Qara, where in Grigorovich-Barsky's time there were very few Christians, there stood the Monastery of St John, "now narrow but recognized by its beautiful structure," and by that time also abandoned.[193]

Among the other monasteries of the Syrian interior, we cannot but mention Dayr Samʿan, the Monastery of Simeon Stylites, 60 kilometers northwest of Aleppo, the jewel of early Byzantine architecture. It was already deserted in the Ottoman period, but it apparently remained in fairly good condition. According to the testimony of Paul of Aleppo, the metropolitan of Aleppo would regularly go there on pilgrimage accompanied by Christians and serve liturgy in the monastery's cathedral church.[194]

To this same group of monasteries of inner Syria should be added a special category of urban monasteries. If we exclude bishops' residences, which were often referred to as "monasteries," in terms of urban monasteries we know of a Monastery of Mar Elias in Homs and monasteries of St George in both Mhardeh and Kafr Buhum. They can be assessed only from the colophons of manuscripts, which do not give us a clear idea about the history of these monasteries. The manuscripts from the monastery in Mhardeh go back to the end of the nineteenth century and the earliest dated manuscript from Kafr Buhum was written by a local deacon in 1805.[195] In the Monastery of Mar Elias of Homs, there is a quite large collection of thirty-eight manuscripts, but it is unclear when and how they arrived there. The only manuscript clearly marked as an endowment to the monastery dates to February 1613.[196] This means that Mar Elias existed at least from the beginning of the seventeenth century.

Dayr al-Balamand

In the second coastal group of monasteries stands the Balamand Monastery of the Dormition of the Most-holy Theotokos, three hours southeast of Tripoli.[197] Here stood the ruins of a Cistercian abbey from the Crusader era. The founding of the Orthodox Monastery of Balamand goes back to September 1602[198] and is associated with the names of the then-metropolitans of Beirut and Tripoli, as well as the influential Orthodox Sheikh Sulayman al-Yaziji, the same person who in 1618 would attempt to obtain the patriarchal throne for Cyril Dabbas.

Through Sulayman al-Yaziji, his secretary, the Pasha of Tripoli Yusuf Sayf authorized the monastery's construction and changed the status of the surrounding land from *timar* (a conditional holding allocated for military service) to a *waqf*. The monastery's records preserve the names of Christian sheikhs who were the first benefactors of Balamand—Sheikh Abu Salih, the aforementioned Sheikh Sulayman, and the village notables Fiʾa Farhat and Hajj Butrus. The list of benefactors also includes Yusuf Pasha, the governor of Tripoli.[199]

It is worth remembering that most monasteries, especially in the early Middle Ages, arose spontaneously around the dwelling place of a well-known ascetic.

In other cases, monasteries were established by Christian princes, members of the aristocracy, and the upper clergy. Dayr al-Balamand belongs to this second type of monastic establishment, which may seem somewhat strange for a Muslim state. In Northern Lebanon, however, with its numerous and concentrated Christian populations, this sort of establishment of a monastery by the Christian elite was entirely normal.

As is typical, Balamand's founders encountered the problem of choosing brethren for the monastery. Around this time, the *khuri* Makarius al-Dayrani, originally from the village of Darayya in Northern Lebanon before becoming abbot of the Monastery of Kaftoun, appeared in Tripoli. As Patriarch Makarius wrote,

> And its [Tripoli's] inhabitants tried to populate Dayr al-Balamand with monks, because there were not then monks there. And when they found amongst themselves a certain Simeon, they were exceedingly delighted and others dwelt with him, and pursued a good life there, and become the reason for the development of that monastery.[200]

The monastery was built up and renovated. A number of buildings from the Cistercian period were decorated and they took him and lodged in Dayr al-Balamand and erected new buildings. The most detailed description of Balamand belongs, once more, to Grigorovich-Barsky (1728). The Church of the Dormition of the Theotokos was, in his words, "grandiose and great," with elongated proportions,

> sufficiently high. . . and with simple and smooth construction, not having a single pillar inside, from below to the cupola above, bent inside, just as smooth outside, and out from above the altar they have a cupola slightly above with four windows, and from these light carries into the church, but it is only beautiful thanks to its construction. The church has one altar and inside are icons, candles and censers.[201]

The Church of the Dormition occupied the entire northern side of the monastery. The smaller Church of St George abutted the eastern walls. It was surrounded by cells and outbuildings, including wine cellars. The long, irregular southern wall encompassed hostels for pilgrims and by the west wall stood the kitchen, trapeza, and residential buildings. "Above are all the cells, where the monks live," described Grigorovich-Barsky, "and below in the middle of the wall are three gates ... and over there is a well for drinking, in which is rainwater, as there is no streaming water there."[202]

The monastery was closely associated with the regional Orthodox elite and became one of the district's chief places of worship. Clearly, it was from the Christian sheikhs of Tripoli that Dayr al-Balamand obtained the fig groves and vineyards mentioned by Grigorovich-Barksy.[203] In spite of the constant political turmoil in Lebanon, the monastery remained an island of relative stability. Feudal clans vied with each other to patronize Balamand.[204]

Balamand Monastery became one of the most important cultural centers of Orthodox Syria. Its library holds nearly two hundred manuscripts, second only to the patriarchal manuscript collection. Numerous notes in the margins of books saying "read" or "viewed" testify to their intense use.[205] A significant proportion of the manuscripts were copied by the monks of Balamand, while others were donated to the monastery.

The donors' geography is extensive: in addition to Tripoli and its surroundings (Amioun, Batroun, and so on), there are also natives of Beirut, Damascus, Aleppo, and even Palestine. In January 1618, the head of the Orthodox community in Tripoli, Sheikh Sulayman ibn Jirjis al-Yaziji, brought a magnificent gift to the monastery, the complete Arabic text of the Bible, a masterpiece of Melkite calligraphy.[206] For the next two hundred years, that manuscript served the monks of Balamand something like a recordbook of honored guests, in which many pilgrims and hierarchs who visited the monastery left their signatures (e.g., there are twenty-eight dated records for the years 1617–1618). Several of the records have the character of a chronicle, noting events from Lebanese political history, the affairs of the monastery, a plague of locusts, and severe frosts. Of the surrounding hierarchs, most closely associated with the monastery were the metropolitans of Tripoli. In the Bible are registered Metropolitan Joachim (February 1636); the priest Joachim al-Halabi, nephew of the metropolitan at the time (1671); another Metropolitan Joachim (1679); and Metropolitan Gerasimus (1786). On December 19, 1671, Deacon Hananiya, grandson of Patriarch Macarius al-Zaʻim mentioned his stay at the monastery. In September 1806, the famous scribe of that time, Metropolitan Athanasius of Beirut, left an admiring comment about the manuscript's medieval creator,

> May God have mercy on the copyist and transcriber because he copied the book so carefully ... compared to other manuscripts. It is better than all the books written in Arabic ... in modern times [?] and it is better than the printed Gospels—whether the old, the Aleppan, or the new one from

the Monastery of Mar Yuhanna al-Shuwayr.[207] Its handwriting is better than all existing manuscripts.[208]

Among the occasional additions to the monastery's books, there appear names of monks and abbots of Balamand, which allows us to trace out the lines of its history. The first abbot of the monastery, Macarius al-Dayrani was elevated to the metropolitan see of Saydnaya by Patriarch Dorotheus around the year 1608. Taking the name Simeon, he headed the diocese for more than a quarter-century.[209] Leadership of Balamand Monastery was then taken up by the *khuri* Yuhanna for seven years, from 1608 to 1615. Under Yuhanna, the number of brothers at the monastery, which in 1602 was nine, reached twenty-five[210] and in 1620, under the abbot the *khuri* Boulos, it was twenty.[211]

In January 1642, in a note by Trad ibn Jurjis from the village of Amioun, there is the first mention of the abbot Saba, son of Yusuf, son of the Deacon Ya'qub, son of Hajj Mikhail from the village of 'Afsadiq near Tripoli. His own signature is preserved in various assemblies from September 28, 1649, and May 12, 1654.[212] Saba accompanied Patriarch Macarius on his journey to Russia in the 1650s. Although the egotistical Paul of Aleppo ignores almost all of Macarius's entourage, he makes an exception for Saba, and Russian archival documents are full of references to "the Lebanese mountains of the Monastery of the Dormition of Archimandrite Saba."[213]

In the Russian State Archive of Ancient Acts (RGADA), there is a letter from 1652 from the brothers of the Balamand Monastery of the Dormition to Tsar Alexei Mikhailovich "about neglecting to give them alms."[214] The text itself of the letter is in Greek, but the five signatures below it are in Arabic: the *khuri* Musa, the *khuri* Hanna, the *khuri* Macarius, the *khuri* Serapion, and the *qass* Yusuf. This letter was brought to Moscow by Archimandrite Saba who came as part of Macarius's entourage. The patriarch of Antioch repeatedly requested—from the tsar, the tsarina, and from Patriarch Nikon—alms for Saba personally, and in March 1656, as mentioned, he obtained charters for three Syrian monasteries for the right to send delegations seeking alms once every seven years. The charter commanded

the boyars and voivodes of the cities near the borders and all officials to let pass the archimandrite and monks of this Dormition Monastery of Lebanon to us in Moscow and from Moscow without detention and give [them] carts and food and guards against foreigners ... and with them impose no fees or trade duties ... and whoever would take from or somehow insult them or their servants, they will be in our disfavor, and twice the amount of whatever is taken from them shall be given back.[215]

When he stopped in Wallachia on his return journey from Russia, Macarius sent part of the gifts from the tsar with baggage to Istanbul under the supervision of Archimandrite Saba. Later, something unexpected happened, because after that Paul of Aleppo assails Saba with curses in his book, saying that after the continuous alms to him, he "turned out to be a son of adultery" (as Georgii A. Murkos translated this curse). "May God repay him and may He be the judge between us and them!" wrote Paul.[216] One might assume that Saba appropriated the treasure and disappeared, but that is completely illogical behavior for the distinguished abbot of a famous monastery.

We probably will never know what conflict occurred between Macarius and Saba, but it seems to have ended in failure for the archimandrite. In Balamand's manuscript collection, there is a euchologion copied by Saba on May 4, 1666.[217] In the colophon, Saba called himself the "former abbot of Dayr al-Falamand." That is, he lost his job. Further on, Saba reported that he wrote the book "in Beirut, during the archpastorate of Metropolitan Kyr Phillip, where he stayed and wrote for six years and two months after his departure from his monastery."[218] It seems that for him his whole life was divided into "before" and "after" the time of his abbacy and the period of "disgrace," which he almost numbers to the day. Thanks to this, we can determine the approximate date of Saba's removal: March 1660, ten months after Macarius's return to Syria. The patriarch was in no hurry to settle scores with his enemies, but nevertheless Macarius did not forget his grievances.

Even as a private citizen, however, the former-abbot Saba retained a certain amount of influence at his monastery. Abbot Neophytos of Balamand went as part of Macarius's next embassy to Moscow (1662), bringing, among other things, a letter to the tsar from Archimandrite Saba.[219]

The colophons of manuscripts from Balamand contain the names of several other heads of the monastery. As we have seen, Neophytos, who succeeded Saba to the post of abbot in 1660, was soon sent to Moscow. It seems that he died on his return journey or shortly after returning, as he no longer appears in the sources. In Neophytos's absence, the monastery was headed by the *khuri* Jeremiah from Hama, first as a vicar (he was referred to as such in April 1663) and then as a full-fledged abbot (as he appears several times in colophons from 1663 to 1675).[220] There is a synaxarion copied by Jeremiah in 1667 in which he says that the brothers of the monastery in his day number twenty-five and he names several of the most authoritative priests.[221] Among them is mentioned the *qass* Farah, a new rising star of the monastery. In 1667, Farah leaves a note in the Bible of Pimen of Damascus in which he calls himself the "servant" (*khadim*) of

Dayr al-Balamand.[222] In May 1675, he orders a new manuscript, a contribution to the monastery, together with the abbot Jeremiah,[223] while in colophons from 1680–1690, he is called "abbot" (*al-ra'is*).[224]

During the schism between Patriarch Cyril and Neophytos (1672–1681), Balamand, along with the coastal dioceses, supported Neophytos. In the monastery's library are preserved manuscripts donated to Balamand by Neophytos al-Saqizi (one of these inserted writings from April of 1682 was stamped with the patriarch's seal).[225] Characteristically, Neophytos continued to call himself patriarch despite having already renounced his claim to the patriarchal throne. A prominent figure at the end of the seventeenth century and beginning of the eighteenth century was the abbot of Balamand, the *khuri* Philotheos. Under his guidance, large-scale construction was undertaken at the monastery in 1695. A narthex was added to the Church of the Dormition,[226] the space between the two churches was closed by an arch, and a number of buildings, known as the "Aleppo wing," were constructed.[227]

During this period, the first foreign traveler visited Balamand, the English merchant Henry Maundrell (March 1697). He left a detailed description of the monastery church and of worship, which was exotic for a Protestant observer. "The monks of this convent were, as I remember, forty in all," wrote Maundrell.

> We found them seemingly a very good natured and industrious, but certainly a very ignorant people.... Nor is this ignorance much to be wondered at; for what intervals of time they have between their hours of devotion, they are forced to spend, not in study but in managing of their flocks, cultivating their land, pruning their vineyards, and other labors of husbandry ... This toil they are obliged to undergo, not only to provide for their own sustenance, but also that they may be able to satisfy the unreasonable exactions, which the greedy Turks, upon every pretense they can invent, are ready to impose upon them. But that it may be the better guessed what sort of men these Greek [i.e., Orthodox] monks are, I will add this farther indication, viz. that the same person whom we saw officiating at the altar, in his embroidered sacerdotal robe, brought us the next day on his own back, a kid, and a goat's skin of wine, as a present from the convent.[228]

At the turn of the seventeenth to the eighteenth century, Balamand was involved in the struggle between the Orthodox and the Catholic Unia. In 1698, there appeared at Balamand two monks from Aleppo, Gerasimus and Sulayman, who had studied with the Jesuits at Tripoli. The Aleppans carried out propaganda in favor of union among the brothers of Balamand. Failing to achieve much success, they left Balamand with a group of supporters and founded their own pro-union Monastery of St John the Baptist in the village of Shuwayr, not far from Beirut.[229] Balamand, along with the surrounding areas of North Lebanon, remained a stronghold of Orthodoxy. A typical example: the monastery houses an ancient manuscript of the "Interpretation of the Gospel" that was brought there in the eighteenth century from the cathedral of Damascus because of the threat of it being seized by the Catholics.[230] That is, Balamand was perceived by the Orthodox as a safe area.

Colophons of manuscripts at Balamand contain the names of several of the monastery's abbots from the early eighteenth century. After the death of Philotheos in 1707, the monastery was headed by the *khuri* ʿAbd al-Masih, according to notes in a few manuscripts.[231] His name also appears on the epitaphion embroidered with the scene of the "Laying in the Tomb" donated to Balamand Monastery by Patriarch Cyril in 1712 "during the abbacy of the *khuri* ʿAbd al-Masih al-Tarablusi," as evidenced by the inscription on its edge.[232] Certainly this is the same "*muʾallim khuri* ʿAbd al-Masih" whose death in October 1716 is reported in one of the notes in the Bible of Pimen of Damascus.[233]

The new abbot was the priest Mikhail ibn ʿAkrut.[234] Under his guidance, there was a new phase of construction work at the monastery. In particular, a hostel for pilgrims was erected, along with a number of other buildings that were later included in the so-called patriarchal wing.[235]

Balamand's situation in the late 1720s was described in detail by Grigorovich-Barsky. There were a few more than thirty monks

> sometimes there was a great number of people, diminished by the oppression of Turkish tributes on any given day, thanks to this they could not maintain perfectly the monastic rites, and in addition to this did not eat in the refectory, but each sorted out his own meal in his cell, church reading and singing they did in fact accomplish.[236]

That is, the cenobitic rule was not completely respected at the monastery.

The history of Dayr al-Balamand during the second third of the eighteenth century is more poorly recorded in the sources than in the previous period. A colophon from 1740 mentions as abbot the *khuri* Philotheos.[237] In one of these entries Farah, son of Yusuf ʿIsa from the village of ʿAfsadiq (the same village from which came Archimandrite Saba, the companion of Patriarch Macarius) tells of his arrival at the monastery in August 1756, his subsequent adoption of the monastic life on April 13 (the year is not mentioned), and his service with the abbot the *khuri* Jirjis al-'Ibrani. Farah is proud to announce his elevation to the rank of deacon and then priest by Metropolitan Sophronius al-Kilizi and Metropolitan Parthenius of Tripoli, respectively.[238] In a note from 1773, Farah already refers to himself as abbot of Balamand.[239] At the end of the eighteenth century, Qustandius, son of the prominent theologian of that time Elias Fakhr, appears in the ranks of the monastic brotherhood. In 1788 and 1790, Qustandius copied two books at the order of the abbot Farah, which then were donated to the monastery.[240]

After a hiatus of almost a quarter-century, there is a series of notes about the abbot Simeon (1813 and 1815).[241] It seems that he soon resigned his post, according to the final entry in the Bible of Pimen, made in July 1817, "in the days of the abbot 'Abdallah ibn Badura from the district of Antioch."[242] Simeon, however, lived for a long time: a manuscript of his is known that was copied in October 1831.[243] With the beginning of the Greek uprising in 1821 and the severe persecution of Orthodox throughout the empire, the monastery was completely empty; its possessions were plundered or fell into disorder; the church was abandoned; and, according to Porphyry Uspensky, it was "more like a prison than a house of God."[244] However, starting in the late 1820s, the monastery began to rise anew on account of the change of the political situation in Syria and the vigorous activity of the abbot Athanasius al-Qusayr,[245] but these events are beyond the time frame of this study.

The Mountain Monasteries Above Beirut

Other monasteries located on the western slope of the Lebanese mountains or on the coast were much inferior to Balamand in size and influence and so are also less frequently mentioned in the sources.

The southernmost of the Lebanese monasteries described by Grigorovich-Barsky, St Elijah (Mar Elias), had stavropegial status and was located six hours from Beirut, high in the mountains by the village of Shuwayr.[246] The exact date of the monastery's founding is unknown, but Grigorovich-Barsky confidently assigned its appearance to the post-Byzantine period based on the fact that the structure of the monastery was from the early eighteenth century and had not decayed. Mar Elias was small and cramped, "however exceedingly welcome to monastic silence." Grigorovich-Barsky wrote of the monastery's economy, "they have few cultivated trees and vineyards, they live off their own labor, working silk. In these lands the monasteries store silk with difficulty."[247]

In the monastery, there was a fairly large collection of about sixty manuscripts. Notes in the margins of a number of manuscripts add details to the history of

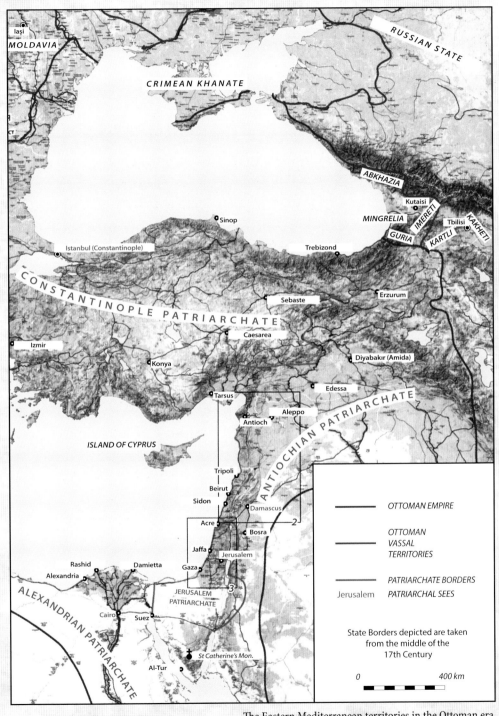

The Eastern Mediterranean territories in the Ottoman era.

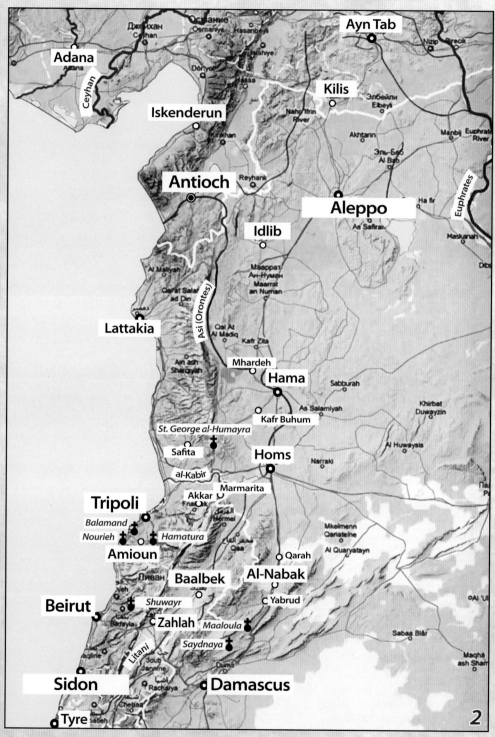

The Antiochian Patriarchate in the XVI-XVIII centuries.

The Jerusalem Patriarchate in the XVI-XVIII centuries.

Our Lady of Balamand Patriarchal Monastery, www.balamandmonastery.org

Eighteenth-century icon of the Aleppo School depicting the 7th Ecumenical Council, the acts of which preserved the epistle of Patriarch Theodore of Jerusalem to the patriarchs of Alexandria and Antioch, justifying the veneration of relics and icons.

The Arabic text in the center of the icon is taken from a history of the council and begins "In the name of our Lord, God and Master Jesus Christ, one hundred and fifteen years after the Sixth Council, the Seventh Holy Council was held in Nicaea..."

Watercolor of Mar Saba (the Lavra of St Sabbas the Sanctified), painted in 1839 by David Roberts, a prominent Orientalist painter. Mar Saba was central among the monasteries of the Judean Desert and the Jordan Valley.

© Mauro77photo | Dreamstime.com

Thirty kilometers north of Damascus, prevalent on the local summit, stands Saydnaya, the most famous monastery in Syria.

1728 drawing, by Vasily Grigorovich-Barsky, of Saydnaya monastery dedicated to the Dormition of the Theotokos

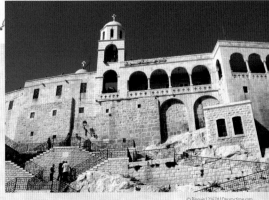

© Pingvin121674 | Dreamstime.com

An interior staircase at Balamand monastery. The monastery stands on the ruins of a Cistercian abbey from the Crusader era.

Balamand Monastery at Evening ©2009 Hector Abouid | creativecommons Attribution 2.0 Generic | www.flickr.com/photos/21536074@N00/3573515887

Above: The coastal monastery of the Dormition of the Most-holy Theotokos at Balamand is 13 kilometers southeast of Tripoli.

Next page, bottom left: In the sixteenth century, Grigorovich-Barsky counted five priests and three churches in Maaloula. Among them was the Monastery of St Thekla. To this day it is a holy place for the people of Qalamun and Christians throughout the Near East.

Next page, bottom right: The Holy Well of St Thekla. The Arabic script states that this water is sacred and asks that it be treated as such.

© Valery Shanin | Dreamstime.com

Maaloula is one of the last centers of the Aramaic
language, which was spoken by Jesus.

© Skifenok | Dreamstime.com

The Church of the Holy Sepulchre. In addition to the Orthodox, over time, Armenians, Syrian Jacobites, Nestorians, Coptic Egyptians, Ethiopians, and Georgians, each have had their own area in the Church of the Holy Sepulchre.

Monks from St Catherine's Monastery. Watercolor, 1839 by David Roberts. It is likely that the monks depicted here would have looked similar to the monks of the Holy Sepulchre in Jerusalem.

Engraving by Edward Revich, 1483, "The Syrians". One of the first depictions of Near Eastern Christians.

Mar Elias. An Euchologion copied in 1654 at the request of this monastery mentioned its abbot the priest Hanna and, apparently, his successor the priest ʿAbdallah.[248] An extremely passionate bibliophile by medieval standards, the priest Sophronius al-Sayqali of Beirut from 1756 on donated book after book to the monastery, buying them or ordering their texts copied. From 1762, Sophronius is referred to as the monastery's abbot in colophons. The last time he is mentioned is before 1778. The next abbot, the priest Neophytos al-Bayruti, appears in a note from 1792.[249] A new surge of interest in the monastery's library is connected to the name of the monastery's economos, the priest Mikhail al-Hawi from Shuwayr. First appearing in July 1809 in the colophon to a kontakion that he copied, and then in the years 1824–1825 under the abbots Macarius and Euthymius, the priest Mikhail re-bound old books that were kept in the monastery.[250]

It seems that the Hieromonk Macarius, installed as metropolitan of Beirut in the early 1680s, came from this monastery.[251] In a crypt under the monastery was the tomb of hierarchs. When visiting it, A. Krymsky described the relics of Metropolitan Macarius, who had died 120 years earlier—that is, around 1780—with excessive naturalism.[252] If you had in mind Metropolitan of Beirut Macarius Sadaqa, the date is wrong as he died later.

In 1728, Grigorovich-Barsky found five or six brothers in the monastery. In the 1840s, Porphyry found eight monks and an equal number of servants.[253] At the end of the nineteenth century, the number of monks remained almost unchanged. A. Krymsky wrote, "There are many cells; obviously, for example in the eighteenth century, many more monks could live here [as we know, it was not so]. However, some of the cells are given out in the summer on lease to people important to the monastery."[254] In the nineteenth century, Shuwayr became a popular mountain resort where many Christian families of the Beirut middle class and foreigners living in Lebanon would spend the summer. For this reason, Mar Elias came to be associated with the names of the famous Russian diplomat and writer K. M. Bazili, who spent time there in the 1840s, and the Orientalists A. E. Krymsky and I. Yu Krachkovsky,[255] who left colorful descriptions of monastic life and popular festivals around the monastery on the Feast of St Elijah.[256]

Likewise not far from Beirut was the Monastery of St Simeon the Wonderworker (Mar Samʿan al-ʿAjaʾibi). In the 1540s, it abbot, Athanasius, held the See of Beirut after Joachim ibn Jumʿa. In chronicles of Beirut, it is noted that in those years it was a large monastery with many monks and teachers.[257] Judging by the tone of statements made by chroniclers starting in the eighteenth century, in those years the monastery was noticeably impoverished. In 1724, the monastery's abbot, Polycarpos ʿAjimi, placed his signature among those electing Uniate Patriarch Cyril

Tanas.[258] The Monastery of St Simeon was one of the few old monasteries of the See of Antioch to adopt the Unia at the beginning of the eighteenth century. Porphyry wrote that at this time the monastery was the see of the Uniate bishop of Beirut.[259]

Also belonging to the Diocese of Beirut were the Monastery of St George (Dayr el-Harf) in the Metn and the Monastery of the Archangel Michael in Biqʿata, which are mentioned by Porphyry but absent from the descriptions of Grigorovich-Barsky. In the former is kept a small collection of manuscripts, some of which have dated records of their donation to the monastery. The abbot Nasrallah made the earliest donation in 1719.[260] That is, the monastery already existed in the time of Grigorovich-Barsky, but it was not described. The library of the Monastery of the Archangel in Biqʿata does not give any basis for dates. Most of its manuscripts are later (the oldest are from 1784 and 1785) and do not contain additional notes. The atypically large amount of Muslim, Maronite, and Uniate literature in the monastery's collection is noteworthy.[261]

The Monasteries Around Tripoli

Farther north, around Tripoli, was located an entire constellation of monasteries. Besides Balamand, there was, in particular, the Monastery of St James the Persian (Mar Yaʿqub). Its core became the cemetery church for Tripoli's Christians,[262] and toward 1600 it was gradually overgrown with monastic buildings. In the words of Grigorovich-Barsky, "The interior [the church] was well built with pillars and towers, having three side-chapels and a uniform gate, few windows, and due to this it was dark, since it stands together between other buildings."[263] Twelve cells, a hostel, and outbuildings surrounded the church and around the monastery were vineyards and an olive grove. Among the abbots of Mar Yaʿqub was the famous priest Zachariah al-Qibrisi (the Cypriot) who was consecrated by Patriarch Ignatius as the last metropolitan of Apamea.[264] Grigorovich-Barsky wrote that in the old days the monastery's monks were many, but in his day they numbered five or six, "who are not able to multiply on account of the tribute [due] to the Turks." The monastery's difficult conditions of existence led to the abandonment in practice of the principles of cenobitic life:

but now, due to the scarcity of monks and many hindrances from the Turks, the monastic rule is not followed, but they eat wherever they want [i.e. not in the refectory together], since even those monks are not always found in the monastery but disperse to do the monastic obedience.[265]

In the 1840s, Porphyry mentions only three monks in the monastery.[266]

Not far from Mar Ya'qub, an hour south of Tripoli on a steep bank of the Qadisha River is the Monastery of the Dormition of the Most-holy Theotokos, called by the name of the neighboring village, Kaftoun. Grigorovich-Barsky wrote that its buildings were ancient and partially dilapidated. The monastery "was deserted on account of the many hindrances and mischief of the Hagarenes," perhaps because it lies on a busy road to Tripoli, "and many," in Grigorovich-Barsky's words, "eat its bread. ... The church there has two altars, vast and beautifully built ... and two gates from the west with a small parvise."[267]

The first known mention of the monastery is in 1596 when it appears in the will of the priest Rizqallah from Tripoli that was certified by two metropolitans.[268] Patriarch Athanasius II Dabbas was buried in the monastery in 1618.[269] In 1696, during the time of Metropolitan Macarius of Tripoli, the monastery was restored under the leadership of the priest Iliya.[270] As is the case with other monasteries, Grigorovich-Barsky noted the reduction in the number of monks to five or six. The same number was found there by Porphyry Uspensky more than a century later.[271]

Within an hour's walk from Balamand and a four-hour journey from Tripoli by the seashore lies the Monastery of the Presentation (according to other sources, the Dormition) of the Most-holy Theotokos, called Natour. Smaller than other Lebanese monasteries, like others, it emerged under the Ottomans and a half-dozen monks lived there. It seems that Natour was an important economic center. Grigorovich-Barsky mentions "a stable for their own and others' horses and donkeys" and a large garden flanking the monastery to the east. Porphyry found only three inhabitants there in the mid-nineteenth century.[272]

The Monastery of the Annunciation of the Most-holy Theotokos, known as Nouriya, amazes travelers with the rare beauty of its location and layout. It clings like a swallow's nest to a steep wooded mountain slope overhanging the sea. "It is terrible to look out onto the vale from the monastery; it is with great labor that the monastery walls and buildings are fixed there on unwieldy clefts and on stony precipices," wrote Grigorovich-Barsky.[273]

The monastery had only one wall, on the northern side facing the sea. Along it stood the monks' cells. From the other sides, rocks surrounded it and the church was located in a cave deep in the mountains. It seems that the monastery was already founded in the Ottoman period. According to Grigorovich-Barsky, "a small and cramped building, however very beautiful, with the same silence, solitude, and tenderness quite befitting monastic residence."[274] Near Nouriya, at the top of the mountain, was the Church of St Simeon the Stylite. In caves behind it were a few cells and outbuildings. On the plain below it, the monastery had farms and vineyards.[275]

The founding of the Monastery of Kaftoun is shrouded in legends of the Bishop of Batroun, Simeon's vision of the Theotokos in a cloud of light, and her request that he establish a monastery. "And he obeyed this light," wrote Macarius, "so he built at his own expense Dayr Kaftoun ... which lies by the Nahr al-Jawzi. He built it in the name of Our Lady and many miracles have occurred there."[276] Curiously, the See of Batroun ceased to exist long before the time when Macarius made his list of Antiochian hierarchs and so the patriarch was unable to report anything about it, but this tradition is imprinted in the collective memory of the Melkites.

Popular memory retained another striking episode in the history of the monastery. The aforementioned Simeon, the first abbot of Balamand, was at the beginning of his ecclesiastical career abbot of Dayr Kaftoun. Sternly ascetic, he tried to make the monastic brethren live by the strict rules of the ancient ascetics. However, Lebanese monks at the end of the sixteenth century were not prepared to endure such harsh discipline. The monks hated Simeon and decided to get rid of him in a rather unusual way. Once when the abbot, as was his routine habit, went down into the dark crypt to read a prayer over the monks buried there, out from a coffin popped a dead man in a white shroud (a monk in disguise) and rushed at Simeon screaming. The abbot fainted and then lay sick in his cell for seven months. Once he recovered, he did not want to share a roof with the monks of Kaftoun and so he left the monastery.[277] Macarius's report on the monastery's founding is not entirely accurate. Syro-Arabic manuscripts from 1256 and 1284 are originally from the Monastery of Kaftoun. It seems that after this monastery had been in a state of disrepair for a time, the bishop of Batroun in the sixteenth century rebuilt a monastery on the ancient ruins.[278]

Grigorovich-Barsky also visited the monastery at the darkest moment of its history, when it had been abandoned for some time and had partially collapsed. "A great number of monks were found in there," wrote the traveler, "but later due to Turkish tributes and oppressions they have fled elsewhere."[279] However, Grigorovich-Barsky linked the monastery's decline not so much to Ottoman authority as to its absence. Kaftoun stood on the border of the district of Keserwan, which belonged to Lebanese emirs and was virtually outside of Ottoman control. Gangs of bandits came down from the mountains and held sway over the monastery. "On account of this monks cannot settle there," the traveler concluded.[280] In the monastery two churches survived. That of St Sergius and St Bacchus was "great and beautifully built ... with pillars and recognizable for its decorated marble." At night, the bandits would light a fire in it, so what remains of its frescoes are covered with a layer of soot. The second church, that of the Most-holy Theotokos was small and unassuming standing off at a distance on a cliff. Unlike the first, it was not desecrated because its doors were locked. On Sundays, the liturgy was served there. "The others are all empty and ruined, and all the cells have fallen," reported Grigorovich-Barsky.[281] It seems, however, that the monastery saw better times both before and after Grigorovich-Barsky's visit. Sometime around the 1630s, Metropolitan Parthenius of Beirut was buried there, which means that the monastery was inhabited at that time.[282] Porphyry Uspensky[283] and later authors habitually list Kaftoun among other Lebanese monasteries without indicating it as being desolate.

Hamatoura

Four hours from Kaftoun and Tripoli, in one of the valleys of the Lebanon Mountains is the Monastery of the Dormition of the Theotokos, Hamatoura. "It stands on a high place near the Lebanon Mountains," described Grigorovich-Barsky, "over a terrible valley, which reduces man to tears, tenderness and amazement, which is very deep and a fast stream … flows there."[284] The small, frescoed church was in the depths of a unique double-leveled cave, occupying its lower level. "They have only two large windows in the southern wall and it is never entirely light inside, but it is illuminated by the lighting of lamps and chandeliers," Grigorovich-Barsky wrote of it.[285] In the cave's upper gallery, to which stairs carved into the rock led, were placed cells. Outside of the cave, the monastery's walls, which were uneven due to the rough terrain, protected the bakery, refectory, storehouse, hostel, stable, and other buildings. As in other monasteries, the gates were "covered with iron with a solid encasement." Higher up on the mountain was the daughter monastery of St George. Previously, the monks had lived there during the summer months, but at the time of Grigorovich-Barsky's visit, it had been abandoned "on account of the many malefactions of the Hagarenes, especially the bandits."[286] The upper monastery stood on a convenient path, while the lower one was difficult to reach and life was quieter there. When describing Hamatoura, Grigorovich-Barsky repeated the standard phrase, "There sometimes the brothers are of sufficient number, now though there are few, as also in other nearby monasteries of Tripoli."[287] This monastery was poorer than all the others. It fed itself from alms and raising silkworms. On the stream in the gorge the monks kept a mill where they ground grain for the surrounding residents.[288]

It seems that before the founding of Balamand, Hamatoura was the cultural and religious center for the district. At the monastery is preserved a remarkably large number of books copied in the sixteenth century by people close to Antiochian hierarchs of the time: the monk Ibrahim, a disciple of Metropolitan Dorotheus of Tripoli (1574); the *khuri* Musa from the village of Marmarita, a disciple of Patriarch Joachim ibn Jum'a (1569, 1580); and others.[289] In marginal notes in the manuscripts there are reports of donations made to the monastery in the late sixteenth century of books, priestly vestments, silk of various colors, plantations of mulberry trees in neighboring villages, and so on.[290] During the years 1589–1592, the Monastery of Hamatoura was chosen as a place of residence by Metropolitan Joachim of Bethlehem who, in 1579, had contested the See of Jerusalem with the Phanariots and afterward apparently did not get along well with Patriarch Sophronius. Joachim, formerly a monk at the enormous and half-empty Mar Saba, found Hamatoura too cramped and so arranged the construction of a new cell that was largely cut from the rock.[291]

Syrian metropolitans also paid the monastery attention in the seventeenth century. Hamatoura holds books donated by Metropolitan Joachim of Beirut in 1600 (the colophon mentions the abbot Ioannicius) and by Metropolitan Meletius Karma of Aleppo from 1627.[292] In 1650, Metropolitan Joachim of Tripoli took refuge in the monastery from "the great oppression that has occurred in Tripoli and its district."[293] The metropolitan and his attendants stayed at Hamatoura for more than eight months and so had the time to become acquainted with the monastery's library and leave notes in its books. In one of them, reference is made to the leaders of the monastery, the "venerable fathers" Elias, the *khuri* Rizqallah, and Matthew.[294]

Several manuscripts were donated to the monastery in the late seventeenth century. A note at the end of one of them mentions the vigorous activity of its abbot, the *khuri* Jirjis, who in 1685 organized the planting of mulberry trees, built new cells, and paved the courtyard of the Monastery of St George, which at that time was still inhabited. A record from December 26, 1689, announced the death of Jirjis. The next abbot, the priest Parthenios al-Batrumani, is mentioned in December 1691.[295] Colophons from the eighteenth and nineteenth century provide information about the visit to the monastery by Metropolitan Parthenios of Tripoli and the *khuri* Nikiphoros, abbot of the Monastery of Nouriya, in May 1762. Mentioned as abbots of Hamatoura are the priest Hanania in 1767 and the deacon Daniel in 1812.[296] Notes from 1821 to 1823 tell of the persecution of the Orthodox by the pasha of Acre, 'Abdallah, when monasteries and churches were plundered and Christians, fleeing extortion, fled to the mountains and gorges.[297]

Ra's Baalbek and the Monastery of St George Humayra

On the other side of the Lebanon Mountains, in the northern part of the Bekaa Valley was the Monastery of the Nativity of the Theotokos in the town of Ra's Baalbek, on the banks of the Orontes. Much less about it is known than about other monasteries. Catholic writers from the early twentieth century date the monastery's foundation to the twelfth century without, in our opinion, sufficient grounds.[298] In ecclesiastical affairs, the monastery was subject to the metropolitan of Homs. In June 1628, at the Monastery of Ra's Baalbek, a council of Syrian metropolitans met, putting an end to ten years of turmoil in the Church of Antioch when the patriarchal throne was contested between Cyril Dabbas and Ignatius 'Atiya.[299] By the beginning of the eighteenth century, the monastery was abandoned and its buildings, curiously, were not put at the disposal of the metropolitan or other church structures, but instead to the sheikhs of the Christian community of Ra's Baalbek, which is not the only example of this arrangement in Syria. In 1722, this local Christian community invited monks from the Uniate Shuwayrite Order to inhabit the monastery once more and so it was restored, but not as a part of the Orthodox Patriarchate of Antioch.[300]

To the north of the monasteries around Tripoli, halfway between Tripoli and Homs on the southern slopes of Jabal 'Alawi, is the Monastery of St George al-Humayra (Mar Jirjis).[301] In its size and importance, it was comparable to Saydnaya and Balamand. Travelers described the monastery as a massive square building standing on a steep hillside with an inner courtyard at the level of the second story and its perimeter surrounded by a stone terrace. The foundational wall of large stones and the bars on the windows gave the monastery the appearance of a sort of fortress; local tradition preserved the memory of repeated attacks on the monastery. In Grigorovich-Barsky's time, Mar Jirjis had only one small gate, a little over a meter in height, locked by a monolithic slab of basalt. Nevertheless, it was necessary to drive camels and horses through this space.[302] According to the traveler, the monastery church was "quite long and high, but very narrow, however beautiful and there were icons painted entirely from top to bottom."[303] Later observers spoke more skeptically of it. "It is very small, with a vaulted ceiling. Everything in it is poor and miserable" (in the late 1830s another church was built in the monastery, larger and richer than the first).[304]

The monastery was famous for the miracles at the icon of St George, the most revered saint of the Middle East. Pilgrims came there even from outside the Patriarchate of Antioch, and not only Christians but also neighboring Muslims and Alawites. The busiest pilgrimage came on the Feast of the Exaltation of the Cross. Then the monastery could not accommodate all the faithful and they stayed in tent camps around the monastery. Merchants would flock to the monastery and the fair would last about two weeks.[305]

Mar Jirjis fed at its own expense all the pilgrims arriving, including all different creeds; merchant caravans making their way from Tripoli to inner Syria;

and the poor, orphans, the infirm, and so on. Grigorovich-Barsky described how the monks took turns cooking meals in two large pots around the clock and distributed them to those arriving. In his words, despite these expenses, the monastery lacked for nothing and was full of "bread, oil, wine, honey, and all sorts of different flours. And from nowhere did they possess any sort of possessiveness, personal gain, or greed, only from each is rationed offerings of alms," and Muslims also gave alms "on account of the saint's miracles."[306] Other, more recent sources report the monastery having extensive possessions, including herds of cattle and olive and mulberry trees. The peasants of the two neighboring villages worked the monastery's lands in exchange for one quarter of the yield. Additionally, the monastery kept forty servants on its payroll in the 1840s.[307] An early-twentieth-century observer wrote of the monastery's lands: "[t]he plowed and terraced hillsides planted with trees, the vineyards, the stone fences everywhere—everything bears the mark of great diligence."[308]

The Monastery of St George was one of the oldest in the patriarchate, its foundation dating back to the pre-Ottoman period and perhaps even to the Byzantine period. An important treasure in the monastery was a charter given to it by the Caliph 'Umar. Although surely counterfeit,[309] it nonetheless reliably guaranteed the safety of the monastery, its inhabitants, and property—land and a certain number of sheep, cows, donkeys, and horses.[310] As mentioned, in 1656 in Moscow, Patriarch Macarius requested charters for the receipt of alms for it along with other Syrian monasteries, and the Monastery of St George was given a charter in the name of the abbot Isaac and its brothers.[311] Grigorovich-Barsky wrote that the monastery had been renovated and rebuilt in 1700 by Patriarch Athanasius (this date seems to be erroneous, as Athanasius was patriarch from 1686 to 1694 and from 1720 to 1724). During his visit to the monastery in 1728, Grigorovich-Barsky noted that there were about forty monks, both Arab and Greek. "At that time, the abbot was a Greek from Cyprus by the name of Peter, a man of reason and virtue."[312] Porphyry wrote of the restructuring of the monastery in the years 1837–1838. In his time, thirty monks lived there, all of Arab origin.[313]

OTHER MOUNTAIN MONASTERIES

In addition to these monasteries that existed during Grigorovich-Barsky's visit to the Levant, a number of other monasteries are known that were mentioned by Porphyry Uspensky in his history of the Syrian Church in the 1840s. Two of them, Dayr al-Harf and the Monastery of the Archangel in Biq'ata have been mentioned. Two others clearly were founded after Grigorovich-Barsky's travels: St George in Souq al-Gharb to the south of Beirut, which was built in 1841 (it was probably not a monastery, but rather a country residence of the metropolitan of Beirut)[314] and St Elias (Dayr Mar Elias al-Rih) near the village of Burj Safita, not far from the Monastery of St George Humayra, which was rebuilt on the ruins of an old monastery in 1806.[315] The dates of the founding of the Monastery of St Damiana (Dayr Mar Dumit) in Husn al-Akrad (Diocese of ʿAkkar) and St Demetrius in the village of Kousba (two monks were living there in 1840) are unknown.[316] The latter monastery houses a small collection of manuscripts, which would likely indicate that it had been founded recently. None of the books, most of which were copied from the late eighteenth century to the first half of the nineteenth century, were written at the monastery or donated to it. They arrived there from different churches in Keserwan and Tripoli.[317] Among the few manuscripts that deserve attention are a commentary on the Gospel in Ottoman Turkish and excerpts from the Synaxarion rewritten by Metropolitan Hierotheos of Diyabakir who, by his own admission, abbreviated the text "so that the people will not be bored by it."[318]

Finally, for unclear reasons, both writers missed the Monastery of John the Baptist (Mar Yuhanna) in the village of Douma in the district of Batroun. This monastery is quite old. A famous Typicon was copied there in 1594 by the Deacon Saba from Beirut, a disciple of Metropolitan Joachim of Lattakia.[319] Most books in the monastery's collection, apart from a few prize examples that came to Mar Yuhanna from Hamatoura, are much later. They were copied or bought in the period from 1769 to 1790 by the *khuri* Euthymius from Amioun, who first called himself a "servant" and then "abbot" of the monastery.[320] Euthymius was a contemporary of the bibliophile Sophronius, abbot of the Monastery of Mar Elias in Shuwayr in the 1760s and 1770s. It is possible that Euthymius himself came from that monastery, according to the first of his colophons.[321]

Additionally, Patriarch Macarius mentioned the *khuri* Azariah, "abbot of the Monastery of Our Lady, called al-Ruʿus al-Kaʿin in the village of Bturram in Koura, Tripoli," whom he appointed metropolitan of Baalbek in 1651.[322] This monastery is not known from other sources. Thus, it is possible that there were still more monasteries in Antioch beyond the written evidence.

The Monasteries of the Patriarchate of Antioch: Rhythms of Development

The extant sources provide some idea of the dynamics of the Syro-Lebanese monasteries. In his description of almost each of them, Grigorovich-Barsky repeated a refrain about the prosperity of the (relatively recent) past and present impoverishment. Although such a pattern is typical of human psychology, in this case it may have a real basis. It was in the Ottoman era, approximately during the seventeenth century, that the last monasteries of Inner Syria died out apart from the Monastery of the Dormition of the Theotokos in Saydnaya and, at least to some extent, the Monastery of St Thekla in Maaloula. This can be attributed hypothetically to demographic processes within the Orthodox community, namely the migration of Christians into cities and the disappearance of many Christian villages from the Syrian hinterland.[323] On the coast, in Lebanon, during a period of prosperity for Tripoli's Christians there arose new monasteries. Given the date of the foundation of Dayr al-Balamand and Mar Ya'qub as well as the boom in manuscript copying at Hamatoura, it is possible to speak of the sixteenth and seventeenth centuries as perhaps the high point of flourishing of monasticism in North Lebanon. During the first third of the seventeenth century, Tripoli's economic and political role faltered and centers of trading activity shifted to the south. The Lebanese Emir Fakhr al-Din Ma'an crushed the local feudal clan of Sayf, who had earlier overseen the Pashalik of Tripoli. This weakened the Orthodox community of Tripoli, who previously had enjoyed the patronage of the Sayf and so dominated the Patriarchate of Antioch in the late sixteenth century, and it lost its position after the Council of Ra's Baalbek. This was also followed by a period of decline in the monastic life: the monasteries deteriorated, the monks split apart, and the cenobitic rule was not respected. In the early eighteenth century, most monasteries had five or six inhabitants. The situation later stabilized, however, and by the middle of the nineteenth century, all these monasteries in the Patriarchate of Antioch survived with about the same number of monks, alongside several new monasteries. It is noteworthy that the majority of Orthodox monasteries (as well as almost all Uniate monasteries) were concentrated in Mount Lebanon, a region with a large and compact Christian population that was poorly controlled by the Ottoman authorities. Later, in the second third of the nineteenth century, as a result of official implementation of the principles of religious tolerance in Ottoman policy during the Tanzimat period and the weakening of financial pressure on Christians, there was a new upsurge of monasteries. Somewhat beyond the scope of this study, it is possible to add that at the beginning of the twentieth century, the Lebanese monasteries were again in a state of severe decline caused by economic difficulties as well as the general secularization of the Orthodox Arabs' way of life.[324]

Practically all the monasteries owned some land and carried out economic activity. Monks and peasant tenants cultivated grapes, vegetables, and olive and mulberry trees. For a long time, the monasteries had a monopoly on growing high-quality tobacco as well as watermills. A monastery with good land and the necessary equipment and manpower was economically more effective than small farms.[325] An additional source of income was pilgrims' offerings and alms collected in big cities. At the same time, however, observers often noted poverty and dilapidated monasteries. There were apparently not enough funds for the monasteries, given the extortion of the Ottoman pashas and Lebanese emirs as well as other expenses, including charity. Only three monasteries played a really serious socioeconomic role in the Patriarchate of Antioch: Saydnaya, Balamand, and St George Humayra. These monasteries were powerful economic structures with vast possessions, famous places of worship, important educational centers for the Church, and institutions of social support for poor members of the Christian community. Monasteries were closely associated with regional Orthodox elites, from whom they received endowments: Saydnaya with Damascus and the Christian enclave of the Qalamun Plateau and Balamand with Tripoli and ʿAkkar.

The moral authority of monasteries—and especially of famous wonderworking relics—was high not only among Christians but also among the Muslims (especially the Shiites and Alawites) of the surrounding population. "Folk Islam" easily absorbs elements of other religions, especially worship at local shrines.

While playing an important role in maintaining the Christian cultural tradition, the monasteries were not active centers of cultural creativity, with the possible exception of Balamand.

During the era of the proliferation of Catholic propaganda in the Middle East and the emergence of the Melkite Uniate community, monasteries in the Patriarchate of Antioch generally rejected the union (we can recall the example of Balamand). Only one of the patriarchate's old monasteries went over to the side of Rome, Mar Simʿan near Beirut. No wonder, then, that the strong monastic movement in the Uniate milieu resulted in the creation of dozens of new monasteries in the seventeenth and first half of the eighteenth centuries, which originally were philo-Catholic in orientation. At the same time, Orthodox monasticism in Syria was not a real force in opposition to the union, as it had been, for example, in fifteenth-century Byzantium or in Ukraine at the turn of the sixteenth to the seventeenth century.

Syrian Monastics as a Social Group

Our information about the composition of the monasteries is fragmentary, and it does not allow us to draw reliable conclusions about the regional and social origins of monastic clergy. A more-or-less representative picture can be made only with regard to the Lebanese monasteries. Among those who mention their origins as being from Damascus or Aleppo, there often appear natives of Beirut and Tripoli, but for the most part they are natives of the mountain villages of Lebanon. As regards their social origins, we can only speculate or resort to questionable analogies to Lebanese Uniate monastics of the eighteenth century,[326] many of whom came from a peasant background.[327] In terms of ethnicity, Arabs naturally dominated among the monks, and it was only starting in the eighteenth century, along the lines of the general Hellenization of the Patriarchate of Antioch, that a Greek element becomes evident in the monasteries.[328] On the other hand, Syrian Arabs of the sixteenth through eighteenth centuries sometimes took monastic vows outside Syria, especially in Palestine.[329]

Despite the fact that a considerable proportion of metropolitans and patriarchs came from the monastic environment, monastic clergy did not have a monopoly on positions in the upper hierarchy of the Church in Ottoman Syria. Many bishops came from the secular clergy and even from laity who, of course, took vows before episcopal consecration. According to Carsten Walbiner,[330] in the seventeenth century, only about half of the metropolitans whose origins are known can safely be said to have been monks before their consecration. Identifying the backgrounds of the others is complicated by the fact that during the episcopal consecration all, whether monks or not, changed their name (i.e., a name change does not indicate entrance into monasticism) and the fact that in the sources the terms for priest, "*khuri*" and "*qassis*," are widely used not only for secular clergy but also for hieromonks.[331] Orthodox monasticism in Syria during the Ottoman period produced almost no famous ascetics or mystics and monastic rules did not differ in severity. On the other hand, it attracted to the monasteries many Christians who desired to escape the social oppression and political instability of worldly life. In the words of the abbot of the Uniate monastery at Shuwayr to Volney (all of which equally applies to Orthodox monasticism),[332]

> It is difficult, perhaps, to close oneself in the monastery, but living there is very peaceful, although every day some sort of shortage happens, but it is not as necessary as … in the world. Consider the state of our local peasants. Everything that they have, we have, and even more; we are better dressed than them, and are better supported, we drink wine and coffee. And what does that mean for our monks? For the most part [they had been] peasant children.[333]

In the early twentieth century, Ignaty Krachkovsky made a similar observation about the monks of the Orthodox monastery of Shuwayr, "Everyone came to the monastery for the most prosaic motives."[334]

It does not seem that monastics in the Patriarchate of Antioch were a particular social group with a strong group consciousness and interests. The monks were too few in number—by an approximate estimate, they made up about 0.15 percent of the entire Orthodox population. Among the Melkite Catholics and especially the Maronites, the proportion was much higher. Within Orthodox monasticism in Syria, groups like the Greek Catholic religious orders or the brotherhoods of the Holy Sepulchre and Sinai were unknown. Of course, the monasteries, especially those in the region of Tripoli, had to work closely with each other, but this communication did not take on organized forms.[335] Nevertheless, monasteries played an important social, and to some extent cultural, role in the life of the Patriarchate of Antioch. This role does not diminish the fact that cultural creativity developed primarily in cities rather than within the monastic environment. Monasteries were centers for the preservation and reproduction of the Christian tradition; of the most important structural parts of Church organization; and, therefore, of the Christian community as a whole. In those places where monasteries, and afterward other Church institutions, fell into decay— we can take Eastern Anatolia in the sixteenth and seventeenth centuries as an example, to not go too far afield—this was almost inevitably followed by the degradation and extinction of the local Orthodox community. The fact that this did not happen in Greater Syria is largely because of the existence of local monastic communities.

CHAPTER 6

A State Within a State: Intra-Imperial Connections in the Orthodox East

The people by this time became furious; they were worn out with standing in such a crowd all night, and as the time approached for the exhibition of the holy fire they could not contain themselves for joy. Their excitement increased as the time for the miracle in which they all believed drew near. About one o'clock the Patriarch went into the ante-chapel of the sepulchre, and soon after a magnificent procession moved out of the Greek chapel. It conducted the Patriarch three times round the tomb; after which he took off his outer robes of cloth of silver, and went into the sepulchre, the door of which was then closed. The agitation of the pilgrims was now extreme: they screamed aloud; and the dense mass of people shook to and fro, like a field of corn in the wind.

—Robert Curzon, 1834

A mong the most important consequences of the Ottoman conquest for Arab Orthodoxy was the breaking of its relative isolation from the rest of the Eastern Christian world, the inclusion of Jerusalem and Antioch in the Rum *millet*, and the close interrelationship between all the local churches of the Orthodox East. The domain of the Ottoman Empire almost precisely coincided with the territory of the Byzantine Empire at its height. Finding itself under the sultans' rule was approximately half the Orthodox world, which before had been divided by state borders and political conflicts. Cultural and political contacts between the Orthodox peoples of the Eastern Mediterranean became an order of magnitude more intense than in the previous century.

Pilgrimage Routes

One manifestation of this was the active development of Christian pilgrimages to the holy places of Palestine.[1] The annual rhythm of pilgrimage largely determined the life of the Patriarchate of Jerusalem.

226

Representatives from all parts of the Orthodox world met in the shrines of the Holy City. Vasily Poznyakov, describing a church procession on a feast day in the Church of the Holy Sepulchre, noted that behind Patriarch Germanus of Jerusalem there were "Greeks, Serbs, Iberians [i.e., Georgians], Russians, Arnanites [Arnauts, that is, Albanians?], and Vlachs."[2] Almost two hundred and fifty years later, Melety gave a more detailed account of the "ethnography" of Orthodox pilgrimage: Greeks, including Turkish-speaking Christians of Anatolia who could only conditionally be counted as Greeks; Arab Orthodox of Palestinian, Egyptian and Syrian background; Slavs, including Bulgarians, Serbs, natives of Russia, Vlachs, and Moldavians; Georgians; Chalcedonian Armenians; and, finally, Orthodox "Syrians" or "Chaldeans."[3]

Among the pilgrims who came to Palestine by sea, the majority were Greeks. Additionally, a much larger number of Orthodox Arabs from various regions of Syria, Palestine, and Transjordan gathered at Easter in Jerusalem. Balkan Slavs and Romanians were less common among the mass of "hajjis."[4] During some periods, Georgian pilgrimages were fairly numerous and sometimes included bishops and members of the royal houses.[5] The pilgrimages of the Eastern Slavs, who came from Muscovy and Ukraine, were the fewest of all,[6] something at which the Greeks, according to Grigorovich-Barsky, were very surprised.[7]

Interestingly enough, Ottoman statistics from the sixteenth and seventeenth centuries specify the regions from which pilgrims came to Palestine because the size of the fees levied on them depended on their origin.[8] In the 1581/1582 season, the bulk of pilgrims (about 29 percent) came from the vilayets of Aleppo and Sham, whereas 20 percent came from various areas of Palestine and Transjordan (the district of Gaza, 'Ajlun, Nablus, and Salt). If we add to these groups residents of the area around Jerusalem (around 16 percent), it becomes apparent that two-thirds of pilgrims were Orthodox Arabs. Unfortunately, for the sake of convenience, Ottoman documents combine into one category of travelers those coming from Bilad-i Rum (the Balkans and Western Anatolia, who were primarily Orthodox) and from Bilad-i Sharq (Eastern Anatolia, Iraq, and Iran, who were primarily Armenians, Syrian Jacobites, and Nestorians). In sum, they constituted 17 percent, but within this group it is not possible to separate the Orthodox from the non-Orthodox. Egyptians, primarily Monophysite Copts, represented a signification proportion of the pilgrims (13 percent). Around 4 percent were impoverished pilgrims of all confessions, whose fees were paid by their wealthy coreligionists. In the Ottoman records, the poor are listed as a group and not broken down by region. Franks (Europeans) represent a little over 1 percent. Somehow, Maronites are listed in their own column, even though they represent only 0.25 percent of the total pilgrims.[9] The only thing lacking in order to complete the picture are the Georgians and Ethiopians, who were exempt from duties and therefore were not taken into account by the Ottoman officials.

Such ethnolinguistic diversity created some difficulties for the clergy of the Holy Sepulchre in terms of providing spiritual care to pilgrims. Melety, not without sarcasm, describes the situation when a hierodeacon in the patriarchal monastery of Jerusalem delivered a sermon in Greek to newly arrived pilgrims: "but ... hardly five out of seventy could understand this teaching. For almost all of them were from Bithynia, knowing only the Turkish language."[10] It was only at the solemn Easter service that it was possible (with the involvement of clergy from among the pilgrims) to organize the reading of the Gospel in four languages: Greek, Arabic, Slavonic, and Turkish.[11] Sermons were very long and only given in Greek "on account of which the people, more than half of whom do not understand Greek, are not pleased," wrote Melety.[12] The language barrier also arose when Slavic pilgrims did not understand the language of their confessors.[13]

Pilgrims traveled to Palestine along two main routes. Some arrived by sea from the west—the Greeks of the Balkans, the archipelago, and Western Anatolia; and Serbs, Bulgarians, Moldavians, Wallachians, Ukrainians, and Russians. On the final stage of the journey they were joined by Egyptian Christians. The rest came by land from the north—Arabs of the Patriarchate of Antioch; the Greek-, Armenian-, and Turkish-speaking Orthodox of Eastern Anatolia; Georgians and Laz; and, occasionally, Russians from the Volga region.

The western route began in the port cities of the Balkans, to which came pilgrims from the hinterland. As a rule, the transport of pilgrims was undertaken by Christian ship owners, sometimes in coordination with the metochion of the Brotherhood of the Holy Sepulchre in Jerusalem. In the mid-eighteenth century, transport to Jaffa cost 15–20 thalers, while the poor managed to obtain it for less. Ships were filled to the limit with people. As Serapion described it, "There was a great squeeze and confusion because there was no more space where it would be good to sit," the places for passengers were determined on the basis of "only as far as it was possible to kick."[14] The navigation route was standard, with minor variations: from Istanbul or Thessaloniki, with a stop on Athos, to Mytilene, then Patmos-Chios (Saqiz)-Rhodes and sometimes the ships stopped along the way in Smyrna and Ephesus. From Rhodes, they sailed to Jaffa via Cyprus or Alexandria.[15] The way was unsafe, and almost all travelers give a colorful description of a storm during which passengers bid farewell to life and fervently pray, each to his own god.[16] In November 1805 alone, two ships sank off Acre and Tripoli, with 150 pilgrims.[17] No less dangerous were there Maltese pirates who attacked unarmed Greek ships: "they stripped the Turks to their last rags," wrote Grigorovich-Barsky, "and carried them off in bonds."[18] Many pilgrim writers saw the sails of pirate ships along their way, but it did not always come to pitched battle. Sometimes pirates did not dare attack on account of the numerical superiority of Turkish ships, and sometimes they were driven away by adverse winds.[19] The captains of many pilgrim vessels were Europeans ("Franks," as Serapion calls them), and the Maltese did not target these ships.[20]

Upon arrival in Jaffa, the pilgrims stayed at the metochion of the Brotherhood of the Holy Sepulchre. It apparently continued to exist for a long time, but in 1723, Patriarch Chrysanthos organized large-scale construction works there, as part of his developing pilgrimage infrastructure. To accommodate the travelers, many new homes and cells were built, with a capacity of up to 500 people.[21] The pilgrims staying at the metochion ate at their own expense, although the abbot invited the wealthiest to dine at the trapeza with him so that he could obtain from them payment for the remembrance of their souls, set at 5 thalers per person.[22] A little later, when Ivan Lukyanov visited Palestine, the prices varied: upon the pilgrims' arrival in Jaffa, a hieromonk of the metochion gave them dinner "and at the dinner he walked with a dish and took from [each] man a gold coin [*chervonoe*], a thaler, he took no less."[23]

Because the journey through Palestine was dangerous on account of attacks by Bedouins and other bandits, the Ottoman authorities undertook the defense of the pilgrims' caravans in return for substantial fees. The metochion of the Brotherhood of the Holy Sepulchre, as well as analogous institutions for the Catholics and Armenians, served as a sort of holding tank for pilgrims. When a sufficient number gathered there, the governor of Jerusalem was informed, and from there a convoy arrived with mounts.[24] A collection was made from the pilgrims to pay for protection. Even in the time of Arseny Sukhanov in the early eighteenth century, the sum amounted to 7 thalers or *efimki*—calculated in hard currency, its price did not change over time. There was a gradated pay scale according to which laypeople paid twice as much as monks. "The unbelievers have no consideration for poverty, they hold mercy in low regard, and only count heads," Grigorovich-Barsky complained.[25]

The movement from Jaffa to Jerusalem of a pilgrimage caravan of several hundreds or thousands of people was a colorful spectacle. It maintained a regular formation. Going ahead of the group were Janissaries with banners and behind them were riders on camels and an Ottoman *agha* with his entourage. Behind him came the crowd of pilgrims on camels, horses, and donkeys surrounded by armed guards. Standard-bearers brought up the rear. The whole journey took twelve hours, a two-day journey with an overnight stay in Ramla, where there were Armenian, Frankish, and Greek metochia. "There along the walls many pilgrims write their names, who was coming from where, and in which year," recalled Matvei Nechaev, "the walls are completely covered in writing—you find little empty space—written in Greek and Bulgarian and Serbian."[26] Another fee was levied in Ramla.

On the second day of travel, three hours past Ramla, the caravan entered the Judean Hills. This was the worst part of the way. It was necessary to go single-file through a narrow crevice overgrown with fig trees and many fell from their mounts and were injured on the crumbling stones. The caravan stretched along for several kilometers. The Janissaries could not provide reliable protection and gangs of robbers attacked the travelers. According to many authors, this one day was as much hardship as the rest of the journey. Because pilgrim writers were unfamiliar with the realities of Palestine, it is unclear who those robbers were that they encountered. By surveying the observations of witnesses, in particular the information from Ivan Lukyanov, it can be argued that most of these attackers were not nomadic Bedouins, but rather *fellahin* from neighboring villages.[27] In the case of armed conflict between the Ottoman authorities and nomadic tribes, when the Bedouins would block the mountainous section of the road to Jerusalem, it was impossible for caravans to pass and no guards would dare accompany them. Therefore, for example, the pilgrimage caravan of 1701 remained in Ramla for three weeks waiting for rebellious Bedouins to reconcile with the authorities and only after that could it go along its way.[28] Nevertheless, the caravan's passage through masses of aggressive *fellahin* was also a serious challenge. Grigorovich-Barsky wrote,

> What misery and poverty the Christian people endured from the shameless and damned Ethiopians, until they passed these mountains of Judea, it is truly impossible to speak of … a great many of them were gathered; some with spears, others with staves and, having started off on the path, they would prohibit us from walking, looking for "bakshish," that is, a bribe. This escort greatly impeded us, but no one could comply with them; not fearing anyone, they were below shame.[29]

The most vivid account of this section of the way was certainly given by Ivan Lukyanov:

> Then the Arabs started to beat and rob us, they were swarming around us like bees, they tore at our clothes, shaking us off and dragging us from our

horses, (saying) "give us a coin," (hitting) with a cudger between shoulder blades, and another one sticks his hand in my breast pocket. To give them money is bad, but not to give is bad too: when you take out your purse, lo, another guy snatches it from your hand altogether. If you do not give, they beat you, but if you give, they will not let you leave from that spot for a quarter of an hour, since like wild dogs, you will not be able to beat them off. If you look around: everywhere are cries and moans, beatings and robbings... everywhere a single man is chased by ten to twenty Arabs. Many have dropped their horses and property and are running away from these dogs. But the cabmen, the dogs, steal even more: they already hover around in between those Arabs – but those cabmen are from those same robbers' villages, so they, dogs, take their chance to steal."[30]

"And we walked all day," wrote Lukyanov further on, "we neither drank nor ate because of those dogs.... As soon as you bring a piece of bread to your mouth, some other one jumps from the side and snatches it up; and even amongst themselves they fight for a piece of bread."[31]

There were situations in which a convoy would fail to fulfill its obligations and leave pilgrims along the way toward the mountains, as happened in Lukyanov's case. "A wretched pasha whose only worthy deed was to escort us out of city and pluck 1 *grivna* and about 2 *altyn* from each and violently push through the mountains towards the Arabs," wrote the pilgrim.[32] On their own, the pilgrims could not put up any resistance against the bandits. "How would the Arabs not pillage! [The pilgrims] do not wait for each other at all: one sat down and went, and that is it. When I was being beaten, another [pilgrim] passed by and when they were beating him, I was passing by—and so they will rob them one by one," Lukyanov lamented.[33]

Only a few pilgrims managed to go from Jaffa to Jerusalem without incident as did Melety, who was in Palestine in 1794, during a rare political lull.[34] This author, however, refers to the practice of systematic tributes being collected from pilgrims "for the Arabs who lived along the way and in the areas around."[35] Melety attempted to avoid paying, referring to his *firman* from the sultan for duty-free passage to the holy places on the basis of the relevant article of the Treaty of Küçük Kaynarca. However, it was explained to the pilgrim that the Palestinian *fellahin* "have no interest in *firmans* and no regard for the Turks."[36]

For all its inefficiencies, the Turkish security still restrained the bellicosity of the Arabs to some degree, and fatalities along the road were not typical. Pilgrims who did not have money for protection had it much worse. They had to pass through the mountains in small groups at their own risk, without any confidence in a successful outcome for their journey.[37]

Judging by the available descriptions, the main influx of pilgrims to Jaffa occurred at the beginning of autumn, with the travelers hoping to spend Christmas and Easter in Palestine, but also to arrive in the Holy Land before the winter storms.[38] For this reason, the convoy from Jaffa to Jerusalem only went once a year. In other seasons, the authorities did not protect pilgrims, who had to hire their own guards or pay off the sheikhs of the Abu Ghosh tribe who controlled the "predatory villages" of the Judean hills.[39]

The flow of pilgrims was no less along the northern route, which overlapped the route of the Muslim hajj in the section from Aleppo to the Sea of Galilee. This route was described schematically by two Russian travelers—Vasily Gagara, who took it in 1634–1635, and Arseny Sukhanov, who returned to Russia from Jerusalem through the Caucasus in 1652.[40] From Tbilisi, pilgrims went to Erzurum via Yerevan and Kars, the same route that Patriarch Macarius of Antioch took back from Georgia to Damascus in 1669.[41] From there, they bypassed the Armenian highlands and went to Sebaste (Sivas) and Caesarea (Kayseri). There were a few variants of this route. Eastern Anatolia had a dense network of caravan routes. Groups of pilgrims moved along them going south and southeast from different cities in Asia Minor. This is how Paul of Aleppo describes the departure on pilgrimage of wealthy Christians from Sinope.[42] In 1804, soldiers of al-Jazzar Pasha of Acre robbed a caravan of pilgrims returning to Anatolia near Tiberias. During this, the Trapezon native Hajji-Anton was killed.[43] Streams of pilgrims arrived in Aleppo, where they were joined by local Christians. Paul of Aleppo describes his pilgrimage to Jerusalem in 1642 along with his father, who was then metropolitan of Aleppo, the Georgian Catholicos Maximus, and sixty clergy and laypeople from Aleppo.[44]

It seems that the Orthodox pilgrimage starting out from Aleppo, as in Palestine, acquired its own infrastructure. In 1653, there arrived in Moscow seeking alms the "white Arab priest Michael" from "the Syrian land of Aleppo" who in his petition to the tsar reported

> I, your pilgrim, built along the fine road to Jerusalem a hostel for the Greek pilgrims who come to Jerusalem to worship at the Holy Sepulchre. And the pasha of the city of Aleppo, lord … beat me and imprisoned me and demanded of me, your pilgrim, as payment for protection six hundred rubles.[45]

It was quite common among Syrian Arab Christians to go to Jerusalem on pilgrimage as the journey to the Holy Land was not long. In the sources, many names of natives of Syria are prefixed with "hajj." Describing the beauty of the newly built patriarchal residence in Damascus, Paul of Aleppo urges his readers (who seem to be his fellow Aleppans) to make a pilgrimage to Jerusalem and to go and see the patriarch's palace along the way.[46] In his phrasing, pilgrimage seems like a commonplace event, almost just an excuse to visit the patriarch's palace.

Despite the short distance from Aleppo and Damascus to Jerusalem, the journey was relatively expensive. Arseny Sukhanov methodically listed the endless tariffs along the way from Jerusalem, which had to be paid almost daily at the gate of every town and on the ferries across the Jordan and Euphrates, ranging from 2 *altyn* to 10 *efimki*. Sometimes these fees were accompanied by beatings from the Turkish guards.[47] The main gathering point along this route was the post of Fandaqumiya, along the road between Nablus and Jenin.[48]

The final stage of the journey after Damascus passed through Hawran toward the headwaters of the Jordan. Pilgrims crossed the river on a bridge above the Sea of Galilee, and then farther along, they went through Capernaum, Nazareth, and Samaria, arriving in the holy city from the north.

Pilgrims at the Holy Places of Palestine

As the pilgrim caravan was approaching Jerusalem, local Christians would come out to meet it—"they greeted each other with kisses and congratulated them."[49] At the gates of the patriarchal monastery, the pilgrims were met by bishops and monks who took them to their cells. For three days, the pilgrims stayed at the monastery and were treated to the trapeza.[50] The pilgrims gave alms to the monastery "according to their strength" and their names were entered into the book for commemoration. Authors of travelogues describe with special feeling the ritual of members of the Brotherhood of the Holy Sepulchre washing the feet of pilgrims for which the pilgrims also wore traditional dress.

The central event of the first day of the pilgrims' stay in Jerusalem was a visit to the Church of the Holy Sepulchre. Following longstanding tradition, the Muslim authorities charged a special tax for this. An admission fee into the church was officially established by Sultan Suleiman and was different for different ethnolinguistic groups.[51] The system of taxing pilgrims copied a similar practice of the Mamluk era. Even the original amounts for the fees originally were stated in Ottoman legislation in the Mamluk-era *altyn* of Qaitbay.[52] In addition to the fees common to all pilgrims (amounting to 47.5 *para*), Franks had to pay 7 gold ducats each (totaling 372.5 para). Pilgrims from Bilad-i Rum (the Balkans and Western Anatolia) and Bilad-i Sharq (Eastern Anatolia and Mesopotamia) were subject to a fee of 3 gold coins of Qaitbay (in sum, 154 *para*). Natives of Syria (the *vilayets* of Aleppo and Sham) paid 2 gold pieces (119 *para*) each and Egyptians paid 1 gold piece (84 *para*). Natives of Palestine and Trans-jordan were exempted from tolls and only paid 25 *akçe* (14 *para*), whereas residents of areas the nearest to Jerusalem paid 4 *akçe* (2 *para*). Georgians and Ethiopians were not subject to any levies.[53] Oded Peri accurately observes that the privileged status of these last two groups, as well as the low taxes imposed on Egyptians, clearly indicates the legal heritage of the Mamluk period, which was centered on Cairo. The Ottomans simply reproduced the already-existing system of levies.[54]

The increasing inflation of Ottoman currency led to a drop in real income from the pilgrimage and losses to the treasury. In the late seventeenth century, the Ottoman authorities tied the amount of the fees to a fixed rate of exchange with European gold, thus almost doubling the amount collected from pilgrims.[55] It seems that the fee also increased in the eighteenth century: in 1726, Grigorovich-Barsky paid 7 thalers, and in 1745, Serapion paid 16 thalers.[56]

By the sultan's command, the money collected was spent on the maintenance of the Qur'an reciters in the Dome of the Rock. In 1552, by special decree, Suleiman forbade the imposition of any additional fees on pilgrims but, of course, this command was not respected. Proceeds from pilgrims in 1526/1527 amounted to 40,000 *akçe*, in 1538 the amount doubled, and in 1553 it tripled,[57] which indicates an increase in the number of pilgrims. Each pilgrim received a certificate of having paid the fee "a card with a stamp signed with a Turkish hand," which was closely checked at the entrance to the church. Those who did not possess such a document were beaten and chased away "with great shame, and with an extra slap."[58]

After three days in the patriarchal monastery, the pilgrims were taken to other monasteries of Jerusalem, where they lived until Easter. It seems that in this way the pilgrims were divided up according to ethnic and geographic background. Slavs traditionally were placed in the former Serbian Monastery of the Archangel Michael, whereas Anatolian Greeks and the Laz of Trapezon were housed in the Monastery of St Demetrius.[59] They had to pay for these places. Serapion, for example, reported that the pilgrims who lived at the Monastery of St Theodore Stratelates paid 12 thalers each, for which "each one there pays to eat … with his own money."[60] It appears that the patriarchate fed the very poor. This also seems to have been what happened in Jerusalem with Grigorovich-Barsky, who made friends with the Greek monks and enjoyed their patronage.[61]

Temperamental Georgian pilgrims caused many problems for the patriarch-ate, demanding food for themselves and fodder for their horses. In letters to Georgian rulers, Dositheus specifically stipulates that the Iberians in Jerusalem maintain themselves without requiring food and loans from the patriarchate.[62]

As a rule, the pilgrims stayed in Jerusalem from autumn to late spring, going around the monasteries and praying in the holy places. On great feasts, meals were arranged for the pilgrims at the patriarchal monastery. The Hieromonk Makary described how the patriarchal vicar instructed the pilgrims in 1705: "Go everywhere without hindrance, except the Jordan."[63] Traveling about Palestine, however, was quite dangerous. Many pilgrims describe encountering bandits who, according to Ignaty Denshin, "rob you even down to your last scrap of fab-ric and leave you naked."[64] He was not particularly lucky in this respect. Ignaty fell into the hands of Bedouins several times: "they beat us mercilessly and robbed us, stripped us naked" and "the Arab barbarians committed every abuse against us and beat us with rocks and sticks."[65] At times, fighting between Palestinian clans prevented visits to the holy places. Thus, pilgrims could not visit Bethle-hem at Christmas 1810 because armed clashes had broken out between groups of townspeople there.[66]

Sometimes members of the Brotherhood of the Holy Sepulchre would lead pilgrims through the holy places in an organized manner, announcing it the night before. Serapion wrote, "And they gather in droves and go with the Turks, on account of the danger of brigandage."[67] In addition to the Via Dolorosa and the other places of worship in Jerusalem, the pilgrims visited Gethsemane, the Mount of Olives, Bethany, and the Pool of Siloam and went to Bethlehem, Mar Saba, and the Monastery of the Holy Cross. Having made the rounds of all these shrines, pilgrims visited the Lavra for a second time on December 5, in memory of Mar Saba, and Bethlehem on Christmas.[68]

Christian pilgrimage was one of the most important sources of income not only for the Ottoman authorities and the church structures, but also for the Arab population of Jerusalem. According to the estimates of Constantin-François Vol-ney, 1,500 pilgrims (the average figure for the late eighteenth century) left more than 1.5 million livres in Jerusalem over the course of their five- or six-month stay.[69] In fact, this is the minimum possible figure. According to Volney himself, the simplest journey to the holy places cost 4,000 livres and with heavy spending on alms the cost of the pilgrimage could reach 50,000 to 60,000 livres.[70]

About a third of these sums was handed over to locals who sold the hajjis "food and water at otherworldly prices."[71] Renting horses and mules to pilgrims, often compulsorily, also brought in significant revenue. "The accursed Arabs strongly insist on the horse; and they beat whoever does not want to travel by horse; the great violence!" complained Lukyanov.[72] "They are dogs robbing us fiercely with the [price of] transit," said another pilgrim, reporting rates of 50 kopecks for 10 versts.[73]

Ivan Lukyanov, one of the most skeptical observers, wrote a great deal about everyday, sometimes unpleasant details of pilgrimage, which were not always recalled by ecstatic authors. Thus, when pilgrims visited a monastery, alms were collected from them at a fixed rate: from the important ones, 5 to 8 ducats, and from the poor, no less than 5 thalers. "And whoever would be obstinate," wrote Lukyanov, "would want to give four thalers, he [the monk collecting money] would speak in his face: such a bad [i.e., pilgrim] you are! Such is the way of the Greeks."[74] At the monastery trapeza, the pilgrims were treated with copious amounts of wine, according to the cynical Lukyanov, "so that the pilgrims will eagerly give more money."[75] With this Old Believer writer, rapture at the contemplation of the famous shrines alternates with sarcastic Grecophobic comments. Thus, departing from the Monastery of Mar Saba, the pilgrims passed by a recluse standing on a stone pillar. Lukyanov wrote that "the Greeks went to bow to him and ask forgiveness from him."[76] We can assess this observation as sensational because pillar-dwelling as a form of asceticism had disappeared by the fifteenth century. Lukyanov does not seem to know this, but he nevertheless started to ask one of the elders:

> What kind of a wonder and a holy thing is this? But he laughed—
> continued the pilgrim—[saying] this is a stylite for an hour for as soon
> as the pilgrims depart from the monastery, it is as if the wind will blow
> him off the pillar.... Such are the stylite-deceivers of the Greeks![77]

Most difficult of all was the journey to the Jordan, which was organized on Epiphany, January 6. The *mutasallim* of Jerusalem guarded the pilgrims with several hundred horsemen and foot soldiers. During the time of Gagara and Sukhanov, the cost of this guard was 3 *efimki* per person and in Grigorovich-Barsky's time it was 4 thalers. Serapion gives a colorful description of this journey:

> Then everywhere along the streets and especially from the monasteries,
> where the pilgrims were sitting, there was a great cry and confusion; for
> there were Arabs everywhere from everywhere in great number with
> camels, horses and donkeys, a great multitude, and they occupied the
> entire street ... and each one of the Arabs [seizes] the pilgrims which are

coming out [of the church] and one puts them on his camel, another on his horse, another on his mule, trying to get there before the other and to snatch and to make the pilgrim sit on his animal for the sake of his own gain, and there was seen among the Arabs a great quarrel and infighting and great cry ... and those [pilgrims] who did not want to sit ... on the camel, wanting to walk with their own feet, were forcibly held by the Arabs and hit with the stick on their sides and sometimes over the head, and were made to sit on their animal by force, unless someone managed to sneak out of the church early into the city.[78]

On the road, the pilgrims were grouped by ethnic and confessional affiliation, with the Orthodox headed by bishops of the Brotherhood of the Holy Sepulchre.[79] The Ottoman convoy, with arms, banners, and tambourines, moved at the head of the caravan, "other armed Turks ran near to the pilgrims ... and forced them to line up and there was a lot of press and cry among the people."[80]

The most difficult leg of the journey began just outside Jerusalem when it was necessary to cross a mountain range teeming with Bedouin bandits, "they were everywhere they live like mice throughout the mountains and rocks."[81] Once it crossed over the mountains, the caravan descended into the Jordan Valley, stopping for the night in Jericho and reaching the river the next day. Serapion describes how at the sight of the Jordan the pilgrims shouted and raced each other and jumped into the river. Those who did not know how to swim entered the river on camels. Stretching for a mile along the shore, each confessional group separated from the others. The pilgrims bathed in the water of the Jordan and collected it in vessels. Serapion recalled:

> The Turks, all with guns and on horseback, stood along the banks, so that the Arabs could not attack us from there; we washed for half an hour in that river and the Turks would not give us more time; the older Turks did not want to wait and drove us all out at once.[82]

Not wanting to lose the income from protecting the caravan, the Ottoman authorities prohibited pilgrims from going to the Jordan alone without an escort. For this reason, monks and the poorest pilgrims made their way there from the Lavra of Mar Saba at night. This is the route that Grigorovich-Barsky took. Out of fear of bandits, he wore "only decrepit rags that would repulse anyone."[83] Travelers sat out the day in the thickets of tamarisk along the edge of the water, "for by day the Arabs walked here and there" not missing out on the profitable trade of catching pilgrims arriving illegally at the river and delivering them to the judge in Jerusalem, who imposed a fine of 50 thalers on the offender's confession.[84]

The central event of the pilgrimage was the celebration of Pascha. On Holy Friday, the Janissaries admitted pilgrims into the Holy Sepulchre, checking their lists for the payment of fees for the journey to Jordan "and those who did not pay were violently chased away."[85] During this, the *mutasallim*, the agha of the Janissaries, and all the upper administration of Jerusalem were present, sitting side by side in the shade under a pitched tent. Ignaty Denshin claimed that on Good Friday the pasha would again collect a fee from the pilgrims of 2 ducats per person: "on that day the sultan's great collection took place, for many thousands of Christians of all creeds were gathered to worship."[86]

Pilgrims and Christians of Jerusalem were in the church from Good Friday to Pascha. We will not describe here the Paschal liturgy in Jerusalem and, in particular, the rite of the coming down of the Holy Fire on Holy Saturday. All this is described in detail in the centuries-old pilgrimage literature, including the Russian literature, from the Igumen Daniel on.

Varlaam wrote that after Easter, the pilgrims made a farewell visit to Jordan.[87] On the second Monday after Easter, heralds with banners walked along the streets, announcing the departure for Jaffa the next day. Once again, crowds of Arabs with mounts thronged the pilgrims, "and whoever did not want to go by foot was beaten mercilessly … and was forcibly planted on their beast for their [the Arabs'] gain."[88] Residents of Jerusalem stood along the road, watching the pilgrims, as bishops gave a blessing. Outside the city, the *agha* began to line up the caravan, collecting a fee of 3 thalers.[89] This same return journey took places in different ways for different people. For Grigorovich-Barsky, for example, it was extremely successful and safe, compared with the first time "since we were with a famous pasha with many soldiers who escorted us."[90] On the other hand, at times of unrest and disorder in Jerusalem, there was no one to protect the movement of pilgrims. Thus, in one season in the early nineteenth century, the Abu Ghosh tribe blocked the pilgrims' way back to Jaffa and demanded that the Christian and Jewish clergy of Jerusalem facilitate the return of one of their kinsmen who had been seized by al-Jazzar Pasha of Acre.[91] In April 1805, the former mayor of the city, who had been exiled by the people of Jerusalem and was seeking to return, also blocked the way to Jaffa, causing unrest among the pilgrims in Jerusalem who blamed the patriarchal vicar and the dragoman.[92]

To conclude the topic of pilgrimage, it is worth providing figures on the number of pilgrims who came to the Holy Land during the first three centuries of Ottoman rule. We have at our disposal two sets of sources: Ottoman financial statements and the testimonies of pilgrims. Oded Peri examined Ottoman documents regarding revenue from pilgrims for twenty-three years from the period 1565 to 1673. The most complete data are from the late sixteenth century, whereas information about the flow of pilgrims from the seventeenth century remains extremely sketchy. The first thing that catches the eye is the abrupt and inexplicable fluctuations in the number of pilgrims. The number of pilgrims coming to Palestine over two or three years may vary by several times. The average number of hajjis proposed by Peri is 585 people per year, varying by about 370 people in either direction. In the years 1580/1581, 1586/1587, and 1663/1664, the number of pilgrims reached 1,200–1,300 people, whereas in 1567/1568 and 1583/1584, the number did not exceed eighty.[93]

When comparing these data with the reports of the pilgrims themselves, it seems that the figures in the Ottoman registries underestimate the numbers by three to four times. One Western author wrote that in 1609 there gathered six thousand Eastern Christians and eighty Latins.[94] In 1636, Vasily Gagara went to the Jordan with 1,700 pilgrims of all confessions, and in 1651, Iona went with 1,500.[95] According to Peri's estimates, incidentally, the number of pilgrims in 1650/1651 should have been 135 people.[96] At the same time, not all pilgrims were able to afford the journey to the Jordan. Of the six thousand people mentioned in 1609, four thousand went to the Jordan.[97] In 1709, Ippolit Vishenski went to the Jordan with two thousand pilgrims, whereas on Easter of that year, there were more than ten thousand people in the Church of the Holy Sepulchre, including, of course, the Ottoman soldiers who were there to maintain order.[98] Similarly, in 1794, Melety went to the Jordan with two thousand pilgrims, whereas in Jerusalem, a total of five thousand devotees had gathered, including neighboring Arabs.[99]

Returning to the issue of the total number of hajjis, we will now present a few more figures. In 1726, Grigorovich-Barsky went from Jaffa to Jerusalem with a caravan of 1,500 travelers and returned the following year with three thousand Greeks, Catholics, Armenians, Copts, and others.[100] This does not count all of the pilgrims who took the northern route. In 1784, Constantin-François Volney counted two thousand pilgrims in Jerusalem.[101]

The dynamics of pilgrimage depended on the political situation in the Eastern Mediterranean. Wars and turmoil naturally limited the circulation of pilgrims. This was the case amid the unrest of the sixteenth and seventeenth centuries, and then, a century later, during the era of the war between the Ottomans and the Holy League. The same situation existed during the Greek uprising of the 1820s and the Russo–Turkish War of 1828–1829, when Orthodox from the Balkans completely ceased visiting the Holy Land. For three to five thousand Armenians, there were 250–300 Greeks from Egypt and Anatolia.[102] The unimpeded flow of pilgrims only resumed in 1830, when there were as many as ten thousand people in Jerusalem for Easter.[103] It seems that many foreign writers did not perceive Syrian and Palestinian Christian Arabs as pilgrims. Most of them only came to Jerusalem for Easter. For this reason, the figure of 1,500 to 2,000 pilgrims, which appears consistently in the sources for the seventeenth and eighteenth centuries, doubled or tripled during Holy Week.

How should the tenfold difference be explained between the number of hajjis that appear in the Ottoman documents of the sixteenth century and the number of devotees attested to by travelers of the seventeenth and eighteenth centuries? Archival materials about tax revenues from the port of Jaffa (in which a special section is allocated to pilgrims' fees) shows a significant increase in the flow of pilgrims over the centuries, from 40 people per year in the late sixteenth century to 350 in 1698 and almost five times more than that in the eighteenth century.[104] Nevertheless, even with this trend, it seems that the Ottoman tax records are not entirely accurate, probably because of official corruption. Preference should be given to the testimony of pilgrims, who cite figures between two thousand for those who came to Palestine from far away and stayed there for six months and five thousand for those who assembled for the celebration of Easter.

The Romanian Lands and the Orthodox East

As mentioned, even more important than pilgrimage for the Church of Jerusalem as a source of revenue were the landholdings donated to the Holy Sepulchre by the rulers of Moldavia and Wallachia, the so-called venerative properties. This story, however, pertains more to Balkan than to Middle Eastern history and a detailed examination must make recourse to Romanian historiography.[105] Here we will give only a brief outline of ties between the Levant and Romania during the Ottoman era.

Financial support for the Orthodox East by the rulers of the Danubian principalities began in the fifteenth century and dramatically increased when both the Middle East and Moldavia and Wallachia became part of the Ottoman Empire.[106] In the sixteenth century, patriarchs of Jerusalem of Greek origin spent time in Istanbul and the Balkans and so, naturally, received alms from the rulers of Moldavia and Wallachia. Patriarch Sophronius explicitly states that he traveled even as far as Moldavia seeking financial assistance.[107] The scale of donations to the clergy of the Holy Sepulchre must have increased under rulers of Phanariot origin. Without being able to make use of Romanian sources, it is difficult to track the dynamics of donations of land in terms of when this practice began and when it reached its peak. The earliest donation of this kind that is known to us was made by that Moldavian ruler Peter the Lame (1586–1592) who donated a metochion in Iasi to the Monastery of Mar Saba.[108] This metochion was mentioned by Trifon Korobeinikov and Arseny Sukhanov.[109] From the sources it appears that the monastery granted to Mar Saba was not the only donation made by Peter the Lame. Half a century later, the metropolitan of Bethlehem describes the procedure for the election of the Patriarch Paisius by the abbots "of the estates of the Holy Sepulchre and the monastic buildings of the voivode Peter and the voivode Barnovschi."[110] "Monastic buildings of the voivode Peter" appear in the plural. The second benefactor of the Holy Sepulchre that is named, Miron Barnovschi, built Barnovschi Monastery in Iasi in 1627, which he donated to the Church of Jerusalem.[111] According to the available information, the surge in contacts between Palestine and Moldavia can be accounted for by the rule of Patriarch Theophanes (1608–1644), who had an active foreign policy and traveled to Georgia, Moscow, and Ukraine and, it seems, spent more time in the Balkans than in the Holy Land. Under Theophanes, the metochion of the Brotherhood of the Holy Sepulchre was established in Constantinople and an entire network of churches, monasteries, and estates in the Danubian principalities were designated for the Patriarchate of Jerusalem.[112]

It seems that of the two Danubian principalities, during the seventeenth century, Jerusalem had closer relations with Moldavia. A contemporary of Patriarch Theophanes was the Moldavian ruler of Greek origin, Vasile Lupu (1634–1653), a political figure of international weight and boundless ambition. After each outbreak of costly struggle for possession of the holy places of Palestine, the bishops of Jerusalem went to pay homage to Vasile in Iasi and ask him for alms to cover their expenses. According to Andrei Muraviev, "few of the Eastern emperors rendered as many services to the Holy Sepulchre as this pious Moldavian voivode."[113] It was before him that Theophanes made a performance described in the chronicles, when he appeared suddenly in the ruler's palace with a noose around his neck and gave Vasile the end of the rope with the words "hang me, my son, for the Turkish creditors are strangling me."[114] All the patriarch's debts were paid immediately by the ruler. In turn, Vasile was an influential politician who permitted himself a great deal with regard to the church. He installed and overthrew patriarchs, and resolved disputes between bishops. Some of his letters to patriarchs look like directives for immediate execution, containing explicit threats in case of disobedience.[115] In March 1645, in the Moldavian capital with the support of Vasile, Paisius—who had formerly been abbot of the Brotherhood of the Holy Sepulchre's Ascension Monastery in Iasi—was elected patriarch of Jerusalem.[116]

Paisius spent a considerable portion of his patriarchate on the territory of Moldavia. He lived there in 1648, before traveling to Moscow, and again upon his return from Russia, in 1649–1651, when he did not dare go to Istanbul out of fear of the intrigues of his enemy, Patriarch Parthenius of Constantinople. In the end, Parthenius was killed in 1651 through the intrigues of the rulers of Moldavia and Wallachia.[117]

There came to be established within the Orthodox *millet* a stable structure of economic relations, in which Moldavia and Wallachia were financial donors to Athos, Palestine, Sinai, and other cultural and political centers of the Orthodox world, a heavy burden for the Moldavians and Wallachians. The rulers, especially those of Phanariot origin, squeezed the very last juices out of their subjects for the needs of their clan, which included the patriarch of Jerusalem. This is one of the reasons for the uprising of the Moldavians in 1653, which overthrew Vasile and unleashed a terror against the local Greeks. Paul of Aleppo, who was in Iasi at the time, wrote,

> The Greeks … did not come out of their homes because of the strong hostility between them and the Moldavians, for Vasile's archons were Greeks … and they greatly enslaved and humiliated the Moldavians.… Day and night they were forced to work to pay the Greeks, just as we are in relation to the Turks.[118]

However, the ethnic origins of rulers did not particularly influence their relations with the Orthodox East. Moldavian rulers continued to donate estates to the Holy Sepulchre, while the patriarch lived for long periods of time in the monasteries of Iasi. The Moldavian ruler Ducas took part in the elections of the patriarchs of Jerusalem, Nectarius in 1661 and Dositheus in 1669.[119] Nectarius lived in Iasi from 1663 to 1665, collecting donations from the Danubian lands.[120] Immediately after his election, Dositheus also went to collect alms in the Danube principalities. As he wrote from Bucharest to his friend the Greek archimandrite Dionysius, the future metropolitan of Ugro-Wallachia, at Cheesefare 1670, "The Lord has brought to these places … His Beatitude Patriarch Kyr Dositheus and he was greeted with full honors and pleasantries."[121] The voivode donated 5,000 groschen to the Holy Sepulchre and the same amount was given "on their own account" by the metropolitan, notables, and monasteries. Despite the fact that at that time they were "very poor and powerless because of great debts and tributes to the king, still again they did not leave the Holy Sepulchre without care and help. After ten days, the most blessed [Patriarch Dositheus] will set out from there and will take the path to Iasi with the Ducas voivode, a great friend of the Holy Sepulchre and of his beatitude (the patriarch)."[122]

During his thirty-five-year patriarchate, Dositheus only visited Jerusalem four times, spending a total of about two years there. He spent all the rest of his time in the Balkans and the Danubian principalities, with the exception of his travels to Georgia. Dositheus's stays in Moldavia and Wallachia are repeatedly mentioned in the sources from the 1670s to the 1700s and local rulers continued to give him churches and monasteries and to secure *firmans* for the reconstruction of places of worship. The foundation of the printing press of the Jerusalem Patriarchate at Iasi in 1682 was of paramount importance. Dositheus personally supervised its activities and, in the late seventeenth and early eighteenth centuries, he published a series of anti-Latin treatises. According to some reports, the Catholics sought from the Sublime Porte to close the press, but to no avail.[123] What the Jesuits achieved in Constantinople in the 1620s, when the first printing press of Cyril Lucaris was destroyed, was impossible in Moldavia.

Dositheus's nephew Chrysanthos began his ecclesiastical career in the Danubian principalities in the 1690s, having returned there after his visits to Moscow and education in Western Europe. Chrysanthos's election as patriarch of Jerusalem took place in 1707, once more with the participation of the ruler of Moldavia. The patriarch at times closely collaborated with the Wallachian ruler Constantin Brâncoveanu. As mentioned, Chrysanthos's preference for the abbots of the Brotherhood of the Holy Sepulchre's monasteries in Moldavia and Wallachia led to a conflict between him and the members of the Brotherhood in Palestine. The publishing activity of the Patriarchate of Jerusalem continued in the Danubian principalities and so, for example, Chrysanthos published the *History of Dositheus Notaras* in Bucharest in 1715.[124]

After the first third of the eighteenth century, there is a dramatic reduction in the volume of sources on the history of the Patriarchate of Jerusalem. Consequently, much less is known about relations between Palestine and Romania during this time. Nevertheless, it is logical to assume that they only became stronger because the patriarchs no longer lived in Jerusalem, but rather in Constantinople, sufficiently close to Iasi and Bucharest. There exist fragmentary references to the patriarchs visiting the Danubian principalities. For example, Patriarch Ephraim was caught there at the beginning of the Russo–Turkish War of 1768–1774, at which he hastily departed to Istanbul for fear of repression against the Orthodox near the front. It is also reported that Patriarch Abraham (1775–1787) visited Moldavia and Wallachia seeking alms.[125]

By the 1840s, twenty-four monasteries and sketes in the Danubian principalities along with their landholdings (fifteen in Moldavia and nine in Wallachia) belonged to the Holy Sepulchre.[126] At some point, the Romanian aristocracy started to tire of being the donor to the Orthodox East and to contemplate regaining the bloated estates of the Holy Sepulchre, Athos and Sinai, which, in the early nineteenth century, constituted almost a fifth of the cultivated land in the Danubian principalities.[127] Ultimately, the presence of the Brotherhood of the Holy Sepulchre in Romania ended with the confiscation of the dependent properties in 1863, but these events already belong to another historical era.

The Arab Church of Antioch, standing somewhat apart from the Greco-centric Orthodox *millet* and not possessing famous places of worship, was not so closely linked to the Danubian principalities. Apart from Joachim Daw, who traveled through the Romanian lands in the 1580s on his way to and from Moscow, it was not until the 1620s that a patriarch of Antioch would go there. This was Cyril Dabbas, who was directed to Moldavia and Wallachia by his patron, Cyril Lucaris, to collect the monetary donations that were so needed in Dabbas's confrontation with his Syrian opponents.[128] In the 1650s, Patriarch Macarius spent a total of more than three years and was close with several successive rulers of Moldavia and Wallachia. Becoming acquainted at first hand with the enormous landholdings of the Patriarchate of Jerusalem, Macarius started to make plans to obtain one of the Danubian monasteries for the Church of Antioch.[129]

Patriarch Athanasius III Dabbas, who was almost at home among the Phanariot clergy, like his Greek brethren spent considerable time in the Romanian lands. It was there that with the support of the Wallachian ruler Brâncoveanu, in 1701, he established the first Orthodox Arabic printing press.[130] When Greeks stood at the head of the Patriarchate of Antioch, the connections between the Orthodox of Syria and the Danubian principalities significantly strengthened. As it happens, Patriarch Sylvester was absent from Damascus for ten years as he traveled around the Balkan and Danubian lands collecting alms. In the 1740s, Sylvester resumed printing activity in Arabic in Iasi. The rulers of Moldavia granted the See of Antioch estates and the Monasteries of St Spiridon in Bucharest and St Nicholas Popăuți in Moldavia.[131]

The principalities were not the only financial donors to Middle Eastern Orthodoxy. Occasionally, other areas of concentrated Christian population within the Patriarchate of Constantinople also played this role. The Patriarchate of Jerusalem, burdened by the costly struggle over the holy places of Palestine, frequently relied on their coreligionists in the Balkans. In critical situations in which the Brotherhood of the Holy Sepulchre was required to make lavish payments to the Ottoman authorities, patriarchs of Constantinople and the Phanariot elite levied a special tax, as was done by Cyril Lucaris in 1633 and Ioannicius in 1653.[132] Such assistance was provided less often to the Patriarchate of Antioch, which was fighting Catholic expansion in the eighteenth century.[133] Thus, Patriarch Neophytus of Constantinople wrote to the metropolitans of Asia Minor in 1736 that, having fallen into serious debt, Patriarch Sylvester of Antioch was headed to their dioceses "first of all, to bless, to pray and to sanctify all of you ... and then to request of you with paternal boldness fitting assistance according to the strength and prosperity of each of you."[134]

Sometimes the financial support went in the opposite direction—from Syria to Constantinople. It seems that this practice was established starting in the eighteenth century, after the Hellenization of the Patriarchate of Antioch and its close encounter with the Greek world. There is, for example, a message from the patriarch of Constantinople to his Syrian coreligionists in 1735 in which he complains of poverty and debt and requests assistance, noting that exarchs previously had not been sent to the Church of Antioch to collect alms.[135] According to the chronicle of Mikhail Breik, during the mid-eighteenth century, alms collectors often came to Damascus from Constantinople. The chronicler even mentions a con artist who posed as a metropolitan from Rumelia and managed to collect a considerable number of donations, purportedly for the Patriarchate of Constantinople before eventually being unmasked.[136]

Relations between Orthodox nations within the empire were also important from a cultural point of view. In these contacts, it was the Balkan lands that once again took the lead. The first attempts to establish a printing press for the needs of Middle Eastern Orthodoxy were taken, as has been noted, in the territory of the Danubian principalities, where the Orthodox clergy felt much more comfortable than in Syria and Palestine. Artists and architects came to Syria from the Balkans. Skilled craftsmen and building materials for the restoration of the Church of the Holy Sepulchre in 1809 were selected in Constantinople and then shipped to Palestine by sea.[137] This is to say that within the framework of the Rum *millet* a complex system of political, economic, cultural, and religious centers closely interacted with each other without interference from the Ottoman authorities.

This is particularly evident in the holding of joint councils by the heads of the Orthodox churches of the empire to address various canonical and theological issues.

REGIONAL CHURCH COUNCILS

The first of these regional councils was held shortly after Syria and Egypt were incorporated into the Ottoman Empire. In 1523, for the first time in many centuries, the patriarch of Constantinople made a pilgrimage to Palestine where he met with his Middle Eastern counterparts, the patriarchs of Alexandria and Jerusalem. During this time, there was once again unrest in the Church of Constantinople, and while Patriarch Jeremiah was visiting the holy places, he was deposed by the metropolitan of Sozopolis, Ioannicius, who seized the patriarchal throne. Then the patriarchs, in turn, gathered in Jerusalem and announced the deposition of Ioannicius, and he was removed from power with the active participation of the Christians of Istanbul.[138]

Often the Middle Eastern patriarchs tried to enlist the support of neighboring local churches to give more weight to their decisions. As mentioned, after Patriarch of Antioch Joachim ibn Jum'a established the order for the marriage of Christians in 1573, he received letters from the other Eastern patriarchs confirming its provisions and threatening violators with excommunication.[139]

In some cases, patriarchs' enthronements took place with the participation of the primates of neighboring sees. Thus, the enthronement of Patriarch Theophanes of Jerusalem in 1608 was attended by the patriarchs of Antioch and Alexandria, who came to Jerusalem on pilgrimage.[140]

Starting in the second half of the sixteenth century, the patriarchs of Alexandria and Jerusalem often visited Istanbul and spent long periods of time there. During such periods, they took part in local church affairs and local councils, even presiding over them as Patriarch of Jerusalem Germanus did in 1545, when he presided over the selection of the successor to Patriarch of Constantinople Jeremiah.

One of the largest regional councils was held in Istanbul in February 1593, at the initiative of Patriarch of Alexandria Meletius Pegas. It was attended by Patriarch Jeremiah II of Constantinople and Patriarch Sophronius of Jerusalem, whereas Meletius also represented the Church of Antioch. The council adopted a number of resolutions about purifying the morals of the clergy, ordering monastic life, forbidding clergy from taking secular positions or interfering in worldly affairs, prohibiting simony, and condemning luxury among the bishops. In addition to this, the council confirmed the earlier decision of the clergy of Constantinople rejecting the Gregorian calendar that had been introduced by the Catholic Church.[141]

The regional councils often considered theological issues and the problem of mutual relations with Western confessions. In the late sixteenth and seventeenth centuries, the Orthodox East became a battleground of influence between the Catholic and Protestant worlds. For the entire seventeenth century, the Greek Church was shaken by the controversy surrounding the ideological legacy of Cyril Lucaris (1572–1638). This prominent church leader and writer was seriously attracted to Calvinism and wanted to reform the Orthodox Church in the spirit of Protestantism.[142] His circle of students and associates included Protestant-oriented theologians and writers. Their opponents defended Orthodox doctrine on the basis of patristic writings and isolated elements of Latin scholasticism. Cyril Lucaris's *Confession of Faith* was condemned with the participation of clergy from the Middle East at councils in Constantinople and Iasi in 1638, 1641, and 1642, although Lucaris's authorship of the work was not officially recognized. By contrast, the confession of faith formulated by Metropolitan of Kiev Peter Mogila was adopted by the Eastern Church.[143]

In the early 1670s, there was another burst of interest in Protestant issues. Western diplomats in the Ottoman Empire, especially the French, formally inquired from the heads of the Eastern Christian churches about their attitude toward Protestant doctrine and especially about their interpretation of the sacrament of the Eucharist. Patriarch Dositheus of Jerusalem wrote a refutation of Calvinism in this regard and even the Patriarchate of Antioch, far removed from the passions raging in the Greek Church over Protestantism, sent a statement of the dogmatic and canonical principles of Orthodoxy to France.[144]

In March of 1672, Patriarch Dositheus convened an imposing council in Bethlehem that once more condemned Calvinism and rejected any resemblance between it and Orthodoxy. Dositheus was critical of Lucaris's person, but for political reasons, he did not acknowledge his authorship of the scandalous *Confession*. The patriarch of Jerusalem made his own statement of the foundations of the Orthodox faith, which became famous under his name.[145]

The Orthodox patriarchs, who were also concerned with Catholic expansion in the Eastern Mediterranean, made joint denunciations of Catholic doctrine, particularly at a council in Constantinople in 1722, which was attended by Ecumenical Patriarch Jeremiah II, Patriarch Chrysanthos of Jerusalem, and Patriarch Athanasius of Antioch.[146]

Within the context of the relationship between Catholicism and the Orthodox East, there were periodic discussions of second baptism for Catholics and Armenians entering Orthodoxy. One outbreak of this discussion took place in the 1750s when the patriarch of Constantinople adopted a doctrine of not recognizing non-Orthodox baptisms and expelled dissenting bishops from the capital. The patriarchs of Alexandria and Jerusalem accepted only the validity of Orthodox baptisms, whereas Patriarch Sylvester of Antioch hesitated and avoided the issue. They threatened to boycott him, but he did not put his signature on a declaration sent from Constantinople.

Mikhail Breik al-Dimashqi wrote about all this in detail,[147] which is further evidence of the deep involvement of the Orthodox Arab East in the internal affairs of the Rum *millet*. Breik also reports in his chronicle about the struggle for the holy places in the neighboring Patriarchate of Jerusalem, personnel changes in the Churches of Alexandria and Jerusalem, and many other events that had no direct relationship to life in Damascus.[148] Other Arab historians also report about the vicissitudes of the struggle over the holy places of Palestine. For example, semiliterate notes in the margins of a bible at Balamand Monastery tells of the Franks "taking away" places of worship in Jerusalem from the Orthodox in 1688 with a list of bishops from the opposing sides and the Ottoman administrators who ruled on the litigation.[149] That is to say, the Arab Orthodox of the Patriarchate of Antioch felt themselves to be not only Syrian but also part of the general Orthodox *millet*.

Relations Between Local Churches

From time to time, conflicts broke out between the local churches of the Orthodox East on account of rivalry for supremacy or spheres of influence. The Patriarchates of Alexandria and Jerusalem inherited border disputes going back even to the Crusader period, when some Palestinian dioceses went under the patriarchs of Alexandria. Patriarch Joachim of Alexandria (1486/1487–1565/1566) had previously been a monk on Mount Sinai and had close ties to the Monastery of St Catherine and enjoyed considerable influence there. The patriarch waited out repeated periods of unrest in the Church of Alexandria on Sinai and, in 1529, he even built the Church of the Holy Archangel Michael at the monastery with his own funds.[150] In 1530 and 1542, however, under pressure from the patriarchs of Constantinople and Jerusalem, Joachim of Alexandria recognized Jerusalem's rights to Gaza, Sinai, Kerak, and other border dioceses.[151] Nevertheless, rivalry between the two patriarchs over possession of the famous and wealthy Monastery of St Catherine continued for decades. After the patriarch of Alexandria was forced to renounce his claims to the monastery, in 1540, the patriarch of Jerusalem regained the episcopal see of Sinai to further limit Joachim's ability to interfere in the monastery's affairs. However, in 1557, taking advantage of the bishop's misconduct, Joachim insisted on a conciliar decision to abolish the bishopric of Sinai and again acted as patron of the monastery. There are, however, references to bishops of Sinai in sources from the 1560s and 1573. The question of the bishopric of Sinai was finally settled at a council in Constantinople in 1575. The council legitimized the status of the bishop of Mount Sinai, who would be elected by the monks of St Catherine's Monastery and approved by the patriarch of Jerusalem.[152]

With the incorporation of Cyprus, which previously belonged to Venice, into the Ottoman Empire in 1570, an Orthodox hierarchy was fully restored on the island. Soon, however, there was a struggle for the archbishop's throne, which attracted intervention from the neighboring patriarchs. In the 1590s, Meletius Pegas, patriarch of Alexandria and lucum tenens of the See of Constantinople, obtained the deposition of Archbishop Athanasius of Cyprus, who was accused of various abuses. The patriarch of Antioch Joachim ibn Ziyada intervened, seeking to return the Church of Cyprus to the jurisdiction of the See of Antioch. Joachim reinstated Athanasius and unrest broke out with renewed vigor. Relations between the two patriarchs reached a critical point in 1599, when Meletius threatened Joachim in a letter: "Flee from these foreign affairs, so that ... tomorrow ... you do not meet danger in your own midst."[153]

The conflict between Meletius and Joachim aggravated the problem of the Monastery of St Catherine on Sinai. The monastery was greatly revered in the Christian world and, having received donations from everywhere in the Christian world, it was wealthy and independent in its actions and strove for real autocephaly. In 1592, when Meletius Pegas attempted to install his disciple Paisius on the episcopal see of Sinai,[154] the monks rejected his intervention and elected as abbot a certain Laurentius (1593–1617). Meletius sought to depose the bishop of Sinai, pointing to his uncanonical consecration by two rather than three bishops and accusing him of dealings with Rome. For his part, Patriarch Joachim of Antioch supported Laurentius, whether out of ambition or not wanting to quarrel with his powerful bishops. As Meletius Pegas angrily wrote to him in 1599,

> You went to Jerusalem, led the poor [patriarch] Kyr Sophronius of Jerusalem into temptation and established a new rule with five or six souls, some priests whom I do not know, with two deacons, with a notary and a sexton; calling them a council you made rules against the rule of the Fathers and of so many councils which condemn ... the consecration by two (bishops).[155]

In the end, Meletius managed to win the Eastern patriarchs over to his side and to force Laurentius to repent, after which he was installed in the See of Sinai for a second time in 1600, this time in accordance with all the canons.[156]

In the early seventeenth century, another conflict emerged over the Monastery of St Catherine. The Sinaites opened a chapel at their metochion in Cairo and held services there, attracting parishioners and depriving Patriarch Cyril Lucaris of Alexandria, who lived nearby, of income. The patriarch attempted to stop the Sinaites' services in his jurisdiction and appealed to the primates of the other local Orthodox churches.[157] With Cyril's accession to the See of Constantinople, the Sinaites chose to stop fighting and reconcile, but during the reign of Patriarch Nicephoras (1639–1645), who was long absent from Egypt to collect alms, they resumed services at the Cairo metochion. Nicephoras and his successor Ioannicius (1645–1657) forbade service of the liturgy at the metochion several times and excommunicated Bishop Joasaph (1617–1660). The struggle continued with mixed results. Joasaph managed to win the patronage of influential people in the Orthodox community of the empire, especially the ruler of Moldavia, Vasile Lupu. Under pressure from Lupu, in 1651, the ecumenical patriarch authorized services to be held in Cairo. In response to complaints from the Sinaite monks, Patriarch Ioannicius was persecuted by the Ottoman authorities and was even detained for a few days in August 1652. However, the following year the situation changed as the Sinaite metochion in Cairo was turned into a mosque (Patriarch Ioannicius denied any involvement in this). Next, the ruler Vasile was overthrown. After that, the See of Constantinople ceased to support Sinai and, in 1654, Joasaph was forced to reconcile with the patriarch of Alexandria and renounce his claims.[158] Russian pilgrims of the early eighteenth century reported that the inhabitants of the Sinaite metochion in Cairo

> [had] no church, but they have a separate cell instead of a chapel, and whenever they want to celebrate the divine service, they go to the (church) of the Nativity of the Most Holy Theotokos of the Patriarchate of Alexandria. And they do not have the freedom to build churches, and what was their church the Turks converted into a mosque, and the courtyard is small.[159]

Apart from the problems of the Cairo metochion, the claims of the Monastery of Sinai increased in other spheres. Bishops of Sinai rejected its subordination to the See of Jerusalem, wore patriarchal vestments, signed their letters with the title "His Beatitude" used only by autocephalous bishops, and generally behaved as a local church completely independent of the other patriarchs. The most ambitious of the bishops was Ananias, who headed the monastery from 1661 to 1671 and then retired under pressure from the patriarchs of Constantinople and Jerusalem, although he continued to informally supervise the monks' activities. According to Ecumenical Patriarch Callinicus, one of the enemies of the "second Arius" Ananias,

> the righteousness of God hurled upon him [Ananias], like the torrents of hail, everyone's chastisements, conciliar condemnations, and the church's *epitimias* [interdicts].... But he, as if he were made out of stone or out of copper, was not ashamed and did not repent of his iniquities ... but like the devil remained unrepentant.[160]

In the 1680s, Ananias and Archbishop Ioannicius of Sinai made for a cunning political duo, putting the monastery under the patronage of the Russian tsars and the patriarch of Moscow. Thus, Sinai passed out of the control of Jerusalem and into the nominal jurisdiction of Moscow, provoking a storm of indignation from Patriarch Dositheus of Jerusalem.[161]

In 1690, Ananias was almost defeated by his main opponent, Dositheus. In the absence of the sultan and the grand vizier, the Sinaites tried to bribe the vizier's *qaimaqam* and arranged with him for the arrest of Dositheus if he refused to recognize Sinai's autocephalous status. Ottoman guards and Sinaite monks burst into the Brotherhood of the Holy Sepulchre's metochion in Constantinople searching for the patriarch, who at the last moment managed to escape, hid somewhere for three days, and fled by night to the sultan's headquarters in Edirne (Adrianople), where he could depend on reliable patrons. In his letters, the aforementioned Ecumenical Patriarch Callinicus described the Sinaites' actions in the metochion of the Brotherhood of the Holy Sepulchre in very colorful terms: "And then you could see the anchorites, the riasophore demons, how they set off running like bloodthirsty wild beasts or wild bears ahead of the people's leader so that they could sooner catch their patriarch and put him to death."[162] "And this displeased them," continued Callinicus, "but they opened their vile mouths, like open coffins, and released their poisonous tongues and spewed forth countless insults ... at the patriarchs and bishops."[163]

In January 1691, Dositheus held a council in Constantinople that not only once more condemned Sinai's claim to autocephaly but also reduced the rank of the archbishop of Sinai to that of a simple bishop. It was only in 1696 that the patriarch, through the intervention of the voivode of Wallachia, reconciled with the bishop of Sinai and restored him to the rank of archbishop.[164]

A no less heated conflict erupted between the Orthodox patriarchates in a dispute over supremacy and influence in the Orthodox East. Although the Ottomans had made the patriarch of Constantinople head of the entire Orthodox *millet*, other patriarchs were also eager to conduct independent policies and at times managed to significantly narrow Constantinople's sphere of influence. Within the Church of Constantinople itself, various groups formed on a regional, clan, or political-ideological basis competed for power. Here a great deal depended on the individual talents and ambitions of a given primate as well as the political situation in the country. In the late sixteenth century, when the Ecumenical Patriarchate entered into a period of unrest and decline and suffered under Ottoman oppression, the leading position in the Rum *millet* went to the patriarchs of Alexandria. Both Meletius Pegas (1590–1601) and Cyril Lucaris (1601–1620) sought to give real meaning to the title of Ecumenical Judge that was attached to their see. They actively interfered in the affairs of neighboring churches, eagerly presided at the enthronement of new hierarchs, and admonished them in their letters, sometimes in an authoritative tone. With the transfer of Cyril Lucaris to the See of Constantinople, the center of power in the Orthodox *millet* also moved there. But despite the fact that Lucaris was undoubtedly one of the most influential ecclesiastical figures of the first third of the seventeenth century, his authority was not without limits. Patriarch Theophanes of Jerusalem represented an independent center of power. Lucaris's intervention in the ecclesiastical strife in the Church of Antioch between 1619 and 1627 caused by the rivalry between Athanasius Dabbas and Ignatius 'Atiya[165] was a failure for the party supported by the patriarch of Constantinople. Lucaris could only ignore the objectionable patriarch who was installed over the See of Antioch.[166]

For many years, there was a feud between Patriarch Parthenius II of Constantinople (1644–1651, with interruptions) and Patriarch Paisius of Jerusalem (1645–1660), who claimed to be the spiritual and political leader of the empire's Orthodox. Parthenius wrote denunciations of Paisius to the grand vizier, the tsar of Muscovy, and the rulers of Moldavia and Wallachia. It was no accident that Paisius, as he was returning from his journey to Moscow in 1649, spent several years in the Danubian principalities, afraid to appear in Istanbul on account of the intrigues of the Ecumenical Patriarch. That conflict ended in 1651 when, as previously mentioned, Parthenius was put to death through the machinations of the rulers of Moldavia and Wallachia.[167] The patriarch's killing made a painful impression on the Christians of the empire, which is reflected even in Russian sources.[168]

Patriarch Dositheus of Jerusalem (1669–1707) was even less tolerant of any intrusion by the See of Constantinople into the affairs of local churches, even when the stance of the Ecumenical Patriarch coincided with his own position.[169]

Constantinople's influence over the life of the Orthodox East markedly increased during the eighteenth century. Patriarchs of Jerusalem lived almost continuously in the capital of the empire and did not separate themselves from the circle around the Ecumenical Patriarch. Weakened by the Catholic onslaught, the Church of Antioch was vitally interested in the Phanar's support, especially because all of the patriarchs of Antioch after 1724 were Greeks more closely connected to the Greek world than to their Arab flock.

Greeks versus Arabs in the Church of Antioch during the Sixteenth and Seventeenth Centuries

The relative proportion of Arab and Greek elements in the Patriarchate of Antioch is an extremely important question for understanding the environment of Middle Eastern Christianity. Unfortunately, this issue is often incorrectly interpreted in foreign historiography. At some point during the nineteenth century there developed a myth of permanent and total Greek domination in the Church of Antioch, which was believed to have been one of the reasons for a significant number of Orthodox Arabs defecting to the Unia. This notion was originally formulated by Catholic authors and was adopted by Orthodox Arabs who at that time were fighting their Greek patriarchs for the Arabization of their church. In the twentieth century, this idea of overwhelming Greek hegemony in the Church of Antioch during the Ottoman era was repeated by many Arab and Western historians.[170] It is only recently that this stereotype has been revised in European scholarship.[171]

We will attempt to determine how serious Greek influence was in the Church of Antioch. According to the available information, the first radical intrusion by Greeks into Antioch's affairs happened under Patriarch Dorotheus III (1541–1543). A rather mysterious figure, Dorotheus began his reign with an unprecedented attempt at union with the Maronite Church. He proposed to the Maronite patriarch that they begin to hold joint services and permit intermarriage between the two communities, while preserving each one's dogmatic integrity.[172] During the sixteenth century, such "ecumenical" projects were possible in the Arab East because of the general decline of theological knowledge among the Orthodox and Maronites and a misunderstanding of the dogmatic differences between the two churches.

Arab chroniclers report that Dorotheus was soon deposed for uncanonical acts by a conciliar decision of the other Eastern patriarchs—Jeremiah of Constantinople, Joachim of Alexandria, and Germanus, who gathered in Jerusalem. Joseph Nasrallah and, following him, Robert Haddad see at work here the anti-Latin mood of the Greek patriarchs and, perhaps, the fears of the Ottomans, who were mindful of the Maronites' formal union with Rome.[173] To make such conclusions, however, we must first verify that the conciliar deposition in fact took place. Porphyry Uspensky, for example, denies that a council of three patriarchs took place in Jerusalem in 1543 and believes that there was confusion in the Arabic chronicles with a similar council of Jerusalem in 1524, when Ioannicius of Sozopolis was deposed for illegally usurping the See of Constantinople.[174]

The almost total correspondence of motive and participants for the two councils is obvious. Moreover, Jeremiah was already quite old in 1543, and it would not have been easy for him to go to Palestine for a second time. However, these arguments are not sufficient to unequivocally accept Porphyry Uspensky's point of view. It is not yet possible to verify information about the council of 1543 from any other sources, and so the question of the circumstances of Dorotheus III's deposal remains open.

Patriarch Joachim Jum'a, who took the throne after Dorotheus III, is seen in the Western literature as the most obvious case of Greek intervention in the affairs of the Church of Antioch. However, much of what has been written about Joachim is something of a scholarly curiosity. Cyrille Karalevskij splits Joachim Jum'a into "Joachim III," who is referred to in two documents from 1527 and 1531 regarding the privileges of a monastery on Lesbos, and "Joachim IV," who was at first an antipatriarch no later than May 1540 (his signature appears on acts of the Synod of Constantinople at the time regarding the rights of another monastery) and then was the legitimate patriarch from 1543 to 1576.[175] In time, all three documents were published by Afanasy Papadopoulo-Keramevs. Joseph Nasrallah went further, combining the two Joachims into one, and hypothesized that already by 1516, after the Ottoman conquest of Syria, Joachim Jum'a was made patriarch of Antioch in Constantinople, where he spent all the years up to 1543 as a titular bishop.[176]

This account, however, contradicts the Arabic sources, which state that before becoming patriarch, Joachim spent eleven years as bishop of Beirut.[177] Neither Karalevskij nor Nasrallah took the trouble to actually examine the three aforementioned documents. Otherwise, they would have seen alongside the signatures of Patriarchs Jeremiah of Constantinople (1522–1546) and Joachim of Antioch the signature of Patriarch Sylvester of Alexandria, who ruled from 1569 to 1590. In the description of the published letters, it is explicitly stated that the signatures of the patriarchs of Alexandria and Antioch were added later, to give the documents additional authority.[178] It is not difficult to posit when this was done. In 1587, Patriarch Joachim Daw returned from Istanbul to the Middle East, possibly together with Patriarch Sylvester of Alexandria, who is known to have gone from Istanbul to Rhodes shortly before 1588.[179] It is more than likely that both stopped on Lesbos on their way. Thus, the "antipatriarch" Joachim (1516–1543) is the fruit of the excitable imagination and excessive credulity of the two respected authors.

With the exception of the not entirely clear story of the deposition of Dorotheus III, the Phanariots of Constantinople first came to be involved in an internal conflict among the Syrian Arabs just sixty-five years after the Ottoman conquest of Syria, during the confrontation between Michael VI Sabbagh and Joachim Daw.[180] As stated, Greek support was of little help for Michael. Damascus ignored the sultan's decrees in his favor and he died in oblivion. Joachim Daw managed to come to terms with the Greeks, living for a time (1584–1585 and 1587) in Constantinople and thereafter maintaining close contacts with the See of Constantinople, for example, with regard to recognition of the Patriarchate of Moscow.

Later on, Syrian bishops also appeared in the capital. Thus, there are repeated mentions in the sources of Metropolitan Macarius of Aleppo staying in Istanbul in the 1590s.[181] Patriarch Athanasius II and Metropolitan Meletius of Aleppo visited Constantinople in the 1610s to plead their cases about the division of authority between them.[182] The first patriarch of Antioch to be consecrated in Constantinople was in 1618.[183] Even the involvement of Ecumenical Patriarchs in the multiyear conflict between Cyril Dabbas and Ignatius 'Atiya, lasting from 1618 to 1627, cannot be regarded as a manifestation of Phanariot diktat. The candidates for the patriarchate were put forward by rival Arab factions and the Greeks only installed one candidate or another. Their support did not mean much, however, as illustrated by the case of Cyril, who was deposed and executed by order of Fakhr al-Din. How would Cyril's patron in Constantinople, Cyril Lucaris, have been able to take revenge on Damascus? He could only delay the alms that were sent through him from Moscow to the See of Antioch in 1628.[184]

The first Greek to appear upon the See of Antioch in the Ottoman period, Euthymius III al-Saqizi (of Chios), was installed as patriarch at the behest of his precursor, Euthymius II, and with the consent of the Arab clergy and flock. During his patriarchate (1653–1647), he performed twelve episcopal consecrations, only one of which was of a Greek.[185] Even this Greek, the priest Pachomius from Chios who became metropolitan of Saydnaya, wrote the notes of ownership and dedication of his books in Arabic, which is to say that he was fluent in that language.[186] Of course, Euthymius al-Saqizi did indulge in some tribalism. Like the Arab patriarchs, he surrounded himself with compatriots and relatives. Euthymius also brought along several natives of Chios, but in general, he defended the interests of the people of Aleppo, whose protégé he was. The

Arabs felt no hostility toward him or his compatriots. Euthymius's syngelos was his nephew Neophytus, who was later made metropolitan of Hama by Patriarch Macarius ibn al-Za'im.[187]

A curious moment—when Macarius approached Istanbul in 1652, he sent the usual letter to the patriarch of Constantinople asking permission to stay in his jurisdiction. According to Paul of Aleppo, Patriarch Paisius of Constantinople and his metropolitans "were extremely satisfied that [Macarius] did not follow the example of his predecessors and gave them due consideration."[188] That is, according to this account, previous patriarchs of Antioch did not show special reverence for the See of Constantinople. The attitude of Macarius and Paul toward the Greeks was ambivalent. On the one hand, the Arabs were conscious of belonging to the Byzantine tradition and identified themselves with the Greeks against other Orthodox peoples, and hence the support of the Arab clergy for Nikon's reform, which standardized the Russian rites according to the Greek model. On the other hand, their attitude toward the Greeks could be quite critical.[189] However, the numerous attacks on the Greeks that are scattered in the *Journey of Macarius* reveal no more than the ordinary degree of prejudice, which was, in fact, not entirely incompatible with admiration for Greek culture and education. It is no surprise, then, that when Paul finished renovating the patriarchal residence in Damascus, he placed on its wall a porphyritic board with an Arabic inscription in verse about the time of its construction and then put the same text in Greek on a yellow slab "so that the sons of Greece might also read it."[190] It was during Macarius's patriarchate that extensive efforts were undertaken to educate the Arabs in the Greek cultural heritage. Greeks often were part of the patriarchal entourage[191] and Macarius was in constant contact with the Balkans.[192] Between 1654 and 1658, he penned a number of letters to the Russian tsar with requests for assistance to the Greek monasteries in Rumelia.[193]

The Greek influence in Syria was exclusively cultural rather than ecclesio-political. In 1666, when the patriarch of Constantinople arbitrarily deposed the patriarchs of Alexandria and Antioch, who had traveled to Moscow,[194] he appointed a new patriarch only for the See of Alexandria and did not even attempt to install someone on the See of Antioch, knowing that the Phanar was still unable to impose its decision on the Arabs.

Very soon, however, an occasion presented itself. In the summer of 1672, a group of bishops gathered in Beirut to challenge the election of Cyril al-Za'im to the patriarchate, declaring that it had taken place under pressure from the pasha of Damascus and without having consulted the other Eastern patriarchs. Apparently not having sufficient influence in Syria, Cyril's opponents appealed to the Ecumenical Patriarch of Constantinople and asked members of the synod, "you there choose a man who fears God and make him our patriarch."[195] Most likely, there was already a preliminary agreement between the plotters and the Phanariots of the capital to choose in place of Cyril the metropolitan of Epiphania (Hama), Neophytus of Chios, who before this had been elected locum tenens by Cyril's Syrian opponents. Communication between Beirut and Constantinople was established by Patriarch Dositheus of Jerusalem, who, during the turmoil, traveled through Syria on his way to the capital, apparently bringing along Neophytus. The young Patriarch Cyril of Antioch did not make a good impression on Dositheus, and the authoritative primate did everything he could to secure his deposition. Then the Synod of Constantinople proceeded to elect a new patriarch. In accordance with tradition, they named three candidates—Neophytus and two Greek metropolitans from Constantinople's jurisdiction.[196] Even if Neophytus's election was prearranged with his Syrian supporters, this was nevertheless the first time that the See of Constantinople formally assumed the power to appoint a patriarch of Antioch.

In the ensuing conflict over this, the two opponents, Cyril and Neophytus, alternately traveled to Istanbul to receive the sultan's *berat* for the patriarchate, with the assistance, of course, of corrupt Phanariots.[197] As mentioned, Cyril emerged from this fight victorious and Neophytus's Greek origins did not help his cause. However, the circumstances of Syrian church history in the late seventeenth century indicate rising Greek influence. The pretenders to the patriarchate (to whom should be added Athanasius in 1686) sought to enlist the support, first of the Phanar and then, accordingly, of the Sublime Porte. Of the ten metropolitans of Greek origin known in the Patriarchate of Antioch during the seventeenth century, six were consecrated in the last decades of the century, including four by Cyril al-Za'im.[198] Despite his Arab origin, Athanasius was largely a man of Greek culture who spent many years in Constantinople and the Danubian principalities, and at one point was archbishop of Cyprus. Out of a total of sixteen patriarchs of Antioch from the sixteenth to early eighteenth centuries—from Dorotheus II to Athanasius III—only eight involved some manner of Greek intervention, which they themselves usually provoked.

The Greek Xenocracy in Damascus

Athanasius is believed to have named his own successor, his protosyngelos the Greek Cypriot Sylvester (1724–1766), who stands at the origin of the Greek xenocracy in the Church of Antioch.[199] The establishment of Greek hegemony is closely associated with the expansion of the Catholic Unia in Syria. The Phanariots hoped that Greek patriarchs would be able to repel the Roman onslaught and keep the Arabs in the bosom of Orthodoxy. In this context, as noted by Thomas Philipp, Sylvester paradoxically enjoyed the support of the pro-Latin Christians of Aleppo against the philo-Catholic Cyril Tanas, who had been elected in Damascus in 1724.[200] Here, once more, the rivalry between the regional power centers of Syria was at play, with little concern for doctrinal issues. The people of Aleppo were ready to submit to Sylvester until he intervened in their internal affairs. As soon as the patriarch intervened, he was expelled, and the community of Aleppo started to seek autocephalous status for itself.[201]

Sylvester, however, proved to be in demand from that portion of Syrian's Christians who rejected union with Rome. For all his personal shortcomings, he was the rightful patriarch and enjoyed the support of the Phanar and the Sublime Porte. Did the Cypriot patriarch seek to impose Greek influence on Syria, to Hellenize the Church of Antioch? During the reign of the first four Greek patriarchs in Damascus (1724–1813), of twenty-four metropolitans of the See of Antioch, most of whom belong to the time of Sylvester, eleven are clearly Arabs and the ethnic background of six is difficult to establish. Seven are of undoubtedly Greek origin, including two bishops of Aleppo in the eighteenth century, which in the eighteenth century was transferred into the jurisdiction of Constantinople. Four metropolitans were Greek Cypriots, compatriots of the Patriarch Sylvester, including his nephew Sylvester, who was metropolitan of Lattakia in the 1760s.[202] According to Grigorovich-Barsky in 1728, Metropolitan Timothy of Hama had ruled there for many years, and so had most likely been installed before Sylvester.[203] The Cypriot Ioannicius was installed as metropolitan of Beirut in 1745 with the consent of the local congregation.[204] Even if we add to this the Cypriot abbots of monasteries met by Grigorovich-Barsky in the late 1720s, it is in no way possible to speak of a total Hellenization of the Church of Antioch in the eighteenth century. Most metropolitans, including such illustrious figures as Sophronius al-Kilizi, Macarius Sadaqa, and Athanasius al-Khabbaz, were Arabs. As it happened, Sylvester was absent from Syria for many years, collecting alms in the Danubian principalities and entrusting the management of church affairs to his Arab *wakils*, such as Tripoli native Mikhail Tuma, who was patriarchal vicar for around thirty years,[205] or Macarius Sadaqa. Sylvester himself knew Arabic and translated a great deal from Greek into Arabic to serve the spiritual needs of his flock. It is enough in this context to recall his efforts to revive Arabic printing.

Shortly before his death, however, Sylvester attempted to play the same game as the first Greeks on the See of Jerusalem, namely, to transfer his hierarchical authority during his own lifetime to his nephew, the metropolitan of Lattakia.

Perhaps this was motivated not so much by a desire to Hellenize the Church of Antioch as by the desire to establish a theocratic dynasty, which was not an unusual phenomenon in the Christian East. However, the metropolitans and laity did not agree with Sylvester's wish. Quarrels broke out, and the metropolitans left for their dioceses without any decision being made.[206] The bishops' infighting and outsized ambitions and the inability of the regional elites backing them to come to a consensus were the main causes of the establishment of the Greek xenocracy. The level of ethnic identity among the Arab metropolitans and *a'yans* in the eighteenth century did not allow them to see the Arab Orthodox as a particular subethnicity with interests different from those of the Greeks. In addition to this, there was the weakening of the Orthodox community in Syria in the face of the Catholic onslaught and its interest in Ottoman and Greek support. For their part, the Phanariots, led by Ecumenical Patriarch Samuel, actively sought the complete submission of the local churches of the East to Constantinople.

After the death of Patriarch Sylvester in March 1766, the metropolitans started to correspond with each other about his successor, each one proposing himself. The contenders were only reconciled by the candidacy of the former metropolitan of Aleppo, Sophronius al-Kilizi. Of Arab background and a respected church leader, he had lived for many years in Palestine and Constantinople and was not associated with any of the Syrian regional elites. Sophronius, however, refused the heavy burden of patriarchal authority and the Synod of Constantinople, headed by the three Eastern patriarchs, elevated the Greek metropolitan of Aleppo, Philemon, to the patriarchal throne.[207]

The mere fact that Constantinople installed a Greek patriarch did not arouse any protest in Syria. Moreover, the Christians greeted him with enthusiasm, expecting a new patriarch who would improve the community's situation, but they were quickly disillusioned with him. Philemon, "a poorly educated man who loved honors," failed to find a common language with his flock. They were irritated both by the undue financial burdens he placed upon them and by his violations of the rules of monastic life, such as eating meat. With his *wakil* Jiryus, he removed decorations from the Monastery of Saydnaya and sold them to cover his expenses. Making the rounds of his patriarchate, Philemon arrived in Lattakia, where he died suddenly on July 6, 1767. The Christians did not mourn his death and said that it was God's punishment for looting Saydnaya.[208]

As mentioned, during the reign of Philemon, there was a church council that determined, among other things, that the election of a patriarch should take place only with the consent of the synod of bishops. The acts of the council were confirmed by Ecumenical Patriarch Samuel, but after the death of Philemon, he rushed to consecrate a new patriarch of Antioch in Constantinople, without the knowledge of the Syrian metropolitans.[209] While in Syria, candidates for the patriarchate were being discussed (including Greek Metropolitans Ioannicius of Beirut and Parthenius of Tripoli and Macarius Sadaq, who claimed that Sylvester had already appointed him as his successor).[210] In Constantinople, they learned of Philemon's will, in which he wrote about the calamities of the Church of Antioch because of Catholic machinations and about "the great fear that anything could come about from the Arabs and put out the bright beacon of Orthodoxy."[211] Ecumenical Patriarch Samuel, referring to the will of the deceased and the ancient tradition of the primacy of the See of Constantinople over the other Eastern patriarchates (a notion that Samuel tried with all his force to implement), installed over the See of Antioch his protosyngelos Daniel of Chios on August 6, 1767.[212]

Daniel also came to have a difficult relationship with his clergy and laity. His prestige was greatly undermined by his involvement in usury. In addition to this, the patriarch oppressed the Christians in all sorts of ways. The buildup of tensions led to an open rupture between him and the Orthodox of Damascus in 1777. Daniel was in Constantinople at the time (perhaps his departure from Syria had been caused by the conflict with his flock). The residents of Damascus complained to the ʿArab Ecumenical Patriarch Sophronius about Daniel's tyranny, avarice, and greed, allowing for his return to the city under certain conditions. In 1779, the parties were reconciled, at least superficially, "but inwardly, only God knows," according to the skeptical Mikhail Breik.[213] Incidentally, it appears that, at a greater distance from Damascus, the compiler of the Beirut Chronicle was much less emotional about Daniel than was Breik. Under Daniel, the important See of Beirut went from the Greek Ioannicius to the Arab Macarius, which, once again, is not consistent with there having been a policy of Hellenization in the Patriarchate of Antioch. The metropolitan of Tyre and Sidon at the time, the Greek Anthimus al-Saqizi (before 1793–1813) was famous as a translator of Greek theological literature into Arabic. That is, he had a perfect command of Arabic language and writing. Reporting his death, the Beirut Chronicle added, "And all the Christians sorrowed over him."[214] The same chronicle refers to Daniel as "a good man" and "a meek and humble person." It is reported that he incurred heavy debts in the fight with the Uniates and in 1792,[215] the Synod of Constantinople invited him to abdicate on account of old age and his inability to manage his financial affairs and curb the Uniates.[216] The kindly image of the patriarch contrasts sharply with the extremely hostile description of him in the Uniate chronicle *Tarikh Hawadith al-Sham wa-Lubnan*.[217]

Daniel chose as his successor the Cypriot Athanasius, a metropolitan of the Church of Constantinople. He was installed as patriarch with the name Anthimus and went to Damascus.[218] Some authors, such as Foma Dibu-Maluf and Joseph Nasrallah, describe subsequent events as follows: parallel to the installation of Anthimus, the metropolitans of Syria made an attempt to recover the right to elect the patriarch. They nominated as patriarch the metropolitan of Homs, Anthimus al-Khabbaz, a native of Damascus and prominent church leader and scholar. When Anthimus arrived in Syria with the sultan's *berat*, he renounced all claims to the patriarchate for the sake of the peace of the church and reassured the people, who were angered by Constantinople's intervention.[219]

In our opinion, this story is of dubious reliability. Athanasius attempted to contest the patriarchal throne in 1813—this is well documented by ʿAbdallah Trad. But what was the basis for Dib-Maluf's story about Athanasius's rivalry with the Greeks in 1792? Is this not an error, attributing the events of 1813 to the previous patriarchate? On purely practical grounds, an Arab "revolt" in 1792 is unlikely. Daniel left Syria as acting patriarch and abdicated while in Constantinople. The Arabs could not have known anything about the schemes conceived in the Phanar and simply were presented with the fact of the arrival of the new patriarch in Syria.

Nevertheless, under that Greek patriarch, Arabs continued to occupy the most important episcopal sees and play an active role in the life of the church. In 1804, as a result of conflicts with the Muslim authorities, Athanasius al-Khabbaz, a powerful and ambitious leader, left the metropolitan See of Homs and was elected to the See of Beirut, where he became famous for his scholarly works and pastoral activities.

Patriarch Anthimus died on July 20, 1813, during an epidemic of the plague that claimed a quarter of the population of Damascus. Metropolitan Athanasius, "full of ambition and proud of his scholarship and wealth," as the chronicle says of him, started to seek election to the patriarchate. However, while the Syrian metropolitans debated who among themselves was the most worthy, in the Phanar, they acted extremely quickly. Already by August 10, a metropolitan of the See of Constantinople, the Bulgarian Seraphim (1813–1823), was enthroned on the See of Antioch. The Beirut Chronicle of ʿAbdallah Trad, whose portrayal of interethnic relations in the patriarchate is uniformly politically correct, strongly emphasizes the love of the newly elected patriarch for his chief rival, Athanasius al-Khabbaz. Seraphim was impressed by the metropolitan's scholarship and his perfect command of Greek. Even in Trad's account, however, one feels the conscious Arab identity when he says of the sudden death of Athanasius in April 1814, "the Arab Church [*sic*] mourned the setting of this sun."[220]

In sum, we can say that the scale of the influence of the Ecumenical Patriarchate on the life of the Middle Eastern churches and the degree of their Hellenization is often exaggerated in the scholarly literature. Historians mistakenly project on the sixteenth and seventeenth centuries the situation in the eighteenth and early nineteenth centuries, which is indeed characterized by a high degree of Phanariot hegemony over the Orthodox *millet*. The Greek domination in the Patriarchates of Jerusalem and—partially—Antioch had both its plusses and minuses. The latter include the fact that the Arab Orthodox of Palestine were deprived of their own elites and for centuries were barred from having an active role in history and were transformed from the subject to the object of policy. In Syria, the situation of the Arab Christians was much better. They always had their own higher clergy, intellectuals, theologians, teachers, and preachers and developed their own Arabic-speaking Orthodox culture. On the other hand, the rapprochement between the Middle Eastern churches and the Orthodox world of the Balkans led to an influx of "new blood" into the Patriarchates of Antioch and Jerusalem. This is reflected in the regular "replenishment of personnel" in the clergy of Syria and Palestine coming from Greece who were sometimes energetic, highly educated, and—most important—respected in the Orthodox *millet* and throughout the empire. Their influence contributed to the material support of the churches of the Arab East by their coreligionists in the Balkans and, especially, the Danubian principalities. Constant financial investment, cultural cooperation, and a replenishment of human resources allowed the clergy of the Levant not only to survive and defend their interests in the holy places of Palestine, but also to have an unprecedentedly active role in the history of the foreign policy of the Orthodox Middle East.

CHAPTER 7

The Holy Places

The Latin ecclesiastic ... threw the Gospel from the Orthodox altar onto the ground.... Both candle-lighters were already fighting each other with candle-sticks, while the Latin priest stood silently in white vestments at the Manger. Metropolitan Dionysius, not entering into the Grotto, urged the worshippers to go in there to beat the Latins, a hieromonk took out sticks and clubs from the cathedral sanctuary and gave them to the worshippers.... One Greek seized our Gospel forged from silver, jumped at the priest in white clothing and shouting out, "so you dishonor our Gospel," began to beat him on the head with that very book with all his might and bloodied his head.

—Porphyry Uspensky, 1848

CHRISTIAN COMMUNITIES AROUND THE HOLY PLACES

Throughout the history of Christian civilization, the Holy Land, Palestine, has been at its sacred center as the object of reverent veneration and the aspiration of millions of pilgrims. The places associated with the life and death of the Savior and other monuments of biblical history were an age-old bone of contention between the Christian churches. Possession of the holy places of Palestine by a particular denomination greatly increased its weight in the Christian world, reinforced its claims to right belief, "birthright," leadership, and direct continuity with the illustrious era of early Christianity. By virtue of this, the struggle between Christians of various sects for the holy places became almost the chief content of the history of the Orthodox Church in the Arab East for centuries.

The main objects of rivalry were the Church of the Holy Sepulchre in Jerusalem and the Church of the Nativity in Bethlehem. In the Ottoman period, the Church of the Holy Sepulchre (also called the Church of the Resurrection) was a chaotic cluster of buildings, over which dominated the half-ruined bell tower of the Greek Patriarchate and two domes, the rotunda of the Church of the Holy Sepulchre, and the Greek Church of the Resurrection (the Katholikon) adjacent to the rotunda to the east. The entrance into the Church of the Holy Sepulchre was from the south side. Immediately behind it was the marble slab Stone of Anointing, decorated with oil lamps and multi-meter-long candlesticks. To the right was the hill of Golgotha, the site of the Crucifixion, where there were thirteen steps. Golgotha was divided into two chapels, the Catholic Chapel of the Nailing to the Cross to the south and the Orthodox Chapel of the Elevation of the Cross to the north. Northwest of Golgotha was the main sanctuary, the Holy Sepulchre, placed inside a small chapel, the Holy Edicule, consisting of two rooms, the outer Chapel of the Angel and the actual chapel of the Holy Sepulchre. The Holy Edicule was covered by the giant dome of the rotunda, along the perimeter of which were located the chapels of the various Christian confessions, mostly to the west. Along the north and southeast, there are a number of places of worship (the Prison of Christ, the Pillar of Reproach, the Chapel of the Separation of Robes, etc.). To the east, the Holy Edicule was bordered by the Greek Basilica of the Resurrection, the largest and most luxurious of all the churches belonging to the complex of the Holy Sepulchre. Abutting the northern part of the rotunda was a Franciscan monastery and several chapels belonging to the Catholics. In the eastern part of the church lay the underground Armenian Church of Sts Constantine and Helen. In its southeastern part, even deeper underground, was the chapel of the Finding of the Cross, the place where, according to legend, the Empress Helen found the cross on which Christ was crucified. Outside, on the side of the gates, toward the church were the Coptic and Abyssinian structures (to the right) and the building of the Greek Patriarchate (to the left).

Among the most important shrines located in the vicinity of Jerusalem include the hill of Holy Sion, the place of the Last Supper, the Dormition of the Theotokos, and other memorable events from Old Testament and Christian history. The church that had at some point been erected over the place of the Dormition of the Theotokos had lain in ruins since at least the fourteenth century. Farther up the hill, at the site of the upper room of the Last Supper and the Descent of the Holy Spirit upon the Apostles, a Franciscan monastery had existed since the 1330s. However, in the mid-sixteenth century, the Muslim authorities seized the site from the monks, under the pretext of the tombs of Kings David and Solomon, who are revered in the Muslim tradition, being located there.

In Gethsemane, at the bottom of the Mount of Olives, adjoining Jerusalem from the East, located in the underground Church of the Dormition of the Theotokos was her tomb. At the top of the Mount of Olives was the former Church of the Dormition, facing a mosque.[1] The remaining Christian monuments of the Mount of Olives had disappeared or fallen into ruin by the Early Ottoman era.

The Basilica of the Nativity in Bethlehem, built by Justinian and the oldest church in Palestine, amazed travelers with its not yet fully lost Byzantine splendor. Adjoining the church from different sides were Greek (from the southeast), Armenian (southwest), and Latin (from the north) monasteries. Under the altar of the Church of the Nativity lies the Holy Grotto, the place where Jesus was born. In the grotto were several doors (from the north, south, and west) belonging to various Christian denominations.

The Christian shrines of Galilee did not spark competition between the Catholic and the Orthodox, because the Western and Eastern Christian traditions locate the sites of the Annunciation and the Transfiguration in different places. Other areas of Palestine that are important for Christians for commemorations, such as the Judean Desert and the banks of the Jordan, were controlled by Bedouin bandits and a permanent Christian presence there was impossible.

It appears that mutual contact between Christian confessions in the holy places was itself sufficient cause for tensions between them. The presence of Christians of other confessions and their unusual liturgical customs at the Holy Sepulchre often irritated fanatical worshipers. In the early fifteenth century, the Greek metropolitan Daniel of Ephesus wrote that the heretics built their chapels around the Holy Sepulchre "in order to chant, or rather to anger the Godhead."[2] The caricature of the Ethiopian and Coptic church processions in the Holy Sepulchre by Vasily Poznyakov is well-known: "and beating on tamborines, jumping and dancing around like minstrels; and some were going backwards, walking and jumping. And we wondered at God's love for mankind how he bears such things: it would be impossible for a person to see such madness even in a market."[3] Only a few pilgrims were able to revise their religious stereotypes through personal contact with members of other confessions, as was noticeably the case with Ivan Lukyanov, who wrote,

and having seen the Armenians and the Armenian women: how great was the surprise to me, a sinner … how they weep in the Holy Sepulchre, for their tears lie in puddles on the slabs of the tomb; … wonder of wonders! Although their faith is heretical, we are astonished by their zeal.[4]

In cases of simultaneous worship at Palestinian shrines by clergy of various confessions, worshippers perceived the neighboring, "heretical" service as a provocation. Porphyry Uspensky mentions that at the Feast of Nativity in 1842, the Copts were so noisy in their chapel at the basilica in Bethlehem that they drowned out the Greeks' singing and reading. "The Metropolitan of Bethlehem twice sent his monk to them and ordered them to be quiet. At first they felt silent, but then they once again started shouting."[5] The third time, the patriarchal *kavas* bodyguard was sent to the Copts and he dispersed them with a whip and scattered their "heretical" garments on the floor. As the *kavas* (bodyguard) told Porphyry, the metropolitan gave him his hand to kiss and "could not have been more pleased" with him.[6] In the early 1830s, a chronicler from the Brotherhood of the Holy Sepulchre complained that during the Greek liturgy in the Church of the Holy Sepulchre the Armenians "began to do the same thing in their place, but loudly, as was their custom, and with disorderly and inharmonious shouts."[7] Forty years earlier, Melety described the Armenian liturgy in similar terms:

> The Armenians annoyed me with their singing.... They shouted with all their might, with extraordinary strain: ... At Matins my hearing was met with a great unrest and heaviness from the sound of the Armenian simandron which went on from the second of our kathismas until nearly halfway through the canons.[8]

Grigorovich-Barsky, describing a similar occurrence of simultaneous worship by different confessions, remarked, "The Romans cover up and drown out all voices with their soulless organ; the Arabs of the Greek faith at the transfer of the gifts always ... cry out with all their strength in opposition to the Romans: the universal faith of the Orthodox Christians."[9] The Catholics perfectly understood the power of the aesthetic impact of organ music[10] and used it as an element of religious propaganda. Ivan Lukyanov recalls his visit to the Church of the Holy Sepulchre, "then no one [from the Orthodox pilgrims] could resist listening to these organs; those dogs played so smoothly and sweetly, and by their playing many in Jerusalem turned away from the Greek faith and to the papist faith."[11] The Eastern Christians strongly fought against locating an organ in the church, not missing the opportunity to request in the Muslim court that the instrument be disassembled or at least that its volume be reduced.

The only asymmetric response that the Orthodox could give to the organ was a simandron of iron and wood, which produced even more of a rumble. However, the time for rapping on the semantron was clearly negotiated with the Ottoman authorities and did not coincide with the Latin masses; to drown out the mass, the Greeks would have to occasionally purchase permission for extra time.[12]

It was only among the later pilgrims with a European education and a somewhat-cosmopolitan mentality that the parallel Orthodox and Armenian liturgies evoked positive emotions: "And the spectacle of these two faiths was majestic, in foreign languages, with various ceremonies glorifying … the same wonderful resurrection of their common God."[13]

However, almost all these negative comments belong to pilgrims unaccustomed to the ethnographic realities of Jerusalem. Monks who lived for a long time in Palestine became accustomed to the presence of "heretics" and peacefully coexisted with them on the everyday level. Despite the struggle between confessions, the bishops of various persuasions always considered it necessary to maintain outwardly friendly relations among themselves, exchanging visits, venerating icons in "heretical" churches, holding meals together, and, even during the bitterest conflicts, disingenuously trying to convince each other of their own irenicism.[14] Conflicts over the holy places were not caused by everyday xenophobia but rather by higher religious–political considerations.

The Origins of the Conflict: Who Is at Fault?

From ancient times, all the Palestinian shrines were in the possession of the Orthodox Church. V. V. Barthold proved that during the Early Arab period this fact was widely perceived as a given and no competition over the places of worship arose.[15] After the Crusader conquest of Jerusalem, control over the places of worship passed, naturally, to the Catholics. Subsequently, to strengthen his alliance with Byzantium, the king of Jerusalem returned some sections of the Church of the Holy Sepulchre to the Orthodox. At the same time, apparently expecting to conclude unions with various Eastern Christian churches, the Latins allocated altars in the church for the Syrian Jacobites, Armenians, and Nestorians.

After Salah al-Din regained the city from the Crusaders, the Catholics lost their privileged position in the Holy Sepulchre. However, the Byzantine emperor's desire for the church to return to being the undivided property of the Orthodox Church was also not satisfied. Under the Ayyubids and Mamluks, the picture of the Christian presence in the Holy Land was even more complicated: the "Greeks" (as the sources call the multiethnic clergy of the Patriarchate of Jerusalem) had the Basilica of the Resurrection, one of the main elements of the complex of the Holy Sepulchre, as well as a number of other sections of the church. The Georgians were a separate community within the Orthodox Church, with their own possessions in the church. Among the Monophysite communities represented at the Holy Sepulchre, the Ethiopians enjoyed a privileged status in the Mamluk state and received generous alms from the kings of Ethiopia. The Armenians had a strong position in Jerusalem and owned the enormous Monastery of St James and many sections of the Church of the Holy Sepulchre. The Catholics, who seem to have lost their possessions in Palestine under Baybars, had the opportunity to return to the Holy Land in 1333 or 1335. At the request of the king of Aragon, Franciscan monks obtained possession of the Monastery of Mount Sion, as well as a number of prestigious sections of the Palestinian places of worship. Apart from the aforementioned ethnoreligious groups, in the Church of the Holy Sepulchre, there were areas for Copts, Syrian Jacobites, and Nestorians, with altars for Maronites (from the fourteenth century) and Serbs (from the fifteenth century) appearing later.[16] In the early Ottoman period, the Nestorian community of Jerusalem gradually died out and lost its possessions in the church, while the section for the Maronites was absorbed by the Latins.

From the evidence of pilgrims from the fourteenth century, it seems that the Edicule of the Holy Sepulchre was the common property of all Christians and did not belong to any one confession.[17] In the fourteenth and fifteenth centuries, the main feast in Jerusalem was the receiving of the Holy Fire on Holy Saturday by the Orthodox Patriarch, from whom the heads of the other confessions received the fire.[18]

Contrary to popular belief, according to which it was under the Ottomans that the problem of the holy places became a source of endless conflict, there is no doubt that the struggle between Christians for the revered holy places or primacy in liturgy took place in the pre-Ottoman period. Already in the decrees of Sultan Baybars, attempts by the "Greeks" to prevent the Latin liturgy in the church are mentioned.[19] Because of the scarcity of sources, we can identify only a few episodes of inter-Christian rivalry, such as the struggle for possession of Golgotha.

During the fourteenth and fifteenth centuries, this shrine repeatedly changed hands. In 1333, it was held by Georgians; in the middle of the fourteenth century, it was held by the Armenians. Pilgrims describe the same situation in the last quarter of the fourteenth century, until Ignaty Smolnyanin in 1395 and an anonymous Greek *proskynetarion* from the end of the fourteenth century, who again describe Golgotha as belonging to the Georgians. After 1396, there are mutually conflicting decrees from the *qadi* of Jerusalem and Sultan Barquq, the former confirming the right of the Armenians to possess Golgotha and the latter protecting the Franciscans' right to Golgotha from the encroachments of the Greeks and Georgians without mentioning the Armenians. Here there is an obvious analogy to the situation in the Ottoman period, when rival confessions obtained from Muslim court the documents in support of their rights that in no way canceled similar documents held by other churches. The reality of the situation is not reflected in the legal regulations, but rather in the evidence from the pilgrimage literature. The Latin pilgrim Fra Noe (turn of the fourteenth and fifteenth centuries) and the Russian monk Zosima (1420) wrote about the Armenian presence at Golgotha. A new surge in the Armenian-Georgian rivalry occurred in the 1420s. By 1439, according to some accounts, the Armenians refused to continue the fight and lost Golgotha to the Georgians. However, in the sources there are vague notions that during the fifteenth century the Georgians lost Golgotha and then regained it one last time in 1475.[20]

The second most important shrine, the Basilica of the Nativity in Bethlehem, was also divided among the Christian confessions. The Franks attached their monastery and its church to Justinian's basilica from the north. The Orthodox held their services at the main altar of the basilica, while in the church's other chapels there were Ethiopians, Nestorians, and Jacobites (by which the sources most likely mean the Copts) and outside the church in the 1330s there were Georgian and Maronite altars. The Grotto of the Nativity, under the altar of the basilica, was held by the Franciscans. Although Ignaty Smolnyanin claimed in 1395 that "Franciscan" services were held at the Holy Manger and Greek services at the Holy Grotto, all other sources of the fourteenth and fifteenth centuries only speak of Catholic services in the Grotto.[21]

The Tomb of the Theotokos in Gethsemane was similarly divided among the different communities, with Latins, Orthodox, Ethiopians, Copts, and others serving on its altars in turn.[22]

If we correctly interpret the accounts of Western pilgrims at the turn of the fifteenth and sixteenth centuries, it is possible to conclude that during this period there was a sharp increase in Latin influence in the holy places: the Franciscans decorated the Edicule of the Holy Sepulchre on their own and controlled access to it by clergy of other churches. There are also mentions of a Catholic altar and lamps at Golgotha.[23] It is possible that these successes on the part of the Franciscans were due to the progressive decline and impoverishment of their Orthodox rivals.

According to Catholic historiography, at the time of the Ottoman conquest of Palestine, the Holy Sepulchre, the Holy Grotto of Bethlehem, the southern portion of Golgotha, the Stone of Anointing, the chapel of the Appearance of Christ to the Myrrh-Bearing Women, and the chapel of the Finding of the Cross all belonged to the Franciscans. The Catholics controlled these holy places throughout the sixteenth century and it was only in the 1630s that the Greeks upset the status quo and undertook a massive campaign to return the Palestinian shrines to their possession.[24]

The Orthodox version of events, naturally, has nothing to do with the previous account. It was formulated at the turn of the seventeenth and eighteenth centuries by Patriarch Dositheus of Jerusalem and repeated by the Greek chroniclers active in Palestine in the early nineteenth century, Maximus Simais and Procopius Nazianzen. Another prominent Greek historian from among the clergy of Jerusalem of that era, Neophytus of Cyprus, wrote independently of Dositheus and his vision of interconfessional relations in Early Ottoman Palestine is markedly different in detail from the other authors' account.

According to the Greek version, when Salah al-Din expelled the Crusaders from Jerusalem, the holy places were placed under the control of the Orthodox. The Syrian Jacobites, Maronites, Copts, and Ethiopians also retained (or regained) their possessions in the Church of the Holy Sepulchre. During the Mamluk era, the Georgian and Serbian presence in Palestine especially stands out, although the Greek chroniclers do not like to recall the Georgians' possessions in the Church of the Holy Sepulchre. Under the Mamluks and the Ottomans, the Orthodox Church enjoyed primacy in the holy places guaranteed by a decree supposedly issued by the Caliph 'Umar and confirmed by *firmans* of the sultans Mehmed the Conqueror (to whom the patriarch made a special visit for this purpose in 1458), Selim I upon the capture of Jerusalem, and Suleiman the Magnificent in 1528.[25] Orthodox authors emphasized the absence from pre-Ottoman Palestine of their rivals, the Franks and Armenians, who did not dare to appear in the holy places on account of the hostility of the Muslims and the political instability in the Middle East. The Latins and Armenians only appeared in Palestine after 1516 (in another variant, after 1453) and, at that time, they showed deep respect for the Orthodox patriarch, but they did not possess any areas of the Church of the Holy Sepulchre. Subsequently, however, through a series of treacherous intrigues, these communities managed to gain a foothold in the holy places, bribing the Ottoman administration and putting significant pressure on the Greeks. The chroniclers attribute the beginning of the conflict between the Orthodox and the Latins to the middle of the sixteenth century. In 1580, the Franciscans, who had given "an immense amount of money to the judges in Jerusalem," obtained possession of the Holy Sepulchre, Golgotha, Bethlehem, and other places of worship.[26]

A similar historical mythology existed among the Armenians, starting with the legendary agreement between Emperor Constantine and King Tiridates and Gregory the Illuminator and ending with *firmans* of early Ottoman sultans granting privileges to the Armenian Church in the holy places of Palestine.[27]

Catholic authors call the *firmans* of the sultans of the fifteenth and sixteenth centuries crude forgeries, fabricated in the 1630s to substantiate the claims of the Orthodox to possession of the holy places. They are, according to Oded Peri, "replete with so many factual inaccuracies, as well as historical, stylistic and textual anachronisms, that there can be no doubt as to their being fake."[28] It seems that this statement is close to the truth. The *ashtiname* of the Caliph 'Umar and the *firman* of Mehmed the Conqueror are indisputably apocryphal[29] and the decrees of Selim I and especially Suleiman the Magnificent are full of absurdities and anachronisms. Thus, the document given by Sultan Suleiman (1520–1566) to Patriarch Germanus (1534–1579) at his (the sultan's?) accession dates back to the year 933 AH (=1528). Three blunders in a single sentence.

Thus, the Greek chronicles of Dositheus and Neophytus of Cyprus, which, for all their subjectivity, describe the course of the struggle for the holy places from the second third of the seventeenth century to the beginning of the nineteenth century in sufficient detail and apparent accuracy, clearly cannot be considered reliable sources for the pre-Ottoman period. It is not clear how trustworthy these chronicles are for the period from 1517 to 1630.

The Sixteenth Century

Turning to other sources, we see quite a contradictory picture. In the late 1530s, Patriarch Germanus wrote to Russia about his construction activities in Jerusalem, "And now I … again we have constructed two church roofs: the first at the Holy Sepulchre we have covered [the church] of the three-day Resurrection, and the second—also at the [church of the] Resurrection where Mary Magdalene met the Lord."[30] In the first case, he is clearly talking about the Holy Edicule. This document confirms the report of later chroniclers about Germanus's reconstruction of the Edicule, which he fortified with marble columns and covered with a lead roof.[31] Around the same time, in 1555, the head of the Franciscan monastery, Bonifatius Crassi, in turn, renovated the Holy Edicule, in spite of opposition from the Greeks.[32] It appears that control over the Holy Sepulchre was contested and passed from hand to hand.

The Greek chroniclers' assertions of the primacy of the Orthodox Church among the other Christian communities are partly supported by Ottoman documents of the sixteenth century, which identify the Orthodox patriarch as the chief of the Christian bishops in Jerusalem. On one occasion, he is even referred to as *bitriq al-Nasara* ("patriarch of the Christians").[33] The Orthodox patriarch conducted the main ritual of the annual cycle of worship in Jerusalem, receiving the Holy Fire on Holy Saturday.

This is confirmed both by a *proskynetarion* of the fifteenth century[34] and by Vasily Poznyakov, who left a vivid description of the Paschal liturgy in 1560. When Bonifatius's Franciscan guardians attempted to enter the Edicule before Orthodox Patriarch Germanus, the Sinaite elders Joseph and Malachi and the Sabbaite elder Moses, according to Poznyakov, "grabbed him [Bonifatius] and did not let him into the tomb."[35] This elder Malachi appears in Poznyakov's description of going up Mount Sinai, when Malachi carried on his shoulders the feeble Patriarch Joachim of Alexandria for the entire way.[36] That is, he was a physically strong man capable of stopping by force the "heretical" hierarch from encroaching on the privileges of the Orthodox. A curious detail to the ethnocultural picture of the Christian presence in the holy places is that the elder Moses, who served as an interpreter for Vasily Poznyakov, was a Serb, and Bonifatius's guardian came from the area of Ragusa (Dubrovnik).[37] Grappling in front of the doors of the Edicule, they may have exchanged insults in their shared native tongue.

The Greek chronicles have preserved some echoes of the struggle for the holy places under Patriarch Germanus. The Armenians encroached on the Ethiopians' section in the northern corner of the chapel of the Finding of the Cross.[38] The Franciscans received from the Jerusalem authorities the right to hold services on the site of the Descent from the Cross (the Stone of Anointing), where they established a wooden altar, which the following year they replaced with one in bronze that was so heavy that rivals would not be able to move it. Patriarch Germanus was absent from Jerusalem at this time. According to Dositheus, he was in Transjordan, where there remained a compact and prosperous Christian population. Upon returning to the holy city, Germanus personally removed the Frankish altar from the church and then went to Istanbul, where he received a *firman* from the sultan about the privileges of the Orthodox.[39] According to Neophytus, at the time that the Latin altar was installed, Germanus was in Istanbul, from which he returned to Palestine with the sultan's decree "granting the church to his disposal" and, gathering together the Orthodox, he commanded them to remove the Frankish altar.[40] This first Greek evidence for conflict with the Latins is not dated, but from the context, it is clear that it took place before 1551. Germanus is known to have stayed in Constantinople in 1543–1544 and the stay may have lasted longer.[41] Apparently, then, in the mid-1540s, there was a conflict around the site of the Descent from the Cross. In 1551, the Franks nevertheless established their altar in the Maronite section, in the northern part of the church by the Chapel of the Apparition.[42]

Once again in 1551/1552 or 1561, the Franks were expelled from Mount Sion by the Muslim authorities. According to the Greek chronicles, they appealed for help to the Orthodox patriarch, who leased them the Monastery of St John the Theologian, which was renamed the Monastery of the Savior. Later, in 1590, the Catholics obtained full ownership of the monastery and ceased payments to the Greek patriarch.[43] As mentioned earlier, according to Greek information, the decisive battle for the holy places took place in 1580. The chronicler from the Brotherhood of the Holy Sepulchre wrote that the Latins, "having given an immense amount of money to the judges in Jerusalem" took from the Orthodox all of Golgotha, the Chapel of St Helen, the Greek part of the church in Bethlehem, and the right to hold services in the Holy Grotto. The new patriarch of Jerusalem, Sophronius, spent a great deal on gifts to Ottoman officials in Istanbul but was only able to regain half of Golgotha.[44] It seems, in fact, that the Latins had already controlled most of these places of worship for no less than a century. At the same time, the Eastern Christians kept the right to worship in the holy places and the Orthodox patriarch, as before, was the first to light candles from the Holy Fire. However, with the introduction of the Gregorian calendar by the Catholic Church in 1582, the Catholics declared the Holy Fire to be a hoax and ceased to participate in the ceremony. As the pilgrim Serapion wrote in 1751 about the Franks, "When the grace ... of the Holy Spirit comes by Greek prayer in the form of fire ... then they, incapable of looking upon such holiness, are like bats and hide themselves in cubbies out of shame and blasphemy."[45]

THEOPHANES AND PAISIUS: A GREEK TRIUMPH

The struggle for the holy places continued over the following decades. In 1607, the Orthodox Patriarch Theophanes, with the assistance of the Sublime Porte, removed the Latins from the southern half of Golgotha, but in 1611, he lost both that half of the hill and possession of the church in Bethlehem, as the Franks won the Jerusalem authorities over to their side, "reinforcing their petition," in the words of Neophytus, "with plenty of gold and gifts."[46] In 1614, the Catholics' privileges were reaffirmed by the Ottomans at the request of Western rulers.

Blind mutual hostility between the Christian confessions in the holy places, skirmishes, and mutual complaints over impediments to the administration of worship were a constant phenomenon. Periodically, this smoldering confrontation developed into large-scale conflicts with a radical redistribution of properties in the holy places. One of the most heated decades in Jerusalem was the 1630s, when Patriarch Theophanes went on a decisive offensive against the Franks. In 1628, the patriarch was able to regain the Holy Grotto in Bethlehem. Perhaps associated with this confrontation was the arrest of Theophanes by the pasha of Jerusalem because of a denunciation by the Catholics around 1629.

Greek chronicles report that the pasha threw the patriarch into prison and was even preparing to execute him. However, the local *qadi* prevented this and released the prisoner. He lived for some time secretly in his cell and then fled the city dressed in women's clothes. The pasha ordered that Theophanes be caught and killed. The patriarch was caught in Acre, but he bought off his pursuers and reached Istanbul where he was able to exonerate himself.[47]

The office of pasha, however, changed often, as did the alternating successes and failures of warring confessions. According to Latin sources, in 1631, the *qadi* and two successive pashas (one of them a Greek renegade) supported the Orthodox and persecuted the Catholics such that the abbot of the Franciscans was forced to flee to Damascus. In early 1632, because of bribery and the influence of the Venetian ambassador, the pro-Latin Muhammad Pasha was appointed in Jerusalem. In the summer of the same year, he returned to the Catholics all rights to Bethlehem and threw the Orthodox patriarch into prison (the pasha was angry that over four months the patriarch had brought the former governor more gifts than in the previous twelve years, which is why the *sanjak* had become more expensive in Istanbul). In late 1632, the secretary of the patriarch of Constantinople came to Jerusalem to help the Orthodox and after him came another *qadi* who had already been bribed by the Greeks. The litigation began again and the key to the Holy Grotto of Bethlehem changed hands four times. "Seeing the failure of his mediation," reported the Latin source, "Muhammad Pasha, who had grown tired of all this strife, refused to continue the proceedings and permitted the disputing parties to appeal directly to Constantinople."[48]

On May 31, 1633, the patriarch of Jerusalem arrived in the capital to participate in the proceedings. Grand Vizier Ibrahim and the Rumelian *qadi 'askar* vacillated in their preferences depending on the size of the bribes offered by the opposing parties. While Ecumenical Patriarch Cyril Lucaris imposed a special tax on his community to bribe the authorities, the French and Venetian diplomats were more parsimonious and the Franciscans eventually lost in July 1634.[49] According to the Greek authors, the grand vizier was inclined to support the Franks, but after he departed to war with Iran, the *qaimaqam* (deputy) of the vizier, the Albanian Mustafa Pasha, "a friend of the Greeks," helped the Orthodox to prevail.[50]

The scales of Ottoman justice swung several times thereafter. Gregory, the nephew of the Patriarch Theophanes, who at one time had studied at Rome, converted to Catholicism after a quarrel with his uncle and wrote a denunciation of the Greek patriarchs, accusing them, among other things, of illegal contacts with Moscow. Perhaps because of the influence of the Sublime Porte, the Franks regained all rights to the Holy Grotto and Golgotha in March 1636. But by October 1637, the Orthodox succeeded in obtaining final confirmation of their predominance in Bethlehem, and a little later, they regained possession over the jewel of Palestinian shrines, the Holy Sepulchre.[51]

At the same time, another knot of contradictions was tied: the Armenians began to claim primacy in Jerusalem. In 1633, with the support of the Jerusalem authorities and then the Sublime Porte, they secured for themselves some monasteries claimed by the Greeks.[52] The following year, the Armenian community launched a direct challenge to the Greek bishops, demanding primacy in the administration of the rite of receiving the Holy Fire on Holy Saturday.

The struggle of the various confessions for priority in worship at the Holy Sepulchre was one of the most important facets of the problem of the status of the holy places. Claims to precedence in worship at the shrines flowed into the struggle for possession of these places and vice versa. As mentioned, after adopting the Gregorian calendar, the Catholics lost interest in the phenomenon of the Holy Fire. However, the differences between the Gregorian and Julian calendars and the church festivals did not solve the problem of the coexistence of the competing confessions. Often the Catholic Easter corresponded with the Orthodox Palm Sunday, and so once again, the question would arise of accommodating two services in the confined space around the Edicule in the Holy Sepulchre.[53]

The Armenian Church celebrates Easter according to a calendar that almost entirely coincides with the Greek calendar apart from four times in a 532-year cycle, when the Greek and Armenian Easters are separated by a gap (occurring on April 6 and 13, respectively).[54] In Armenian church terminology, this situation is called a "curved Easter." In such a year when passions escalated to the extreme, the Holy Fire acted as proof of the truth of the doctrine of the church on whose Easter it made its appearance. The Armenians and the Orthodox had clashed on this basis since the twelfth century. The next such discrepancy in the date of Easter took place in 1634. According to the Greek chroniclers, the Armenians convinced the Jerusalem authorities with generous gifts that theirs was the true calendar. On the eve of the Greek "curved Easter," Janissaries cordoned off the Edicule and drove away the Orthodox worshippers; in another version, they were not even allowed into the church. As Patriarch Theophanes wrote to Moscow in November of the same year,

> and so foreigners with arms guarded the yard ... and drove out the Christians, who stood in sorrow with tears and at that hour arose something like a certain voice and an earthquake, and the holy fire appeared from the crevices of the roof of the Holy Sepulchre and illumined the entire church and blinded the enemies, and the infidel people guarding poured out water lest the fire flares up and they could not manage anything and the fire appeared three times ... and then the Armenians saw that the

Lord appeared in Holy Fire and they, covering their shame, gave out bags of money to the infidels so that no one would say that the holy fire appeared.[55]

From the Orthodox perspective, it was the most significant event in the entire centuries-old struggle over the places of worship. Later pilgrim writers embellished it with bright colors and fictional details, sometimes very far from the reports of primary sources. In particular, they transmitted the story that after they expelled the Greeks, the Armenians attempted themselves to receive the Holy Fire "by their accursed faith they conjured and they walked with a cross near to the edge of the Tomb of the Lord ... and there was nothing."[56] When it finally descended, the fire exploded around the church like ball lightening, hitting the Turkish pasha in the chest and knocking him over. It passed through the wall of the church and with a roar split a column at the entrance (the left column at the gate of the church is indeed cracked). It then ignited a censer standing on the ground or a bunch of candles in the hand of the Greek patriarch (a century later, few remembered that Theophanes was not in Jerusalem at the time).[57]

According to a late legend, the Ottomans, terrified of the miraculous phenomenon, returned primacy in the Holy Sepulchre to the Greeks. "The Armenians," wrote Ippolit Vishenski, "were driven from the church, and the vicar of the Armenian patriarch and whoever was in his rank—they were all stripped naked ... and from that hour the Armenian had no honor."[58]

In fact, the Armenians do not seem to have felt defeated. They moved their dispute with the Greeks to Istanbul, where they were able to rely on their compatriot the Grand Vizier Ibrahim as well as a long association with the Armenians of the sultan's favorite Abaza Pasha, who was promised 60,000 ducats. Taking the side of the Greeks was the Rumelian *qadi 'askar* (one of the main Islamic judges) and the former Christian *bostanji bashi* (the head of one of the elite Janissary units), who arranged a meeting between Murad IV and Greek monks, who informed the sultan of Abaza Pasha's having been bribed by the Armenians. According to the Greek chroniclers, once Murad made sure of the truth of the charges, he executed his favorite and three Armenian elders.[59] In fact, the true reason that the pasha was executed had little connection to this. A recent rebel and opponent of the Janissaries' domination, Abaza Pasha already had too many enemies at court.[60] In any case, the Greeks won this round of the fight, and in August 1634, they received a *firman* from the sultan for their primacy in the worship at the Holy Sepulchre.[61]

Ten years later, in 1644, the Armenians renewed their claims to the holy places and received a plot in the Grotto of the Nativity in Bethlehem. Three months later, the Greeks managed to cancel the sultan's *firman*, but the Armenians continued the struggle for a presence in the shrines of Bethlehem. Then, in the 1640s, there began a long legal case between the Greeks and Armenians over inheriting the Palestinian property of the Ethiopians, whose community had almost entirely died from the plague. The Greek patriarch, who by that time had just gained control over the Serbian legacy in the Holy Land, pointed to his status as the head of all the Eastern Christian Churches in Jerusalem. The Armenians referred to the common Monophysite faith that they shared with the Ethiopians.[62] During those years, there did not cease to be disputes over primacy at the Paschal services. Arseny Sukhanov, who was in Jerusalem at Easter in 1652, wrote that Patriarch Paisius first pushed his way into the Edicule, but that the Copts and Armenians tried to join him, "and not a little they tousled with the church warden, and the warden held the doors as such with his comrades, and did not let the Armenian patriarch in, but stood, pressed against the door."[63]

As a counterbalance to the *berat* that Paisius possessed from the sultan, granting him leadership over the Serbian, Georgian, and Ethiopian communities, in 1653, Armenian Patriarch Astvatsatur received a *berat* subordinating to him all the Monophysite communities of the holy city, and in 1654, he took possession over the legacy of the Ethiopians in Bethlehem and Jerusalem.[64] The dispute between the Armenians and Greeks over the Ethiopians' possessions, the Holy Grotto of Bethlehem, and the reception of the Holy Fire reached its peak in 1655–1657, when the disputed areas changed hands several times. Greek chroniclers claim that the Armenians reported to the Sublime Porte about the Patriarch Pasius's contacts with Russia and his creating the "Crown of the Emperor Constantine" for the Russian tsar. The story of this mitre nearly cost Paisius his head.[65]

In the end, the Greeks received a decision in their favor from the sultan. This was made possible by the support of Grand Vizier Mehmed Köprülü, an Albanian from an Orthodox family who had only converted to Islam at the age of twenty. However, the vizier's protection was costly. The Armenians, in turn, bribed Köprülü's old enemy, the ruler of Gaza and Jerusalem, Husayn Pasha, who, along with the pasha of Damascus, long hindered the implementation of the vizier's decrees. In 1657, the Greeks finally managed to push the Armenians out of the Holy Grotto of Bethlehem and to retain the majority of the Ethiopians' possessions. However, taking advantage of internal strife among the Greeks (Patriarch Pasius's feud with his vicar in Jerusalem, Anthimus, and the grand dragoman of the Porte, Panagiotis), in 1660, the Armenians secured their rights to the Monastery of St James, which until then the Greeks had considered to be their property, which was on loan to the Armenian patriarch.[66]

At the same time, the Ottomans were prepared to meet the Armenians' demands for equality with the Greeks in participating in the ritual of receiving the Holy Fire. In April 1657, having grown tired of fruitless struggle, representatives of the Greek and Armenian churches in Jerusalem entered into an agreement to host the ritual jointly.[67] At a later point, the date of which is uncertain, the Greeks were once again able to assert their primacy in this most important ceremony. At Easter 1697, the English traveler Henry Maundrell witnessed the litigation of the Greeks and Armenians before the *qadi* of Jerusalem, when "the former endeavor[ed] to exclude the latter from having any share in this miracle."[68] The Protestant observer was very skeptical toward Eastern Christians and did not believe in the miracle of the Holy Fire. This explains the hostile tone of his description:

> Both parties having expended (as I was informed) five thousand dollars between them, in this foolish controversy; the cadi at last gave sentence, that they should enter the Holy Sepulcher together, as had been usual at former times [...] The Greeks set out, in a procession round the Holy Sepulchre, and immediately at their heels follow'd the Armenians. [...] Toward the end of this procession, there was a pigeon came fluttering into the cupola over the sepulcher; at the sight of which, there was a greater shout and clamor than before. This bird, the Latins told us, was purposely let fly by the Greeks, to deceive the people into an opinion that it was a visible descent of the Holy Ghost.[69]

The Greek patriarch's vicar and the Armenian bishop entered the Edicule together. "The exclamations were doubled as the miracle drew nearer its accomplishment," Maundrell continued,

> and the people press'd with such vehemence towards the door of the sepulcher, that it was not in the power of the Turks to guard it, with the severest drubs to keep them off. [...] The two miracle-mongers had not been above a minute in the holy sepulcher, when the glimmering of the holy fire was seen, or imagin'd to appear, thro' some chinks of the door; and certainly Bedlam it self never saw such an unruly transport, as was produc'd in the mob at this sight [...] It must be own'd that those two within the sepulcher, perform'd their part with great quickness and

dexterity: but the behavior of the rabble without, very much discredited the miracle.[70]

That is to say, as is evident from this description, at the end of the seventeenth century, the Orthodox and Armenians were still participating in the ceremony on an equal footing. However, eleven years later, according to Ippolit Vishenski, only the Greek patriarch entered the Edicule and then, coming out with three bundles of burning candles, he gave one to the Armenian patriarch and another to the Coptic patriarch, who had come to Jerusalem on pilgrimage that year.[71] A half-century later, Serapion testifies that on Holy Saturday only one Greek hierarch was allowed into the Holy Sepulchre and the Armenian patriarch was admitted only into the little outer room of the Edicule, the Chapel of the Angel, "and he [the Armenian patriarch] bought off the Turks so that, standing amidst the people, so that it would not be shameful for him, for it was impossible for him to ask for such grace from the Lord, like the ignominious."[72]

THE RISE AND FALL OF DOSITHEUS NOTARAS

In the second half of the seventeenth century, there was a long hiatus in the confrontation between the Greeks and Armenians. Meanwhile, relations between the Orthodox and Catholics were strained. Minor skirmishes between the Brotherhood of the Holy Sepulchre and the Franciscans over priority in worship at the Holy Sepulchre happened constantly, sometimes erupting into pitched battle with the use of weapons and many wounded.[73] In 1697, the guard of the Franciscan monastery in Jerusalem showed Henry Maundrell a scar on his hand—the trace of wounds inflicted by a Greek priest in one such clash.[74]

In the early 1670s, the Patriarch Dositheus undertook extensive work on the reconstruction of the Basilica of the Nativity in Bethlehem. The church was once again covered with a lead roof and decorated with an iconostasis, which a master from Chios took four years to carve. With this construction, Dositheus sought, among other things, to perpetuate the rights of the Greeks to the church of Bethlehem. It was not without reason that during the interior alterations the passage leading to the Holy Grotto from the Franciscan monastery was walled up. The Latin monks, of course, perceived the restructuring as a challenge. At their instigation, the Arab Catholics of Bethlehem tried to kill Dositheus. He barely escaped, riding away from his attackers on horseback.[75]

Tensions rose again in 1674, with the arrival from Istanbul of the French ambassador to Jerusalem, demanding the transfer of the holy places to the Latins. "The Franciscans became arrogant," Neophytus of Cyprus wrote about those days. There was once again a bloody clash between the Greeks and the Franks and one Orthodox monk was mortally wounded. Bribed by the ambassador, the Jerusalem authorities kept silent. The following year, the dispute over possession of the holy places moved to the capital.[76] To prove his case, Dositheus made reference to the decrees of the caliphs and the Mamluk sultans, and *hatt-i sherifs* of the Ottoman sultans, while in response, the Franks could essentially only point to the decisions of local authorities in Jerusalem. The grand vizier ruled in favor of the Greeks and ordered the Franks expelled from the court. In October 1675, a *firman* was issued granting undivided possession of most of the Palestinian shrines to the Orthodox. It was Dositheus's finest hour, the greatest Orthodox triumph in the struggle for the holy places. Taking advantage of his position with the Sublime Porte, Dositheus won many privileges for the Orthodox at the expense of rival confessions, in particular a limitation of the number of Franciscans in Jerusalem. However, not all of these orders were carried out by the local administration in Jerusalem.[77]

For their part, the Franciscans tried many times (in 1682, 1684, 1686, and 1688) to persuade the Sublime Port to revise the privileges given to the Greeks. Western diplomats in Istanbul, especially the Polish ambassador who had arrived in 1679 to make peace with the Ottoman Empire, intervened in the dispute over the holy places on the side of the Franciscans but, in the words of Dositheus, "it was like hitting and shattering eggs of hard stone."[78] However, the Catholics' arguments began to sound much weightier after the defeat of the Ottoman army at Vienna in 1683 and the empire's subsequent defeat in a war with a coalition of European powers. France was the only state to remain friendly with the Ottomans and the Sublime Porte granted it concessions for the Catholics in the Holy Land. Already, in 1686, a commission from Istanbul arrived in Jerusalem to examine the complaints of the Franciscans and to look into the buildings that were taken from them after 1637. The commission's opinion was inclined toward the Latins in the dispute over the holy places, but Dositheus prevented the government from changing the situation four times.

In the mid-1690s, Grand Vizier Mustafa Pasha Köprülü handed over to the Franciscans ownership of the Holy Edicule, half of Golgotha, the place of the Finding of the Cross, and the cathedral in Bethlehem along with the Holy Grotto and other sites. In June, the decree was carried out by which the Catholics took control of the holy places. Orthodox altars and iconostases were broken apart and icons and lamps were discarded. It was ordered that there should be no interference in the transition of Eastern Christians to the Latin Church.[79] As Ivan Lukyanov wrote ten years later when visiting Bethlehem,

The Turks took [the church] from the Greeks and gave it to the Frenchmen, and to the Greeks they gave a side chapel on the side of that church;
and whatever the Greeks had built in that church, it was all taken out by
the Frenchmen: the deisis, the gilded and carved iconostasis ... and this
structure lies today at random; and this structure that cost the Greeks
many thousands in money, now it perishes for nothing.[80]

Dositheus made desperate attempts to induce the Ottomans to return the shrines
to their loyal Greeks. Grand Vizier Husayn Köprülü explained to the patriarch
that he would at the first opportunity, but Turkey's defeat in the war with the
Holy League proved this to be an illusion. Under the terms of the Treaty of
Karlowitz in 1699, the holy places of Palestine remained in the possession of the
Latins. Interestingly, in their petition to the Austrian emperor, the Franciscans
insisted that one of the conditions for concluding the treaty with the Porte be that
Dositheus be deposed, along with any of his successors who "might also persist
in their anger."[81] Apparently, this item was rejected through the great efforts of a
dragoman from the Mavrocordatus family.

Aware of the increased power of foreign diplomatic interventions,[82] Dositheus
tried to use Russian influence to oppose the pressure of Western ambassadors.
Starting in November 1690, the patriarch repeatedly appealed to the Russian
authorities to stipulate the return of the holy places to the Greeks as a condition
for reconciliation with Turkey. Dositheus particularly actively urged Peter I to
intervene in the question of the holy places during the peace talks in Istanbul
undertaken by Yemelyan Ukraintsev (1699--700). Dositheus wrote to the tsar,

In as much as these [i.e., the Turks] are proud and want a petition with
supplication, then give it to them with subtle words, it would seem to be a
small kindness. Because of this they are waiting for the greatest effort and
the warmest supplication, so that they may appear as if they are fulfilling
the desire of Your... Serenity as something great and wonderful.[83]

He sent to Moscow specimens of the required letters to sultan, the grand vizier,
and the mufti.[84] At the same time, the patriarch of Jerusalem went on the attack
with reproaches against his colleague, Patriarch Adrian of Moscow, who did not
put sufficient pressure on the tsar, as a result of which the issue of the holy places
was not included in the negotiation of the treaty—"and because of this we were
saddened and are weeping much."[85] In fact, Peter I was interested in Dositheus as
a valuable informant and agent of influence, but the tsar was not going to sacrifice

peace with Turkey for the interests of the church of Jerusalem. Only the clerk Yemelyan Ukraintsev, to meet the wishes of the patriarch, privately petitioned the vizier to return the holy places to the Orthodox. The Ottoman dignitaries agreed with all the arguments in favor of the Greeks and promised to return to them rights to the places of worship as soon as there was a favorable political moment.[86] Dositheus did not cease waiting for that moment, although in 1704 and 1705, he again tried to win the sultan's government over to his side. The only thing he managed to achieve was to block the petition of the Franks to the Sublime Porte to restore the dilapidated Church of the Resurrection.

The patriarch understood that, as in the case of his own restoration of the church of Bethlehem thirty years earlier, any construction or decorative work establishes the rights of the confession that performs the works to the holy places.[87]

The Eighteenth Century: The Pendulum Swings

The condition of the dome, however, became more and more dangerous and this forced the rivals to compromise. After intense negotiations between the Orthodox Patriarch Chrysanthos, the French ambassador, and the Latin procurator of the Holy Sepulchre, it was decided in 1718 to hold joint repairs, and in 1719, the necessary approval was obtained from the Ottoman government.[88] In the 1730s, there are accounts of revived hostility between the Greeks and Armenians associated with a radical rearrangement of power in the Ottoman elite. In 1730, an uprising in Istanbul led to the overthrow of Sultan Ahmet III and the rise of a grand vizier of Armenian background, ʿAli Pasha. "Madness was held in high esteem and impudence prevailed," wrote a Greek chronicler.[89] Even before these events, the Armenians protested against another "curved" Greek Easter in 1729, arguing for the truth of their calculation of the date of the feast. Patriarch Chrysanthus obtained a *firman* from the sultan forbidding further discussion of the issue and putting an end to the disputes.[90]

Now, with the support of the vizier and the Ottoman elite, the Armenians renewed their claim to primacy over the Monophysite communities of Jerusalem and for equality with the Greeks in performing the Paschal services. According to the Greek authors, the Armenians attempted a grandiose fraud, forging decrees by the sultan from the sixteenth century regarding the primacy of the Greeks in the holy places, inserting "Armenians" in the place of "Rum."[91] In fact, the Armenian Church had such documents in its possession no later than the seventeenth century. Depending on the political circumstances, the Ottoman authorities gave credence to these *firmans*, and then declared them fake (dealing with the same way with analogous documents held by the Greeks).[92] The Armenians also enlisted in their favor the testimonies of the bribed judge of Jerusalem and more than two hundred local residents who sold their voices for 50 piasters. Metropolitan Parthenius the Athenian, a contemporary of the events, wrote,

> the Arabs sell anything you like for money; this is the ancient custom of the population of Judea. I do not think that the Arabs are reprehensible. They are poor people and when they are presented with the occasion to enrich themselves, they attach their seal, I do not blame or judge, there is enough evidence of a witness, because he has need of money; it is not difficult to get testimony from the lips of a witness, it is much harder to treat such money with contempt and return it.[93]

As a result, in 1730, 1731, and 1734, the Armenian lobby in Istanbul achieved the issue of the sultan's decree granting the Armenians of Jerusalem the requested privileges.[94]

Having waited for the disgrace of ʿAli Pasha and his Armenian associates in 1735, Patriarch Meletius managed, after a trial at the highest level, to take revenge and regain the Greeks' lost rights. The chief intermediary and protector of the Greeks who brought them victory was the vizier's *kehaya-bey*, Osman Khalis Efendi, to whom the Orthodox chronicles dedicate flowery panegyrics.[95]

The year 1756 marked when nearly seventy years of Catholic predominance in the Palestinian shrines came to an end. On Palm Sunday, which fell on Catholic Easter, there was a mass brawl between the Orthodox and the Catholics, with each side accusing the other of hindering their worship. Arab Catholics from Bethlehem and ʿAyn Karem, who carried swords, stones, and sticks into the church under their clothes, participated in the fight on the side of the Latins. The Greeks found out about the looming conflicts and, in advance, the clever *skevophylax* of the Holy Sepulchre replaced the silver lamps and censers with glass. When the fight started, all the healthy monks from the Greek patriarchate rushed to the aid of their fellow believers. The Orthodox Albanians, of which there were many in the Brotherhood of the Holy Sepulchre, were distinguished by a particular audacity. The doors of the church were locked and monks descended on ropes from the roof of the patriarchate to the window of the church. All the Orthodox censors had been dumped in a pile, and the silver utensils of the Latins were pulled down and plundered by Arabs of both confessions.[96]

The proceedings of the conflict were reported to the Porte's court, "which," according to Muraviev, "were always viewed with displeasure due to the fact that everyone was forced to give into the demands of the Franks and give up their ancient given rights."[97] The positions of the Orthodox in the Church of the Resurrection, Gethsemane, and Bethlehem were restored. In November 1757, the sultan's *hatt-i sherif* was carried out: a Greek monk stood guard at the Holy Edicule, the Latin lamps were carried out of the Church of the Theotokos at Gethsemane, and the Greeks took possession over the Basilica of the Nativity in Bethlehem and two doors leading into the Holy Grotto. The northern door remained in the possession of the Catholics. So as to not irritate the Franciscans to an extreme degree, Greek Patriarch Parthenius allowed them to hold services at the Holy Manger and to have a few lamps there. It should be noted that the possessors of one place of worship or another were, as a rule, very jealous of the services of rival churches in these shrines and tried, when possible, to obstruct their opponents. During their predominance in Bethlehem, the Franciscans once forced the same Patriarch Parthenius on the Orthodox Feast of the Nativity to stand outside the basilica with its doors locked and did not allow him inside.[98]

As mentioned in Chapter 6, a detailed description of these events is contained in the Damascus chronicle of Mikhail Breik.[99] Similarly, information about Dositheus's fight with the Franciscans in the 1680s was recorded by an anonymous monk of Balamand in the margins of one of the monastery's manuscripts.[100] Orthodox Syria closely monitored the situation in the Palestinian shrines.

In 1768, taking advantage of the outbreak of war between Turkey and Russia, the Catholics again tried to regain lost possessions, but even under such circumstances Patriarch Ephraim and his future successor Metropolitan Sophronius managed to convince the sultan and the Sheikh-ul-Islam of their right.[101] After the French Revolution of 1789, the Franciscans' position in the Holy Land was sharply weakened: Europe was no longer behind them.

The Fire at the Church of the Holy Sepulchre

In the sixteenth through eighteenth centuries, the main disputes over possession of the holy places were between the Catholics and the Orthodox, whereas the Armenians primarily laid claim to precedence in worship and primacy over the "lesser" Monophysite churches. Starting in the early nineteenth century, the Armenian Church began to claim joint ownership over the major places of worship.

A surge of intrigue occurred in the autumn of 1799, following Napoleon's Syrian campaign. The Ottoman army, led by Grand Vizier Yusuf Pasha, pursued the French, stopping at Gaza. The Armenians took advantage of the presence in Palestine of the head of the Ottoman administration and asked him for permission to serve the liturgy in the Holy Grotto of Bethlehem. In May 1800, they secretly received a *firman* granting them equal rights with the Greeks to hold services in all the places of worship. Just at that moment, the chief lobbyist for Greek interests, the grand dragoman of the army George Karaca, died. However, the position of the Orthodox was defended by Russian Ambassador Vasily Tomara. The support of Russian diplomacy, of which Patriarch Dositheus had once dreamed, had finally been triggered a hundred years later.[102] The Greek chronicler Procopius Nazianzen noted with satisfaction that after this defeat, the Armenian patriarch fell ill with grief and "gave up his wicked soul."[103] The infighting over the holy places had its own real casualties.

According to the chroniclers, the eighty-year-old Orthodox patriarch, Anthimus, also died on November 30, 1808, from the nervous shock caused by the news of the fire in the Church of the Holy Sepulchre. That year was the point of maximum influence of the Armenians in the Ottoman Empire. In the circle of Mustafa Pasha Bayraktar, there were many Armenian advisors and bankers. Right at the same time, on the night of September 30, 1808, an enormous fire broke out in the Church of the Holy Sepulchre.

The Greeks accused the Armenians of deliberately setting fire to the shrine to obtain from their patron Mustafa Pasha—the actual master of the empire—the right to restore the entire church and thus, in the future, to gain possession over it.[104] According to another, less sinister account, the fire was started by two Armenian monks who had somehow been wronged by their ecclesiastical superiors and wanted to take revenge. However, the flames went beyond what was planned.[105] One way or another, a fire broke out in the Armenian section of the Church of Sts Constantine and Helen and from there it spread around the Church of the Holy Sepulchre, full of wooden structures and cloth curtains.

There remain vivid eyewitness accounts. According to Procopius Nazianzen,

Around the sixth hour of the night they [the Armenians] set fire to their space in the choir loft. When the flames had broken out enough, they began to scream … our people and [the Franks] ran to their aid, but the damned ones would not let them enter into their quarters, saying that there was no need and that they could put out the fire themselves. So they said, but in reality … they poured on the fire whole pitchers of vodka, oil and other easily flammable substances.… Seeing that the fire and flames were flaring up more and raging like an angry lion, and like a chameleon changing color, they began to wail and cry out, calling on the help of the remaining priests who were in the patriarchate.… Until the Turkish gatekeepers were awoken and then they came and opened the door of the church ... flames ... had spread throughout the entire church ... and it became impossible to put out the fire.[106]

Maximus Simaius was at the patriarchate, adjacent to the Church of the Holy Sepulchre, when the alarm sounded. "Hearing this and wondering what it was," he wrote,

> we ran and saw how the flames were coming out of the windows and devouring the frames which were all made out of wood. Greatly frightened, lest suffer ... the dome of the Most Holy Sepulchre, all us monks, small and great, ran, taking lots of water in different containers and poured it from the highest window of the church against the belfry. But we labored in vain due to the great distance. We could not pour water on the flames, not from the high windows mentioned, nor from the windows of the altar. The gate-keepers shouted. But when did they arrive and open the holy gates? In an hour, when the flames had already engulfed the entire Armenian section. Then ... the flames rose to the dome which was completely devoured ... the fire and such great flames came out of the uncovered part of the church [i.e., the hole in the roof of the rotunda] that it lit up all of Jerusalem.[107]

Procopius summarized,

> First the areas of the Armenians were burned, then the church of Golgotha and the rooms around it. The flames rose and engulfed the large wooden dome covered in lead, destroying everything wooden in the church and the dome and the great lead dome melted. The entire katholikon burned [still in reference to the Church of the Resurrection within the church complex], the great altar, the fine iconostasis, two wooden sacristies at the altar, the exquisite works of patriarchal *synthronon*, two large cupboards with various sacred relics in them. The marble columns that stood under the arch of the altar turned to ash and the entire dome was destroyed. The fire melted wax and destroyed icons, holy garments, chandeliers, lamps and various holy and precious vessels ... only the holy door of the Holy Edicule ... was not harmed.[108]

The Greek chroniclers claimed that in the vizier's circle *firmans* were already prepared for the transfer of all the holy places into the undivided possession of the Armenians. It only remained for the decrees to be sealed with the sultan's *tuğra*, but at the last moment, on November 3, 1808, Mustafa Pasha was killed by rebelling Janissaries, the *firmans* were burned along with his home, the Armenians' position was shaken, and the right to rebuild the church went to the Greeks.

Construction work began in the summer of 1809 and was accompanied by ceaseless conflict and litigation with the Franks and Armenians, who were supported by the mufti of Jerusalem and the Janissaries of the city. The Greeks received the patronage of the pasha of Damascus, Genj Yusuf, who, seeking to consolidate his power in Jerusalem, infringed upon the ancient liberties of the local Janissaries. Specifically, he drove them out of the citadel of the city, where their garrison was located.[109]

In December 1809, the city's Janissaries rebelled against the pasha, took the *mutasallim* captive and, at the prompting of the Armenians and Franks, vented their anger against the Greeks, whom they considered to be the instigators of all Genj Yusuf's actions. The rebels struck their first blow at the Church of the Holy Sepulchre, which was still under construction. The architect and some of the workers managed to flee. Of those who remained, one mason was killed on the spot and three were wounded and locked in cells. "Approaching the church armed like wild, rabid wolves," wrote the chronicler, "some hacked at the marble and columns, others stripped the marble paneling of the Holy Edicule and still others opened the monks' cells in the church and plundered them just like thieves."[110] The rioters broke into the monasteries, plundered their property, and searched for Patriarchal Vicar Misael, the dragoman, and the Greek hierarchs. All, however, managed to hide—some with neighboring Muslims, some in a septic tank, and some in the dungeons. The rebels controlled the city for a few weeks. They laid siege to the citadel and every day beat and robbed the Orthodox. In January 1810, the pasha's army appeared suddenly under the walls of Jerusalem, entered the city, and crushed the rebels' resistance. The next day, twelve leaders of the rebellion were strangled.[111]

Construction work on the church continued. At the same time, the Greeks took the opportunity to eradicate all traces of the presence of non-Orthodox confessions in the church, throwing out the lamps and icons of other groups, decorating the buildings with Greek inscriptions, and so on. It was only with the help of the Egyptian Pasha Muhammad 'Ali that the Copts managed to defend their chapel adjacent to the Holy Edicule. The Greeks had to rebuild it against their will, albeit on a smaller scale.

Finally, on September 13, 1810, construction was completed and the church was consecrated.[112] Of course, the struggle for the holy places had not ended. Communities whose interests were frustrated continued to deluge the Sublime Porte and the Jerusalem authorities with complaints and gifts, and the balance swung back toward the Latins and Armenians. In 1811–1812, they once again pushed the Orthodox out of possession of the holy places, relying on decisions of the Porte; the support of the pasha of Sidon and Damascus, Sulayman; and the governor of Jerusalem. Sulman was angry with the Greeks because they did not give him a loan. The Porte had been turned away from the Orthodox by the intrigues of the Armenian *sarrafs*, who accused the grand dragoman and his brother from the Phanariot Mourouzi clan of treason (both were executed in the autumn of 1812). In fact, the grand dragoman and ethnarch of the Greeks, Demetri Mourouzi, fell victim to his pro-Russian and anti-French orientation. After Napoleon's occupation of Moscow, the sultan tried to gain the favor of the French emperor in exchange for the head of his dragoman.

In May 1811, the Franciscans obtained at their disposal all the disputed places of worship in the Church of the Holy Sepulchre and installed an organ in the church, which was irritating to the Orthodox. The Latin monks discarded the "schismatic" lamps, crosses, and candlesticks, covered over the Orthodox icons, and wanted to scrape off the Greek inscriptions, but they were deterred from this by the *mutasallim*. In January 1812, the Armenians were given completely equal rights to the Greeks. The smaller Monophysite churches were given the right to choose their own protector and so went under the protection of the Armenian patriarch. The Sublime Porte ordered the Armenians to pay the Greeks 37,500 piasters in compensation for the restoration of the Armenian sections of the church. Thus, the Greeks lost the basis to claim possession of those areas. The stipulated amount was significantly lower than the actual costs, but the Armenians avoided even paying that. The *qadi* of Jerusalem, who attempted to protect the rights of the local Greeks, was exiled. After that, the Armenians received half of the Tomb of the Theotokos in Gethsemane and one of the keys to the Holy Grotto in Bethlehem.[113]

During the years from 1812 to 1820, the Greeks gradually recovered their lost rights, despite opposition from the governor of Jerusalem. This time, the Orthodox were helped by Sulayman Pasha of Sidon, who had grown cold toward the Franks. In December 1817, the Greeks were allowed to worship in the Holy Edicule on equal footing with the Franks and, in 1820, they were made equal to them in all other rights of possession to the Holy Sepulchre (decoration, maintaining order, and so on).[114]

However, the Greek uprising of 1821, and then the Russo–Turkish War of 1828–1829, once again undermined the position of the Orthodox Church. Under these conditions, there began a new upswing for the Armenians, who won rights equal to the Greeks to use the Holy Edicule and the Stone of Anointing.[115]

Somewhat beyond the chronological framework of this work, we will mention that the Armenians achieved their greatest influence in the holy places during the Egyptian occupation of Syria. The Armenian lobby was powerful in the circle of the Egyptian ruler Muhammad 'Ali and Armenian bankers had great influence in Istanbul. Under these circumstances, the Orthodox and Latins seem to have united for the first time against the Armenians and, with European support, obtained a decree from the Sublime Porte in 1839 invalidating the Armenians' privileges. After that, the Church of the Assumption, which the Armenians had built at the top of the Mount of Olives, was destroyed by Arab Christians of both confessions. In the 1840s, competition for possession of the holy places took place chiefly between the Greeks and the Latins. It was at this time that the dispute over the keys to the Holy Grotto of Bethlehem broke out, which became the pretext for the beginning of the Crimean War.

AN ATTEMPT AT INTERPRETATION

As we see, during the centuries-long struggle, the Porte was very fickle in its sympathies, supporting one confession then another, and this made the situation in Palestine confusing and unstable. As Konstantin M. Bazili wrote in the nineteenth century,

> Each competing side possesses hundreds of contradictory documents of its people; each one of them at one time or another won their process to have control over the holy places ... and as was the custom for the Turkish Chancellery the most recent executive order did not alter the earlier, contradictory decision, and so quite often at the very same time, the government granted to one side and to another the very same rights and benefits, which resulted in a legal chaos where in each claim, every suit, could present, according to the guidelines, irrefutable grounds.[116]

Observers and researchers have long wondered: how significant was the Ottomans' attitude in the struggle over the holy places? Did the Turks have any stable sympathies or antipathies toward any of the various churches?

In the Russian literature of the nineteenth century, it was widely believed that the Turks preferred their Orthodox subjects.[117] At the same time, some authors, especially writers of the late nineteenth century of an anti-Turkish persuasion, thought differently:

> Is not the reason that the Latins have firmly established themselves near the holy places of Palestine, which were earlier in the control of the

Orthodox, due to the indulgences of the Turkish government? … In general, the Porte until recently sided more with the Latins, more favorably and graciously, in direct harm to its loyal subjects.[118]

There is also an intermediate perspective, according to which the Ottomans were neutral between the competing Christian confessions. According to I. N. Berezin, in the early eighteenth century one Ottoman minister said (albeit in a different context), "There is little need [to distinguish] whether the pig is white or black; they are all pigs and the Sublime Porte makes no difference between Armenians, Roman Catholics and Greeks."[119] Such thoughts were expressed by many Ottoman officials in a variety of periods.

The inconsistency of the Porte can be explained by the age-old principle of "divide and rule," of which it has been constantly accused by diplomats and historians. On closer examination, however, one can note the repeated attempts by the Turks to reconcile rivals or to preserve the status quo. Petty bickering over every lamp in front of the Holy Sepulchre at times seemed pointless to the Ottomans: during one of the biggest legal cases between the Greeks and Armenians in the presence of all the luminaries of Ottoman law, a dignitary resented that so many respectable men should waste their time on account of the quarrelsome infidels.[120] Sometimes the judge would entreat the defendant to make voluntary concessions by threatening that the process would be delayed indefinitely.[121] The frequent zigzags in the policy of Mahmud II, many times varying between anger and mercy with respect to each confession, can be explained as simply an attempt to find a mutually acceptable status that would put an end to the countless conflicts.

One of the most recent attempts to identify the Ottomans' motivation and preference was made by the Israeli historian Oded Peri. He is inclined to believe that Ottoman policy, for all its inconsistency on the surface, in fact, was carefully calculated, was rational, and had distinct goals. Evidence for the Ottomans' rational approach to the fight over the holy places included, among other things, the Sublime Porte's distinguishing in its attitude toward possession of a place of worship and rights to hold services there. In the first case, the Ottoman authorities' position was deliberately ambiguous. They shied away from giving undivided support for any of the churches, leaving themselves maximum freedom to maneuver. The Porte simultaneously recognized mutually exclusive "ancient" *firmans* on the privileges of the Orthodox and Armenian churches, while the status of the Franciscans in the holy places was guaranteed in the capitulations, which were formulated in vague and imprecise terms. According to Peri, "maneuverability was tantamount to neutrality, which to the Ottomans meant maintaining a constant harmony with a rather inconstant reality."[122] At the same time, in the question of freedom of worship in the holy places, the Ottomans held a clear position on the right of all confessions to have access to the shrines, regardless of who the owner was.[123] In reality, there was never equality in worship. Peri's exclusive reliance on archival sources does not allow him to see the discrepancy between the real situation and juridical prescriptions, such as in the issue of the Armenians' participation in receiving the Holy Fire.

The position of the authorities was determined by a number of factors and it was difficult for the Ottomans to maintain objectivity. According to Nikolai Skabalanovich, a Russian scholar of the second half of the nineteenth century, because of the constant hostility of Turkey and Catholic Europe,

> the entire business was caused by the art of intrigue, the size of bribes and the degree of pressure of foreign embassies. But if the Porte rejected these external incentives and acted more or less independently of them, then … the Catholic community suffered losses and profited from lesser arrangements and less patronage from the Porte than the other communities.[124]

It is obvious that money was a major driving force in the struggle over the holy places. Peri tends to downplay the role of bribes in determining Ottoman court decisions regarding places of worship. He believes that most monetary relationships were settled at the grassroots level of Ottoman administration, before reaching the imperial center, and indicates only three occasions when cash sums paid by Christian confessions for the transfer to them of a given place of worship appear in the archival sources of the seventeenth century.[125] The exclusive commitment to the archives again fails the Israeli author. If he had turned to the Christian chronicles, he would have found that there are not three examples of bribes for the entire eighteenth century, but three such examples on every page.

However, there were other factors that also influenced the struggle over the holy places. The Jerusalem regional elite—the 'ulama, sharifs, and other local notables—had a certain weight at in Ottoman courts. This opinion, however, was easy to sell and resell for short-term changes of 180 degrees. Moreover, according to Peri, the imperial authorities made their final decisions primarily on the basis of their own preferences, sometimes in defiance of the local notables.[126]

A more important role in disputes over the holy places was played by high officials in the capital, many of whom were converts to Islam from Christian backgrounds. It is usually assumed that these neophyte Muslims were distinguished by greater religious fervor and that what they most feared was being suspected of sympathizing with their former coreligionists. However, the behavior of many Ottoman bureaucrats refutes this opinion: after having accepted Islam, they continued to live according to their previous system of values. Former Orthodox supported the Greeks and former Armenian Gregorians supported the Armenians. Even more important than the support of viziers and other officials was the patronage of influential people of the harem—eunuchs or the wives and favorites of the sultan. Ottoman officials sometimes supported one confession or another because of personal rather than ethnic ties. Those in a position of power were very often influenced by Christians in their entourage, especially bankers and doctors (these positions were practically monopolized by *dhimmis*). The external factor, pressure from foreign diplomats, was also important.

Peri is inclined to believe that the transfer of the holy places to the Catholics was an unprecedented, extraordinary event in which the holy places became the object of foreign policy rather than of the internal politics of the empire.[127] However, at least from the beginning of the seventeenth century, one can note repeated attempts by Western diplomacy to win from the Porte concessions for the Catholic community. That is, European ambassadors long acted as one of the centers of power in the struggle over the holy places. It is just that 1690 marked the first great success of these external factors. Later, however, when the status of the holy places was debated in 1757 and 1768, the Porte, as we have seen, did not look to the opinions of foreign diplomats. After the French Revolution, external support for the Catholics in Palestine came to an end and Russia's protection of the Greeks was equally ineffective because of the almost-constant Russo–Turkish wars. Great power diplomacy only began to play a really important role in determining the status of the holy places no earlier than the 1830s.

In our opinion, the aggravation or attenuation of the struggle over the places of worship and the success or failure of a particular church was determined by each confession's relationship with the patrons of its group in the Ottoman administration—that is, on the balance of power in the imperial elite, as well as the ability of rival churches to pay because one was required to pay generously for all the authorities' services.[128]

In the most general terms, the course of the struggle could be represented be a gigantic sine wave. The strong positions maintained by the Catholics in the places of worship throughout the sixteenth century were radically shaken by the Greek patriarchs from Theophanes to Dositheus in the second and third quarters of the seventeenth century. The Phanariot factor was fully at play in this: the connection between the Brotherhood of the Holy Sepulchre and the Greek elite of the empire had its leverage over the Ottoman administration. Starting in the late seventeenth century, a new era began in the history of the Ottoman state and, consequently, of the Orthodox East, as well as an era of progressive decline in Ottoman power and strengthening European influence in the region. The first victim of this was not Islam, but Orthodoxy. The Latins successfully carried out propaganda for the Unia and won a preeminent position in the holy places. The strengthening of the Catholic presence also came to be the dominant feature of the history of the Christian East in the eighteenth century, although it is true that the Orthodox *revanche* in 1757 does not fit with this trend. The causal link between high politics and the status of the holy places in the sixteenth and eighteenth centuries should not be exaggerated. On the whole, it is not possible to discern consistent Ottoman support for any community or a clear commitment to the strategy of divide and rule.

Given the incapacity and corruption that distinguished the Ottoman authorities of this era, especially at the provincial level, it is difficult to speak of a conscious policy toward the conflict between Christian confessions.

In the second third of the nineteenth century, the great powers would use the problem of the holy places for their own political consolidation in the Middle East. The Brotherhood of the Holy Sepulchre and the Franciscans would be pawns in this game, but nothing would be said of the independent position of the Sublime Porte.

CHAPTER **8**

Foreign Relations

*When [the soldiers] are at war, as many of them as will remain alive, will learn
the art of war, but when they just sit, they do not wage war, and in the time of
need they are not useful to anyone. But if such people exist who hope that military instruction is done without trouble, without labor, without death—such
people should put on a kamilavka and set off to live in a monastery and flip
through their prayer beads.*

—Patriarch Dositheus to Peter I, 1706

Historians quite rightly call the Ottoman Rum *millet* "a state within a state."
Indeed, the Orthodox ethnoconfessional community possessed many of the
attributes of statehood, including its own foreign policy, which at times had a
marked impact on foreign relations in the Mediterranean and Eastern Europe.
The Orthodox East's vectors of foreign relations spread out in a wide fan from
Georgia, Muscovy, the West Russian lands of the Polish Commonwealth, the
Orthodox countries of the Danube region to the Catholic and Protestant states
of the West. In this chapter, we turn to an analysis of Middle Eastern Christians'
contacts with the countries of the Eastern Christian world, which was based on
religious-cultural affinities and at times led to closely interwoven destinies both
for individuals and for whole peoples separated by thousands of miles.

Of course, the Orthodox *millet* of the Ottoman Empire was not a monolithic
political entity. Within this framework, it is possible to distinguish half a dozen
independent "players"—the heads of all the local churches and of the most influential monasteries. The clergy of the Orthodox East was divided into several
competing factions, and it is not always possible to establish their structure and
interests. These factions were unstable, their membership was fluid from one
group to another, they often changed political orientations, and their actions often
were vague and their behavior contradictory. But despite the fact that Greek
familial and compatriotic structures in the Ottoman era have been little studied,

it is possible to make a preliminary attempt at outlining the pattern of interaction among these ecclesial factions.[1]

Even if the patriarchs of Constantinople played an incomparably bigger role within the Ottoman state than the patriarchs of Jerusalem and Antioch, on the outside, in the sphere of contacts with their coreligionists to the North, the tone was often set by bishops from the Arab East. The foreign policy activity of the Ecumenical Throne was not helped by frequent changes of patriarch and the atmosphere of intrigue and denunciations in the Phanar. When the bishops' every effort was spent on internecine struggles, it left them no possibility of properly dealing with the needs of the Church. The patriarch of Jerusalem, ruling in an atmosphere of greater stability, was more able successfully to develop and implement a long-term political strategy. In any case, however, the foreign relations of the Orthodox of Syria and Palestine can be considered only in the general context of all Eastern Orthodoxy.[2]

North–South: Making Contacts

Under Ivan III and Vasily III, Muscovy's growing political ambitions, founded in their awareness of being successors to the Byzantine Empire, determined their extensive relations with their Balkan coreligionists and regular alms packages to Athos, Serbia, and the Patriarchate of Constantinople.[3]

The incorporation of Syria and Egypt into the Ottoman state greatly simplified contacts between the Middle Eastern Christians and the new Orthodox empire that arose to the North.[4] The monks of Sinai sent their first delegation to Moscow in search of alms on November 16, 1517, the year of the Ottoman conquest of Egypt.[5]

Because embassy documents for the years 1519–1549 were lost, disappearing in the Moscow fire of 1549 and other disasters, relations between Russia and the East during this period can be judged only from indirect and incomplete data in terms of sources. In particular, in 1533, Patriarch Joachim of Alexandria sent his first letter to Russia, in which he described in vivid terms the plight of Egyptian Christians "among the godless and in destitution because of the wicked, especially many are their abuses and unendurable torments."[6] Among other things, the patriarch requested assistance for the nun Macrina, abbess of the Monastery of the Theotokos Hodegetria in Jerusalem, who came to the Russian lands "for the sake of her own needs and poverty, to beg for alms" from the Russian tsar.[7] This is the first evidence in Russia of alms seekers from Palestine in the Ottoman period.

Within a few years Patriarch Germanus, as soon as he was elected, sent his representatives, the elders Arsenius and Dositheus, to Russia. In March 1541, they met with Archbishop Makary of Novgorod, the future metropolitan of Moscow, and told him about the needs of the Church of Jerusalem. The patriarchal decree reported Germanus's efforts: the restoration the dilapidated Church of the Holy Sepulchre, the construction of the dome of the Church of the Resurrection and other works on which "we have spent much." The construction apparently was not sanctioned by the Muslim *qadi* and so Germanus wrote that "the impious and godless Arabs and Turks did not remain silent in their jealousy, and they went and slandered me in front of the godless governor, the *sanjak-bey*."[8] The *sanjak-bey* (local governor) sent his men to destroy the newly built parts of the church, "and," wrote Germanus, "they took me and bound me in chains and in fetters brought [me] to the godless *sanjak-bey*." It was only at the cost of making large bribes that the patriarch managed to save the church, but to cover the debt, he had to send alms collectors as far as Novgorod.[9] The monk Arsenius even received alms from the sovereign himself: among other gifts for the patriarch is mentioned the fur coat of Basil III.[10]

Thus, the view of Nikolai Kapterev is not entirely correct when he states that Patriarch Germanus's first contact with Russia was in 1543 when he, while in Istanbul, signed the letter of the clergy of Constantinople to the Russian sovereign requesting the release of Maximus the Greek.[11] It is curious that a similar letter was soon dispatched to Moscow by Patriarch Joachim of Alexandria.[12] In contrast to the brief and exceedingly humble tone of the messages sent from the patriarchs of Constantinople and Jerusalem, Joachim issued a sharp sermon that "neither the Orthodox Christians, nor the tsars who are honored with great respect, act in this way toward a poor man, and especially not toward a monk."[13] It seems that no Eastern patriarch ever wrote to the Russian tsar in such a sharp tone: "It is just to imprison those who do not fear you ... and to bind those who wish you evil, but it is not good and not just to hold by force and to insult the poor ones and especially a teacher, such as that poor Maximus." Joachim concluded his lengthy letter by saying, "I have never written to you and I have not asked for any consolation for myself [the aged patriarch seems to have forgotten about his letter of 1533]; do not offend me in this and do not force me to write another letter to your kingship."[14]

Maximus the Greek, as is well known, was never released from Russia, but positive contacts between Russia and the East continued. In 1548, Patriarch Germanus sent a new embassy to Russia—the elders Daniel and Gabriel, who reported a powerful earthquake in Palestine, during which the bell tower of the Holy Sepulchre collapsed onto the dome of the Church of the Resurrection and destroyed it. The bell tower of the church in Bethlehem was also destroyed and other churches as well as the Edicule of the Holy Sepulchre were affected. The patriarch sought assistance for rebuilding the churches, explaining that "we do not have the strength from the daily assaults of impious foreigners and from violence."[15] The amount of alms sent was small, about a hundred rubles. The government of Ivan IV, it seems, was not at that moment (1550) completely conscious of its interests in the Holy Land.

The Mission of Vasily Poznyakov

Recognition came a bit later. An ever stronger Muscovy gradually laid claim to political leadership in the Orthodox world. From the end of the 1550s, Muscovite diplomacy began to work out the question of the recognition of the Russian sovereign's imperial title in the Orthodox East. The respective embassy was dispatched with gifts to Constantinople and to Mount Athos. In turn, the Greek bishops, interested in a strong patron, embraced the sovereign aspirations of Ivan IV with full approval. In 1562, a delegation arrived from Constantinople from the patriarch with synodal decrees in recognition of the title of the tsar assumed by the Russian autocrats.[16]

Closely connected to these events was an action of Russian foreign policy unprecedented in scale to enhance prestige in the Middle East: the mission of Archdeacon Gennady and Vasily Poznyakov to the Eastern patriarchs. The immediate reason for this mission was the arrival in January 1558 of the monks Joseph and Malachi from Sinai with a letter from Patriarch Joachim of Alexandria and Bishop Macarius of Sinai dated September 26, 1556. The message from the patriarch and the archbishop was filled with hyperbolic elegies to the Russian tsar, who was called the "second sun" and the future deliverer of the East from the yoke of the infidels, and it contained a humble request for alms for the dilapidated monastery of Sinai, which remained "like a small spark in this wilderness, mocked and fading on account of our sins."[17]

Taking advantage of the opportunity, in October 1558, the Russian government sent out a large embassy to the Orthodox East with many gifts for the patriarchs and monasteries. The leaders of the mission, Archdeacon Gennady and Vasily Poznyakov, received, among other objectives, the directive to "describe the customs of these countries."[18] As we shall see, Russia was beginning to take a closer look at the post-Byzantine area.

Archdeacon Gennady died at the beginning of the journey, in Istanbul, and so further leadership of the embassy passed to Poznyakov. In October 1559, he reached Alexandria, where he met with Patriarch Joachim and told him about the greatness and victories of the Russian tsar. The patriarch was crossing himself toward the icons and was recalling the prophecy "indeed a king will rise from an Orthodox land of the East and God will subject to him many kingdoms," and the Eastern Christians will be spared "by his hand from the godless Turks."[19]

Together with the patriarch, Poznyakov visited Cairo and, in November, the Monastery of Sinai, leaving a touching description of his meeting with the monks: "The abbot came toward us and kissed us, choking with tears and said, 'Thanks be to God, for granting us to see the messengers of the Orthodox tsar!' Then the brothers began to embrace and kiss us, and lovingly they shed tears from joy."[20]

Having returned at the end of 1559 to Alexandria, Poznyakov sailed from there to Palestine. Patriarch Joachim conveyed with him the letter addressed to the Russian tsar, in which he told "of the great sorrows, needs and misfortunes, and the disgraces and abuses," which he himself and his flock endured "from unmerciful rulers and wild beasts, the ungodly sons of Hagar" and sent up prayers that the Lord may trample the enemies of the tsar, and scatter them on the ground, as the dust from the face of the wind.[21] As we can see, Joachim made a notable evolution from strict exhortation in connection with the case of Maximus the Greek, toward humble praises to the tsar and the desire to behold "the magnificent form" of his face.[22] In the shifting political conditions, the patriarch took stock and recognized in Muscovy a powerful patron of Middle Eastern Christians.

On Easter Sunday, April 14, 1560, Poznyakov arrived in Jerusalem, where he stayed until July. Patriarch Germanus received alms from the tsar: on the list was a sable coat, miscellaneous property worth 400 gold Hungarian coins, the same amount donated to the Holy Sepulchre, and 200 gold coins for Golgotha. When the patriarch received the alms, however, 400 rubles were missing, for which he blamed Joseph, head of the Sinaite delegation. "How he squandered them," Germanus wrote to the tsar, "you yourself find out."[23] From then on, the patriarch asked him to send alms only with monks from Jerusalem. Among other things, Germanus asked the tsar for a mitre, "because many here," as the patriarch explained, "at the Holy Sepulchre wear mitres—Armenians, Ethiopians, and others. It is only we who do not have one."[24]

Probably after the visit to Jerusalem, in the summer of 1560 Poznyakov arrived in Damascus, where he delivered alms from the tsar to Patriarch Joachim ibn Jum'a, and thus began relations between Antioch and Russia. Joachim also sent a letter to the tsar, full of grandiloquent praise. "Would that God grant us to see your royal form, that is your image," wrote the patriarch, "and would that we could hear your divine and most-sweet voice. We bless, we give thanks, and we bow down, we kiss you for your almsgiving and compassions."[25]

The government of Ivan the Terrible twice sent special missions to the Eastern patriarchs: the embassy of Semen Barzunov in 1571 with alms for the patriarchs of Constantinople and Alexandria, to Athos and Sinai, and the embassy of Ivan Mishenin (accompanied by the famous Trifon Korobeinikov) in 1582–1584 with an enormous amount of alms for the remembrance of the soul of Tsarevich Ivan. The gifts were distributed among the monasteries of Mount Athos, Patriarch Jeremiah of Constantinople, and Patriarch Sylvester of Alexandria, who at that time was in Istanbul.[26] It is notable that at that time the patriarchs of Antioch and Jerusalem were not portrayed as so trustworthy to Moscow and in the dispatching of monetary donations to the East they often were not taken into account.

In this situation, the Palestinian clergy took the initiative themselves. In summer 1582, Metropolitan Joachim of Bethlehem along with a group of Arab Christians went seeking alms with the permission of the patriarch of Jerusalem. In autumn 1583, Joachim arrived in Moscow and was received by the sovereign, and in September of the following year, he was sent home with gifts. He was the highest-ranking representative of the Patriarchate of Jerusalem to have appeared in Russia up to that time. Among those who left Moscow with the metropolitan are mentioned elders from Mar Saba and Archimandrite Isaiah from the Antiochian patriarchal cathedral, who perhaps was the first Syrian envoy to Moscow in the Ottoman period.[27]

The Middle Eastern Policy of Fyodor Ioannovich

After the pious Fyodor Ioannovich came to the throne in Moscow, financial assistance to the Eastern Churches increased even more. In August 1584, the tsar sent the envoy Boris Blagoy to Istanbul with notice of his accession to the throne and alms for the patriarch of Constantinople and the monasteries of Athos. In April 1585, Boris Blagoy met with Patriarch Theoleptus, as well as with the patriarchs of Alexandria and Antioch, who were in the Ottoman capital at the time. On several occasions after that Patriarch Sylvester of Alexandria invited the envoy to meals, where he spoke at length about the Russian Tsar's impending acquisition of "Emperor Constantine's inheritance," only lamenting that, because of his very old age, he would not live to see those days.[28] As he left the embassy, Sylvester gave a letter for the tsar with lengthy instructions about how to run the state and preserve Orthodox principles; relevant advice was also addressed to the metropolitan of Moscow, Dionisy.[29] Sylvester, it seems, was trying out the role of spiritual mentor for Muscovy.

Patriarch Sophronius of Jerusalem also sent Fyodor Ioannovich general instructions about righteous kingship and love for the poor and needy, churches, and the Holy Sepulchre: "where two chandeliers are lit for the sake of the many years of your kingdom, and we pray for your kingship all day and night during the sacred liturgies….]."[30] The patriarch's letter was brought to Moscow by Archimandrite Joasaph, who returned with the significant sum of 900 rubles, along with charters for the free passage to Moscow of monks from Jerusalem for alms.[31]

Communication with Boris Blagoy, as well as perhaps with the metropolitan of Bethlehem, prompted a third patriarch, Joachim Daw of Antioch, to travel to Moscow in person to seek monetary assistance. In the winter of 1585–1586, he arrived in Kiev, where, with the approval of the patriarch of Constantinople who was troubled by the pro-Catholic sentiments of the bishop of the Kievan metropolia, he took an active part in the ecclesio-political struggle. In particular, Joachim authorized the establishment of the Orthodox Brotherhood of Lvov and encouraged it in its conflict with the local bishop, in addition to issuing a series of canonical decisions ordering the everyday life of the clergy.[32]

In April 1586, while in Lvov, Joachim sought the tsar's permission to visit Russia, and in June of that year, he arrived via Smolensk in Moscow, where he would remain until August. The unprecedented arrival of an Eastern patriarch caused a major stir in Moscow society. Russian authorities used the occasion to raise the topic in discussions with Joachim of establishing a patriarchate in Moscow.[33] Joachim Daw declined to address the issue of autocephaly, but he promised to bring it to the consideration of the Eastern churches. The *podyachy* (assistant clerk) Mikhail Ogarkov was sent back with Joachim to Constantinople with alms and letters for the patriarchs.

The subsequent course of events has been described in detail by historians: the arrival in Moscow of Patriarch of Constantinople Jeremiah and his prolonged stay in Russia (1588–1589), the elevation of Metropolitan Job of Moscow as patriarch, and the councils held in Constantinople in 1590 and 1593, which confirmed the establishment of the Patriarchate of Moscow on the part of the entire clergy of the Christian East. The process of recognition was not entirely smooth, and it faced in particular the resistance of the new patriarch of Alexandria, Meletius Pegas, who was not present at the council of 1590.[34]

To encourage the Greek bishops to recognize speedily Moscow's ambitions, the Russian government sent new embassies to the East with plentiful gifts: the *dyak* (clerk) Grigory Nashchokin in May 1591; Ivan Koshurin in 1592; and, probably the most famous of the diplomatic missions, the *dyaks* Mikhail Ogarkov and Trifon Korobeinikov in 1593. Reaching Istanbul in April, the ambassadors distributed alms to the patriarch of Constantinople and to the monasteries of

Athos and gave the funds due to Patriarch Meletius of Alexandria and Patriarch
Joachim of Antioch (the latter of whom was at that moment with Metropolitan Macarius of Aleppo in the capital). On September 28, the embassy arrived in
Jerusalem, where it distributed among the patriarch and all the monasteries furs
and money in excess of 4,000 gold pieces. In February of 1594, Trifon sent 430
gold pieces and forty sable furs to the Monastery of Mount Sinai.[35]

Godunov and the Time of Troubles

The interval between 1594 and 1602 is another gap in our knowledge of contacts
between Russia and the East, as the archival materials have been lost for these
years. On the basis of circumstantial evidence, it is possible to assume that there
were several decrees at the end of the sixteenth century giving alms to Mar Saba
in Palestine.[36] Mention is also made of a completely missing embassy from Jerusalem, headed by Metropolitan Germanus of Caesarea. Boris Godunov, perhaps
sensitive to the feeble legitimacy of his power, greatly valued the position of the
Eastern patriarchates and eagerly sent alms to the Orthodox East. Between the
years 1603 and 1605, there was a number of delegations in Moscow from Mount
Athos, Serbia, the Patriarchate of Constantinople, and a delegation from Mar
Saba headed by Archimandrite Gregory. Following the latter, in December 1603,
an embassy arrived from Patriarch Sophronius of Jerusalem, headed by Archimandrite Theophanes, the future patriarch. In his letters, Sophronius complained
of the lengthy hiatus in almsgiving and the severe need of the See of Jerusalem.
He asked in particular for money to buy a vineyard and an olive grove for church
purposes. Even though Godunov's authority was already wavering and the False
Dmitri was advancing toward Moscow, it had no effect on the splendor of the
reception and the generous alms bestowed upon the Eastern clergy. According
to Kapterev, this was all in order to make a strong impression on Archimandrite
Theophanes, who would play a prominent role in the later history of Russian–
Palestinian contacts.[37]

    The last Eastern embassy to come to Godunov's court was set by the Monastery
of Mount Sinai with letters from the patriarchs of Alexandria and Jerusalem, and
Bishop Laurentius of Sinai, telling of the monastery's "great poverty" on account
of "the Hagarene tribute" and "plundering by the Arabs" which forced the monastery to sell holy vessels and vestments for 4,000 gold pieces.[38] Sinai was unlikely
to have been able to receive alms from Tsar Boris. The False Dmitri would soon
enter Moscow and the cataclysms of the Time of Troubles broke off political ties
between Russia and the Middle East for a long period. During this period, only
once, in 1605, did Patriarch Sophronius of Jerusalem attempt to establish contact

with Moscow, turning to the False Dmitiri for financial assistance, while congratulating him for his miraculous escape and accession to his ancestral throne. Church historians justify Sophronius on the grounds that he did not know with whom he was dealing.[39]

Not all envoys from Middle Eastern Churches were able to get out of Moscow safely before the start of the Time of Troubles. There is preserved in the archives of the Foreign Ministry a petition dated April 1619 from the elder Sophronius of Mar Saba, who had come to Moscow for alms under Tsar Boris, "in what year, I do not remember."[40] Stuck in Russia during the Time of Troubles, the elder received "daily sustenance" under Boris—1 *grivna* per day and a bucket of honey, while under "Rastriga [the defrocked monk]," the False Dmitri, and Tsar Vasily only 1 *altyn* per day and a bucket of beer. One senses how the agonizing state cut foreign spending but had not yet resolved to completely abandon relations with the Orthodox East. After the Polish occupation of Moscow the issuance of "daily sustenance" ceased, and in 1611, when the Poles burned Moscow (was it perhaps then that the records of the 1590s were lost?), Sophronius left "for the camps" of Prokopy Lyapunov's volunteer army.[41] From there, the elder moved to Yaroslavl, then to Kazan, where he was fed in the monasteries. Once he felt that the situation was stable, he appeared in Moscow begging for his "daily sustenance," "so that … he would not die of hunger."[42]

The Era of Theophanes

All the same, starting in 1619 there was a period of renewed contact between Russia and the East. Already in 1613 and 1615 the government of Mikhail Romanov sent letters to the patriarch of Constantinople announcing the end of the Time of Troubles in Muscovy and requesting the prayers of the Eastern clergy for the tsar and for Russian power.[43] In 1619, Patriarch Theophanes of Jerusalem arrived in Moscow. In the Russian literature of the era, there is a beautiful legend that Theophanes came on account of a decision by the Eastern patriarchs, to help the Russian Church to overcome the painful aftermath of the Time of Troubles and, above all else, to provide assistance in the election of a new patriarch of Moscow. Later historians have discerned more prosaic reasons for Theophanes's mission: he came seeking alms and only by chance did this coincide with the election of Patriarch Filaret Romanov, and thus the patriarch of Jerusalem presided at Filaret's consecration.[44]

Having received ample alms, more than 2,000 rubles ("despite the ruin of the state," as Kapterev caustically remarks[45]), Theophanes left Moscow for Kiev in February of 1620.[46] Ukraine was no less important than Moscow as a field of activity for hierarchs of the Orthodox East, especially because the Metropolia of Kiev was part of the Patriarchate of Constantinople. For this reason it was the Patriarchate of Constantinople and the Greek world of the Balkans that were primarily involved in the dramatic struggle leading up to the Union of Brest and the continued confrontation between Orthodoxy and Catholicism in Ukraine.

Clerics from the Middle East participated in these events less often, but at times they managed to play a prominent role in Ukrainian political and cultural history. It is sufficient to recall the activities of Patriarch Joachim Daw of Antioch in Lvov during the years 1585–1586, as discussed previously. Cyril Lucaris headed the Orthodox academy in Vilnius and was present as exarch of the Patriarchate of Alexandria at the alternative Orthodox Council of Brest in 1596. The Patriarch of Alexandria at the time, Meletius Pegas, who wanted to play the role of spiritual leader of the Eastern Christian world, sent dozens of letters to the leaders of the Orthodox party in Ukraine.[47]

During the course of these events, Theophanes decided to stay in Kiev (March 1620 to the beginning of 1621). By this time in Ukraine, during the establishment of the Unia, there was not a single Orthodox bishop and Catholic circles considered their final victory to be at hand. At the Phanar, and in Moscow, they were exploring various ways to restore the Orthodox hierarchy in Western Russian lands. Theophanes received the necessary authority to do so from the Ecumenical Patriarch. In Ukraine, the church brotherhoods and the local clergy insisted on the consecration of bishops as soon as possible, but Theophanes hesitated for some time out of fear of a reprisal from Polish authorities. It was only the defeat of the Polish army by the Ottomans in September of 1620 that gave him a mostly free hand to act. Relying on guarantees of security from the Cossacks, in October of that year, the patriarch of Jerusalem consecrated several bishops and a new metropolitan of Kiev. It was a veritable act of sabotage against the Polish authorities. The king declared Theophanes to be an impostor and a Turkish spy, but the patriarch had already been evacuated to Moldavia under the protection of three thousand Cossacks.[48]

It is no exaggeration to describe the next quarter-century in the history of the foreign policy of the Orthodox *millet* and, in particular, of ties between Russia and the East, as the "Era of Theophanes." The patriarch of Jerusalem was the central figure in the system of contacts between the Orthodox Levant and Russia under Patriarch Philaret and Tsar Mikhail Romanov, whose reign ended almost simultaneously with Theophanes's time as patriarch. Apart from him, perhaps only Cyril Lucaris enjoyed similar diplomatic attention and tender mercies from the Russian authorities.

The Patriarchate of Jerusalem accounted for a significant, if not the principal, share of the alms that Moscow sent to the East. These donations came both through Russian embassies arriving in Istanbul (the missions of Kondyrev and Bormosov in 1622, Begichev in 1624, Yakolev and Evdokimov in 1629, and so on) and through envoys sent to Moscow by the patriarch of Jerusalem. One of the most prominent of these embassies arrived in 1625. It was headed by a relative of the patriarch, Archimandrite Cyril, and by the archimandrite of Mar Saba, Gregory, who brought letters from Theophanes, Metropolitan Athanasius of Bethlehem, and monks of Mar Saba, with the usual complaints of "losses" and the Holy Sepulchre's "great debt," which had reached 50,000 gold pieces. It is noteworthy that, in addition to letters to the tsar and the patriarch, the messengers also brought similar letters to a number of influential princes and boyars. Theophanes learned how to deal with the domestic political situation in Moscow and sought to ingratiate himself among the boyar aristocracy using lobbyists for his interests.[49]

In Moscow, there was another lobby from the Orthodox East—Greek clergy who had settled in Moscow and served as advisors to the Posolsky Prikaz about Levantine affairs. Theophanes's interests were represented by the Greek cellarer of Novospassky Monastery, Ioannikii (d. 1631), who had come to Moscow in 1619 as part of the patriarch's retinue. Ioannikii's task was to direct the flow of Russian alms to the Patriarchate of Jerusalem. However, this was not always possible for him, due to competition from other Greek "experts" in eastern affairs, especially Metropolitan Averkios of Veroia. Particularly linked to Averkios's intrigues were Theophanes's setbacks following the embassy to Russia from the Holy City in 1629, headed by Metropolitan Athanasius of Bethlehem. The metropolitan went back with little more than scant alms, which prompted Theophanes to launch an active propaganda campaign, sending to Patriarch Filaret of Moscow denunciations of Averkios and addressing Averkios with bitter reproaches: "You have offended all and took away our alms, saying that I gave away the tsar's alms to the Christians here and appointed my own people as metropolitans. It was not so, but I sent everything that was collected to the churches of God."[50]

Archimandrite Cyril, Theophanes's nephew, once again appeared in Moscow in early 1635. In the patriarchal letters, which he brought, there can clearly be heard a new motif, connected with the struggle with the Armenians and "Latins" for possession of the holy places of Palestine, and the resulting losses.[51] After Cyril, who was placated with rich alms, another nephew of Theophanes, Paisius, a hegumen from Iasi (in present-day Romania), arrived in Moscow for the first time in January 1636. Carrying out a series of financial and political errands for the Russian government, Paisius went to Istanbul that same year, returning once more to Moscow in December, and then in early 1637, he was sent with gifts to Iasi, where at that time Patriarch Theophanes was located.[52]

The example of this episode shows that Theophanes's relations with Moscow were not limited to importune requests for alms and the sending of money and furs to Jerusalem. Even during his stay in Moscow, the patriarch of Jerusalem took an active part in the affairs of the Russian Church and the disputes of the Russian clergy over the correction of the liturgical books according to Greek models, supporting in particular the Grecophile-oriented abbot of the Holy Trinity–St Sergius Lavra, Dionisy, who was being persecuted by church authorities.[53] Theophanes, who maintained a constant correspondence with Tsar Mikhail Romanov and Filaret, was, according to Kapterev, the most respected of the Eastern bishops in Russia: during his lifetime, the Russian Church again began to submit to Greek cultural influence.[54] Additionally, Theophanes and his men served Muscovy's political interests in the Ottoman Empire, primarily by providing Russia with information about the situation in Eastern Europe and the Mediterranean.

The Eastern patriarchs' cooperation with Russian intelligence (the functions of which were performed by the Posolsky Prikaz and the governors of border towns) began at the end of the sixteenth century. The patriarchs acted as advisors to the tsar's ambassadors in Istanbul and collected information of interest to Moscow. This activity was well compensated (alms to eastern coreligionists often were veiled payment for services) and thus senior hierarchs of the Rum *millet* willingly became political agents for Russia. Among them was Patriarch Theophanes. However, he made for a poor spy because he feared the Turks and avoided risk. This in particular is demonstrated by his letter to the tsar in 1638:

> We write and make known [to you] concerning what is going on in Constantinople, but because of this, we experience great fear—of which you also are aware. Solely our great love for your piety and for your charity, which you have for us, motivates us to write and to make known [these things to you]."[55]

Despite his service to the Tsar of Muscovy, it seems that Theophanes was generally loyal to the Ottoman authorities. This sentiment is found in many of his letters, where the patriarch speaks reverently of the austere justice of Sultan Murad IV ("and here the sultan rules and ushers in a great fear and the wicked people have no power ... and in all of Constantinople there is calm")[56] and of his support for the Orthodox in the struggle over the holy places "as soon as the enlightenment from God was given to the heart of the long-living tsar, sultan Murad, he justly dealt with us, Christians."[57] Theophanes dreamed of a Russian–Ottoman alliance against Catholic Poland. In 1634, at the time of the Smolensk War, he wrote to Moscow:

> And here we see how well the Turkish kingship helps you: he sent Abaza Pasha[58] and repaid the Poles with great suffering … … And whoever of the important people we know, we always encourage them for the help to your kingdom, and we see that good things came out of our work.[59]

In this, Theophanes's political orientation coincided with that of another prominent Greek church leader of that era, Cyril Lucaris. He too was loyal to Ottoman authority, hostile to the Catholic world, and sympathetic to the Protestants, and so he lobbied for a union between Russian, the Ottomans, and Sweden against the Polish–Lithuanian Commonwealth. However, the similarity of their policies did not prevent these two church leaders from quarreling for personal or some other reasons.[60] Representatives of other parties, called the "Greco-Venetians," opposed those groups of Greek clergy who were centered around Lucaris or Theophanes. Among the Greco–Venetians, for example, was Athanasius Patelaros (d. 1653), who twice briefly held the See of Constantinople. These groups were characterized by pro-Western sentiment and negative attitudes toward the Ottoman authority. Vera Chentsova is inclined to explain this position through the origins of these people in Corfu, Chios, or Crete, the islands that had long been under Venetian control and had been exposed to the strong cultural influence of the West.[61]

In addition to the patriarchs, intelligence was delivered to Moscow by other clergy, as well as by the laity, who acted as trusted agents of the patriarchs or independently. From 1630 to 1660, this role was performed by ten Greek metropolitans (among them those of Nazareth and Bethlehem) and many archimandrites and monks, among whom the names of the clergy of the Holy Sepulchre often appear. Russia's chief "resident" in the East was for a long time Archimandrite Amphilochius, who once lived in Jerusalem and then changed sides to join the circle of the patriarch of Constantinople, Cyril Lucaris. After Amphilochius's death in 1653, a veritable competition broke out among Greek secret agents for the position of Russia's main informant.

Mutual denunciations generally accompanied Greek intelligence activities. In 1641, Theophanes informed Moscow about Amphilochius: "He writes and sends to you … messages with many lies, do not believe him." In 1667, Gabriel, a Greek from Constantinople, reported:

When those Palestinian bishops, archbishops, metropolitans, and patri-archs write that they care for the affairs of your royal majesty, and this they write and, having come, they tell this verbally, your royal majesty should not believe it. Everything they write and say is a lie, because being there they do not know of any genuine affairs or news, for they are not allowed to know anything and are treated like dogs.[62]

This mutual enmity among the spies is explained by the struggle for attention and favor from the Muscovite authorities, who did not skimp on payment for services. On the whole, it should be noted that the Greek agents often supplied unproven or outdated information. Usually these men were not serving as spies for long and at the slightest danger stopped all communication with the Rus-sians. The main incentive for most agents was money; few served for ideological reasons, but this was just the sort that proved to be the most loyal and valuable informants. These included, for example, Cyril Lucaris, who was executed by the Ottomans in 1637 on account of the intrigues of his enemies among the Phanariot clergy, led by Metropolitan Cyril Contaris of Veroia. Theophanes, a careful per-son and not as charismatic as Lucaris and for this reason not possessing as many enemies, safely outlived his Constantinopolitan confrere and in 1638 reported to Moscow about Cyril's death:

They slandered the old patriarch Cyril and denounced him as a traitor before the vizier Bayram Pasha … And then they took the patriarch … and imprisoned him in the tower by the Sea of Marmara.[63] And after a few days they put him to death and flung him out to sea … And that for-mer metropolitan of Veroia [the new patriarch Cyril] sent word to us that we should serve with him, and we did not want to serve with him, and he began to threaten us with the godless Hagarenes.[64]

After the execution of Cyril Lucaris by the Ottomans and the accession of the pro-Catholic Cyril Contaris to the patriarchal throne, Lucaris's group broke apart: many of his people fled from Istanbul and were for a long time in hiding.[65]

Following the fall of Contaris in 1639, a new center of power formed in Con-stantinople, which could be termed "the heirs of Lucaris." It was represented by the patriarchs Parthenius I (1639–1644) and Parthenius II (1644–1651, with inter-ruptions), who were loyal to the Sublime Porte and hostile to the Western world. Simultaneously, in Iasi under the patronage of the ambitious Moldavian ruler Vasile Lupu (1634–1653), an alternative center of influence formed, headed by the Greco-Venetian Athanasius Patelaros and Gabriel Vlasios, the metropolitan of Nafpaktos and Arta. Vasile Lupu, as mentioned, provided generous financial assistance to the Orthodox churches of the Ottoman world, including to Patriarch Theophanes of Jerusalem, who spent many years in the Moldavian monasteries belonging to the Holy Sepulchre. At the same time, the ambitious ruler sought to control the Orthodox hierarchs and actively intervened in ecclesiastical affairs. He intrigued against Parthenius II and attempted to place on the Patriarchal See of Constantinople his client Athanasius Patelaros.[66]

Envoys with letters from Theophanes also arrived in Moscow in 1641 and 1643. The second of these embassies, led by Archimandrite Anthimus and a cousin of the patriarch, Archdeacon Neophytus, received, among other gifts, icons in silver frames for the churches of Jerusalem, and a hierarchal hat for the patriarch valued at 880 rubles.[67] The last letter from Theophanes, delivered by the Greek agent Foma Ivanov, was written in Constantinople on December 10, 1644, and the patriarch already had died on December 15, as Foma informed the Posolsky Prikaz.[68]

The Patriarchate of Antioch, more insular and remaining somewhat aloof from the Greek world of the Levant and its foreign policy, was practically not involved in the relations between Russia and the East of that time. Moreover, after the victory of Ignatius ʿAtiya over Cyril Dabbas in 1628, relations between the See of Antioch and the Phanar were irreparably damaged[69] and Cyril Lucaris, acting as the main intermediary for the distribution of Russian alms for the East, cut Damascus off from them. In 1633, Patriarch Ignatius of Antioch attempted to complain to Moscow,

> May it be known to your kingship that we are poor and needy in the present times ... I have found out that your kingship does not forget us and sends [us alms] ... but they keep [them] in Constantinople and do not send these to us ... And even now we wish that you show us mercy and not forget us.[70]

Of course, details of Russia's wealth and generosity penetrated into Syria. In the 1620s to the 1640s, several priests of the Patriarchate of Antioch journeyed of their own initiative to Moscow to seek alms.[71] In 1646, Patriarch Euthymius III also tried to enter into contact with the Russian government, sending an embassy to Moscow headed by Metropolitan Jeremiah of ʿAkkar. However, at Putivl on the Russian border, the embassy was delayed pending further instructions from Moscow. In Russia, there were periodic attempts to restrict the excessive influx of alms seekers from the Christian East, stopping them at the border and sending them back with a few alms. In early 1647, during the correspondence between the governor of Putivl and the Posolsky Prikaz, Metropolitan Jeremiah died and his companions were sent home from Russia practically empty-handed.[72]

PATRIARCH PAISIUS'S FINEST HOUR

In the next quarter-century, ties between Russia and the East seem to have reached their highest state of development. This was stimulated by a sharp change in the geopolitical situation in Eastern Europe. In 1644, the War of Candia[73] began between the Ottoman Empire and Venice and the European powers supporting them over Crete, the birthplace of many of the Greco-Venetians. The war sharply polarized the positions of the Greek bishops. The Iasi group spun anti-Ottoman intrigues in support of the project of an alliance between the Moldavian ruler Vasile and the Polish–Lithuanian Commonwealth, which was seen as the striking force in the Christian world's confrontation with the Ottomans. The plan was to bring Russia into this anti-Turkish (and likewise anti-Swedish) union. In connection with this, a plan was discussed in Moscow for the marriage of the daughter of Tsar Mikhail Fedorovich with the son of the king of Denmark, Sweden's traditional enemy. For his own part, Patriarch Parthenius II of Constantinople attempted to thwart this dynastic union by pointing out the need to rebaptize Protestants, something unacceptable to the Danish side.[74]

During this period, in both Russia and the Ottoman Orthodox *millet*, a new generation of people came into power who were more interested in each other. The young Tsar Alexei Mikhailovich, who ascended to the throne in 1645, was an exceedingly religious person who was convinced of his messianic vocation as patron of the entire Orthodox world. Under his rule, financial assistance to the Orthodox East reached its apex. During a short period in the late 1640s and early 1650s, four Eastern patriarchs visited Moscow, as well as many bishops, abbots of monasteries, and other clergy.

At the same time, Patriarch Theophanes was replaced as the central figure in Russian–Middle Eastern relations by his successor to the See of Jerusalem, Paisius, a much more energetic and ambitious person. As mentioned, he twice went to Russia when he was still an abbot in Iasi, undoubtedly forming a clear idea of the military, political, and financial resources of the Russian state. Therefore, despite his close relationship with the Moldavian ruler Vasile, Paisius—a completely independent political actor—began from the very first days of his patriarchate to emphasize his pro-Moscow orientation.

In July 1645, Paisius sent notification of his election to Moscow, along with the usual complaints about the Hagarenes' oppression and requests for assistance. It should be mentioned that previously the Eastern patriarchs had no tradition of informing Moscow about their accession to the throne.[75] In September, Paisius sent a letter of condolence on the death of Tsar Michael in which he recalled the generosity of the deceased toward his Ottoman coreligionists and asked the new tsar to multiply his alms for them.[76]

In the early years of the Candian War, the anti-Ottoman element of the Greek clergy was prepared to set their hopes on Polish King Wladyslaw IV, whom they regarded as the future liberator of the Balkan Christians from Hagarene slavery.[77] However, the plan for the Polish–Lithuanian Commonwealth to act against Turkey was rejected by the Polish magnates in the Seym in 1646. The only ally of King Wladyslaw proved to be the Zaporozhian Cossacks, who were ready to go to war with the Ottomans. This is how some scholars explain the sympathy of the Iasi Greeks for Bogdan Khmelnitsky.[78] It seems, however, that with the beginning of the uprising in Ukraine in 1648, the cossacks ceased to be a potential force against the Turks and dreams of the Polish–Lithuanian Commonwealth entering into war against the Porte had to be abandoned. What happened in Eastern Europe in the late 1640s was the struggle of two entirely different civilizations, Orthodox and Catholic, which did not touch on the dispute between the Ottomans and the Venetians over Crete. The support in the Greek world for the Ukrainian uprising can be explained by the total shift in priorities for all ecclesiastical groups in the new political environment. Now the Greek bishops encouraged Russia to accept the allegiance of the Zaporozhian Host and then to expand toward the southwest, with the prospect of having an outpost on the Ottoman border.

In 1648, Paisius left Palestine and went to Moscow in person. While in Moldavia in October, the patriarch secretly entered into negotiations with Bogdan Khmelnitsky, urging him to fight the Poles and reunite with Russia. Then, while passing through Ukraine, he stopped in Kiev to meet with the hetman in person. From January until June of 1649, Paisius stayed in Moscow, where he was received several times by the tsar. He conducted negotiations with the Posolsky Prikaz, repeatedly calling on the Russian autocrat to take back the throne of the Emperor Constantine and to liberate the Eastern Christians from the "wild beasts that mercilessly devour [us]."[79] Simultaneously, Paisius acted as Bogdan Khmelnitsky's mediator in the discussion of Ukraine's entry into allegiance with the Russian tsar. As is well known, the Russian government at first greeted Khmelnitsky's offer unenthusiastically, not wanting to breach the peace with the Poles.

As for the distress of the Eastern Christians under Ottoman rule, as the Duma *dyak* Mikhail Volosheninov said to the patriarch in the tsar's name,

> we hear this with pain in our soul and heart, but no one can resist the will of God … However we unceasingly care for this, that the Lord God may avert his righteous anger and return the Holy Sepulchre and the holy city of Jerusalem into the hands of pious kings.[80]

After receiving lavish gifts, Paisius left Moscow on June 10. He was accompanied by a number of Russian clergy, including Arseny Sukhanov, who already had diplomatic experience in the East.

On his way back through Ukraine with a long stop in Moldavia, Paisius continued to be actively engaged in Ukrainian affairs. He corresponded with Bogdan Khmelnitsky and sent him his representatives, Arseny Sukhanov and Metropolitan Gabriel of Nazareth, who had come to Moldavia from Palestine. In December 1649, Arseny arrived in Moscow, to be followed a year later by Gabriel and other emissaries of Paisius, with letters from the patriarch in which he explained the political situation in Southeast Europe and the Ottoman Empire in particular and continued to lobby for the idea of receiving Ukraine into Russia. Huge efforts were needed on Paisius's part to persuade the authorities in Moscow who did not want trouble with the Poles and to keep the frustrated Zaporozhians from taking reckless, unfriendly measures toward Russia that might derail the plan. Encouraged by the growing power of the Orthodox peoples, in late 1649, Paisius promoted the grandiose geopolitical project of a Muscovite-Zaporozhian-Moldavian-Wallachian coalition against the Turks, who were bogged down in the war with the Venetians. An assault on the Ottoman Empire from the north was to be supported by a revolt of Greeks and Serbs behind Ottoman lines. The plan, however, was rejected by cautious Muscovite politicians.[81] It is worth recalling that Paisius's diplomatic activity aimed at Russia and Zaporozhia was not only the political strategy of the Patriarchate of Jerusalem but also part of the overall effort of the Greek world to consolidate the Orthodox peoples of Eastern Europe. At the same time, there remained internal rivalries among the Greeks. Some of the Iasi Greeks, such as Gabriel Vlasios, found themselves in the entourage of Paisius of Jerusalem. Athanasius Patelaros remained an independent actor to a significant degree, but he also encouraged Russia to act in the Black Sea region and to liberate Constantinople from the infidels. Paisius's rival, Patriarch Parthenius II of Constantinople maintained no less close and friendly ties with Bogdan Khmelnitsky and Tsar Alexei Mikhailovich.[82]

At a time when Russia felt like never before that it was an integral part of the Eastern Christian world, Nikon's ecclesiastical reform, which harmonized Russian liturgical rites with those of the other Orthodox Churches, was natural. It is believed that Paisius encouraged the tsar and the patriarch to undertake this reform, which was meant to be a necessary step toward a future unification of the Orthodox peoples under the scepter of the autocrat of Muscovy and all of Byzantium. Nikon was also seduced by the idea of theocratic authority modeled on that of the hierarchs of the Rum *millet*.[83] Chentsova argues that is was not only Paisius of Jerusalem who urged the Russian authorities to take this step; Parthenius II of Constantinople, Paisius's old enemy, also proposed his own version of reform. Unfortunately, now it is difficult to understand precisely the difference between the two programs. It is obvious, however, that the two Greek patriarchs fought for influence at the Muscovite court. Associated with these intrigues was an accusation of unorthodoxy and the exile of Arsenius the Greek who was involved in the revision of liturgical books and originally was left behind in Moscow by Paisius in 1649.

It is precisely in connection with plans for church reform that Arseny Sukhanov, the monk of the Trinity–Sergius Lavra was sent from Moscow to the East with the task of collecting liturgical and theological manuscripts, recording the differences in ritual between the Orthodox churches in Russian and Levant, and discussing a series of theological questions with Eastern bishops. Those Muscovite statesmen who sent Arseny also do not seem to have approved of Paisius's version of the plan for church reform. While being in Iasi in the spring of 1650, Sukhanov held a debate about the faith over multiple days with Patriarch Paisius and his entourage, defending the correctness of the Russian variations in liturgical rites.[84] No wonder, then, that Paisius made every effort to prevent Sukhanov from meeting with his rival Parthenius II. The patriarch of Jerusalem got his way: in May of 1651, a few days before Arseny Sukhanov arrived in Constantinople, Parthenius was deposed and killed, presumably through the machinations of the rulers of Moldavia and Wallachia.[85]

By late summer, the Russian emissary reached Egypt and met in Cairo with Patriarch Ioannicius of Alexandria. In September, he went via Damietta to Palestine, arriving in Jerusalem on October 6.[86] It is quite obvious that the objectives set before Arseny in Moscow went well beyond church issues: along the way, he was keenly interested in the state of fortifications and of the Ottoman armed forces, in news from the front of the Candian War. Sukhanov secretly sent all of his correspondence to Moscow through the previously mentioned Archimandrite Amphilochius, the main Muscovite informant in Istanbul.[87] When describing the fortifications of Jerusalem, Arseny demonstrated knowledge of fortifications and ballistics, quite unexpected for his ecclesiastical rank, giving professional advice in case of a possible siege of the city.[88]

Arseny stayed in Jerusalem until late April 1652, making many interesting observations about the life of Palestinian Christians.[89] Unlike the ecstatic letters of pilgrims who did not notice anything around themselves other than venerable relics and holy places, Sukhanov prefigured Porphyry Uspensky in the role of the meticulous "observer of the East," recounting the local population's way of life.[90]

Sukhanov was critical toward the Greek clergy in Palestine, again being the precursor of Russian anti-Phanariot publications of the nineteenth century. Otto-man Christians had opportunities for careers almost exclusively within the insti-tution of the Church, which led to the "overflow" (as Malyshevsky terms it) of clergymen who did not have an inner calling to the religious life.[91] This became one of the perennial causes of unrest and intrigue among the clergy that often shocked Russian observers. A certain difference in mentality, which was strik-ingly evident when there was even a slight degree of close acquaintance between the Russians and their coreligionists, did not help to create mutual sympathy. Levantine clergy were not distinguished by piety and asceticism in the Byz-antine and Old Muscovite spirit. Eastern patriarchs who came to Russia were easily wearied of the long services and harsh fasts of the Muscovites. "Knowl-edgeable people have told us," wrote Paul of Aleppo, "that if someone wants to reduce his life by fifteen years, let him go to the country of the Muscovites and live among them as an ascetic, demonstrating constant abstinence and fasting, reading [prayers] and getting up at midnight. He should stop all jokes, mirth, and undue familiarity," stop drinking or smoking, and so on. "God knows," Paul continues, "that we behave like saints among them ... though of necessity and not voluntarily."[92] Similarly, in the papers of Arseny Sukhanov, one encounters many indications of deviations from monastic discipline by Patriarch Paisius and other members of the Brotherhood of the Holy Sepulchre. This "espionage" greatly unnerved the clergy of Jerusalem. "That very day," Sukhanov wrote, "the *daskal* (i.e., *didaskalos*, teacher) reports, I heard how the cellarer said, Arseny sits there in the cell, he writes everything about us, monks, he wants to present this book to the tsar; it would be good if the patriarch took his books and burned them."[93]

According to Kapterev, the theological discussions with Sukhanov in Iasi once more caused Paisius to worry about the future political and spiri-tual unity of the Orthodox peoples. The patriarch of Jerusalem decided to remind his Muscovite counterpart Nikon about his plans for church reform. For this purpose Paisius sent Metropolitan Gabriel of Nafpaktos and Arta, a prominent theologian who knew the Slavic languages, to Russia. Gabriel stayed in Moscow from October 1652 to February 1653 and had several conversations with Nikon, explaining the correctness of the Greek rituals and the need for an appropriate revision of the Russian services. Shortly after the metropolitan's departure in the spring of 1653, Patriarch Nikon proceeded with his reform of the Russian church. Even in his letters to Nikon, Paisius persistently supported the reform initiatives in the Russian church.[94]

Undoubtedly, the patriarch of Jerusalem was a great statesman, an outstanding politician and a skilled, and often successful, diplomat. He showed himself to be a master of subtle intrigue, overcoming his enemies and emerging victorious even in the most impossible situations. It seems that Paisius made up for his lack of a strong education with a keen intellect, guile, and an expansive geopolitical vision. Notable in the patriarch's worldview is his heightened sense of the divine election of the Greek Church and messianic ambitions. "The faith came out of Sion and all that is good originated with us. For we are the root and the source for everyone in faith, and we had the Ecumenical Councils," said Paisius to Arseny Sukhanov in 1650.[95] However, during his theological disputes with Sukhanov, the patriarch mostly kept silent, letting his highly educated advisors speak. Not being a refined theologian, Paisius, it seems, was similarly indifferent to piety. From the denunciations of Arseny Sukhanov, it is clear that the patriarch took a careless attitude toward conducting services in the Church of Holy Sepulchre, allowed himself to breach the fasting discipline, and played the role of an ascetic only before the Moscow envoy.[96] By character, he was a coarse and imperious person. In 1646, he suppressed the unrest of the Arab Christians, instilled fear in many of his bishops, and treated the laity harshly.[97] Paisius did not hesitate to step over dead bodies. It is enough to recall the execution of Patriarch Parthenius II of Constantinople who was a similar kind of a "predator," only a less fortunate one because of his intrigues.[98] However, when Paisius found himself in a similar situation, arrested by the Turks in 1657 and sentenced to death, even with the noose already around his neck, he found the strength to act with dignity and retain the presence of mind that perhaps saved his life.[99] Overall, he appears to have been in spirit not only a churchly figure but also a secular figure, a rare sort of Orthodox theocratic leader and certainly one of the outstanding personalities in the history of the Orthodox East.

THE JOURNEY OF MACARIUS

A quite different man was Paisius's contemporary, Patriarch Macarius of Antioch, who also played a prominent role in the history of Russian–Eastern relations.

In the summer of 1652, Macarius made a long journey to the courts of Christian princes, hoping to receive alms for his see. In October, he reached Istanbul where he received letters of recommendation from the Ecumenical Patriarch, and in early 1563, he arrived in Iasi where he stayed for a time at the court of the voivode Vasile Lupu. However, Macarius's hopes for generous Moldavian alms were dashed when in the spring of 1653 Vasile was overthrown by the local aristocracy, after which the country became the scene for a devastating war between rival factions of Moldavian boyars that involved the Zaporozhian Cossacks, Hungarians, and Crimean Tatars.[100] Making it out of Moldavia only with difficulty, Macarius moved to Wallachia, where in the spring of 1654 he witnessed the death of the voivode Matei and the election of a new ruler.[101] Leaving Wallachia and crossing the Dniester on June 10, 1654, Macarius made his way across Ukraine shortly before its liberation from Polish rule.[102] After a ceremonial meeting in the camp of Bogdan Khmelnitski and a visit to Kiev, on June 20 the patriarch reached Putivl.

Macarius's triumphal procession into Russia was interrupted by an epidemic of the plague that kept him in Kolomna for almost half a year. It was only on February 2, 1655, that Macarius and his retinue managed to reach Moscow, where only a few days before the tsar and his army had returned from the Polish campaign.[103] The magnificent reception that Macarius received from Tsar Alexei Mikhailovich and the Patriarch Nikon surpassed all similar ceremonies during visits to Moscow by other Eastern hierarchs. Nikon utilized the authority of the Antiochian primate to the full extent for enforcing his church reform. The most decisive steps toward standardizing the rituals were made by Nikon during Great Lent of 1655 with even more radical reforms in winter–spring 1656. The patriarch of Antioch was an active participant in all activities related to this. With Macarius's support, Nikon spoke out against icons in the Frankish style, established the new way of making the sign of the cross, issued a new edition of the Sluzhebnik, "corrected" according to Greek models, and proclaimed the first anathemas against opponents of church reform.[104] After a visit in August–September 1655 to Valdai Monastery and Novgorod, in January 1656, Macarius had another audience with the tsar in Savvino–Storozhevsky Monastery.

Impressed with this meeting, Alexei Mikhailovich made a promising statement: "I pray to God that before I die I will see him [i.e., Macarius] among the four patriarchs serving in Hagia Sophia, with our patriarch the fifth among them."[105] A little later, the tsar spoke even more explicitly about the liberation of the Greeks:

My heart grieves over the enslavement of these poor people … God will ask this of me on the Day of Judgment, because even though I have the possibility of redeeming them, I neglect this. And I have made a commitment that, God willing, I will sacrifice my army, my treasury, and even my own blood in order to deliver them.[106]

Perhaps speaking here was Alexei Mikhailovich's euphoria from his first triumphs in the war with the Poles, when all geopolitical dreams seemed easily obtainable for him.

In spring 1656, at his own insistent request, the patriarch of Antioch was allowed to return home. "God only knows what longing and great anguish we felt," wrote Paul of Aleppo about the prolonged stay in Russia. Undoubtedly, most visitors from the Christian East felt uncomfortable in Russia, despite the generous alms and the honor surrounding them in Moscow. The sharp difference in lifestyle and system of government between the Muscovites and the peoples of the Eastern Mediterranean certainly had an impact, and Paul of Aleppo expresses such feelings.[107]

Macarius brought back almost unprecedented gifts—money and furs valued at three thousand rubles, as well as icons, church vessels, vestments, and special letters to the See of Antioch and prominent Syrian monasteries, allowing for the regular delivery of alms from Russia.[108] Macarius's belongings were loaded onto sixty carts. For comparison, scholars cite the information that in 1634 the embassy of Holstein left Moscow with eighty carts.[109] On June 12, 1654, the caravan arrived in Putivl and then went through Kiev and Chigirin, reaching Iasi on August 21 and Wallachia in November. Throughout this time, the patriarch maintained an active correspondence with Moscow about theological issues and also interceded on behalf of this or that Greek petitioner going for alms to Russia.[110]

In the mid and late 1650s, it appears that Macarius became the key figure in relations between Russia and the Middle East. The patriarch of Antioch possessed neither the strong will nor the political acumen of Paisius, but (perhaps for this very reason) he enjoyed a special position with Tsar Alexei Mikhailovich. Macarius almost never intervened in politics of his own volition. He did not impose his own view, preferring to "go with the flow." He appears to have been the complete opposite of the tyrannical Paisius: a kind but weak man who always sympathized with the suffering and the oppressed. Perhaps it is because of these qualities that the people of Damascus so loved him, as evident in the chronicles.

On the basis of Russian archival documents, however, a somewhat-different image of Macarius is revealed. It is quite clear that he was eager for money, and Muscovite diplomacy actively played on this, especially in the 1660s, during the trial of Nikon. On the one hand, this miserliness had an objective explanation.

A thousand years of oppression and extreme poverty had a corrupting effect on the Eastern clergy. Once, Patriarch Macarius saw in the refectory of the Valdai Iviron Monastery luxurious vestments captured from Polish Jesuits casually spread on the floor, and he was barely able to restrain himself from asking for these garments "desecrated" by heretics as a gift for himself. Had he tried to speak of it with the Muscovites, wrote Paul of Aleppo, "and they would[have said], 'Look how small their faith is!' However, if God wills, let Him allow that they become angry with us, that through them He may enrich us!"[111] The archives confirm this trait in Macarius: he submitted endless petitions (an especially large number were filed in spring of 1656, before his departure from Russia) in which he asks for more and more gifts for himself, his see, or his entourage: from about four pounds of whalebone and two pounds of mica to velvet *epimanikia* for Archdeacon Paul.[112] The most characteristic episode, however, involved the story of the horses carrying the patriarch's baggage, part of which Macarius had left in Putivl when he arrived in Russia and part in the Spassky Monastery near Kaluga. A year later, seeing that his stay in Russia would be prolonged, Macarius remembered about the horses and decided to sell them. As it turned out, two of his horses at the Spassky Monastery had been stolen. The Russian authorities launched a rigorous inquiry into the incident and decided to recover the cost of the missing horses from the monastery's peasants. Patriarch Macarius was required to report the amount of the damages and, sensing that he had the upper hand in the situation, he demanded the exorbitant price of 15 rubles for each horse (for comparison, the patriarch's servants were only with great difficulty able to sell the horses remaining in Putivl for a price of 3–9 rubles each).[113]

At the same time, the patriarch of Antioch could show compassion and mercy when it cost nothing. Thus, on the way back from Moscow, when passing through Putivl, Macarius took the pain to write a lengthy petition to the tsar asking for the pardon of two horsemen who had been convicted on a complaint from the "Circassians from Konotop" and sentenced to death for sodomy and child molestation.[114]

For all his desire to avoid being drawn into politics, on several occasions, Macarius was drawn into large-scale historical dramas, although perhaps not of his own initiative. One such episode occurred just as the patriarch was returning from Moscow, when he was staying in the Danube principalities from August 1656 to September 1657. After the Council of Pereyaslav and the reunification of Ukraine with Russia, the geopolitical position of Moldavia and Wallachia changed dramatically. The overthrow of Vasile Lupu in 1653 prompted the Greek bishops who were oriented toward him to seek a new political patron, namely the Russian tsar, who was able to act as the leader of an anti-Ottoman coalition. Patriarch Paisius of Jerusalem and other Eastern bishops began to make plans for the next push by the Muscovite kingdom toward the Orthodox East. The idea of a Russian–Moldavian alliance also found support with the voivode of Moldavia, Gheorghe Ştefan. In October 1655, the patriarch of Jerusalem sent a letter to Moscow asking for Moldavian lands ravaged by the Hagarenes to be placed under protection. In spring of 1656, a Moldavian embassy, headed by Metropolitan Gideon, arrived in Russia to conclude an alliance against Poland that would place Moldavia under a Russian protectorate. In autumn of 1656, Patriarchs Paisius and Macarius sent letters to Moscow kindly asking for the acceptance of the Moldavian embassy's offers and the protection of this country from Hagarene threats.[115]

GATHERING CLOUDS

The protectorate treaty was not realized because of a sharp reorientation of Moscow's foreign policy. In 1656, Russian authorities made the most fatal geopolitical mistake of the seventeenth century, opting for reconciliation with Poland to combat Sweden for access to the Baltic Sea. For a time, the Eastern hierarchs attempted to pursue an independent game, supporting the anti-Catholic alliance of the Danube principalities, Hungary, Sweden, and Bogdan Khmelnitsky, even though this alliance no longer suited Moscow's plans. At that point, Macarius was at the court of the Wallachian voivode Constantin. Paul of Aleppo gives a curious description of the feast arranged by Constantin for Epiphany 1657: the voivode gave toasts for the health of all the political and spiritual leaders of neighboring countries except Russia and, of course, Poland.[116]

The clergy of the Orthodox *millet*, however, had not abandoned their attempts to once more open Russia toward Southeastern Europe. Greek informants sent letters to the Posolsky Prikaz, urging the Russians to make peace with Sweden and resume the offensive against Poland with the prospect of an outlet to the Ottoman borders. Thus, for example, in April 1658, a messenger arrived from the Greek patriarchs who relayed in particular a message from Patriarch Ioannicius of Alexandria that stated, "It does not become you, a pious sovereign … to fight with Swedes from both sides. For you began, great sovereign, the war with the Polish king, and it must be committed to the end."[117] The patriarch urged the king not to believe the Polish oaths and the truce agreement because, as he wrote, the Poles

> are lying to you, great sovereign, but I, who prays to God for you, have discovered the truth, that the Pope of Rome sent letters of pardon to the

king of Poland, [saying,] pray to God, … and you will be forgiven by me, but only do not yield to the enemy.[118]

Patriarch Paisius of Jerusalem also wrote to Russia in the same vein.

On Easter 1657, Paisius planned to consecrate solemnly upon the Lord's Tomb the so-called Mitre of the Emperor Constantine, prepared at his request, which then was supposed to be sent to the Russian tsar as a symbol of imperial continuity and his rights to the Byzantine legacy.[119]

However, the openly pro-Moscow activities of the Orthodox clergy caused the Ottoman authorities to lose their temper. In March 1657, the energetic Grand Vizier Mehmet Köprülü began a radical eradication of the "fifth column." According to some reports, they demanded that the Moldavian voivode extradite the church hierarchs associated with the plans for a Russian–Moldavian alliance, including Metropolitan Gideon and Patriarch Macarius of Antioch.[120] The voivode refused, and in response on March 24, the Ottomans executed Patriarch Parthenius III of Constantinople who was accused of having secret links to Russia. Mass arrests began of Greek merchants and clergy suspected of pro-Russian sympathies. Patriarch Paisius of Jerusalem was also captured while in Istanbul and accused of manufacturing the aforementioned mitre.[121]

Paisius was accused of treason, including conspiring with the Muscovite tsar to capture Constantinople. The grand vizier, who was Paisius's patron, and the sultan were absent from the capital and so the investigation was led by the *qaimaqam* (the deputy vizier). On his orders, the patriarch was thrown in prison and then led in chains through the city, stopping several times to simulate preparation for execution. With the noose already around Paisius's neck, they asked him to give ransom money in exchange for his life. The patriarch denied all allegations and refused to pay. Finally, he was returned to prison and then the vizier acquitted the patriarch and dismissed the *qaimaqam*.[122]

In view of these daunting events and at the insistence of the voivode Constantin, Macarius avoided leaving Wallachia.[123] However, by late autumn of 1657, Wallachia also ceased to be a safe haven. News came from Istanbul that the voivode had been deposed (a little earlier the Moldavian voivode Gheorghe Ştefan had also been deposed) and the Ottoman and Crimean hordes were invading the country. Constantin fled to Hungary without putting up a fight and the Tatars plundered Târgovişte. Macarius and his companions hid in forests and mountain monasteries. "Our horses were under saddle night and day," Paul wrote, "and we were ready to flee to the high mountains for fear of chancing upon attack from the Tatars, especially in view of our fame."[124] Fortunately for

Macarius, the new voivode Ghica, appointed by the Turks, was friendly to the patriarch. In April 1658, Macarius was able to return to Bucharest and even led the coronation ceremony for the voivode on Pentecost.[125] In Paul's notes there suddenly appear critical comments about the former ruler Constantin who had lost the Arabs' respect after his cowardly flight from the country and who now, as it turned out, was in debt to the patriarch and was in general "extremely stingy and not all that honest."[126]

The situation in Wallachia, however, remained troubling and the Turkish military operations against the Hungarians did not cease, so Macarius sought any ways that he could get out of the country. Finally, in October 1658, he managed to hire a ship in Galati and sail to Sinope. The patriarch's caravan then crossed Anatolia, and in April 1659, he arrived in Aleppo.[127]

By 1658, Russia's war with Sweden proved to be inconclusive and Muscovite diplomacy once again turned to Ukrainian affairs. However, over the years, the pace of the advance toward the Southwest had been lost. Poland had received respite to continue the struggle and in the late 1650s Russia lost many positions in Ukraine. This undermined all of Tsar Alexei Mikhailovich's plans to liberate his Middle Eastern coreligionists.[128]

THE AFFAIR OF NIKON: LIGARIDES AND NECTARIUS

Over the next decade, relations between Moscow and the Orthodox East were marked by the affair of Nikon, a conflict between secular and religious authorities in Russia that began in 1658 with the patriarch's resignation and ended eight years later with his official deposition and exile. Nikon's fall caused a painful reaction in the East because the patriarch had been the chief conduit for Greek influence in Russia. Nikon, in turn, refused to recognize his deposition by a synod of Russian clergy in 1660, claiming that only the four Eastern patriarchs were entitled to judge him. Thus, the conflict could not be resolved without the participation of the Christian East.

A key role in Nikon's overthrow was played by one of the most striking and controversial figures in the Greco–Oriental world, Paisius Ligarides (d. 1678), the metropolitan of Gaza, a brilliant intellectual with a dark past. A Greek from Chios and a graduate of a Catholic college in Rome, he easily changed religious and political orientation. At one time, he was close to Patriarch Paisius of Jerusalem, from whom he received the metropolitan's title, and in February 1662, he was in Russia, having been invited by Nikon himself a long time ago. Navigating quickly in this environment, Ligarides went over to the side of Nikon's opponents and, as a person of highly educated talent, he rendered valuable services to the tsar in his struggle with the patriarch. It was Ligarides who, becoming Alexei Mikhailovich's favorite for a time, took it upon himself to support Nikon's trial ideologically and to involve the hierarchs of the Orthodox East in this affair.[129]

At the end of 1662, an embassy was sent from Moscow to Istanbul headed by Hierodeacon Meletius the Greek, a close friend of Paisius Ligarides. Meletius had to persuade the Eastern patriarchs to come to Moscow to participate in Nikon's trial, for which they were advanced a sum of 3,000 ducats. In Istanbul the tsar's envoy met with Patriarch Dionysius of Constantinople and the newly elected patriarch of Jerusalem, Nectarius. The patriarchs were by no means sympathetic to the plans to depose Nikon and so they avoided the invitation to go to Moscow. With regard to the conflict between the tsar and Nikon, they prepared an evasive epistle in the form of questions and answers about the relationship between secular and spiritual authorities, in which Nikon's name did not even figure. Copies of the letter were sent for the signatures of the patriarchs of Alexandria and Antioch. Resentment grew among the clergy in Constantinople against Nikon's persecutors, Meletius and Paisius Ligarides. In connection with this, a certain Antiochian archimandrite is mentioned who openly reproached the Eastern patriarchs for corruption and searched around the city for Meletius, with clearly hostile intent. Meletius himself wrote of this, "This Antiochian archimandrite uttered (belched forth) these things not only in the absence of the patriarchs, but also before them in their presence, and he was going around the whole of Constantinople, seeking to denounce me."[130] In September 1663, Patriarch Nectarius moved from Istanbul to Iasi. There he met again with Meletius, who was on his way back to Russia. Nectarius expressed even sharper opposition to Nikon's disgrace and later, in March 1664, wrote a special epistle to the tsar with an appeal to reconcile with the patriarch. At the same time, Archimandrite Dositheus, the future patriarch, who was in Nectarius's entourage, wrote to Paisius Ligarides, condemning him for the position he took in the affair of Nikon. These letters did not at all please the Russian authorities and Nectarius's messenger stayed in Moscow for two years, practically under arrest.[131]

The tsar was also displeased with the results of Meletius's embassy (he had returned to Moscow in May 1664) and in September of that year Meletius was sent to the East for a second time, with new personal invitations for the Greek patriarchs to come to Moscow to oversee Nikon's trial. A separate embassy, headed by the Greek Stephanus Yuryev visited Patriarch Nectarius in Moldavia in January 1665. After a long deliberation, Nectarius refused to go to Moscow, realizing that his peacemaking efforts had come to naught and Nikon's fate was sealed.[132]

Nikon's disgrace led to a marked cooling in the Russian–Greek relationship during the time of Nectarius's patriarchate (1661–1669). Nikolai Kapterev links the reduction in the activity of the Levantine clergy to the personality of this patriarch who "was a very sickly person, not very energetic or enterprising, but was rather more inclined to calm and bookish activities."[133] In our view, such a characterization is rather one-sided. Other sources describe Nectarius's personality differently and, importantly, in such a contradictory way that one gets the impression that they are talking about completely different people. A brilliant intellectual, like many of the clergy from Crete, Nectarius began his career at the monastery on Mount Sinai where he played a key role in the 1640s and 1650s. In the Sinaites' struggle with the patriarchs of Alexandria, he acted as a bold adventurer, an intelligent and energetic planner of political moves and complicated intrigues, and an influential figure in circles of powerholders. Such things were only rewarded with curses in the memoirs of his enemy, Patriarch Ioannicius of Alexandria, who called him "an instrument of the anti-Christ creating temptations," "an excommunicated teacher of lies," "an accomplice to the lawless ones," and so on.[134] In 1653, the patriarch anathematized Nectarius, accusing him of planning to seize the See of Alexandria.[135]

Already by those years the Sinaite hieromonk was famous as a prominent writer and scholar, and the author of works on church history that were reprinted many times in the seventeenth and eighteenth centuries. However, even in his scholarly research, Nectarius remained under the influence of Sinaite group solidarity, "preferring benefit to the truth," as one of his contemporaries said of him.[136] Emperor Justinian's novella, granting autocephaly to the Monastery of Sinai, forged by Nectarius, made waves in church circles, despite the fact that Dositheus subsequently proved it to be a fabrication.[137] Echoes of this legend about Justinian's novella can still be found in the pages of some works of church history.

Nectarius's passionate struggle for the interests of his own group were highly appreciated by the monastic brotherhood, and, after the death of Bishop Joasaph of Sinai in 1661, Nectarius was elected in his place and sent to Jerusalem to be consecrated. At this moment when the newly elected bishop had probably reached the furthest limits of his dreams for his career, fate played a trick on him, lifting him even higher. On his way to the Holy City, Nectarius learned that, by decision of the Synod of Constantinople, he had been elected patriarch of Jerusalem. Thus, Nectarius found himself faced with the need to wage a merciless struggle against his own home monastery of Sinai, which was seeking independence from Jerusalem. Upon becoming patriarch, Nectarius became consumed with the interests of his own see and he started to look once more into the Sinaites' claims. In his writings, Dositheus noted, not without satisfaction, that everything done by the Monk Nectarius for the glory of the Monastery of Sinai was undone by the Patriarch Nectarius. He undoubtedly felt pained by this duplicity and so, to compensate somewhat for his "betrayal," he granted the bishop of Sinai the rank of archbishop and bargained for new awards and donations for the Monastery of St Catherine. But in the end, Nectarius was hardly able to rid himself of his feeling of guilt and, perhaps, was it this feeling that forced him to resign in 1669?

Judging from what is available in the sources, it does not seem likely that Nectarius had a lust for power. However, it is not this lack of political ambition that predetermined Nectarius's refusal to take an active part in grand politics and international relations. In the 1660s, during the escalating conflict between the tsar and the Patriarch Nikon, the Russian government emphatically sought support for its actions from the Eastern patriarchs. However, as noted, Nectarius sympathized with Nikon and made every effort to convince the tsar to come to terms with the disgraced patriarch and to return him to his see. "Have zeal for the Orthodox faith," Nectarius implored the Russian autocrat in his letter of March 1664,

> so that during the time of your sacred kingship there may not have been laid down an evil and perilous custom to remove those of your patriarchs who are Orthodox and believe rightly about the dogmas of the faith.... This is the beginning of the destruction of the church in Constantinople; it has served and serves to this day as the source of many evils and causes us to be disgraced before the Western church.[138]

In Moscow, such exhortations were received with displeasure, as the Muscovites desired to see the Eastern hierarchs as servants and not judges of Russian policy. However, in Nectarius's diplomatic activity, he demonstrated integrity and dignity not typical of the Phanariots. Even though he was struggling hard against his church's growing debt, he never asked Russia for financial assistance, as he knew that afterward he would have to act according to Moscow's dictates.

Macarius's Second Journey

Meletius the Greek had accomplished nothing in Istanbul, as the patriarch of Constantinople was strongly opposed to Ligarides and to Nikon's trial. However, upon arrival to Egypt, Meletius managed with generous promises to persuade Patriarch Paisius of Alexandria and Archbishop Ananias of Sinai to go to Moscow. Leaving Egypt with Meletius on May 25, 1665, they went through Tripoli to Damascus, where they learned that Patriarch Macarius of Antioch had gone to Georgia to collect alms. Meletius and his companions followed after Macarius and arrived in Tbilisi in October. At the time, Macarius was in Imereti. After long correspondence and entreaties, which caused Meletius much stress, Macarius finally agreed to go to Moscow after Easter. Meletius and the patriarch of Alexandria wintered in Shemakha, where Macarius joined them in the spring of 1666. Together, they traveled to Derbent, and there ships coming from Astrakhan met them. After a difficult voyage, on June 19, the caravan dropped anchor at the mouth of the Volga River.[139]

The patriarchs' reception in Russia was planned as an event on a national scale, with an enormous amount of effort and resources. The patriarchs, surrounded with all honor and luxury and accompanied by the metropolitan of Astrakhan and a few bailiffs, including the *podyachy* (assistant clerk) of the Department of Secret Affairs (*Prikaz taynykh del*), slowly went up the Volga to Simbirsk and from there overland to Moscow via Arzamas and Vladimir. Deposited in the archives is an abundant interdepartmental correspondence about the preparations for meeting the patriarchs. By autumn 1666, the correspondence takes on an urgent and a frenetic character. In the guests' chambers they hastily upholstered the walls and furniture with cloth and chose attendants (*yaryzhnye*) for the maintenance of the patriarchal embassies "so that they not be thieves or drunkards."[140] Ceremonial riassas were sewn for Paisius and Macarius out of fox and squirrel fur.[141] The tsar periodically sent the guests gifts and grandiloquent letters of welcome.

At the same time, around these Levantine guests there brewed energetic work of another kind, not always apparent to the untrained eye. The tsar needed a prerehearsed trial against Nikon, and the patriarchs could not be allowed to form their own opinion regarding him, different from Moscow's official opinion. The authorities took strict measures to isolate the patriarchs from unnecessary contact with the outside world. The metropolitan of Astrakhan was advised not to disclose any details of Nikon's case to the patriarchs, on the grounds of his lack of awareness because of his distance from Moscow. Particular attention was paid to the interception of possible letters from Nikon to the patriarchs. Nikon in fact did periodically attempt to convey to the Eastern hierarchs his vision of the conflict between secular and religious authorities in Russia. Similarly, the bailiffs were ordered to "firmly guard" against the patriarchs "sending any letters to anyone." In particular, Meletius the Greek was advised to recruit Paul of Aleppo to keep an appropriate watch over Patriarch Macarius.[142]

On October 20, the patriarchal convoy, numbering five hundred horses, was met by Colonel Artamon Matveev, a rising star on the Russian political horizon in the last years of Alexei Mikhailovich's reign. Matveev was also instructed to find out whether the patriarchs were angry with Paisius Ligarides and to send Meletius the Greek to Moscow ahead of the convoy for necessary consultations ahead of the tsar's meeting with the patriarchs.[143]

On November 2, 1666, Paisius and Macarius triumphantly entered Moscow, and two days later, they had an official audience with the sovereign in the Palace of Facets. There was plenty of magnificent ceremony and flowery speeches. The tsar likened the patriarchs to the Apostles Peter and Paul, recalling his guests' long journey. He compared Macarius and Paisius to holy martyrs and passion-bearers, as they appeared as "imitators and accomplishers" of their labors. Macarius in particular was named as "the glory of the church, the exalted eagle, the spiritual flute … the Master's vessel."[144]

The following day, November 5, Alexei Mikhailovich unofficially received the patriarchs in his dining quarters. No minutes of the meeting were taken, but it is easy to assume that no magnificent speeches were recited. The tsar and the patriarchs spoke privately for four hours. It was at this time that Nikon's fate was finally decided and the roles for the upcoming trial were assigned.

It is not our task here to describe the trial, which took place from December 1 to 12, 1666, as it has been thoroughly analyzed in the scholarly literature. It is perhaps, however, our task to examine the behavior of the Eastern patriarchs at the hearings, especially that of Macarius, who was in a rather awkward position given his former friendship with Nikon and the dozens of petitions he wrote to the patriarch of Moscow at the time, requesting various benefactions. However, even during the patriarch of Antioch's first visit to Moscow, it was evident that the Arabs feared and disliked Nikon but were deeply committed to the tsar.[145] And now, at the Council of 1666, Macarius properly earned his royal alms, taking an active role, himself attacking Nikon and, with feigned outrage rejecting all of Nikon's reproaches against the tsar and his circle.[146] Macarius's zeal once caused Nikon to lose his composure: "You are great here," he told him, "but what answer will you give before the patriarch of Constantinople?"[147]

After Nikon's condemnation, the Eastern patriarchs participated in the subsequent meetings of the council in January 1667. There they discussed questions about the relation between secular and spiritual authorities and the delimitation of the scope of their authority. The patriarchs presented their judgment on the issue, again at the prompting of Paisius Ligarides and based on the previous agreement with the tsar and the boyars. Counting on plentiful royal alms, the patriarchs were prepared to use their authority to sanctify the most radical caesaropapist positions, but due to the resistance of the Russian episcopate, the council adopted a compromise solution regarding the limits and prerogatives of royal and episcopal authority. From April to June 1667, the council once more addressed the issues of church reform and of the Old Believers. The Eastern patriarchs themselves had little understanding of Russian realities and were completely under the influence of Paisius Ligarides and his supporters from among the Greeks resident in Moscow. As a result, the council adopted radical formulations condemning the entire previous Russian church tradition, especially the decisions of the Stoglav Council of 1555 and the Messianic claims of the "Third Rome." The doctrine of the Old Believers was equated with heresy, subject to ruthless eradication. According to most historians, the Greek hierarchs' involvement in an internal Russian conflict had fatal consequences, exacerbating the conflict between the Nikonians and the Old Believers a hundredfold and giving it an irreversible and bloody character.[148]

However, the authority of the council's decisions passed with the participation of the Eastern patriarchs came into question when it was revealed that Patriarch Parthenius of Constantinople had deposed Paisius and Macarius for their unauthorized trip to Russia. A new patriarch had even been put in Paisius's place. The tsarist government was once more forced to make serious efforts to convince the Phanariots and the sultan's authorities in Istanbul to revoke this decision. Already starting in December 1666, when the first rumors of the patriarchs' deposition appeared in Russia, in Moscow, they began to prepare an appropriate appeal to the sultan and the hierarchs of Constantinople for the rehabilitation of Paisius and Macarius. After clarifying all the circumstances of the patriarchs' deposition, final versions of the tsar's letters were prepared and sent to Istanbul in July 1667 with the embassy of Afanasy Nesterov and Ivan Vakhromeev. This task was made easier by the deposition of Patriarch Parthenius of Constantinople in November. In January 1668, the embassy was allowed into Adrianople (Edirne), where the issue of the patriarchs was discussed with senior administrative and judicial functionaries of the Empire. "For the sake of friendship" with the Muscovite tsar, the sultan agreed to return the deposed patriarchs to their thrones. Relevant *berats* were prepared and presented to the ambassadors in April.[149]

Then, in April 1668, Patriarch Macarius left Russia with lavish royal gifts. Taking the same route via the Volga as he took on his way to Russia, Macarius left Astrakhan on September 3, reaching Derbent by sea and from there he went to Shemakha. Cargo and gifts for the Khan of Shemakha cost Macarius several hundred rubles. Later in Moscow, Macarius's messenger Ivan Kuzmin reported,

And the khan, having taken these gifts, sent his man to the patriarch to ask and to see, if the patriarch has any of the Muscovite precious items, which are suitable to be among the shah's possessions which are suited for the daily life of the shahs ... and that khan's man ... took ... sables, atlases, damasks, wool ... squirrel and ermine furs, a large and priceless amount of whalebone, and having taken [all these things], he told the patriarch: if the khan fancies it, then he will take it, but the rest he will send back.[150]

The khan, however, did not return anything but rather assigned it the absurdly low value of 5,000 rubles and issued Macarius a promissory note for that amount.

After spending six weeks in Shemakha, Macarius and his retinue moved to Tbilisi, to the court of the king of Kartli, Shah-Nawaz Khan, who had favored Macarius since his first visit to Georgia. "And they arrived in the Georgian lands in the city of Tbilisi on the first of January," recounted Ivan Kuzmin,

and they received him with honor in that city, meeting him with the signs of power. And the khan [Shah-Nawaz] did not give the patriarch a fare [i.e., a daily monetary allowance], he simply sends food and even that not too often. And he lives in that city, buying everything [himself].[151]

It was at this time, on January 30, 1669, that Macarius's only son, Paul of Aleppo, died in Tbilisi. From Tbilisi, Macarius repeatedly appealed to the khan of Shemakha to repay the debt, but the latter suggested waiting until the next silk harvest. Despairing, the patriarch wrote to Moscow on August 24, 1669, "We have been living now for ten months in Tiflis. And as I live with many of my men and horses, I spend all my money on food, for everything is so expensive. Every day, I give out 10 rubles for all the provisions."[152]

Finally having received, through the mediation of the king of Kartli, reimbursement from the khan of Shemakha for the value of their goods, Macarius returned home in autumn of 1669. The patriarch then wrote to Russia about his misadventures,

"As ... we had arrived in the Persian land in the city of Shemakha, as many sables as we had were taken at half their price. And in place of money they gave us silk, at twice its value. And they helped us in the Iberian lands for an entire year because of this silk. And what we had with us was from the charity of your royal majesty, all was lost in the Georgian land. And as we left the Iberian land and came to the Turkish lands, we were seized by the Turkish pasha and tax-collector and they took from us two thousand *efimki* in the city of Erzurum, in addition to giving many great gifts to the judges and chiefs of that city. And when we arrived at our see in Damascus, we owed seven thousand *efimki*.[153]

Macarius repeatedly complained to the tsar about his misfortune, both from Tbilisi and from Damascus, asking him to reimburse the losses he incurred. However, Macarius's last embassy to Moscow, headed by Metropolitan Nectarius, which arrived in Moscow in May 1671, received fewer alms than was expected (money and furs worth 1,000 rubles), along with delicate hints that the patriarch's appetites were excessive. In the official letter to Macarius, it said,

> And we were not a little sorrowful for such poverty and losses of Your Beatitude. Meanwhile, may Your Beatitude know of the state expenses (?) of our royal majesty, since we, the great sovereign, have also distributed ... an innumerable [amount of] ... salaries. And even now we still give away [money] to our ... large army, and also for the redemption of the captives.[154]

According to Kapterev, the persistent requests of the patriarchs, particularly Macarius, for alms made "a very hard and unpleasant impression" on the Russian authorities. In Moscow, they realized that they had become the object of "shameless exploitation."[155] However, it seems that the government of Alexei Mikhailovich did not allow for excessive altruism. Macarius was paid so long as he was needed. Once he had fulfilled his task, it was inadvisable to continue to spend gold and furs on him. Besides that, it is obvious that at the end of his reign Alexei Mikhailovich had begun to lose interest in Middle Eastern politics, and consequently in the Levantine patriarchs. Having just finished a protracted war with Poland, the Russian state had substantially exhausted its military and economic resources and did not have the strength for the large-scale expansion into the Orthodox East of which Alexei Mikhailovich was still dreaming at the time of Macarius's first visit.

THE ERA OF DOSITHEUS

In the last quarter of the seventeenth century, Patriarch Dositheus of Jerusalem took the leading role in the system of relations between the Orthodox East and

Russia. Coming from the lower classes, he was able to make a brilliant career in the Church of Jerusalem, becoming its patriarch at the age of twenty-eight. His strong will, energy, and political and scholarly talent all set him apart from the rest of the Eastern bishops. Dositheus considered his Church of Jerusalem to be the pillar and beacon of true faith and himself to be the guardian of piety throughout the Orthodox world. His interests were on a continental scale, and he was actively involved in church politics stretching from Serbia to Georgia, but he paid special attention to Russia.

At the first opportunity, in July 1679, Dositheus sent letters to the tsar and the patriarch of Moscow through the Russian ambassador in Istanbul. They contained discourses in the biblical and Byzantine spirit, and reflections upon the monarch's duty to observe strict piety and not to allow heretical innovations into the Church. Dositheus instructed the Russian sovereign, "A tsar is even greater than a bishop.... Read the Holy Scriptures often, ... for what is a pious tsar, if not an apostle of Jesus Christ?"[156] Once again, Kapterev noted that Dositheus's letters are not ordinary complaints about poverty and persecution. He does not ask for anything for himself and the tone of the letters is "authoritative and edifying" not "humbly obsequious."[157]

Dositheus waited two years for a reply. It was delivered by the ambassador Prokopy Voznitsyn, who had arrived in Istanbul in connection with the conclusion of the Treaty of Bakhchisarai. The gifts sent to the patriarch seem quite modest compared with those received by his predecessors. Nevertheless, acting at the request of the tsar and Patriarch Ioakim of Moscow, Dositheus actively helped Voznitsyn in the negotiations with the Porte, unlike the other Greek hierarchs who, fearing the Ottomans, avoided communication with the Russian ambassador. In Voznitsyn's opinion, Dositheus was "a most intelligent man, a true servant to God and to our great sovereign; and he warns [us] from those who render a false service to him, the great sovereign."[158]

Dositheus assisted the Russian embassy and, as he was performing such tasks, the young Tsar Fyodor Alexeyevich hoped for a rehabilitation of the former patriarch Nikon, whom he deeply respected. This could not have been but attractive to Dositheus, considering the Patriarchate of Jerusalem's attitude toward Nikon's trial during the reign of Nectarius. At that time, Dositheus had been the right hand of the elderly patriarch and personally oversaw the negotiations with Moscow about Nikon's case. Now, in 1682, he was taking upon himself correspondence with the other Eastern primates about rehabilitating the disgraced patriarch. The text of "letters of absolution" was also drafted by Dositheus personally and sent to the patriarchs, who reacted to this undertaking without enthusiasm and only "after much pestering gave those letters of absolution," as Voznitsyn reported.[159]

From that time, Dositheus became Russia's chief political agent in the East. The Russian government used him to resolve various kinds of problems. In 1685–1686, he acted as a mediator in the negotiations on the transfer of the Metropolia of Kiev to the jurisdiction of the Patriarchate of Moscow. In 1685, Dositheus selected teachers, the famous Likhud brothers, for the early model of a university, that was being created in Moscow, which later became known as the Slavic-Greek-Latin Academy.

The Turkish army's disaster near Vienna in 1683 and the subsequent defeat for the Ottomans in the war with a coalition of Catholic powers—with which Russia joined in 1687—clearly demonstrated the weakness of the Ottoman Empire, which had now set out on a path of drastic decline. In the Orthodox East, pro-Russian sentiments were once more revived, spurred on even more by the threat of Catholic expansion. On territory reclaimed from the Ottomans by the Holy Roman Empire and the Venetians, the Orthodox were subjected to many pressures to persuade them to join the Unia. As the Athonite Archimandrite Isaiah said in Moscow in 1688, "all of great Christendom tearfully begs the sovereigns [Ivan and Peter Alexeyevich] so that they may not allow them to be released from the infidel bondage to a greater and more bitter bondage."[160]

Dositheus had a similar point of view. He saw Russia as the Third Rome, destined to liberate the Christian East from the "infidels."[161] For many years, Dositheus collected military and political information through his own network of informers and passed it to the tsar's ambassadors in Istanbul or directly to Moscow. Moreover, the patriarch, according to Kapterev,

> not only reported to Moscow what he learned and heard, like other agents ... but, like a Russian statesman, he always accompanied his reports with his own explanations and considerations. He gave our government advice and guidance, sometimes very emphatically. He sought to guide Russian foreign policy in the direction that he thought was best ... additionally, he showed very little inclination to endorse those steps taken by Russian policy that differed with his own plans and instructions.[162]

In the early 1690s, Dositheus seems to have thought that the end of the Ottoman Empire was drawing near. He did his best to prevent Russia from "prematurely" reconciling with the Turks[163] and to persuade Russia not to trust the peaceful assurances of the Porte. "Now ... [the Turk] takes care to deceive you, while it is possible to defeat the Austrians, and then he will not count you as men, because he is quite deep and cunning," Dositheus warned his Russian correspondents in 1692.[164] Dositheus even devised a plan for Russia's operations in the war: oust the Turks from Ukraine, then together with the Poles crush Crimea, eliminate the Budzhak Horde, and move toward the Danube, and then Moldavia and Wallachia would go over to Russia's side, about which Dositheus had a secret agreement with the Moldavian voivode.[165] In 1693, Dositheus obtained a draft of the Catholic Holy League's peace treaty with Turkey and sent it to Russia with his own caustic comments:

> When the Austrians make the Danube their border and prevail over the lands of Serbia, Hungary, and Transylvania, while the Poles will take over Ukraine, Podolia, and the lands of Wallachia and Moldavia ... then they will be the first enemies of Moscow, and there will always be war with them.[166]

At the same time, continued Dositheus, the Orthodox Slavs and Romanians will be forced to convert to the Unia and the Greeks will remain forever in Turkish slavery. This was another part of Dositheus's strategy, to set up Russia against the Catholic West, the future rival for the Ottoman inheritance.[167]

The Holy League's peace negotiations with the Ottomans in 1698 seriously disturbed Dositheus, who feared that Russia might join this agreement. The patriarch passionately urged Peter I not to reconcile with the Turks by any means and to continue the war to total victory, promising him divine favor:

> Do not be afraid of the heathens, instead recall the words of Moses: one drives out a thousand, and one hundred drives out the tens of thousands. If God is with us, who is above us? And do not take care that the Papists reconcile, but remember two things: God preserves these things for your holy kingdom, for God wants the Orthodox kings to be victorious over the enemy ... and does not want the heretics to have power.[168]

Dositheus's efforts were unsuccessful, and Russia also went on to reconcile with the Ottoman Empire. The terms of the peace agreement of 1700 went through a long and difficult negotiation between the tsar's ambassador Yemelyan Ukraintsev and Ottoman officials. Dositheus found ways to advise the Russian diplomat secretly, urging him to stand firm and not to make any compromises, given

Turkey's internal weakness.[169] It seems that Dositheus was one of the first to create the image of the Ottoman Empire as a "sick man." In particular, he wrote,

> For while in his youth, a lion is fearsome and of great strength, in his old age he is useless and lacking teeth and nails ... but ... to some he seems to be as strong as he used to be before. Thus [also], the local sovereigns, while being most useless and pitiful, and lacking in military force, hide their lack of strength and poverty ... through lies, craftiness, boastfulness, and pride.[170]

Despite the goodwill of a number of officials of the Porte toward Dositheus, his attitude toward the Ottoman Empire was more than critical. "Three things are now lacking in this kingdom: intelligence, oneness of mind, and money," wrote the patriarch in one of his dispatches.[171] The motives driving Dositheus are clear: he was hoping for the fragility of the peace and he was pushing Russia toward a new confrontation with the Turks by pointing out that the Ottomans did not abide by the treaty and were capable of a treacherous attack. The patriarch warned,

> By the command of their false prophet, the Turks, if they could, would have at once taken the whole world for themselves and in one hour ... would have slaughtered all Christians who did not submit to them. But since they are unable to bring about these things, they agree to make peace, but once they are strong again, they will disregard oaths and treaties.[172]

In the early 1700s, Dositheus continued his close cooperation with Russian diplomats, advising the ambassadors on the issues of Ottoman policy and providing them with intelligence reports. In his letters to the tsar, the patriarch even justified his absence from Istanbul and Edirne, citing a political lull when the Russian ambassador was not in urgent need of his advice.[173] At the same time, Dositheus pretendedly stated that he did not need any reward for his labors: "Working for the Orthodox state, we serve God Himself, and from him we hope for recompense ... and we seek again in this our thanksgiving from God, but we do not ask for anything from you."[174] All this did not prevent the patriarch from enjoying ample Russian alms. However, it should be recognized that he fully earned it.

Out of considerations for secrecy, the patriarch avoided writing to Russian recipients directly from Istanbul[175] and passed along the necessary information orally through ambassadors. When he was in relative security in the Danube principalities, however, Dositheus regularly sent his own reports to Russia about the mood at the Sublime Porte and the movements of the Ottoman army. While somewhere in Wallachia, the patriarch reported in detail on, for example, the performance characteristics of frigates in Ottoman shipyards or the circumstances of the massacre of the 1700 Hajj caravan by the Bedouins.[176] In his last letter to Peter I, from October 1706, Dositheus wrote, "we have the rank of informant under your God-protected power."[177] "And so we will act," he wrote three years earlier, "while we live, for not only are we the most fervent intercessors for your power, but also zealous laborers, and most of all we hold your decree as a holy word and the voice of God."[178] It is noteworthy that Peter and his entourage, who generally were skeptical about the Eastern clergy, highly valued Dositheus's services. In his letters, Peter I refers to him as "beloved father and shepherd."[179]

Needless to say, all this geopolitical advice and intelligence activity put Dositheus at a huge risk. The smallest leak could subject him to a death sentence. In Dositheus's reports, there is a constant motif: "My lord, the times are exceedingly difficult and very terrifying and we fear for our lives and for our people."[180] In that year, Dositheus and his entire spy network of agents was on the brink of being unmasked when one of the employees of Pyotr Tolstoy, a Greek with access to all secret intelligence, decided to convert to Islam. The ambassador managed to poison the traitor and then received an admonition from Dositheus, "We advise you to give heed to us and to have people faithful to Moscow for this service, but stay away from the Greeks, for the Greeks do not keep secrets."[181]

Dositheus's interests cannot be reduced to geopolitics and Russian–Turkish relations. The patriarch actively interfered in the internal politics of Russia. He addressed the tsar with lengthy exhortations and instructions about military development, urging continuous vigilance and readiness with regard to the Ottomans. Dositheus paid particular attention to the Cossacks, whom he regarded as the chief shield against the Ottoman–Tatar threat. The patriarch of Jerusalem urged Peter I to cultivate the Cossacks' warlike spirit and not to forget them in the division of the spoils of war, citing the example of the appropriate procedures among the Janissaries and the Crimean Tatars. Dositheus demonstrated his erudition by making a clever historical parallel between the Cossacks and the Ghassanids or Mardaites,[182] urging him not to repeat the mistakes of the Byzantine emperors by leaving open the steppe borders of their empire.[183]

Dositheus made curious suggestions about the development of the newly annexed Azov region, where the patriarch offered to create a free trade zone and thereby to divert to Azov the flow of trade coming up the Balkans and through Poland to Russia. Moreover, the patriarch advised that "poor Greeks" who could not afford to pay the *jizya* be encouraged to resettle in the Azov region. With this in mind, he was asking permission in advance to build a church in Azov for services in the Greek language, because, in his words, "Even though there is one God ... and one faith, nevertheless may a person of any faith hear it in his own language, for that is the cause of salvation."[184]

Complaining about the increased tax burden on Christians in the Ottoman Empire, Dositheus proposed that Peter impose an analogous poll tax on the Muslims in Russia and thus, following the example of the Ottomans, to convert the people of other faiths who would be unable to pay an "Orthodox *jizya*." "And even if such a one becomes a bad Christian," wrote Dositheus, "nevertheless his son will be a good Christian."[185] The patriarch clearly relied on his personal observation of the process of Islamization in the Balkans and wanted to see Russia as a mirror image of the Ottoman state, with Christianity and Islam switching places. Seeing that one of the factors of Islamization was close casual contact between members of the two religions, he advised against permitting the segregation of Russian Muslims: "It is necessary to live together with them in order to compel them to be Christians."[186]

As well as military–political and socioeconomic issues, the patriarch of Jerusalem was interested in ecclesiastical–ideological issues. He was an ambitious man who considered himself to be the bearer of a divine mission. Rigorously fanatical, he was devoted to the idea of the greatness of Orthodoxy. The long struggle for the holy places as well as the general atmosphere of intolerance prevalent in the Orthodox *millet* made the patriarch of Jerusalem staunchly hostile to all manifestations of Western culture. He perceived himself to be a central figure in a civilizational struggle and responsible before God for the entire Eastern Christian world. Therefore, Dositheus sought to prevent the penetration of European science and customs into Russia, believing that close contacts with foreigners would result in the destruction of Orthodoxy. "And above all endeavor," wrote Dositheus to his Muscovite colleague Ioakim in 1679, "that not one of the faithful ... may read or keep for himself such books which contain the foul and godless doctrines of the Pope-worshippers and or the Godless and foul teachings of Luther and Calvin, for they are filled with falsehood and deceit."[187] In a letter to the patriarch of Moscow in 1682, Dositheus emphatically repeated, "Keep pure Christ's flock from Latin writings and books," citing decrees of Byzantine emperors for burning heretical books and executing their owners.[188]

However, it would be a mistake to present Dositheus as an ignorant xenophobe. Although the patriarch did not know Latin (while at the same time knowing Ancient Greek, Turkish, and perhaps some Arabic), he was familiar in translation with all the developments in European theology and with the works of Greek Uniate authors. Apparently, Dositheus also did not mind his nephew and heir Chrysanthos studying in Western universities. The patriarch apparently believed, however, that only a select few can become acquainted with Western culture and jealously guarded his flock from it. "There are some who slander you in this way as unlearned," the patriarch wrote to his Russian coreligionists,

> but you say with [the apostle] Paul: "we are not ashamed of the Gospel of Christ, for it is the power for salvation unto every believer" (Rom 1:16) and again: "our whole faith is not in the wisdom of men, but in the power of God" (1 Cor 2:5).[189]

Dositheus recognized only the Byzantine cultural tradition and sought to oppose it to Western science and culture. "If anyone is looking for learning," he wrote to Russia in 1682, "study the Greek language and not any other."[190]

Under conditions in which not only the Eastern Mediterranean and Ukraine but also Russia itself fell inside the orbit of Western Christian spiritual influence, Greek and Russian priests actively exchanged books and manuscripts with anti-Latin content. Dositheus himself largely coordinated such contacts.[191] In the early 1690s, he dreamed of creating in Moscow a strong center for the revival of Byzantine culture and anti-Latin polemics. With this purpose in mind, he repeatedly sent works of Greek polemical literature to Russia for translation and publication.[192]

The policy for selecting personnel in the Russian Church caused Dositheus particular anxiety. He advised the tsar not to choose as metropolitans and patriarchs Ukrainians (who studied in the Latin schools), Serbs, or Greeks (here Dositheus goes against his own Hellenic patriotism), because these people "are greatly mixed and intertwined with schismatics and heretics,"[193] from which innovations and unrest can enter into the Church. "Although we profess the Cossacks to be Orthodox, nevertheless many of them have corrupt morals," warned Dositheus after the Metropolia of Kiev was annexed by Moscow.[194] In his opinion, the only person worthy to be a bishop is a "native Muscovite," even if he is poorly educated, because Muscovites "are protectors ... of their dogmas, ... not being lovers of disputations nor deceitful people."[195] The ideal option for organizing the Church, according to Dositheus, would be the unlettered but steadfast-in-faith Muscovite patriarch, pious and advanced in years, who has under his pastoral direction Greek, Serbian, and Ukrainian scribes and teachers. For this reason Dositheus so disliked the Ukrainian Stefan Yavorsky, who served as *locum tenens* of the Patriarchal See of Moscow at the beginning of the eighteenth century.[196]

To strengthen the influence of the Church, Dositheus repeatedly advised the Russian authorities to increase the number of episcopal sees. To avoid placing a heavy burden on the royal treasury, he proposed reducing the costs of maintaining bishops, citing the example of humility and poverty of the clergy in the East:

> Patriarchs here in Constantinople ... go about on foot, the hierarchs are beggars.... Expensive clothes are not fitting for clergy, for the iconoclasts wore such garments.... Our expenses are equal to those of one of one abbot of the smallest monastery, and on our clothing not more than 500 kopecks are spent.[197]

Needless to say, Dositheus, the staunch guardian of Byzantine piety, was greatly shocked by Peter I's reforms. The patriarch could not accept the Russian tsar's involvement with the Great Embassy and passionately urged him not to send his son to study in Vienna. "The ever-memorable fathers and forefathers of your holy kingship ... did not study customs and science from any Franks, but they ruled and still rule nearly the entire universe, being strong, great, fearsome, and invincible."[198] It was apparently under Dositheus's influence that the patriarch of Constantinople spoke out against Peter's plan to marry his son to a European princess, asking rhetorically, "Or are there so few chosen, honorable, noble and pious maidens there in Moscow?"[199] Nevertheless, Dositheus continued to serve the idea of Third Rome, which had already ceased to exist. Moreover, the patriarch did not entirely realize the full depth of the changes and the break with Byzantine tradition that was occurring in Russia. He had long been blinded by a certain mythical image of Peter I as a "new Constantine and Theodosius," sovereign defender of the Orthodox Church, and executor of Dositheus's strategic plans. The patriarch was not able to give up on his cherished myth and seems to have turned a blind eye to many things that were not in keeping with it.

Patriarch Dositheus is undoubtedly the most outstanding figure of the Orthodox Middle East and perhaps, along with Cyril Lucaris, of the entire Greek and Eastern Church in the Ottoman era. Unlike his predecessors to the patriarchal throne—the brilliant politician Paisius and the outstanding writer and theologian Nectarius—Dositheus combined the qualities of both a skilled political actor and prominent scholar. He was a man of exceptional ability and irrepressible ambition. Dositheus's most irreconcilable enemy, Bishop Ananias of Sinai, wrote of him, "He ... does not think about the judgment, nor about the recompense or the laws of God, but he exalted himself above Lucifer and wants to have everyone under his feet."[200]

Most of all, Dositheus resembles Dostoevsky's depiction of the Grand Inquisitor. The patriarch's personality is clearly revealed in his letter to Peter I in 1706 about strategy in the Great Northern War. Dositheus advises the tsar to wage a war of attrition, regardless of losses, because manpower will nevertheless run out earlier for the Swedes. They should not regret their own losses since they will go to heaven as martyrs for the faith. "I write first of all—to your excellency, that you do not mourn those who will die in war, if it is useful," Dositheus suggested to Peter. "Why do you pity the Cossacks, if they die? For if they die, they are martyrs."[201] In these words, all of Dositheus is summed up. He was of the breed of a charismatic leader standing beyond good and evil, above ordinary morality, regarding himself as entitled to rule over thousands of lives. However, unlike many charismatic leaders who send their followers to their deaths while themselves remaining safe, Dositheus risked not only the lives of his informers, but also his own head. He spent forty years on the edge, with any slip threatening him with immediate execution. Against the background of such figures of the Greek East as Paisius Ligarides and Meletius the Greek, educated and talented people who were completely amoral, Dositheus stands in marked contrast. He was a man with no less talent and an iron will while at the same time having clear principles that he did not change under any circumstances.

To play the role of spiritual leader of Orthodox civilization, Dositheus needed the second member of the symphony, a strong Christian ruler with capable military power to support his geopolitical dreams. Dositheus chose Peter I for this role but, as it turned out, unsuccessfully, as Peter's interests were oriented toward the West. According to Kapterev, Dositheus, who was dependent on post-Byzantine Greek learning, dreamed that the Greeks would play the same culture-bearing role in Russia as they did in Europe during the Renaissance.[202] However, Dositheus was two hundred years too late. The Greek world could not compete with European science and culture in quantity or quality. This had fatal consequences for the relationship between Russia and the Middle East.

THE POSITION OF THE GEORGIANS

As mentioned, Dositheus kept a close look on the situation throughout the Orthodox world, not only paying attention to Russia but also, in particular, to the Georgian lands. Georgia was one of the most important areas of interest for the Levantine patriarchs and is worthy of special consideration as a vector of their foreign policy.

Again, the Georgians' cultural relations with Syria and Palestine go back to the Early Byzantine period. In the tenth and eleventh centuries, Georgian monastic communities flourished in the environs of Antioch, on Sinai, and in Palestine. In the Mamluk period, the time of greatest decline for Christianity in the Middle East, the Georgian kings invested in the Palestinian monasteries, which has prompted some later historians to a somewhat-exaggerated idea that the role of protector of the Orthodox East, which previously had belonged to the Byzantine emperor, was assumed by Georgia in this period.[203] Alongside the visible Georgian presence in Palestine, one should not forget the continuing links between Georgia and the Church of Antioch.

According to Christian tradition, it was precisely Eustathius, patriarch of Antioch, who performed the baptism of Georgia in the fourth century and ordained the first Georgian priests and bishops. A significant proportion of Georgian lands belonged to the jurisdiction of the Patriarchate of Antioch. Subsequently, the East Georgian Church received autocephaly (apparently in several stages between the seventh and eleventh centuries), but the catholicoses long continued to commemorate the name of the patriarch of Antioch at the liturgy and to pay them some tribute.[204] The special character of the relationship between Antioch and Georgia is highlighted by the fact that one of the Syrian clergy held the title of "Exarch of Iberia." Patriarch Macarius appointed one such exarch in 1649 and sent him as his representative to Georgia.[205] Georgian pilgrims on their way to the holy places passed through Syria, which helped to maintain constant close contacts between the Orthodox Arabs and their Georgian coreligionists.

In the Ottoman era, Georgia could no longer act as protector of the Orthodox East because it was itself in a state of severe decline. It was divided into several parts—the kingdoms of Kartli, Kakheti, and Imereti and the principalities of Mingrelia and Guria—which for many decades were subject to the rivalry between the Ottoman Empire and Safavid Iran. In 1639, Istanbul and Isfahan agreed to divide the Caucasus: the western part of Georgia went into the Ottoman sphere of influence and the eastern part into the Iranian sphere. As vassals of Iran, the kings of Kartli were forced to convert to Islam, but the influence of the Orthodox Church in Georgian society remained unshakeable. For this reason, the Eastern patriarchs were able, as before, to receive financial assistance from the Georgian sovereigns.

As mentioned in Chapter 4, in the late seventeenth and first half of the eighteenth century, Georgian kings donated estates, similar to the Romanian dependent properties to the Holy Sepulchre and to Georgian monasteries in Palestine. In the words of N. Khutsishvili, "This model of land ownership grew quite rapidly and within fifty to sixty years it became a well-developed system of feudal landholding."[206] This scholar believed that before that time, the Georgian colony in Palestine hardly possessed any property.[207]

It is possible that the campaign of donations in the early seventeenth century was associated with a sharp weakening of the Georgian community in Palestine and the loss of landholdings there that had belonged to the Georgians in the Mamluk period. In that situation, the Georgian villages and vineyards had to become an alternative stable source of income for the Palestinian monasteries. The patriarchs of Jerusalem, especially Theophanes, who was in Georgia around 1612 or 1613, may also have stimulated this wave of donations.[208]

Prominent among the Iberian landholders who aided the Holy Sepulchre was the ruler of Kakheti, Teimuraz (1589–1663), who played a key role in Caucasian history at that time. He belonged to the part of Georgian nobility who, maneuvering between the Ottomans and Iran, sought to engage a third regional power in the affairs of the Caucasus: the Russian state. Teimuraz was the most active supporter of Russia and, in 1639, he formally went over to Russian allegiance. Russia, however, despites its pan-Byzantine ambitions, soberly assessed the balance of forces in the Caucasus and shied away from direct military intervention in Georgian affairs. As a result, in 1648, Teimuraz was defeated by the king of Kartli and took refuge in Imereti. From there, seeking further patronage from the Russian tsar, Teimuraz sent his grandson Irakli (in Russian sources, Nikolai Davidovich) to Moscow, and in 1657–1658, he himself went to Russia. When he did not receive the anticipated military assistance, he returned to the Caucasus and, in an attempt to come to terms with the Persians, capitulated to the shah. Refusing to convert to Islam, Teimuraz finished his days in captivity in Astrabad.[209]

Teimuraz's name was well known in the Middle East. Macarius and Paul of Aleppo paid him the highest respect and Macarius called him a "new martyr."[210] It is possible that, while he was king of Kakheti, Teimuraz maintained some contacts with Macarius. It is well known that ambassadors from the patriarchs of Antioch were sent to Georgian lands. Metropolitan Zacharias of Apamea was sent there by Patriarch Ignatius 'Atiya and the metropolitan of Saydnaya was sent there by Euthymius III.[211] These embassies can be roughly dated to the 1630s. The sources are silent about the purpose and results of these Antiochian missions. While still metropolitan of Aleppo, Macarius met with the Georgian catholicos Maxim during a pilgrimage to Jerusalem for Easter 1642.[212] While in Moscow in 1655, the patriarch of Antioch met with Queen Helen, Teimuraz's daughter-in-law, and his grandson Nikolai, the future king of Kartli, Nazar 'Ali Khan.

"We often visited them on account of their great love toward our master the patriarch," wrote Paul of Aleppo, "since they knew of him when he was still in Aleppo [i.e., before he was installed as patriarch].[213]

As he was returning home in 1656, Macarius sent a letter to the Russian tsar from Wallachia. In it, among other things, he urged him to help Teimuraz return to the throne:

> Again we remember ... Khan Teimuraz, the Georgian king ... may he not be forgotten until the end, but may your kingship be his helper in all things, so that through your help he may recover his throne, so that Orthodoxy may be strengthened and the Christian race may be exalted and not diminish, for your kingship will receive a great recompense from God who renders each one what is due.[214]

At almost the same time, in 1658–1659, Patriarch Paisius of Jerusalem visited the Georgian lands. Undoubtedly, he hoped to receive alms to cover the costs of his struggle for the holy places that had become more intense in the 1650s. Recall that during this time there was a certain cooling in Paisius's relationship with Moscow, but the Danubian principalities were ravaged by war, and the patriarch had nowhere else to go to obtain financial aid.

The road to Georgia was long trodden by Greek alms collectors. According to Patriarch Macarius of Antioch, under conditions in which the local clergy were uneducated—when, for example, most Mingrelian deacons could not read and repeated prayers memorized by heart—Greek priests who were under suspension from the patriarch of Constantinople or conmen posing as bishops felt themselves at liberty in Western Georgia.[215] Of course, real Greek bishops also visited Georgia. In particular, a journey there by Patriarch Nicephorus of Alexandria is known to have taken place in the early 1640s.[216]

A young Dositheus Notaras accompanied Paisius on a journey to the Georgian lands, and it is to Dositheus that we owe our knowledge of the patriarch's route. From Istanbul they went by sea to the port of Kontozi (modern Gagra) near the Cape of Adler. From there, in June 1658, they sailed along the coast until they reached the Kodori River and then went overland until they reached the monastery of the bishop of Mokfi (Mokva). In Zugdidi, the patriarch met with the ruler of Mingrelia, Levan Dadiani, and then rested from the hardships of the road for a time in the neighboring village of Kotskheri, which belonged to the Monastery of the Cross. From Mingrelia, Paisius moved on to Imereti, to the court of King Alexander, and wintered in Gelati Monastery. It is noteworthy that the Greeks avoided appearing in the Safavid zone of influence and even declined an invitation from the king to go to a village bordering Kartli for the feast of Theophany. The patriarch firmly identified with the Ottoman world and feared that the Persians would capture him and lead him off to Isfahan. In western Georgia, however, Paisius moved freely and was a welcome guest at the courts of all the local nobles, despite their mutual wars. With the opening of navigation, he went down the Mingrelian River Khopi to the Rioni, which forms the border with Guria. He met with the Gurian prince Kai-Khosro and in May 1659 he returned to the Balkans via Trebizond.[217]

Dositheus does not write about the amount of alms that Paisius received in Georgia, but we can assume that the patriarch was not mistaken in his expectations. The same calculations motivated Patriarch Macarius of Antioch to go to Georgia in 1664. Although Macarius himself wrote that he was primarily driven by his desire to honor his Georgian flock with his attention and to guide it along the true path, and was only secondarily motivated by the See of Antioch's debt problem,[218] it is clear that the patriarch's actual priorities were in the reverse order. No wonder that among Georgians' praiseworthy qualities, Macarius notes their generosity in giving charity, by which, he says, they differ sharply from "all the other Christians of the world."[219]

Two major sources telling us about the patriarch of Antioch's stay in the Caucasus have survived. Macarius himself composed one of them, apparently soon after his return to Syria.[220] That text, written by the elderly patriarch, is in some places monotonous and confused, with constant repetitions. It contains a description of Georgian history and the general political situation in the region, and it goes into great detail about the manners and customs of the people.

The second source for Antiochian–Georgian contacts during that time is considerably less well known. It is the *Description of Georgia* composed by Paul of Aleppo during his stay in Moscow as part of Macarius's entourage. Paul submitted this text to the Office of Secret Affairs on February 27, 1667. The document was written in Greek and then translated into Russian. The original is apparently now lost and the only known copy of the translation is preserved at the Russian State Archive of Ancient Acts (RGADA).[221]

On the basis of these sources, it is possible to establish in broad terms the route and circumstances of the patriarch of Antioch's journey to Georgia. Macarius set out from Syria in 1664.[222] His path led through Aleppo, Marash, and Erzurum. In the past, we speculated that the patriarch began his tour of the Georgian lands with Tbilisi, the capital of Kartli.[223] Carsten Walbiner did not agree with this opinion, since from the dates of the colophons of Macarius's manuscripts, it appears that he began his journey with Western Georgia. In this case, Macarius apparently went through Trebizond and then on by sea to Mingrelia. The route over dry land through Guria is less probable, because in the *Description of Georgia* the little that is reported about Guria is clearly hearsay.

Macarius and his companions spent the second half of 1664 and 1665 in Mingrelia and Imereti. Paul described the land in the most glowing terms:

> Mingrelia is also a blissful place: there is much silk, iron, grapes on the trees, and all sorts of animals.... Imereti is the glorious royal throne, having great grace, because it stands above all of the Georgian land. The air is good, the land is beautiful, rich in all fruits and vegetables. There are fortified cities built of stone, much silver and iron ore, only they do not advertise this out of fear of the impious.[224]

Although still quite positive, Macarius's view of Georgia was still nevertheless somewhat more critical. The patriarch wrote much in condemnation of the internecine wars between the local princes and the sale of Christian captives into slavery.[225] "And no one gives them good counsel and guides them along the path of truth,"[226] lamented the patriarch, clearly taking on the role of the Georgians' spiritual mentor. Macarius subjects the Georgian clergy to particularly sharp criticism for being completely fused with the secular nobility. According to the patriarch, the bishops could barely read and sometimes were so young that they had not yet even sprouted beards, but they ruled over their serfs like real princes, going with the king to war at the head of their own armies, waging war against each other, and selling the captives as slaves to the Muslims.[227] The lower clergy were illiterate, not knowing the rites or the canons, and the bulk of people in Mingrelia were not even baptized. "This is because," repeats Macarius, "there is no one to watch over them, to teach and instruct them."[228] Neither their own bishops nor any of the foreign bishops who come to Georgia from all the ends of the earth teach anything to the local priests, "instead, they collect money from them and leave without doing anything useful for them."[229]

Macarius clearly considered himself to be an exception to this rule. He often and, it seems, exaggeratedly wrote about his educational and administrative activities: training priests, punishing slave-traders, and correcting rituals.[230] The way in which Macarius described the population of the Georgian borderlands—"Christians in name only," without churches or priests—very closely resembles the state of his own Antiochian patriarchate a century earlier. In Macarius's time, it was already too late to revive Orthodoxy at the headwaters of the Euphrates and "kitchen Orthodoxy" was transformed into a quasi-pagan "folk Islam." However, in the foothills of the Western Caucasus, Macarius attempted to do what he had not had time to do in Eastern Anatolia: halting the degradation of Orthodox culture, preaching, and holding mass baptisms. "You should have seen how enormous was the crowd of people following us ... begging us to baptize them," wrote the patriarch.[231] Abkhaz and Svan chieftains came down from the mountains and called on the patriarch to baptize their fellow tribesmen, but Macarius did not risk going deep into the mountainous region. About the missionary activities of his father, Paul of Aleppo wrote,

> Of their [Georgian] hierarchs no one went into those mountains, nor have they seen anything out of fear. But we were there in the flesh and went and baptized many thousands of souls, male and female, young and old, even eighty years and older. And they ran [toward us] with great piety, and were baptized with fervent love, counting both snow and frost for nothing.[232]

It should be noted that the stay in Georgia turned out to be fruitful for Macarius's and Paul's literary activities. Not burdened by concerns of ecclesiastical administration and with considerable leisure, the patriarch and deacon wrote many of their works at this time.

On October 1, 1665, while Macarius was in Imereti, Alexei Mikhailovich's envoy, Meletius the Greek, arrived in Tbilisi from Syria along with Patriarch Paisius of Alexandria. They were on their way to Moscow to participate in the trial of Nikon. Meletius sent a similar invitation to Macarius. He hesitated and postponed his decision on the grounds that "[he] acquired fixed possessions and does not have anyone to hand [them] over to or with whom to send [them] on his way home to repay his debts."[233] Because of these negotiations, Meletius was stuck in the Caucasus until the next spring. Macarius's vacillation was put to an end by the king of Kartli Vakhtang V (Shah Nawaz Khan, 1658–1667) and his son Archil (Shah Nazar Khan), at that time the ruler of Kakheti. They convinced the patriarch of Antioch to go to Russia and to act as their secret mediator in contacts with Moscow, with the goal of persuading the Russian government to penetrate more actively into the Caucasus and to assist their Georgian coreligionists in their fight against Muslim expansion.[234]

Thus, in the *Description of Georgia* that Paul presented to the Posolsky Prikaz, there appear many stories related to Archil, Kakheti, and its strategic fortress of Sioni:

> And that governor [Archil] ordered us many times ... that we write to your royal majesty to make it known that if you wish to establish the city of Terek and other Russian Cossack towns, so that the Orthodox Christians in Georgia may be kept safe from Lezgian evil-doers, may your royal majesty send for that city to be built ... and may he firmly establish it with its own troops. And then you will have control over the crossroads, and the eyes of the enemies will be blinded, and, moreover, the path of the Lezgians to Crimea will be severed. For, had this city been established and fortified, the Lezgians would not have come every day with such many thousands of Russian people, captured by Tatars, whom they sell to Qizilbash.[235]

It seems in this case that Paul was acting not only in the diplomatic interests of Kartli and Kakheti, but also expressing his own geopolitical perceptions and beliefs about Russia's historic mission. "And it will be a great reward to your royal majesty from God and benefit to the kingdom," wrote the deacon,

> and all Georgia beseeches your royal majesty so that this be done ... and the road will be clear from Georgia up to Terek by dry land.[236] Those states, of which we wrote, which are up in the mountains, do not have a ruler and have lost the Orthodox faith, beseech your royal majesty that you may be their ruler—so that they may bow down before you, and accept the Christian faith.[237]

In his overview, Paul wrote extensively about the mountain peoples of the Caucasus. Some of them, such as the Abkhaz, Paul lists as being potentially Orthodox: "And these peoples all keep the Great Fast, have big churches and venerate the holy icons, and yet because they do not have good bishops and priests to correct them, they have become savage."[238] The Muslim tribes that Paul calls "Lezgians" are particularly demonized:

> And they have no other business than to steal and enslave Georgian Christians in Kakheti and Russians from Terek ... When they see a Christian sick and infirm ... they kill him as a sacrifice to their foul god ... thus

also these people do, which is even worse than what Tatars do: not only do they slaughter Christians, but first they drink their blood, and second, they wash their faces with this blood for the sake of their godlessness.[239]

Paul was especially uneasy about the growing Islamization of the peoples of the Caucasus where Muslim preachers, "sow their deadly poison."[240] He wrote, "God is our witness that due to our fear of them [the Lezgians], we have lived such a long time in Shemakhi, because it was impossible to pass."[241]

Paul relates a curious episode in connection with the voyage of the Eastern patriarchs over the Caspian Sea from Derbent to Astrakhan:

And since we were for such a long time on our boats upon the sea, and were nearly dead of thirst, with great fear we have sent a small boat with men to get some fresh water, but they [the Lezgians] awaited us so that we may fall into their hands. And they attacked our men whom we sent with arms, and nearly captured them. But we were like dead men from thirst and from the sea storms, and there was a great multitude of them gathered, and they prayed to their god, so that our boats would be thrown to the shore by the storm, so that they may take us captive.[242]

Macarius's second stay in the Caucasus in 1668–1669 was recounted previously, and we will not revisit that story here.

A place comparable to that of Macarius in the history of Georgian–Levantine relations belongs to Patriarch Dositheus of Jerusalem. Twenty-two years after his journey to Georgia as an obscure cell-attendant in the entourage of Paisius, Dositheus reappeared in the Southern Caucasus as patriarch, in whose hands lay the fate of the Iberian monasteries of Palestine.[243] It seems that this time he started his route in Tbilisi, where King George XI of Kartli paid him the principal sum for redeeming the monasteries. Dositheus did not describe this journey in as much detail as that of Paisius, but on a few points it is possible to establish his subsequent route. In the summer of 1681, the patriarch was in Kutaisi, and from there he went to Guria. Somewhere along the border between the two states, Dositheus met with the nobility and clergy of Imereti and Guria, apparently to encourage them to make donations. In September, the patriarch went through Lazia and then on by sea to Istanbul.[244]

Later, Dositheus would continue to have active contact with Georgian kings and catholicoses. Porphyry Uspensky published the texts of five epistles of the patriarch to Georgia, composed between 1699 and 1706. We can assume that it is only a small part of Dositheus's correspondence with the Georgians during his thirty-eight-year patriarchate. Unfortunately, the patriarch's other letters are inaccessible, if they survive at all. However, what was published proves to be typical for Dositheus's global scope and desire to intervene in all the temporal and ecclesiastical affairs of his coreligionists. He wrote not only about the problems of the Georgian monasteries in the Holy Land but also of the properties of Palestinian monasteries in Georgia. The patriarch undoubtedly had immense spiritual authority in Georgia, as the catholicos of Lower Iberia asked him about the permissibility of a dynastic marriage between the ruling families of Mingrelia and Imereti, who were to some degree interrelated, while the king of Kartli, Nikolai (Nazar ʿAli Khan, 1688–1703), appears to have repented before him for his forced apostasy. Dositheus was prepared to forgive both incest and apostasy in exchange for extensive financial support for the holy places in Palestine and the cessation of the slave trade in Georgia.[245]

The patriarch wrote long discourses to the kings about the duties of a Christian ruler, directly encouraging them to intervene in the affairs of the Church, to correct the rituals and root out the theocratic ambitions of the bishops, to encourage them

> to take meals, to sleep, and to ride on horseback in a way that befits a bishop and not the aristocracy ... And the laymen should be forbidden to sell Christians, to shave the beards of the dead ... to put on them leather shoes and to mourn them like Hellenes [pagans] do.[246]

Georgia also became another theater for Dositheus's battle against Catholic expansion. During the reign of Shah Nawaz, Jesuit missionaries were admitted into Kartli to preach among the local Armenians, bringing them, in the words of Dositheus, "out of fog and into darkness."[247] Dositheus believed that "the heresy of the Armenians is vastly more bearable than the heresy of the Papists," since "the Armenians, however they might be, only look after their own affairs."[248] That is, they do not seek to proselytize. The Papists, however, "are worthy of hatred and rejection," they "name one impure and corrupt man the second God on earth, they ruined the kingdom of the Orthodox, they strengthened the Hagarenes.... Whoever loves them does not love God.... They are worse than the Hagarenes."[249]

Already in 1681, Dositheus attempted to persuade King George to expel the Jesuits from Kartli and to return the churches given to them by Shah Nawaz to the Armenians. George promised Dositheus that he would grant his request, but he did not. The patriarch of Jerusalem's particular ire was raised by letters from the missionaries to Rome that he intercepted in 1688, in which they claimed the Georgian princes and bishops' conversion to Catholicism.[250] In a letter to King Vakhtang VI (1703–1724) in 1706, Dositheus urged him to guard the Church against the "Latin wolves" and to avoid all contact with them. "Having anticipated their evil tricks, avoid conversations with them in advance and do not love them.... They know worldly wisdom and deceive people with beautiful words, falsely explaining the Holy Scriptures and wrongly interpreting the Holy Fathers."[251] For all his many years of labor to save the Georgian monasteries of Palestine, Dositheus asked for one thing: the banishment of Latin monks from Georgia, "that the world might be freed of their evil."[252]

No less interesting is the story of Dositheus's attitude toward the Islamization of the kings of Kartli. Among the members of the Georgian nobility who were commemorated at the liturgy at the Holy Sepulchre was the Muslim Nazar 'Ali Khan (Nikolai Davidovich). Dositheus acknowledged that the king had only formally embraced Islam while remaining a Christian at heart. The patriarch instructed the Georgian ruler on how he should behave with the Persians:

> Deceive them, smile at them, tell them lies … if only to benefit Christians. Do not love them … even if they love you.... Forbid your nobles to sell Christians to Muhammadans.... Give alms to the churches.... And when death approaches … then, as much as you can, appear as if you are melancholy or in a trance in order to avoid saying the confession of faith of the impious; but often repeat: "I believe in one God," and in this way die.[253]

ANTIOCHIAN STRENGTHENING IN THE EARLY EIGHTEENTH CENTURY

The last years of Dositheus's patriarchate, during the period of his most active contacts with Russia, Antiochian–Russian relations experienced a noticeable recovery. This had been preceded by a long hiatus of almost three decades. The reasons for the attenuation of contacts, in addition to the previously mentioned cooling between Greeks and Russians in the 1670s and the Russo–Turkish wars, were related to the internal situation of the Church of Antioch. The death of Macarius and Paul of Aleppo, a generational change in church leadership, and the subsequent turmoil and schisms, when the legitimacy of Patriarch Cyril seemed doubtful to many, all worked against any active foreign policy. Only once does the Church of Antioch figure in the history of contacts between Russia and the East in the late seventeenth century, when both patriarchs of Antioch— Neophytus, who had just abdicated, and Cyril, who had just consolidated his position—signed letters deposing Patriarch Nikon of Moscow. As we may recall, the initiative in this matter was entirely Russian and the Eastern patriarchs simply signed identical letters that were drawn up for them by Dositheus of Jerusalem.[254]

Contacts between Antioch and Russia were renewed through the efforts of Patriarch Athanasius Dabbas. Unlike his rival Cyril, who had a somewhat provincial outlook, Athanasius had spent many years in Constantinople in the early eighteenth century. He had moved in circles of Greek clergy and, like Dositheus, was involved in contacts with the Russian embassy. Some alms came his way, and Athanasius came to realize the advantages of Russian patronage and Russian financial capabilities. He wanted to obtain money from the tsar for a special project, his lifelong dream: organizing a printing press for Orthodox Arabs. In January 1707, Athanasius enlisted the support of the ambassador Pyotr Tolstoy and sent his *protosyngelos*, the Cypriot Leontius, with letters for the tsar and Chancellor Gavril Golovkin.[255] Passing through Ukraine, Leontius presented the letters to the hetman Ivan Mazepa, who sent them on to Peter I in Poland and ordered Leontius to wait for a response in Nizhin. The Antiochian messenger would remain there for two years, through Charles XII's campaign against Ukraine and the Battle of Poltava. It was only in 1709 that he was able to go to Moscow. Apparently, during all this time, Leontius was engaged in commerce, as evidenced by the twelve carriages of possessions that he brought with him. In February 1710, there followed a royal decree granting a salary to Athanasius's embassy. The amount of alms was modest: money, furs, and cloth totaling less than 200 rubles, of which the patriarch was personally due 70 rubles.[256]

If Athanasius's later statements are to be believed, even this money did not reach him because the *protosyngelos* Leontius died on his way back. In August 1714, the patriarch repeated his attempt, sending to Russia from Aleppo another messenger, the hieromonk Parthenius, whom he referred to as his "deputy in the affairs of the printing of books."[257] Parthenius arrived in St Petersburg in June 1715, but no information about the results of his embassy survives.

Ukraine and the Orthodox East

Leontius's journey reflects another vector of the external contacts of the Orthodox East: Ukraine. Relations between Ukraine and the Levant have been touched on repeatedly earlier. We can recall, for example, the stays in Ukraine of Joachim Daw and Theophanes of Jerusalem, as well as the contacts of various Eastern hierarchs with Bogdan Khmelnitsky. During the period of Ukraine's political agency during the second half of the seventeenth century and the early eighteenth century, hetmans and Cossack leaders, like the Moldavian, Wallachian, Georgian, and Muscovite rulers, considered it their religious duty to support the Orthodox East.

All embassies of Ottoman Christians making their way to Moscow passed through Ukrainian lands and, naturally, communicated with local clergy and the hetmans' administration. Those hetmans who broke with Moscow hindered the Eastern hierarchs' passage into Russia. Thus in 1662, the messengers of the patriarch of Antioch were detained in Chigirin by Yury Khmelnitsky and sent back to Wallachia, from which they made their way to Putivl bypassing the territory of the rebellious hetman.[258] By contrast, Cossack leaders loyal to Moscow acted as intermediaries for contacts between Russia and the East. Among the documents at the RGADA, in the general mass of papers, scribbled in the characteristic cursive of the Moscow scribes, are the "tailed" letters of the travel charters that the Ukrainian hetmans issued to the Middle Eastern petitioners for alms. Presumably, the Cossack leadership also gave alms to the Levantine Christians on his own behalf, but there is no information about this in the available sources. There is only a trail of fragmentary evidence, such as the grants given to the Monastery of Sinai by Ukrainian nobility in the 1680s.[259]

In the 1690s, the future patriarch of Jerusalem, Chrysanthos, then still an archimandrite, repeatedly visited Moscow on behalf of his uncle Dositheus. As he was going through Ukraine, he was in close contact with Hetman Mazepa, discussing with him the issues of church politics and promising to provide information about the affairs of the Ottoman Empire.[260]

The Ukrainians had also purely domestic and personal contacts with the Orthodox East that were much closer than those of the Muscovites. Characteristically, the majority of the pilgrims coming to the Holy Land from the Russian Empire in the first half of the eighteenth century were of Ukrainian provenance.

Ukrainian aid to the Orthodox East reached an especially wide scope in the early years of the eighteenth century. Ippolit Vishenski described the silver altar tablet that he saw at the Golgotha chapel, which was "procured" by Hetman Mazepa. It is possible that this is the same tablet with an embossed image of the Descent from the Cross and the inscription "By the generosity of the illustrious Ivan Mazepa, the Russian Hetman," that Porphyry Uspensky mentions one hundred and fifty years later among the vessels of the Church of the Holy Sepulchre.[261] Porphyry also found in the archives of the Holy Sepulchre copies of letters from the patriarchs of Jerusalem to Mazepa, thanking him for his zeal for the Holy Sepulchre and generous donations.[262] In 1830, Andrei N. Muraviev saw an oil portrait of Mazepa with his coat of arms and inscription in Latin at Mar Saba. Apparently the *parsuna* (a portrait in iconographic style) was sent to the monastery along with contributions and requests for prayers for the salvation of the hetman's soul.[263] According to the pilgrim Ivan Ignatiev (1708), at the solemn liturgy in front of the Lord's Tomb on the Sunday of Orthodoxy, the Jerusalem hierarchs commemorated Ivan Mazepa immediately after the Russian monarch and before the Moldavian, Wallachian, and Phanariot nobility.[264]

In 1707, Patriarch Athanasius of Antioch also received via the *protosyngelos* Leontius large Ukrainian donations for the printing press in Aleppo. For that occasion, in 1708, an additional printing of the Arabic Gospel was issued along with thanksgiving verses in honor of Mazepa and the depiction on the front page of the Russian Order of St Andrew, whose recipient was the Ukrainian hetman. The printing was issued partially at the expense of Colonel Daniel Apostol from Mirgorod. These copies had a more modest cover and contained Daniel's coat of arms and a poetic dedication addressed to him.[265]

Mazepa's philanthropy was closely tied to some of his political interests in the Orthodox East. Among these interests, significant place was given to Dositheus's successor as patriarch of Jerusalem, Chrysanthos, whose name is associated with the most dramatic changes in the relations between Russia and the Christian East.

Chrysanthos: A Changing World

Patriarch Chrysanthos is an emblematic figure in the history of relations between Russia and the East. After two hundred years of lively contacts between Moscow and the Christian East, these ties were almost instantly severed by Chrysanthos and would remain virtually moribund for over a century.

Nothing presaged this turn of events at the time that Chrysanthos ascended to the See of Jerusalem. In the first year of his reign, the new patriarch warmly assured Peter I of his readiness to serve Russia according to Dositheus's example. However, the patriarch's letters sound grandiloquent to the point of ringing false, and Chrysanthos sometimes goes overboard with singing the praises of his Russian correspondents. Thus, having received a letter from the tsar in September 1707, Chrysanthos wrote, "I received such a joy on that day, which I never had since I began to live."[266] "The entire Orthodox people," the hierarch further continued, "hopes … to see its liberator … your invincible and sovereign majesty … not from the hands of Pharaohs or tormentors but from those of the perceptible demons and beasts."[267] In the autumn and winter of 1707, Chrysanthos collected alms in Moldavia and Wallachia. Returning to Constantinople in January 1708, the patriarch cautioned that he would not often write to Russia from there and promised to maintain contact through the Russian ambassador Pyotr Tolstoy.[268]

At that point, Chrysanthos's relationship with Russia rapidly started to be phased out. In the summer of 1708, Tolstoy reported to the Chancellor Golovkin with a certain degree of vexation, "The Patriarch of Jerusalem resides in Constantinople, however he corresponds with me exceedingly rarely."[269] The ambassador, on the other hand, was ready to explain that this was out of Chrysanthos's fear of incurring the wrath of the grand vizier, who "is fiercely unkind toward Christians."[270]

Chrysanthos sent his final letter to the Russian chancellor in September 1708. He apologized for his long silence, motivated by fear of Ottoman persecution, and announced his imminent departure for Jerusalem. From there, Chrysanthos maintained only sporadic contact with Tolstoy, who tried once more in the spring of 1709 to raise the question at the Porte of returning the holy places to the Greeks.[271]

How can Chrysanthos's cooling toward his northern coreligionists be explained? In contrast to his uncle, this patriarch was completely loyal to the Sublime Porte and, as a cautious and shifty personality, he was unwilling to irritate the Ottomans by maintaining a relationship with Russia. This was even though the relationship between the two countries was not hostile at that time: the Ottomans were waiting to see the outcome of Charles XII's campaign in Russia and did not want to take any drastic measures. It is worth noting that Chrysanthos did not rely heavily on St Petersburg financially, as he had a generous patron in the Wallachian ruler Constantin Brâncoveanu. The ruler assisted in Chrysanthos's accession to the throne and subsidized many of the projects of the patriarchs of Jerusalem in the eighteenth century, from the restoration of Mar Saba to the work of the Holy Sepulchre's printing house in Bucharest. Compared with such charity, the few sable pelts sent as an advance by Peter I[272] to Chrysanthos did not seem impressive.

However, it became increasingly difficult for Chrysanthos to maintain friendly relations with all of the patrons of the Church of Jerusalem simultaneously. The course of history put these patrons into conflict each other and the patriarch was forced to make an unambiguous choice. Events were starting to snowball: Charles XII's invasion of Russia, Mazepa's treason (October 1708), the Battle of Poltava (June 27, 1709), the flight of the king of Sweden and Mazepa to the Ottoman border, and finally the rapid deterioration of Russian–Ottoman relations and the Ottoman declaration of war against Russia on October 20, 1710.

Chrysanthos sat out the beginning of these events in Palestine. The pilgrim Ippolit Vishenski repeatedly mentions the patriarch's presence in the Holy City between January and April 1709.[273] In April 1709, the ambassador Pyotr Tolstoy optimistically informed Chrysanthos, "The affairs of the most divine one [i.e., of Peter I] are in considerably better shape. ... The traitor Mazepa abides in his final despair."[274] At this time, Chrysanthos was serving the liturgy on the silver tablet donated by Mazepa. Unfortunately, Vishenski is silent about the identity of the Christian rulers for whom Chrysanthos intoned "Many Years" on the Sunday of Orthodoxy of 1709. In April, however, the pilgrim left Jerusalem and our sources of information about Chrysanthos are greatly reduced.

The outbreak of the Russo–Turkish War put the Wallachian ruler Constantin Brâncoveanu in a difficult position, as he was bound to Russia by a secret alliance but eventually sided with the Porte. During the early part of the Prut campaign in June 1711, the Wallachian ruler outwardly supported friendly relations with Russia, writing letters to Peter I that the latter called "a kiss of Judas."[275] Chrysanthos's position seems to be entirely in agreement with the orientation of the Wallachian prince.

In 1712, Greek agents reported to Russian authorities that it was the patriarch Chrysanthos who had acted as an intermediary in putting Brâncoveanu in contact with the Porte. The agents denounced Chrysanthos as someone

> who is not a Christian, but an atheist and Turkish *shpeg* [spy] from the old days. When the vizier of the previous year was in Adrianople, he visited the vizier incognito every night. And when the Turks went on a campaign, he sent with the vizier his trusted monk, who was incognito in Turkish dress with the vizier and who almost daily reported to the vizier the news from the Moldavian ruler concerning our sovereign's troops.[276]

Russian sources mention a project that is not yet fully understood, which is Chrysanthos's appointment in 1712 as "Patriarch of the Cossacks."[277] Pylyp Orlyk, chosen by the Cossack emigrants to be the new hetman after the death of Mazepa, maintained a correspondence with Chrysanthos. However, Orlyk's letters, dated 1710, 1711, and 1725, have not been published and their contents remain unknown. It is possible that the hetman and the patriarch met in Moldavia or Wallachia and reached some sort of agreement.[278] We can assume that Chrysanthos was given (or promised) a *berat* from the sultan sanctioning his spiritual jurisdiction over the lands of the Zaporozhian host, although from the perspective of church canons, this seems quite bizarre.

In the summer of 1712, Chrysanthos again started to be in contact with Russian diplomatic representatives. He struggled to deflect suspicion from himself and from the Wallachian voivode, swearing eternal loyalty and willingness to serve the Russian people and sovereign.

And since the things did not proceed in accordance with our desire, wrote the patriarch,

> this was due to the will of God and to the reasons unknown to us. And after this I heard many unexpected words concerning the suspicion not only against me, but also against some long-time and righteous friends [i.e., Constantin Brâncoveanu] who were loyal to his royal majesty … and of all the sorrows this was to me the greatest sorrow.[279]

For a time, relations were restored. Russian ambassadors to the Porte corresponded with Chrysanthos and Brâncoveanu and recommended that the Russian government show the patriarch and the voivode a certain grace, "for although it is impossible to trust them, nevertheless it is better that they were not open enemies."[280] However, by autumn of 1713, Chrysanthos was finally convinced that confidence in him was lost and ceased all contact with Russia.[281]

Why did everything stop with this? Already Nikolai Kapterev raised this question but did not find a response and later generations of historians have had little to add. Westernized Petersburg Russia shifted its cultural and political interests, and contacts with the Orthodox East lost their former value. Additionally, with the establishment of a permanent diplomatic mission in Istanbul, Russia eliminated the need for costly and unreliable Greek informants.[282]

If we turn to an analysis of these diplomatic representatives during the eighteenth century and the correspondence of the Russian resident in Constantinople with the Collegium of Foreign Affairs, we are struck by their focus on solving purely practical questions of Russian–Ottoman relations. The diplomats write about mutual border claims, issues of trade and navigation, the demarcation of borders, and the exchange of prisoners after the preceding war, Crimean and Polish affairs, and Turkey's international position. The geographic area of Russian interests was limited: an arc from the southern Caspian Sea and Georgia through Kabardia, Kuban, and the Crimea to the Danube. Only after the Treaty of Küçük Kaynarca in 1774 did Russia begin to pay attention also to the Mediterranean. However, this attention amounted only to gathering information on the situation in Egypt and other Ottoman provinces or purely situational responses to the seizure of one or another Russian ship by North African pirates. The Christian East is entirely absent from this picture.[283] It seems that less attention was paid to all the issues of Syrian and Palestinian Orthodoxy during the entire eighteenth century than to disputes about rights to salt extraction in the lakes of the Kinburn Peninsula near Ochakov.

Once more, Petersburg Russia's Middle Eastern policy was determined by pressing political questions. Everything rested on real possibilities and practical interests. The political line was pragmatic and cynical, without the ideological framework that was characteristic of the Muscovite tsardom, which never forgot its status as the leader and defender of universal Orthodoxy. Despite the fact that the possibilities available to the tsars of the sixteenth and seventeenth centuries were much less than those available to the empresses in the eighteenth century, the ambitions of Third Rome far exceeded those of St Petersburg.

With regard to the reasons for Russia's alienation from the Christian East, Derek Hopwood also mentions the series of Russo–Turkish wars that made contact with Russia unsafe for the Eastern patriarchs.[284] In fact, exactly twenty-five of the hundred years following Chrysanthos's death were taken up with wars between the two empires. Although Dositheus, in his own time, was not stopped by such obstacles, his successors, if they ever entered into contact with Russia, did not address the reigning monarch but rather the Holy Synod, with the sole purpose of requesting alms.[285]

THE SUSPENDED ANIMATION OF THE EIGHTEENTH CENTURY

The nature of contacts between Russia and the Middle East in this period somewhat resembles the sixteenth century, when the Eastern patriarchs also turned to Russia for financial assistance without promising to perform services of a political nature. However, where Muscovy had readily provided such assistance, the Petersburg Empire showed less interest in the Orthodox East.

The patriarchs of Jerusalem had strong incentives to ask Russia for financial support. Dositheus took control of a patriarchate over which hung a debt of 150,000 piasters. This the patriarch was able to repay with Georgian alms and other income. However, the large-scale reconstruction of five monasteries at the end of Dositheus's reign and apparently falling revenues from pilgrimage during the crisis of the Ottoman Empire in the late seventeenth century led to an increase in new debt, which reached 100,000 piasters at the time of Dositheus's death.[286] Chrysanthos spent no small sum on the reconstruction of the dome of the Holy Sepulchre, building the guest house for pilgrims in Jaffa, and restoring the burned metochion of the Holy Sepulchre in Constantinople. Continued disruption of pilgrimage and the Ottomans' execution of Constantin Brâncoveanu in 1714 possibly affected the amount of Wallachian alms to the See of Jerusalem. According to the Holy Sepulchre's sources, Chrysanthos's debt rose to 200,000 piasters.[287]

In such a situation, the patriarch was forced to address the Russian Synod with a desperate plea for help in March 1728. Placed at the head of the embassy to Russia was a certain Archimandrite Germanus. For reasons that remain unclear, the embassy's departure seems to have been delayed for three years. In addition to Chrysanthos's letter of 1728, he is known to have sent another letter on September 29, 1730, which was transmitted to the Holy Synod by this same Germanus.[288] Undoubtedly, Germanus went with an embassy only once. He set off after Chrysanthos's death on February 7, 1731, carrying, among other things, letters from the new patriarch, Meletius.

As is typical, Meletius complained about the disasters that had befallen the Church of Jerusalem: the violence of the Bedouins who lay siege to monasteries, spending on gifts for the Muslim elites of Jerusalem, and "papist malice," on account of which the patriarch was forced to pay taxes for the Orthodox Arabs, lest the Latins pay the taxes and attract them to their faith. As he claimed, alms from pilgrims to the Holy Sepulchre were failing, "from the evil-bearing tyrant yoke" as well as from "Arab malice." That is, the Bedouin and *fellahin* who were robbing pilgrims on their way to Jerusalem.[289]

Archimandrite Germanus arrived in St Petersburg in November 1731. It is likely that a similar embassy from Patriarch Sylvester of Antioch arrived in Russia at the same time with similar requests. On December 7, there followed an imperial decree to issue 2,000 rubles "to Jerusalem for the sake of the health of her imperial majesty for the necessary demands of that place," as well as a thousand more to the patriarchs of Jerusalem and Antioch personally. The summer of the following year, the Russian resident in Istanbul, Ivan Neplyuyev, handed the money over to the patriarchs' representatives.[290] This was the last time in the eighteenth century that the Russian government paid such sums to petitioners from the Orthodox East.

In 1735, the decree of the Empress Anna Ivanovna established the so-called Palestinian roster (*palestinskiie shtaty*), which established a fixed amount of alms due to various patriarchates and monasteries. The share for the patriarchates of Jerusalem and Antioch came to 100 rubles per year, essentially a symbolic amount.[291] Funds were paid every five years, for which it was proposed that patriarchal representatives in the person of archimandrites be sent to Russia (who, it was clearly stipulated, could be accompanied by one hierodeacon and three lay servants). In the case that the envoys went through Kiev, they were guaranteed supplies and money for fodder. They also were granted a monetary stipend during the embassies' stay in St Petersburg.[292]

The Church of Jerusalem's demands were much higher. In June 1743, an embassy arrived in Moscow from Patriarch Parthenius with a request for assistance with paying off a debt of 350,000 piasters. For the first time, Russian authorities started asking the patriarchal envoys tough questions about how such colossal debts were incurred. Not satisfied with their standard complaints of Bedouin plundering, the pashas' "greediness," problems with heretical denominations, and the Ottoman Christians' "extreme poverty," the government requested explanations from the envoy at the Porte, Alexei Veshnyakov. "We do not want ... for our alms to serve in vain for vainglory or any advantage of the Turks," and thus the new priorities of Near Eastern policy were formulated in St Petersburg.[293] The ambassador was reminded, "in no way [to] keep our treasury for the giving away to the local patriarchs, and not [to] spend it in vain."[294]

In the winter of 1745, Veshnyakov sent to St Petersburg a composition by the patriarch himself, "A Brief Account" of the vicissitudes of the struggle for the holy places since ancient times and the costs associated with this struggle. The Collegium of Foreign Affairs remained dissatisfied and demanded concrete information about the causes and dimensions of the debt. Veshnyakov was unable to obtain such accounts from anyone. The patriarch of Jerusalem's envoy, Archimandrite Agapius, also presented a report on the circumstances of the increase in patriarchal debt.[295] All this paperwork dragged on for more than three years. Meanwhile, in 1746, Patriarch Parthenius anxiously wrote to Agapius, "Your tarrying is grieving us," and reported about new debts and total disarray in the patriarchate.[296]

In the end, they gave Agapius what was due for ten years according to the Palestinian roster and granted him permission to collect alms in Russia. In the fall of 1747, the archimandrite's financial abuses were revealed and he was expelled from the country. The money he had collected, totaling 8,745 rubles, was seized and sent to the patriarch separately.[297]

PARTHENIUS, A MISUNDERSTOOD ALLY

It is noteworthy that the resident Alexei Veshnyakov used all his forces to play along with Patriarch Parthenius, attempting to convince St Petersburg to provide financial assistance to the Church of Jerusalem. Reporting on the debt that was hanging over the patriarch, Veshnyakov wrote,

> By local standards, [the debt] is rather moderate, and not great, by God's blessing, ... that the patriarchs of this see are not changeable [i.e., they do not change as frequently as in Constantinople], and nearly all ... are pious people, because they do not attain it by avarice or by cunning, and not from the Turks.... For this reason it is so small, if we compare it to the one here [i.e., to the debt of the Ecumenical Patriarchate], which is more than 900,000, considering that he is subject to incomparably lower taxes ... and does not have enemies like the [Patriarchate] of Jerusalem.[298]

Veshnyakov concluded by comparing the corrupt and avaricious schemers of the Phanar to the Church of Jerusalem: "There is only this house and church administration here which can be called a Christian [patriarchal] throne. For this reason, when [Parthenius] himself declares that he owes 353,000 thalers, in good conscience, I cannot raise any doubts."[299] Perhaps in this way Veshnyakov wanted to repay the patriarch for his services of a political nature.

Parthenius represents an exceptional phenomenon in the history of the Christian East in the eighteenth century. Alone among all the patriarchs, he attempted to continue Dositheus's line of political cooperation with Russia. Like Dositheus, Parthenius collected intelligence about the state of the Ottoman Empire and tried to influence Russia's consciousness of its strategic priorities in the region. The specific details of the patriarch's cooperation with the Russian resident are buried in the depths of diplomatic documentation and still await researchers.[300] Only once after the death of Alexei Veshnyakov in the summer of 1745 did Parthenius make direct contact with St Petersburg.

The patriarch's report on the internal situation in the Ottoman Empire,[301] transmitted through Lieutenant A. Nikiforov, was similar to the messages sent by Dositheus. We see there the same relish in describing the military weakness of the Ottoman Sick Man, the sultan's incapacity, the impoverishment of the treasury, the collapse of its naval forces, and the constant expectation of rebellion in the capital. Parthenius warned that the Ottoman official sent to Russia with the diplomatic mission was actually "sent more for espionage, for it is always suggested to the Porte through the French and the Papist Jesuits that Russia begins to organize military preparations against the Turks."[302] More interesting are the geopolitical reasonings of the patriarch. "When Russia will intend to start the war against the Turks in order to liberate the Christians who find themselves in the Turkish infidel state, and in order to secure its borders," wrote Parthenius,

> in this case it would not be bad to place a defensive force near its borders on Crimea's side, but in actuality to go with a greater army toward the Danube, where the road is more plentiful and healthy for the troops. And it would be more reliable to seek assistance there, for the majority of inhabitants near the Danube are Christians.[303]

By gaining a foothold on the Danube, Russia could cut the Ottoman Empire off from the Crimean and Budjak Tatars who then, according to Parthenius's thinking, would have no choice but to submit to Russian allegiance. "If there would be such divine mercy, that Russia will acquire the territory up to the Danube River," dreamed the patriarch, the next step should be to build a Russian Black Sea Fleet, which would easily be staffed with sailors from coastal Christian nations. Then Russia would be able to have for itself "a great and very profitable commerce" and, most important, be able to protect its southern borders.[304]

Unlike Dositheus, Parthenius did not try to give instructions for the policies of the Russian Church concerning appointments, but he did provide such recommendations with regards to the diplomatic corps. The patriarch requested that his opinion be related to

> highly entrusted lords the ministers … so that in place of the deceased resident Veshnyakov they may send to Constantinople a Russian man who is intelligent, experienced and trustworthy in these affairs, … and that he may have with him from now on the interpreters who are Russians, and not taken from the foreigners.[305]

"And if they are foreigners who are in the service, although they may show themselves to be loyal and willing," Parthenius warned, "but the reality of the matter is that they will never have zealousness in favor of Russian interests, but in a crafty way they take more to heart their own interests," and as such, it is with a very high probability, they could be bought out by the Ottomans or someone else.[306]

It is worth asking why Parthenius's efforts, unlike Dositheus's similar activities, went unappreciated in St Petersburg. If Dositheus's relations with his northern coreligionists formed an entire era in the history of both Russia and the Greek world, Parthenius's work as a Russian political agent was not noticed by his contemporaries and was completely forgotten by later historians. The answer, apparently, is that Parthenius was not perceived as a most holy patriarch, but rather as an ordinary informant. The St Petersburg officials were not interested in his spiritual dignity and authority, but only in the information he provided. Moreover, although Dositheus headed the whole network of Russian agents, Parthenius was only one of its links, and not always the most valuable. In parallel with him, there were people in Istanbul who were actively passing on much more important and confidential information about events at the Ottoman court. These people were not called by their own names even in coded messages. As an ordinary informer, Parthenius was too expensive. His services were not comparable to paying the debts of his see (which in the Russian currency of that time exceeded 230,000 rubles).[307] The sums that St Petersburg was willing to spend on Middle Eastern coreligionists were three to four times smaller.

ALMS SEEKERS

In fact, in reality Russian authorities did not always succeed in restricting the scarce appraisals of the Palestinian roster. Patriarch Sylvester of Antioch was particularly successful at obtaining additional financial assistance. In 1752, his envoy Archimandrite Ignatius received, in addition to the fixed alms for 1745–1753, another 3,000 rubles on account of the patriarch's special letter of supplication to the Empress Elizabeth.[308] In 1760, Sylvester's new representative Archimandrite Anthimus collected the "salary" for 1753–1761 and asked for the amount owed to his see for a further five years. This was refused on account of the archimandrite lacking suitable authorization from Sylvester. Then Anthimus appealed to the Holy Synod with a special appeal for alms and the highest decree from February 28, 1763. The Patriarchate of Antioch received another 1,000 rubles "to pay off debts."[309] It seems that, contrary to the usual stereotype, even in the eighteenth century, Russian authorities were not entirely indifferent to the problems of Middle Eastern Christians.

In July 1765, Sylvester appealed to the Holy Synod to transfer the alms accumulated over five years through the Greek merchant Hajji Nikolaos Angelos.[310] The decision was made in 1766, but it seems that it was not put into force on account of the Synod's move from Moscow to St Petersburg and subsequent bureaucratic confusion.[311]

What is the most striking in the subsequent history of the relations between Antioch and Russia is that the patriarchs who reigned after Sylvester no longer petitioned Russia for alms. It was only in May 1792, almost thirty years later, that Anthimus wrote to the Russian representative in Constantinople that his see did not receive the alms since 1763, "either because the letters [granting privileges] were in Antioch, or because of other circumstances,"[312] and requested the provision of assistance. The patriarch received the requested alms only in 1800, when the Collegium of Foreign Affairs sent, via two Greek merchants, 3,900 rubles that had been "accumulating" since 1761.[313]

The same unexplained hiatus[314] is also observed in contacts with the See of Jerusalem. As many as thirty years passed after Agapius's mission before Patriarch Abraham addressed the Holy Synod with a request for aid in 1776. It was decided to send him 2,800 rubles through the Russian representative in Istanbul from the means allocated for the Palestinian roster. Six years later, the patriarch wrote that the money had never been received. As it turned out, it had been used for other purposes by the Moscow Office of Foreign Affairs, which led to a lengthy correspondence between the Collegium of Foreign Affairs and the Holy Synod.[315]

There was once more a long pause in Russian–Palestinian relations. The next time the patriarch of Jerusalem appealed to the Holy Synod for aid was only in 1815. By that time, there were more than 90,000 rubles in the State Treasury that had not been claimed since 1780 by the various beneficiaries of alms according to the Palestinian roster.[316]

The end to this constant stream of official financial assistance was partially offset by the permission to the monks of the Patriarchate of Jerusalem to collect alms in various dioceses, usually in Ukraine. Similar permissions were given to the monks of the Monastery of Sinai, who came to Russia in 1723, 1735, and 1745 and in subsequent years. In addition to payments according to the Palestinian roster (at a rate of 70 rubles annually), Sinai received substantial amounts of private donations from St Petersburg, Moscow, and Ukraine. Relations between Sinai and the Slavic world in the late seventeenth and eighteenth centuries are reflected in the so-called Sinai Book of Commemorations, which recorded the names of donors for commemoration at the monastery.[317] In 1744, the monastery founded its own metochion in Kiev with the Church of St Catherine.[318]

Perhaps some alms from private individuals also made it to the Church of Antioch. In 1733 and 1740, Grigorovich-Barsky sent letters to his parents in Kiev through the Greek merchant Spandones, who, in addition to his commercial activities in Russia, served as representative and advisor to Patriarch Sylvester of Antioch and easily could have sent him donations from Russian philanthropists.[319]

At the same time, the Russian government was even more zealous than it had been in the seventeenth century in seeking to prevent the "unauthorized" collection of alms by Greek monks. The procedure for the transfer of money was carefully stipulated by the Palestinian roster: the patriarch's envoy had to show a copy of the letter of patent and a certificate signed and stamped by the patriarch with a list of all persons in the embassy. Measures were taken to prevent conmen with stolen letters or forged certificates from entering Russia. "It seems to us not to be unbeneficial," the Synod wrote to Patriarch Sylvester of Antioch, "and if your holiness would not seem opposed, to request also from our resident in Constantinople and, in the regions where Alexandria and Antioch are, from the British or Dutch consuls ... a letter which would certify the authenticity of those sent by you."[320]

Other petitioners for alms were to be turned away, as the Russian diplomatic representatives in Constantinople were regularly reminded.[321] Around 1743, a group of self-styled collectors of alms for the Holy Sepulchre were unmasked, who were caught because they had "the nerve to come to not only Ukraine, but to other places in the All-Russian Empire, and even to appear to her imperial majesty's most sublime court under the pretext of begging for alms."[322] Once the patriarch of Jerusalem confirmed that he had no connection to these alms collectors, "these monks were put under arrest and confessed in the course of the most thorough investigation that was conducted that they were actually imposters."[323]

After the Treaty of Küçük Kaynarca in 1774, Russia's position in the Eastern Mediterranean was dramatically strengthened. One consequence of these geopolitical shifts was the project of a network of Russian consulates in the cities of the Levant, including Beirut, Damascus, and Acre. In this way, the Middle Eastern patriarchates might have appeared to be in closer contact with Russia. However, concrete decisions to appoint consuls in these cities were only made in 1785, and while bureaucratic formalities were still dragging on, the new Russo–Turkish War of 1787–1791 broke out. Those consuls who had managed to begin working were forced to flee outside the Ottoman borders. However, those at the Collegium of Foreign Affairs directing the Russian representatives in the Levant thought least of all about reaching out to the Orthodox East. Completely contrary to the wishes of Patriarch Parthenius, most consuls were appointed from among foreigners who barely knew any Russian. The consulates' range of concerns was limited to commercial and political issues. They were expected to avoid communication with their Eastern coreligionists as much as possible. As the ambassador in Constantinople Yakov Bulgakov wrote in his circular of March 1787,

> By most high rescript of Her Imperial Majesty, from January 27th of this year I was ordered to appoint all dependencies of the local mission to the comprising leaders of general consul, the consul, and the vice-consul, in order that they by no means whatsoever give out passports to foreign monks of the Greek confession who want to travel to Russia, that they might not beg under any condition.[324]

Georgia and the Orthodox Levant in the Eighteenth Century

In the eighteenth century, communication between the Orthodox Levant and Georgia was also drastically reduced. After Dorotheus Notaras's tour of the Georgian lands in 1681, only one Middle Eastern patriarch visited the Southern Caucasus. This was the Antiochian primate, Cyril ibn al-Zaʻim, who appeared there almost immediately after Dositheus in 1682–1683.[325] This journey may have been connected to the recently concluded struggle for the throne of Antioch between Cyril and Neophytos al-Saqizi. Because of the complete disorder of Patriarch Cyril's finances, he attempted to cover his debts with the help of Georgian charity.

After that, relations between the Middle East and Georgia can only be traced in dotted lines. In 1692, Metropolitan Gregorius al-Halabi of Erzerum was in

Tbilisi.[326] At the beginning of the eighteenth century, the bishop of Maaloula went to Georgia, apparently for alms, and remained there. After this, in July 1724, Patriarch Athanasius attached the widowed diocese to the metropolitan of Saydnaya.[327] The illuminated manuscripts of the translation of the Greek Chronograph, which belonged to Paul of Aleppo and remained in Georgia after his death (we know of the additions to this manuscript made in 1737 by King Vakhtang of Kartli), somehow returned to Syria and in 1762 belonged to a certain Arab Christian.[328] Georgian monks and nuns appeared from time to time in the monasteries of Syria and Palestine in the eighteenth century.[329] However, the intensity of contacts clearly waned and Patriarch Parthenius of Jerusalem wrote to the Georgian catholicos in 1755 that the kings of Georgia had not sent anything to the Holy Sepulchre in twenty-five years and no one came on pilgrimage from the Georgian lands.[330] Parthenius was not entirely accurate: nineteenth-century researchers mentioned among the treasures of the sacristy of the Holy Sepulchre utensils offered by queens of Kartli in 1723 and 1752 and an icon in the sanctuary of the Church of the Resurrection that was restored by the prince of Mingrelia in 1770.[331] Among Georgian pilgrims of this century two major figures are known: the writer and Archbishop of Tbilisi Timothy (Timot'e) Gabashvili who visited Palestine in 1758 and Jonah, metropolitan of Ruisi, who had been deposed from his see by King Irakli II and attempted in the 1780s to appeal this decision to the Eastern patriarchs.[332] There remained in Georgia some property belonging to the Holy Sepulchre, from which the Patriarchate of Jerusalem periodically received some income. Between 1800 and 1812, Archimandrite Athanasius, who would go on to be patriarch of Jerusalem from 1827 to 1844, managed these properties.[333]

However, the weakening of ties between Georgia and the Syro–Palestinian Orthodox world is obvious. In the literature, the decline in Antiochian–Georgian contacts is explained by the establishment of Phanariot dominance over the Church of Antioch, after which all of the patriarchate's external relations were restricted to the Phanar.[334] This does not appear to be convincing. Patriarch Sylvester of Antioch maintained active contacts with the Danubian principalities. The aforementioned Metropolitan Jonah of Ruisi freely toured Palestine, Syria, and Egypt to enter into direct contact with the primates of the Eastern sees.

The synchronicity of the collapse of ties between the East and Russia and of those between the East and Georgia after Dositheus Notaras is striking. However, none of the arguments offered to explain the decay of Russia's ties with the Orthodox East applies to Georgia. The decline of Georgian–Levantine relations had their own particular reasons that apparently should be sought within internal Georgian dynamics.

IN PLACE OF AN EPILOGUE

During the Russo–Turkish and Napoleonic Wars of the early nineteenth century, Russia had no time for the Orthodox East and the Eastern patriarchs, and the patriarchs did not try to remind Russia of their existence. However, in 1814–1815, there began a distinct renewal of contacts. After the Congress of Vienna, the power of the Russian Empire was at its peak and the authorities of the Church of Jerusalem, burdened by the costly struggle for the Holy Places, actively sought St Petersburg's patronage. The establishment of contacts was facilitated by the addition to the empire of Bessarabia, where several metochia of the Holy Sepulchre were located.

In 1814, a Greek merchant founded a metochion of the Patriarchate of Jerusalem in Taganrog. Four years later, imperial assent was granted to open another metochion in Moscow.[335] In response to demands for financial aid from Patriarch Polycarpus of Jerusalem, in 1816, the Holy Synod awarded the Holy Sepulchre the amount of 25,000 rubles from the sums allocated in the Palestinian roster.[336] Archimandrite Arsenius, the rector of the Jerusalem metochion in Moscow, transferred even more funds to the patriarch.[337] Polykarpus and his successor Athanasius (r. 1827–1844) were in constant correspondence with the Russian ecclesiastical hierarchy.

After the Treaty of Adrianople in 1829, Russia's penetration into the Orthodox East became explosive. The pilgrimages of Andrei N. Muraviev in 1830 and of A. S. Norov in 1835 awakened Russian society's interest in their forgotten coreligionists. The establishment of a Russian consulate in Beirut in 1839 and of the Ecclesiastical Mission in Jerusalem in 1847 became visible cultural and political milestones of Russia's consolidation in the region.

It appears that Russia's "rediscovery" of the Orthodox East, a surge of interest in the Palestinian holy sites and the affairs of Middle Eastern Christians became possible because of evident interior changes in the Russian Empire. Russian society, which had just recovered from the cultural shock of the Petrine reforms, began to remember its roots and to recover its forgotten identity. One manifestation of this identity was the irrational yearning for the Holy Land, the same yearning felt by contemporaries of Vasily Poznyakov and Arseny Sukhanov.

In the nineteenth century, the Orthodox East appears as an almost passive object of Russian policy. However, this policy's priorities were formulated in the seventeenth century with the participation of Middle Eastern hierarchs like Paisius and Dositheus.

CHAPTER 9

The Catholic Unia

[Patriarch] Cyril managed things very well and pastored the flock of Christ in peace and tranquility. He is worthy of all praise, except that he conspired with the Franks and turned a blind eye to their doings, such that he elevated their status. Their contemporaries ate unripe grapes but we have got the sour taste in our mouths.

—Mikhail Breik, 1767

O woe is me who in such an inopportune time find myself your bishop and pastor!

—Patriarch Sylvester of Antioch (1724–1766)

THE CATHOLIC PRESENCE IN THE LEVANT

The seventeenth and eighteenth centuries, a time of active economic and religious expansion of the Catholic world in the Levant, was one of the key periods in the history of the Christian East. Arab Christians were faced with a historic "call" from Western civilization. The contact between these cultures led to a dramatic rift in the Middle Eastern Christian communities. A segment of the Eastern Christians abandoned their old identity and passed into union with Rome. These shocks stimulated an enormous release of spiritual energies by all the warring parties—Eastern Catholics of various sects and followers of traditional Orthodoxy—understanding their own identity, justifying their historical choice, and developing new methods of ecclesio-political struggle. It is no exaggeration to say that the Catholic spiritual expansion into the Levant and the establishment of an Arab Unia were the chief events in the cultural and political history of Syrian Christians in the late seventeenth and eighteenth centuries.

Active contacts between the Latin West and the Middle Eastern Christian world took place during the Crusades, but with the expulsion of the Crusaders from Syria and Palestine, communication between Rome and the East sharply weakened. As mentioned, in the 1330s, Mamluk authorities allowed a group of Franciscan monks to return to Jerusalem and Bethlehem. With time, a network of monasteries and inns serving European pilgrims developed in Jaffa and Ramla. In the seventeenth century, the Catholics were able to establish several monasteries in Palestine: in Nazareth, Mount Tabor, ʿAyn Karem, and Mount Carmel near Haifa. It is traditionally thought that the Franciscans, "the custodians of the Holy Sepulchre," were not inclined to proselytism, being more concerned with control over the holy places and organizing pilgrimage than preaching among the local Christians.

Nevertheless, even in the Mamluk period, there was a small community of Arab Catholics of the Latin rite in Bethlehem and several other areas of Palestine that by the seventeenth century played a prominent role in Palestinian history. In everyday terms, however, the Arab Latins did not differ from their Orthodox neighbors in Bethlehem; their way of life was characterized by the tribal system and rather vaguely-held religious notions.[1] The existence itself of Arabs of the Latin confession in no way posed a threat to the integrity of the Orthodox community. The position of many Arab Catholics under the authority of the Franciscans was not any more attractive than the status of the Arab Orthodox under the rule of the Phanariots. In regard to this issue, Constantin-François de Volney wrote,

> The Spanish monks in Jaffa and Ramla treat the Christians belonging to them with a cruelty that does not in the least agree with the Gospel. ... The Christians ... are not happy, but they dare not but submit to this condition. Experience has taught them that the good fathers' indignation entails dire consequences.[2]

In addition to Palestine, a Franciscan mission was established in Beirut. Officially, its mission was to provide pastoral care to European merchants. Additionally, the Catholic monks maintained close ties with the Maronite community in Lebanon and acted as intermediaries in its dealings with the Vatican. It was largely through the efforts of Franciscan missionaries at the turn of the fifteenth to the sixteenth century that there occurred a final accession of the Maronites to the Church of Rome.

The confrontation between Catholic Europe and the Ottoman Empire, as well as the Portuguese expansion into the Indian Ocean, stimulated the papacy's renewed interest in the Christian East. The Portuguese alliance with Christian Ethiopia and the increasing strategic importance of Egypt led to a series of attempts by the Vatican at rapprochement with the Coptic Church in the six-teenth century. In 1553, Catholic missionaries managed to persuade one of the lines of Nestorian patriarchs in the mountains of Kurdistan to enter into union.

The Latin *Drang nach Osten* reached a particular extent during the Counter-Reformation when the Catholic world, recovering from the impact of Protestant-ism, went on the offensive in all directions, hoping, in particular, to recoup losses in Northern Europe by calling Eastern Christians to union. A number of schools were opened in Rome, such as the Greek and Maronite Colleges, which focused on training agents of papal influence among representatives of the Eastern Chris-tian peoples. In 1583, a permanent Jesuit mission was established in Istanbul. The continental scale of the papacy's missionary plans can be outlined from almost simultaneous events such as the Union of Brest in 1596 in Ukraine; the Synod of Diamper in 1599, which consolidated the bringing into union of the Mala-bar Christians in India; the adoption of the Gregorian calendar by the Maronite Church in 1596; and the violent controversy that shook the Coptic Church from 1594 to 1597 over relations with Rome.[3]

In 1625, a Catholic mission was established in Aleppo, Syria's largest eco-nomic center with a Christian population in the thousands. Already in 1656, part of the Syrian Jacobite community in Aleppo passed into union, forming their own church structure. According to an agreement between France and the Sublime Porte in 1673, Catholic priests enjoyed the same diplomatic status as consular officers serving French subjects in Aleppo. Thus, in 1680, the city had twenty-four Latin priests and monks and only fourteen French merchants.[4] In Lebanon, Fakhr al-Din II welcomed Western cultural influence, giving a free hand to the Carmelites, Capuchins, and Jesuits. With the support of Lebanese sheikhs and the French consuls, the Latins built monasteries in the mountains and opened missions in the coastal cities of Sidon, Tyre, and Tripoli. In 1643, Catholic missionaries moved into inland Syria, opening a representation in Damascus.[5]

The strengthening of the Catholic position paralleled the massive economic penetration of European countries into the Levant in the seventeenth and eigh-teenth centuries and the composition of an Arab Christian merchant class. From the late fifteenth through the mid-eighteenth centuries, Aleppo was the largest commercial center in the Middle East, a crossing-point of trade routes between Central and South Asia and Western Europe. Traditionally, Aleppo's trade was controlled by Sephardic Jews and Armenians native to Jolfa, who monopolized the trade in Iranian silk. Powerful internal solidarity and a diaspora scattered across many countries helped these communities to have a strong position in international trade. Arab Christians, who had neither sufficient capital nor a diaspora outside of Syria, could not compete with the Jews and Armenians.[6]

Starting in the mid-seventeenth century, however, there was a sharp rise in the economic activity and prosperity of Arab Christians. This was partially because of the rapid development of sericulture in Lebanon and cotton in Palestine and the increasing importance of the port cities of the Eastern Mediterranean. Additionally, during this period, France, which was in need of silk for its factories, actively established itself in Levantine markets. According to the conclusion of Thomas Philipp, there was a coincidence of interests between Arab Christian and French entrepreneurs: they were both relatively new players in the Levantine market (before then, England had been dominant) and worked in new, nontraditional sectors of the economy associated with the production of silk and cotton. Syrian Christians specialized in the silk trade and acted as intermediaries of Levantine companies who preferred to have local Arab Christians as their partners, rather than Jews and Armenians whom they saw as competitors.[7]

The growing Christian merchant class was interested in securing the protection of the European consulates, who could provide protection from the extortion of the Ottoman pashas and the attacks on merchant ships by Maltese pirates. Such protection presupposed entering into union. In this way, the formation of the Uniate community was a consequence of the formation of the new merchant class that served France's interest in the Middle East and acted as an intermediary between the Syrian and European economies.[8]

Of course, we should not lose sight that this schema (trade–consular patronage–Unia) is a simplification and is conditional in many respects. The success of the Unia in Damascus was achieved without the presence of any European consulates and many merchant families successfully engaged in business for generations before entering into union. Finally, in Aleppo, more people were under the patronage of Protestants—the English and Dutch consuls—than under representatives of Catholic powers.[9] Although the Ottoman authorities were generally tolerant of the Latin presence in the cities of the Levant,[10] the creation of Uniate communities was not in the interest of the Porte. Despite its broad internal autonomy, the Orthodox Church was partially integrated into the Ottoman state structure, with the patriarch being something like a government official equal to a pasha of three tails.[11] By contrast, the organization of the Catholic Church remained subordinate to the Vatican. Although Catholics in Turkey paid the *jizya* to the sultan's treasury, they were politically and spiritually tied only to Europe, which for centuries had been the main enemy of the Sublime Porte.[12] For a Syrian Christian to become a Frank meant falling out of the existing *millet* system and to be practically outside the law. Therefore, Catholicism's successes in the Levant in the seventeenth century were rather modest, and cases of directly entering into union number fewer than a dozen people per year.[13] What proved to be more effective was another of the missionaries' activities: the establishment of schools in which the younger generation of Arab Christians, more susceptible to Catholic influence, was enrolled. Missionary schools with dozens of students are known to have been active in Damascus, Aleppo, and other cities during the seventeenth century. Thus, by the beginning of the eighteenth century, there had developed a significant class of pro-Catholic Orthodox Arabs. Using the experience of the Union of Brest, the Latin monks made a special effort to appeal to the Orthodox clergy, especially the bishops, hoping that by bringing the upper hierarchy over to the side of union, the entire community would follow their pastors.[14]

THE CHURCH OF ANTIOCH AND THE VATICAN: A CHRONICLE OF CONTACTS

Antiochian Orthodox clergy of the sixteenth and seventeenth century did not view the Western missionaries with any hostility. As Robert Haddad has written, the Orthodox Arabs had long forgotten the horrors of the Crusades, and the decline in their theological expertise left no room for doctrinal controversy with the Franks.[15] Additionally, living in a religiously and ethnically diverse society led to tolerance for people of other faiths among the Christians of the Middle East, if not on a theological level, then on an everyday level. Many Middle Eastern Christians dreamed of a cultural and spiritual revival in their communities through a reliance on European education and the achievements of Western science. The missionaries' monetary assistance to Eastern Christians during times of famine and epidemics was gratefully accepted. The hierarchs most inclined to cooperate with the missionaries also received personal subsidies.[16]

Repeated statements by Western missionaries of the sixteenth and seventeenth centuries about the readiness of the Orthodox Syrians to reunite with the Apostolic See of Rome and accept Latin dogmas seem to have been far from reality. Catholic historiography, distinguished by its exalted historical optimism, was inclined to declare all Middle Eastern bishops to be supporters of union except those who officially declared Latin dogma to be anathema. At the same time, Arab Christian chronicles do not say a word about contacts with Catholics from the sixteenth to the mid-seventeenth century, and the missionaries' two-hundred-year-long conversation with Orthodox bishops about unifying the churches produced no concrete results. Perhaps Latin missionaries exaggerated their success in dealing with the Orthodox East. Perhaps they were mistaken, taking at face value the refined Middle Eastern sense of respect, etiquette of dialogue, and code of hospitality. Additionally, interchurch contacts in the Ottoman world of the sixteenth and seventeenth centuries cannot be measured by the same standards as Eastern Europe during the time of the Unions of Florence and Brest, during which time it was possible to observe a significant and uncompromising confrontation between Byzantine and Western civilizations. In the Arab East, relations between Christian communities were far less conflicted. Suffice it to recall the strange attempt at a Melkite–Maronite union under Patriarch Dorotheus III[17] or the sharing of churches by Orthodox and Maronites mentioned in the sources from the late sixteenth century.[18] According to the Arab Uniate historian of the eighteenth century, Yuhanna al-'Ujaymi, Patriarch of Antioch Joachim ibn Jum'a (1543–1576) took a positive attitude toward Catholics and, in 1560, sent an encyclical letter to his bishops forbidding them from calling the Franks heretics or blaspheming the pope.[19]

Pope Gregory XIII (1572–1584), one of the key figures of the Counter-Reformation, paid special attention to dealings with Middle Eastern Christians. In the years 1578–1579 and 1580–1582, the mission of the Jesuit Giovanni Battista Eliano (1530–1589) was active in Sidon in Syria. Although the main purpose of his visit was to strengthen ties, the legate was ordered to enter into contact with the Orthodox and Syrian Jacobite Churches. The schism in the Patriarchate of Antioch beginning in 1581 between Michael VI and Joachim Daw created an extremely favorable situation for the penetration of Latin missionaries into the Orthodox milieu and for bringing at least one of the rival patriarchs into union.[20] In December 1581, Eliano met with Joachim Daw in Damascus. At the missionary's suggestion, the patriarch sent a letter to the cardinal of Santa Severina[21] who oversaw the Vatican's contacts with the Orthodox churches. However, to the cardinal's dismay, in the patriarch's letter, there was nothing but flowery pleasantries; Joachim declined to talk specifically about union.[22] Eliano's communication with Michael in Aleppo in July 1582 proved to be more productive. Feeling that he was losing his standoff with Joachim, Michael exhibited a willingness for the most extensive possible contacts with Rome and even agreed to go to Italy. "As it stands, not much separates him from the kingdom of God," Eliano summarized his communication with the patriarch in a letter to the superior general of the Jesuit Order.[23] In March 1583, the pope sent a new embassy to the East, led by the Maltese Lionardo Abel. He was ordered to enter into contact with the heads of the Eastern churches and to persuade them to reunite with Rome under the terms of the Union of Florence and with acceptance of the decisions of the Council of Trent and the calendar reform of 1582.[24] Lionardo Abel began his mission in Tripoli, where he presented the local Orthodox with the content of papal letters addressed to them. Part of the Tripoli community supported the idea of union. Later, on September 16, 1584, these people sent the appropriate letter to Pope Gregory XIII.[25] This letter, as well as the reports of the papal legates, makes it possible to reconstruct the events of 1583–1585. From Tripoli, Abel went to Aleppo where he remained, sending letters to the Christian hierarchs. Both of the rival Orthodox patriarchs, Michael and Joachim, were in catastrophic financial situations and had slim prospects of winning. They could not neglect such an ally as the Catholic Church with its vast resources—including, perhaps, financial resources. In the spring of 1584, Lionardo Abel made a pilgrimage to Jerusalem and, when passing through the Bekaa Valley, made contact with Joachim Daw. They met in the village of ʿAyta, near Zabadani, where the utterly destitute Joachim was hiding from the extortion of the Ottoman officials. The patriarch, daring to appear neither in Damascus nor in Tripoli, was in a situation in which he could not afford another conflict, including with representatives of the Catholic Church, which was rather influential in the Levant. At the same time, he was doubtlessly not a supporter of union. For this reason, in his talks with Abel, the patriarch had to maneuver frantically. The papal envoy presented Joachim with a letter from the Apostolic See calling for the resumption of the union concluded at the Council of Florence and the adoption of the Gregorian calendar. The patriarch replied that he had never heard of the Council of Florence. This statement has been quoted in the scholarly literature as an example of the Ottoman Christians' blatant ignorance of theological matters.[26] It seems that this is not at all self-evident. Joachim quite possibly desired to avoid giving a direct answer and to buy time. Abel gave him a copy of the acts of the Council of Florence for examination. The patriarch of Antioch stated that before making such an important decision about religious and ecclesial unity, he needed to consult with the primates of the other local churches and with the leaders of the Christian community of Syria. Therefore, he agreed to have another meeting with Abel in Tripoli to finalize the agreements. It is possible that Joachim already knew that he would not appear in Tripoli at the stipulated time. He soon set sail for Constantinople, hoping for financial assistance from the Ecumenical Patriarch to get rid of his debts.[27]

In Jerusalem, Abel attempted to persuade Patriarch Sophronius to enter union. He behaved in the same evasive manner as Joachim, referring to the need to discuss the matter with the authority on it in the Orthodox world, Patriarch Sylvester of Alexandria, and leaving for Sinai. Without waiting for an answer, Abel returned to Aleppo, learning along the way that his meeting with Joachim would also not take place.[28] After the failure in negotiations with the patriarchs of both Antioch and Jerusalem, in 1585, Abel turned to Michael al-Hamawi, who had lost the struggle for the patriarchate and lived in Aleppo as a private person. He had nothing to lose and moreover was severely offended by the other Orthodox patriarchs who "betrayed" him in favor of Joachim. It is no wonder that at his meeting with Abel, he complained at length about the misery that he suffered at the hands of Joachim and his supporters, later writing to Rome about the same thing. The ex-patriarch told the papal legate of his readiness to accept Catholic dogmas and the primacy of the pope. Michael drew up the relevant letters and certified them with his seal, but nothing is known about any response to them from the Vatican.[29] It appears that in the papal curia, they decided that Michael did not have any real power and negotiating with him was pointless. Interestingly, in the Catholic historiography, Michael is considered to be the only legitimate patriarch of Antioch at that time, while Joachim Daw appears as a usurping anti-patriarch.

With regard to Joachim Daw's negative attitude toward union with the Catholics, one cannot but give the example of his activities in Ukraine in 1585–1586, when the patriarch of Antioch supported the laity of the Lvov Brotherhood, the future source of resistance to the Unia, in their conflict with their pro-Latin church hierarchy.[30] In Syria itself, Joachim's name was firmly associated with the anti-Catholic faction of Antiochian clergy. There is an Arabic polemical treatise from that time in the form of a response to the papal letter addressed to Patriarch Joachim. This *Response* was written by Metropolitan Anastasius al-Marmariti ibn al-Mujalla, the closest associate of, or, as he styled himself, the "disciple of our master Patriarch Kyr Yuwakim al-Antaki."[31] Anastasius's treatise, despite its polemical nature, was written with exquisite politeness. The author speaks a great deal about the joy it caused the Antiochian Christians that the pope was striving to overcome the differences "sowed between … [them] by the devil." After such a hopeful start, Anastasius begins to examine the theses of the papal letter and demolish them. The Gregorian calendar reform, which the papal legate suggested to the Orthodox to adopt, was subject to particular attacks. Anastasius was skeptical about the research of European astronomers and mathematicians, pointing out that the dating of Easter and other feasts was established by the Apostles under the inspiration of the Holy Spirit and that any change to the basic elements of the Christian tradition is cause for excommunication and damnation. The author appealed to the universal view of the entire Orthodox world,

Also, our community, our bishops, our kings and all our people, scattered in the four cardinal directions—Greeks, Russians, Georgians, Vlachs,

> Serbs, Moldavians, Turks [the Turkish-speaking Christians of Anatolia?], Arabs and others ... from the time of the Holy Apostles and the God-bearing fathers of the Seven Ecumenical Councils down to this day recognize one faith, one confession one Church and one baptism ... and all our nations agree in the four corners of the inhabited world with one word and one affair ... and we did not receive the confession and the holy tradition which is in our hands ... from unknown people, like other, foreign communities.

"But we pray," he continues,

> with the Holy Apostles and the 318 fathers [of the Council of Nicaea] whose signs and miracles shine forth from them manifestly. And so how can we change the tradition of such holy fathers and follow after unknown people who have no other trade but to observe the stars and examine the sky?[32]

Without taking up the task of presenting a detailed analysis and commentary on the treatise of Anastasius ibn al-Mujalla in this current work,[33] we simply point out that even among Arab hierarchs of the sixteenth century who were considered "ignorant" and "theologically illiterate," there were plenty of people with a clear understanding of their Orthodox identity who were able to assert that identity articulately.

The Seventeenth Century: The Embrace Gets Tighter

After the 1580s, there was a three-and-a-half-decade pause in ties between Rome and Antioch. The next attempt to conclude a union probably took place under Patriarch Athanasius II (1611–1618) who, according to several authors of the first half of the seventeenth century, in particular the Jesuit missionary Jacob Galtieri, openly sympathized with the Catholics and even called a council of bishops in Damascus in 1617 or 1618 that recognized the Union of Florence and sent an embassy to Rome with a request to enter into communion.[34] These results of this demarche are not known, and it is odd that the Vatican archives are silent about it. At the same time, information has been preserved about what happened in the 1614 conflict between Athanasius and the Maronite patriarch, who sought to introduce the Gregorian calendar in the Maronite community in Damascus, against the wishes of Athanasius.[35] For an adherent of union, such a position would seem to be illogical.

Philo-Catholic sentiments are also attributed to Athanasius's brother Cyril, who, according to Yuhanna al-ʿUjaymi, "was a Catholic, just like his brother, and always opposed the schism."[36] Mindful of the ruthless, nine-year struggle between Cyril and Ignatius ʿAtiya, Catholic authors gave the role of antihero to Ignatius, "Ignatius was rich, but he did not have praiseworthy qualities. The emirs of the Maʿan family supported him and he persecuted Cyril, causing him great expenses."[37]

The real picture is much more complicated. It is difficult to imagine that Cyril Dabbas would have advertised his pro-Catholic sympathies (if indeed they were such) as long as he enjoyed the unwavering support of Cyril Lucaris, the staunchest and most passionate opponent of Rome. Dabbas's longstanding conflict with Meletius Karma, whom Catholic historiography counts in the ranks of supporters of union, also does not fit with his alleged Catholicism. Finally, Cyril's antagonist, Ignatius, who was residing in Beirut, also caught the attention of the local Capuchin missionaries, who established contact with him. Ignatius was upset by his involvement in the killing of Cyril Dabbas, and in 1631, he appealed to Rome asking for absolution as well as alms for the impoverished Church of Antioch. The patriarch's request was considered by the Congregation de Propaganda Fide, and as a precondition, he was encouraged to accept union with Rome.[38] That is, the confrontation between Cyril and Ignatius cannot be explained by the Catholic expansion in the Middle East when put together with these contradictions. The missionaries cast a wide net and immediately reached out to all parties in a conflict. On the other hand, some hierarchs of the Orthodox East also reached out to all possible patrons, simultaneously seeking financial assistance from both Rome and the Russian tsar, as Ignatius himself did in 1633. And, as has already been noted, the Arabs did not invest the same meaning in their words of fraternal unity with the See of Rome in these statements as Catholics saw in them.

Metropolitan Meletius Karma of Aleppo, later Patriarch Euthymius II of Antioch (1572–1635) is one of the major figures of the Arab literary renaissance. All of his translation and ecclesial activities were aimed at further familiarizing the Arabs with the Byzantine cultural tradition. However, being broad-minded and realizing the full power of the technical and intellectual potential of Western civilization, Meletius readily entered into contact with the missionaries and attempted to extract the maximum benefit from this for his cultural projects.[39] Thus, he welcomed the establishment of a missionary school in Aleppo in 1627 and, once patriarch, he offered to open a similar school in Damascus.

Starting in 1617, Karma negotiated with the Vatican for the publication in Italy of Arabic liturgical texts and periodically made statements about the desirability of church unity and the acceptance of union by the Arabs, for example, through his envoy Pachomius who arrived in Rome in 1635.[40] It is possible that the value of these statements was less than was thought in Rome. However, even in Rome, Karma was not trusted. It was not without reason that seventeen years of talks about an edition of Arabic books came to nothing: the Vatican did not want to lose the monopoly on Arabic printing.[41]

Catholic historians of the nineteenth and twentieth centuries, without going into the intricacies of these relationships, referred to Karma in the words of the missionaries of the seventeenth century as a "good Catholic." They explained the patriarch's sudden death as a result of being poisoned by "Greek monks" who disagreed with his pro-Catholic orientation. They blamed the absence of evidence for this in Arabic sources, particularly in the annals of Karma's disciple the Patriarch Macarius, on considerations of political correctness that Macarius followed when producing an official history of the patriarchate.[42] Generally speaking, in the history of the Church of Antioch, the seventeenth and early eighteenth centuries were marked by an unprecedented concentration of real or imaginary poisonings. Of the twelve patriarchs and anti-patriarchs who lived during this period, five of them are held by various accounts to have been poisoned and only four of them died a natural death. In any case, it is evident that Karma's efforts were focused on integrating the Orthodox Arabs into the Byzantine cultural sphere and that what he wanted from the Catholic world was technical assistance for this process.

Much the same can be said of Patriarch Macarius al-Za'im's (1647–1672) relationship with the Catholic world. According to the author of the Beirut Chronicle, Macarius "out of the purity of the intentions of his heart" allowed the missionaries to settle in the patriarchal metochion and did not prevent them from communicating with his flock.[43] The chronicler attempted to justify the patriarch's contacts with the missionaries by referring to his naiveté. The Beirut Chronicle was compiled in the late eighteenth century and was marked by the fierce struggle between Orthodoxy and the Unia. Thus, from the chronicler's viewpoint, communication with Catholics by a respected prelate had to be justified. In Macarius' own time, such contacts appear natural. The missionaries spoke of the patriarch in condescending terms, saying that he was a good pastor who had no idea about theology.[44] In 1661–1664, on several occasions Macarius conveyed his messages to Rome through European missionaries. In them, he once more raised the issue of publishing Arabic liturgical literature and welcomed the efforts of the "Mother Church" to restore the original unity of Christians. On December 14, 1663, the patriarch secretly signed a Catholic confession of faith.[45] In late 1664, a curious Greek adventurer from Chios named Symeon appeared in Rome, calling himself the metropolitan of Isfahan and presenting a letter of recommendation from

Macarius. Presumably, the patriarch of Antioch had intended to use Symeon to further the negotiations with the Congregation de Propaganda Fide.[46]

In the case of Macarius, later historians automatically applied their notions of religious identity characteristic of the nineteenth and twentieth centuries to the seventeenth century. It seemed obvious that if Macarius signed a Catholic confession of faith, then he was a Catholic. It is not at all the case that this would have been obvious to Macarius himself. The religious consciousness of the Christians of the Levant at that time was blurry and did not resemble modern religious notions. Curiously, Macarius' first letter to the pope was written on September 30, 1661, three days after he wrote a letter of gratitude to the Russian tsarina (one of the letters brought to Moscow by the embassy of Archimandrite Neophytus in 1662). Macarius's Catholic confession of faith was certified by his signature in Greek, made by someone in the patriarch's entourage. In the opinion of paleographers, it is the same hand to which belongs Macarius's Greek signature under an Orthodox confession of faith in the acts of the Council of Constantinople in 1652, which Macarius attended.[47] In 1670–1671, Carmelite and Capuchin missionaries reported to Rome that the Patriarch Macarius was a "crypto-Catholic" who was wary of openly declaring his true religious sympathies because of his close relations with the Russian tsar.[48]

Undoubtedly, in informal conversation with the missionaries, Macarius told them exactly what they wanted to hear. The patriarch's true views can be found in the book of his son, Paul of Aleppo, Macarius's alter ego. We note, incidentally, that Paul of Aleppo and, later, his sons did not study with the Western missionaries even though a missionary school existed in that time in Aleppo. Paul's *Journey of the Patriarch Macarius* is permeated with harshly anti-Latin sentiments. Most famous in this context is the passage about the forcible imposition of Catholicism on Ukraine by Jesuit priests whom Paul rhetorically compares to Yezidis, the Kurdish sect of "devil-worshippers."[49] There is no doubt that Macarius remained in the bosom of the Orthodox tradition. Thus, like many Eastern bishops, he was not averse to receiving alms from all possible patrons, as when he simultaneously addressed letters full of praise and pleas to Alexei Mikhailovich and Louis XIV. Thus, for example, the patriarch sent a letter to the French king on February 15, 1663. Almost half the text is filled with grandiloquent praise and good wishes for the addressee. Perhaps Alexei Mikhailovich would have been unpleasantly surprised to learn that it was not only he whom Macarius called "the greatest of all the Christian kings" and it was not only to him that he wrote "we trust in help from the Lord and from you."[50] However, the letter does not contain any indications of the patriarch's willingness to change religious orientations. Macarius complains of the wretchedness of the Antiochian Christians and requests financial assistance, in return only promising the mercy of the Lord and that the king would be seated with the assembly of saints in the kingdom of heaven.[51]

In everyday life, Macarius had no hostility toward the non-Orthodox. It is no surprise that when discussing relations with heterodox confessions with Russian clergy in 1656 and later, in correspondence with the tsar and Nikon, Macarius insisted on recognizing the reality of the Catholic sacrament of baptism.[52] In this case, the patriarch of Antioch followed the canonical tradition common to the Orthodox churches of the Eastern Mediterranean. Thus, although Macarius's position toward the Latins was more lenient than that of the people of Muscovy, there is no doubt about his commitment to Orthodoxy.[53]

Passing the Point of No Return

The half-century after the death of Macarius was a key period in the development of the Melkite union with Rome. In the last quarter of the seventeenth century, the Levant Company was organized, strengthening the position of European merchants in Syria. According to a number of agreements, consuls received broad authority to grant their protection to Ottoman subjects. Finally, in the ecclesio-political arena, there had formed a critical mass of graduates from the missionary schools. However, most probably the main factor behind the success of the movement for union was the shifts in the international balance of power. The international position of the Ottoman Empire suffered dramatically when it suffered severe defeats in the war of 1683–1699 with a coalition of European powers. The prestige of the Catholic powers in the Middle East increased significantly and the Sublime Porte's control over the Arab provinces loosened. All this contributed to a pro-union sentiment among Christians, oriented toward the new political and cultural centers of power.

The first of the graduates from the missionary schools to reach the top of the ecclesiastical hierarchy was Neophytus al-Saqizi, nephew of the Patriarch Euthymius III, who himself aspired for the patriarchal throne from 1672 to 1681.[54] However, he is not known to have had any contacts with Rome during this period.

A much more valuable asset for the missionaries was Euthymius al-Sayfi (1643–1723), a native of Damascus who became metropolitan of Tyre and Sidon in 1682. He was also educated at a missionary school and had the reputation among his contemporaries as a "vessel of learning."[55] Euthymius, like much of his flock, was involved in trading Lebanese silk, and this brought the metropolitan closer to the French merchants, diplomats, and missionaries. In December 1683, he secretly converted to Catholicism and, for four decades, remained the main conduit of Roman influence in the Arab East. Euthymius received regular subsidies from Rome and was engaged in active missionary activity and promoting Catholicism among pilgrims passing through Sidon and the Christians of Mount Lebanon, Hawran, and Palestine. For this purpose, in 1685, he established the Arab al-Mukhallisiya monastic community, known in European literature as the Salvatorians. In 1701, Euthymius was appointed administrator of the Melkites in union with Rome in the Levant. On the basis of joint commercial interests, the metropolitan worked closely with the Lebanese emir and the pasha of Sidon, Usama Abu Tawuq, attempting to use his assistance to incorporate Acre, a new and growing center of Christian commercial activity, into his diocese.[56] The patronage of the Lebanese emir and the pasha of Sidon allowed Euthymius to feel safe from possible reprisals from the Orthodox Patriarch Cyril and the anathemas periodically imposed on al-Sayfi by the Synod of Constantinople.[57]

For the most part, however, Patriarch Cyril had no time for the metropolitan of Sidon. From 1686 to 1694, the Church of Antioch was split by an internecine struggle for the patriarchal throne between Cyril and Athanasius Dabbas. In this struggle, Athanasius, an alumnus of the Catholic school in Damascus, tried to rely on the support of the Western missionaries. For many years, Athanasius played a double game, presenting himself to Rome as a supporter of Catholicism. In April 1687, he secretly sent messages to the pope and the French consul in Damascus declaring his recognition of Catholic dogma. In 1694, the rival patriarchs reconciled, and Athanasius Dabbas abandoned his claims to the patriarchal throne in exchange for the diocese of Aleppo. Aware of the growing pro-Catholic sympathies of the Christians of Aleppo, Athanasius tried not to clash with the Western missionaries residing in the city.

Among the Orthodox, there existed suspicions about Athanasius. Already in 1686 the bishop of Beirut, Sylvester Dahhan, stated, "Our patriarch is a Frank."[58] Mikhail Breik was of the same opinion in his chronicle. The authors of the Beirut Chronicle and other sources believed that Athanasius, seeing the missionaries' influence on his flock, was simply forced to maneuver and turn a blind eye to canonical deviations, particularly with regard to fasting, in hopes of keeping the people of Aleppo within the Orthodox Church through tolerance.[59] In any case, Catholic missionaries operated openly in Aleppo without any interference from Athanasius and, by the end of the seventeenth century, their influence was firmly established.[60]

In the pro-Catholic milieu of Aleppo in the early eighteenth century, there was a young deacon named ʿAbdallah Zakher (1680–1748) who actively cooperated with the Jesuit mission. He edited Arabic translations of Latin theological literature and wrote his own polemical treatises in refutation of Orthodox polemical writers. Thus, ʿAbdallah rose to prominence in Athanasius's circle and, according to some, was his secretary and worked in the Aleppo printing press organized by the patriarch.[61]

At the turn of the seventeenth to the eighteenth century, several bishops of the Patriarchate of Antioch (the bishops of Beirut, Baalbek, Tripoli, and Sidon) secretly converted to Catholicism. A group of pro-Catholic monks left Balamand Monastery and founded the Uniate Monastery of Mar Yuhanna (St John the Baptist) in the village of Shuwayr in the mountains above Beirut. In 1708, Euthymius al-Sayfi built the monastery of Dayr Mar Mukhallis (Holy Savior), which became a center of Uniate propaganda and sheltered its preachers during times of persecution.[62]

In his convert's zeal, Euthymius al-Sayfi tried to reform the Melkite liturgy on Latin models and innovated new church rituals. Even the Catholic missionaries felt this was unnecessary, to say nothing of the Eastern Christians (for more details, see Chapter 10). Euthymius disseminated pro-Catholic literature in Arabic. He himself wrote a polemic about the primacy of the pope, *al-Dalalat al-Lamiʿat (The Brilliant Proofs)*, written at the beginning of the eighteenth century and published in Rome in 1710.[63]

Among supporters of union, in addition to the graduates of the missionary schools in Aleppo and Damascus, increasing numbers of students had studied in Italy. Prominent among them was the nephew of Euthymius al-Sayfi, Seraphim Tanas. In Orthodox sources, Seraphim receives even more imprecation than Euthymius. He is called a "cunning fox," a "viper spewing deadly poison," and a "devil in human flesh, the firstborn of Satan, a monstrous beast, a sower of the wily seeds of wickedness."[64] Ordained a priest in 1711, he led the propaganda for union in Acre and had his eye set on the local bishop's throne.[65] Upon the death of the bishop there around 1713, Euthymius al-Sayfi attempted to achieve the transfer of Acre into his own jurisdiction to remove the city from the "anti-Catholic atmosphere" of the Patriarchate of Jerusalem. From the very first, this did not work. Patriarch Chrysanthos of Jerusalem installed his own bishop in Acre, the previously mentioned Arab Photius (ʿAbd al-Nur). After Photius's death in 1721, Euthymius renewed his claim to the city. For 1,000 piasters, the governor of Sidon, ʿUthman Pasha, arranged the transfer of Acre into the control of his protégé. In 1722, however, Chrysanthos managed to buy over the pasha, although it seems also that British diplomacy was not sympathetic with the Catholics' success. Acre was again transferred to the Patriarchate of Jerusalem and the local Catholic community was persecuted and partially moved to Sidon.[66]

Euthymius al-Sayfi's activities caused growing irritation in Orthodox circles, especially among the Greeks. There is mention of the fact that at the beginning of the eighteenth century the patriarch of Antioch excommunicated Euthymius. In late 1714, Patriarch Chrysanthos of Jerusalem promulgated an encyclical condemning the treatise *al-Dalalat al-Lami'at*. In October 1718, the patriarch of Constantinople anathematized Euthymius and sentenced him to deposition and exile. This patriarchal decree was signed by the other Eastern patriarchs, including Cyril V and Athanasius Dabbas. Euthymius, however, was under the protection of Uthman Pasha Abu Tawuq and French diplomacy and so he was able to ignore any decisions from the Phanar.

Patriarch Cyril was unable to stop the Catholic onslaught in Syria. Backing the pro-Catholic metropolitans were local pashas, European consuls, influential parishioners, and the Lebanese emirs. The Antiochian primate did not feel the support of the Sublime Porte and this situation was unaccustomed and painful. As Robert Haddad has written, Cyril could not have understood that the weakening of the Ottoman system of authority of which he was a part was due to European expansion in the Eastern Mediterranean. Backed into a corner, the patriarch tried to fight his enemies with their own weapon—through rapprochement with Rome.

His intermediaries for contact with the Vatican were the Franciscan friar of Damascus, Biagio da Salamanca, and the nephew of Euthymius al-Sayfi, Seraphim Tanas. Cyril's first letter to Pope Clement XI, written on August 20, 1716 (Gregorian), was of a fairly streamlined character. Cyril referred to the pope as his "elder brother," declared his adherence to the teachings of the Seven Ecumenical Councils, and indicated among the conditions for a rapprochement between Antioch and Rome the protection of the French consuls for Syrian Christians and the termination of European corsairs off the Levantine coast. Upon reading the contents of the letter, the French consul in Sidon, Poulard, found its wording unacceptable and requested that the patriarch compose a new one, suggesting an appropriate model. Cyril's second letter, dated September 8, was strikingly different from the previous one: the patriarch wrote of recognizing the primacy of the pope and accepted the decisions of the Council of Florence and all Catholic dogmas.

Cyril's correspondence with Rome was kept a closely guarded secret to avoid confusion among the Orthodox and repression from the Ottoman authorities. Various centers of power in the Latin East challenged each other's prerogatives to determine Rome's policy in relation to the Church of Antioch. The Franciscan missionaries of Italian and Spanish background patronized Athanasius Dabbas and sought to sideline Euthymius al-Sayfi and Cyril Tanas, whose interest were often in conflict with the Franciscans' plans. However, they were outweighed by the influence of Euthymius, who was supported by French diplomacy, and further contact with Cyril was carried out by monks of the Salvatorian Order. Euthymius expected to inherit the patriarchal throne after Cyril and insisted that Rome annul its recognition of Athanasius Dabbas as patriarch of Antioch. In October 1717, Seraphim Tanas delivered to Cyril a new text for him to sign with a Catholic profession of faith, which would be the final approval of the patriarch's reunion with the See of Rome.

However, shortly thereafter Cyril's relationship with Rome rapidly started to cool. In the opinion of his contemporaries, Cyril was not interested in the theological peculiarities of Western and Eastern Christianity and sought rapprochement with Rome for the purely pragmatic reasons of consolidating his power. Not having received the expected benefits, he began to reproach his Catholic correspondents over the imposition of Latin canons and rituals on the Syrian Christians and their inability to rein in the Maltese pirates. The Uniate emissaries Seraphim Tanas and Gabriel Finan, in contact with the patriarch in Damascus in the spring of 1719, reported to Rome about the duplicity of Cyril, who spoke like a "schismatic" with the "schismatics" and refused to continue contacts with the Vatican.

In April 1719, Cyril received news of Euthymius al-Sayfi's deposition by a synodal decision of the patriarchs of Constantinople, Jerusalem, and Alexandria. To avoid conflict with French diplomacy, the patriarchs did not mention Euthymius's pro-Catholic orientation among the reasons for his deposition but rather he was charged with various canonical offenses. After some hesitation, Cyril made public the document excommunicating Euthymius. He had accumulated his own mass of grievances against the metropolitan who was outside the control of his authority, ranging from his nonpayment of tithes to his performing noncanonical weddings. One of the Franciscan missionaries in Damascus, Tomaso Díaz Campaya, brokered a reconciliation between the hierarchs. He persuaded Euthymius to go to Damascus and repent to Cyril in exchange for the removal of the charges against him. The formal reconciliation between Cyril and Euthymius occurred in late November 1719, but latent hostility remained. Many believed that it was at Euthymius's instigation that the patriarch was accused by the authorities in Damascus of secretly performing the marriage of a Christian man to a Muslim woman and had to pay 3,000 *qurush* in his defense.[67]

Despite Cyril's contacts with Rome, Orthodox chroniclers generally speak sympathetically of the patriarch. In particular, Mikhail Breik wrote that he had ruled his community "very well," decorating churches and the patriarchal compound and having an enormous influence over both Christians and Muslims. Nevertheless, he did not interfere with the strengthening of the Catholic missionaries in Damascus who, in the 1720s during a period of rapprochement between the patriarch and Rome, made significant progress in the struggle over the souls of the Christians of Damascus. Two generations later, Mikhail Breik illustrated Cyril's nonresistance and lack of will with a proverb: "They ate the sour grapes but we got the stomach-ache." They ate the unripe grapes but we got the sour taste in our mouths.[68]

Cyril died in January 1720 of gangrene probably caused by diabetes, as reported to Rome by the Franciscan missionaries and Euthymius, or from being poisoned by Tomaso Campaya who was present with him, as reported by Breik.[69] Euthymius al-Sayfi expected to gain the patriarchal throne but was confronted with competing claims from Athanasius Dabbas. Euthymius's position was complicated by the fact that he did not receive absolute support in the Catholic world. The metropolitan could rely on the Jesuits and French diplomacy, whereas the Franciscan monks, who were mostly of Spanish and Italian backgrounds and were influential in the Middle East, stood with Athanasius. Moreover, Athanasius Dabbas had extensive connections with Orthodox circles in the Balkans and enjoyed a degree of support from the Phanar. All of this resulted in victory for Athanasius who became the new patriarch. His relationship with Euthymius was hopelessly ruined.[70]

The personality of Patriarch Athanasius seems much more complex and contradictory than that of Cyril. Intelligent and educated but unprincipled and spineless, he vacillated between his pro-Latin flock (Athanasius continued to live in Aleppo, even after consecrating the nominal metropolitan of Aleppo, Gerasimus) and pressure from the Phanar, which demanded that he combat Catholic influence. The Synod of Constantinople urged Athanasius to take real steps against union and so, in 1721, he translated from Greek into Arabic the polemical treatise the *Rock of Offense*[71] and wrote several treatises expounding Orthodox doctrine (see Chapter 10). Similar anti-Catholic literature and a previous synodal decision were sent to Syria, along with the requirement not to read and to burn the pro-Latin materials published by Euthymius al-Sayfi.[72]

Although Athanasius avoided contact with the Vatican after his elevation to the patriarchal throne, he was not trusted in the Phanar, and in 1722, he was summoned by the Synod of the capital, where he was required to publicly make his confession of Orthodox faith. Then Athanasius signed a joint encyclical condemning Catholic dogmas. As a result of all these declarations, in 1723, the Sublime Porte sent instructions to the pashas of Damascus and Aleppo for the arrest of a number of persons involved in the movement for union. Even earlier, in November 1722, 'Abdallah Zakher had fled from Aleppo to Mount Lebanon fearing persecution on account of his polemical activity.[73] The patriarchs appealed to the Sublime Porte to ask that Euthymius al-Sayfi be exiled to Adana. After the transfer of 'Uthman Pasha from Sidon to Damascus, Euthymius's position was weakened. He was arrested and spent three months imprisoned in the citadel of Sidon. Once freed, the metropolitan moved to Damascus under the protection of Uthman Pasha.[74]

The octogenarian Euthymius al-Sayfi died in November 1723.[75] The author of the Orthodox Beirut Chronicle states that the empty see was claimed by Seraphim Tanas, who became the leader of the pro-Catholic party in the Patriarchate. Athanasius, who returned from Aleppo around that time, refused Tanas's claims. Then Tanas appealed for help to the Lebanese Emir Haydar Shihab. Tanas managed, with generous gifts, to win over the emir and his entourage, who were already sympathetic to the Catholics. The emir's servants brought the Armenian Catholic bishop and Bishop Neophytus of Beirut and forcibly compelled them to consecrate Seraphim as a bishop, contrary to the canons.[76] Of course, this story is a fiction of later Orthodox polemicists who wanted to demonstrate the illegitimacy of the Uniate hierarchy. In fact, Seraphim remained a priest until the autumn of the following year. In 1723, Ignatius al-Bayruti was made metropolitan of Tyre and Sidon. Although sympathetic to the Catholics, he was weak-willed and did not seem dangerous to Athanasius.[77]

The struggle between Orthodox and Catholics for the soul of Patriarch Athanasius continued until his last days. On his deathbed, Latin missionaries visited the patriarch and offered him absolution in the name of the See of Rome. In Catholic circles, the common version of the story is that the missionaries succeeded in getting the dying patriarch to renounce his schismatic errors. Orthodox chroniclers inform us of their own interpretation of events.[78] Mikhail Breik claimed that Athanasius, like Cyril, was rumored to have been poisoned by the Latins,[79] whereas the Beirut Chronicle states that the patriarch, wanting to clarify his religious orientation, several times before his death defiantly confessed to the abbot of the Monastery of St George, the priest Peter who was known for his hatred of Catholics.[80] The eighteenth-century Uniate historian Yuhanna al-'Ujaymi also acknowledged that Athanasius refused to make a confession of faith before the Jesuits and states, "They say that he died as a schismatic."[81]

Athanasius died on July 25, 1724. The last of the participants in the events of the previous fifty years had died, and the history of the Church of Antioch began a new phase, in which the Catholics began to reap the fruits of their centuries of work.

The Schism

Subsequent events fit quite well into the scheme described previously of the confrontation between regional centers of power. Damascus, which had had a long association with Euthymius al-Sayfi, supported the claims of his nephew,

Seraphim Tanas, to the patriarchate. Aleppo, which for many years had been oriented toward Athanasius Dabbas, was prepared to accept the man designated to succeed him. This was Athanasius's deacon, the Greek Cypriot Sylvester, who previously had served in Aleppo and at that time was on Athos. The Aleppans wrote to Constantinople to express their desire to see Sylvester as patriarch. Seraphim acted swiftly. On his side, in addition to the pro-Catholic part of the congregation, was the governor of Damascus 'Uthman, Pasha Abu Tawuq, who previously had patronized his uncle, Euthymius al-Sayfi. One of the French merchants in Sidon gave Seraphim the money to pay for official approval for his being named patriarch.[82] Documents pertaining to the election of Seraphim, who took the name Cyril upon acceding to the patriarchate, have been preserved. Among the names of the electors' signatures are 29 priests, 11 notables (a'yan al-ta'ifa), 3 deacons, and 287 people who refer to themselves as a'yan. For the small Christian community of Damascus, the number of a'yan seems inflated; most likely, they are simply the heads of families.

Seraphim/Cyril was also supported by six bishops (Tyre-Sidon, Homs, Aleppo, Saydnayna, Banyas, and a bishop of the See of Furzul, newly created for the occasion) and three abbots (Dayr Mar Mukkhallis, Mar Yuhanna in Shuwayr, and Mar Sam'an near Beirut).[83] On September 19 or 20, 1724, Cyril Tanas occupied the patriarchate with the assistance of the pasha. In later Orthodox chronicles, these events were embellished with many details meant to highlight Cyril's uncanonical actions. According to the Beirut Chronicle, two Orthodox bishops who were in the city at that time as well as some priests and laity boycotted the pro-Catholic patriarch. Then Cyril sent his men as well as the pasha's Muslim police to catch these bishops and priests. They seized them and dragged them through the streets "offering them up for all kinds of humiliation before the people passing by."[84] In the church, which was filled with soldiers, Cyril made the Orthodox clergy exclaim "Many Years" for him.

An interesting feature distinguishes the Orthodox and Catholic interpretations of the election of Cyril Tanas. Orthodox authors argue that from the very beginning Cyril expressed his submission to the pope and received ordination from the head of the Capuchin missionaries, representing the See of Rome.[85] However, this seems to be another polemical overreach.[86] Initially, Cyril did not set himself in opposition to the Orthodox *millet*; he wanted to be the legitimate patriarch of Antioch, recognized by the Phanar and the Sublime Porte. It was only five years later, when he realized that he would not receive legal status in the empire, that the patriarch appealed to Rome for support and recognition. At the council of Uniate clergy at the Monastery of al-Mukhallis in 1730, the Capuchin missionary Dosithée de la Sainte-Trinité declared on behalf of the pope the recognition of Cyril as patriarch of Antioch.[87] Even by the autumn of 1724, Cyril was, if not supported by the Porte, at least supported by the pasha of Damascus and so felt sufficiently strong. For its part, the Synod of Constantinople immediately after the death of Athanasius informed the Sublime Porte of the catastrophic situation of Orthodoxy in Syria and received an order from the sultan to select a patriarch "alien to Latin error." The decree stipulated that the candidate for the patriarchate should not be from Syria (this, of course, was a suggestion of the Phanariots), so much was the purity of Orthodoxy among the Syrians in doubt.[88] According to the will of Athanasius, the new patriarch should be the aforementioned Greek Cypriot Sylvester (ca. 1696–1766). He was summoned to Constantinople and consecrated on September 27, 1724. From this moment began the Greek xenocracy in the Patriarchate of Antioch, against which Arab nationalists fought so hard in the second half of the nineteenth century. However, the fact is that something that in the late nineteenth century looked like absolute evil looked entirely different in the early eighteenth century.

In the recollection of Mikhail Breik, who knew him personally, Sylvester was "a holy and God-fearing man," something recognized even by the Muslims, "but he did not have political tact and his opinions were fickle."[89] Sylvester waited for more than a year in Constantinople until a favorable political climate developed. Finally, in October 1725, he went to Syria with a decree from the sultan accepting him as patriarch and ordering the arrest of Cyril. The field had already been cleared for Sylvester. By this time the patron of the Uniates, 'Uthman Pasha, had died. Without waiting for the arrival of Sylvester, in January 1725, Cyril looted the patriarchal compound in Damascus and fled to the Lebanese Emir Haydar in Dayr al-Qamar.[90] Was it not at this time that the Uniate Monastery of Mar Yuhanna in Shuwayr was decorated with a collection of old Russian icons, about which nineteenth century travelers wrote?[91] It is likely that many of the gifts given to Patriarch Macarius by Alexei Mikhailovich were stored there.

Sylvester arrived in Aleppo from there went to Damascus, and then made a tour of several dioceses and finally settled in Aleppo.[92] Historians have long noted the surprising paradox: the most pro-Catholic city in Syria willingly accepting a Greek patriarch supplied by the Phanar. Then there was the regional rivalry between the two Syrian metropolises; the people of Aleppo did not want to obey a patriarch from Damascus chosen by the people of Damascus.[93]

Thus, two parallel hierarchies began to take shape in the Patriarchate of Antioch: Orthodox and Uniate. The greatest successes achieved by the propaganda for union were in Aleppo, as well as in the coastal and mountainous regions of Lebanon south of Beirut. In 1728, Grigorovich-Barsky found no Orthodox faithful in Sidon apart from a few visitors. According to his account, the Uniates did not obey the local Orthodox bishop, but rather had their own bishop and followed Eastern rites with an admixture of Latin elements, with services conducted in a both Arabic and Greek "where they know but do not only know Arabic."[94] The main center of the Uniate Church was in the mountains above Sidon, where the residence of Cyril and the Monastery of Dayr Mar Mukhallis were located. Cyril Tanas gathered together loyal monks there, around twenty in 1728. There in the Lebanese mountains, other Uniate monasteries were founded at the turn of the seventeenth to the eighteenth century—Mar Yuhanna at Shuwayr with fifteen monks and St Isaiah, which was smaller in size and joined together with the Maronite Monastery of St George, a day's journey from Beirut. It was there in 1728 that Grigorovich-Barsky met Patriarch Cyril and later wrote, "There were many debates with me over the articles of faith, praising the Uniates, but calling all the Greeks together with the most holy patriarch heretics."[95] However, the majority of Syrian monasteries remained faithful to Orthodoxy, including the largest—Balamand, Saydnaya, and St George.

At that time, the Orthodox predominated in Beirut, something that Grigorovich-Barsky tied to the piety of its bishop, Neophytus. Somewhat later, in the mid-eighteenth century, a Uniate community was formed in Beirut, led by the influential Dahhan family. Remaining on the side of Orthodoxy were the communities of Tripoli, Homs, and Sidon, from which the congregations expelled bishops who had fallen into union, such as those of Antioch, Alexandretta, and other cities. A number of regions were engulfed in a permanent struggle between the two confessions. Thus, Grigorovich-Barsky wrote of the Christian community of Baalbek,

> All there is the devil's own chaff, and raised up by Uniates ... half are of the old Greek Orthodox faith, and got a rise out of the holy Church; they have among themselves hatred and strife for all the days, united in deeming the others heretics. ... There from long ago is the episcopal throne known, along with the Archbishop who does not pass all his time there these days, for when the Orthodox are overcome by the Uniates, then there will be the bishop on their throne, when the Uniates defeat the Orthodox, then they will expel the bishop.[96]

Acre, at the junction between Syria and Palestine, became another battlefield between Orthodoxy and Catholicism.

Grigorovich-Barsky describes the position of Orthodoxy in Damascus, the center of the patriarchate, in pessimistic terms. In Damascus itself, the traveler found only four hundred Orthodox men, who constituted the smallest of all the city's communities "but those were not altogether strong in faith and fasting."[97] There were twice as many Uniates, and they did not go to the Orthodox church, preferring the Roman Catholic one.

However, Grigorovich-Barsky's bleak assessment of the situation ("having crossed Syria where few Orthodox are discovered, there are Uniates everywhere") seems exaggerated.[98] The Orthodox hierarchy, supported—albeit inconsistently—by the Ottoman authorities, succeeded in stabilizing the situation in the interior of Syria, where Uniates were in the minority. This applies to Damascus, in contrast with Aleppo, where the Uniates almost completely dominated. In this way, the ancient rivalry between Damascus and Aleppo took on religious overtones.[99] The Uniate community operated freely only in Mount Lebanon, which was not controlled by the Ottoman administration.

THE ALEPPAN EPICENTER

The main events of that time were played out in Aleppo, Syria's largest city, where Patriarch Sylvester settled in early spring of 1726. Although most of the people of Aleppo were supporters of union, as has been mentioned, they tried not to spoil relations with the patriarch and received him with honor. Sylvester, however, did not possess political tact and attempted to eradicate Uniatism with an iron fist. When, during a solemn reception for the patriarch on a Wednesday, fish was served at mealtime, he knocked over the table legs and angrily cursed the people of Aleppo as "fish-eaters." Then, in the church, Sylvester threatened to excommunicate those who ate fish during fasts. Apparently because of the fact that it was the elites of the Christian community who determined its pro-Catholic sympathies, Sylvester deliberately treated influential members of his flock coldly and, much to their humiliation, rendered honor to the lower classes and ordinary people. His threats attained the opposite result: the people of Aleppo were embittered, stopped going to church, and plotted a conspiracy against him. At first, Sylvester enjoyed the total support of the pasha and of prominent Muslims, which allowed him to imprison notables found guilty of Catholicism, to impose exactions on them, and so on. In the court archives of Aleppo, there are preserved lists of local Christians suspected of having pro-Latin sympathies. These documents are dated March 24 and July 1, 1726. The latter list included hundreds of names. Many of those on the lists were arrested and imprisoned. On August 24, the Uniates of Aleppo put forward a counterclaim against Patriarch Sylvester, meticulously enumerating all of his exactions, which were on the order of thousands and tens of thousands of *qurush*.[100]

Sylvester realized that oppression alone would not be able to halt the onslaught of Uniatism. The spiritual assault of Catholicism had to be countered with an assault at no less of an intellectual level. The patriarch appealed to Makarius Kalogeras, scholarch (rector) of the Academy of Patmos, at the time the largest center of education for the Ottoman Greeks. Makarius (ca. 1689–1737) who possessed an encyclopedic education and was pious to the point of fanaticism, was one of the most prominent figures of the Orthodox *millet* at that time. He immediately responded to Sylvester's request and sent his best disciple, James of Patmos, to Syria. There, with the patriarch's support, in early August 1726, he opened a school in Aleppo, "that despite the many times over intelligent and verbose men and skilled philosophers, they could have been able to oppose the enemies of the church of Christ."[101]

Nevertheless, Sylvester's struggle with the Uniates of Aleppo ended with his defeat. The people of Aleppo were able to win over the Muslim authorities of the city with lavish gifts. The French consul, who originally remained neutral, could not forgive the patriarch for rounding up pro-Catholic Arabs, which occurred in the French church, violating its diplomatic immunity. The French were also irritated by the close (including commercial) ties between Sylvester and the British consulate.[102] Perhaps the Orthodox, searching for a counterweight to the French–Uniate tandem, fumbled toward a rapprochement with British diplomacy, which was not pleased with French Catholic expansion in the Levant. The dragoman of the British consulate in Aleppo during the 1720s was Elias Fakhr, later logothete of the See of Antioch, the leading Orthodox polemicist of the eighteenth century.[103] However, by the beginning of the eighteenth century, France had pushed Britain out of the leading economic and political positions in Aleppo. Thus, Sylvester found himself surrounded by enemies.[104]

According to Orthodox accounts of subsequent events (which occurred, approximately, at the end of August 1726), a Uniate mob attacked the patriarch, plotting to kill him, but he escaped by swimming across the river and managed to reach Constantinople.[105] The dramatic cast of this story could be attributable to the polemical bent of the author of the Beirut Chronicle, but Mikhail Breik, a much more balanced narrator, also notes that the people of Aleppo rebelled against the patriarch "out of anger and stubbornness" and, taking advantage of the local authorities, wanted to kill him, on account of which Sylvester had to flee the city by night.[106] According to other information, the Ottoman authorities imposed a crushing fine on the patriarch and failure to pay it would result in imprisonment. Fortunately, the British consul helped Sylvester to leave Aleppo in secret.[107] Catholic authors omit these details, saying only that the patriarch was forced to leave the city, feeling that the *qadi* and Muslim notables had gone over to the side of the Uniates. After that, there was a crackdown on the Orthodox in Aleppo. Sylvester's vicar and priests appointed by Sylvester were thrown into prison and the Uniates seized the city's church. In the first half of 1728, James of Patmos was briefly arrested and his school was closed.[108]

At the same time, the people of Aleppo sought to leave the Patriarchate of Antioch and be placed nominally under the authority of the See of Constantinople. They sent the Phanar complaints about Sylvester's cruel and unreasonable actions. To verify this, the Synod of Constantinople sent Bishop Gregorius, who spent two years in Aleppo and upon his return reported that the residents of the city were firm in their faith, except that they kept fasts poorly. The Uniates tried not to arouse Gregorius's suspicion and strongly expressed their loyalty to him. Additionally, as is evident in Uniate sources, they bribed him with 10,000 *qurush* and so the bishop did not interfere in the affairs of Aleppo's Christians. For this reason, when Grigorovich-Barsky visited the city on Christmas Day, 1728, he could not find an Orthodox priest to whom he could confess in all of Aleppo, and so he was forced to go to a village two days' journey from the city. The Uniates of Aleppo, according to Grigorovich-Barsky, "exceedingly hate the Orthodox and give them no mercy."

The Orthodox in the city were "of little number and the Uniates were innumerable in that place."[109] After Gregorius's departure, the people of Aleppo asked the Synod of Constantinople to bring back from exile Metropolitan Gerasimus, a secret Uniate who had been installed and later exiled by Patriarch Athanasius. In Constantinople, they believed in their trustworthiness and agreed to it, all the more so because all of Syria remained without a pastor as Patriarch Sylvester had spent six years in the Danubian principalities to raise funds for his impoverished see.[110] When Gerasimus arrived, he commemorated Sylvester in the prayers, behaved carefully, and did not advertise his Catholic views. At the same time, the people of Aleppo, supporters of union who were backing him, spun a new intrigue and attempted to achieve complete independence from the See of Antioch. A special role in the conspirators' plans was played by the monk Michael of Mar Yuhanna in Shuwayr, brother of the sultan's doctor Mansur, an Aleppan who had converted to Islam and had great influence at the court. With Mansur's help, the Uniates managed to obtain their demand for autocephaly upon payment by Aleppo of the same taxes that were levied on any patriarchate. The elderly

Gerasimus, who long refused to go into retirement, was eventually forced by the people of Aleppo to install the bishop Michael (who took the name Maximus) and to go into exile in a monastery in Lebanon where, according to the Beirut Chronicle, he soon died.[111] However, according to the Uniate chronicler Hanania al-Munayyir, Metropolitan Gerasimus did not die so soon after his retirement, but rather a quarter-century later, in 1754.[112] That is, he was not sent to retirement on account of senility but because of some internal struggle among the Catholics of Aleppo. Orthodox authors strongly relished the compromising story of the Uniates' forcible overthrow of Gerasimus. Strangely, the Aleppan Catholic chronicle of Ni'ma ibn Khuri Tuma does not mention Gerasimus, stating only that the Lord dealt bountifully with the city when, for forty-five cases paid to the authorities of Aleppo and Istanbul, Aleppo was withdrawn from Sylvester's jurisdiction and transferred to Metropolitan Maximus, who arrived on April 13, 1730.[113]

Such a radical redrawing of the church's boundaries failed for the Uniates, not least because the Sublime Porte had no time for them then. In the autumn of 1730, Istanbul was engulfed in an uprising that ended with the execution of Grand Vizier Ibrahim Nevşehirli and a change of sultans. In such an unstable environment, it was easier for the Catholics to buy the right decision from the Ottoman authorities. Orthodox hierarchs tried several times to return Aleppo to their control. Three complaints are known to have been made to the sultan by the Eastern patriarchs between 1730 and 1732, with the request that he put an end to Catholic expansion in the Levant. It was first and foremost about Aleppo where, according to the patriarchs, there were only fifty diehard Catholics and about a hundred people who were partially attached to the heresy. This group, with the support of thirty to forty Frankish priests, kept under their control a silent majority of Christians of Aleppo, "who remain faithful in their soul to the true church and their sultan."[114] However, this time the Catholics managed to win Istanbul over to their side, recalling the support of Maximus through the pasha and *qadi* of Aleppo and upheld their arguments with new cash offerings.[115]

The autonomy of Uniate Aleppo lasted from 1730 to 1746. Only one time, from 1733 to 1734, did Sylvester manage to briefly return Aleppo to his administration. Maximus fled to Mount Lebanon but then bribed the *qadi* and the pasha and was able to return. During these years, the people of Aleppo openly professed Catholicism. Those who remained loyal to Orthodoxy, in the words of Mikhail Breik, "they handed over to the judicial authorities," threatened with chains and executions and bribed the poor with money and gifts. Many Christians fled the city. Orthodox chronicles rhetorically compared Maximus's actions to the ancient heretics' persecutions of the faith.[116]

The position of Orthodoxy was slightly better in the rest of Syria. In the early 1730s, Patriarch Sylvester went to Damascus and immediately there were clashes between the Orthodox and the Uniates. Grigorovich-Barsky, who was living there in 1733, wrote of the adherents of the union, "on any day they were ready to kill and murder the Most Holy Patriarch Sylvester, defiling and betraying whom they please and because of this we were in constant fear ... and prepared for flight on any given day."[117] In 1728, James of Patmos transferred his school from Aleppo to Tripoli and then in 1733 to Damascus, trying to influence the Uniates with passionate sermons and denunciations, but without success. As Grigorovich-Barsky explained, "their hearts were corrupted by the teachings of the Jesuits."[118] The preacher, however, did not know Arabic and this prevented him from entering into contact with his audience. Attempting to prevent the onslaught of the Unia, Sylvester sent James to preach in Syrian cities. In his absence, the school withered because the *didaskalos* had not been able to find a worthy successor. James returned from his mission broken and disillusioned after having witnessed the widespread success of the Uniates. Seriously anxious about the collapse of his near decade of efforts, he left Syria forever in 1735.[119] Sylvester visited the dioceses then went to Constantinople and returned to Damascus. In 1744, he sent his *wakil* Michael Tuma to Wallachia to seek alms to pay off debts. Cyril Tanas took advantage of his absence and, with the help of Western diplomats in Constantinople and well-placed Armenians sympathetic with the Latins, obtained a *berat* for himself as patriarch of Antioch from the Sublime Porte over the head of the Synod. On July 21, 1745, Cyril's representative arrived in Damascus and occupied the patriarchal residence. Pasha Asʿad al-ʿAzm ordered that the church be given to him and Sylvester's representative be thrown into prison. Cyril sent a command to all the dioceses that he be commemorated at prayers, threatening disobedience with punishment. Cyril himself appeared in Beirut where, as already mentioned, by that time there was an influential group of Uniates led by the aristocratic Dahhan family. With the help of the Lebanese Emir Mulhim Shihab, the Uniates seized the Orthodox church and Cyril consecrated the priest Theodosius from the Dahhan family as bishop of Beirut. The elderly and ailing bishop of Beirut, Neophytus, was forced to attend the ceremony. Meanwhile, the Syrian bishops wrote to Constantinople, requesting Sylvester's return. The synod recalled Sylvester from Wallachia and had the Porte cancel the decree for Cyril's recognition. The patriarchal vicar went to Syria in the retinue of the newly appointed pasha of Sidon with a document confirming Sylvester's authority.

Cyril and Theodosius fled to the mountains under the protection of the Lebanese emir. In Damascus, Cyril's representative was arrested by the governor and imprisoned along with some of the Uniate clergy. The Orthodox walked through the Christian quarter with music. Many Uniates fled the city because they were being persecuted by the local Janissaries even more than by the pasha. In 1746, Sylvester's messenger, Metropolitan Nicophorus, arrived in Damascus with the sultan's decree for the return of Uniates to Orthodoxy. As'ad Pasha seized many Christians praying in a Catholic monastery and literally ordered them to pray with the Orthodox and cease communicating with the Franks. A little later, the Uniates bribed the pasha and regained the right to pray in the monastery of the Latins. Arriving in Damascus in 1754, Sylvester found that over half the congregation had fallen away into union, but took no action, fearing another attack. An uneasy truce was established in Damascus.[120]

Ironically, Western authors, who generally stress the successes of Uniate propaganda, write that it was greatly reduced during the second half of the eighteenth century as Jesuit missionaries were repeatedly expelled from the city and their activities were severely restricted by the watchful eye of the Orthodox clergy. All of this is connected with the absence of European consuls from Damascus and, consequently, an institution of consular patronage for missionaries and supporters of union.[121]

THE BATTLE FOR ALEPPO CONCLUDES

In 1746, Sylvester managed at great cost to secure the repeal of Uniate Aleppo's independence from the patriarch of Antioch. This was made possible by the resignation of the Aleppo Catholics' patron, the sultan's doctor Mansur. The patriarch's determination encouraged Cyril to rely even more on assistance (including material) from the people of Aleppo for his response. Sylvester sent an Ottoman official to Aleppo with orders to seize the church building and to throw a number of prominent Catholics into prison. Metropolitan Maximus managed to escape to Cyril Tanas in Keserwan.

In 1746, the Orthodox metropolitan Gennadius entered the city accompanied by twelve priests. They were intended to replace the Uniate clergy. Subsequent events are described differently in the Catholic and Orthodox sources. The Catholics complain of Gennadius's cruelty and write that he arrived with broad powers in the name of the grand vizier commanding that anyone who does not recognize the metropolitan's authority be punished, tortured, and imprisoned. According to the Catholics, Gennadius unleashed a reign of terror against them, and the people of Aleppo had to spend tens of thousands of *qurush* to bribe the authorities to temper the metropolitan's enthusiasm.[122] However, according to the Beirut Chronicle, out of credulity or a weak will, Gennadius allowed the Catholics to once again gain control over the church and, on account of his incompetence, was replaced two years later by Metropolitan Sophronius.[123] The Orthodox version is apparently closer to the truth. Gennadius was not able to bring the Christians of Aleppo under his control and so left the city, as is evident from the Catholic sources (Ni'ma ibn Tuma even uses the verb "fled" in this regard).[124] As for the description of the persecutions organized by him, they consist of literary clichés that were typical of the period and should not be taken literally.

It seems that among the Christians of Aleppo there remained a group of adherents to Orthodoxy. The sources mention that the arrests of Catholic priests under Gennadius were accompanied by street clashes between Christians of various denominations.[125] One of the most influential Christian merchants of the city was the Orthodox Yusuf al-Dib, dragoman of the British consulate. In 1749, Patriarch Sylvester made him his *wakil* in Aleppo. Using his new powers, Yusuf returned the city's church to the Orthodox and secured the arrest of the city's Uniate clergy and many of the Christian a'yans. However, he often settled personal grudges with commercial competitors, such as George 'Aida, a prominent Uniate merchant also in the service of the British consulate who was arrested in 1750 on charges of financial mismanagement.[126]

In the autumn of 1749, the Uniates attained the promulgation of a decree returning Metropolitan Maximus to power, but this decision was successfully challenged by Patriarch Sylvester. He once again gained control over the city and installed Metropolitan Sophronius, the former bishop of Acre.[127] It was in all respects a strong move by Sylvester. Sophronius, a native of the town of Kiliz near Aleppo, could be perceived by the community of Aleppo as one of their own. Moreover, Sophronius was a prominent figure in the Orthodox *millet* by virtue of his education, knowledge of languages, literary talents, and future career—in 1771, he would become the patriarch of Jerusalem and in 1774 he would go on to be ecumenical patriarch.

Arriving in Aleppo in 1750, Sophronius, unlike Sylvester, tried to act on the basis of exhortations and beliefs and, thankfully, his intellectual level allowed him to engage in theological debates. For a time, to avoid conflicts with the Aleppo community, the metropolitan posed as almost supporting the Uniates. He talked with them about the dogmas of the faith, trying to determine who the most insistent Catholics were and who were wavering. A Uniate chronicle calls Sophronius a "snake in the grass," adding that he was even worse than Gennadius.[128] However, Sophronius's attempts to convince the Uniates of Aleppo with words did not find success and so the metropolitan, like many Eastern hierarchs, succumbed to the temptation to solve the problem quickly, drastically, and effortlessly—to have the Unia suppressed at the hands of the Ottomans. In April 1752, the governor of Aleppo, Sa'd al-Din Pasha, who supported Sophronius, imprisoned the leaders of the local Catholics and demanded that they return to Orthodoxy. Although the metropolitan denied his involvement in the repression, the Catholics believed that he was to blame for the incident. Mutual hostility reached the point that the Catholics sent their children to throw stones at Sophronius as he exited the church. The metropolitan seized the cathedral from the Catholics and drove out their priests. The people of Aleppo waited for the pasha's departure from the city to go meet the caravan of pilgrims on their way to Mecca, and then they paid off his deputy, the *qadi*, and the notables of the city and thus gained a free hand to crack down on the metropolitan. On September 24, 1752, a mob of Catholics attacked the metropolitan's compound and Sophronius was arrested, beaten, and imprisoned.[129]

The metropolitan spent four and a half months in captivity, subject to daily vilification and harassment. Finally, upon the pasha's return, Sophronius was released with a written promise to never return to Aleppo. The predominance of the Catholics was once again established in the Diocese of Aleppo. Metropolitan Maximus returned to the city in 1754. The few remaining Orthodox prayed in the house of the English dragoman Elias Fakhr along with two priests who hid their status as clergy from outsiders.[130] However, in 1755, Raghib Pasha became governor of Aleppo. Sympathetic to the Orthodox, his doctor was Athanasius Ypsilanti Comnenus, an influential Phanariot and author of a historical work that is a valuable source for the history of the Unia in Syria. Comnenus demanded from the Uniate Metropolitan Maximus the paper prohibiting Sophronius from returning, so that he could freely enter the city. The pasha initiated proceedings for the transfer of the church building in Aleppo to the Orthodox and denounced the commitment of the people of Aleppo to papism before the grand vizier. The following year, in 1756, the vizier issued a decree exiling Maximus to Adana and returning the diocese to Sophronius. Meanwhile, Raghib Pasha was transferred away from Aleppo and Sophronius, neither a fighter nor a fanatic by nature, categorically refused to return to Aleppo and expose himself to new dangers. The patrons of the Catholics of Aleppo, the sultan's doctors Mustafa Efendi and Maximus's brother Mansur, used the sultan's hostility toward the vizier and, threatening them with death, prevented Comnenus and the ecumenical patriarch from acting and so facilitated Maximus's return from exile in April 1757.[131]

However, after the death of Sultan Osman III that same year, the Orthodox once again gained the upper hand. Athanasius Comnenus and the Synod of Constantinople suggested that Sylvester transfer the Diocese of Aleppo to the control of the ecumenical patriarch. Sylvester, who, according to one chronicler "had become very sluggish and cowardly on account of the Aleppans' wrath, having suffered so much on account of them over thirty years," agreed.[132] The new metropolitan installed by the Phanar, Philemon, arrived in Aleppo in May 1758 along with a Turkish official who had the authority to hand the church over to Philemon and arrest Maximus. Maximus, however, already had not been sure of his safety and so had fled to Lebanon several months earlier.[133]

Philemon's reign in Aleppo was relatively quiet. The Catholics were afraid to resist actively the representative of the powerful ecumenical patriarch. During this period, the Catholics turned to new methods of confronting the Orthodox hierarchy. Without entering into open conflict with the metropolitan, they boycotted the Orthodox church and conducted services in private homes or in the Maronite church.[134] Philemon, in turn, did not pursue the Uniates and limited himself to obtaining a set fee from them. He found only pitiful remnants of the Orthodox community—one elderly priest and a few laypeople who did not know the practices of the Church.[135]

Over the decades, as the situation in Aleppo stabilized, the patriarchs of Antioch raised the issue of returning the diocese to their jurisdiction. Appropriate resolutions were issued by the Synod of Constantinople from 1766 to 1792, but for unclear reasons, Aleppo remained under the jurisdiction of the patriarch of Constantinople until the nineteenth century.[136]

THE MELKITE UNIATE CHURCH

During same decade, simultaneous to the struggle for Aleppo, the basic structures of the Uniate Church took form in Mount Lebanon. As mentioned, Cyril's patriarchal rank was officially recognized by Rome in March 1729. Having ascertained the truth of the patriarch's assertion of full acceptance of Catholic doctrine and unconditional obedience to the Holy See, in February 1744, the pope and the Congregation de Propaganda Fide sent Cyril the pallium[137] as a token of special honor.[138] Accepting Catholic dogmas, the Arab Uniates preserved the Byzantine rite with—at least during that time—minor additions of Roman elements. The services were conducted in Arabic and Greek and the clergy's vestments remained the same as those of the Orthodox, so the less educated segment of the Christian population often could not ascertain the difference between the two confessions.[139]

By the middle of the eighteenth century, the Uniate Church included about a half-dozen episcopal sees, mainly along the coast from Jubayl to Acre and in

Mount Lebanon. The metropolitans of Aleppo also remained in Mount Lebanon for the most part. There were also several Uniate monasteries, the most important of which were the aforementioned Dayr Mar Mukhallis near Sidon and Mar Yuhanna in Shuwayr.

Among the Uniates, as among the Maronites, the monastic movement played a greater role than it did among the Orthodox. A significant proportion of the Uniate urban intellectual elites migrated to the Lebanese monasteries, where they had the opportunity to express themselves freely. The monasteries also attracted the sons of the surrounding mountain peasants, some of whom received an education and rose to prominent roles in the community. Almost all Uniate metropolitans and patriarchs came from the monastic environment. In contrast to Orthodox monasticism, religious orders existed among the Uniates, bringing monasteries together into two congregations: the Mukhallisiya, led by the monastery of Dayr Mar Mukhallis, and the Shuwayriya, centered on the monastery of Mar Yuhanna.[140]

Grouping around the Monastery of Shuwayr were six monasteries, including one for women, located on the slopes of Mount Lebanon and the Bekaa Valley on lands donated by local sheikhs and emirs.[141] In 1785, the order numbered 178 people.[142] The congregation's heyday came in the time of its rector Nicholas Sayigh (1692–1756), a prominent religious figure and poet who headed the monastery from 1732 until the end of his life. Nicholas instituted monastic regulations on the model of the Rule of St Basil and in 1754 sent them to Rome for approval, which would come after his death.[143] A decade earlier, in 1745, the Vatican approved the charter for the congregation of Dayr Mar Mukhallis.[144]

A prominent member of the Shuwayrite order was the aforementioned deacon ʿAbdallah Zakher who settled in the monastery of Mar Yuhanna after retiring from Aleppo in 1722. Along with his literary and propagandistic activities, he is known as the founder of Uniate printing. There was an active printing press at Shuwayr from 1734.[145]

There was a strong rivalry between the Shuwayriya and Mukhallisiya congregations because of regional differences (Shuwayr was dominated by immigrants from Aleppo and Mar Mukhallis by immigrants from Damascus), and this was expressed in debates over rituals and the relative severity of monastic rules. These debates gave rise to ample polemical literature on both sides. There were several councils at which the rivals attempted to bridge the gap.[146]

Confrontation between the two religious congregations reached its peak when, shortly before his death in December 1759, Cyril Tanas handed the patriarchal throne over to his nephew, Athanasius IV Jawhar, a native of Damascus.

Several bishops and the Shuwayrite community opposed his candidacy and, in August 1761, elected the metropolitan of Aleppo Maximus al-Hakim, and then, after his death in November of that year, the bishop of Beirut Theodosius V Dah- han (patriarch from 1761–1788). The feud lasted for several years. Athanasius Jawhar entrenched himself at Dayr Mar Mukhallis, benefiting from the patron- age of the Druze feudal Jumblatt clan, whereas Theodosius went to Acre under the protection of the ruler of Galilee, Dahir al-ʿUmar. The pope took the side of Maximus and Theodosius. Although he personally went to Rome to defend his rights, after a long struggle, in 1768, Athanasius was forced to renounce the rank of patriarch and agree to become metropolitan of Tyre and Sidon.[147]

The deaths of Cyril Tanas, Maximus, and their antagonist Sylvester, who died in 1766, marked an epochal change in the relations between Orthodoxy and the Uniate Church. The period of bitter struggle in inner Syria as a whole ended. In Aleppo, the Uniates retained their victory, remaining subordinate to the Orthodox metropolitan only formally. In Damascus and most other cities, the Orthodox hierarchy remained in control and the Uniates were in the minority. From time to time, the Orthodox patriarchs started to persecute the Uniate com- munity. For example, in 1784, Patriarch Daniel secured the arrest of a Uniate sheikh and three priests in Sidon for the murder of an Orthodox priest and then took four churches from the local Uniates. Some of them, however, were soon returned to the Catholics at the insistence of Ghandur al-Khuri, a lieutenant of the Lebanese Emir Yusuf.[148]

THE BEIRUT EPICENTER

The center of gravity in the confrontation between the two faiths then shifted to Lebanon. The strengthening of political separatism in several parts of the Ottoman Empire in the second half of the eighteenth century led to a conver- gence between local Muslim rulers who aimed to achieve independence from the Sublime Porte (such as Yusuf Shihab in Mount Lebanon, Dahir al-ʿUmar in northern Palestine, and ʿAli Bey al-Kabir in Egypt) with the Uniate merchant class who, unlike the Orthodox and other traditional confessional communities, were not incorporated into the empirewide administrative system and were not recognized by the central Ottoman authorities and therefore were vitally inter- ested in the patronage of regional Muslim leaders. The Uniates supplied cadres of officials for the semi-independent rulers of the Middle East and so controlled trade in many areas of the Levant and tried to influence the political situation in the Eastern Mediterranean.[149]

The favorable position of the Uniate communities in Mount Lebanon and parts of the Levantine coast led to mass migration to these areas by supporters of union from regions of inland Syria where Catholics were persecuted. During the eighteenth century, the Christian population of Damascus and Aleppo fell by almost half, but this coincided with an equally dramatic increase in the number of Uniates along the Syro–Palestinian coast. In 1815, there were four thousand five hundred Uniates in Sidon, almost a third of the city's population of fifteen thousand. They made up two thousand of the seven thousand five hundred inhabitants of Acre, as well as most of the inhabitants of Tyre, Haifa, and Zahle.[150] Involvement in maritime trade favored the migration of Uniates to the cities of Egypt, where by the beginning of the nineteenth century they numbered four thousand people. The cohesive and dynamic Uniate community of Egypt successfully integrated itself into the country's economic system, displacing competing ethnic and religious groups. Uniates took positions as the advisers, financiers, and tax farmers for the Mamluk rulers of Egypt. Starting in 1768, the Uniates had full control over the Egyptian customs office, disposing of enormous cash flows. In the informal structures of the self-governing Melkite community led by the merchants and customs officials, the clergy took an unusually subordinate position. Generally speaking, the secular elite, represented by merchant clans connected through marriage, played a vital role in the life of the Uniates.[151]

In the early 1770s, when Turkey suffered defeats in the war with Russia and the Mediterranean was dominated by the Russian navy, the Uniates actively supported the anti-Ottoman policy of the separatist leader of the Egyptian Mamluks, 'Ali Bey (d. 1773) and Sheikh Dahir al-'Umar. Thus, the leading place in the circle of Dahir was taken by his advisor and steward, the Uniate Ibrahim Sabbagh, who placed fellow Uniates in all key positions in the administration. In the historical literature, a negative image of Sabbagh has developed—a tyrant, oppressor, and bribe-taker who because of his avarice was thwarted. After the fall of Acre and the death of Dahir in early 1776, Sabbagh was captured by the Ottomans and strangled, because he was someone who knew too much about the sheikh and about what wound up in the hands of the Kapudan Pasha.[152] Catholics also played an important role in the administration of the Lebanese Emir Yusuf Shihab, especially Ghandur al-Khuri, the emir's lieutenant from 1782. The Beirut chronicler wrote of Ghandur, "As for his power, he was very great…. The Emir Yusuf wrote to him, 'Dear brother!' and the rulers of the country and citizens struggled to even write him."[153] Even the Uniate chronicler, for all his sympathy for Ghandur, admitted his arrogance, "he behaved …

as though he were emir."[154] Ghandur was a Maronite, but he fully supported the Melkite Uniates in the fight against Orthodoxy and, according to the Beirut chronicler, used his authority "to raise up a persecution against the Orthodox Christians, disturbing the tranquility of their lives, oppressing them with extortion and mercilessly harming them. He sought that as a result of such treatment they would give up their true Orthodox faith and accept the false Catholic faith."[155] To those who apostatized, he promised privileges, and to those who stood firm in faith, he threatened death, killing some of them. He seized Orthodox churches and handed them over to the Uniates.[156]

The Uniate metropolitan of Beirut, Ignatius, and the Catholic missionaries were particularly zealous in persecuting the Orthodox. Just as in the interior of Syria, the Orthodox hierarchy periodically resorted to persecuting the Uniates, in Mount Lebanon the inverse situation occurred. The Orthodox were vulnerable to pressure from secular authorities and could not appeal to the Sublime Porte. "At this time," we read in the Beirut Chronicle, "His Holiness the [Orthodox] metropolitan of Beirut let out mournful sighs and we lifted up continuous prayers to the Lord with bitter tears, begging Him to stop the persecution."[157]

In 1789, Yusuf Shihab waged war against the pasha of Acre, Ahmad al-Jazzar, and was defeated, captured, and hanged along with his lieutenant Ghandur. When the Orthodox of Beirut learned of this, they rejoiced and "gave great thanksgiving to God Most High"[158] because if he had been victorious over al-Jazzar, Yusuf had promised to put Beirut under rule of Ghandur, and the city was fraught with the persecution of the local Orthodox community. After Ghandour's execution, churches confiscated by him were returned to the Orthodox and many who had been forcibly converted to Catholicism returned to Orthodoxy.[159]

Unlike the separatists Dahir and Shihab who were associated with the Uniates, the Pasha of Acre, Ahmad al-Jazzar, consistently demonstrated loyalty to the Sublime Porte. This is why, according to Thomas Philipp, he preferred to use Orthodox officials in his administration, the most famous of whom were the Sarruj brothers.[160] However, upon closer examination of the pasha's personnel policy, it appears that he was indifferent to the religion of his advisors. Ahmad Pasha readily employed the services of Orthodox, Uniates, and Jews and then, when necessary, threw them in jail, executed them, and seized their property. Having looked favorably upon and taken into his service the sons of Ibrahim al-Sabbagh in 1779, the pasha threw them in his dungeon a year later. The Sarruj brothers' longstanding service to the pasha ended with their disgrace and execution in 1794.[161] The senior Uniate official Mikhail al-Bahri managed to get out of al-Jazzar's prison alive in 1789, but with his nose and ears cut off and after having sworn to never again deal with the powerful people of this world. His sons, however, did not follow their father's example, and in the early nineteenth century, they held prominent positions in the *eyalets* (administrative divisions) of Sidon and Damascus. They built the Uniate church in Damascus and later served the Egyptian Pasha Muhammad 'Ali and had great influence during the Egyptian occupation of Syria in the 1830s.[162]

Returning to the era of Ahmad al-Jazzar, it should be mentioned that in the administration under his power in Beirut, the pasha also exploited the rivalry between the two powerful merchant clans led, respectively, by the Orthodox Yunus Niqula and the Uniate Faris Dahhan. Economic competition between these two poles of Beirut society was aggravated by the religious enmity and political rivalry between Yunus and Faris when the pasha alternately farmed out the city's customs office to them and then imprisoned them and demanded the payment of enormous fines. Yunus generally enjoyed more respect from al-Jazzar, which ensured the dominance of the Orthodox Christian community of Beirut until the sheikh's death in March 1789. Yunus Niqula, almost the only member of Ahmad Pasha's circle who managed to die a natural death not in disgrace, bequeathed control over the city's finances to his brother Selim.

However, in March 1791, the situation deteriorated for the Orthodox group. Faris Dahhan, a man whom the Beirut Chronicle characterizes as "very proud, stubborn, vindictive, vengeful, a fanatic for his religion," gained the post of head of the Beirut customs office by promising to pay al-Jazzar a thousand purses from the city's Christians.[163] Selim Niqula was convicted of a shortfall of 2 piasters and imprisoned. After Niqula, all of the more or less wealthy Orthodox of Beirut were imprisoned, and were presented with unbearable demands for cash payments. As the chronicler wrote,

> their arrest lasted for three days…. They began to search in hiding-places, cellars and wells. If someone was not found, then his son was taken and thrown into prison, even if he was a child. Anyone whom the Almighty preserved changed his clothes and fled into the mountains. However, his name was listed [on the arrest list], his shop was sealed, and the debt-collectors were in his house [demanding payment] from his household.[164]

If we are to believe the Beirut Chronicler, Faris Dahhan managed to paralyze all commercial activities of his Orthodox competitors, who spent many months in prison, were subjected to torture and extortion, and were forced to sell all their property for a pittance to pay even a fraction of the taxes. The Sarruj brothers tried to intercede for the Orthodox, but al-Jazzar was not inclined to agree to a reduction of his revenue. Then the pasha had the idea to expand the fines to all the Christian confessions of the city. There was a new wave of arrests of the merchants of Beirut; the overcrowded prisons could not accommodate the prisoners who were already there.

Al-Jazzar was of course aware that much of the money that had been shaken out of the Christians had found its way into the pockets of Faris and his henchmen. Waiting until they were sufficiently enriched, the pasha ordered the high administration of Beirut arrested and their property confiscated. Dahhan was seized in the *diwan*, throne into the dungeon, and required to pay 100 purses. However, al-Jazzar had barely managed to get half that amount before Faris died in prison in April 1792, either from beatings or from the plague.[165]

THE LAST BATTLE

Thereafter, in the history of confrontation between the Orthodox and the Uniates, there was a lull that lasted for almost three decades. The sources do not contain any information about significant intercommunal conflicts. Bruce Masters believes that this very problem of the Ottoman authorities ignoring the Uniates was beneficial to them. Their church continued to exist, quasi-underground in inland Syria and openly in the mountains and along the coast. The permanent bans on contact with Latin monks or worship in private homes issued by the sultans were easily ignored by corrupt pashas and *qadis* on the ground. However, the centralization of the state ruthlessly pursued by Sultan Mahmud I (1809–1837) still gave the Orthodox Church a chance to put an end to the Uniates at the hands of the Ottoman authorities.[166]

The final offensive against the Uniates in the Ottoman Empire was undertaken in January 1818 when, at the initiative of the Armenians of Constantinople, the Porte ordered Uniates of all persuasions to go to the churches of their ancestors. The governor of Aleppo, Khurshid Pasha, received similar instructions. On March 14, the Orthodox metropolitan Gerasimus al-Turkuman arrived in the city. He was a native of Aleppo, as the Phanar's policy of appointing clergy had become more thoughtful. On April 17, 1818, the metropolitan announced before thousands of Uniates the Porte's decree that they submit to Orthodox clergy and that recalcitrant Uniate priests be imprisoned. The leaders of the community tried to talk to the pasha to bring him over to their side, but he turned a deaf ear to the Uniates' theological arguments. According to some reports, the pasha, "who had a relentless hatred of Catholics,"[167] even arrested and deported a number of Uniate priests for noncompliance with the decrees. After that, the city's Uniates rioted against Metropolitan Gerasimus, whom they blamed for the persecution. The agitated mob marched on the metropolitan's residence. The metropolitan managed to escape under the protection of the *qadi*. Then, the Uniates laid siege to the court building, an open challenge to Ottoman authority. The *qadi* fled along with the metropolitan to the pasha and presented the affair to him in the darkest colors: "the infidels came to kill us."[168] The Uniate mob went to the pasha's residence, but was dispersed by soldiers. Thirteen of the instigators were beheaded on the spot.

Gerasimus, however, could not hold onto the city and, after surviving two assassination attempts, abandoned his see. In May, the Uniate community, having brought the pasha an appropriate sum of money to apologize for the recent riots, had the opportunity to restore the status quo ante.[169]

Around the same time, Patriarch Seraphim of Antioch sent one of his metropolitans to bring the Uniates of Sidon into submission. However, a powerful Uniate lobby had developed in the Pashalik of Sidon, as Uniates predominated in the bureaucracy of Acre, Sidon, Tyre, and Beirut, and they were closely associated with 'Abdallah Pasha and the powerful *sarraf* Haim al-Yahudi. Thus, the pasha expelled the metropolitan from his territories.[170]

Patriarch Seraphim, who is portrayed in Uniate sources as a fanatical ascetic who pathologically hated Catholics, obtained a new decree at the capital on subordinating the Syrian Uniates to him but, as usual, obtaining a new decree (he arrived in Damascus in June) was easier than seeing it implemented. The Uniates, supported by the *qadi* of Damascus, did not recognize the patriarch's orders. The Orthodox also managed to gain to their side the *mutasallim* Salih Agha. According to the Uniate chronicle, the Rum attacked Patriarch Seraphim in the market of Damascus, tearing his clothes and breaking his staff. The Ottomans used this as a pretext to accuse the Uniates of political disloyalty and conducted mass arrests of Catholics and other Christians, only releasing them after receiving lavish ransoms.[171]

The initial outbreak of this conflict was followed by a six-month lull, but then, in early 1819, all the Uniate priests of Damascus were arrested in one night. At the patriarch's insistence, the authorities banned Frankish, Maronite, and other non-Orthodox clergy from entering the houses of the Uniates and talking to them about matters of faith. They arrested the Uniate priests and sent them into exile. Apparently, there was a plan to put them on a ship and send them to the Balkans or Anatolia. The prisoners were taken through Homs and

Tripoli via a detour through Mount Lebanon, where the Maronites were able to free the convicts. At the insistence of the Uniates in his entourage, the Pasha of Sidon, 'Abdallah, convinced the ruler of Tripoli, Mustafa Berber, to release the exiled priests and send them to Acre, under 'Abdallah's protection. The Uniate Chronicle reports that upon having learned of this, Patriarch Seraphim fell into a rage and swore before an icon of the Theotokos to fight the Catholics until the end.[172] However, he failed to fulfill this promise.

In 1821, after the start of the Greek uprising and the Ottoman persecution of the Orthodox, the Uniates resumed their worship. Upon hearing of this, the patriarch, however, "did not dare say a word, as he was in disgrace."[173] It was now no longer the Uniates, but rather the Orthodox, who appeared to the Porte to be potential traitors and rebels. It is no wonder that in April 1821, at the beginning of the Greek uprising, a delegation of Uniates of Aleppo rushed to assure the Ottoman authorities of their loyalty and to disassociate themselves from the Greeks. Shortly thereafter, the Uniates of Aleppo were recognized as a *de jure* autonomous Catholic *ta'ifa* within the Rum *millet*.[174] In 1827, motivated by harassment from the authorities, the entire Diocese of Amida (Diyabakir) of the Patriarchate of Antioch passed into union with Rome, hoping for the protection of France.[175] Finally, in 1829, with the end of the persecution of the Orthodox, the Porte officially issued a decree on religious freedom for Uniates.[176] During the Egyptian occupation of Syria (1831–1840), the Uniates used the full protection of the authorities to build cathedrals in the cities. In 1837, the Sublime Porte recognized the Melkite Uniates as a separate *millet* with all the rights of autonomy.

In this way, a century and a half of dispute between Orthodoxy and Uniatism came to an end. Relations between the two communities gradually stabilized during the nineteenth century and movement back and forth between the union and Orthodoxy disappeared. However, the Orthodox community had lost about a third of its members, including the most dynamic and advanced. Therefore, to summarize, it would not be an exaggeration to say that Orthodoxy lost this fight.

Why Did the Unia Succeed? Uniate Identity

What was the reason for this outcome of events? Why were the structures of the Orthodox Church ineffective before the Uniate challenge, even as they enjoyed support from the Ottoman authorities?

The Orthodox authors of the eighteenth and nineteenth centuries have given a superficial treatment of the Unia's successes. The chroniclers tended to explain them by "God's acquiescence" as well as the fact that the Jesuits, according to

Neophytus of Cyprus who was not without Phanariot snobbery, "knew Arabic and had a lot of gold, valuable clothes and things like this, which seems sufficient to lure the base Arabs."[177] "The only reason for the [Uniates'] propagation," said Neophytos, is that the Catholic missionaries allowed their followers to eat fish during fasts and recognized the legitimacy of marriages in the fourth and fifth degree of kinship "because," in the author's words, "the Arabs indulge in gluttony and therefore the rest of the passions."[178] The authors of the Beirut Chronicle also believe that Christians accepted Roman dogma "in their simplicity and because there was nothing to eat during fasts."[179] That is, in the opinion of the Orthodox Church, the Jesuits worked on the basest human instincts—gluttony and lust—which explained all their successes. Only in passing does Mikhail Breik hint that the Catholics' successes occurred "by God's allowance on account of the strife of our spiritual leaders."[180] The assessment of the Uniate movement was self-evident to Orthodox authors: there is the true Orthodox faith, inheritor of the apostolic tradition, and the ecumenical councils; and there is malicious heresy introduced from the outside. But how did the Uniates themselves understand their transition to union with Rome?

Unfortunately, we have few such assessments dating back to the first and second generation of the Uniate movement. Early examples of historical interpretations of the nature of the Syrian Unia can be found in the Vatican's declarations associated with sending the pallium from Rome for Cyril Tanas in 1744 and in the annals of the first Uniate chronicler, Yuhanna al-'Ujaymi (1756).[181] Uniate historiography formed under the strong influence of Catholic scholarship and Roman officialdom. Al-'Ujaymi, who was born in a remote village in Lebanon, received such a profound Jesuit education and spent so many years in Europe, that he was in fact the Arabic-speaking representative of the Roman Catholic historiographical tradition. In the writings of the Uniate historians, it is sometimes difficult to distinguish original thoughts from the suggestions of the College of St Athanasius or of the Syrian missionary schools.

The Melkite Catholics did not have the strongly pronounced historical inferiority complex found among most Uniates at that time. For many people, adopting union with Rome meant crossing out the entirety of their former historical identity and recognizing their ancestors as heretics burning in hell. From this, for example, derives the frantic polemical ardor of Maronite historiography which, against all evidence, attempts to prove the perpetual orthodoxy of its church or the radical destruction of all the community's manuscripts from the pre-union period, as was done by the Malabar Church, as well as presumably the Maronites, to destroy the evidence and delete their non-Catholic past.[182]

By contrast, the Melkite Uniates were proud of the glorious past of the Apostolic See of Antioch and presented its history after 1054 as a series of attempts to enter into communion with the Roman Mother Church. This historiographical trend gained particular strength during the nineteenth century. Catholic writers remembered Peter of Antioch's rejection of the "Cerullarian Schism," the signature of the exarch representing Antioch on the acts of the Council of Florence, and the seventeenth-century patriarchs' contacts with missionaries. All the pathos of Melkite Catholic historiography came down to the fact that the Melkite Uniate Church did not begin in 1724, but rather with the Apostle Paul.[183]

Thus, al-ʿUjaymi was not a fanatic and recognized "as holy men" even those patriarchs of Antioch who were not in the diptychs of the pope.[184] Uniate chroniclers writing in the Lebanese mountains wrote about the Orthodox in much calmer terms than the chronicles written in major cities, which were the epicenters of religious confrontation. The fact that the Orthodox Church of Antioch, from the point of view of Rome, remained in schism but not in heresy, allowing Melkite scribes to look down on their fellow Catholics from other Middle Eastern churches. This, however, did not prevent close everyday contact between Melkites and Maronites and personal friendships between many of the bishops of both churches. In the context of the rejection of the Arab Catholic ecclesiastical hierarchy by the Ottoman authorities, Melkites in large cities were often forced to go to Maronite churches, the only Eastern Catholic churches to enjoy legal status. There were even transfers of Melkite Uniates into the Maronite community, about which Cyril Tanas complained to the See of Rome. At the same time, the rapprochement of the Melkites with the Maronites led to some friction between them, particularly regarding their attitude toward the revered founder of the Maronite community, Yuhanna Maroun, whom the Melkites regarded as a Monothelete heretic. When they sent Patriarch Cyril Tanas a printed icon of St Maroun, he defiantly tore it into shreds. Yuhanna al-ʿUjaymi dedicated an entire treatise to denouncing the heretical origin of the Maronite community.[185]

The ethnic identity of the Uniates initially remained as it had been. They called themselves Romaians—*al-Rum, al-Rum al-Kathulik*—and their Orthodox opponents they called "heretical" or "schismatic" Rum—*al-Rum al-aratiqa wa-l-mashaqqin*.[186] Toward the middle of the nineteenth century, Uniate bishops and scribes managed to adopt for themselves the traditional self-designation of the Orthodox community, "Melkites," and thereby claimed the ancient heritage of the Middle East and put themselves in opposition to Orthodox Christianity on the level of ethnic identity.[187]

With time, the ethnic component of conflict between Uniates and Orthodox played an increasingly important role in the development of a Melkite "national myth." In the nineteenth century, in an era of widespread awakening of national-ist movements and ideologies, many historians and commentators interpreted the schism of 1724 and the emergence of the Melkite Catholic Church as a Greco–Arab national struggle, a struggle between Greek (Orthodox) and local (Catholic) parties.[188] In Chapter 6, we attempted to demonstrate the illegitimacy of such an interpretation.

Let us once more summarize the considerations of an ethnic nature for the union with Rome. First, there was no Phanariot domination of the Church of Antioch in the sixteenth and early seventeenth centuries. It preserved its fully Arab character. Greek bishops were few in number and did not attempt to Hellenize the Syrian church. Interventions into the affairs of the Patriarchate of Antioch by the Patriarchate of Constantinople usually failed.

Second, the Arab Christians did not view the Greek xenocrats of the eigh-teenth century as a foreign oppression. Their religious consciousness prevailed over their ethnic consciousness. In the corpus of chronicles, letters, memoirs, and declarations by members of the Syrian church, only a very few times are disputes implied to have ethnic motivations. Bruce Masters correctly noted that the Dama-scene chronicler Mikhail Breik never expressed dissatisfaction with the Greek origin of the Patriarch Sylvester, "the undisputed hero" of Arab Orthodox histo-riography.[189] The resentment among Syrian hierarchs by the installment of Greek patriarchs in 1767 and 1813 was more a manifestation of thwarted personal or family ambition than a conscious national protest. Even in the eighteenth century, the Greek hierarchs did not seek to Hellenize their flock. This was discussed in Chapter 6, but we will give another example here. When the Cypriot Greek metropolitan of Beirut, Ioannicius (1745–1774), decided to abdicate, he advised the people to invite to the metropolitan see the famous preacher from Tripoli, Macarius Sadaqa. Ioannicius pointed out that the Arab Macarius would be close to his flock, unlike a Greek who would be "alien to you both in language and in nature."[190] That is, even this Cypriot bishop was alien to Hellenic chauvinism and religious solidarity seemed to him to be more important than national solidarity.

Third and finally, there is something about which no one seems to have spo-ken yet. In terms of religious independence, the only advantage that the Uni-ates had over the Orthodox was that all of their patriarchs and metropolitans were of Arab origin. In all other respects, the Melkite Catholic Church was more tightly controlled by the Vatican than the Orthodox Patriarchate of Antioch was by the Phanar. Rome sanctioned the election of each Uniate patriarch, and in the case of a disagreement between candidates for the patriarchate, it independently determined the winner. This decision was not subject to appeal, unlike similar interventions by the Phanar in the See of Antioch in the sixteenth and seventeenth centuries. It was in Rome that monastic charters and the acts of Uniate councils were or were not approved. These councils themselves often were held at the initiative of papal legates. Uniate canons and rituals underwent increasing Latin influence culminating in the mid-nineteenth century with the introduction of the Gregorian calendar. Roman pressure at the end of the eighteenth century began to provoke resistance among Uniates desiring to defend their Middle Eastern identity and independence from the steamroller of Latin unification. Similar sentiments were particularly reflected in the activities of Germanus Adam, metropolitan of Aleppo from 1777 to 1780, and the most prominent of the Melkite Catholic patriarchs of the nineteenth century, Maximus Mazlum.[191]

To summarize, we repeat that the opposing religious parties in Syria in the eighteenth century were almost completely unaware of nationalism, and this did not play a prominent role. It is significant that a serious writer such as Bruce Masters—for all his credulity to stereotypes and the inadequacy of his sources— came to similar conclusions, noting in particular that parts of the Jacobite and Armenian Churches, in which there were no ethnolinguistic conflicts, also came into union with Rome.[192]

Alongside the nationalist interpretation of the rise of the Unia in Syria, there is a regionalist interpretation. According to this interpretation, union with Rome was the result of Christian Arabs' desire for independence and autonomy in church life, not in the nationalist sense of Arabs versus Greeks, but rather in the regionalist sense of Aleppo versus Damascus, Damascus versus Constantinople, and so on.[193] Such an interpretation appears more convincing, because, in contrast to the other theory, it does not contradict the obvious lack of national consciousness among Syrian Christians of the eighteenth century and it explains, for example, such a paradox as the Uniates of Aleppo supporting the Orthodox Greek Sylvester in 1724 against the Catholic Arab Cyril. The leading proponent, if not the originator, of this interpretation in terms of regional separatism was Thomas Philipp, who claimed that the prosperous Arab Christian middle class began to seek a greater role in the affairs of their own communities and this gave rise to their conflict with the church authorities of the Phanar. According to him, in 1724, the first patriarch was elected by the community of Damascus and not appointed by Constantinople. Orthodoxy was identified with centralism and Catholicism symbolized local interests. "Local autonomy was a key question in the genesis of Uniate society," concluded the researcher.[194]

A similar view was held by Bruce Masters. He calls the pro-union mood of Middle Eastern Christians "a populist, reform movement with strong localist tendencies,"[195] and argued that, "a strong mercantile middle class dominated all three sects [i.e., the Orthodox, Jacobites, and Armenians who were still suffering from Catholic expansion] and a locally based hierarchy would best serve its political interests."[196] Masters was also not without factual errors, attributing to the Uniate churches the introduction of the intelligible local language of Arabic instead of the traditional Greek and Syriac.[197]

However, this "regionalist" interpretation also raises objections. What was written shows how strong regional bonds were in the sixteenth and seventeenth centuries.[198] Those very people of Aleppo from generation to generation determined by their own will the candidates for the patriarch of Antioch, not the metropolitans of Aleppo. At the same time, the motives for the election of one person or another to the bishop's throne are not fully understood. It is noteworthy that a candidate's origins did not play a decisive role here. Of the seven metropolitans of Aleppo from the end of the sixteenth century to the beginning of the eighteenth century, two were natives of Aleppo, the origin of one is not clear, and the remaining four were from other cities. Of these four, Meletius Karma, born in Hama, was elected unanimously in 1612 by the clergy and laity of Aleppo. The native of Hama Athanasius was installed in 1648 by the Patriarch Macarius, who is known to have been from Aleppo, whereas the Damascene Athanasius Dabbas was, paradoxically, put forward in 1686 by the community of Aleppo in opposition to Patriarch Cyril al-Za'im, who was born in Aleppo. Too many contradictions do not fit in with the monodimensional explanation on the basis of regional preferences.

In our opinion, the roots of the Unia should be sought in another sphere.

Summarizing the views of Western scholarship, Bruce Masters highlighted two explanations for the success of Catholic propaganda: a material explanation put forward by Robert Haddad and a spiritual explanation put forward by Bernard Heyberger.[199]

With regard to the importance of material factors, the Syrian economy's close contacts with Europe and the involvement of Arab Christian business circles within the Catholic cultural and political spheres of influence have been mentioned in this chapter. The Unia's triumph in Syria was largely a consequence of the weakening of the Ottoman Empire and the strengthening of European influence, when Syrian Christians preferred to focus not on the Sublime Porte and the Phanar but on Versailles and the Vatican. It is symbolically significant that the first Uniate, the metropolitan of Tyre and Sidon Euphymius Sayfi joined with Rome in the same year that the Ottomans were defeated near Vienna and entered upon their path of protracted decline. Robert Haddad even noticed that the speed with which Patriarch Cyril joined with Rome in 1716 coincided with the rate of advancement of the European armies during the Austro–Turkish War during that time. According to Haddad, Orthodoxy was the first victim of European expansion into the Ottoman Empire.[200] Bruce Masters believes that the Uniates, by keeping the Eastern rituals, "were protected by that all-important façade of tradition, while committing themselves to a place in a new economic and political world order, increasingly dominated by the West."[201]

Bernard Heyberger, in turn, wrote about the importance of religious and cultural factors. According to him, ossified tradition and corrupt Eastern clergy failed to meet the spiritual needs of their flock. Catholicism stimulated the spiritual revival of Arab Christians. The missionaries' preaching especially had an influence on women, who held a higher social status in the Catholic tradition.[202] If we set aside the confessional bias of the author—who relies almost exclusively on Catholic sources and idealizes the Uniate Church, whose internal defects were no less than those of the Orthodox—it should be recognized that the missionaries' policy in the cultural and educational spheres became an important factor in the success of Catholic propaganda. The decline of Middle Eastern Christianity and the cultural degradation and ignorance of both the flock and the clergy were acutely felt by Orthodox, Coptic, Jacobite, and Armenian clergy. Within each of the Levantine churches, there were sizeable groups of clergy who, to have a chance for spiritual renewal and the revival of their churches, were ready to enter into union with the Catholics and to make use of their system of education and learning. As Ignaty Kratchkovsky wrote, the advantage that the Maronites and Uniates had over the Orthodox lay in the fact that the Western-oriented elements of society

> could rely … on a long tradition and serious assistance both in schools and in the development of writing…. The Orthodox clergy did not have such opportunities…. In its ideological aspirations oriented towards Greco-Byzantine writing, it did not have any center analogous to Rome to which it could gravitate.[203]

At the same time, it must be admitted that Orthodox culture had sufficient vitality to rapidly evolve over the seventeenth century and that the Catholic challenge of the eighteenth century stimulated a further rise in creative activity among the Arab Orthodox, as will be discussed in the following chapter.

CHAPTER 10

The Culture of the Orthodox Orient

A General Background

Throughout their history, the Orthodox Arabs never had their own state and found themselves in a foreign environment and highly complex sociopolitical conditions. Nevertheless, the Melkite community demonstrated considerable resilience and strength of identity. This was facilitated by the presence of a rather complex and rooted cultural tradition capable of sustainable reproduction and creative development.

In the first centuries of Ottoman rule, this culture experienced a distinct ascent, in marked contrast to the hibernation in which Middle Eastern Christians had remained during the Mamluk era. However, before discussing the causes and forms of the Melkite cultural revival, it is necessary to understand the situation of the Arab Orthodox cultural tradition within the broader context of related cultures and subcultures which at times had a strong influence on it.

The culture of the Orthodox world of the sixteenth to eighteenth centuries was generally uniform for all its peoples, albeit separated into several regional variants. Balkan–Mediterranean, East Slavic, and perhaps Caucasian cultural groups should be distinguished, all more or less self-sufficient but remaining in close contact with each other. A leading role was played by the Greeks, who had a strong influence on the development of the Southern Slavs, Romanians, and Christian Arabs.

If we look closer and turn directly to the region of Syria and Egypt, we will notice there the parallel existence of several subtypes of Orthodox culture. Levantine Greeks represented the dominant Greek culture in the Eastern Mediterranean. In Syria, as well as parts of Palestine and Egypt, there developed a "provincial" Arab Orthodox culture. Also in Syria, islands of Syriac Melkite literary culture were gradually melting away. In the dioceses of Eastern Anatolia, there remained an underexamined Armenian-speaking Orthodox subculture. For the sake of comprehensiveness, we can mention the literary cultures of the

Georgian and Slavic monastic cultures in the Holy Land during the sixteenth and seventeenth centuries. The Patriarchate of Antioch included part of the lands of Georgia proper (the Pashalik of Akhaltsikhe), which, however, we will not consider here as it belonged to Georgian rather than Middle Eastern cultural traditions.

The Greek cultural elite who were active in Palestine, Sinai, and Egypt were oriented toward the Greek-speaking cultural area of the Balkans, the Archipelago, and the Greek diaspora in Europe. They were more closely associated with Constantinople, Mount Athos, or Venice than with the local Arab population. The spiritual needs of the "natives" were served by the Arab Orthodox elite of Syria and Lebanon. The development of the two main Orthodox cultures of the Middle East—Greek and Arabic—proceeded in parallel, without merging. At the same time, the Arab Orthodox culture was strongly influenced by the Greek culture. In the seventeenth and eighteenth centuries, multiple eras can be identified as times of "cultural infusions," associated with the names Meletius Karma, Macarius al-Za'im, Patriarch Dorotheus of Jerusalem, and the Patriarchs of Antioch Athanasius III Dabbas and Sylvester. For an educated Christian Arab, knowledge of Greek was compulsory. Translations from Greek into Arabic were widespread, including translations of the latest historical and theological treatises. As an example of the close intertwining of these two cultures, one can evoke the emergence of Arab printing in the Greek monasteries of Wallachia and the activities in Syria of the educator James of Patmos, discussed in the previous chapter. Particularly significant in this context was a bilingual cultural "borderland," the creation of cultural-linguistic intermediary figures, the Hellenized Arabs of the eighteenth century, such as Sophronius al-Kilizi, Patriarch Anthimus of Jerusalem, and others who wrote in both languages and played the role of intermediaries between the Arab and Greek worlds.

The creative energy of the Orthodox East was primarily embodied in literature, books, and texts. Architecture and fine arts were much less prominent. Nevertheless, it seems appropriate to start with precisely these genres and then to go on to the topic of literature. At the same time, we will set aside the vast, anonymous folklore, legends, and stories of miracles associated with the holy places and the great ascetics' and we will only consider the "top floor" of the culture.

It should also be said that we do not intend to provide an exhaustive list of all the figures and works of Middle Eastern Orthodox culture. Georg Graf and Joseph Nasrallah have composed those guidebooks. Within the framework of the present work, we would like to provide an outline of the main trends and

developments that shaped the cultural creativity of the Orthodox peoples of the
region of Syria and Palestine.

ARCHITECTURE

The first three centuries of Ottoman rule were not marked by any vibrant construction activities on the part of Middle Eastern Christians. The reason for this,
on the one hand, was that the *shariʿa* ban on the construction of new and expansion of old churches was maintained. Nevertheless, such actions as the destruction of churches or their transformation into mosques or sufi lodges, as often
occurred in the Mamluk era, happened only exceptionally under the Ottomans.[2]
However, on the other hand, the difficult economic situation of many Christian
communities made constructing church buildings a scarcely feasible task.[3] It was
more a question of preserving crumbling churches and monasteries—sometimes
even Byzantine buildings—than of new construction and architectural creativity.
In the sources, there are many references to restoration works undertaken by the
patriarchs of Jerusalem at the holy sites of Palestine. In these accounts, almost
no targeted building campaigns appear. Rather, the patriarchs act on a situation,
guided not by ambitious architectural projects but by the urgent need to prop up
this or that collapsing wall.

Already in the late 1530s, Patriarch Germanus had restored the domes about
the Church of the Resurrection and the Church of St Mary Magdalene. The construction was carried out without the *qadi's* permission. "And those who hate our
faith," the patriarch wrote, "the impious Arabs and Turks in their jealousy did
not keep silent about us, but went and slandered me before the godless ruler the
sanjak-bey."[4] The *sanjak-bey* threw the patriarch in chains and wanted to destroy
the illegally constructed buildings. It was only at the cost of large bribes that this
was avoided.

In January 1545, there was an earthquake in Palestine with its epicenter at the
Dead Sea. The strength of the aftershocks (7.0 on the Richter scale) was not much
smaller than the notorious earthquake of 749 that destroyed dozens of Umayyad
towns on both sides of the Jordan.[5] However, over the subsequent eight hundred
years, there were significantly fewer towns and buildings, so the damage was
not as enormous. Among other things, the bell towers of the Church of the Holy
Sepulchre and the Basilica of the Nativity in Jerusalem collapsed. During the collapse of the former, the dome of the Church of the Resurrection was damaged.[6]
It is symptomatic that the bell tower had not been restored for several centuries
because of the scarcity of church funds. During the earthquake, the Edicule over
the Holy Sepulchre was also damaged. Despite the violent protests of the Greeks,

permission for its reconstruction was granted to the Franciscans.[7] In the Holy Land, architecture was closely intertwined with politics.

Under Patriarch Sophronius, the nearly collapsing vaults of the church in Bethlehem were repaired and during his patriarchate the Church of Saints Constantine and Helen was constructed.[8] Paisius and Nectarius erected hostels for pilgrims in Jaffa and Ramla and rebuilt dilapidated monastery walls.[9]

Patriarch Dositheos undertook a large-scale reconstruction of the Basilica of the Nativity in Bethlehem in the early 1670s. The construction was accompanied by some changes in the internal layout (the corridor from the Latin monastery to the Holy Cave was blocked), and consequently, there were clashes between the Catholics and the Orthodox.[10]

Refurbishing the rotunda over the Holy Sepulchre was a serious political problem. Representatives of the Greek and Latin churches contended for this honor until finally, in 1718, fearing for the hazardous condition of the dome, they agreed on restoring it jointly.[11] Various patriarchs throughout the eighteenth century made repeated repairs to monasteries and hospices.[12]

Finally, the biggest event in the architectural history of the Holy Land was the restoration of the Church of the Holy Sepulchre after a fire in 1808. During the course of the work, carried out from 1809 to 1810 by the Greek architect Chelebi Komnenos, the layout of the building was retained but the interior was somewhat "corrected" with the removal of elements of Gothic design left by the Crusaders.[13]

Thus, the current appearance of the Holy Sepulchre is to some degree an example of the architecture of the Orthodox East of the early Ottoman period. Other good examples include the Church of the Archangel Gabriel in Nazareth, which goes back to the early 1760s (the current bell tower was added later) and the Monastery of the Holy Cross (now in Jerusalem), which was radically rebuilt in the mid-seventeenth century.

The *shari'a* restrictions on religious construction were easier to bypass in remote monasteries. Suffice it to recall the construction of the bell tower of the Monastery of St Sava by Serbian monks in the seventeenth century. The tower itself was an entire monastery complex with its own church. However, it is worth emphasizing that for legal purposes, the construction of the tower was presented formally to the Ottoman authorities as the restoration of dilapidated buildings that had supposedly existed under the previous plan.[14]

In general, there are few Orthodox architectural sites in Palestine that have retained their appearance from the sixteenth to eighteenth centuries. Almost all the churches and monasteries were rebuilt in the nineteenth century, when

restrictions on Christian worship and church construction were lifted and the
financial position of the Patriarchate of Jerusalem was much stronger.

Because of the limited number of authentic monuments from the sixteenth
to eighteenth centuries, written sources play an important role in reconstructing the external appearance of Middle Eastern churches during that time.
However, the authors of these texts, pilgrims with "tunnel vision," were interested mainly in the prestigious churches and famous holy sites. As a rule, the
appearance and decoration of these churches is presented by observers as rather
splendid. The only things causing regret were the ragged marble floors and
obstructed gates of the church in Bethlehem. Only a few travelers pay attention
to the poor appearance of the churches in villages and small towns, standing in
sharp contrast with the colored marble and carved iconostases of the famous
monasteries.

Thus, Grigorovich-Barsky testifies that "it seemed [to him] that it is nowhere
worse, more wretched or more poor to see the churches," that is, those situated
along the road not far from Jaffa:

> I do not even say that it does not have any adornment inside: no icons,
> no lamps, nothing, but what is painful that [the church] had neither roof,
> nor doors or windows. What did it have? Only three stone walls, and
> even those not whole, but the fourth wall, which was on the side of the
> entrance, has fallen apart even unto the ground, and the upper part has
> also fallen through. Only above the sanctuary, it is covered a bit with
> wood.[15]

The most emotional descriptions of this sort belong to Porphyry Uspensky.
Although they are somewhat beyond the timeframe of this study, it is safe to
assume that the conditions of the churches seen by the archimandrite would not
really have changed that much over the years. Thus, he found the churches in Bir
Zeit, on the Cisjordanian Ridge,

> Mother of God! Holy Angels! The church is a long pit, covered with
> withered branches, Dositheos the light of God is not evident in it.…
> There is nothing there: not an icon, no iconostasis, no vesssels, no vest-
> ments. To mark the place of the royal doors there are two curved, fitted
> pillars, plastered with clay mixed with husks. If it were even, at the very
> least, swept up in this pit, then the soul could mourn less severely for the
> desecration of the great sanctuary of the Lord.[16]

Even the newly built village churches had no domes, altars, or iconostases. "In place of a throne," wrote Porphyry, "some sort of stone column was set up and on it lay filthy rags with which something was wrapped up, most likely, a handwritten Gospel; out of pity I did not even want to unfold them."[17]

The same contrast between the cathedrals and the churches in the rural hinterland can be observed in the Patriarchate of Antioch. According to the testimony of Porphyry, "The church … in the name of the Forerunner [in Maaloula]. The horror: sheep excrement, the stench, all sorts of garbage, bunks on the shelves, piled high with rubbish. A tavern is better than this church."[18] Construction activity in Syria, as in Palestine, was chiefly limited to refurbishing and reconstruction. In most rural areas, there was no need for new church buildings. Recall the urbanization, reduction in the number of Christians, and the abolition of dioceses in rural areas described in Chapter 3.

Sometimes the organizers of construction works attempted to circumvent *shari'a* restrictions, relying on the distance from Ottoman administrative centers or taking advantage of a period of unrest when the Muslim judiciary was paralyzed. However, such ventures often ended badly for Christian bishops and architects. We can recall the sad story of the priest Moses who attempted to repair Saydnaya illegally in the 1640s.[19] Similarly, in 1759, the pasha of Damascus imprisoned Patriarch Sylvester and his vicar Michael Tuma, levying them with a fine of fifty sacks for having arranged two years earlier for the illegal repair and decoration of the Church of Saints Cyprian and Justina.[20]

Opportunities for large-scale church construction were rare, and as a consequence, Christian architects' lack of experience sometimes had tragic consequences. In 1767, a newly built church in Beirut collapsed, burying eighty-seven parishioners in the rubble. It was hurriedly built and its pillars were "thin and not proportionate," as explained by the chronicler.[21]

It seems that the construction of bishops' residences met with fewer obstacles. Meletius Karma built a new metropolitan's residence in Aleppo "with great amenities, solid construction, high walls … and strong foundations," as Paul of Aleppo described it.[22] Paul of Aleppo described the complex of buildings of the patriarchate in Damascus, built by the Patriarch Macarius with Muscovite money in the late 1650s in such detail and color that, to avoid overly lengthy quotations, it is best to refer the reader to the original source.[23]

Among the few examples of original architectural creations by Syrian Christians can be listed the construction of monasteries near Tripoli at the turn of the sixteenth to the seventeenth century, including first and foremost the construction of Balamand Monastery, where the remains of a Cistercian monastery built by the Crusaders were supplemented by a number of buildings in the seventeenth and eighteenth centuries.

FINE ARTS

In recent decades, art history has occupied an increasingly prominent place in studies of the Christian East, displacing traditional fields, such as philology, theology, and history. Not being an expert in issues of art history, the author cannot claim any particularly detailed coverage of artistic production in the Orthodox East. Therefore, we will offer the reader a quick sketch of the fine arts of the Orthodox of the region of Syria and Palestine, leaving the writing of foundational works on this subject to future researchers. Middle Eastern iconography, like the rest of the Orthodox culture of the Levant, can be divided into two branches, Greek and Arab. However, this division is more than convention. It only seems legitimate at first glance to single out any cultural or geographic areas: Palestine and Sinai, where Greek art dominated, and Syria, where Arab artistic traditions prevailed. In fact, many Arab artists worked in Palestine and entire schools of art were formed. Alongside this, in the Arab (Melkite) iconographic tradition there rank a number of artists of Greek origin who painted icons in Syria for Arab churches.

So, it would seem correct to classify the art of the Middle East on the basis of the subculture of the audience to whom the artistic production was oriented, whether it was the Greek monasteries and multinational pilgrims or the autochthonous Arab Christian communities. However, this criterion seems blurry. Well-known artists painted churches both in the Greek monasteries and the Arab villages, and in these Arab churches, the Melkite icons were sometimes lost in the mass of imported Greek and Russian images.

Icons in the churches of Jerusalem, Bethlehem, Sinai, and other famous holy places were also for the most part imported, painted by the Greek artists of the Eastern Mediterranean. Predominant there were the products of the Cretan school, the principal legislator of the post-Byzantine world from the sixteenth to the mid-seventeenth century. Apart from these, other Greek regional styles of fine art were represented. For example, the "beautiful"—according to contemporaries—iconostasis of the church in Bethlehem installed by Patriarch Dositheus in 1672 and torn down by the Franciscans twenty years later was made by artists from Chios.[24] The current iconostasis of the church of the Monastery of Our Lady of Balamand was created in Macedonia in the late seventeenth century.[25]

Additionally, icon-painting Greek monks also were encountered within the territory itself of the Arab East. The major artistic center was the Monastery of

Sinai, where for the most part visiting Cretan artists worked. The Sinaite school of icon painting was capable of creative innovations. such as the creation of an original iconographic type of St Catherine sitting on a throne. This icon, first made in 1612 by Ieremias Palladios for the monastery's new iconostasis was copied in subsequent decades throughout the Eastern Christian world.[26] Meletius of Chios (the future Patriarch of Antioch Euthymius III al-Saqizi) was renowned as an icon painter and began his ecclesiastical and artistic career in the Palestinian Mar Saba.[27]

In parallel with the production of local and Greek icons, European and Muscovite icons also circulated in the Orthodox East. Arseny Sukhanov mentions with displeasure one of the images in Mar Saba: "The church's altar and the screen and the local images and festivals are well done, only the cross of the Crucifixion, which stands above the royal doors, was done according to Latin convention."[28]

Arab Christian artists worked alongside the Greek artists in Palestine.[29] Most of them were artisans who focused on providing services for pilgrims. From their studios came icons—painted, etched on mother-of-pearl, or simply colored engravings—with pictures of the Palestinian holy sites and scenes from the Gospel, which were distinguished from other schools of icon painting by their unusual attention to the topography of the Holy Land.[30] Mass-produced icons, characterized by a low artistic level[31] apparently corresponded to the unassuming needs of pilgrims. As Meletius wrote of them in the late eighteenth century,

> In Jerusalem, there are painters and silversmiths from among the Arabs. Of the former the work is very poor, however it is satisfactory when they paint on cloth the city of Jerusalem with all the holy places for the pilgrims, and they gain [money] for their labors; there is mastery of other things as well, candelas and they fashion other things fairly well.[32]

However, even the quality of Greek painting started to rapidly deteriorate after the extinction of the Cretan school in the mid-seventeenth century.[33] At the same time, in quantitative terms, iconographic production was very high. The work of Orthodox artists even "infiltrated" foreign territory: in the 1830s and 1840s, the iconostasis of the Uniate monastery in Jaffa was fitted with icons painted by an Arab Orthodox deacon from Jerusalem.[34]

It is worth mentioning the traditional craft of the people of Bethlehem: carving mother of pearl and producing crosses and icons from it.[35] This craft has been known since almost the time of the Crusades, but in museum collections, there are only recent examples from the nineteenth century or rarely from the eighteenth century.

The growth of pilgrimage stimulated intensification in the production of appropriate souvenirs—rosaries, crosses, belts, lambs, models of churches, and so on. During the time of Constantin Volney, the export of similar products from Palestine reached three hundred crates a year, bringing monasteries of different denominations a total income of 50,000 piasters. "The preparation of these holy things," wrote a French traveler, "supports the largest part of the Mohammedan and Christian families in Jerusalem, also those situated in nearby lands; men, women and even children do all the carving of images, lathe work with wood, stringing of coral and embroidering with silk, pearls, gold, and silver."[36]

In the same group of arts and crafts tied to servicing pilgrimage, it is worth mentioning the specific branch of fine arts represented by tattooing. Many pilgrims wanted to leave with a visible and lasting sign of their pilgrimage exploits. This tradition gave rise to the emergence of the corresponding craft specialization. The earliest description known to us of the technology used for tattooing in Jerusalem goes back to the seventeenth century. The artist placed a stencil on the pilgrim's hand, made a silhouette of the drawing with coal powder, and then cut away its outline with needles dipped in ink made from gunpowder mixed with cow bile. The finished drawing was washed with wine for disinfection.[37] So far as we know, the images of the tattoos themselves have not been preserved since the material to which they were applied is less resilient than wood and stone. We are left with having to refer to verbal descriptions of the figures. Henry Maundrell mentions the great variety of symbols used by the tattoo artists.[38] Constantin Volney wrote of images of the cross, spears, and the intertwined names of Jesus Christ and Mary.[39]

Both authors primarily interacted with pilgrims of the Catholic confession. However, the paucity of Western pilgrims suggests that they could not have provided a steady demand for tattooing. It is more likely that a similar tradition existed among followers of the non-Chalcedonian churches and the Orthodox Arabs.

Over the course of its development, the painting of the Syrian Melkites naturally experienced the same ups and downs as the Arab Christian community in the region. The era of the High Middle Ages, the eleventh to fourteenth centuries, left a number of monuments of fine art, the largest group of which being the frescoes of churches of the Qalamun Plateau in the area of Sidon-Maaloula-Nabak. Melkite painting was based on the rules of Byzantine visual art, with the inclusion of elements from Syrian and Western aesthetics. Later Arab Christians took inspiration from the Crusaders and the Kingdom of Cyprus. For example, in Middle Eastern frescoes and icons, St George and other holy warriors are portrayed in the typical Byzantine style dressed in Balkan plate armor, but at the same time, they are invested with typical crusader banners of a red cross on a white field.[40]

However, in the Later Middle Ages, the tradition of icon painting was interrupted among Arab Christians. With only a few exceptions, Arab icons from before the sixteenth century have not generally been preserved. Only a handful of icons have come down to us even from the sixteenth century, most of which were imported from Greek lands.[41] It is difficult to understand how for centuries an entire people lost the ability to express themselves through visual art.[42]

Therefore, the most impressive achievement in the history of Melkite art was the revival of the tradition of painting in the seventeenth century. This took place within the broader context of the cultural development known as the "Melkite Renaissance," about which see more in the following. The initiator of this renaissance is traditionally considered to be Metropolitan of Aleppo Meletius Karma (1572–1635). In his youth, Karma spent many years in Palestine, where he had the opportunity to become acquainted with Greek icon painting. He invited his fellow monk from Mar Saba, Meletius of Chios, to Syria where he painted, in particular, the cathedral in Damascus.[43] The artist from Chios played the role of a catalyst in reviving interest in painting among the Arab Orthodox.

One of Karma's disciples, the priest Yusuf (late sixteenth century–after 1667), later nicknamed al-Musawwir ("the artist"), learned painting from Meletius. He was known not only as a painter, but also as a translator, calligrapher, and miniaturist. His earliest works date from 1641. Nineteen icons with the signature of Yusuf al-Musawwir are preserved from the years 1645 to 1647. We also know of manuscripts decorated with miniatures by him, including a psalter and a translation of the Greek chronicle of Matthew Kigalas.[44] Yusuf's works are characterized by a strong Greek influence. We do not find in them anything particular to the Middle East, apart from the Arabic inscriptions on scrolls held by saints and prophets. Sometimes marginal figures are depicted with long Arab robes (*jalabiyyas*) and turbans.[45] Yusuf can be counted as one of the artists of the international post-Byzantine style, but hardly the best of them. However, the icon of the Ascension from the Cathedral of Lattakia that is attributed to Yusuf would have done honor to the best masters of the Cretan school.

The works of Yusuf al-Musawwir were relatively few in number and this explains the large-scale importation of icons to Syria in the mid-seventeenth century. During his first visit to Moscow, Patriarch Macarius eagerly bought Russian icons.

In his petition to Alexei Mikhailovich, he wrote, "I have exchanged your very large royal donation for… thirty gilded icons of different saints, so that I could give them as blessings to distinguished Orthodox Christians, when God will bring me to my own realm."[46] Macarius asked for stipends for icons at the expense of the royal treasury.

On his next visit in 1668, he directly asked for gifts of Russian icons to decorate the churches of his impoverished see: "And because of the number of years, sir, the local icons in those churches became dilapidated, and we, sir, have no good iconographers, and no one to paint or restore [icons]."[47] Macarius ordered icons on specific themes, which were made in short time by artists from Kostroma, Yaroslavl, and Nizhny Novgorod.[48]

The Orthodox East was characterized by an aesthetic omnivorousness clearly expressed in the artistic judgments of Paul of Aleppo. For him the standard was the products of the Cretan school, which incorporated a number of elements from Italian Baroque. Perhaps it was European Baroque painting that most impressed Paul, hence his famous assessment of Ukrainian iconography: "Cossack painters have adopted the beauty of the painting of faces and the color of clothes from the Franks and Polish painters … and now they paint Orthodox images, being trained and skilled."[49]

Frankish influences were only starting to penetrate into Muscovite iconography at that time, provoking protests from zealots. However, Paul also liked the non-Western style of Muscovite painting. "Know," he wrote, "that the iconographers in this city have no equal on the face of the earth when it comes to their art, their fine brush and their skill in craftsmanship…. It's a pity that people with such hands are mortal."[50]

Yusuf al-Musawwir is considered to be the founder of the Aleppo school of iconography, represented primarily by four generations of his family. One of Yusuf's sons, the priest Niʻma al-Musawwir (active 1675–1722) inherited his father's vocation. He was perhaps the most prolific Arab painter of icons, and among the large churches of Syria and Lebanon, it is rare to find one that does not have one of his icons.[51] The style of Niʻma contrasts sharply with that of his father's more graphic quality and rigid lines. His best work, in our opinion, is an icon of Saints Symeon the Elder and the Younger (1699, Balamand). The two ascetics atop their columns against a background of angular mountains are surrounded by a kaleidoscope of figures of clergy, Bedouin Arabs and the infirm and poor, many of which are real types from that era, preserved for us by the painter's brush.[52]

Art historians believe that Niʻma al-Musawwir had a propensity for artistic experimentation and tried his hand at two different styles. One was a restrained and severe style reminiscent of the Cretan school, the other characterized by a supersaturated golden radiance that turns the icon into a piece of jewelry. This has led to the attribution to Niʿma of many anonymous icons of various styles, sometimes, in our opinion, baselessly. For example, the icon of St Juliana at the Lebanese Monastery of St Michael in Zouq,[53] which artfully expresses the dimensions of faces and hands, even to the eyes of a layman has nothing to do with Niʿma's style manner of painting. It seems, then, that there were more Arab Christian artists than we thought. Many of them have remained anonymous, their works attributed to other artists.

From the beginning of the eighteenth century, there was a growing European influence on the works of Melkite artists. However, it is not clear whether it is possible to speak of direct borrowings from Baroque painting or whether the Arabs through Greek iconography, which experienced the same Western influence, received Baroque elements. Then, with Niʿma's son Hanania (late seventeenth century–ca. 1740) and grandson Jirjis al-Musawwir (d. after 1777), there are themes and motifs unusual for the Orthodox canon.[54] For example, it is possible to point to the floral theme in Hanania's[55] icon "Our Lady of the Rose" (1721)[56] or Jirjis's icon "The Immaculate Conception" (1762), inspired by the painting of the same name by Murillo.[57] However, in spite of these imitations, the overall style of the Aleppo school generally followed the post-Byzantine style common to the entire Orthodox East. Also by Jirjis is an icon of St John the Baptist (1755) that is absolutely Byzantine in style and spirit.[58]

Hanania and especially Jirjis al-Musawwir worked during an era of bitter struggle between Orthodoxy and Catholicism for dominance in Aleppo. Art historians have attempted to speculate about the Arab icon painters. Jirjis, for example, is considered to be philo-Catholic on the basis of his Baroque predilections and the fact that most of his works adorn Uniate churches.[59]

From these arguments it is clear that there is no specifically Uniate iconography. Proponents of the Unia fully shared the Orthodox aesthetic sensibility. Icons of the Aleppo School are now kept in both Orthodox and Uniate churches, as well as sometimes even in Armenian and Maronite churches. We can clearly identify the Catholic confession of an artist only in those cases in which he identifies himself in his signature on the icon as belonging to one of the Uniate monastic congregations. This is the case with Jirjis's disciple, the Basilian monk Cyril al-Dimashqi (d. 1789). His style is no different from that of the Aleppo school, apart from some primitive, simplified forms and decorative motifs.[60]

In Russian scholarship, there has been an attempt to identify another style of Melkite iconography, the Grecophilia of the School of Tripoli and Beirut in the first half of the eighteenth century, which focused on copying the Cretan style of painting. The Arab origins of the painters of the icons from Tripoli are notice-able only in their Arabic-language inscriptions, flashy colors, and overabun-dance of decorative details.[61] However, the idea of a singular, highly professional "coastal" school standing in contrast to the "vernacular" Aleppo school is based, it seems, on a misunderstanding. The best icons of Balamand Monastery, located near Tripoli, on which the particulars of the Tripoli school are judged are precisely donations of Aleppine Christians painted by the brush of Niʿma al-Musawwir.[62] Non-Russian art historians attribute the few painters who worked on the coast (such as the previously mentioned Hanna al-Qudsi)[63] to the Aleppo school.

To this should also be added Greek artists living in Syria, such as Patriarch Sylvester and Bishop Parthenius of Tripoli.[64] Several works dating from the 1760s belong to Parthenius, who did not imitate the Baroque, but rather his icons had a style more like the Paleologan proto-renaissance. Parthenius's icon of the prophet Elijah killing the priests of Baal[65] is, in our opinion, one of the pinnacles of Middle Eastern art. If one is to discuss a naïve proto-folk school in Syrian iconography, one should speak of a group of artists who worked for churches in the Qala-mun Plateau situated between Homs and Damascus. About a dozen artists can be identified in this region, mostly of the Orthodox confession. Their icons date to the period from 1702 to 1792. Identifying these artists as a particular "school" is conditional, because the style of each one is quite individual. The only thing that unites them is their common Arab origin and that which is characteristic of all naïve, primitivist, provincial art.[66] The most prominent regional artist of the eigh-teenth century, Mikhail Najjar al-Dimashqi, was a prolific artist who between 1705 and 1743 worked for the Church of Saints Constantine and Helen in Yabrud and the churches of Saydnaya and Dayr Attiya. His work is characterized by the bright, *lubok*-esque (*lubok* is a woodblock print), more graphic manner of brush-work, which nevertheless has the particular charm of naïve art.[67] Another artist of this circle worth mentioning is Yusuf ibn Mikhail Elian (1770s),[68] whose icons are considered some of the best in the collection of Sidon.

We would tend to classify in this same group of provincial artists the Leba-nese iconographer Butrus ʿAjaimi, active between 1806 and 1845. Although art historians classify ʿAjaimi's painting alongside the works of the nineteenth-century artist Niʿma Naser al-Homsi as belonging to a special "neo-archaic" style,[69] on its own aesthetic merits, it is close to the icon painting of the Qalamun Plateau of the eighteenth century and represents an extreme form of *lubok*-esque primitivism. Experts nevertheless highly value this childlike art and refuse to consider it "decadent." This "grand style" of Melkite iconography of the sev-enteenth and eighteenth centuries reminds them of the European avant-garde of the twentieth century.[70] We must admit that 'Ajaimi's homely icons have a strange, primal energy not possessed by the urban artists imitating the Baroque or the Cretan school.

In the early nineteenth century, Middle Eastern iconography received more powerful Greek momentum in the person of the Cretan-born artist Michael Poly-chronis (Mikhail al-Qariti, as he was called by the Arabs). He received his artistic education on his home island and then, in the second decade of the nineteenth century, he worked in Syria and Lebanon, decorating the churches of Maaloula, Saydnaya, and Tripoli with many icons. Experts call his post-Byzantine style a synthesis of Baroque and Arab Christian art.[71]

Compared with contemporary European paintings, the icons of Michael Polychronis may seem too saccharine, lacking perspective and dimension, and often with theatrically frozen figures. The decorative aspect of icons interested him no less, and he slowly and carefully worked to perfect his characters' cloth-ing. However, in comparison with the Arab artists of the eighteenth century, it seems that Michael reached the heights of realism in Melkite iconography.[72]

The Cretan artist had a noticeable impact on contemporary Arab painters, so that experts consider it possible to speak of a "School of Polychronis."[73] However, the level of his imitators was markedly lower than that of the examples on which they relied. There is an impression of decline in Arab iconography of the nine-teenth century. This is clearly demonstrated in the production of the so-called Jerusalem school in the second half of the century.[74] However, its activities go beyond the timeframe of this study and so it is unnecessary for us to analyze the works of the later painters of Jerusalem.

In concluding the topic of Melkite iconography, we must recognize that these aesthetic judgments are inherently subjective. The qualitative characteristics of Orthodox art are hardly possible to determine because of the lack of common standards of evaluation.

It is curious that observers from the first half of the nineteenth century, accustomed to classicism in painting, spoke of Middle Eastern Christian art with a great deal of skepticism. Visiting the Monastery of St George near Beit Jala, Russian traveller Avraam Norov commented, "The art of the icons is very bad, similar to the Suzdal style, although the icon of St George is very ancient."[75] He was echoed by Porphyry Uspensky, who, in describing the Church of the Annunciation at Mar Saba said, "The icon style is extremely bad. It is remarkable only that faces are depicted as very stern and severe. It is frightening—or rather, unpleasant—to look at them."[76] Other travelers dealt with the naïve, *lubok*-esque pictures of rural churches. In this case, Porphyry's sarcasm is evident when he observes a mural with a scene of the Sacrifice of Abraham in the Palestinian village of Tayba: "Abraham holds his son by the hair … who [the son] thanks to the peculiar artistic skill of the painter looks like a foal."[77] In describing the village churches of the Patriarchate of Jerusalem, Porphyry often has comments such as, "Old icons of the roughest sort of painting sent here from the Monastery of the Holy Sepulchre," "the icons are very dilapidated, almost without faces," and "Two or three faded icons make up all the decoration of the sanctuary."[78]

GREEK LITERATURE IN PALESTINE: SIXTEENTH TO MID-SEVENTEENTH CENTURY

It is rather difficult to write about the cultural activity of the Greeks of Palestine because of their close connection with the rest of the Greek world and organic access to pan-Hellenic culture. Some bishops of the Holy Land spent the greater part of their lives in Istanbul or Moldavia and Wallachia so their literary works have only an indirect relationship to the Arab East. Not being a specialist in Modern Greek topics, the author, again, cannot claim to provide a complete picture and must confine himself to a schematic overview of the cultural activity of the Greek clergy in the Holy Land.

Certain characteristic features can be identified in the literature of the Greeks of Palestine. Above all, this is an interest in Middle Eastern history—especially of the Church—and geography. Monks of the Holy Sepulchre made a notable contribution to the genre of the *proskynetarion*, the guide to the Holy Land. Although literature of this type was intended primarily for "external use," for pilgrims coming to Palestine from the Balkans, the compilation of these guides would hardly have been possible without the participation of the local clergy of the Holy Sepulchre. Texts of *proskynetaria* were copied and stored in the Palestinian monasteries.

One of the most interesting examples of this genre is that *Proskynetarion Containing All the Miraculous Signs Revealed by Our Savior in the Holy City of Jerusalem*.[79] Unlike other guides, whose authorship and dating is vague, this text undoubtedly belongs to a monk of the Holy Sepulchre writing between 1582 and 1586. In the text, there is possibly the earliest mention of Catholics' denial of the phenomenon of the Holy Fire in connection with the transfer of the Western Church to the Gregorian calendar. When believers light candles from the fire, the author wrote, "The Franks are in great perplexity. They do not believe in this miracle and repeat that it is all a fraud. They remain in their faith, we remain in ours and you have faith in everything, that we may pray for you."[80]

This work was written in verse and is rather large in size, replete with fine detail and outpourings of emotions, whether it is sorrow for shrines that have been destroyed or reverence for the sanctity of the ancient ascetics. The author was not without a sense of humor and so he conveys to us some of the details of his everyday life. Thus, at the end of his work, he says, "And you know why this story ends ... because I wrote it at night by candlelight; the cat jumped (it was black and young), a mouse ran past, the cat jumped again, putting out the light without asking me."[81]

To the authors of *proskynetaria* can be added the prominent diplomat and associate of the Patriarch Paisius, Archbishop Gabriel of Nazareth (d. between 1652 and 1657). While he was in Moscow on a diplomatic mission in 1651, Gabriel quickly mastered the Church Slavonic language, made translations from Greek, and composed a number of original works of didactic literature, as well as his most famous work, "The Story of the Holy and God-Protected Places of the Holy City of Jerusalem," a geographic overview of Palestine and especially of its ecclesiastical antiquities.[82]

Starting in the mid-seventeenth century, the era of Paisius and Gabriel, there begins a flowering of Greek culture in the Holy Land. Belonging to the retinue of Paisius for some time was one of the most brilliant Greek intellectuals of that era, Metropolitan of Gaza Paisius Ligarides (1609/1610–1678). A fine European education and scholarly talent combined in him with a rare and unprincipled opportunism. For many years, Ligarides played a double game, maneuvering between the Orthodox Church and the See of Rome. Invited to Moscow by Patriarch Nikon in 1662, Paisius was close with the tsar, went over to the side of Nikon's enemies, and became his chief persecutor. The zigzags of Ligarides's political biography are described in detail in Chapter 8. As for the literary works of this author, some of his theological and historical works should be mentioned, the most important of which is devoted to Palestinian church history, becoming the basis for Dositheus's classic work, *History of the Patriarchs of Jerusalem*.[83]

The fame of Paisius Ligarides transcended the bounds of the Greek cultural sphere. His works were highly esteemed in the Arab Christian environment. When Patriarch Macarius of Antioch and Paul of Aleppo met with Ligarides in Wallachia in 1657, they were simply astounded by the intellect of this Greek scholar. Paul wrote of him with awe and describes how earnestly he begged for Paisius's permission to copy the book composed by him about the prophecies of sages and saints about future events in the East, "until his consent was obtained using gifts and he thus grew ashamed before us."[84]

Enjoying no less fame in the Orthodox East was the work of Nectarius (1602–1676), a monk of Mount Sinai and later, from 1661 to 1669, patriarch of Jerusalem. The founder of Near Eastern archaeology and epigraphy, a collector of ancient inscriptions, and author of famous works of church history, he dedicated his literary talent to the exaltation—sometimes to the detriment of scholarly objectivity—of the Monastery of St Catherine, for which he received sharp criticism from Patriarch Dositheus. However, Dositheus never allowed himself to apply such derogatory characterizations to his predecessor as he did to other Sinaites. He realized that condemning Nectarius would cast a shadow over the entire See of Jerusalem. Nectarius penned a number of anti-Latin polemical treatises, dealing with papal authority, the circumstances of the Union of Florence, and so on. Some of these works were subsequently published by Dositheus. Nectarius's writings were in high demand in Arab circles during the struggle with the Catholic Unia in the Patriarchate of Antioch. The anti-Latin treatises of the patriarch of Jerusalem were translated into Arabic in the 1730s and subsequently published.[85]

Dositheus Notaras

The literary activity of Patriarch Dositheus Notaras (1641–1707) represents the apex of Greek Palestinian culture. The patriarch was himself the greatest scholar of his time throughout the post-Byzantine space. He was always at the center of the spiritual and intellectual life of the Orthodox *millet*, which during this time was experiencing a marked influence from Catholic and Protestant thought.

The seventeenth century was a time of serious enthusiasm for the ideas of Calvinism among Greek philosophers. The most important figure of this milieu was the patriarch of Constantinople, Cyril Lucaris (1572–1638), author of the scandalously famous "Confession of Faith" that was Protestant in spirit.[86] These ideas were further developed by several of his disciples and followers, such as Theophilus Corydalleus (1563–1646), one of the mentors of the future Patriarch Nectarius, and John Caryophillus (d. ca. 1693), a friend and ally of the bishop of Sinai, Ananias. Alongside this orientation, there was an active anti-Protestant movement, whose representatives relied on the authority of the Greek Fathers of the Church and disparate elements of Latin scholasticism. Church leaders, seeking to dissociate themselves from the Calvinist sympathies of Cyril Lucaris, held a number of local councils condemning the Protestant faith. The last of these councils was held by Patriarch Dositheus in Bethlehem in 1672.[87]

Dositheus was critical of Cyril Lucaris, calling him a "secret heretic" and writing of him that "he proved himself to be evil-minded and unworthy of his throne and rank."[88] However, for political reasons, the participants in the anti-Protestant councils avoided personally condemning Cyril Lucaris, a famous member of the church hierarchy, and instead preferred to question the authorship of the "Confession of Faith." Dositheus had an equally negative impression of other Protestant theologians. The last of them, John Caryophillus, great logothete of the Church of Constantinople, endured a great deal of persecution from Dositheus and was even the object of a polemical treatise, "The Sword Against John Caryophillus." Largely because of the efforts of the patriarch of Jerusalem, the "Protestant troubles" in the Greek Church in the late seventeenth century came to naught.[89]

Dositheus was no less hostile to Catholicism. If the struggle with Protestant influences was the subject of abstract theological polemic, Orthodoxy's relationship with Catholicism often spilled over into political confrontation. It was also a struggle for possession of the holy places of Palestine, with which Dositheus was directly concerned, and the military, political, and religious expansion of Catholic powers in the Balkans and the need to confront Catholic ideological and cultural influence in Russia and Georgia. In previous chapters, we discussed Dositheus's various organizational and propagandistic activities to prevent Latin penetration in all parts of the Orthodox world. Here, it is worth mentioning the patriarch's intellectual activity. He polemicized against contemporary Latin theologians, writing commentaries on the anti-Catholic writings of Byzantine and modern Greek authors.

The same passionate temperament and unbending fanaticism spilled over into the pages of Dositheus's historical works. As Nikolai Kapterev rightly remarks,

> although not remarkable for the accuracy of their treatment of the material or their scientific independence, they frequently suffer from long-windedness, but on the other hand they are striking due to the enormous erudition of the author,[90] the diversity and extensiveness of his knowledge, the remarkable scholarly diligence, and by its own special objective.[91]

Dositheus's purpose was entirely practical—promoting Orthodoxy and denouncing the enemies of the true faith and of the See of Jerusalem.

Dositheus's chief work was the fundamental *History of the Patriarchs of Jerusalem*, one of the first attempts taking a scholarly approach to Palestinian Orthodoxy's past. In early Byzantine historiography, events are described in sufficient detail, as is the case for the first centuries of Christianity and the era of the ecumenical councils and so up to the period of the Arab Conquest, Dositheus should not have had any problems with the sources. Further along, however, he had to fumble about almost blindly. The period from the seventh century to the fifteenth century was a continuous blank spot and in filling it, Dositheus paved the way of generations of later researchers, many of whom mechanically repeated the main points of his work. In his own work, Dositheus made use of the archives of the patriarchate, all available Byzantine sources, some Latin chronicles, and the writings of Arab Christian authors, especially Eutychius of Alexandria, whose chronicle was translated for him by Archbishop Christodoulos of Gaza. The chronology of the patriarchs of Jerusalem proposed by Dositheus was imperfect, due to the fact that "the chroniclers differ, but more often are completely silent."[92] Particularly outrageous for the historian, this caused gaps and absurdities in the Jerusalem diptychs. Dositheus himself realized the shortcomings of his work, allowing for its correction by "wiser" scholars. Among statements of facts, the author interspersed sermons and historiographical and propagandistic digressions, often of an anti-Latin character. Thus, Dositheus subjected the Crusades to harsh criticism: "The Franks, even more than the pagans, are the enemies and persecutors of Orthodoxy," and "The French captured Jerusalem in due time, but their guilt lies in the fact that native Christians were killed and pagan rule prevailed and grew six times over."[93]

One of the main tasks of Dositheus's historical research was to justify the rights of the Church of Jerusalem to possess the holy places of Palestine and to refute her inevitable rivals, the Catholics and Armenians. The patriarch successfully completed this task. For centuries, Orthodox writers on inter-Christian relations in the Holy Land have relied on Dositheus's arguments, and often continue to do so today. At the same time, it must be recognized that he often sacrificed objective truth for his propaganda objectives. In support of the rights and privileges of the Greek Church, Dositheus fabricated many historical facts and repeated other apocryphal stories that had been circulating among monks of the Holy Sepulchre already before him. For this reason, even with events of the sixteenth century that seem as if they were not too far off for him to assert, it follows that Dositheus's narrative should be treated with caution.[94] Allowing for his emotional excesses, Dositheus's chronicle becomes truly detailed and reliable starting with his description of events of the seventeenth century. Here the patriarch relies on archival documents and his own recollections—he had much to remember from the fifty years he spent at the center of the ecclesio-political life of the Christian East.

Dositheus also composed a number of other historical works, the most accessible of which for Russian readers is the *History of the Bishopric of Mount Sinai*.[95]

This book is also the by-product of the patriarch's many years of struggles, in this case with the ambitions of the monastic brotherhood of Sinai.[96] In the pages of this work, the reader does not encounter the unctuous descriptions of the holy places of Sinai that would seemingly be mandatory for any author venturing to write about the Monastery of St Catherine. Dositheus is interested in much more mundane issues—the monastery's juridical status, evidence for its immemorial subordination to the See of Jerusalem, and exposing the intrigue and pride of the "evil bishops" and "false monks" of Sinai. It is not oil but bile that oozes from Dositheus's every line. It is not without reason that historians have described the book as "relentlessly vindictive."[97] In it, the patriarch pours out his soul, taking revenge in the pages of the book for all the defeats he had suffered from the Sinaites in real life.

In his ideological and political struggles, Dositheus sought to use the advanced technology of his time, the printing press. In this domain, the Latin West was far ahead of the Orthodox East. Dositheus wrote,

> Seeing that ... cursed papism ... wants to deceive certain parts of the Orthodox ... Church with sophistry and false words of worldly wisdom, the Orthodox though, although they bravely battle against malefactors ... however they do so with great labor, because the books of old Orthodox saints and other wise men ... they have not prepared [anything] in one single place that can answer to every trick of the wicked ... we wanted to gather from all these Orthodox works, old and new, and print them.[98]

Although Greek typography had existed, particularly in Venice, since the sixteenth century, with his grandiose plans and objective, Dositheus required his own "publishing house." With the support of the ruler of Moldavia, the patriarch founded a printing house in one of the monasteries of Iasi in 1680. In 1682 and 1683, the printing house published the anti-Latin treatises of Patriarch Nectarius of Jerusalem, along with other works of the same orientation. However, during the war between the Ottoman Empire and the Holy League, Moldavia was devastated by the Poles and the printing house in Iasi was destroyed. Dositheus was only able to resume publishing seven years later in Bucharest, under the patronage of the ruler Constantine Basarab. In 1690, there was issued a compilation denouncing Calvinist doctrine that included works by Meletius Syrigus.

In parallel to this, the patriarch attempted to find a more powerful patron for his publishing projects. In 1692, Dositheus's nephew, Chrysanthos, was sent to Moscow with a request to arrange an edition in Greek of anti-Latin polemical literature, to protect the "simple Christians" from "the papal infection that is more pernicious than the plague and destroys the flock of Christ."[99] Although Dositheus's initiative was well received in Russia, there was a delay in the establishment of the print shop, and the patriarch quickly lost interest in the project. In 1694, he recalled Chrysanthos from Moscow, having need of him in the East, as well as finding himself at odds with the Likhudov brothers, the only people in Moscow who could arrange Greek typography.[100]

The situation was not completely clear. Although Dositheus was an impulsive man, he had enough of a sense of purpose and was capable of following through on his intentions. Perhaps the tasks that Dositheus had set were partially fulfilled by the printing press operating in Wallachia. Throughout the 1690s, anti-Latin polemical treatises were fairly regularly published as well as texts both by Dositheus himself and works of Byzantine ecclesiastical authorities starting with Photius, which he edited.[101]

Dositheus was concerned with education in the entire Eastern Christian world, particularly in Palestine. In 1704, through the assistance of Phanariot sponsors, he established a network of schools in Jerusalem, Gaza, Ramla, Kerak, and other cities. The patriarch developed the curriculum for these schools himself, focusing on the study of Greek and Arabic letters.[102]

THE EIGHTEENTH CENTURY

Many of Dositheus's activities were continued by his successor Chrysanthos (1707–1731). As mentioned, he received an excellent education in Venice, Padua, and Paris and was close with many scholarly luminaries, among whom should be mentioned the Dominican Le Quien, one of the first European specialists in Middle Eastern Christianity. Chrysanthos's encyclopedic education and scholarly talent is visible even just on a list of his works, which cover mathematics, astronomy, theology, philosophy, and—most interesting to us—historical and geographic works. Part of them deal directly with the Christian East, reviewing the Orthodox dioceses and patriarchates. Thus, Chrysanthos's work *A History and Description of the Holy Land and the Holy City of Jerusalem* (1728) contains a topographical sketch of Palestine with numerous discursions into the history of the country. Already, the range of sources involved shows that the author was educated on the level of Dositheus. Chrysanthos relied not only on the Old Testament and Byzantine writers, but also on ancient historians and geographers as well as contemporary Western scholars. At the same time, the refined intellectual Chrysanthos did not have so strong and integral a nature as his uncle. On the pages of Chrysanthos's works, one does not feel furious passions and emotions.

His writing style in general is dispassionate and somewhat abstruse.[103] Chrysanthos kept pace with Dositheus in terms of giving patronage to schools and libraries and vigorous publishing activities. Apart from his own works, in 1715, he published in Bucharest Dositheus's *History of the Patriarchs of Jerusalem*, which Chrysanthos shortened and sometimes radically altered, it is said, for fear of displeasing the Ottomans. This patriarch was much more loyal to the Sublime Porte than his predecessor.[104]

For a long time after Chrysanthos, there did not appear on the See of Jerusalem people of such a high intellectual level. Nevertheless, a certain literary revival continued among the Palestinian Greeks in the second third of the eighteenth century. Thus, even when he was metropolitan of Caesarea in Palestine, Patriarch Parthenius (1737–1767) wrote the narrative *On the Feuds Between the Orthodox and the Armenians*, which took place in the first half of the 1730s. This work, with a pompous, flowery style, was composed between 1734 and 1737 with a practical purpose, enriching his successors with the experience of struggle with rival confessions.[105] In the previous chapter, Parthenius's correspondence with the Russian Synod about the reasons for the See of Jerusalem's debts and the problem of the status of the holy places was mentioned. At the request of St Petersburg, the patriarch personally wrote a historical overview of the state of the Church of Jerusalem and its relations with rival confessions. Although this text largely goes back to Dositheus's *History*, it nevertheless deserves to be mentioned in the general context of historiographical works of the Palestinian Greeks.[106]

A prominent figure in the Orthodox culture of Palestine at that time was the educator James of Patmos, who was discussed in Chapter 9 in connection to the struggle against the Catholic Unia. After leaving Syria in 1735, James stayed briefly on Patmos and then moved to Jerusalem in the autumn of 1736 at the explicit invitation of the clergy of the Holy Sepulchre. There he founded the fourth and final theological school in his life, where he taught until his death in 1765. In addition to providing primary education to the children of Christian Arabs, this school had as its purpose the training of educated clergy to fill important positions in the Brotherhood of the Holy Sepulchre. The curriculum included languages (Hebrew, ancient Greek, Arabic, and Latin) and Greek literature from antiquity to the post-Byzantine period, as well as logic, philosophy, and mathematics. Particular emphasis was placed on preparation for preaching. The school became famous far beyond the borders of Palestine; many of its graduates and teachers had successful ecclesiastical careers. Thus, James's collaborators, the Athenian Ephrem and the Syrian Sophronius, went on to occupy the Patriarchal See of Jerusalem (in 1766–1770 and 1770–1774, respectively).[107]

James of Patmos was not the only Greek "culture-bearer" sent to the Middle East to confront the Catholic onslaught. In the year of James's death, there appeared in Palestine the monk Nicephorus Theotokis (1731–1800) who at one time had studied in Italian universities and taught at the gymnasium in Corfu. From Palestine, he went to Constantinople and then later headed the gymnasium in Iasi. In 1776, he moved to Russia where he held a series of episcopal sees. According to Russian sources, in the 1760s and 1770s, Nicephorus was engaged in preaching work in Palestine, where he "attracted many Muslims and heathens."[108] This implausible assertion cannot but provoke skepticism about the results of Nicephorus's preaching. It is equally unlikely that his anti-Latin treatise, published in Greek in Germany in 1775, brought about any great benefit.[109] To denounce the Unia in Greek while addressing himself to an Arab audience was unproductive. However, it cannot be excluded that Nicephorus had some knowledge of Arabic. He is listed among the translators (along with the priests Antun Elias Sabbagh and Elias Nicholas Fakhr, about whom more will be said later) of the work "Khabar Muluk al-Rus" ("Accounts of the Russian Tsars"), whose appearance in an Arabic version in 1773 was clearly due to the Russo–Turkish War.[110]

A far greater role in Greek and Arabic culture was played by James's colleague at the Patmos academy, the *didaskalos* Ephraim. In the 1740s and 1750s, he had been a teacher and preacher on Cyprus. Even then, James worked with him to prepare the works of Macarius of Patmos for publication. Collections of Macarius's sermons were published several times in Europe between 1755 and 1768. The first edition was detained in Venice and destroyed by order of the Inquisition. Around 1760, Ephraim was elected archbishop of Cyprus but, for unclear reasons, he declined this honor and left the island. In 1761, he was in Beirut and Damascus, the chief centers of the confrontation between Orthodoxy and the Unia. At the request of one of the Arab Orthodox writers, the priest Yusuf Morcos, Ephraim wrote an anti-Catholic treatise, "The Code of Heretical Innovations Introduced by the Latins." In it, the author lists 170 deviations from the Orthodox faith that had become established in the Catholic Church in the time since the Great Schism of 1054. Most likely, this text was originally written in Greek and then translated into Arabic, as Ephraim was unlikely to have known Arabic. Ephraim was also the author of more than a dozen theological, canonical, and homiletic works, most of which were published during his lifetime, but these were published in Greek and are not directly connected to the Arab East.

Shortly after 1761, Ephraim moved to Palestine. For a time, he was the assistant to James of Patmos in his school and, according to some sources, he led the school after James's death. The *didaskalos* Ephraim had a meteoric career in the Church of Jerusalem, quickly becoming one of the most influential members of the synod, and was soon consecrated metropolitan of Bethlehem. It is possible that his common origin with Patriarch Parthenius the Athenian played a role in his fate, if we remember how strong the ties were among members of the Brotherhood of the Holy Sepulchre from the same country. In October 1766, the elderly Parthenius, living in Istanbul, presented the Ecumenical Patriarch with an act of abdication in favor of Ephraim, who was elevated to the patriarchate in December of that year.[111]

Perhaps the most famous graduate of the school in Jerusalem was the future patriarch Anthimus (ca. 1718–1808). He came from a Mesopotamian Nestorian background, was captured as a child by Bedouins, and was bought by members of the Brotherhood of the Holy Sepulchre, converted to Orthodoxy, and was given a Greek education. A disciple of James of Patmos and Sophronius, he was widely known for his erudition and his great knowledge of Greek, Arabic, Turkish, and Persian. Anthimus served for a while as secretary of the Brotherhood of the Holy Sepulchre and, after the death of James, led his school, accepting a position as a priest and preacher of the See of Jerusalem. Over a period of twenty years, from 1788 to 1808, he stood at the head of the Church of Jerusalem and was one of the most authoritative hierarchs of the Orthodox *millet*. Anthimus was known as a brilliant orator capable of preaching in three languages, and a patron of education who did not neglect the Jerusalem school. At its head he put Archimandrite Maximus, a writer, theologian, philologist, and translator who knew Arabic. Anthimus wrote his own compositions, a *Commentary on the Book of Psalms* and a commentary on Christian dogmas entitled *Correct Instruction in the Christian Faith*, in Greek and then translated them into Arabic. Despite his assimilation to the Greek milieu, the patriarch did not forget about the needs of his fellow Arabs. Anthimus's polemical and educational writings, which were published in Vienna in the early 1790s, continued to be used by Arabs many decades later.[112]

The patriarch's most interesting work, in the genre of the propaganda manifesto, rare in Christian Arabic literature, is the *Didaskalia Patrike* (*Fatherly Instruction*), published in 1798. In it, Anthimus praises the Ottoman Empire as an instrument in the hands of God designed to protect the Eastern Christian world from the aggression of Latin Europe.[113] This idea, shared by a large proportion of Orthodox clergy from the time of the Council of Florence of 1439, if not earlier, rarely finds so candid and emotional an expression as in the treatise of Anthimus.

THE CONSTELLATION OF HISTORIANS

The turn of the eighteenth to the nineteenth century was marked by a new burst of creative activity among the Greeks in Palestine. During these years, there were a number of historians and chroniclers of the Church of Jerusalem. The first of these that should be named is the already-mentioned Archimandrite Maximus Simaius (d. after 1810), a disciple of Patriarch Anthimus and head of the Jerusalem school. The Russian pilgrim Melety, who visited Palestine in 1794, complained that in all the Brotherhood of the Holy Sepulchre one could scarcely find two scholarly monks. One of the two men he named was Maximus Simaius. In the words of Melety, "the *protosingelos* [Maximus] leads the life of silence, from which however he devotes some time to the education of five or six men in the sciences."[114] Alongside works on Hellenic grammar and the geography of the Holy Land, Maximus left a valuable treatise on the history of Jerusalem.[115] Maximus almost mechanically copied Dositheus's chronicle, which was no small service to modern scholars, for whom his work is much more accessible than Dositheus's book, which had already become a rarity in the nineteenth century. Maximus Simaius does not seem to have drawn on additional sources. Turning to the events of the eighteenth century, especially its second third, when it is impossible to rely on the works of Dositheus and Chrysanthos, the author became laconic. It is only with Napoleon's expedition in Egypt that entries begin to acquire the character of a diary.[116]

Known through his literary works is the Cappadocian Procopius Nazianzen (1776–1822), called "Araboğlu" (son of the Arab) by the Turks for his brilliance in Arabic. Procopius served as the dragoman of the Patriarchate of Jerusalem and patriarchal vicar and was always in the thick of ecclesio-political life. During the long-term absence of the patriarch, the dragoman was one of those who led the Orthodox community in Palestine and as such was repeatedly subjected to repression by the Ottoman authorities after the start of the Greek uprising. Procopius penned a poem about the fire in the Church of the Holy Sepulchre in 1808 and a chronicle, "Downtrodden Jerusalem," largely based on Dositheus's *History*. Writing a chronicle was a foundational moment for Procopius. It begins with a list of the patriarchs of Jerusalem up to the beginning of the nineteenth century. Next are alternating presentations of the struggle for the holy places with the Catholics and the Armenians (from 1517 until the second decade of the nineteenth century, while three times more space is dedicated to the machinations of the Armenians than to the intrigues of the Catholics). It concludes with a translation of thirty-two decrees of Muslim rulers, starting with the legendary *ashtiname* (decree) of the Caliph 'Umar, regarding the privileges of the Orthodox

Church in Palestine (especially well represented were the *firmans* of Mehmet II). Procopius's works pursued the same pragmatic goals as the work of Parthenius the Athenian, namely, enriching readers from the Brotherhood of the Holy Sepulchre with experience in combatting "heretics" and giving them arguments for their disputes about the status of the holy places.

Although Procopius did not say much about events before the end of the seventeenth century, he describes the eighteenth century better than Simaius and independently of him. In particular, the author clearly made use of Parthenius the Athenian's narrative. In places, Procopius's presentation of the material is emotional, especially because he was a direct participant in the events of the first two decades of the nineteenth century. He depicts certain scenes from the perspective of an eyewitness:

> Hajji Khalil Efendi cast a fierce and angry glance at us. Shaking his head and wanting to frighten us, he said, "So, you want to destroy the command and judgment of the king?" To this we responded, "For many years we have been servants and slaves of the king, may he be in good health, and we can not conceive of such an absurdity."[117]

Already after the death of Procopius, the librarian and secretary of the Brotherhood of the Holy Sepulchre, Anthimus of Anchialus (d. after 1851) completed a continuation of the chronicle. "I finished this book and added what I myself experienced and what I myself had been an eyewitness of,"[118] he said in the preface. Anthimus's work described in detail events from 1818 to 1828, "the recent decade filled with turmoil," as he called it.[119] Anthimus lived at a time when Palestine had become quite safe and affordable for foreign travelers, some of whom refer to him in their notes. Thus, Avraam Norov, describing the patriarchal library, observed, "The library is under the care of the first secretary, the kind and learned priest Anthimus … he knows the French language."[120] Andrei N. Muraviev appended to the first edition of his notes on his journey to the Holy Land statistics about the Orthodox population compiled by Anthimus. Porphyry Uspensky, however, held a low opinion of that statistical description, which was full of errors. According to the acerbic archimandrite, "the author has never traveled through Palestine and has no clear idea about the location, distance, and population of the Orthodox villages."[121] In the 1840s, Porphyry met with Anthimus on more than one occasion and left a colorful description of him: a very old man, already retired, but retaining an interest in church politics, with a stormy temperament; all the clergy of the Holy Sepulchre feared Anthimus's heavy staff.[122]

The most prolific writer of the first half of the nineteenth century was Neophytus of Cyprus (d. after 1844), secretary of the patriarchate and, for a time in the early 1830s, abbot of the Lavra of Mar Saba. Among his works stands out "The Account of Neophytus of Cyprus About the Christian Denominations in Jerusalem and their Quarrels Among Themselves About the Places of Worship," a history of Palestine from the foundation of Jerusalem to 1843, and a chronicle, "Twenty Years, or a Continuation of What Has Happened in the Orthodox Church of Jerusalem from 1821 to the Present 1841." Of all the chroniclers of his generation, Neophytus was the most creative. He was the only one who was not crushed under the authority of Dositheus's *History* and did not rewrite it. Neophytus, of course, used this source but alongside it he employed many other documents, particularly copies of Ottoman judicial decisions kept in the archive of the patriarchate. As a result, there is more of a description of events of the sixteenth century with Neophytus than in Dositheus's chronicle. However, Neophytus almost skips the first half of the eighteenth century and details only recommence with Napoleon's Egyptian expedition. Neophytus wrote a number of other works, in particular the narrative "On the Arab Catholics or Uniates," dedicated to the Catholic expansion in the East. However, Neophytus had little idea about what had happened in Syria in the eighteenth century. His scholarly interest is only in describing contemporary events.

As we can see, all of these chronicles—those of Maximus, Procopius, and Neophytus—are distinguished by a number of common features. Their main focus was the struggle for the holy places and they covered certain other aspects of the life of Palestinian Christians much less. The chroniclers were not able to avoid the distortion of proximity. The pre-Ottoman period is treated with extreme brevity. Slightly more is said about the sixteenth century. On the other hand, the seventeenth century is described with an abundance of detail, thanks to the chroniclers' reliance on Dositheus's *History*. The eighteenth century is less well known to the authors than the seventeenth. It is only from the beginning of the nineteenth century that entries once again become detailed and reflect the historians' personal experiences and memories.

THE LIBRARIES OF THE HOLY LAND

The literary activities of members of the Brotherhood of the Holy Sepulchre and centuries of donations of liturgical manuscripts to Jerusalem contributed to the accumulation of significant collections of books in the monasteries of the Patriarchate of Jerusalem. Even by the end of the nineteenth century, despite significant losses, around one thousand five hundred manuscript folios remained in the

Palestinian monasteries. The largest libraries existed in the patriarchal residence in Jerusalem and the Monastery of Mar Saba.[123] It is also worth mentioning the collection of Georgian manuscripts in the Monastery of the Holy Cross.

In 1652, Arseny Sukhanov described the library of the Monastery of the Archangel, a metochion of the Lavra:

> There are countless books—Greek, Latin, Slavic, printed and handwritten, all sorts of wise philosophical ones, precious books, but also many books have decayed, and were eaten through by moths. In olden days Serbs lived here … and as they hated the Greeks, because of this they neglected this place.[124]

In 1834, the British traveler Robert Curzon left a description of the library of Mar Saba:

> In one part of the church I observed a rickety ladder leaning against the wall, and leading up to a small door about ten feet from the ground. Scrambling up this ladder, I found myself in the library of which I had heard so much. It was a small square room, or rather a large closet, in the upper part of one of the enormous buttresses that supported the walls of the Monastery. Here I found about a thousand books, almost all manuscripts, but the whole of them were works of divinity. One volume in the Bulgarian or Serbian language was written in uncial letters; the rest were in Greek, and were for the most part of the twelfth century.… There were about a hundred other MSS. in the apsis of the church: I was not allowed to examine them.[125]

Porphyry Uspensky brought the best specimens of his collection of manuscripts of the Christian East from the library of the Lavra. It is enough to look at the catalog of Porphyry's collection to get an idea of the quantity and quality of the manuscript treasures stored at Mar Saba.[126]

No less important was the library of the Patriarchate of Jerusalem. The patriarch Dositheus took great care for its preservation and replenishment, even including a special clause in the charter of the Brotherhood of the Holy Sepulchre of 1689:

> The library of the patriarchate should have a good door and lock and the books should be dusted once every three months. The key to the library

must be kept with a trustworthy brother so that no book should disappear
or be withdrawn. Each brother who desires to take a book shall register and return it after reading. No person outside of Jerusalem is by any
means allowed to take a book from the library.[127]

It seems that these instructions were carried out in part and a century and a half
later Robert Curzon noted that

It contains a good library, the iron door of which is opened by a key as
large as a horse-pistol. The books are kept in good order, and consist of
about two thousand printed volumes in various languages; and about
five hundred Greek and Arabic MSS. on paper, which are all theological
works. There are also about one hundred Greek manuscripts on vellum:
the whole collection is in excellent preservation.[128]

ORTHODOX PALESTINE: MARGINAL SUBCULTURES

Alongside the highly developed Greek literary culture, there also remained in
the Patriarchate of Jerusalem the self-sufficient culture of the Arab Orthodox.
However, it should be stated that it would be wrong to single out a particularly
Palestinian Arab Christian subculture. The boundaries within the Arab Orthodox world were not just "transparent"—they did not exist. Over the whole space
of Syria, Palestine, and Egypt, there was a free movement of people and books.
The Arab Orthodox of Palestine were fully familiar with the literary works of
their Syrian coreligionists. In 1846, Porphyry Uspensky found in the library of
the metropolitan of Bethlehem editions from all the Arab Orthodox presses—
Bucharest, Aleppo, Iasi, Beirut—for the whole of the eighteenth century, starting with the first examples of Arabic printing in Wallachia in 1701 and ending
with the Viennese publications of Patriarch Anthimus.[129] Many of the Christian
Arabic manuscripts circulating in Palestine were copied in Damascus or Aleppo
and then donated by pilgrims to Bethlehem or the Church of St James in Jerusalem, dedicated to Arabic services.[130] However, against this background, actual
Palestinian book production appears rather modest.[131]

The cultural life of Orthodox Palestine is distinguished by a marked rise
in the late seventeenth century. It was directly tied to the efforts of Patriarch
Dositheus and his vicar Archbishop Christodoulos of Gaza to revive Arab
Orthodox culture and literacy. Christodoulos, who seems to have been some-
thing of an advisor on Arab affairs to Dositheus, translated a great deal from
Greek into Arabic and encouraged other translations (including from Church

Slavonic) and ordered the copying of Arabic liturgical books, especially for the churches of Transjordan.[132] One such manuscript, given to the church in the village of Fuheis in the ʿAjlun Mountains, is held at the Russian National Library of St Petersburg. The priest Neophytus, who refers to himself as "*wakil* of father Kyr Dositheus ... Patriarch of Jerusalem," made the donation."[133] The book had a difficult fate. It had been immersed in something, dirty fingers soiled it, and the edges of the pages were worn by constant use and glued. The winding paths of worms ate many sheets. One sheet that fell into complete disrepair was replaced by a new one of a different size, with the text written in a much worse hand. In the margins there are sometimes notes by the Transjordanian priest, written in a clumsy hand with cheap, faded ink. The record by the sponsor about the donation of the book was attested by "*raʾis al-kahana* [Arabic for 'hierarch'] Khristufulis, Metropolitan of Gaza."[134] Dositheus, for his part, also arranged for books to be copied and sent to rural parishes where they were needed, albeit at the parishes' expense.[135]

During the eighteenth century, a new urban center developed in the territory of the Patriarchate of Jerusalem, Acre. In the city, there was a large and influential Christian community, consisting primarily of immigrants from Syria, who were in a better situation than the Christians of the patriarchate's Palestinian hinterland in terms of their educational and cultural needs. During the era of Dahir and al-Jazzar, Acre became an important center of Arab Christian culture.

During the Ottoman era, the Georgian and Serbian monastic communities of Palestine ceased to exist. Their decline, particularly that of the Georgian colony, is told in the cessation of manuscript copying in the Monastery of the Holy Cross. There remain, however, a large number of undated paper manuscripts of low quality that belong to the fourteenth to sixteenth centuries. However, they may be for the most part offerings from pilgrims rather than local products. The last recorded date of a book being copied is from 1502. After that, there are no notes in the colophons about copying new texts, only rebinding worn-out codices. The Kakhetian dignitary Beena Cholokashvili, who came on pilgrimage in 1512, and the archbishop of Urbnisi, Blas, who came in 1570–1572,[136] were particularly active in the restoration of books. The dwindling Georgian community did not need new service books, but attempted to save the perishing legacy of its past. The previously mentioned, somewhat grandiose reconstruction of the Monastery of the Holy Cross in the 1640s appears dissonant against this background, but this was the swan song of the Georgian presence in the Holy Land.

ARAB ORTHODOX OF THE SIXTEENTH CENTURY: A PROTO-RENAISSANCE?
In discussing the traditional culture of the Arab Christians in the sixteenth and seventeenth centuries, Bernard Heyberger used terms such as "Dark Ages" and "decadence." Small numbers, poverty, and religious disunity led to the decline of their cultural creativity, which degenerated into the compilation and copying of ancient manuscripts.[137] It is only possible to agree with the French historian as regards the first half-century of Ottoman rule, which continued the inertia of cultural decline that engulfed the Christian East during the Mamluk period.

The paucity of information about Melkite culture during those decades indicates its low productivity. Almost no original works appeared. The language and style of church documents testify to the absence of literary education even among the hierarchs.[138]

The previously mentioned attempt by Patriarch Dorotheus II to agree to an ecclesiastical union with the Maronites in 1543 could only have been made by both parties ignoring their own religious dogmas. Even in 1628, in the acts of the Council of Ra's Baalbek when enumerating the various vices of the Christians, it mentions that "[p]reviously they had the custom, due to ignorance and lack of knowledge, of introducing heretical books into the Church and, believing them to be Orthodox books, reading from them stories, legends and sermons."[139]

Nor was knowledge of canon law up to standard. Patriarch Meletius Pigas of Alexandria, who waged a long dispute over canonical issues with Patriarch Joachim of Antioch, wrote to him in 1599, "I wonder how you ventured to refer to the forty-second canon of the First Council. Do you know that the Orthodox Church has no more than twenty-one canons from the First Council?"[140]

In the Arab Christian environment, scholars of the exact sciences were almost completely extinct. In 1539, differences in the tables for determining the date of Pascha between the various Middle Eastern churches gave rise to the complicated problem of calculating the date of Pascha. Patriarch of Antioch Michael ibn al-Mawardi called a church council to discuss this issue in the village of Qara, but its participants were unable to understand the calendrical and astronomical intricacies. To be fair, it should be noted that calculating the date of Pascha requires serious mathematical training and is not possible for everyone. However, in the early Middle Ages, there was a sufficient number of such specialists, whereas in the Patriarchate of Antioch in the sixteenth century, there could be found only one man (whose name, unfortunately, is not extant) who could correctly calculate the date of Pascha 191 years into the future.[141]

Reading the ungrammatical texts of Arab Christians sometimes annoys the modern researcher; however, we cannot forget that the grammatical errors and dialecticisms of Christian scribes are not necessarily indicative of intellectual weakness on the part of these people. The Melkites' creativity remained and it only required a few external stimuli for the Orthodox community to begin a cultural revival.

Chief among these external stimuli was the Greek influence that was constantly increasing after the incorporation of the Arab East into the Ottoman Empire. Knowledge of Greek was mandatory for educated Melkites. Many monks from the Balkans and the Archipelago pursued asceticism in Palestine and Sinai. Greek books—including printed ones—entered Syria in increasing numbers. Moreover, the Arabs came into contact with the inhabitants of the European factories and Catholic missionaries. Journeys by Middle Eastern clergy to Constantinople and Eastern Europe on church business or for alms dramatically expanded their cultural and geographic horizons.

For centuries, scholars have written of a so-called Melkite Renaissance (Arab. *al-Nahda*), a cultural revitalization among the Arab Orthodox of the seventeenth century. After several centuries of creative decline and stupor, Middle Eastern Orthodoxy, which seemed to have fallen hopelessly into a coma, experienced a real cultural reawakening and a sharp intensification of cultural life. Scholars tend to explain this revival by the close connection of the Melkites to Greek post-Byzantine culture and their awareness of their marginality within the pan-Orthodox cultural space. The basic content of the "Melkite Nahda" was the desire of the Arab Orthodox to overcome their cultural isolation within the Eastern Christian world, to all at once "catch up" with the post-Byzantine culture of the Balkans, and to become familiar with the latest achievements of Greek erudition. In the Arab East, the Nahda was possible because of relative tolerance towards Christians living under Ottoman rule and the barriers to communication between peoples of the Eastern Mediterranean had been removed.

However, this long process of awakening is somewhat surprising. One hundred years passed from the inclusion of Syria into the Ottoman Empire before the first literary work appeared by a representative of the Nahda, traditionally considered to be Metropolitan of Aleppo Meletius Karma. At the same time, a careful study of the sources leads to the conclusion that the cultural revival of the Melkites began a generation earlier.

In the early 1580s, European influence on Christians in the Middle East abruptly increased in connection with the missionary "*Drang nach Osten*" of Pope Gregory XIII.[142] The missions of Giovanni Battista Eliano and Lionardo Abel became, in the terminology of Arnold Toynbee, a historic "challenge" for the Arab Orthodox for the first time in many decades, if not centuries, forcing them to reflect on their ethnic and religious identity within the Christian world. The Antiochian hierarchy and scribes had to formulate an attitude toward issues such as the Union of Florence and the Gregorian calendar. The Catholic onslaught stimulated a wave of ideological and literary activity among the Arabs, some of whom were in favor of and others against rapprochement with Rome. Philo-Catholics wrote letters to the Vatican about brotherly love. Along these lines are known the letters of the Melkites of Tripoli in 1584 and that of ex-Patriarch Michael VI al-Hamawi.[143] Supporters of Eastern Orthodoxy composed polemical anti-Latin treatises. Earlier mention was made of the treatise by Anastasius ibn al-Mujalla, the future metropolitan of Tripoli.[144] Most striking of all in this text is the geopolitical outlook of the author, who perceives his people as part of a vast Orthodox world. This does not fit well with the notion of total ignorance among the Christian Arabs of the sixteenth century. Anastasius's missive was the most prominent, but not the only, product of the anti-Latin polemic. The Damascene priest Yuhanna ibn Musallim wrote his own response "to the Frankish priest Battista,"[145] and an anonymous anti-Latin treatise of the 1580s has also been preserved.[146]

It cannot be ruled out that Anastasius ibn Mujalla, who was close to Patriarch Joachim Daw, accompanied him on a journey to Eastern Europe in 1584–1586 and that it is from this that Anastasius derived his geopolitical concepts and preferences. The journey of Joachim Daw had a direct impact on the development of Arab Christian culture. One of the patriarch's companions, 'Isa, later metropolitan of Hama, composed a poetic description of Muscovy, the first in the Arab world. The *qasida* of 'Isa is small in size—seventy-two verses, around four or five handwritten pages. This emotional and enthusiastic account of the curiosities of the Muscovite kingdom captured the Arab's imagination: bells ringing, golden domes, solemn liturgies and the mighty power of the Muscovites. For three generations of Melkites, the *qasida* remained the main source of information about their northern coreligionists, until this was changed by Paul of Aleppo's book.[147]

It is worth remembering that Joachim Daw and his companions were not the first Arabs who ventured on a journey to Muscovy. The way was paved for them by Metropolitan of Bethlehem Joachim, a native of Keserwan, who in 1579 aspired to the patriarchal throne of the Holy City. Even from this time, Metropolitan Joachim was already known to Dorotheus Daw, the future Patriarch Joachim, then still metropolitan of Tripoli, who came to Jerusalem for the proceedings related to the conflict as exarch of the Ecumenical Patriarch.[148] In 1583–1584, Joachim of Bethlehem had been in Moscow waiting to receive alms.

On his journey home, he met with Joachim Daw in Constantinople, undoubtedly, and inspired him to journey to the Orthodox lands of Eastern Europe. After returning to Palestine, Metropolitan Joachim left Bethlehem, probably because of friction with his former rival, Patriarch Sophronius, and, unbefitting to his dignity, settled in the Monastery of Hamatoura near Tripoli. There he retranslated into Arabic the Typicon, the basic liturgical manual. Joachim anticipated the similar work of Meletius Karma, just as Metropolitan 'Isa represented a predecessor of Paul of Aleppo. The metropolitan of Bethlehem also composed a description of the topography of Constantinople: here can be made out the geographical contours of the future works of Macarius ibn al-Za'im. All trajectories of the Melkite Renaissance of the seventeenth century go back to the works of the Syro–Lebanese scribes of the 1580s.

Moreover, Joachim of Bethlehem, who returned to Palestine in 1591/1592, must surely have known the young monk of Mar Saba, 'Abd al-Karim (Meletius) Karma. Similarly, there is no doubt that even earlier Karma, the son of a priest from Hama, had communicated with his diocesan bishop, Metropolitan 'Isa, the author of the description of Muscovy. It was precisely 'Isa and Joachim, people with enormous life experience and uniquely broad-minded for their environment, who were among those who discovered the vast world of Orthodox civilization and inspired efforts to integrate Antiochian Christians into the pan-Byzantine cultural space.[149]

However, the cultural rise of the Melkites in the 1580s was succeeded by two decades of apparent stagnation. This can be explained by the general sociopolitical crisis in the Ottoman Empire at the turn of the sixteenth to the seventeenth century, the era of the so-called Jelali Revolts. Political anarchy and economic ruin did not contribute to cultural creativity.

Nevertheless, some examples of literary activity even go back to this period, especially poetry in the colloquial dialect, which was widespread among Christians during the Ottoman era.[150] A significant amount of verse was devoted to spiritual topics and various cultural events in the Orthodox community—lamenting a departed patriarch, a panegyric welcoming a new prelate, and so on.[151] This poetry, whose most prolific practitioner was the priest Yuhanna ibn 'Isa Uwaysat (d. 1663), was of no particular aesthetic or intellectual value, rather represented the release of emotions, alternating calls of "arise!" and "weep!" The names of some other poets of that era are known. Ibrahim al-Antaki, who lived in Aleppo around 1520, composed an apology for Christianity against Islam. The Aleppan priest Bulus ibn al-Za'im, father of the future Patriarch of Antioch Macarius, composed religious verses. Verse notes can be found in the colophons of manuscripts and in the texts of historical works, indicating the popularity of the poetic genre.[152]

THE SUNSET OF ARAMAIC WRITING

In the early Ottoman era came the final decline among the Orthodox of Syriac liturgy and writing. The German semiticist Anton Baumstark presents data about fifty-two Melkite Syriac manuscripts preserved from the sixteenth century, which is comparable to the number of manuscripts from the previous century, whereas the number of manuscripts is markedly reduced during the last three decades of the century. From the seventeenth century, he reaches a total of nine manuscripts, of which six are from the first two decades, with the latest from 1654.[153]

Some Antiochian hierarchs continued to sign official documents in Syriac or garshuni[154] —examples of this are known until the 1630s.[155] Often, however, this was just a tribute to ancient traditions and the signatories themselves had a weak knowledge of Syriac and poorly remembered the alphabet. In two garshuni signatures on a letter from Antiochian clergy to Tsar Fyodor Ivanovich in 1594, some forgotten Syriac letters are replaced with Arabic.[156]

However, there is evidence indicating that Syriac writing continued in use even after the mid-seventeenth century. The Syriac liturgy was preserved in the in the area of Maaloula and surrounding villages up to the present day, so accordingly, Syriac liturgical texts were copied.[157] However, the scope of the use of Syriac writing shrank to the narrow limits of the liturgical literature and thus acquired a marginal character.

THE MELKITE RENAISSANCE

The second decade of the seventeenth century was marked by a new wave of cultural revival among the Arab Orthodox. This moment is traditionally considered the beginning of the Melkite Renaissance. Earlier, we attempted to demonstrate that a literary revival, sharing all the characteristics of the Melkite Renaissance of the seventeenth century, was already noticeable in the region of Tripoli in the 1580s. However, the activity of the second generation of Arab Christian writers, grouped in Aleppo around Metropolitan Meletius Karma (1572–1635), later patriarch of Antioch under the name Euthymius II, was much more massive and consequential.

A native of the city of Hama, Meletius (his first given name was ʿAbd al-Karim), in his youth, became a monk in the Palestinian Lavra of Mar Saba. There he became acquainted with Greek culture, determining the entire course of his future career. A renowned ascetic and preacher, he was elected to the See of Aleppo in 1612 and held it for more than twenty years (1612–1633). Meletius's militant asceticism was combined with rare oratorical talent and a deep knowledge of Greek language and theological literature. Noting the numerous discrepancies between the Arabic and Greek liturgical books, the metropolitan of Aleppo undertook the enormous task of producing new, high-quality translations of liturgical texts. He took as his model the standard edition of the Greek Venetian printers, aiming to bring about uniformity in the liturgical practices of the Orthodox peoples. Meletius's translations and corrections of church books belong to two or three dates: in 1612, he put into use his own version of the Hieratikon, Synaxarion, Sticherarion, and Typikon; sometime before 1628, the Horologion; and, in 1633, the Euchologion.[158] Undoubtedly, each of these books required years of painstaking work and examination of the numerous translations of church literature that were in use in the Arab milieu. Along with his translations, Meletius also composed a number of his own works, mostly sermons and missives.[159]

To standardize the liturgical texts and replace corrupted versions in use, Meletius wanted to take advantage of the opportunity of printing. At that time, typesetting in Arabic script existed only in Catholic countries. Meletius established ongoing communication with the Vatican through Maronite clergy and the Franciscan missionary Tommaso de Novara, who worked in Syria from 1612 to 1622. In 1621, Meletius sent his protosyngelos, Absalom, to Rome to discuss printing in Italy Arab Greek liturgical books for Middle Eastern Christians. For more than ten years, Meletius continued to correspond with cardinals from the Congregation de Propaganda Fide about this publishing project and the technical details of its realization. In particular, Meletius was critical of the Catholic edition of the Arabic Gospel, which was full of errors ("for Arabic is not your tongue," wrote the metropolitan) and insisted on the publication of texts that he himself had verified. In Meletius's letters, his manner of presentation and its graceful style betrays an inner composure, a discipline of thought not always evident among his compatriots. Not waiting for progress, in the early 1630s, Karma sent another messenger, Pachomius, to Rome. He returned with new assurances from the cardinals that the preparations for the publication of the Arabic Gospel were already close to completion. After Karma's death, the project stalled.[160]

Thus, Meletius's activities appear to be a Syrian prototype for the church reforms of the Patriarch Nikon of Moscow. However, Meletius's innovations did not result in such bloody excesses as the schism in seventeenth-century Russia and generally were unopposed. On the contrary, Meletius's liturgical texts received wide distribution among Melkites and quickly replaced other versions of the texts. In the manuscript collections of monasteries of the Patriarchate of

Antioch, books translated by Meletius occupy the largest place in terms of numbers, alongside translations of the Bible and the patristic translations of ʿAbdallah ibn al-Fadl of Antioch.

MACARIUS AL-ZAʿIM

The most prominent disciple of Meletius Karma was Patriarch Macarius al-Zaʿim. He was born in Aleppo at the turn of the sixteenth to the seventeenth century to the family of a priest. The first steps in the career of Macarius (who then bore the name John) were made under the auspices of Metropolitan Meletius, of whom Macarius said, "I am a humble student of his, was honored to be worthy of the priesthood, and also instructed morally."[161]

In his early thirties, John was widowed and became a monk. Meletius Karma, who was elected to the patriarchal throne, intended for his disciple to occupy the See of Aleppo. In view of the patriarch's impending death, John (who at his episcopal consecration took the name Meletius in honor of his teacher) was installed as metropolitan by the next patriarch, Euthymius III in September 1635. Upon Euthymius's death, Meletius al-Zaʿim, now under the name Macarius, took the patriarchal throne, which he occupied for a quarter-century. Macarius had never received a formal education. In his youth, it seems, he had only acquired some fragmentary knowledge by serving Meletius Karma. Western missionaries in Aleppo spoke rather condescendingly of Macarius's level of education. He had a mediocre knowledge of Greek, having only learned it in adulthood.[162] Nevertheless, Macarius had an instinctive thirst for knowledge and understood the need to educate his compatriots.[163]

Macarius spent all his life zealously making up for lost time, filling the gaps in his education. The earliest texts known to have been written by him date from the 1630s, when he was already on the See of Aleppo. The last were composed at around the age of seventy and are characterized by the same avid interest in the world. Macarius's autograph manuscripts, texts on various topics numbering hundreds of pages, have been preserved, written in a fine, barely legible hand. The randomness of the entries (for the most part, translations and compilations) is striking. Under a single cover are found lives of saints; acts of councils; lists of Frankish kings; lists of episcopal sees; tables for calculating Pascha; and historical, geographical, theological, and liturgical texts. Sometimes the entries are dated, and it gives the impression that the patriarch wrote constantly, during his every free hour.

On the basis of his rough notes, Macarius compiled a number of collections with historical, hagiographical, liturgical, and canonical content. These incorporate, in varying proportions, translations from Greek, compilations, and Macarius's original compositions. The contents of the collections are not always stable; some texts are included several times over in different books. The dating of many of these works is difficult to determine. It is evident, however, that both of Macarius's great journeys, especially his prolonged stays in Kolomna in 1654 and Kutaisi in 1665, proved fruitful for him.

So what interested Macarius and what did he want to convey to his compatriots? The history of Byzantium, the Seven Ecumenical Councils, and the four patriarchates, with a particular interest in the history and geography of the Church of Antioch, were at the center of his attention.

Macarius's historical writings form the basis of modern Arab Orthodox historiography (more will be said in the following in connection with the work of Paul of Aleppo). However, apart from these texts that have long been published, historical notes by Macarius remain in the unpublished manuscripts. The most interesting unpublished autograph manuscript of the patriarch is the historical-canonical content of St Petersburg Manuscript B 1227. There, alongside materials borrowed from other sources and the author's version of the history of the Patriarchate of Antioch, is a treatise by Macarius from 1665 about the metropolitans and dioceses of the Church of Antioch. In the context of the decline of the tradition of chronicles among the Arab Orthodox, the patriarch had to pay more attention to oral tradition than to written sources. The rather short memory of a semiliterate, largely agrarian society preserved information about what happened during the course of approximately no more than two generations. Along with a sparing list of bishops, interspersed into the narrative are belletristic stories about some of the most vivid events connected with a personality of a particular bishop. Macarius's text represents the mold of the Melkites' collective memory, a reflection of the ways of forming a quasi-historical mythology.[164]

Among Macarius's other original works, the best known is his description of Georgia, which the patriarch visited in 1664–1666 and 1669. It provides an overview of the political and ecclesiastical history of the country and some geographical and demographical information. The greater part of the work is devoted to describing Macarius's educational activities among the Georgian clergy, who had fallen into disarray. The narrative, however, is full of self-promotional exaggerations.[165]

Another important aspect of Macarius's literary activities was hagiography. Using his administrative capabilities, he identified, collected, and transcribed rare ancient manuscripts, most often kept in remote villages of the patriarchate.[166] A manifestation of the Antiochian regional patriotism characteristic of the Melkite

Nahda was Macarius's collection *Lives of Saints from Our Land*, composed in the 1650s. In the preface, the patriarch laments the fact that Syrian Christians did not know their ascetics, which is what prompted him to compile this work. The collection includes, among other things, biographies of theologians, writers, and scholars of the eleventh through thirteenth centuries who had not been added to the list of saints. Macarius wanted to prove to himself and to everyone that the Church of Antioch was by no means marginal in the Orthodox world.

Along with this, the patriarch and his collaborators translated from Greek the lives of dozens of early Christian and Byzantine saints unknown in the Arab East. After Meletius Karma's translation of the Synaxarion, Byzantine saints invaded the Antiochian cultural space. Macarius contributed to this process in an effort to enrich Melkite culture by the addition of Greek ascetics and martyrs to the circle of saints traditionally venerated in the Middle East.[167]

From Macarius's pen also came several books of a liturgical character, mostly translations of Greek commentaries on the Divine Liturgy as well as extracts from Greek canonists, particularly concerning marriage and inheritance, and a number of dogmatic and didactic texts, homilies, a polemical anti-Protestant essay (in response to a request from the French consul in Aleppo), and other works.[168]

PAUL OF ALEPPO

Macarius's literary work is difficult to consider in isolation from the activities of his son and close associate, Paul of Aleppo (Bulus al-Za'im), a figure equaling Macarius in his importance to Arab Christian culture. As the son of a bishop, gifted with linguistic and scholarly talents, Paul of Aleppo (1627–1669) had far more opportunities for self-education and self-expression. From earliest childhood, he was always in the middle of church life, "always inseparable" from his father, attending services, taking part in pilgrimage to the Holy Land, and so on. At the age of fifteen, Paul was made a subdeacon, and at twenty-one, he was ordained archdeacon of Damascus, Aleppo, "and all the Arab countries."[169] He was something of a secretary to Macarius, drawing up official documents and signing them after the patriarch, among other confidants. Incidentally, Ignaty Krachkovsky noted that Paul's beautiful calligraphic handwriting was rare among the Arab Orthodox.[170]

Paul accompanied his father on the journey to Russia in 1652–1659, personally knew Tsar Alexei Mikhailovich, and was well received in the highest circles of Russian society. He was offered an opportunity to stay in Moscow and work as a translator in the Posolsky Prikaz, but he refused, citing homesickness and the children he left there (in 1644, Paul married, and by the early 1650s, he already had two sons). Upon his return to Syria, Paul was actively involved in the ecclesiastical affairs of his father. During the patriarch's absence, he remained his deputy in Damascus, traveled on errands to Aleppo, and so on. During these years, the archdeacon appears before us as a major administrator and an outstanding public figure. He organized the construction of the new patriarch's residence in Damascus, decorated the church, sought to regulate the activities of the clergy, and interceded before the local Ottoman authorities on behalf of Christians. Paul had undoubted diplomatic talent. He was able to find a common language with the Ottoman pashas and knew when it was necessary to "open the hand of generosity." According to Paul, he had such authority in the eyes of the Ottomans that "his word had weight for each and above all, that which the deacon said, was universally recognized."[171]

Chroniclers who lived generations later wrote of the love and respect that the Orthodox inhabitants of Damascus had for Paul. His education was supplemented by his life experience and wide range of interests. The Syrian deacon perceived his Church of Antioch not only as part of the empirewide community of Orthodox peoples, but also, more broadly, as part of the entire Eastern Christian civilization, stretching from the Arctic Ocean to the Sinai. He admired Russia, but he did not lose his sense of reality and remained loyal to the Ottoman Empire. If not for his early death, Paul would have become one of the most outstanding patriarchs of Antioch—there is no doubt that he was intended for the patriarchal throne after Macarius. Fate, however, did not favor Paul. On the return leg of Macarius's last journey, he died under mysterious circumstances in Tbilisi[172] on January 30, 1669, at the age of forty-two.[173]

However, during the period of time allotted to him, Paul did much for Arab Christian culture. He had received a more systematic education than his father. There survive copies from his hand of theological works of Byzantine and Syrian authors. He was well oriented in geography, Greek, Arabic, Ottoman, and Russian history, and he had a fine artistic taste. Paul knew a great deal about painting, preferring the European realist school. As for architecture and design, Paul had the opportunity to put his ideas about beauty into practice during the construction of the luxurious patriarchal residence in Damascus and the renovation of the church, both of which the deacon supervised personally.

Paul's chief legacy is the literary work representing the pinnacle of Arab Christian culture of the Ottoman period. Paul's best work, *Rihlat Makariyus* (*The Journey of Macarius*), describes the journey his father undertook in the 1650s. In this book, Paul gives a vivid picture of the history, geography, life, customs, and political events unfolding before his eyes in the Danubian principalities, Ukraine, Russia, Anatolia, and Syria. During the journey, he wrote as events happened, creating a rough first edition of the book. On the return home, he wrote a second, expanded version of the work on the basis of these diaries. Paul's strong personality and ambition are noteworthy, as he did not have the self-effacement characteristic of most medieval chroniclers. "All my desires lie in this," he wrote about the occasion of writing his book, "that during my life I may myself create a monument, that subsequently when someone finds it, he would say, 'Yes, God have mercy on him!'"[174]

In direct connection with Macarius's first journey appeared Paul's work, *The History of Vasile Lupu, Voivode of Moldavia, and His Wars*, which he composed in Kolomna in 1654. Later, Paul composed more geographical descriptions, in part based on translations from Greek.[175] During Macarius's second journey, possibly by order of the clerks of Moscow, Paul composed a description of Georgia where he stayed with Macarius in 1664–1665. This text is preserved only in Russian translation.[176]

No less than Patriarch Macarius, Paul of Aleppo worked for the revival of the historiographical tradition among the Arab Orthodox. Macarius and Paul established a cycle of works entitled "The Names of the Patriarchs of Antioch from the Time of the Holy Apostle Peter to Our Own Time." The problems of authorship of individual parts of this work have not fully been resolved. Scholars include the text of *The Names of the Patriarchs* among a number of Macarius' unpublished manuscripts. Preliminary versions (one dating to 1657) are preserved within the collection *al-Majmuʿ al-Latif* (The Elegant Collection), while the latest compilation, from 1665 is in manuscript. St Petersburg, Institute of Oriental Manuscripts B-1227, the copy of which is known to be found in the Vatican collection as manuscript. Vatican Arabic 689.[177] However, in places this version also looks like a haphazard collection of excerpts from primary sources. Macarius did not have time to complete his work.

Parallel to this work, there is a list of patriarchs of Antioch of the thirteenth to sixteenth centuries as amended by Paul of Aleppo, which he included in the preface to the *Journey of Macarius*. The collection of histories of the patriarchs of Antioch compiled by Mikail Breik al-Dimashqi (d. after 1781), whose chronicle has long been in scholarly use, made use of both Paul's work and one of the early versions of Macarius's work. Breik attributed the compilation of the early history of the patriarchate, from the Apostle Paul to the Crusaders, to Macarius. G. Murkos did not agree with this attribution, pointing to a phrase from Paul of Aleppo in the *Journey of Macarius*:

I tried … to compose … successive chronicles, similar to that, which I earlier had composed with such diligence about the first patriarchs of

Antioch from the time of St Peter … until the time of Elias and Christian, the Latin patriarchs who were made patriarch in Antioch when it was conquered by the Franks.[178]

Joseph Nasrallah, however, believes that this chronicle has not come down to us.[179] With the manuscript St Petersburg B 1227 available for scholarly use, doubts about the authorship disappear completely. Antiochian church history is described by the patriarch in his own hand, with some remarks in the first person. They are preserved even in the compilation made by Breik, who did not attach much importance to thoroughly editing the texts that he used. There are phrases like "this letter exists in the Hellenic language. I, the humble one, translated it into Arabic"[180] and "which [books,] having found whole, I, the humble one, transcribed for myself."[181] It is obvious that only the patriarch could have been speaking of himself in this way.

Syrian church history up to the seventh century is described in sufficient detail on the basis of works by Byzantine authors. Later, Macarius bases himself on information gleaned from the writings of Theophanes the Confessor and Eutychius of Alexandria, sometimes adding information from other sources, apparently Nikon of the Black Mountain. Incidentally, it is known that Paul of Aleppo himself made a copy of Eutychius's chronicle.[182] Macarius rewrote entire pages of the chronicle of Yahya of Antioch in his *History*. When the description of the period covered in this source is completed, the presentation becomes lapidary.[183] The historian occasionally refers to Kedrenos, Nikon of the Black Mountain, and the works of the eleventh-century Arab Christian authors 'Abdallah ibn al-Fadl of Antioch and the monk Michael. Starting with the period of the Crusades, the account is reduced to a dry list of the patriarchs of Antioch, mainly the Latin ones. The list ends, in fact, with Elias and Christian, whom Paul mentions, summarizing his historical works. Perhaps somewhere Paul retold Macarius's chronicle of the first one hundred patriarchs of Antioch, just as he duplicated Macarius's history of the patriarchs of the sixteenth to early seventeenth centuries.

There is a list composed by Paul of Aleppo of the patriarchs of Antioch during the Mamluk period. The text is included in the preface of the *Journey of Macarius* and, with slight differences, in the chronicle of Mikhail Breik. Paul's attempt at reconstructing the succession of patriarchs of the thirteenth through the first half of the fourteenth centuries ends in failure; this century simply falls out of the chronicle. Paul believed that the patriarchal see moved to Damascus almost immediately after Baybars destroyed Antioch. The campaign itself of Baybars is described by Paul in some detail because this event is well recorded in Muslim chronicles. As for particularly Christian history, then, as Paul wrote, "from that time, information about the patriarchs has entirely ceased in the absence of a new historian.... The reason for this was the increase in worries and sorrows, captures and constraints, that plagued the children of baptism."[184] The only coherent historical narrative of the Mamluk era belonged to Patriarch Michael of Antioch, who lived at the turn of the fourteenth to the fifteenth century. His chronicle has come down to us only in Paul's transmission. This source, however, is nothing more than a short list of names and dates, from the relocation of the patriarchs to Damascus in the mid-fourteenth century to the year 1404. Further investigations by Paul turned into a hunt for colophons: "After him [patriarch Michael], it [was] written about him by a different hand that he died," "I found at last the donated writing of an old Book of the Epistles," "I also found at last the following from an ancient book," "in another book I found ..." and so forth.[185] Subsequent historians have praised Paul's manner of working. He almost always indicates his sources and subjects them to scholarly criticism.[186]

The next part of the chronicle, covering the years 1543 to 1647, was composed by Patriarch Macarius, largely relying on his own memories, oral traditions, and documents that were subsequently lost. This historical narrative has come down to us in two versions, in the eighteenth-century chronicle of Mikhail Breik and mentioned in Paul of Aleppo's preface to the *Journey of Macarius* under the title "List of the Patriarchs of Antioch." The list covers events from 1268 to 1650. Macarius's information about church history of the sixteenth and seventeenth centuries is retold in brief, sometimes with noticeable differences in detail. However, from the patriarchate of Euthymius III (1635–1647), Paul's edition, in turn, becomes much more detailed than the versions of Macarius and Breik and contains unique information about different aspects of the life of Syrian Christians. To this it is also possible to add the ending of the *Journey of Macarius*, which resembles diary entries about the life of the Orthodox community in Syria from the spring of 1659 to July 1661.

THE CULTURAL MILIEU OF THE ERA

Of course, the activities of Macarius and Paul were only possible under conditions of a favorably disposed environment and the existence of a large group of "consumers" of the cultural values that they produced. The compositions of Arab Christian writers were actively read and copied over the next few generations. A number of lesser-known writers and translators worked alongside Macarius.

A circle of Melkite scribes had already formed in Aleppo around Meletius Karma. This included the artist, translator, and calligrapher Yusuf al-Musawwir (d. before 1667) who, among other works, produced translations in conjunction with Paul of Aleppo.[187] Karma's archdeacon, the *oikonomos* Mikhail Baja (d. at the beginning of the eighteenth century) was famous as a preacher, translator, and lecturer. In his later years, he became friendly with Catholic missionaries and influenced the formation of a number of Uniate intellectuals in the first half of the eighteenth century.[188] Although Patriarch Euthymius III al-Saqizi did not leave his own literary works, he contributed to Melkite culture as a painter and patron of education. Geographical literature of the era, in addition to the classical work of Paul of Aleppo and the writings of Macarius, is represented by a number of descriptions of the holy places in Palestine as well as Rome, Constantinople, and Alexandria. For the most part, these texts are anonymous and secondary. Against their background stands out the original compositions of the Deacon Ephrem, who described the Monastery of St Catherine on Mount Sinai (precise dating is difficult)[189] and the story of the journey of the Aleppan Ibn Raʿad to Venice in 1656.[190]

The historical works of Melkites are also not limited to the books of Macarius and Paul. A few more authors wrote on historical themes in Aleppo during the seventeenth century. In 1641, Yuhanna ibn Salih al-ʿAzar collected stories about the miracles that had taken place in the churches of Aleppo and around 1671 Tuma ibn Sulayman compiled a history of the city. Anonymous authors left a diary of a stay in Aleppo of Patriarch of Antioch Euthymius III in 1641, a biography of Patriarch Macarius (which has come down in a manuscript from 1676), and a poetic description of Aleppo (1655).[191]

Alongside this, in such diocesan centers as Beirut and Homs, historical writing began to develop in the form of fragmentary records of certain events of church life. There were also patrons of education, such as the priest Farah, who, in 1651, became bishop of Beirut under the name Philip and established a large library in the city.[192]

Most historical records of this kind are found in manuscript colophons. These are often notes left by prominent church hierarchs, such as the metropolitans of Aleppo, Marmarita, and Tripoli.[193] However, the largest collection of historical records is not found in the urban book collections, but rather in the monastic libraries, especially at Hamatoura and Balamand.[194] Sometimes a few scattered notes are found on the margins of a book, forming a sort of spontaneous chronicle. In addition to information about the installment and repose of hierarchs and abbots, donations, construction work, and lists of the names of the inhabitants of the monasteries, the monks also wrote about natural anomalies—frosts, locusts, years of famine, and political discord in the country. In most cases, these sources remained unutilized by later chroniclers. One exception is the Beirut Chronicle of ʿAbdallah Trad, which incorporates fragmentary records of local clergy from the sixteenth and seventeenth centuries.

Worthy of special mention is the micro-chronicle compiled in Balamand Monastery around the turn of the seventeenth to the eighteenth century. Apart from fragmentary entries about events during the Mamluk era, the manuscript contains a coherent account of the succession of patriarchs of Antioch and other events of church history from the death of Joachim Jumʿa in 1575 to the reconciliation between Cyril al-Zaʿim and Athanasius Dabbas in 1694.[195]

The popularity of poetry in the colloquial dialect among Christians has been mentioned. There are more than two dozen authors of books of poetry from the seventeenth century. Unlike other literary movements that developed in Aleppo and, to a lesser extent, in Damascus, the practice of poetry was ubiquitous. This is illustrated by the *nisbas* of the poets, coming from Egypt, Hama, Homs, and even Raʾs Baalbek. Several of the poets were monks or priests, but most of them were laymen. Poems are known to have been written by the previously mentioned clerics, the preacher Mikhail Baja, Metropolitan Philip/Farah of Beirut, and Metropolitan Euthymius Saifi.[196] One gets the impression that versifying was, almost without exception, a hobby.

The subject matter of poems was both spiritual—praising the Lord and the saints, panegyric expressions of repentance, didactic instruction—and secular. The Russian reader can become acquainted with a sample of the poetry of the era in the book of Paul of Aleppo. Appearing there is a *qasida* (which Joseph Nasrallah, however, calls rhymed prose)[197] composed in 1660 by the Damascene priest Yuhanna ibn al-Dib about the consecration of myrrh by Patriarch Macarius. The panegyric contains a biography of the patriarch and addresses Macarius, Paul, and (just in case) his sons with lavish praise.[198] Flattering the patriarchal grandchildren was farsighted: twelve years later, Yuhanna ibn al-Dib was involved in installing one of them as patriarch.[199]

In contrast to the medieval Arab scholars, the Melkites were almost exclusively attracted to the humanities. Other sciences were in decline. There are only a few examples of works on astrology, alchemy, and dream interpretation. Medicine was slightly more developed. Two Melkite doctors from Aleppo, Mikhail Yuwakim and Jibraʾil al-Mukarram, who were active in the first and second thirds of the seventeenth century, respectively, wrote a series of treatises on diseases, medicines, hygiene, and methods of diagnosis.[200]

THE EIGHTEENTH CENTURY: ORTHODOXY VERSUS THE UNIA

The Beginning of the Struggle

The schism in the Patriarchate of Antioch of 1724 and the fierce opposition between the Orthodox and Uniate branches became the chief subject, not only of the church-political history but also of the cultural history of the Arab Christians of the eighteenth century. Both communities passionately attempted to assert themselves in order to justify their civilizational choice and to realize their identity. The Arab Orthodox found themselves facing a historic challenge from the Catholic world, an adversary with overwhelming material and intellectual superiority. The survival of Arab Orthodoxy depended on the effectiveness of the answer to this challenge. Therefore, it seems appropriate to continue to focus precisely on the ideological confrontation between the two churches. That is, on the various domains of polemic and apologetic, setting aside other genres of Arab Christian literature, such as poetry and geographical literature, even though they represent a large number of texts.[201]

Religious polemic in the Middle East was launched by European missionaries who translated into Arabic a huge body of Latin theological and propagandistic literature. Particularly prominent in this field was Pierre Fromage, the head of the Jesuit mission in Aleppo at the beginning of the eighteenth century. The translations prepared by Europeans were for the most part incoherent. They were edited by philo-Catholic Arabs such as ʿAbdallah Zakher and put into circulation in the edited version. It is characteristic that of the seventeen nonliturgical books published at the first Uniate press at Shuwayr, eleven were translations of works by Western theologians.[202]

Note, however, that only a small proportion of the translations of Western authors represented direct anti-Orthodox polemic. The bulk of the translated literature was devoted to discussions of soul-saving themes, Christian apologetics, demonstrations of the vanity of the world, asceticism, meditative experiences, problems of knowledge of God, and so on.[203] They acquainted Arab readers with all genres of Western theology, introducing them to the Catholic view of Christianity. Along with this development, philo-Catholic literature in Arabic also existed among the Maronites. Thus, the first generation of Uniate scribes "stood on the shoulders" of their Latin teachers, utilizing their intellectual experience and established arguments.

What was the starting position of the Orthodox? We have already quoted Ignaty Kratchkovsky that the Orthodox literary tradition "focused on Greek Byzantine writing ... did not have a center, more or less analogous to Rome, to which it could gravitate." Greek Constantinople "did not provide a solid base and could not clearly ascertain the aspirations associated with Arab Christian cultural currents."[204] That last phrase echoes conventional wisdom regarding the alienation between Greeks and Arabs and Phanariot chauvinism. In fact, it is doubtful that the Spanish or Italian Jesuits would have understood "Arab cultural currents" better than the Greeks of Constantinople. The era of the Melkite Nahda provided many examples of how the Arabs selected and adapted the best of Greek literature to their spiritual needs. In the context of the Catholic onslaught, Orthodox Syrians willingly drew on the achievements of Greek polemicists. One such work, the *Catechesis* of Zacharias Gerganos, was translated into Arabic in 1704, immediately provoking the appearance of the first Arab Uniate polemical treatise. This was written by Euthymius al-Sayfi (1643–1723), metropolitan of Tyre and Sidon and administrator of the Middle Eastern Catholics, about whom much was said in the previous chapter.

In addition to his tireless activism and organization activities, which left a huge epistolary legacy, Euthymius's creative nature sought expression in reforming the Melkite liturgical tradition. Sayfi's ritual innovations provoked sharp criticism in Orthodox circles. It was not only the Russian Old Believer I. Lukyanov who experienced a shock when, in 1701, he observed the liturgical service of the metropolitan of Sidon,[205] but also the broad-minded former Patriarch of Antioch Athanasius, who around 1718 instructed his secretary 'Abdallah Zakher, then still Orthodox, to write a denunciation of Euthymius's innovations.[206] Sayfi's liturgical reforms were not even understood in the Catholic milieu. The temperamental metropolitan sent letter after letter to the Congregation de Propaganda Fide, demanding support for his endeavors. Rome kept a diplomatic silence for many years, and it was only after Euthymius's death that his innovations were condemned.[207]

The metropolitan's creativity was more in demand in the field of religious polemic. At the beginning of the first decade of the eighteenth century, he wrote a treatise *Kitab al-Dalalat al-Lami'a* (the *Brilliant Proof*) in which, over the course of more than four hundred pages, Euthymius justified the primacy of the Apostolic See of St Peter in the Christian world and denounced Orthodox dogmatic misconceptions about the Filioque, purgatory, and the nature of holiness.[208] The book was published in Rome in 1710 and a proportion of the printing was sent to Damascus and Aleppo. The following year, the keeper of the papal library, the prominent Maronite scholar Joseph Assemani, translated the treatise into Latin. In correspondence with the Congregation de Propaganda Fide in 1718, Sayfi insisted on the need to prepare a Greek translation of his book.

It seems that the *Brilliant Proof* had considerable resonance in the Arab East, because in December 1714, Patriarch Chrysanthos of Jerusalem, who was in Moldavia and Wallachia, opposed this treatise with a special encyclical, referring to Sayfi as a "heretic" and "blasphemer." In 1717, the metropolitan of Sidon requested that Rome send another three hundred copies of his book.[209] In 1722, the Synod of Constantinople imposed an anathema on Euthymius, specifically warning the Orthodox against reading his works and offering as an alternative the Arabic translation of the Greek anti-Latin treatise, the *Rock of Offense.*[210] Patriarch of Antioch Athanasius Dabbas who, by virtue of his position, was able to act as the main opponent of Euthymius al-Sayfi, made the translation.

To what degree did Euthymius's contemporaries, Patriarchs of Antioch Cyril al-Za'im and Athanasius Dabbas, correspond to that role? Cyril, a childhood friend of Euthymius, unlike his father and grandfather, had no inclination to literary activity. "His person and converse promis'd not any thing extraordinary," the British explorer Henry Maundrell summarized his impression from being in contact with him in 1697.[211] Cyril's literary legacy includes only a few letters and official documents, including a "forgiveness letter" in the case of Patriarch Nikon, the text of which was composed by Dositheus of Jerusalem; it only remained for Cyril to sign it. There are interesting autobiographical notes by Cyril about his being made patriarch and additions made by him to his grandfather's treatise on the diocesan bishops of Antioch. In this text, Cyril continued the list of metropolitans, naming the ordinations carried out by him and by his rivals, the "anti-patriarchs" Neophytus and Athanasius Dabbas. In the lines of the patriarch's terse entries, unremitting hatred for his old enemies comes through.[212]

Attributed to Cyril is an Arabic translation of the encyclical of the patriarch of Constantinople against Euthymius al-Sayfi. Joseph Nasrallah, however, doubts this, pointing out that the patriarch did not know Greek.[213] Cyril had neither the education nor the inclination for conducting anti-Latin polemic. As for Athanasius Dabbas, he was in no way inferior to Euthymius al-Sayfi in terms of education and intelligence. The patriarch knew Greek brilliantly and was well oriented in Byzantine and contemporary literature. Athanasius wrote a number of works of a canonical and homiletic character and translated from Greek sermons of John Chrysostom, the acts of the councils, instructions for priests, and commentaries on the Divine Liturgy.[214] The initiative to organize Arabic-language printing precisely belongs to Athanasius (see the following details). Spending a long time at the court of the Wallachian voivode Constantin Brâncoveanu, Athanasius made an attempt to introduce his Romanian patrons to the history of the Church of Antioch and composed a work on this in Greek. However, a researcher would look in vain for any original information or significant opinions of the author. Most of Athanasius's work is copied from Macarius's *History of the Patriarchs of Antioch*, with details that seemed unnecessarily removed in some places. Only the description of the eighteenth century is of definite interest, as Athanasius had to express his own version of events. The ex-patriarch's bias is even more pronounced than that of his rival Cyril. At the same time, Athanasius recognized with captivating frankness that certain unseemly events in the life of the Church of Antioch were "impossible to put down in writing."[215]

In 1705, the ex-patriarch prepared a translation of a philosophical treatise that had just been published in 1698 by the Moldavian aristocrat Dimitrie Cantemir (1673–1723), the future ruler of Moldavia and associate of Peter I. Cantemir's work, *The Dispute of the Wise Man with the World*,[216] devoted to problems of Christian ethics and the relationship between spiritual and material values in life, is more a work of virtuoso intelligence than the fruit of a serious spiritual quest by the young aristocrat. For Cantemir, publication of the treatise was part of his political game, what would now be called a "PR campaign." The questions the author raises and the answers he suggests also struck a chord with Athanasius. Athanasius brought the Arabic translation of the treatise to Aleppo, where the text was edited and finalized by the Maronite priest Gabriel Farhat, later known as Germanus Farhat, Maronite bishop of Aleppo and a major figure in early modern Arabic literature. In the cosmopolitan atmosphere of Aleppo, there was still the possibility of such creative collaboration between hierarchs of different confessions.

Athanasius himself was also somewhat cosmopolitan; his cultural and religious identity appears somewhat "blurry." The patriarch's decades-long double game between Orthodoxy and Catholicism indicate that he lacked a clear position in life or a fundamental orientation of values. One of the patriarch's Catholic contemporaries referred to him in irritation as "homo politicus." Athanasius's orientation caused no less concern in Phanariot circles. As mentioned, in the early 1720s, the Synod of Constantinople demanded that Athanasius provide unequivocal proof of his Orthodoxy. This resulted, in particular, in the publication under Athanasius's name of the anti-Latin treatise the *Rock of Offense*, attacking the Vatican's claims to hegemony. In fact, Athanasius was not the author, but rather the translator, expanding on the content of a polemical treatise by the Greek bishop Elias Miniatas published in Leipzig in 1718. The Arabic version was printed in London in 1721.[217]

Catholic authors who have written biographies of Athanasius are still inclined to regard him as one of their own. However, among those historians who have addressed the greatest Arab Uniate writer of the eighteenth century, 'Abdallah Zakher (1680–1748), the patriarch appears to be a fierce persecutor of Catholics. 'Abdallah was close to the patriarch for some time, participating in the printing activity in Aleppo and, as mentioned, acting as Athanasius's secretary. However, Zakher provoked serious anger from Athanasius with his first literary work, written in refutation of the Orthodox polemicist Gabriel, metropolitan of Philadelphia. The appearance in 1720 of Zakher's treatise the *Healing Antidote to the Philadelphian's Poison* coincided with Athanasius's final reorientation toward the Orthodox centers of power. Without waiting for the patriarch's return from Constantinople, 'Abdallah Zakher thought it wise to leave Aleppo and take refuge in the monasteries of Lebanon, where he remained until his death. Of the fourteen original treatises by 'Abdallah Zakher, eight are polemical in nature and (with the exception of two, addressed to the Armenians and the Protestants) are directed against the Orthodox. 'Abdallah analyzed controversial dogmatic positions, defending the Catholic view of the procession of the Holy Spirit and transubstantiation. Some of his works are polemical responses to the books of the Arab Orthodox intellectuals of the time, Elias Fakhr and Sophronius al-Kilizi.[218]

'Abdallah Zakher's literary output, as is generally true in the development of Melkite Uniate culture, was to some degree facilitated by the existence of a network of monasteries established by Uniates in the mountains of Lebanon. The monasteries served as a refuge for Uniate clergy in days of persecution and served as the economic centers of the country, and inside their walls, schools, writers, translators, and printers were all active. According to Carsten Walbiner, the Uniate monastic movement of the eighteenth century was fundamentally different from the earlier monastic tradition of the Middle East, which was focused on withdrawal from the world, contemplation, and asceticism. The head of the Shuwayrite Order, Nicholas Sayegh (1692–1756), a native of Aleppo and a close friend of 'Abdallah Zakher, was the one who managed to turn the face of emerging Uniate monasticism toward the world, transforming monasteries into centers of religious propaganda and education.[219] This was, perhaps, the main contribution of Nicholas al-Sayegh to Melkite culture, a contribution far greater than his theological writing, his editing translations of Jesuit treatises—something that earned him a rebuke from the Synod of Constantinople in 1723—or even his poetry, for which he was revered by his contemporaries most of all.[220]

Thus, by 1730, the balance of power had been definitively delineated: the Uniates formed into a separate church structure and launched a vigorous intellectual assault on the Orthodox. The Orthodox Church, the ground pulled out from beneath its feet, recognized the historic challenge and the need for an immediate response. Confrontation began between the two communities in various spheres of ideological debate and, more broadly, cultural activities.

Competing Educational Systems

> *He [the Uniate patriarch] intends to release small foxes into our vineyard, but Patriarch Cyril and I are preparing jackals [to be set] at the local religious school.*
>
> —Porphyry Uspensky, 1848

Arab Christians' interest in Catholicism and their positive outlook toward the Western missionaries can largely be explained by their awareness of the cultural superiority of the Europeans and the expectation of assistance from them in educating Middle Eastern Christians. Naturally, the Melkites of the seventeenth century had their own mechanisms of transmitting traditional knowledge, but they did not develop into a coherent system of education. The level of learning was limited to basic literacy and dogmatic instruction, with only a few seeking something more.

An estimate of the percentage of adult male Christians who were literate could only be based on massive archival materials, but such sources, unfortunately, are not available to us. To what degree did interest in books extend beyond the clergy? As a sample for analysis, we examined the first fifty manuscripts written before 1831 in the catalog of the patriarchal manuscript in Damascus. Among the copyists, owners, and readers who left notes in the margins of the manuscripts, the numbers of clergy and laity were almost equal: thirty-four (including bishops) and thirty-seven, respectively. If we divide them into groups by century, in the sixteenth and seventeenth centuries, we see that the proportion of clergy to laity was somewhat greater at sixteen to fourteen, while in the eighteenth and early nineteenth centuries, the proportion of laity increased, to eighteen clergymen and twenty-three laypeople.

However, even among the clergy, literacy was not universal. Western travelers of the eighteenth century constantly reproached the Arab monks for their ignorance:

> The young monks were more occupied with field work than with practicing spiritual meditation and solitude, to which they devoted themselves just as little as they did to study. This is the reason that the monks are usually so ... ignorant that in the biggest monasteries you can hardly find such that might at least understand something written in Greek, the

language in which all their services and prayers are written (Monseigneur Grelot, mid-seventeenth century).²²¹

He was echoed by the Englishman Henry Maundrell, who visited Balamand in 1697,

> I found upon inquiry that they could not give any manner of rationale of their own divine service. And to show their extreme simplicity, I cannot omit a compliment made to the consul by the chief of them, viz. that he was glad to see him, as if he had beheld the Messiah himself coming in person to make a visit to him.²²²

Europeans, who misunderstood the national psychology of the people with whom they were dealing, of course, exaggerated the "simplicity" of Arab Christians. Similarly, the Russian pilgrim Leonty, who wanted to sketch a plan of Mar Saba in 1765, faced the problem of a lack of writing materials in the Lavra: "But, they recounted, there has been no paper in the Lavra, almost since the time of the holy father John of Damascus."²²³ One might take all of this seriously if one does not know about the forty-six codices transcribed by monks at the Lavra in the eighteenth century²²⁴ or about the two hundred manuscripts stored at Balamand Monastery. However, one must admit the ignorance of some of the monks, to say nothing of the laity.

Learning to read was sometimes private. In 1645, the metropolitan of Aleppo wrote to one of his alms collectors, "Your son Bishara is already working and producing two units of linen a day. His brother John has learned to read the Psalter and has begun to learn Greek. Your brother, the Deacon Niʿma is teaching him to read [Greek]."²²⁵

Alongside private instruction, there were early forms of parochial schools—circles of students studying with a local priest. In 1706, Patriarch Dositheus attempted to organize primary education in his patriarchate and to place it on a firm financial footing. Having received a donation from a wealthy Phanariot, the patriarch put the annual salary of the *hieropsaltes* of the Church of the Resurrection at 30 qurush, and he would teach church singing to monks of the Holy Sepulchre and to the children of laymen. Another 20 qurush was allocated to priests in Gaza, Ramla, Tayba, Beit Jala, and Kerak to teach Greek and Arabic grammar.²²⁶ It is worth noting that, apart from Gaza, these settlements amounted to large villages. That is, education penetrated somewhat deep into the rural hinterland. In the village of Tayba, as mentioned, in the mid-nineteenth century,

Porphyry Uspensky found an entire library of Arabic apocryphal literature, including records of rare legends and tales of miracles, including some of local origin.[227]

The system of education in the patriarchate functioned even without Dositheus's infusions of money. Already in 1701, five years before the patriarch's instructions, I. Lukyanov described the instruction of Arab children in Ramla,

> And the way they study is different from ours: from the morning until noon he learns the Horologion or the Psalter, then from noon until evening—the stichera in the Octoechos and the Menaion[228] that fall on that day, and then he says them in church.[229]

After mastering Arabic reading and writing, the students switched to Greek, "They know Greek letters well and sing well, but the simple language they do not know, nor [do they have] the knowledge of books, they will not figure out the Greek books."[230] That is, Greek texts and hymnography were learned by heart, without understanding the meaning of the words. It is possible that there were similar primary schools, only much less affected by Greek influence, in the cities of the Patriarchate of Antioch. Needless to say that Roman Catholic education was at a much more advanced level. Since the time of the Counter-Reformation, the leaders of the Catholic Church had realized that the system of education was their main defensive and offensive weapon. The Jesuits in Rome established a number of colleges, including ones aimed at the training of Eastern Christians. These institutions had the highest standard of education in the world. For two hundred years, the mechanism of selecting and training talented young people from the Christian East was tried and tested in the Maronite community.

When, in the second third of the seventeenth century, Western missionaries opened their schools in Damascus and Aleppo, the Orthodox took it quite positively. Far from the religious conflicts in Eastern Europe, the Arab bishops were not even able to imagine the problems that the Catholic presence would cause within two or three generations. The flowers of the Orthodox youth of Damascus—Neophytus al-Saqizi, Euthymius al-Sayfi, and Athanasius Dabbas—passed through the Jesuits' school. In Aleppo, which scholars call the "intellectual and religious center of Arab Christianity" in the seventeenth and eighteenth centuries,[231] Catholic education structures were even more widely represented. In the second half of the seventeenth century, a graduate of the Collegium Maronitarum, Butrus al-Tulani, founded *al-maktab al-maruni*, the Maronite School, in Aleppo on the model of the Roman colleges.[232]

In the late seventeenth century, there formed in Aleppo a circle of young Christian intellectuals, longing for enlightenment. It included the Maronite Gabriel (Germanus) Farhat—the oldest in the group; the future Uniate leaders Maximus al-Hakim, ʿAbdallah Zakher, and Nicholas al-Sayegh; and members of the Maronite and Armenian communities. Aware of the loss of knowledge of literary Arabic among Christians, they turned to a prominent Muslim philologist, Sheikh Sulayman al-Nahawi, who began to teach them Arabic grammar and style. According to some sources, the Melkite priest Michael Baja, who had studied for a time in Rome, taught ʿAbdallah Zakher and his comrades theology, philosophy, and mathematics. Butrus al-Tulawi, himself also an expert in theology and ancient philosophy, introduced his Melkite students to the basics of Western thought and the views of the Catholic Church on many religious and secular issues.[233]

Typically, even if the Christian middle class of Aleppo saw the benefits of education, it was only at the primary level. The father of Nicholas al-Sayegh made sure that his son mastered Arabic letters, but then took him out of school and had him trained in the family trade of jewelry-making.[234] Nicholas, however, made a different choice, going to the monks, and eventually played a decisive role in forming the Shuwayrite Order, with its focus on the world and spreading education.

In particular, the monasteries, especially Shuwayr and Dayr Mar Mukhallis, became the basis for Arab Catholics' educational system. No doubt, primary schools also existed among the Uniates in urban centers, but there is little information about them and the precarious situation of Uniate clergy in major cities did not allow for the creation of serious educational structures. On the other hand, in the Lebanese monasteries, the Uniates felt confident, and Nicholas Sayegh considered one of the main tasks for monastic leaders to be educating their coreligionists.[235]

At the Monastery of Mar Yuhanna, there operated a primary school for children of the laity. Those who wished to do so could continue studying secular subjects, such as medicine, within the walls of the monastery. Its system of training was developed for young monks. It included both the teaching of religious sciences and mastering the rule of the order, as well as worldly knowledge, particularly printing and bookbinding.[236]

Specific information about the educational program in the Uniate monasteries does not survive. On the basis of the Shuwayrite collection of books, Carsten Walbiner has attempted to reconstruct the monks' range of reading and educational interests. Typically, with rare exceptions, the Uniate scribes did not know foreign languages and did not keep European books in their monasteries. The monks used literature in translation extensively, but the translations from Western languages were mainly represented by the genres of theology and historiography. The most popular of the secular sciences was philology, and in the monastery were kept dozens of grammatical treatises by Muslim linguists and their Arab Christian colleagues, especially Germanus Farhat. In terms of philosophical ideas, the Shuwayrites were familiar with commentaries on Aristotle and the Isagoge of Porphyry, as well as the treatises of Bulus al-Tulani and of a student of 'Abdallah Zakher, Joachim al-Mitran (1696–1766). The monks were interested in Muslim literature. Sixteen manuscripts have been preserved there with content related to this, including texts of the Qur'an, hadith, works about fiqh, Islamic dogma, and Qur'anic exegesis. The Uniates also viewed astrology, geography, and medicine through the prism of the Arab Islamic tradition. The monastery in Shuwayr became famous as a center of medical science, which is confirmed by the twenty-two manuscripts preserved there on medical topics. However, the Shuwayrites do not seem to have had any idea of developments in contemporary European medicine. The monks also valued Arabic belletristic literature, including *Kalila wa-Dimna*, the Maqamat of al-Hariri, and the poetry of Abu 'Ala al-Ma'arri. The Christian poets Nicholas al-Sayegh, Germanus Farhat, Hanania al-Munayir, and many others whose works were read and copied in the monastery found inspiration in Muslim poetry.[237]

In other words, the monks took only a little from European science and, generally, remained in the bosom of the traditional culture of the Middle East. Accordingly, European observers looked down on them. Carsten Walbiner mentioned the exceedingly skeptical comments made by Constantin Volney about the Shuwayrites, whom he regarded as just as ignorant as the rest of the Syrians. When the French scholar tried, for example, to explain to the monks that the earth revolves around the sun, some of them accused him of heresy.[238]

However, the upper hierarchs of the Uniate community recognized the superiority of European science and sought to introduce the most talented of their coreligionists to it. The rule of the Shuwayrite brotherhood, developed in the 1730s, specifically states a program of selecting the most capable of the monks between the ages of eighteen and forty for an eight-year course of studies in Rome at the College of St Athanasius consisting of Arabic, Greek, logic, philosophy, theology, and, in cases of obvious ability, Latin. Although the pope approved the Shuwayrites' rule and allocated one of the churches of Rome for the order, funds for training Lebanese monks could be found neither at the Vatican nor in Shuwayr. The project nearly failed. During the entire eighteenth century, only one monk from Shuwayr received an education in Rome, as well as eight monks from Dayr al-Mukhallis[239] and half a dozen other members of the Uniate Melkite community, mostly natives of Aleppo. In the late 1760s, the Melkite patriarch twice appealed to the Vatican with a request to accept a group of monks to study in one of the Latin colleges of Rome. However, the cardinals refused him this, perhaps at the instigation of Melkite students in Rome who feared that Arabs would lose their identity in the Latin schools.[240]

These concerns were not idle, if we take into account the experience of Ukrainian Uniates who studied in Italy in the seventeenth century. They left the Uniate Church in droves and transferred to "full-fledged" Latin Catholicism. A similar attempt was also made by the Melkite priest Dionysius Hajjar (d. 1790), a graduate of the College of St Urban who worked as a translator at the Congragation De Propaganda Fide.[241] However, he was refused permission to enter into the Latin rite: the Vatican had need of proven cadres specifically in the Uniate Church structures.

Is it possible to say that graduates of the College of St Athanasius became the intellectual elite of the Melkite community? Not all of them returned to the Middle East; some chose to stay in Rome. Most worked in the field of translation from Latin and Italian and taught theology at Dayr al-Mukhallis, but they hardly left any original works. Others reached the episcopate, as was the case of the first Uniate patriarch, Cyril Tanas. Only a few of those who studied in Rome became scholars at the European level, capable of advancing Arab Christian scholarship and culture. Among these can be mentioned the historian Yuhanna al-'Ujaymi (1724–1785) and the metropolitan of Aleppo and brilliant polemicist and theologian Germanus Adam (1725–1809).

Overall, however, the students who did their studies in Rome formed the intellectual environment to which Melkite culture owes its high level and large amount of literary production. Thanks to them, Arab Christian society realized the need for its own system of higher education. Eventually, in 1811, the Uniates established their own seminary in the Lebanese village of Ain Traz. The Orthodox undertook a similar effort eighty years earlier. Patriarch Sylvester, who took the reins of the Church of Antioch during a time of deep crisis, was keenly aware of the intellectual superiority of his Catholic opponents. Just as the Arab Uniates sought to rely on the Roman system of education, Sylvester also sought outside support, from the Greek Enlightenment. At that time, the largest Orthodox educational center of the Eastern Mediterranean was the Academy of Patmos, where Macarius Kalogeras taught, usually at the elementary level, grammar, rhetoric, theology, philosophy, Greek, and Latin. Around 1725, Sylvester turned

to Macarius for assistance in organizing a religious school in Syria. Macarius recommended for this task his favorite student and assistant, James, who left for the
Middle East in 1726.

In the previous chapter, we discussed the vicissitudes of the fate of James of
Patmos and his school, which would change its location three times in the period
between 1726 and 1734. James's school was composed of two stages. The lower
stage held general courses for about a hundred Arab children, while the higher
stage was for novices in monasteries, candidates for the priesthood, and clergy.
James taught them theology and philosophy. Presumably, the curriculum replicated that of the Patmos Academy, with the addition of a number of subjects
studied in Arabic and with an emphasis on preaching and anti-Latin polemic.
Education was free and the poorest students received an allowance from the
patriarchate. The school received students from all over Syria and from even
farther afield. Among those known to have studied with James are Philotheus,
the future archbishop of Cyprus (1734–1759); Ioannicius, the future metropolitan
of Beirut (1745–1774); and the Russian traveler V. Grigorovich-Barsky, who left
a laudatory description of his teacher. During the long years of his stay in the
Middle East, James seems not to have learned Arabic. On the contrary, he saw his
mission as introducing the Arabs to Greek culture.

In his letters to James, Macarius Kalogeras praised him for reviving interest
in the Greek "teachers" in the East, whereas, according to him, "previously ...
these works were lying under a bushel, serving as food for moths and covered
with dust."[242] The *didaskalos* worked closely with Macarius, who sent to Syria
textbooks and texts of sermons to help James's students. In his correspondence,
Macarius constantly supported James, urging him not to think about returning home, but to carry the cross of his ministry in Antioch. Thus, after James's
imprisonment in Aleppo in 1728, Macarius wrote to his disciple,

> The news of your exploits and your imprisonment for the truth reached
> as far as to our region and while it induces some to mourn for you, as for
> me—I rejoice and am glad because my lord, James, has already put to the
> test the apostolic labors and has been subject to those very same chains ...
> I am asking you to stay courageous to the end and do not grow weak
> in the line of duty ... because that would be a betrayal of justice to your
> honor, to the hope that many have in you, and to your praise.[243]

As mentioned, James eventually left Syria together with the Patriarch Sylvester. Soon, however, the teacher's knowledge was once again in demand in the

Christian East. Among circles of the Brotherhood of the Holy Sepulchre, the idea ripened to open a theological school in Palestine. Patriarch Meletius of Jerusalem asked James to take the post of scholarch, head of the future institution. In August 1736, James left for Palestine and, by the end of that year, he began to teach at the newly established school. The school, like its Syrian predecessor, had two sections: primary education for the Arab Orthodox youth and advanced training for the educated clergy of the Brotherhood of the Holy Sepulchre. The curriculum consisted of Greek, Latin, and Arabic; the study of the Holy Scriptures and the patristic heritage; ancient, Byzantine, and post-Byzantine Greek literature; and logic, philosophy, and mathematics. Particular attention was paid to preparing graduates for preaching activities.[244] As with James's previous school in Syria, the school in Jerusalem attracted students from all over the Eastern Mediterranean. Some of James's assistants, mostly Greeks, taught alongside him.

The available sources do not permit us to evaluate objectively the quality of teaching in James's schools. A. P. Lebedev once attempted to evaluate the level of instruction at the Patmos Academy,[245] which James sought to emulate, and the historian's evaluation was rather skeptical. He cites a phrase from a letter by Macarius Kalogeras to the Patriarch Sylvester: "Let it be known, that this barren island did not produce and will not produce *didaskaloi* [i.e., people well versed in the sciences], for the feebleness of the teachers [here Macarius attests to him] and only mere copyists of the sciences."[246]

Of course, one should not compare the schools of Macarius and James to the Roman colleges, but by the standards of the Middle East, the level of the Greek schools may have been quite high and comparable to the missionary schools. It should be noted, incidentally, that Grigorovich-Barsky spent many years profitably studying with both *didaskaloi*, Macarius and James, and Grigorovich-Barsky had already studied in the colleges of Kiev and Lvov and could debate as an equal with Uniate Patriarch Cyril, whom he met in one of the Lebanese monasteries.[247]

The *didaskalos* died in 1765. How long did the school continue to operate after James's death? Sophronius and Ephraim, the future patriarchs of Jerusalem, are named as James's successors at the head of the school.[248] In the case of the former, the error is obvious: after his being made a metropolitan in 1740, he is unlikely to have returned to Jerusalem. Even if Ephraim helped an elderly James with teaching, he did this for a brief period of time because of his rapidly progressing ecclesiastical career: in the autumn of 1765, Ephraim became a metropolitan, and the following year, he was elevated to the patriarchate. It seems more convincing to posit that after James's death, the school placed one of its best students, Anthimus, himself also a future patriarch, at the head.[249] Because Arabic was Anthimus's native language, the school must have maintained some connection with the Middle Eastern soil and perhaps there was a certain number of Arabs among the advanced students. Upon becoming patriarch in 1788, Anthimus handed the school over to his former pupil, Archimandrite Maximus Simaius,²⁵⁰ who was also discussed at the beginning of this chapter. Maximus lived until 1810. It is difficult to say whether the school existed up to that time, through such upheavals as Napoleon's Syrian campaign and the fire at the Church of the Holy Sepulchre, with all their disastrous consequences for the Church of Jerusalem. In any case, if any educational activity continued after Maximus, it had to have died out during the period of persecutions in the 1820s, when the very existence of the Brotherhood of the Holy Sepulchre came into doubt.

On the basis of the observations of Porphyry Uspensky, we can conclude that during the first half of the nineteenth century, schooling in the Patriarchates of Antioch and Jerusalem declined to an elementary level. In cities such as Tripoli, Jaffa, and Acre, there were parochial schools with dozens of students. Greek and Arabic were taught there, but Greek was not in demand and it did not take root, all the more so because an archaic and bookish Greek was taught in these schools instead of the spoken language.²⁵¹ In large villages, priests taught the children of *fellahin* to read. Naturally, there was no question of teaching Greek literature. The clergy differed little from the *fellahin* in their lifestyle and level of culture. Porphyry Uspensky recalled meeting a priest and teacher in Beit Jala, "His bare feet were quite black and his head covered with a greasy turban, which is usually worn by the secular Arab priests. 'A fit teacher,' I thought."²⁵²

There is evidence from Porphyry's time for the existence of primary schools in monasteries, although such schools, of course, had existed earlier. Even in the women's monastery of Saydnaya, there were three women who received salaries from the patriarch to teach reading and writing, not only to the nuns of the monastery but also to girls from the neighboring village.²⁵³ There are manuscripts copied by one of these teachers, the nun Thekla. She is apparently the only female scribe in Ottoman Syria.²⁵⁴ In 1830, the abbot of Balamand Monastery, Athanasius, established a school for his monks, which he dreamed of turning into an institution for advanced study. He hoped that this seminary would train Arab clergy worthy of being named bishops and of competing with the Greek higher clergy. The Greek patriarch of Antioch soon put a stop to this dangerous endeavor, removing Athanasius from the monastery and closing the school.²⁵⁵

Both Thekla and Athanasius, however, were already people of another era, when traditional society began to transform in the Middle East and was becoming aware of new values and priorities. "At first, the local Orthodox feared science like the plague. Now, the quest for learning is apparent," the Damascene priest Yusuf Muhanna al-Haddad, one of the leading figures of Orthodox education in the mid-nineteenth century, told Porphyry.[256]

It seems fairly obvious that during the eighteenth century the Uniates succeeded more than the Orthodox in developing a system of education. But is it legitimate to explain the success of the Unia and the intellectual superiority of the Melkite Catholics by the fact that they adopted the latest achievements of European science and culture? The Uniates relied on a legacy of Western thought that was traditional, religious, and medieval in spirit and ignored the Europeans' latest developments in science (which would become popular a century later, during the so-called Arab Nahda). It is not for nothing that from the standpoint of a typical man of the Enlightenment, such as Constantin Volney, the translation and publishing activities of the Uniates started out in the wrong direction, "Instead of translating works containing practical benefit and thus stimulating … a taste for sciences, [the Melkites] translated mystical books, the reading of which produces, rather than morals, only boredom."[257] That is to say, the difference between the Orthodox and Uniate cultures was not one of quality, but of quantity. Some read translations of John Chrysostom, others read Ignatius of Loyola, but all remained equally within the framework of medieval religious consciousness.

From a modern point of view, among both the Orthodox and the Catholics, higher schooling was divorced from the practical necessities of life and focused on abstract theological knowledge. However, such knowledge was the basis of the cultural content of the era, what makes a person a full-fledged personality. Additionally, abstract philosophical disciplines stimulated students' intellectual development, and the ability to think logically and to develop any complex concepts.

Why were the educational activities of James of Patmos in Syria so short-lived and relatively unsuccessful? It appears that the chief problem of the Orthodox high school (although it would be more correct to refer to it as a "middle school") was that it was firmly focused on Greek models and had little connection to its Arab context. James spent forty years in Syria and Palestine and did not attempt to learn Arabic. All sermons and teaching materials had to be translated from Greek into Arabic, and the quality of the translations is unclear. James, no doubt, felt somewhat uncomfortable in an Arab environment. He was well aware of the ineffectiveness of his teaching efforts, which ran into the language barrier. Add to this the fierce opposition of the Catholics and a lack of financial and political support from the Orthodox hierarchy, and James's psychological breakdown and decision to leave Syria with Sylvester becomes clear: without the patriarch's protection, James did not want to stay in Damascus.

Interior of the Basilica of the Nativity in Bethlehem. Built by Justinian, it is the oldest extant church in Palestine. Ancient byzantine mosaics are exposed on the upper walls and under the floors.

Patriarch of Jerusalem Dositheos Notaras (1669-1707). In the early 1670s, Patriarch Dositheus undertook extensive work on the reconstruction of the Basilica of the Nativity in Bethlehem.

The writings of Macarius III (al-Za'im) Patriarch of Antioch, 1647-1672, form the basis of modern Arab Orthodox historiography.

ΟΟΟΙ ΠΑΤΕΡ ΗΜΩΝ
ΑΝΑ5ΑΣΙ ΣΙΝΛ ΟΡΣ

ΑΝΑ5ΑΣΙ ΕΝ ΣΙΝΑ ΜΟΣΗΣ
ΝΕΘ ΚΑΙ ΠΕΝ ΤΛΕΥ ΤΣ
ΤΝ ΘΕΟΝ ΒΛΕΠΕΙΝ
ΕΧΕΙ

17th century icon of St Anastasius of Sinai (d. ca. 700) from St Catherine's monastery. An accurate depiction of a monk of the Near East.

St Sergius, 13th century icon from Sinai. The iconographic style is identical to the frescoes of the 12th and 13th-century Syrian churches of the Qalamun Plateau.

The holy stylites Simeon the Elder and Simeon the Younger. 1699 icon by the hand of the priest Yusuf al-Musawwir.

St Simeon the Stylite the Younger. Pre-1667 icon by Yusuf al-Musawwir. "Al-Musawwir" means "the artist".

© Lukk | Dreamstime.com

Yusuf al-Musawwir is considered to be the founder of the Aleppo school of iconography. Four generations of his family inherited his vocation. The most significant diocesan centers of the Antiochian See were Damascus and Aleppo.

Panorama and details of the Citadel of Aleppo.

© Bluedpp | Dreamstime.com

© Karolina Vyskocilova | Dreamstime.com

© Zoom-zoom | Dreamstime.com

1722 icon of "The Triumph of Orthodoxy", by Yusuf's grandson,
Hanania al-Musawwir.

Mar Saba in a green Judean desert after spring rains

Dome of the Church of the Resurrection over the Holy Edicule containing the Holy Sepulchre.

The Moldavian ruler, Vasile Lupu (1634–1653), provided generous financial assistance to the Orthodox churches of the Ottoman world, including the Holy Sepulchre.

© Aoldman | Dreamstime.com

Constantin Brâncoveanu, King of Wallachia, 1698-1714, was a generous patron of Patriarch Chrysanthos of Jerusalem. Brâncoveanu subsidized the restoration of Mar Saba as well as the work of the Holy Sepulchre's printing house in Bucharest.

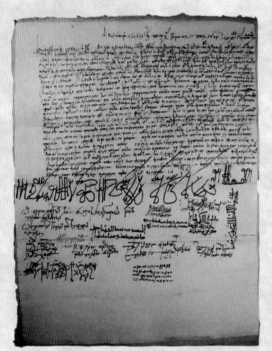

Before his departure from Moscow in the spring of 1656, Patriarch Macarius ibn al-Za'im petitioned the tsar requesting letters for three Syrian monasteries—Saydnaya, Balamand, and St George Humayra—for the right to receive alms from Russia in the future. This is the letter sent on November 1, 1656 from Târgoviște to Tsar Alexei Michalovich. The Greek text is sealed with the Arabic signature, executed by Paul of Aleppo, who's handwriting was far better than his father's.

Above and below: The letter of the Antiochian Patriarch Joachim ibn Ziyada to Tsar Theodore Ivanovich, April 1596. At the bottom of the letter are signatures of Antiochian hierarchs written in Greek and Arabic and Melkite Garshuni script. The majority of signatures, including the patriarch's, are rendered by the same hand, ostensibly by the scribe of the letter.

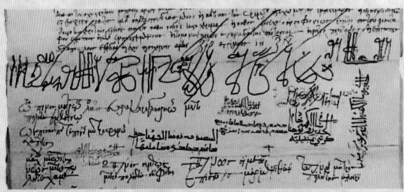

It is noteworthy that the *didaskalos*' activity in Palestine was much more productive. This can be explained by his comfort in a Greek-speaking environment and the absence of any Catholic rivals in the vicinity. In the literature, however, some conflicts are mentioned in the Brotherhood of the Holy Sepulchre in association with James's school. Perhaps the training of young, educated clergy rankled some of the semiliterate metropolitans. Nevertheless, the school operated successfully for decades. But despite the fact that both successors of the *didaskalos*, Anthimus and Maximus Simaius, knew Arabic, the proportion of Arab students at the seminary seems to have remained small.

The Arabs needed a school based on the Greek model of education, but without Phanariote linguistic chauvinism. However, Arab Orthodox intellectuals had not yet reached the critical mass necessary to create their own seminary: they were too scattered in time and space. When Sophronius al-Kilizi was conducting his patriarchate in Constantinople, Anthimus was leading the school in Jerusalem; Masʿad Nashw was preaching in Cairo; Elias Fakhr and Yusuf Mark had already died; and the young Athanasius Khubbaza was still beginning his ecclesiastical career, practicing asceticism in the Monastery of Sinai.

A DUEL OF THEOLOGIANS

Both sides—the Orthodox and the Uniates—quickly mastered the entire set of arguments that had been constructed by the thinkers of the Western and Eastern churches over the previous nine hundred years. The ecclesio-political struggle between supporters of Orthodoxy and Catholicism in Aleppo, Damascus, and Beirut—all the litigation, clashes, boycotts of liturgies, and arrests—was accompanied by a veritable literary battle between theologians of both confessions. Rarely did a year go by in the eighteenth century without the appearance of a new apologetic or denunciatory treatise from the pens of the rival camps' scribes.

Assessing the quality of the polemical literature, the coherence and convincing nature of the arguments, is no less problematic than discussing the quality of Melkite iconography. We are inclined to avoid passing judgments on this question. Perhaps philosophers and theologians are better able to answer this. It is only possible to make an objective judgment about the quantitative parameters of literary production. Joseph Nasrallah gives the names of twenty-five Uniate polemicists for the period from 1724 to 1800 and thirteen names of their Orthodox opponents. Under the label of "Phanariot," the historian includes not only the compilers of polemical treatises, but also those who wrote on any religious themes as well as translators of theological writings. One can add to this list of authors eight Catholic patriarchs (of which only Maximus al-Hakim left a noteworthy literary legacy) and four Orthodox patriarchs of Antioch, two Arab patriarchs of Jerusalem, as well as around ten Uniate and a dozen Orthodox anonymous polemical texts. The final ratio is roughly three to four in favor of the Uniates. The gap in intellectual forces cannot be called large. The high creative output of certain Orthodox authors also should be mentioned.

One of the greatest figures among such Orthodox authors is the Tripolitan Elias Fakhr (1680–1758). The same age as the deacon 'Abdallah Zakher, the deacon Elias appears to be his mirror image from the other side of the barricades. In 1711, while Zakher was serving as secretary to the former Orthodox Patriarch Athanasius, Fakhr converted to Catholicism, an unsurprising move in the context of the pro-Western orientation of Melkite merchants. Elias was certainly an extraordinary man. He immediately attracted the attention of the Vatican and corresponded with cardinals and the pope. The "Knight of St Peter," as Elias referred to himself at the time, produced a series of Arabic translations of treatises by Catholic writers, some with anti-Orthodox content. His knowledge of Greek, Italian, and English and his commercial ties helped him to have a career in the British diplomatic missions of the Levant. From 1724, Fakhr served as dragoman of the British consulate in Aleppo. At that time, the native of Tripoli became friends with Patriarch Athanasius and was elevated by him to the diaconate. Athanasius used Elias's talents in controversies with his opponents, particularly with 'Abdallah Zakher. Such cooperation between a philo-Catholic and an Orthodox patriarch was quite possible in a situation in which the schism had still not received its organizational form and the religious beliefs of many clerics were of a diffuse and unstable character.

However, the ideological position of Elias Fakhr was soon made clear. Around 1725 or 1726, he made a conscious return to Orthodoxy. Patriarch Sylvester named him logothete of the Church of Antioch. In the previous chapter, it was mentioned that in 1726 Elias helped the patriarch avoid prison and leave the city, and in 1727, he secured the release of James of Patmos from prison. From the 1730s to 1750s, Fakhr acted as one of the most influential patrons of the Orthodox community in Aleppo. Thus, after the expulsion of Metropolitan Sophronius al-Kilizi and Aleppo's coming to be under a Uniate metropolitan, the last remaining adherents of Orthodoxy could meet for worship only in the house of Elias Fakhr who, by virtue of his status as the English dragoman, could be unafraid of persecution from the Ottoman authorities. Around 1757, after some blunder in his service, Fakhr was removed from working at the English consulate and sent to Tripoli, where he soon died.

Elias Fakhr was the author of eleven polemical anti-Latin treatises (those of which that are dated come from the period from 1727 to 1752), mostly in the form of refutations of the works of Catholic thinkers. He wrote about all the points of controversy in the doctrines of the two churches: the procession of the Holy Spirit, the understanding of the sacrament of the Eucharist, the circumstances of the Photian Schism,[258] the Union of Florence, and so on. Alongside his original works, Elias translated many Greek polemical treatises about purgatory, the primacy of the papacy, and other dogmatic differences between the Eastern and Western churches. European missionaries and Arab Catholic writers, in turn, wrote refutations in response to a number of Fakhr's writings.[259]

An even greater figure among the Orthodox polemicists was Sophronius al-Kilizi (1710–1781), who was born in a small town north of Aleppo. Sophronius appears in the sources starting in 1730 as a deacon in Aleppo and a little later as Patriarch Sylvester's secretary. Sophronius called himself a disciple of the *didaskalos* James of Patmos. They may have met in Syria, and there is no doubt that Sophronius studied with James in in Jerusalem in the late 1730s. The first translations of Greek theological works by the deacon date from 1733. That is, he composed them at a relatively young age. In 1740, the hierarchy of the Patriarchate of Jerusalem decided to place Sophronius on the episcopal see of Acre. He asked to postpone his consecration for a year so that he could complete his studies with James. However, the Brotherhood of the Holy Sepulchre needed to close a gap in the line of defense against Catholic expansion and in the most vulnerable position. Acre was fast becoming the chief port of the Eastern Mediterranean, had a large Arab Christian population, and was one of the centers of Catholic propaganda. During his time as metropolitan of Acre, Sophronius became a key figure in the ecclesio-political struggle in the region. ʿAbdallah Zakher wrote a treatise against him and Patriarch Sylvester published in Iasi translations of Greek anti-Latin literature made by Sophronius. The most dramatic period of the metropolitan's life is associated with his time on the See of Aleppo (1750–1752), which ended, as mentioned, with a few months of captivity and a few months of harsh imprisonment. This discouraged Sophronius from having any interest in politics for a long time. After moving to Constantinople following his release, he categorically refused offers for him to return to the See of Aleppo or to take the reins of the Church of Antioch after Sylvester in 1766. Nevertheless, as mentioned, in the last decade of his life Sophronius was able to hold two patriarchal sees and became the only Arab to head the Church of Constantinople.

The peak of Sophronius's literary activity came in the 1730s through the 1750s. He prepared Arabic versions of the basic works of Greek polemical literature from the relatively recent—the writings of Patriarch Nectarius of Jerusalem—to documents from the mid-fifteenth century about the Eastern patriarchs' rejection of the Union of Florence. In 1739, Sophronius translated a selection of ready-made polemical texts, the anti-Catholic compilation published by Dositheus in Iasi in 1682. In addition to these works, the future patriarch made a compilation from Greek literature on the subject of Christian pedagogy, translated the catechism of James of Patmos, and wrote original treatises on the differences of belief between Orthodoxy and Catholicism.

The works of Elias Fakhr and Sophronius provoked polemical responses from ʿAbdallah Zakher and a group of his Shuwayrite students, among which were Joachim Mitran (1696–1766) and Sulayman Qattan (d. 1799), Zakher's successor as head of the Shuwayrite printing press. Joachim Mitran was one of the most prolific Uniate authors. In the 1740s and 1750s, he composed numerous polemical writings in defense of Catholic dogma as well as collections of sermons and books on logic and philosophy.[260] The sheer number of Uniate polemicists was quite high. Elias Fakhr alone had at least five Catholic opponents.

Melkite Uniate authors can be divided into geographic groups: the circle of Shuwayrite authors, the Salvatorian (Mukhallisiya) Order, and representatives of the clergy in Aleppo. Among the monks of Dayr Mar Mukhallis, the most striking polemicist was the priest Yusuf Babila (d. 1787), a native of Sidon. He studied in Rome, was the secretary of Cyril Tanas, and taught theology at the Monastery of Mar Mukhallis. Although Yusuf rejected the offer of the episcopal see of Sidon and remained a simple priest, his authority in the Uniate Church was no less than that of the bishops. Babila was actively involved in the polemic between the Shuwayrite and Salvatorian orders and in the struggle to expel Athanasius Jawhar from the patriarchal throne in the 1760s. He also participated in the development of his order's rule, wrote about current affairs, and ruled on legal issues.[261] Babila's chief opponent from the Orthodox camp was Yusuf Mark (d. 1773 or 1774), a native of Tripoli and protosyngellos of the Church of Antioch. His first literary effort, a refutation of the doctrine of papal supremacy, dates to 1748. Living in Beirut in the early 1750s, Mark supervised the Orthodox printing house and opened a school "of linguistic and theological sciences."[262] The author of the Beirut Chronicle was generous in his praise of Yusuf, calling him "the teacher of bibliophiles" and "the best of priests, luminary of the theological sciences, the glory of Arab writers."[263] In the early 1760s, Yusuf Babila was in Beirut where, at the request of the physician Jibraʾil Jilda, he wrote two treatises on the procession of the Holy Spirit from the Catholic point of view. Yusuf Mark immediately reacted to the revitalization of Catholic thought in his city and responded with a treatise addressed "to Jilda and his teacher the priest Babila." Babila then wrote a new work expanding on his theses about the Filioque, entitling it in the manner of Arab scribes "Sharh al-'Aqida al-'Adima al-Dark bi-Dahd Ajwibat al-Khuri Yusuf Mark" ("An Explanation of the Ineffable Dogma in Refutation of the Priest Yusuf Mark"). Yusuf responded with the treatise "Kitab al-Burhan al-Jali al-Mu'taliya li-Dahd Ajwibat al-Khuri Yusuf Bab al-al-Bala'" ("The Book of Clear and Sublime Proof for Refuting the Responses of the Priest Yusuf, Gate of Woe"—here Mark plays on his opponent's name, changing "Babila" to "Bab al-Bala'" or "Gate of Woe"). Both Yusufs seem to have derived a certain degree of pleasure from going over to personal debate. They exchanged another pair of treatises on transubstantiation, composed in the form of rebukes of each other's false beliefs.[264]

Yusuf Mark died during the period of the Russo–Turkish War when Beirut was occupied by Russian troops. Therefore, the famous theologian was honored with a funeral ceremony impossible for *dhimmis* under *shari'a*. "They carried him from his home to the church with lighted candles," wrote the Beirut Chronicler, a stunning and unprecedented ceremony.

> They carried the cross in front and behind this came more priests in their *epitrachelia*, then finally, bringing up the rear, was the metropolitan with Russian officers, junior officers, and a crowd of Christians.... In [Mark] the Christians lost a spiritual teacher and precious writer.[265]

Another Arab Orthodox theologian of the eighteenth century who can be put alongside Sophronius al-Kilizi is his contemporary Mas'ad Nashw. He was born in Damascus and moved to Egypt, where he became economos of the Patriarchal See of Alexandria. Little is known about Mas'ad, despite the large number and prestige of his works. The dates of his birth and death have not been established and so it is only possible to speak of the period of his literary activity as being between 1740 and 1785. During this time, he wrote more than a dozen original polemical works, including a refutation of the Council of Florence entitled "Kitab al-Tafnid didd al-Majmu' al-'Anid" ("The Book of Rebuking the Recalcitrant Council"), as well as sermons, letters, responses to Latinophrones, and a refutation of the doctrine of purgatory. Mas'ad debated this issue with the head of the Salvatorian Order, Mikhail Abu Arraj (d. 1798). Mas'ad translated a great deal from Greek—from works of Saints Athanasius and John Chrysostom to the latest anti-Catholic pamphlets. Patriarch Sylvester published some of these translations in Iasi in the 1740s.[266]

The last major writer of this period was a native of Damascus, Athanasius al-Khabbaz (d. 1814). A man with a tumultuous fate, he was a monk on Sinai, then later metropolitan of Homs who was removed from his see involuntarily, and then finally metropolitan of Beirut with aspirations to the patriarchal throne.[267] He lost the battle for the patriarchate but left a vivid legacy of scholarship and literary works. Possessing a perfect command of Greek, Athanasius was another mediator between two cultural and linguistic worlds. Even Joseph Nasrallah, who was biased against the Orthodox theologians, paid tribute to the excellent education and lively intellect of the metropolitan of Beirut. In his youth when he was on Sinai, Athanasius composed a description of the holy mountain. Later, in the early nineteenth century, he wrote commentaries on difficult passages in the Bible and instructions for priests on liturgical and canonical issues. Athanasius translated some of the sermons of Macarius of Patmos, including texts of a sharply anti-Latin orientation, and a polemical treatise by an unidentified Greek author about the history of persecutions of the Orthodox by the Latins (to which he added several of his own accounts). Quite remarkable is Athanasius's attempt to go beyond translating Greek anti-Catholic literature (which was perhaps already close to exhaustion) and to exploit the untapped potential of European critics of the papacy. He put this to use in the treatise "Ma huwa al-Baba?" ("Who Is the Pope?"), an Arabic translation of the Greek translation of the work of the Austrian professor of canon law, Josef Eybel, "Was ist der Papst?" This scholar analyzed the emergence of the idea of the primacy of the pope in the Christian world and, based on his legal and sociopolitical analysis, demonstrated the illegitimacy of the Vatican's ambitions.[268]

The Arab theologians listed thus far are only the tip of the iceberg of Arab Christian literature. For every author of original treatises, there were several preachers, translators, and compilers whose names we will not mention here. It is worth mentioning, if only in passing, the cultural milieu of Aleppo at the turn of the eighteenth to the nineteenth century, when it was one of the centers of literary activity for the Uniate community. Its central figure was undoubtedly Germanus Adam (1725–1809), metropolitan of Aleppo from 1779. Like the other Uniate bishops, he lacked legal status in the eyes of the Ottoman authorities, and so he lived mostly in the Lebanese monasteries or in Italy. From the long list of Germanus Adam's works, only two are directed against the "schismatics" (i.e., the Orthodox): treatises from 1767 and 1803 outlining the foundations of Catholic dogma. The metropolitan spent much more energy on internal Catholic problems, participating in the internecine struggle among Uniate bishops, organizing church councils, and advocating the independence of the Melkite Church in the face of the Vatican's globalization. The Vatican condemned a number of Adam's works and the acts of councils conducted by him at different times.[269] After the metropolitan's death, his manuscripts were sought in the Lebanese monasteries and, at the pope's request, were sent to Rome for burning.[270]

With the victory of the Unia among the Christians of Aleppo, the city lost its former role in Arab Orthodox culture. In the eighteenth century, the literary activity of the Orthodox shifted to Beirut. A lively maritime trade and the protection of the Lebanese emirs greatly contributed to the prosperity of Beirut's Christian community.

Among the prominent Orthodox intellectuals of Beirut in the second half of the eighteenth century were Cypriot Metropolitan Ioannicius (d. 1776), a pupil of James of Patmos and prominent theologian; his successor to the episcopal see, Macarius Sadaqa (1730–1790), a famous preacher; the deacon Theophilus Halabi, previously a close associate of Patriarch Sylvester, who taught "the Greek and Arabic sciences";[271] and the previously mentioned printer, writer, polemicist, and educator, Yusuf Mark. None of these people were natives of the city, but Beirut was a magnet for the Orthodox intellectual elite. The best examples of the flourishing of Christian culture in the city are the opening of the printing house in 1751 and its emergence as an independent center of historical writing, which will be discussed in later sections of this chapter. One gets the impression that Beirut was significantly superior to Damascus, the seat of the patriarchate, in its intellectual potential.

All the writers and polemicists involved in the struggle over the Unia in Syria appealed to a similar range of issues. Relatively little changed over the generations in the points of theological controversy between the Orthodox and the Uniates. Distinct differences in the degree of interest in various issues are noticeable only if we compare Anastasius ibn Mujalla's *Response* to the pope, written in the 1580s, to the writings of polemicists who lived two hundred years later. Metropolitan Anastasius was most concerned with the calendar reform adopted by the Catholic Church in 1582. In the eighteenth century, this issue is absent from polemic between the Orthodox and the Uniates. There was enough patience in the Vatican to not attempt immediately introducing the Gregorian calendar to the Melkites but rather first to gradually bind them to Rome. The Uniates were forced to accept the new calendar only in the mid-nineteenth century, and even then, this process caused a serious crisis and a schism within the Melkite community. The metropolitan, however, shied away from any analysis of the decisions of the Council of Florence, simply going on the defensive and stating that he and his contemporaries have never heard of such a council from their ancestors, and so in their eyes, it had no validity.[272] Theologians of the eighteenth century were even less interested in the Union of Florence. Although individual polemical texts devoted to the issue were written and translated, the Council of Florence was pushed into the background by more relevant events in interchurch relations.

Conversely, the doctrinal differences between the Orthodox and Catholic churches remained unchanged. Almost every author from both camps spoke of five *haqa'iq*—dogmatic positions—that divide Eastern and Western Christendom. Specific treatises were written about almost every one of these doctrinal positions separately—the Filioque, purgatory, the primacy of the pope, and transubstantiation.

For some reason, the least interest is dedicated to doctrine about the nature of sanctity, which in its Catholic understanding gave rise to the trade in indulgences. Perhaps this is because Levantine Orthodoxy was itself not alien to the idea of selling "certificates of absolution," a document signed by patriarchs guaranteeing the absolution of the recipient's sins.[273]

Upon acquaintance with the content of the polemical treatises, the researcher can hardly escape the feeling that much of it is a sort of scholastic mental exercise, incomprehensible to ordinary people. Even if we set aside uneducated *fellahin* and assume that the polemicists addressed their works to townspeople, it is difficult to imagine that illiterate tinsmiths, commerce-driven silk merchants, and cynical moneychangers really were interested in problems of the procession of the Holy Spirit or the theological understanding of the sacrament of the Eucharist. Perhaps other issues of controversy were more salient to Arab Christians. A person concerned about his fate in the afterlife could not remain indifferent to the question of purgatory, while the doctrine of the primacy and infallibility of the pope is not so much theological as political in nature and even a nonreligious person could not remain indifferent to it.

Nevertheless, it is difficult to get rid of the impression that polemicists of both camps wrote their treatises mainly for each other and for a narrow layer of educated monks and bishops. As for ordinary people, their religious preferences were determined, it seems, by mostly irrational factors, such as the perception of services on an aesthetic level or, conversely, considerations of practical benefits.[274]

Thus, the family tradition of the Arab Catholic Mshak clan has preserved a story about the entrance into the Unia of its ancestor, Jirjis, a merchant's son who lived on the Lebanese coast. His Catholic bride demanded that he go over to her faith. He wondered what Catholicism was and to get acquainted with the faith, he was brought to Dayr Mar Mukhallis, where he observed the liturgy for a few days. As a result, Jirjis concluded that the prayers, the language of worship, and the monastic vestments were no different from what he had been accustomed to from childhood. "The Catholics are Orthodox," he concluded. "Why did you change your name when your confession is the same as mine?"[275]

The ritual aspect of religion was more important for Syrian Christians than the dogmatic aspect, as has been typical for many of their coreligionists in every time and nation. It is no wonder that Orthodox hierarchs spent so much effort on the so-called war of kalymavchis in the 1830s and 1840s, when the Greek patriarch of Antioch attempted to pass legislation through the Porte to codify the differences in headgear between the Orthodox and Uniate clergy. The similarity in the appearance between clergy of both confessions is considered to be a serious factor in the success of Uniate expansion among uneducated people.[276]

No discussion of the theological literature of the Orthodox and Uniates can bypass the question of its originality. We have already said that the two sides mastered the centuries-old heritage of polemic between the Orthodox and Catholic worlds. An enormous number of polemical texts were translated into Arabic: by the Catholics, from Latin and Italian, and by the Orthodox, from Greek. It would be tempted to attempt to calculate the ratio of original works to translations in the Arab Christian literature of the eighteenth century, but this task would be time consuming and imprecise. Nevertheless, it can be asserted with all confidence that there were significantly more translations than original works. It likewise would not be a big mistake to believe that the authors of original works drew their arguments from the works of their precursors, especially because most of these authors knew foreign languages and were engaged in translation.

Moreover, both parties used in their struggle not only the texts of European and Balkan authors of the past, but also contemporary foreign sources. We have mentioned the Greek educators and writers working in the Arab East—James of Patmos, Nicephorus Theotokis, and the *didaskalos* Ephraim—whose works were translated into Arabic and put into circulation immediately after their publication. A number of Greek bishops of the Church of Antioch, such as Sylvester and Metropolitan Anthimus of Tyre and Sidon (d. ca. 1813),[277] knew Arabic and also left original works or translations.

On the other side, Latin missionaries, in particular the aforementioned Pierre Fromage, were active. They wrote refutations of criticisms of Catholicism by Elias Fakhr and other Orthodox writers; deconstructed the history of the Greek Schism from Photius to the Council of Florence; and, in 1709, the Jesuit Claud Sicard even made a mathematical study (*burhan handasi*) of the supremacy of the See of Rome.[278]

It is of interest that some European Protestants acted on the side of the Orthodox. As mentioned, British diplomacy was sensitive to Catholic (read: French) expansion in the Levant. An employee of the British Consulate in Aleppo in the 1720s, Rowland Sherman, not only contributed to the publication in London of the anti-Catholic treatise the *Rock of Offense*, translated by Patriarch Athanasius, but also he himself translated into Arabic a polemical work by Archbishop Gabriel Severos of Philadelphia.[279]

A somewhat anecdotal figure in Orthodox–Uniate polemic is a rabbi who converted to Catholicism and adopted the resounding name of ʿAbd al-Masih (Servant of Christ). In his convert's zeal, he wrote a denunciation of his former coreligionists, *An Epistle Against the Jews*. Further spiritual quests or other factors led him to Orthodoxy and prompted him to write the anti-Catholic treatise *The Book of True Knowledge in Response to the People of the West*.[280]

A Duel of Chronicles

If the polemics of theologians can be called "the battle for the skies," the search for evidence of the right belief, and divine chosenness of one's community, the work of Orthodox and Uniate historians was the "battle for the past," the struggle to claim the heritage of the Middle Eastern Melkites. At the same time, not all chroniclers rose to the point of historiosophical generalizations. Most simply chronicled the course of events but did so, in any event, with a bias toward the positions of their coreligionists. Some of the Uniate chroniclers lived in the major cities and wrote the history of local Christians, sometimes weaving into the narrative a comprehensive political history of the region. The Uniates' Aleppo chronicle is represented by the figure of the deacon Niʿma ibn al-Khuri Tuma (d. 1770). In his youth, Niʿma was secretary to Patriarch Athanasius Dabbas, enjoyed his good graces, and did not hesitate to praise his patron in *qasidas* (the chronicler, among other things, was fond of poetry). Later he converted to Catholicism, was close to Uniate Metropolitans Gerasimus and Maximus al-Hikim, and was Maximus's acting secretary when he became patriarch. Over the course of his long life, amid a heated political environment, the secretary to two patriarchs—Orthodox and Catholic—accumulated many confidential documents pertaining to the ecclesiastical history of the Christians of Aleppo. In 1759, he made these materials public, providing them with an introduction and commentary. A number of documents from this collection were subsequently printed. In particular, the Uniate historian of the early twentieth century, Constantine Bacha, published a complaint by the Uniates of Aleppo written by Niʿma informing the See of Rome of the persecution that the Catholics suffered from Patriarch Sylvester. This text was written, of course, with pathos and emotion, but it abounds in exact dates and figures, particularly the amounts of the fines imposed on the dissidents by Sylvester.[281]

In the early nineteenth century, Mikhail Sabbagh, grandson of Ibrahim Sabbagh, an associate of Sheikh Dahir, wrote historical works. In addition to the political biography that he wrote of the Galilean sheikh, *Tarikh Dahir*, authorship of the initial portions of the chronicle *Tarikh Hawadith al-Sham wa-Lubnan* (*History of Events in Syria and Lebanon*), signed "Mikhail al-Dimashqi" is attributed to him. The chronicle covers the period from 1782 to 1841. It is believed that it has two authors, the second of which has been convincingly posited to be Mikhail Mshaka, a famous figure in Arabic literature of the second half of the nineteenth century. However, the first part of the chronicle is written by someone who is clearly an eyewitness to events that occurred before Mshaka's birth. It includes a detailed secular political history of Damascus and the deeds of local pashas, interrupted occasionally by an emotional account of the persecution of the Uniates by the Orthodox patriarch Daniel and the rebellion of the Uniates of Aleppo in 1818.[282] For example, it is reported that the patriarchal deacon who conducted the trial of the Uniates arrested in Damascus soon thereafter died ignominiously and that people saw a viper on his grave.[283]

Similar in genre to the *Tarikh Hawadis* is a mixed ecclesial and secular history of events in Lebanon and Syria from 1745 to 1800 written by a native of Homs, the Shuwayrite monk Rufa'il Karama (1730–1800).[284] Some later Lebanese historians used this chronicle, particularly Hanania al-Munayyir (1756–after 1830), which can be attributed to a "monastic" group of chroniclers.

Monastic chronicles developed primarily in the Shuwayrite Order. Its basis goes back to monastery archives and records of current events whose foundation was laid in the 1730s by Nicholas al-Sayegh, the most famous of the abbots of Mar Yuhanna. Hanania al-Munayyir used all these records to make a lengthy history of his order, *Tarikh al-Rahbaniyya al-Hannawiya al-Mulaqqaba bi-l-Shuwayriya* (*History of the Monastic Congregation of St John, Called Shuwayrite*). The narrative goes up to the 1804 death of Ahmad al-Jazzar, which to contemporaries seemed to be an event of epochal magnitude.[285]

Hanania garnered even greater fame from his second extensive chronicle, *Kitab al-Durr al-Marsuf fi Tarikh al-Shuf* (*Arranged Pearls of the History of the Chouf*) in which he followed the tradition common to Christian chroniclers of that time of placing the history of their community or order within the broader context of regional political history.[286] The chronicle covers the period from 1697 to 1804, but it only reflects the last third of the eighteenth century though the early nineteenth century in real detail, often from eyewitness reports. In the previous chapter, it was mentioned that Hanania, unlike the authors of the urban Uniate chronicles, is tolerant toward the Orthodox. He gives almost no space to the topic of interconfessional strife and, generally speaking, his *History* is a statement of facts almost devoid of propagandistic digressions and argumentation.

Carsten Walbiner has noted that the library of the Monastery of Mar Yuhanna at Shuwayr contains many translations from Western authors of the sixteenth to eighteenth centuries about ecclesial and world history. However, this did not prompt Shuwayrite historiographers to compile their own works of a similar scale.[287] The interests of the Lebanese chroniclers rarely extend geographically beyond Acre and Damascus and temporally before the eighteenth century.

There was only one Uniate historian who thought globally and attempted to write a complete history of the Church of Antioch. Yuhanna al-'Ujaymi (1724–1785), mentioned more than once in the previous chapter, spent eleven years in Rome and Paris studying languages and theology. Returning to the East in 1750, he took an active role in the internecine struggle between the Uniate hierarchs, wrote learned treatises and traveled twice on church business to Europe, where he ended his days. Yuhanna's main historical work, entitled the *Taktikon*, is a list of the patriarchs and dioceses of Antioch with historical commentary from the Apostle Paul until 1756.[288]

'Ujaymi's narrative is based in no small part on the latest works of Western church historians of the time. "A sensible, respectable work," Porphyry Uspensky said of the esteemed 'Ujaymi's chronicle. "It is much better than the similar work by Antiochian patriarch Macarius ... better in its comprehensiveness and its closeness to the truth of fidelity to the chronology."[289] When comparing 'Ujaymi's text with Macarius's chronicle, the exaggerated attention paid by the Uniate historian to problems of the relationship between the Eastern and Western churches, such as the case of Photius, is striking.[290] In reality, the person of Photius, the Great Schism of 1054, and even the relationship between the Patriarchate of Antioch and the Crusaders had been overlooked or forgotten by medieval Christian Arab chroniclers with their limited geographic horizons and failures of historical memory. The description of the origin of the Unia and the schism in the Patriarchate of Antioch in 1724 registered by 'Ujaymi is quite balanced and does not contradict the objective facts. An entire century would pass before Uniate historiography, at least in a number of its representatives, would degenerate into emotional propaganda unburdened by historical realities.[291]

When we turn to the Orthodox contemporaries and opponents of the Uniate historians, the first figure to attract attention is the Damascene priest Mikhail Breik al-Dimashqi. Information about Breik's life is scarce and can be reconstructed only from occasional references in his writings. He was probably born in the second decade of the eighteenth century,[292] lived in Damascus, was a scribe, and then chose a spiritual career. In August 1740, the vicar of Patriarch Sylvester, Metropolitan Nicephorus, ordained Breik to the deaconate and then, ten days later, as a *qassis*, that is, to the priesthood. There seems to have been a close relationship between the metropolitan and Mikhail. In 1750, Nicephorus left Damascus, leaving Breik as his representative and raising him to the rank of *khuri* and archpriest. The high point in the ecclesiastical career of the Damascene priest was when he became economos of the Monastery of Sidon, a post to which Patriarch Daniel appointed him in 1768. A year later, however, Breik left the post, citing exhaustion from disturbances. Perhaps there were some conflicts with the nuns, aggravated by Michael's misogyny—in his writings, he repeatedly states that all the evil in the world is from women. The date of the Damascene chronicler's death is unknown. It is only clear that he died shortly after 1781.[293]

Mikhail is the author of three works: an unpublished world history *Jami' Tawarikh al-Zaman* (*Compendium of the History of Time*), *al-Haqa'iq al-Wafiyya fi Tarikh Batariqat al-Kanisa al-Antakiya* (*The Comprehensive Truth About the History of the Patriarchs of the Church of Antioch*), and *Tarikh al-Sham* (*History of Damascus*). The history of the patriarchs of Antioch, covering the apostolic era through the consecration of Patriarch Daniel on August 6, 1767, is, in many respects, the final stage in the development of Arab Orthodox historiography. Although historical records were later created in this community, they were either not given a consistent chronological arc or were of a local, provincial character. In his history of the patriarchs, Mikhail Breik mainly relied on the works of Macarius, occasionally supplementing it with other sources. Breik wrote that he had to expend no small effort in looking for the manuscripts of his predecessors in the dust of libraries.[294] Between Macarius and Mikhail Breik there is another transmission link, the priest Farah who lived in Damascus at the end of the seventeenth century and described contemporary events in Syrian ecclesiastical history. Constantine Bacha attributed authorship of a rather large segment of the chronicle, from the death of Macarius in 1674 until 1724, to Farah.[295]

The final part of the chronicle belongs to Breik himself. Breik composed it "likely using the accurate tales of worthy priests and other figures"[296] as well as on the basis of personal impressions. Porphyry Uspensky believed that by this small turn of phrase, "tale," you can believe it.[297] However, when compared with other sources, it is notable that the chronicle includes significant factual errors. It is impossible also not to regret the large gaps in the narrative and the fact that dates are rarely mentioned. Nevertheless, the chronicle of Mikhail Breik is an important source for Syrian ecclesiastical history in the eighteenth century. It should also be added that many texts of Macarius come to us only through Breik's history.

The ecclesiastical and political life of the Levant is reflected far more in the same author's *History of Damascus*. It has been noted by modern researchers that the trend among Arab Christian chroniclers of the eighteenth century to include the history of their community within the broader context of the political history of the region[298] probably originates with Mikhail Breik. In this respect, he was ahead of Rufa'il Karama, Hanania al-Munayyir, and other Uniate historians. The chronicle begins in 1720; starting in the mid-1750s, the entries become regular; and the narrative ends in 1781. The *History* includes both a description of ecclesiastical events in the life of the Christian community as well as sociopolitical chronicle of Syria: wars, riots, changes of rulers, harvests, locusts, epidemics, the prices of bread, and so on. The author pays the lion's share of his attention to Damascus. Nevertheless, space is dedicated in the chronicle to episodes in the history of Lebanon, Palestine, and Egypt. Mikhail Breik was oriented in the position of the neighboring Orthodox churches, changes in the Ottoman sultans, and some international events. He mentions Russia, the Seven Years' War, and the Lisbon earthquake of 1755 and, in such cases, he does not fail to refer to his sources. The author described in greatest detail the events of 1772–1777. Alongside illuminating historical events, the chronicle includes semifolkloric traditions, especially miracle stories common among the Arab Orthodox, especially prophecies about the future fate of the world in the second half of the eighteenth century, culminating in the prediction of the second coming of Christ. Generally speaking, Mikhail Breik's chronicle is one of the main sources for the history of the Arab provinces of the Ottoman Empire in the eighteenth century and is among the greatest achievements of Arab Orthodox historiography.

In European scholarship, Mikhail Breik is considered to be almost the only representative of Arab Orthodox historiography of the eighteenth century.[299] This misconception stems from the fact that the Beirut Chronicle of 'Abdallah Trad belongs to the early nineteenth century and because of the low availability of the text, no Western scholar has attempted to analyze its contents.[300] At the same time, a hundred years ago, A. E. Krymsky demonstrated that the work is a compilation and highlighted some of its components, most of which were written by different authors of the eighteenth century. That is, the Orthodox chronicles of this century are by no means exhausted by the figure of Mikhail Breik.

At the heart of the chronicle is a consistent account of the formation of the Catholic Unia in Syria in the first half of the eighteenth century that is not tied to a chronology.[301] The author's interests are almost entirely limited to events in Aleppo. Apparently, he was a native of the city and, in any event, someone close to Metropolitan Sophronius al-Kilizi, whose ordeal on the See of Aleppo is described with great skill. The text was composed as a propaganda pamphlet. The description of the struggle of Orthodoxy and the Unia is punctuated by passionate polemical digressions and denunciations of Catholicism and the Vatican's claims to supremacy in the Christian world. "We have not received grace from the See of Rome," the author wrote, "and the pope was not crucified for us."[302] In the narratives, there are echoes of the controversies between the Orthodox and the Catholics, including, for example, to whom the last patriarch of the undivided Church of Antioch, Athanasius Dabbas, confessed. The author referred to reliable witnesses who were present at the death of the patriarch and confirmed that, contrary to the missionaries' speculation, he died as an Orthodox.[303] The anonymous polemicist composed colorful legends about the scandalous circumstances of the consecration of Cyril Tanas as metropolitan and patriarch or Maximus Hakim's occupation of the See of Aleppo.[304] For the author, it was important to prove the illegitimacy of the Uniate hierarchs. Carsten Walbiner believes that these stories are propagandistic fabrications, where some real facts are woven into a false context.[305] Nevertheless, in our opinion, it should not be denied that the Aleppine fragments of the chronicle have a certain historical value, all the more so because they were written in the immediate wake of events, in the 1760s.

Another component of the chronicle, the Beirut city history of the 1740s, begins in the 1790s and centers on the figure of the Orthodox Sheikh Yunus Nicholas and the fate of the Orthodox community of the city. The person who wrote this chronicle was clearly a merchant rather than a clergyman, because so much attention is paid to the economic situation there and to the extortion imposed by the Pasha al-Jazzar of Acre on wealthy Christians.[306]

Around 1792, a certain compiler—according to the hypothesis of A. E. Krymsky, a member of the Bustros family of Beirut—combined the two fragments (the excerpt from the history of Beirut from the 1740s was placed in the middle of an Aleppine chronicle). At the beginning of the narrative, the compiler added a list of the bishops of Beirut from the sixteenth–eighteenth centuries; to the middle, information about the change of patriarchs of Antioch in 1766–1767; and, at the end, information about the succession of Patriarchs Daniel and Anthimus in 1792. Porphyry Uspensky published the chronicle in this arrangement.[307]

In the 1820s, the Beirut native 'Abdallah ibn Mikhail Trad revised the text of the chronicle, including in the middle of the Beirut fragment an excerpt from a Lebanese Orthodox chronicle from the 1780s telling of the struggle between

Pasha al-Jazzar of Acre and the Lebanese Emir Yusuf Shihab.[308] The history of Beirut was continued with a description of Napoleon's Middle Eastern expedition and the final years of the rule of Ahmad Pasha al-Jazzar (the period from 1798 to 1804).[309]

The author of this account is a Christian contemporary of the events, most likely not 'Abdallah Trad. Trad seems to have authored the presentation of the ecclesiastical history of the Beirut diocese of the Patriarchate of Antioch from 1798 to 1813[310] and, of course, the description of the final decade reflected in the chronicle, 1815–1824.[311] This version of the chronicle was published in Russian translation, though not completely, by A. E. Krymsky[312] and in the Arabic original by Naila Kaidbey. Thus, the Beirut Chronicle of 'Abdallah Trad is a compilation of at least six historical works, four of which were written in the eighteenth century. In other words, the intensity of chronicle-writing in the eighteenth and early nineteenth centuries was no less among the Orthodox than among the Uniates. Moreover, among all the chroniclers of both branches of the divided patriarchate, it was the Orthodox Mikhail Breik who first attempted to merge the history of his community with general Syrian political history. The unidentified author of an account of the Syrian Unia effectively transformed the historical narrative into a polemical pamphlet, supplying his coreligionists with arguments in disputes with Catholics.

The acute lag in the field of historiographical works by the Orthodox began in the second half of the nineteenth and early twentieth centuries, when Uniate and European historians published a number of works on the history of the Church of Antioch, which the Orthodox were unable to oppose with their own look at the past of Syrian Christianity. However, an analysis of the reasons for this is beyond the scope of the current work.

A Duel of Printing Presses

The clash of civilizations taking place within the Church of Antioch unfolded not only in the field of intellectual conflict, but also in the field of technological competition. The most important such technology was the printing press, the powerful mechanism for reproducing cultural traditions and instrument of spiritual expansion, which appeared in the Middle East at this time.

The first experiments with typography in the Ottoman world, among the Slavs of present-day Montenegro, belong to the end of the fifteenth century, closely behind similar processes in Europe. In the Eastern Mediterranean, however, it seems that printed matter was less popular and printing could not be sustained. Among Orthodox Christians in the sixteenth century, a stable center for printing could be established only in the Greek colony in Venice. At the Jesuits' prompting, the Ottomans suppressed the project of Cyril Lucaris to have a printing house in Istanbul in the 1620s. As mentioned earlier, Greek printing was actively developed in the Danubian principalities at the end of the seventeenth century, including the efforts of the Patriarchs of Jerusalem Dositheus and Chrysanthos.

In the Arab East, the first attempt at book publishing was undertaken in 1610 among the Maronites, at the Lebanese Monastery of St Anthony.[313] The printed Arabic books that circulated in Syria in the sixteenth and seventeenth centuries were the products of European, primarily Catholic, typography.[314] Unlike some other traditional societies, Arab Christians perceived the printed book quite positively. The most advanced leaders of the Melkite Nahda were well aware of the importance of printing, but they did not see a possibility of organizing it on their own. The Arab Orthodox did not have a wealthy diaspora in Europe comparable to the Greeks' colony of Venice and their well-developed bookselling infrastructure.[315] The Arabs were completely dependent on external support and European presses for printing. Earlier, we mentioned the relevant projects of Meletius Karma in the 1620s. A similar sentiment is evident with Patriarch Macarius and Paul of Aleppo.[316]

However, plans for publishing were implemented only by the former Patriarch Athanasius, who found a sponsor in the Wallachian voivode Constantin Brâncoveanu. In January 1701, Athanasius, who was then in Bucharest, requested from the ruler the printing of liturgical books in Greek and Arabic for the impoverished See of Antioch. Snagov Monastery near Bucharest was equipped with a printing press. Arabic letters were produced by the hieromonk Antim Ivireanul, who also managed the publishing process.[317]

The pioneer of printing, Antim was an extremely colorful personality. A Georgian by birth, as a young man, he was bought out of slavery by Patriarch Dositheus of Jerusalem. Antim later became metropolitan of Ugro-Wallachia and was killed by the Ottomans in 1716 on suspicions of political disloyalty. Almost the entire "Byzantine commonwealth"[318] was focused on printing at Snagov: an Arab metropolitan, a Georgian printer, a Greek patriarch, and a Wallachian patron. The financial and technical capabilities of the Orthodox East were far weaker than those of the Catholics. However, in some situations, the Orthodox managed to combine efforts across regional and ethnic boundaries and achieved real results. In 1701, the Liturgikon was published, a year later the Horologion, decorated on its front page with the coat of arms of the voivode Constantin Brâncoveanu and verses in his honor in Arabic and Greek. Both books were intended to be distributed to Arab priests for free.[319]

When Athanasius returned to Syria in 1705, the Wallachian ruler gave him the gift of the printing equipment from Snagov. The press was transferred to Aleppo,[320] and in 1706, the Psalter and the Four Gospels were published—the first printed Arabic books published directly in the Arab East. A total of eleven books were published on the Aleppo press, for the most part during the period 1706–1711.

It seems that a large part of the print run was distributed to parishes for free, so it is not possible to speak of whether the printing operation broke even. Athanasius lacked funds, and he searched for benefactors throughout the Orthodox world, making appeals to the ruler of Wallachia, the Ukrainian aristocracy, Peter I, and Patriarch Chrysanthos of Jerusalem.[321] Most of the press's publications were related to the liturgical literature necessary for everyday church practice, as well as patristic writings. It was only the press's penultimate publication that was brought about by the pressing issue of anti-Latin polemic. The Greek polemical treatise the *Rock of Offense*, as translated by Patriarch Athanasius (entitled in Arabic *Sakhrat al-Shakk*), was published in 1721.[322] However, most researchers tend to believe that *Sakhrat al-Shakk* was published in London. Athanasius's disciple Sulayman al-Aswad, who had been sent to Europe for training, organized in England the republication of three books from the Aleppo press. Apart from the *Rock of Offense*, these were the Psalms (1725) and the Gospel (1727).[323] For the Orthodox Syrians, it was still easier to hire the services of foreign publishing houses than to develop their own printing presses.

The subsequent fate of the Aleppo press is obscure. Its last publication was the Kontakion, which was released in 1725. Not a single copy of this book has been preserved.[324] It is not known when the press finally ceased operations, where its font went, and so on.[325] It is easy to assume that organizational problems (Athanasius's departure to Istanbul in 1722, his death, and then the turmoil on account of the Unia) coupled with an acute shortage of money put an end to this attempt at Arabic publishing. In the Aleppo of the 1720s–1750s, beset with the struggle between the Orthodox and Catholic parties, no one cared about printing books.

However, intellectuals of the time were well aware of the merits of printing and the experiment was continued as soon as possible. This occurred in the Uniate milieu, where the general level of education was higher and the issue of financing the printing was not as acute. The first Uniate printer was the most important churchman of the community, the aforementioned ʿAbdallah Zakher (1680–1755). At one time he worked at Sylvester's press in Aleppo, where he gained expertise in printing. In the early 1720s, the deacon left Aleppo to take refuge in the Uniate monasteries of Mount Lebanon. It was there, first at a monastery in the village of Zouk Mikhail and then at the Monastery of St John in Shuwayr that ʿAbdallah worked to establish a printing press. With the help of the Jesuit missionary Pierre Fromage, he received printing equipment from France. ʿAbdallah, a goldsmith by profession, cut his own letters; all researchers have noted the grace of the early Shuwayrite font. "They [i.e., the words of the printed text] can barely be distinguished from a manuscript," wrote Constantin Volney, "so artfully did one observe in their subtlety neither thicknesses nor blindnesses, there was not a single fused Arabic letter visible anywhere."[326] The printing press went into operation in Shuwayr and on February 26, 1734, its first publication appeared, a philosophical treatise by the seventeenth-century Spanish Jesuit Juan Eusebio Nieremberg entitled in the Arabic version *Mizan al-Zaman* (*The Balance of Time*). The following year, ʿAbdallah issued the Psalms in the same version that Athanasius had published thirty years earlier. Over the next century, the book would see eleven reprints. The Shuwayrite press was active until 1899, issuing sixty-nine titles, thirty-six of which were reprints of previously issued books.[327] Of this total number of publications, thirty appeared during the eighteenth century.

The subjects of the Shuwayrite publications are markedly different from the publications of Athanasius's press in Aleppo. Of course, Zakher and his successors also printed editions of the Holy Scriptures and liturgical texts, but the lion's share of Shuwayrite publications is taken by translations of Western theologians, mainly Jesuits. Only a few books from the turn of the eighteenth to the nineteenth century belong to Arab Uniate authors or contain the acts of councils of the Melkite Uniate Church. It is characteristic that these texts were for the most part subject to condemnation from the Vatican.[328]

The Shuwayrite press also faced financial difficulties and its activities were periodically frozen. Publishing was nearly halted in the 1740s. The most severe trials were endured by Sulayman Qattan (d. 1779), who succeeded ʿAbdallah Zakher as head of the printing press in 1755. Qattan had to face strong opposition from the monastic superiors. In the scholarly literature, it is customary to emphasize the dynamic nature of Uniate monasticism and its orientation toward activity in the world. For all the validity of this assertion, it is somewhat one-sided. Among the leadership of the Shuwayrite Order, there were enough people who considered the work of printing barely compatible with the standards of monastic cenobitic life and the path of asceticism. In 1761, Sulayman Qattan directly demanded from the Order a special indulgence for his employees. That is, probably a release from other forms of monastic obedience that would distract them from publishing work. In February 1762, the two sides made a compromise agreement in twelve points regarding the printing regime in the monastery, but the following year, Sulayman began to seek to completely remove the press and its employees from the jurisdiction of the monastic authorities. The chapter sent a report to the supreme abbot of the Order a thirty-six-page report outlining its version of the conflict, treating the matter in a way that was clearly not favorable to the printer. Qattan replied with a sharply worded letter in which he accused the monastery's leadership of ignorance and of working against the development of printing. He also threatened to stop the printing press and to offer its services to another community (apparently, the Maronites). If the printer intended to frighten this chapter of the Order, he was very much mistaken. In April 1765, the Shuwayrite fathers wrote another twenty-six-page letter to the supreme abbot and terminated the 1762 agreement on the status of the press. The typesetters and bookbinders went to tend the gardens with the rest of the brethren. Qattan left Shuwayr and for two years sought justice from the leading authorities of the Uniate Church and the Latin missionaries. They sided with the printer and persuaded the Order to make concessions. Printing activity resumed in 1767 but friction between Qattan and the monastic superiors continued for many years.[329]

A noticeable decline in printing activity occurred in the last decade of the eighteenth century, causing Constantin Volney to make pessimistic forecasts of the imminent demise of Lebanese printing. "Few books are sold, including psalters, which are made for children as Christian school books," he wrote in 1784. "The costs for these things [a printing press] goes so high because the paper must be gotten from Europe; the labor moreover goes very slowly."[330] It took a lot of time to accurately connect the Arabic letters, which are written together. The various written forms for the same letter, depending on whether it is at the beginning, middle or end of a word, required the manufacturing of an enormous number of letters, "for which there were so many boxes," reported Volney,

> that the printer had no way of getting them all from one place, but had to run to and fro, seeking out the word in almost nine hundred boxes. These things cause a great loss of time, on account of which Arabic typography never has such perfection as it does with us.[331]

Nevertheless, the Monastery of Shuwayr with its printing press remained the largest intellectual center of the Levant and both the Orthodox and the Maronites were guided by its example in trying to establish their own printing presses.[332]

The Orthodox Patriarch of Antioch Sylvester felt uncomfortable in Syria under pressure from the Uniates and chose to implement his publishing activities in the Danubian principalities. In 1744, he departed to Moldavia with Patriarchal Vicar Michael Tuma to establish an Arabic printing press there. This was the main purpose stated for the journey, which would be prolonged for almost ten years.[333] In 1745, a press was started at the Monastery of St Savvas in Iasi, which the following summer issued the anti-Latin treatise of Patriarch Nectarius of Jerusalem, the *Judgment of Truth* (*Qada' al-Haqq*). Attached to the treatise was a verse pamphlet on the subject of the infallibility of the pope, written by Eustratius Argenti from Chios.[334] Sylvester sent the book's print run of one thousand five hundred copies to the church in Syria.[335] In February 1747, in Iasi, in an edition of one thousand copies, Sylvester published another polemical work of Eustratius Argenti in refutation of the Latin doctrine of the Eucharist. Mas'ad Nashw made the translation in 1740.[336]

That is, Sylvester primarily published propagandistic literature necessary in polemic with the Unia and distributed it to parishes for free. Alongside this, the patriarch also printed liturgical texts. The literature mentions his having published an Arabic Horologion[337] and the translation of the Kontakion attributed to Sophronius al-Kilizi.[338]

When Sylvester's publishing activity waned—perhaps for financial reasons—the Christians of Beirut made an attempt to establish an independent printing house. It is interesting that this initiative was not connected to the ecclesiastical hierarchy, but with the initiative of Sheikh Yunus Nicholas, head of the Orthodox community of Beirut. In 1751, the equipment was purchased and the type was made, modeled on the font of the press at Shuwayr. The aforementioned priest Yusuf Mark headed the printing house. The press's first publication was the Psalter (May 21, 1752), the most popular book in medieval Christian culture. At the publisher's request, the text was verified and corrected by the leading theologians of the Arab East, Sophronius al-Kilizi and Elias Fakhr. The book opens with a brief statement of Christian doctrine and ethics. From this, it appears that the publication was intended not only for liturgical and educational needs (the Psalter, we recall, was used for learning to read), but also for maintaining a minimum level of theological knowledge among the Christians.[339] According to piecemeal information, around 1753, the Horologion and Kontakion were also published at the Beirut printing house. After that, the press was stopped.[340] In this regard, the statement circulating in the Russian literature that the printing press was destroyed during the bombardment of Beirut by the Russian squadron in 1772 or 1773 is not entirely clear.[341] Even if the building was destroyed by artillery fire, publishing in Beirut had ceased twenty years before that. Further attempts at publishing books for the Arab Orthodox took place outside of Syria.[342]

Anthimus, the future Patriarch of Jerusalem, composed an interpretation of the Psalms and a presentation of the fundamentals of the Christian faith. On becoming patriarch, he published these works in Vienna under the title *An Explanation of the Psalms* (November 1791) and *A Solid Guide to the True Faith* (May 1792). Anthimus's works were intended for the elementary education of Christians and for the preservation of the basic foundations of religious beliefs, "so that the Arabs," in Porphyry's words, "understand the Psalter, do not yawn while reading it, and are able to respond to heretics."[343]

After Anthimus, there was a strange pause in Orthodox publishing lasting half a century. At a time when the Uniate printing press at Shuwayr published an average of three books a decade, the Orthodox seemed to have exhausted their enthusiasm and material resources. It is possible that a relative lull in the confrontation with the Unia reduced the need for polemical literature. The disasters of the 1820s caused the Orthodox community to focus on survival rather than the development of technology. Finally, Arabic printing was of little interest to the Greek patriarchs. The revival of printing among the Orthodox would only happen in 1842 and only with the active support of the Russian consulate, which financed the opening of a printing house in Beirut.[344]

CONCLUSION

The cultural revival of the Melkites during the generations of Anastasius ibn Mujalla and Meletius Karma is perhaps the most surprising in all the history of this community during the Early Modern period. A people who seem to have fallen into a permanent state of stupor and stasis suddenly found the strength for a spiritual awakening. How can this phenomenon be explained? The Greek influence on Middle Eastern Orthodoxy, which sharply increased after the Ottoman conquest, has been mentioned more than once. But the true reasons for the Melkite Nahda lie deeper than we think. They lie in some unknown mechanisms of the oscillation of the vital energy of the Arab Orthodox. It is also difficult to explain clearly the interruptions in the Melkites' literary activity during the Ottoman period.

After a sharp rise in intellectual activity in the region of Tripoli in the 1580s, there followed two decades of suspended animation that was replaced by the Nahda of Meletius Karma, Macarius al-Zaʿim, and Paul of Aleppo. The main phase of the Melkite Renaissance was from the 1610s to the 1660s. During the last three decades of the seventeenth century, there was a marked decline in cultural production.

Some authors extend the Melkite Renaissance into the eighteenth century, including in that movement both the printing activity of Athanasius Dabbas and the activities of the intellectuals of Aleppo of the early eighteenth century, such as Germanus Farhat,[1] ʿAbdallah Zakher, Nicholas al-Sayegh, and others.[2] In our opinion, this is hardly justified. There was no direct or indirect succession between the figures of the Nahda and the Melkite writers of the following century. They were inspired by different objectives and stimulated by different cultural impulses. Meletius and Macarius sought to integrate the Melkites into the Byzantine cultural space. ʿAbdallah Zakher and his associates looked to Catholic Europe. Accordingly, the Orthodox cultural revitalization of the eighteenth century was a defensive reaction, a response to the Catholic challenge that, once more, was determined by the realities of the age and not by the impetus of the Nahda.

The literary upswing among Arab Christians of both denominations continued for almost all of the eighteenth century. By quantitative indicators, Uniate cultural production was almost a third higher than that of the Orthodox. The Uniates were especially far ahead of their rivals in the fields of education and publishing. This can be explained by the stronger stimulus given to Arab Catholic culture. Behind it lay the powerful intellectual capacity of Latin Europe. The Orthodox could rely only on the relatively modest achievements of Greek literature and education. Additionally, compared with the Orthodox, the Uniate community had a higher material and social level, as the Unia took place primarily among the wealthy commercial and entrepreneurial strata of the Melkites. However, Orthodox writers of the eighteenth century generally were able to perform on an equal footing with the Catholics. Elias Fakhr, Sophronius, Masʿad Nashw, and their followers built up cultural resources sufficient to preserve the community's identity. At the same time, it seems that by the turn of the eighteenth to the nineteenth century, the Orthodox culture of the Levant had run out of steam. Although the writing of history and a number of other literary genres and the development of iconography continued, the Orthodox abandoned their attempts to establish higher education and printing. Perhaps the reason for this was a certain stabilization in Orthodox–Catholic relations in the late eighteenth and early nineteenth centuries. The Catholic challenge was no longer so relevant. The suppression of the Jesuits in 1773 and the revolutionary upheavals in Europe weakened the position of the Middle Eastern Uniates, who were more in need of external support than the Orthodox. Confrontation between the two churches and the transfer of entire villages from one confession to another would continue throughout the nineteenth century, but this did not bring into question the survival of the Orthodox or Uniate communities as such.

What were the future prospects of Arab Orthodox culture? Observing it at the end of the 1840s, Porphyry Uspensky painted a picture of further decline and torpor. On the basis of his words, we can conclude that only Russian financial and intellectual support promoted the development of the Arab Orthodox in the second half of the nineteenth century. This raises the question: what would have happened to them had Russia not come to the Orthodox East? And, a couple centuries before them, if the Jesuits and Capuchins had not come there? As is well known, historical arguments in the conditional mood are speculative. We will refrain from them and shall only state that no external stimulation is able to awaken a culture that is already dead and exhausted. Even at the beginning of the nineteenth century, the Arab Orthodox milieu was capable of producing people who desired education and the development of their people.[3] That is to say, its potential was far from exhausted and carried within itself the possibility of new cultural breakthroughs.

If we imagine two thousand years of the Christian East as a sine wave with highs and lows of prosperity and decline, the first three hundred years of Ottoman rule will appear to be a rather favorable interval of this historic journey. In the first decades of the sixteenth century, at the time of the Ottomans' arrival in the Middle East, Arab Orthodoxy was in a deep crisis. It had begun in the mid-thirteenth century when the war between the Muslims and the Crusaders entered into a decisive phase, after which a series of religious persecutions broke out in the Mamluk Sultanate. The pandemic of the Black Death marked a period of general decline in the Middle East, both for its Christian and Muslim components. The last century and a half of the history of the Mamluk state was marked by increasing depopulation, economic collapse, and the expansion of nomads.

The Christian revival that began in the sixteenth century—first demographic and then cultural—can be explained by the nature of Ottoman society, which was more tolerant of other faiths than was typical of the Muslim-majority Mamluk state, as well as by the general economic recovery and political stabilization characteristic of the "Golden Age" of the Ottomans. An important feature of the demographic processes in the Christian environment was a powerful urbanization—the migration of Orthodox from agricultural regions to cities: Aleppo absorbed the rural population of northern Syria, Damascus absorbed the Christians of the Qalamun Plateau, Jerusalem attracted residents of Bethlehem and Beit Jala, and Gaza was enriched with immigrants from Transjordan. It is possible that this contributed to the economic and cultural dynamism of the Melkite community, but at the same time, it led to a reduction in its area of settlement. On the whole, it by no means strengthened the demographic potential of the Orthodox and their relationship with the soil—that is, the most important criteria for the viability of any of the Arab Christian subethnicities.

One of the most interesting and at the same time least-known phenomena in the life of Middle Eastern Christians during the Ottoman era can be referred to as the social degradation occurring in their environment: the loss of many cultural traditions, the revival of tribal relations, and primordial belligerence. Among the Orthodox, these processes are most evident in Transjordan, Hawran, the Judean Mountains, Mount Lebanon, and the upper reaches of the Euphrates. Sources record among the local Christians the development of traditions of tribal solidarity, blood feuds, the presence of a proper quasi-aristocracy in the person of village sheikhs, and the close involvement of Christian tribal groups in the rivalries of neighboring Muslim sheikhs and tribes. The isolation of peripheral areas of the Middle East from the influence of religious institutions led to the degradation of the religious beliefs of local Christians. Those living in remote mountain villages who might not see priests and liturgies for half a lifetime were deprived of the opportunity to receive basic religious rites. This often led to the loss of a traditional Christian identity and assimilation into the Muslim environment through the adoption of a primitive "folk Islam" mixed with elements of Christian beliefs. Such processes of creeping Islamization reached their greatest scope in the mountain valleys of eastern Anatolia, where between the late sixteenth and the first third of the seventeenth centuries, the Orthodox population disappeared almost entirely.

As part of the Ottoman imperial space, interaction between the Orthodox churches and peoples of the Eastern Mediterranean increased greatly. The holy places of Palestine attracted monks and pilgrims from all over the Orthodox world. Thanks to them, in the Holy Land were preserved monastic tradition, literary culture, icon painting, and so on. Already noticeable during the Mamluk era, Hellenic influence in the Church of Jerusalem culminated in 1534 with the final transition of the patriarchal throne and, subsequently, all higher ecclesiastical positions into the hands of Greeks. This process was not met with serious resistance from the Arab Orthodox, whose ethnic identity was largely overshadowed by their religious identity. Additionally, as mentioned, most of the rural Christian population lived in isolated and semimountainous areas and so were cut off from the cultural influence of religious centers and did not take part in internal church life. There developed a contrasting picture: a semiwild Arab Christian hinterland side by side with the relatively educated monastic and senior clergy of the Patriarchate of Jerusalem, consisting of foreigners.

The Patriarchate of Antioch developed under different conditions. Here factors of social archaism were less pronounced. The strip along the coast and the fertile land along the route between Damascus and Aleppo were firmly controlled by the Ottoman authorities. The two Syrian metropolises, the largest economic units in the Middle East, were centers for the development and dissemination of Christian culture. The higher clergy remained predominantly Arab. Secular elite groups of Christians were an independent center of power, balancing the ecclesiastical hierarchy or even exceeding it with their capabilities of economic and political influence. As a rule, Christian regional elites determined the candidates for local bishops and periodically sought to promote their countrymen to the patriarchal throne.

In the 1580s, contact with the Greeks and the other Orthodox peoples of Eastern Europe, as well as the challenge of the Catholic world of the era of the Counter-Reformation stimulated the first rise in intellectual activity in the Christian Arab environment in many centuries. It was concentrated in the area of Tripoli, at that time one of the leading centers of the Christians of the Levant. The prosperity of the Tripolitan regional elite inaugurated a whole campaign of founding monasteries in the mountains of North Lebanon in the late sixteenth and early seventeenth centuries. Characteristically, these monasteries were not the result of a spontaneous monastic movement but rather were established from scratch by the arbitrary decision of the Christian aristocracy in a manner resembling similar practice in Byzantium or medieval Serbia that was by no means typical of the Muslim world.

The crisis that afflicted the Empire at the turn of the sixteenth-seventeenth centuries affected the Christians' situation. This was most evident in the decline of monasteries, the main custodians of Christian culture and identity. In the first third of the seventeenth century, many Palestinian monasteries went into disrepair and first the Serbian and then the Georgian communities in the Holy Land ceased to exist.

A regrouping of forces occurred in the Patriarchate of Antioch. Tripoli's loss of its trade and economic role led to a weakening of the Orthodox community in the region of North Lebanon and the final movement of centers of power to Damascus and Aleppo. It was there during the second decade of the seventeenth century that there began a cultural revival of Arab Orthodox known as the "Melkite Renaissance." The production of original literary works and translations and adaptations of post-Byzantine Greek literature intensified and Syrian iconography was revived. In the second third of the seventeenth century, the patriarchs of Antioch and Jerusalem played a prominent role in international politics, maintaining close ties with the Danubian principalities, the Georgian kingdoms, the Orthodox lands of Western Russia, and Muscovy. From the early eighteenth century, communication between the Melkites and their northern coreligionists went into decline on account of the cultural and political reorientation of St Petersburg toward the West, as well as the permanent military confrontation between the Russian and Ottoman empires.

During the same period, Catholic influence in the Middle East markedly increased, which led to the schism in the Patriarchate of Antioch in 1724 and a Uniate Melkite church issuing forth from it. Around a third of the Arab Orthodox went over to the Unia. It is evident that this mass change of identity was a painful process predetermined by certain radical social and spiritual shifts.

Two sets of factors encouraged the Melkites toward the Unia: socioeconomic and cultural-psychological. In the first case, it was the contribution of the Arab Christian merchant and business class, which was focused on ties to the European economy and interested in the patronage of the consuls of the Catholic powers, who were increasingly influential in the weakening Ottoman Empire. In the second case, we are dealing with a sort of psychological revolution, the awareness on the part of clergy and laity of the decadence and ignorance of their community and an attempt to breathe new life into it by associating it with the achievements of Catholic thought and education and modern technologies, such as the printing press. We are speaking here about medieval culture in the spirit of the Catholic Baroque. The European intellectual quest of the Enlightenment as well as the newest achievements of medicine and science remained beyond the comprehension and interests of the Uniate intellectual elite. Perhaps for many among the Arab Christian urban elite, the two stimuli—economic and cultural—were intertwined. In the people of the West, they saw (or subconsciously felt) a potency for the future and desired to identify themselves with it. As for the uneducated masses of the common people, the appeal of the Unia was facilitated by the similarity in ritual practice between the Uniates and the Orthodox. In summarizing these features of the history of the Orthodox Levant in the eighteenth century—such as a foreign policy in hibernation; the loss of Greek domination of the holy places; the patriarchates teetering on the edge of bankruptcy; and, finally, the Uniate schism—it is possible to conclude that there was a new crisis in Middle Eastern Christianity. Western scholars do not think so: in the most optimistic spirit, they describe spiritual renewal and the revival of the Arab Christians under the influence of Catholic impetus. Indeed, the support of the West provided the Christian community that accepted the Unia with a significant increase in intellectual and economic prosperity. The price, however, was high: the Uniates' rejection of their former identity and an intra-Christian struggle that would not end for generations.

At the same time, this Catholic factor stimulated as a response the unleashing of the spiritual energy of the Orthodox, including attempts to establish higher education and printing and the development of theological polemic and polemically colored historiography. The confrontation with the Unia led to an increased dependence on the Phanar on the part of the Patriarchate of Antioch. From 1724 until 1899, the occupants of the See of Antioch came from Greek lands. However, the Uniate Church's dependence on the Church of Rome was perhaps even more rigid. The political turmoil that engulfed Europe in the late eighteenth century and the corresponding cessation of active support for Middle Eastern Catholics sharply reduced the scope of Uniate expansion and the competition between the two branches of the divided Patriarchate of Antioch.

Summing up, the overall picture of the development of Middle Eastern Orthodoxy in the sixteenth to eighteenth centuries is highly controversial. The social degradation in the Judean hills and the Melkite Renaissance in Damascus and Aleppo occur in parallel. High points of cultural creativity and political activity are followed by decades of torpor. A certain dynamism in Syro–Palestinian Orthodoxy during the Ottoman era is obvious, but it was stimulated by external factors. Relatively stable and tolerant Ottoman rule created a favorable environment for the survival and development of the Arab Orthodox. A sharp increase in the Greek presence in Palestine helped to preserve the monastic tradition, literary culture, and international contacts of the Patriarchate of Jerusalem. Cultural influence from the Balkans also predetermined the Melkite Renaissance. Moldavian, Wallachian, Georgian, and Russian financial inflows provided for the basic survival of the monasteries of the Holy Land, which had no other sources of income. The historic challenge from the Catholic world prompted the Arab Orthodox to recognize and defend their identity. Undoubtedly, the Orthodox community had its own vitality, so long as it could successfully respond to external stimuli. However, this energy was clearly running out.

The Middle Eastern Christians of the Ottoman era completely fall under Lev Gumilev's description of an ethnos in the phase of obscuration. This applies even to the best representatives of the community, such as Macarius al-Zaʿim or Athanasius Dabbas, whose psychology and motivations are easy enough to reconstruct from the sources. Although a talented and somewhat educated people, they are totally devoid of inner fortitude and firmness of belief or some inner core. They are susceptible to external pressure and willing to trade their beliefs and identity and these qualities grow from century to century. A conflictedness, sometimes obscure, which permeated the whole internal history of the Arab Christians (as well as the post-Byzantine Greeks), and the inability to sacrifice personal ambitions for the sake of abstract goals and values, are also the characteristics of a dying ethnos. Against this general background appear some noticeable exceptions, such as Meletius Karma and Dositheus Notaras, but they do not change the overall picture. And their environment prevented them from this, as happened with Macarius al-Dirani, who tried to force the Lebanese monks of the late sixteenth century to live according to the rule of early Byzantine ascetics.

The position of Middle Eastern Christianity would change most radically during the nineteenth century. The growing influence of the Great Powers in the Ottoman Empire transformed the local Christian community into clients of

France, Russia, or England. Attempts by the Ottoman authorities to negate the autonomy of the *millets* and to grant equal rights to its citizens of various faiths led to an unprecedented scale of religious conflicts and massacres of Christians. The Orthodox Church, like the other churches of Syria and Egypt, faced the challenge of the secularization of its flock and the spread of liberal and nationalist views among them.

In the twentieth century, these trends would result in result in a noticeable change in the self-identification of the Arab Orthodox, who will identify with the Arab world. The demographic indicators of the Middle Eastern Christians, which had been very favorable during the nineteenth century, deteriorated sharply in the early twentieth century. A low birth rate and mass emigration led to a precipitous drop in the proportion of Christians in the region and jeopardized their continued existence as a viable ethnoreligious group.

It is the duty of historical scholarship to preserve the image of that world that is perhaps passing away. Without knowledge of it, our understanding of the historical path and interaction between Christianity and Islam is incomplete.

Appendix: Patriarchs and the Sultans

Eastern Patriarchs and Ottoman Sultans from the
Sixteenth Century to the Early Nineteenth Century[1]

Patriarchs of Jerusalem

Dorotheus/ʿAtallah II (1491–1534)

Germanus (1534–May 3, 1579)

Sophronius (May 3, 1579–1608)

Theophanes (1608–December 15, 1644)

Paisius (March 23, 1645–December 2, 1660)

Nectarius (April 7, 1661–January 19, 1669)

Dositheus II Notaras (January 23, 1669–February 7, 1707)

Chrysanthos Notaras (February 8, 1707–February 7, 1731)

Meletius (February 23, 1731–1737)

Parthenius (1737–October 17, 1766)

Ephraim (December 1766–April 1770/1771)

Sophronius (April 1770/1771–January 24, 1774)

Abraham (June 1775–November 1, 1787)

Procopius (November 2, 1787–October 23, 1788)

Anthimus (October 24, 1788–November 10, 1808)

Polycarp (November 10, 1808–January 3, 1827)

Athanasius IV (January 15, 1827–December 16, 1844)

Patriarchs of Antioch

Dorotheus II ibn al-Sabuni (September 1497?–1522/1523)

Michael V ibn al-Mawardi (before 1522?–July 6, 1540)

Dorotheus III (ca. September 1540–late 1543)

Joachim IV ibn Jumʿa (late 1543–January 20, 1576)

Macarius II ibn Hilal (ca. 1543–ca. 1550)

Michael VI al-Hamawi (1576–1583/1592?)

Joachim V Daw (May 25, 1581–October 7, 1592)

Joachim VI ibn Ziyada (1593–November 1603)

Dorotheus IV ibn al-Ahmar (November 1603–1611)

Athanasius II Dabbas (1612–February/March 1619)

Ignatius III ʿAtiya (May 3, 1618–late 1633/early 1634)

Cyril IV Dabbas (May 3, 1618–June 1, 1628)

Euthymius II Karma (May 1, 1634–January 1, 1635)

Euthymius III al-Saqizi (early 1635–November 11, 1647)

Macarius III al-Zaʿim (December 12, 1647–June 12, 1672)

Cyril V al-Zaʿim (July 2, 1672–January 6, 1720)

Neophytus al-Saqizi (November 1672–1681/1682)

Athanasius III Dabbas (June 25, 1686–October 1694; January 1720–July 12, 1724)

Sylvester (September 17, 1724–March 13, 1766)

Philemon (April 28, 1766–July 5, 1767)

Daniel (August 6, 1767–December 15, 1791)

Anthimus (late 1791–July 20, 1813)

Seraphim (August 1813–February 19, 1823)

Methodius (May 13, 1823–June 24, 1850)

Patriarchs of Alexandria

Joachim I Pany (1486/August 6, 1487–1565/1567)

Philotheus II (?–1523)

Sylvester (April 12, 1569–July 1590)

Meletius I Pegas (August 5, 1590–September 13, 1601)

Cyril III Lucaris (1601/1602–November 4, 1620)

Gerasimus I Spartaliot (November 30, 1620–July 30, 1636)

Metrophanes Kritopoulos (September 1636–May 20, 1639)

Nicephorus (late May 1639–April 1645)

Ioannicius (June 9, 1645–September 15, 1657)

Paisius (October 15, 1657–1677/1678 with interruptions)

Joachim II (1666–April 1668)

Parthenius I (1678–June 30, 1688)

Gerasimus II Palladas (July 25, 1688–January 20, 1710)

Samuel Kapasoulis (January 22, 1710–1712)

Cosmas II (1712–1714)

Samuel Kapasoulis (second time 1714–early September 1723)

Cosmas II (second time September 12, 1723–November 28, 1736)

Cosmas III (March 5, 1737–July 3, 1746)
Matthew Psaltis (September 26, 1746–May 1, 1766)
Cyprian (July 22, 1766–1783)
Gerasimus III Gimaris (June 20, 1783–August 6, 1788)
Parthenius II Pankostas (September 13, 1788–September 9, 1805)
Theophilus II (November 9, 1805–October 14, 1825)

Patriarchs of Constantinople

Jeremiah I (1520–1522)
Ioannicius (1522–1523/1524?)
Jeremiah I (second time 1524–1537)
Dionysius II (1537)
Jeremiah I (third time 1537–1545)
Dionysius II (second time 1545–1555)
Joasaph II (1555–1565)
Metrophanes III (1565–1572)
Jeremiah II (1572–1579)
Metrophanes III (second time 1579–1580)
Jeremiah II (second time 1580–1584)
Pachomius II (1584–1585)
Theoleptus II (1585–1586)
Jeremiah II (third time 1586–1595)
Matthew II (1595)
Gabriel I (1596)
Theophanes I (1696–1597)
Meletius Pegas (Patriarch of Alexandria, locum tenens 1597–1599)
Matthew II (second time 1599–1602)
Neophytus II (1602–1603)
Raphael II (1603–1607)
Neophytus II (second time 1607–1612)
Cyril Lucaris (1612)
Timothy II (1612–1621)
Cyril Lucaris (second time, 1621–1623)
Gregorius IV (1623)
Anthimus (1623)
Cyril Lucaris (third and fourth times 1623–1630/1630–1634)
Cyril II Kontaris (1634)
Athanasius III (1634)

Cyril Lucaris (fifth time 1634–1635)
Cyril II Kontaris (second time 1635–1636)
Neophytus III (1736–1737)
Cyril Lucaris (sixth time 1637–1638)
Cyril II Kontaris (third time 1638–1639)
Parthenius I (1639–1644)
Parthenius II (1644–1645)
Ioannichius II (1646–1648)
Parthenius II (second time 1648–1651)
Cyril III (1652)
Athanasius III (second time 1652)
Paisius I (1652–1653)
Ioannichius II (third time 1653–1654)
Paisius I (second time 1654–1655)
Ioannichius II (fourth time 1655–1656)
Parthenius III (1656–1657)
Gabriel II (1657)
Parthenius IV (1657–1662)
Dionysius III (1662–1665)
Parthenius IV (second time 1665–1667)
Clement (1667)
Methodius III (1668–1671)
Parthenius IV (third time 1671)
Dionysius IV (1671–1673)
Gerasimus II (1673–1675)
Parthenius IV (fourth time 1675–1676)
Dionysius IV (second time 1676–1679)
Athanasius IV (1679)
James (1679–1683)
Dionysius IV (third time 1683–1684)
Parthenius IV (fifth time 1684–1685)
James (second time 1685–1686)
Dionysius IV (fourth time 1686–1687)
James (third time 1687–1688)
Callinicus II (1688)
Neophytus IV (1688–1689)
Callinicus II (second time 1689–1693)
Dionysius IV (fifth time 1694)

Callinicus II (third time 1694–1702)
Gabriel III (1702–1705)
Neophytus V (1707)
Cyprian (1708–1709)
Athanasius V (1709–1711)
Cyril IV (1711–1713)
Cyprian (second time 1713–1714)
Cosmas III (1713–1716)
Jeremiah III (1716–1726)
Callinicus III (1726)
Paisius II (1726–1733)
Jeremiah III (second time 1733)
Seraphim I (1733–1734)
Neophytus VI (1734–1740)
Paisius II (second time 1740–1743)
Neophytus VI (second time 1743–1744)
Paisius II (third time 1744–1748)
Cyril V (second time 1752–1757)
Callinicus IV (1757)
Seraphim II (1757–1761)
Ioannichius III (1761–1763)
Samuel I (1763–1768)
Meletius II (1668–1769)
Theodosius II (1769–1773)
Samuel I (second time 1773–1774)
Sophronius II (1774–1780)
Gabriel IV (1780–1785)
Procopius (1785–1789)
Neophytus VII (1789–1794)
Gerasimus III (1794–1797)
Gregorius V (1797–1798)
Neophytus VII (second time 1798–1801)
Callinicus V (1801–1807)
Gregorius V (second time 1806–1808)
Callinicus V (second time 1808–1809)
Jeremiah IV (1809–1813)
Cyril VI (1813–1818)
Gregorius V (third time 1818–1821)

Selim I (1512–1520)
Suleiman the Magnificent (1520–1566)
Selim II (1566–1574)
Murad III (1574–1575)
Mehmed III (1591–1603)
Ahmed I (1603–1617)
Mustafa I (1617–1618)
Osman II (1618–1622)
Mustafa I (second time 1622–1623)
Murad IV (1623–1640)
Ibrahim (1640–1648)
Mehmed IV (1648–1687)
Suleiman II (1687–1691)
Ahmed II (1691–1695)
Mustafa II (1695–1703)
Ahmed III (1703–1730)
Mahmud I (1730–1754)
Osman III (1754–1757)
Mustafa III (1757–1773)
Abdul Hamid (1773–1789)
Selim III (1789–1807)
Mustafa IV (1807–1808)
Mahmud II (1808–1839)

NOTES

Introduction

1 Broadly speaking, the concept of the Christian East includes all the Orthodox and non-Chalcedonian churches. We are using this term in a narrower sense that has been adopted in Russian and, to some degree, in foreign scholarship: it signifies the Eastern Christian cultures other than the Greek and Slavic elements. That is to say, the Christian East is the extant and extinct churches of Western and Central Asia, Northeastern Africa, and the Caucasus: the cultures of the Syrians, pre-Islamic Arab Christians, Copts, Ethiopians, Nubians, Armenians, Georgians, Sogdians, Christian Turks, the Christians of India's Malabar Coast, and so on. In the Middle Ages, the Christians from Egypt to Mesopotamia were to a greater or lesser extent Arabized, which allows us to conditionally combine them as Arab Christians. As a synonym for this term, we will use the term "Middle Eastern Christians."

2 With the exception, perhaps, of the period from the second third of the nineteenth century until the beginning of the twentieth century, a time of active Russian interest in the Middle East, leaving aside the large amount of documentary sources that consistently have attracted the interest of Russian researchers.

3 Greater Syria (Arabic *Bilad al-Sham*) is a geographic concept that includes the Western part of the Fertile Crescent, along with the adjacent lands of the Palestinian Authority, and Jordan.

4 For more details about all these authors, see Chapter 10 of this monograph.

Chapter 1: The Historical Context: Orthodox Christians Under Muslim Rule from the Sixth to the Fifteenth Century

1 For more on the Arab conquests and the reactions thereto by the people of the Near East, see O. G. Bol'shakov, vol. 2; see also M. V. Krivov, 95–103; for excerpts from sources and essential commentaries, see N. A. Mednikov, vols. 1–2.

2 Melkites means "royal" (from the Syr. *malka* for "king") is a term used to denote Middle Eastern adherents of the doctrine of Chalcedon, that is, the faith of the Byzantine emperors. Later on, the Arab Uniate community took on this self-designation, having broken away from the Orthodox Patriarchate of Antioch. Therefore, as applied to medieval realities, the term "Melkites" means the Orthodox, and for the eighteenth and nineteenth centuries, it designates Arab Uniates of the Byzantine rite. In the present study, the term "Melkites" is used to mean "the Orthodox population of the Middle East," if we are talking about the period before eighteenth century, when the Uniate Antiochian church emerged. Note that the ethnic community implied by this term may have been different from one century to another.

3 For an analysis of this document, see N. A. Mednikov, 1. 556–99.

4 *Dhimmi* (Arabic *ahl al-dhimma* "the protected people") is in Islamic law a term for nonbelievers who were subjects of the Islamic state. For more on the legal evolution of the status of dhimmis, see, for example, N. A. Mednikov, vol. 1.

5 N. A. Mednikov, 1, 566–600; V. V. Bartol'd, "Review of Lektsii po istorii Vizantii by A. A. Vasil'ev," 511; V. V. Bartol'd, "Islam i melkity," 651–652; Hitti, 422–24, 485–86; Atiya, 82, 84, 193, 198, 267–68; Runciman, *A History of the Crusades*, 1.20–23.

6 Under Islamic law, a Muslim man can marry a Christian woman; a Christian man, however, must convert to Islam in order to marry a Muslim woman.

7 Runciman, *A History of the Crusades*, 1.23–25; Fargues, 49–51.

8 A. Atiya, 82, 84, 193, 267, 68; Runciman, *A History of the Crusades*, 1.25–26; N. A. Mednikov, 1.649–650, 841–842; O. G. Bol'shakov, 2.124–127; O. G. Bol'shakov, "Vizantiia i Khalifat"; A. Mets, 44–45, 54–55.

9 N. A. Ivanov, *Programa*, 5.

10 On the status of Upper Mesopotamia in the first decades of the Caliphate, see Robinson, *Empire and Elites After the Muslim Conquest: The Transformation of the Northern Mesopotamia* (Cambridge, 2000). On the situation of the Copts, see Brett, 6–7.

11 Piccirillo, 48, 53–54; Zeyadeh, p. 118ff.; MacAdam, 51; Shick, "Luxuriant Legacy," 86–87.

12   MacAdam, 57–59, 72–74, 76, 82; Zeyadeh, 121–124; Griffith, "ʿAbd al-Masih an-Nagrani," 357; Shick, "Luxuriant Legacy," 86–87.

13   The chapel erected over the Holy Sepulchre, the sacred center of the Church of the Resurrection in Jerusalem.

14   Arculf, 1–12; Willibald, 13–22; Bernard the Wise, 23–31.

15   MacAdam, 77–78, 81; *EAEHL*, 190, 270–285, 384, 927–930, 1035–1050.

16   J. Neale, 67–80; Eutychius, 46; Matveevskii, 229–233.

17   A. N. Murav'ev, *Istoriia*, 1.286, 299–305; Yu. A. Kulakovskii, 197–198; V. Potlov, 40–41.

18   Eutychius, 13, 27; N. A. Mednikov, 2.260–261, 271; V. Potulov, 40; Karalevskij, "Antioche," col. 595.

19   O. G. Bol'shakov, 1.115, 176; N. A. Mednikov, 1.651.

20   Eutychius, 38; (Russian translation: N. A. Mednikov, 2(1).272); V. V. Bartold, "Review of Lektsii po istorii Vizantii by A. A. Vasil'ev," 582.

21   Kekelidze, 144.

22   V. V. Bartol'd, "Islam i melkity," 652; see also K. A. Panchenko, "Rod Ioanna Damaskina," 88–99.

23   V. V. Bartol'd, "Islam i melkity," 653.

24   V. Potulov, 45; K.-P. Todt, 173; Moosa, 101–104; Karalevskij, "Antioche," col. 591–592.

25   Moosa, 114–116.

26   *SCWSC*, 30; O. G. Bol'shakov, 3.116.

27   *SCWSC*, 202–204; N. A. Mednikov, 2(1).273; N. A. Mednikov, 1.683–686.

28   Eutychius, 41 (Russian translation: N. A. Mednikov, 2.273).

29   J. Neale, 80, 86; Matveevskii, 233–235.

30   N. A. Mednikov, 2.89–90; O. G. Bol'shakov, 3.274–282; O. G. Bol'shakov, "Vizantiia i khalifat," 357.

31   Eutychius, 42; For a discussion of this issue, see: N. A. Mednikov, 1.687–699.

32   N. A. Mednikov, 1.701.

33   Eutychius, 43–44; (Russian translation: N. A. Mednikov, 2. 275–276); N. A. Mednikov, 1.704–722; V. V. Bartol'd, "Khalif Omar II."

34   Theophanes, year 6215.

35   Kekelidze, 151–157.

36   Leo III the Isaurian (717–743): Byzantine emperor and initiator of the Iconoclast policy.

37   Theophanes, year 6255.

38   A. N. Murav'ev, *Istoriia*, 1.319–322, 330, 334–337.

39 Eutychius, 45 (Russian Translation: N. A. Mednikov, 2.276–277); N. A. Mednikov, 1.723; V.V. Bartol'd, "Islam i melkity," 653–654; Theophanes, year 6234.

40 Kekelidze, 166; Eutychius, 52; N. A. Mednikov, 2.278, 285, 287, 288, 290, 329–330; K.-P. Todt, 184–185.

41 Theophanes, year 6234.

42 Ibid., year 6248.

43 N. A. Mednikov, 1.775, 2.285; V. V. Bartol'd, "Islam i melkity," 654; K.-P. Todt , 178–79.

44 E. Brooks; K. A. Panchenko, "K istorii pravoslavnogo letopisaniia."

45 Wright, 111; A. Papadopulo-Keramevs, *Muchenichestvo shestidesiati novykh sviatykh muchenikov*, i–iii.

46 Kh. M. Loparev, "Vizantiiskie zhitie sviatykh VIII–IX vv." 76ff.; *Zhitie Romana Novogo*; A. Papadopulo-Keramevs, *Muchenichestvo shestidesiati novykh sviatykh muchenikov*.

47 Theophanes, year 6234; *Zhitie Petra Kapetoliiskogo*.

48 *Zhitie Antoniia/Ravakha*; S.n., "Istoricheskoe skazanie o podvizhnichestve Ilii Novogo"; Kh. M. Loparev, "Vizantiiskie zhitiia sviatykh", XIX.45; S.n., "Skazanie o muchenichestve sviatykh ottsov v lavre prep. Savvy", 47.

49 Griffith, "ʿAbd al-Masih an-Nagrani," 333–335, 351–359.

50 Porphyry Uspenskii, *Pervoe puteshestvie*, 108–119.

51 Willibald, 19.

52 Kh. M. Loparev, *Vizantiiskie zhitiia* sviatykh, 19.28.

53 Ibid., 24.

54 Brett, 6–7.

55 J. Neale, 1.114–118; N. A. Mednikov, 1.736–737.

56 L. Browne, 57–58; Runciman, *A History of the Crusades*, 1.26–27.

57 Theophanes, year 6267. Theophanes clearly borrows this passage from the Syriac Melkite chronicle of 780.

58 Theophanes, year 6272; N. A. Mednikov, 1.744–747; 755–757; 759–760.

59 N. A. Mednikov, 1.720–722, 724, 736, 744–745, 748, 757, 768.

60 Burns, *Monuments of Syria*, 111–112.

61 Zeyadeh, 120; MacAdam, 57, 74–81.

62 Piccirillo, 48; Shick, "Luxuriant Legacy," 87–88.

63 J. Nasrallah, *HMLEM*, 3(1).69.

64 Piccirillo, 47.

65 S.n., "Skazanie o muchenichestve sviatykh ottsov v lavre prep. Savvy", 9.

66 Kh. M. Loparev, *Vizantiiskie zhitiia sviatykh*, 19.32.

67 Finkelstein, 60, 61, 64.

68 Theophanes, years 6301, 6305.

69 A. Atiya, p. 86; M. Brett, p. 7, 15.

70 M. Brett, p. 15.

71 Piccirillo, 53–55.

72 Swanson, 63.

73 M. Hiyari, 134

74 Burns, *Monuments*, 142, 144, 156.

75 Brett, *Population*, 3, 8–10.

76 Brett, *Population*, 18–19.

77 Ibid., 15.

78 Griffith, "The Monks of Palestine," 17–20.

79 Griffith, "Greek into Arabic," 122–23.

80 Ibid., 124–128.

81 For the bibliography on these figures, see: Griffith, "The Monks of Palestine," 22–23; K. A. Boiko, 53–60; K. A. Panchenko, "K istorii pravoslavnogo letopisaniia," 109; K. A. Panchenko, "Kosta ibn Luka," 162.

82 Griffith, 6, 24.

83 Eutychius, 49.

84 K. A. Panchenko, "K istorii pravoslavnogo letopisaniia," 109–120; K. A. Panchenko, "Vospriiatie istoricheskogo protsessa," 82–86.

85 Eutychius, 75 (Russian translation: N. A. Mednikov, 2, 288–289).

86 Eutychius, 55 (Russian translation: N. A. Mednikov, 2.280).

87 Griffith, "Greek into Arabic," 125; Griffith, "The Monks of Palestine," 15–17.

88 Kh. M. Lopaerev, *Vizantiiskie zhitiia sviatykh*, 19.23, 29–30; N. A. Mednikov, 2(1).288–289; Theophanes, year 6255.

89 V. V. Bartol'd, "Karl Velikii i Kharun al-Rashid"; V. V. Bartol'd, "K voprosu o franko-musul'manskikh otnosheniiakh."

90 Bernard the Wise, 26; V. V. Bartol'd, "Karl Velikii i Kharun al-Rashid," 293; A. A. Dmitrievskii, "Tipikony," 63–64.

91 Kh. M. Loparev, "Vizantiiskie zhitiia sviatykh," 17.215; V. V. Bartol'd, "Karl Velikii i Kharun al-Rashid," 291

92 Kh. M. Loparev, "Vizantiiskie zhitiia sviatykh," 17.215–216.

93 Griffith, *"The Life of Theodore of Edessa,"* 152–156.

94 J. Neale, 82–96; N. A. Mednikov, 1.649–650, 683–687, 701–702.

95 "Skazanie o muchenichestve sviatykh ottsov v lavre prep. Savvy", 32–35.

96 Eutychius, 55–56; N. A. Mednikov, 1.762–764, 2.279–282.

97 N. A. Mednikov, 1.778–788; Hitti, 543–545; I. M. Fil'shtinskii, 133–142.

98 N. A. Mednikov, 1.791, 804, 805, 809–810, 813; N. A. Mednikov, 2.291–293, 330–331.

99   A. Mets, 16; V. R. Rozen, 89.

100   V. R. Rozen, 110–122; A. Mets, 17; Runciman, *A History of the Crusades*, 1. 30–31; O. G. Bol'shakov, "Vizantiia i khalifat," 364–365.

101   N. A. Mednikov, 2.335–336.

102   N. A. Mednikov, 1.821–824, 2.335–336, 338–342, 343–346; K. A. Panchenko, "Antiokhiiskii patriarkh Khristofor," 223–227.

103   V. R. Rozen, 32–33, 40–41, 240–259, 309–331; N. A. Mednikov, 1.825–838; Runciman, *A History of the Crusades*, 1.31–34; Kuchuk-Ioannesov, "Pis'mo Tsimiskhiia," 96–100.

104   Eutychius, 88; N. A. Mednikov, 2.294.

105   A. A. Dmitrievskii, "Tipikony," 36, 40, 49, 63.

106   Brett, "Al-Karaza al-Marqusiya," 36–37.

107   N. A. Mednikov, 1.840–841; A. Mets, 57.

108   V. R. Rozen, 35, 295–300; A. Mets, 58.

109   V. R. Rozen, 42–43, 337–338; N. A. Mednikov, 1.839–840, 849, 2, 357–358.

110   N. A. Mednikov, 1.849–853; A. Mets, 58–59.

111   N. A. Mednikov, 1.853–854, 2.360–371; V. R. Rozen, 48.

112   Yahya, 201; V. R. Rozen, 48, 49, 356–357.

113   N. A. Mednikov, 1. 854–857; A. Mets, 59.

114   A significant figure in the history of the late Fatimid Caliphate is the vizier Badr al-Jamali, the *de facto* ruler of the state at the end of the eleventh century. A *ghulam* (slave-soldier) of Armenian ethnicity, thus hardly a sincere convert to Islam, he relied on the forces of Armenian mercenaries, many of whom were Christians. Badr treated Coptic patriarchs with marked respect. At the same time, the church was strictly subordinated to the interests of the state. Christians and Jews had to pay *jizya* without exceptions. The vizier dictated resolutions to the council of Coptic bishops, making use of Biblical terminology, in a manner similar to Christian emperors in the era of the Ecumenical Councils (Brett, "Al-Karaza al-Marqusiya," 50–52).

115   V. V. Bartol'd, "Review of Lektsii po istorii Vizantii by A. A. Vasil'ev," 590–591; V. V. Bartol'd, "Islam i melkity," 655; Yahya, 237, 239; N. A. Mednikov, 1.857–860.

116   V. V. Bartol'd, "Review of Lektsii po istorii Vizantii by A. A. Vasil'ev," 592; V. V. Bartol'd, "K voprosu o franko-musul'manskikh otnosheniiakh," 295; Yahya, 252; A. Mets, 46.

117   Michael the Syrian, 160–161; Matthew of Edessa, 84–85.

118   V. R. Rozen, 1–2, 4, 22, 86–87, 90.

119   The commander-in-chief of the guard units stationed in the eastern part of the empire.

120 V. R. Rozen, 3–11, 24–25, 33, 124–127, 209.

121 Arkim. Leonid, "Tri stati k russkomu palestinovedeniiu," 44–45.

122 Runciman, *Vostochnaia skhizma*, 54–56; Archim. Ledonid, "Tri stati k russkomu palestinovedeniiu," 45.

123 Eutychius of Alexandria. *Eutychii Patriarchae Alexandrini Annales*, edited by Louis Cheikho. 1–2 Vols. Paris: C. Poussielgue, 1906 and 1909; *Histoire de Yahya-ibn-Saʿid dʾAntioche, continiateur de Saʿid-ibn-Bitriq*, edited and translated by J. Kratchkovsky and A. Vasiliev. *Patrologia Orientalis*. 18.5 (1924), 23.3 (1932).

124 See, in excerpt, V. R. Rozen, 36–48; A. Mets, 139–141; I. Iu. Krachkovskii, "Arabskaia geograficheskaia literatura," 266–267.

125 A Byzantine title of middle rank.

126 Habib Zayat, "Vie du patriarche melkite d'Antioche Christophore (d. 967) par le protospathaire Ibrahim b. Yuhanna. Document inédit du Xe siècle." *Proche-Orient Chretien* 2 (1952), 11–38, 333–366.

127 Kekelidze, 119–23.

128 C. Basha and L. Cheikho, "ʿAbdallah ibn al-Fadl al-Antaki."

129 V. V. Bartol'd, "Islam i melkity," 655.

130 M. V. Krivov, "Araby-khristiane," 250–255.

131 V. R. Rozen, 45–47; see also P. V. Kuzenkov and K. A. Panchenko, 5–6.

132 V. V. Bartol'd, "Review of Lektsii po istorii Vizantii by A. A. Vasil'ev," 585.

133 Nicephorus Bryennius, 105–108; F. I. Uspenskii, 3.40–43; Runciman, *A History of the Crusades* 1.64–72.

134 Runciman, *A History of the Crusades* 1.73–75; Michael the Syrian, Part 1, 30.

135 G. Graf, 2.98–100; Nasrallah, *HMLEM*, 3(1).86–89.

136 Bat Yeor, 2.48–49.

137 Runciman, *A History of the Crusades* 1.76–78; Nasrallah, *HMLEM*, 3(1).103–104.

138 Runciman, *A History of the Crusades* 1.195–217, 235–250, 261–287; Runciman, *Vostochnaia skhizma*, 67–9; F. I. Uspenskii, 3.107–115.

139 Runciman, *A History of the Crusades*, 1.222, 252, 257, 277, 289; Runciman, *Vostochnaia skhizma*, 66, 68–69.

140 Runciman, *Vostochnaia skhizma,* 69.

141 Runciman, *A History of the Crusades* 1.288–289; Runciman, *Vostochnaia skhizma*, 69.

142 A. Popov, 227–30; P. Plank, 188.

143 A. Jotischky, 91.

144 P. Plank, 187; Nasrallah, *HMLEM*, 3(1).104–105.

145 Arkhim. Leontii, xxv–xxxvii; P. Plank, 187–188; R. Rose, 241.

146 P. Plank, 186.

147 Runciman, *A History of the Crusades* 1.320; Runciman, *Vostochnaia skhizma*, 69.

148 Runciman, *A History of the Crusades*, 1.257. R. Burns, however, argues that there was an Orthodox bishop in the city before the arrival of the Crusaders (R. Burns, *Monuments of Syria*, 57). In this case, the separation of the Orthodox and Catholic ecclesiastical institutions in the East should be counted from autumn of 1098.

149 F. I. Uspenskii, 3.116–120.

150 Runciman, *A History of the Crusades* 1.305–306, 320–321; Runciman, *Vostochnaia skhizma*, 72.

151 J. Richard, 154–155; Jotischky, 91; P. Plank, 185.

152 P. Plank, 185; Jotischky, 91–92.

153 Jotischky, 85.

154 Daniil, 49, 55, 59, 61; Zevul'f, 286.

155 Daniil, 123; Runciman, *A History of the Crusades,* 1.294–295; Runciman, *Vostochnaia skhizma*, 69–70; J. Richard, 150–60; Pahlitzsch, Georgians, 35–39.

156 Jotischky, 93; Runciman, *Vostochnaia skhizma*, 70–71; J. Richard, 154–155.

157 John Phocas, 46–47, 50–52; Jotischky, 93.

158 M. Sharon, 50–52.

159 Pahlitzsch, 36.

160 Jotischky, p. 93.

161 John Phocas, 49; Jotischky, 90, 92; J. Frenkel, 111–112; Pahlitzsch, p. 36–37.

162 P. Plank, 184; J. Richard, 151–157; R. Rose, 240–41.

163 P. Plank, 183–184.

164 P. Plank, 186; Griffith, "Anthony David of Bagdad," 19.

165 Runciman, *A History of the Crusades* 1.320–321, 3.87–91, 99–100, 135–138, 231; Runciman, *Vostochnaia skhizma*, 71–75; F. I. Uspenskii, 3.149–155, 205–220; Karalevskij, "Antioche," Col. 618–19.

166 R. Rose, 239–249; Pahlitzsch, 37–39.

167 Matveevskii, 365–370; Runciman, *A History of the Crusades,* 3.150–169; Runciman, *Vostochnaia skhizma*, 76.

168 R. Rose, 241; Porphyry Uspenskii, *Vtoroe puteshestvie*, 246. V. Grumel proposes placing the death of Euthymius at 1230 (V. Grumel, "La Chronologie des patriarches Grecs," 197–198).

169 Matveevskii, 367–369; Atiya, 92.

170 Kamal al-Din ibn al-ʿAdim, 163.

171 Michael the Syrian, Part 3, 17–20.

172 Atiya, 94.

173 Michael the Syrian, Part 5, 50.

174 Atiya, 95.

175 Atiya, 94–95; Matveevskii, 367–369.

176 Savva Nemanich, 1–4, 17–21, 30–39; Pahlitzsch, 39; Pahlitzsch, "Athanasios II," 465–474; Grumel, "La Chronologie des patriarches Grecs," 198–199.

177 Runciman, *A History of the Crusades,* 3.306.

178 Ibid., 307.

179 Ibid.; S. Humphreys, 351–356, 360.

180 S. Runciman, *A History of the Crusades*, 3.307; J. Richard, 349–365.

181 S. Humphreys, 358–360.

182 Runciman, *A History of the Crusades*, 3.316–326.

183 Ibid., p. 319–20.

184 Hitti, 622–624; Atiya, 92–93, 194, 397, 400.

185 Bat Yeor, 56–59, 70–73, 75–81; L. Browne, p. 174–178; O. Meinardus, 12; T. K. Koraev, 44–45, 48–49.

186 M. Brett, "Population and Conversion," 25–30.

187 D. V. Shestopalets, 153.

188 R. Irwin, 112–114.

189 Cited in T. K. Koraev, 45–46.

190 For details, see K. A. Panchenko, "Podzhog Kaira 1321 g."

191 T. K. Koraev, 48; D. V. Shestopalets, 156.

192 For details, see K. A. Panchenko, "Zabytaia katastrofa."

193 Atiya, 98.

194 L. Browne, 178.

195 Reifenberg, 58, 99; I. M. Smilianskaia, *Sotsial'no-ekonomicheskaia struktura*, 25.

196 On the disappearance of the settled population in the Syrian steppe in the thirteenth and fourteenth centuries, see O. Grabar, 8, 11, 161.

197 Reifenberg, 59.

198 The last known record of the monastery as active belongs to Sava the Serbian (1235) (Savva Nemanich, 22). In addition, Arsenius, the bishop of Tripoli, and then patriarch of Antioch in 1284–1286 (Savva Nemanich, 22) was in Mar Sam'an in his youth (Nasrallah, "Chronologie, 1250–1500," 7). Arsenius's youth hypothetically can reckoned no earlier than 1240. The only argument against such a dating of the devastation of the monastery could be contained in a Melkite manuscript dating to the fourteenth century, labeled as a donation to the monastery of St Simeon the Stylite (Troupeau, n164). It cannot be excluded,

however, that the dating of the manuscript is not completely accurate or that it is a different monastery of St Simeon, for example, the monastery Mar Sam'an al-'Aja'ib near Beirut (see Chapter 5).

199 Le Strange, 41.

200 D. Korobeinikov, 4–5; Vryonis, 320.

201 L. Browne, 170–71.

202 Atiya, 276.

203 L. Browne, 172.

204 D. Korobeinikov, 9–10, 15.

205 Vryonis, 351–402; D. Korobeinikov, 9, 17–18.

206 T. K. Koraev, 47.

207 Nasrallah, *HMLEM*, 3(2).50, 83.

208 MS Lattakia, 28.

209 Nasrallah, *HMLEM*, 3(2), 99, 108–110; K. A. Panchenko, "Greki vs. Araby," 22–23.

210 Jotischky, 85.

211 Frenkel, 112–113.

212 Savva Nemanich, 3, 4, 17, 34, 37, 59; Agrefenii, 274–275; Ignaty Smol'nianin, 21–22; Zosima, 35–38; Daniel of Ephesus, 54–58; M. Sharon, 3.48–54.

213 Savva Nemanich, 3, 4, 35–36; Agrefenii, 275–276; Zosima, 35, 36; Frenkel, 114–15.

214 Frenkel, 113.

215 Nasrallah, *HMLEM*, 3(2).82–87.

216 Hesychasm is a mystical movement, cultivated in the Orthodox monastic tradition and focused on the participation in the divine energy (the light of Tabor), which is active in the world. In fourteenth-century Byzantium, hesychasm acquired the traits of an ideological and political movement and played a prominent role in public life.

217 A. Tsagareli, 130, 193–240; Porphyry Uspenskii, *Kniga bytiia moego*, 8.47–48.

218 Savva Nemanich, 36; Nasrallah, *HMLEM*, 3(2). 88–89; A. Tsagareli, 222; A. Peristeris, p. 175–176.

219 MS Damascus 433; S.n. *Kratkii obzor sobraniia rukopisei, prinadlezhavshego ep.* Part II, 14.

220 E. Rose, 243; Pahlitzsch, 36–38.

221 Pahlitzsch, 40–45; C. Muller and J. Pahlitzsch, 268–281.

222 A. Tsagareli, 97–106, 116–123.

223 Arkhim. Leonid, "Serbskaia inocheskaia obshchina v Palestine," 42–53; S. Popović, 389–390, 400–406.

224 Runciman, *The Historic Role of Christian Arabs*, 12–13; Nasrallah, *HMLEM*, 3(2).147.

225 R. Rose, 241.

226 Pahlitzsch, 47

227 Nasrallah, *HMLEM*, 3(2).50–51.

228 Pahlitzsch, 48.

229 Pahlitzsch, 46–47; Nasrallah, *HMLEM*, 3(2).52.

230 Maximus Simaius, 34–35; A. N. Murav'ev, *Istoriia*, 2.244–248; Nasrallah *HMLEM*, 3(2).68–69.

231 D. Nicol, 291.

232 Papadopulo-Keramevs, *Opisanie sv. mest bezymiannogo kontsa XIV v,* iii–xi.

233 Troupeau, 147.

234 Zosima, 23.

235 Nasrallah, *HMLEM*, 3(2).49.

236 MS Vostfaka, 677.

237 K. A. Panchenko, "Greki vs. araby," 17–19.

238 Nasrallah, *HMLEM*, 3(2).166–167, 171.

239 S. v., "Evfimii I, patriarkh Antiokhiisii," in *Pravoslavnaia Entsiklopediia*, 17.425.

240 Nasrallah, "Chronologie, 1250–1500," p. 8–10.

241 S. v. "Dionisii I, patriarkh Antiokhiiskii" in *Pravoslavnaia Entsiklopediia*, 15.308.

242 Nasrallah, "Chronologie, 1250–1500," 10–11; Nasrallah, *HMLEM*, 3(2).107.

243 Gregory Palamas (c. 1296–1357)—an Athonite monk and later archbishop of Thessalonica, the spiritual leader of the hesychast movement.

244 Nasrallah, "Chronologie, 1250–1500," 13–18; Nasrallah, *HMLEM*, 3(2).65–66.

245 Nasrallah, *HMLEM*, 3(2).66–71.

246 K. A. Panchenko, "K istorii russko-vostochnykh sviazei," 5–20.

247 Nasrallah, *HMLEM*, 3(2).71.

248 Matveevskii, 261, 266.

249 Matveevskii, 375–381; A. P. Lebedev, Istoriia greko-vostochnoi, 273–275; Nasrallah, *HMLEM*, 3(2).59–62.

250 Nasrallah, *HMLEM*, 3(2).58, 62.

251 Ibid., 62, 148–149.

252 *Kratkii obzor sobraniia rukopisei prinadlezhavshego ep. Porfiriiu,* 138; MS Lattakia 28; Nasrallah, *HMLEM*, 3(2).148–149.

253 Nasrallah, *HMLEM*, 3(2).58.

254 This legend, recorded in Arabic probably in the first half of the sixteenth century, was translated into Greek in 1688, and in the nineteenth century was published by Porphyry Uspensky. Another, later variant of the tale exists, in which all the secondary plot lines were eliminated, and only the central episode with the drinking of the poison remained. This narrative reveals traces of a meticulous literary work and also shows the influence of a ninth-century anti-Jewish polemical treatise *The Life and Labours of St John, Catholicos of Urhay*. This version of the narrative appeared in Rus rather early (its most complete text is found in the *Pilgrimage* of Vasily Poznyakov, dated to 1559) and became quite widespread. See Porphyry Uspenskii, "Aleksandriiskaia patriarkhiia," 15–29; Poznyiakov, 1–31; Kashtanov, *Rossiia i grecheskii mir v XVI veke*, 258–261.

255 A. N. Veselovskii, 14–33.

256 Karalevskij, "Antioche," col. 632; Nasrallah, *HMLEM*, 3(2).72–73.

257 Nasrallah, *HMLEM*, 3(2).73–74; A. Zanemonets, 86–100.

258 Nasrallah, *HMLEM*, 3(2).79; Karalevskij, "Antioche," col. 632–634.

259 D. F. Kobeko, 272–275; K. A. Panchenko, "Patriarkh Ioakim," 229–234.

260 Nasrallah, *HMLEM*, 3(2).79; Nasrallah, "Chronologie, 1250–1500," 34–35.

261 K. A. Panchenko, "Patriarkh Ioakim."

262 L. Eckenstein, 166; Porphyry Uspenskii, *Pervoe puteshestvie*, 140–141.

263 S. v. "Iakov II, patriarkh Ierusalimskii" in *Pravoslavaia Entsiklopediia* 20.514.

264 Nasrallah, *HMLEM*, 3(2).76; Nasrallah, "Chronologie, 1250– 1500," 34; Runciman, *The Great Church in Captivity*, 228.

265 M. Bakhit, 44–45.

266 Daniel of Ephesus, 58.

267 Arkhim. Leonid, "Serbskaia inocheskaia obshchina v Palestine," 53; J. Frenkel, 115; K. A. Panchenko, "Greki vs. araby," 27.

268 L. Eckenstein, 162–163; A. Von Harff, 141; Nasrallah, *HMLEM*, 3(2).85–86.

269 H. Ernst, 210–249.

270 Matveevskii, 369.

271 P. Zhuze, "Eparkhii Antiokhiiskoi tserkvi," 486–92; K.-P. Todt, "Notitia und Diozesen."

Chapter 2: The Political Context: The Ottoman State and the Orthodox Church

1 Mikha'il Burayk, *Tarikh al-Sham*, 118.

2 "Rum" is a medieval name of the Byzantines in the East; it is synonymous with the word "Orthodox."

3 V. V. Bartol'd, "Turtsiia, islam i khristianstvo," 424.

4   Ibid., 426.

5   N. A. Ivanov, "Sistema milletov," 30–31.

6   I. I. Malyshevskii, 34.

7   E. P. Naumov, 119.

8   The earliest evidence of this kind dates back to 1432 (Halil Inalcik, "The Status of the Greek Orthodox Patriarch," 197).

9   Halil Inalcik, "The Status of the Greek Orthodox Patriarch," 196–97; H. Inalcik, "Ottoman Methods of Conquest," 103, 113–14.

10   Halil Inalcik, "Ottoman Methods of Conquest", 104–105.

11   From the Arabic word *milla* ("nation"). It should be recognized that the term "system" as applied to the *millet* is not quite correct. They were created as a result of a number of disparate regulations in different years.

12   B. Braude and B. Lewis, 12–13, 21–26; N. A. Ivanov, "Sistema milletov," 31, 35–39.

13   See, for example, I. N. Berezin, "Pravoslavnye tserkvi v Turtsii"; A. P. Lebedev, *Istoriia*; N. A. Ivanov, "Sistema milletov"; B. Braude and B. Lewis; R. Clogg; Halil Inalcik, "The Status of the Greek Orthodox Patriarch."

14   I. N. Berezin, "Pravoslavnye tserkvi v Turtsii," 6–8.

15   RGADA, Fond 52/1, 1669, no. 11, ff. 29–32.

16   AVPRI, Fond 89/1, 1745, no. 4, ff. 114v–116.

17   I. N. Berezin, "Pravoslavnye tserkvi v Turtsii," 6.

18   Ibid., 7–8.

19   RGADA, Fond 52/1, 1669, no. 11, ff. 30–31.

20   AVPRI, Fond 89/1, 1745, no. 4, f. 115.

21   Runciman, *The Great Church*, 172, 175.

22   I. N. Berezin, "Pravoslavnye tserkvi v Turtsii," 9; A. P. Lebedev, *Istoriia*, 100, 102; Runciman, *The Great Church*, 170–71.

23   I. N. Berezin, "Pravoslavnye tserkvi v Turtsii," 8.

24   I. N. Berezin, "Pravoslavnye tserkvi v Turtsii," 11; A. P. Lebedev, *Istoriia*, 106.

25   I. N. Berezin, "Pravoslavnye tserkvi v Turtsii," 12–13; AVPRI, Fond 89/1, 1745, no. 4. ff. 115–115v.

26   RGADA, Fond 52/1, 1669, no. 11, f. 31.

27   AVRI, Fond 89/1, 1745, no. 4, f. 116.

28   I. N. Berezin, "Pravoslavnye tserkvi v Turtsii", p. 14.

29   Ibid., 14–15.

30   I. N. Berezin, "Pravoslavnye tserkvi v Turtsii," 16.

31   See, for example, I. N. Berezin, "Pravoslavnye tserkvi v Turtsii," 41; I. I. Malyshevskii, 244–265.

32 A. P. Lebedev, *Istoriia*, 249, 303, 324–325.

33 I. N. Berezin, "Pravoslavnye tserkvi v Turtsii," 65.

34 I. N. Berezin, "Khristiane v Mesopotamii i Sirii," 1854, no. 17, 14; 1855, no. 3, 75.

35 *Kharaj* was a land tax in the Muslim East. Sometimes the term is erroneously used as meaning a poll tax levied on non-Muslims.

36 Cited in: N. Skabalanovich, 461.

37 I. N. Berezin, "Khristiane v Mesopotamii i Sirii," 1854, no.17, 8–9; I. N. Berezin, "Pravoslavnye tserkvi v Turtsii," 19.

38 That is, a purse, or sack (see the glossary).

39 K. M. Bazili, 2007, 142.

40 For details, see: I. N. Berezin, "Khristiane v Mesopotamii i Sirii," 1854, no. 17, 7; 1855, no. 3, 68–71; Bat Yeor, 34–36, 76–79, 106–107, 328–329.

41 At least officially, since, in fact, Christians were often the sailors on warships and made up local police and paramilitary border forces. (Runciman, *The Great Church*, 179; I. N. Berezin, "Khristiane v Mesopotamii i Sirii," 1854, no. 17, 9).

42 N. Skabalanovich, 450–452.

43 A. P. Lebedev, *Istoriia*, 125.

44 Runciman, *The Great Church*, 181–82.

45 Halil Inalcik, "The Greek Orthodox Patriarch," 197.

46 N. A. Ivanov, "Sistema milletov," 39.

47 B. Braude and B. Lewis, 13, 17.

48 A. P. Lebedev, *Istoriia*, 130.

49 Runciman, *The Great Church*, 173–176.

50 A. P. Lebedev, *Istoriia*, 110, 114.

51 B. Braude and B. Lewis, 13.

52 A. P. Lebedev, *Istoriia*, 133–135.

53 Ibid., 136–38.

54 V. V. Bartol'd, "Turtsiia, islam i khristianstvo," 427.

55 *Timariot*—a service class, the holders of *timars*—conditional land holdings, given based on military service.

56 Halil Inalcik, "Ottoman Methods of Conquest," 113–117, 119.

57 B. Masters, 42.

58 Ibid.

59 S. A. Frantsuzov, "Pripiska k Arabskoi Biblii."

60 D. E. Eremeev and M. S. Meier, 148–149; T. Iu. Kobishchanov, 5–7.

61 In popular imagination, the word "*raya*" was perceived as a derogatory name for the Christian subjects of the Ottoman Turks. In fact, it did mean "herd," as is often supposed, but "flock," which is almost the same as the term "congregation" in the Church. This concept was also applied to the entire taxpaying population of the empire, regardless of their religious affiliation (B. Braude and B. Lewis, 15).

62 D. E. Eremeev and M. S. Meier, 131–133, 143.

63 Ibid., 147.

64 Ibid., 157–161.

65 Ibid., 161–65.

66 Abdul-Rahim Abu-Husayn, 24–27, 84–86.

67 Abdul-Rahim Abu-Husayn, 16, 17, 19, 78–80.

68 Ibid., 81–84, 87–93.

69 Ibid., 48–55, 93–120.

70 Abdul-Rahim Abu-Husayn. 124–127; T. Yu. Kobishchanov, 14.

71 Cited in Abdul-Rahim Abu-Husayn, 127.

72 D. E. Eremeev and M. S. Meier, 177–178.

73 D. E. Eremeev and M. S. Meier, 166, 174–175; T. Yu. Kobishchanov, 8–9.

74 D. E. Eremeev and M. S. Meier, 179–184, 188–191; T. Yu. Kobishchanov, 15.

75 T. Yu. Kobishchanov, 15–18.

76 For details, see T. Yu. Kobishchanov, "Krest nad Beirutom."

77 Beirut Ecclesiastical Chronicle, 72.

78 K. M. Bazili, 2007, 18–20; T. Yu. Kobishchanov, 68–78, 81–88.

79 Mikha'il Burayk, *Tarikh al-Sham*, 103–118.

80 Ibid., 27.

81 Sharifs are descendants of the Prophet Muhammad, a privileged social group in the Islamic Middle East.

82 al-Jabarti, *'Aja'ib,* 413.

83 Mikha'il Burayk, *Tarikh al-Sham*, p. 112.

84 Beirut Ecclesiastical Chronicle, 69

85 Beirut Ecclesiastical Chronicle, 81.

86 K. M. Bazili, 2007, 79–82, 91–98; T. Yu. Kobishchanov, 20, 22–25.

87 K. M. Bazili, 2007, 98–103.

88 Neophytus of Cyprus, "Rasskaz," 28–30; Maximus Simaius, 87–89.

89 Sabanu, *Tarikh hawadith al-Sham wa-Lubnan*, 21.

90 Clogg, 188–193.

91 Neophytus of Cyprus, "Dvadtsatiletie," 122–135; Procopius Nazianzen, 332–340; K. M. Bazili, 2007, 130; Sabanu, *Tarikh hawadith al-Sham wa-Lubnan*, 68.

Chapter 3: Geography and Demographics

1 In addition to historical Syria, separate groups of Middle Eastern Orthodox lived in Egypt, within the Patriarchate of Alexandria, as well as in Eastern Anatolia, which in ecclesiastical terms belonged to the See of Antioch.

2 Hitti, 30–44; I. M. Smilianskaia, *Sotsial'no-ekonomicheskaia struktura*, 13–15.

3 Volney, 2.489.

4 I. M. Smilianskaia, *Sotsial'no-ekonomicheskaia struktura*, 15–17, 22–30; Hitti, 45–47; Reifenberg, 21–24.

5 I. M. Smilianskaia, *Sotsial'no-ekonomicheskaia struktura*, 31–32.

6 For more on the problem of the veracity of Ottoman statistics see: B. Masters, 53–54; T. Yu. Kobishchanov, 59–62.

7 Paul of Aleppo, 5.169.

8 Ibid.

9 Paul of Aleppo, 5.170.

10 See concrete figures in B. Masters, 53; T. Yu. Kobishchanov, 60.

11 B. Masters, 49.

12 R. Haddad, *Syrian Christians*, 10.

13 M. Bakhit, 25–28; B. Heyberger, 19.

14 B. Masters, 56. In 1697, Patriarch Cyril of Antioch, in conversation with the English traveler Henry Maundrell, counted his flock in Damascus to be greater than 1200 "souls" (i.e., individuals) (H. Maundrel, 491). It is evident that the interlocutors did not understand each other and that the conversation was not about "souls" but about families, households.

15 Philipp, 26.

16 M. Bakhit, 25–28; B. Heyberger, 19; M. Radziwiłł, 4–5; Grigorovich-Barsky, 1800, 314–319.

17 B. Heyberger, 19; Grigorovich-Barsky, 1800, 318–319; Paul of Aleppo, 5.159, 160, 188ff.; Mikha'il Burayk, *Tarikh al-Sham*, 59.

18 Grigorovich-Barsky, 1800, 318; See also Paul of Aleppo's account of the reconstruction and decoration of this church in 1660 in Paul of Aleppo, 5.160.

19 Grigorovich-Barsky, 1800, 318.

20 Nasrallah, *Souvenirs de St Paul*, 53–62. Recalling this church in his chronicle of the 1540s, the Patriarch Macarius adds "when" it "still" belonged to Christians (Nasrallah, "Chronologie, 1500–1634," 36).

21 Grigorovich-Barsky, 1800, 316.

22 Paul of Aleppo, 5.150–152; for a description of the patriarch's residence in 1728, see: Grigorovich-Barsky, 1800, 319.

23 Paul of Aleppo, 5.150–152.

24 I. Vishenski, C. 60.

25 Grigorovich-Barsky, 1800, C. 319.

26 Paul of Aleppo, T. 5, C. 170.

27 I. Vishenski, 60.

28 Mikha'il Burayk, *Tarikh al-Sham*, 124–125.

29 Grigorovich-Barsky, 1800, 319.

30 Mikha'il Burayk, 454.

31 B. Masters, 55–57.

32 A. Raymond, "Une communaute en expansion," 353–357.

33 B. Heyberger, 20–21.

34 Grigorovich-Barsky, 1800, 342.

35 Grigorovich-Barsky, 1800, 292; B. Heyberger, 21.

36 Grigorovich-Barsky, 1800, 292.

37 M. Bakhit, 35, 38; B. Heyberger, 21; Rodionov, 18.

38 B. Heyberger, 24.

39 Macarius, 73; K. A. Panchenko, "Mitropolity i eparkhii pravoslavnoi Antiokhiiskoi Tserkvi v opisanii Pariarkha Makariia III az-Za'ima (1665 g.)," 138; see also C. Walbiner, "Bishoprics," 125.

40 M. Bakhit, 31–39; B. Heyberger, 23; Paul of Aleppo, 5.196–197; Rodionov, 22. According to eighteenth-century reports, the Orthodox Christians of Beirut tried to send their families to mountain villages when there was danger of war or epidemics. The village of Mansuri was especially closely tied to Beirut; it was there that Orthodox *a'yan* of Beirut, Yunus Nicholas, wielded great influence (Beirut Ecclesiastical Chronicle, 69, 70–72, 84).

41 M. Bakhit, 39–40.

42 M. Bakhit, 39–40.

43 Grigorovich-Barsky, 1800, 287–288.

44 Uspenskii, *Skazanie o Siriiskoi unii*, 522, 545–546; Beirut Ecclesiastical Chronicle, 64–65.

45 M. Bakhit, 40; Grigorovich-Barsky, 1800, 284–285.

46 I. Vishenski, 61.

47 M. Bakhit, 23–4; B. Heyberger, 22; Grigorovich-Barsky, 1800, 321; Paul of Aleppo, 5.192.

48 M. Bakhit, 21–23.

49 C. Walbiner, "Bishoprics," 125.

50 Grigorovich-Barsky, 1800, 329.

51 Grigorovich-Barsky, 1800, 327–329.

52 Paul of Aleppo. 5.191.

53 M. Bakhit, 24–25, 29.

54 Paul of Aleppo. 5.169.

55 M. Bakhit, 29–34; Grigorovich-Barsky, 1800, 308–313.

56 Grigorovich-Barsky, 1800, 329; see also: B. Heyberger, 21.

57 L. Cheikho, "Min Rayaq ila Hama," 906–907.

58 Grigorovich-Barsky, 1800, 334–335; B. Heybeger, 21; L. Cheikho, "Min Rayaq ila Hama," 953–954.

59 Mikha'il Burayk, 441. Macarius is apparently speaking about the distant past, the sixteenth century, as Paul of Aleppo gives the figures of the Christian population of Kafr Buhum to be less—two hundred families in the city and the surrounding area (Paul of Aleppo, 5.169). This is yet another example of the reduction in the Orthodox population in rural areas of Syria at the beginning of the seventeenth century.

60 In the absence of the vowels in the source Arabic texts, there may be some mistakes in the reading of these names.

61 Macarius, 75; K. A. Panchenko, "Mitropolity i eparkhii pravoslavnoi Antiokhiiskoi Tserkvi v opisanii Pariarkha Makariia III az-Za'ima (1665 g.)," 140; see also: C. Walbiner, "Bishoprics," 123–124.

62 Macarius, C. 75; K. A. Panchenko, "Mitropolity i eparkhii pravoslavnoi Antiokhiiskoi Tserkvi v opisanii Pariarkha Makariia III az-Za'ima (1665 g.)," 140; see also: C. Walbiner, "Bishoprics," 124.

63 Ibid.

64 Reifenberg, 60.

65 M. Bakhit, 20–21.

66 Grigorovich-Barsky, 1800, 344.

67 Paul of Aleppo, 1.4; Grigorovich-Barsky, 1800, 366.

68 Grigorovich-Barsky, 1800, 337–338.

69 C. Walbiner, "Bishoprics," 125.

70 Paul of Aleppo. 1.6.; Grigorovich-Barsky, 1800, 339–340.

71 B. Masters, 55–56.

72 C. Walbiner, "Bishoprics," 122–123.

73 Nasrallah, "Chronologie, 1500–1634," 49–50.

74 C. Walbiner, "Die Bischofs-und Metropolitensitze," 118–119.

75 Arsenii Sukhanov, 97.

76 C. Walbiner, "Bishoprics," 127.

77 C. Walbiner, "Die Bischofs-und Metropolitensitze," 120.

78 Mikha'il Burayk, 430–431; see also Nasrallah, "Chronologie, 1500–1634," 51–52.

79   Macarius, 76; K. A. Panchenko, "Mitropolity i eparkhii pravoslavnoi Antiokhiiskoi Tserkvi v opisanii Pariarkha Makariia III az-Za'ima (1665 g.)," 141.

80   M. Bakhit, 40–42; B. Heyberger, 23.

81   N. Lewis, 19–20.

82   C. Charon, 916–917.

83   C. Walbiner, "Bishoprics," 122–126.

84   Ibid., 126.

85   For the most complete information about the existence, merger, and abolition of sees, see the article C. Walbiner, "Bishoprics."

86   The table was compiled using M. P. Bakhit, 52; A. Cohen and B. Lewis, p. 84–91. The main criterion in the calculation of the Ottoman statistics was the number of separate households. In addition to that there was a special record of single men who paid a lower tax rate, as well as other categories of people who are exempt from taxation. The table shows only the number of households. Over the years marked "*" the data includes the total number of Christian taxpayers (households plus single men), which is to say, the number of households (families) was a bit less than indicated in the table. It is evident if one adds up the different confessions of Jerusalem that the number of households is lower than what is shown on the general graph of all Christian households. This is due to the fact that the final figure includes not only heads of household, but also single men and also monks, who were included in Ottoman censuses along with other categories of people.

87   Peri, 14.

88   Ibid., 15–16.

89   Ibid., 19. The glaring inconsistencies in these figures are evidence of Armenian pilgrims in the early seventeenth century. Simeon Lekhatsi counted twelve Armenian families in Jerusalem (Simeon Lekhatsi, 197). The constant number of Armenians in Jerusalem was certainly higher because of monks and pilgrims, but the pilgrims were not included in the Ottoman statistics.

90   Peri, 20–23; A. Cohen, 87.

91   M. Bakhit, 50; A. Cohen, 87; Neophytus of Cyprus, "Rasskaz Neofita Kiprskogo," 14.

92   Peri, 23.

93   M. Bakhit, 49. See also Chapter 5.

94   See more on this in Chapter 7.

95   Arsenii Sukhanov, 89; Iona, 13.

96   Arsenii Sukhanov, 53; Grigorovich-Barsky, 1885, 372, 379, 380.

97   M. Bakhit, 52–54.

98 Arsenii Sukhanov, 167; Iona, 20.

99 Peri, 16.

100 Grigorovich-Barsky, 1885, 359.

101 Arsenii Sukhanov, 58.

102 Arsenii Sukhanov, 175; Iona, 20; Grigorovich-Barsky, 1885, 363–65.

103 Peri, 14–17.

104 M. Bakhit, 64; A. Cohen, 109.

105 Gabriel of Nazareth, 21; A. S. Norov 2.72, 83.

106 M. Bakhit, 54.

107 N. Lewis, 21–23.

108 Arsenii Sukhanov, 89.

109 Gabriel of Nazareth, 16.

110 M. Bakhit, 45–46.

111 Gabriel of Nazareth, 15.

112 Vasilii Gagara, 7.

113 Gabriel of Nazareth, 15.

114 Grigorovich-Barsky, 1800, 348; S. Pleshcheev, 61.

115 S. Pleshcheev, 69.

116 S. Pleshcheev, 60.

117 A. S. Norov, *Puteshestvie*, 2.186.

118 M. Bakhit, 45–47.

119 Ibid., 56.

120 I. Luk'ianov, col. 249.

121 SIPPO (Soobshcheniia Imperatorskago Pravoslavnago Palestinskago Obshchestva), 1886, 63.

122 M. Bakhit, 56.

123 Trifon Korobeinikov, 96.

124 Arsenii Sukhanov, 50.

125 Grigorovich-Barsky, 1885, 286.

126 I. Luk'ianov, col. 246.

127 A. S. Norov, *Puteshestvie*, 2.119.

128 M. Bakhit, 31.

129 Ibid.; A. Cohen, 120–23.

130 Paul of Aleppo. 5.168.

131 See details in Chapter 8.

132 SIPPO., 1886, 63.

133 Arsenii Sukhanov, 49.

134 I. M. Smilianskaia, *Sotsial'no-ekonomicheskaia struktura*, 109.

135 Grigorovich-Barsky, 1885, 277.

136 *Beirut Ecclesiastical Chronicle*, 69; al-Jabarti, *'Aja'ib*, 413.

137 A. S. Norov, 2.127.

138 Th. Philipp, 26; A. S. Norov, 2.263.

139 I. M. Smilianskaia, 112–113; Th. Philipp, 26.

140 The data for 1579 and 1582. (A. Cohen, "Jerusalem in the 16 century," 17; RGADA, Fond 52/1, Book 2, f. 4; A. N. Murav'ev, *Snosheniia* 1.128–129).

141 Trifon Korobeinikov, 101; A. N. Murav'ev, *Snosheniia*, 1.276.

142 N. F. Kapterev, *Snosheniia ierusalimskikh patriarkhov*, 17–18, 21.

143 RGADA, Fond 52/1, 1629, no. 22, ff. 8-9.

144 Following the biography of the famous Metropolitan Gabriel of Nazareth, one can conclude that he was ordained during a stay in Palestine by Patriarch Paisius before his trip to Moscow, that is, in 1646–1648 (Gabriel of Nazareth, iii).

145 I. Pomerantsev, "Izbranie ierusalimskikh patriarkhov," 214; I. Pomerantsev, "Dosifei," 4, 25; I. I. Sokolov "Sviatogrobskoe bratstvo," 8.

146 I. Luk'ianov, col. 314.

147 See more on this in Chapter 4.

148 Maximus Simaius, 79.

149 G. Iared, 12; Maximus Simaius, 89; N. F. Kapterev, *Snosheniia ierusalimskikh patriarkhov*, 2.610ff.

150 F. Braudel, 2.65–91; M. S. Meier, *Osmanskaia imperiia*, C. 83.

151 M. S. Meier, *Osmanskaia imperiia*, 83; I. M. Smilianskaia, 32.

152 A. Cohen, 21.

153 I. M. Smilianskaia, 32–33; M. S. Meier, *Osmanskaia imperia*, 85–87.

154 M. Bakhit, 21, 23, 24, 31.

155 R. Haddad, *Syrian Christians*, 10, 20–21.

156 B. Masters, 57.

157 Peri, 17; B. Masters, 58.

158 M. Bakhit, 21, 24, 30, 51, 52; A. Cohen, 84–91, 120–123.

159 B. Masters, 60.

160 M. S. Meier, 84, 89.

161 Of course, the picture of coexistence and relations between settled and nomadic populations in the Middle East was far more complex and included elements of mutually beneficial symbiosis. Nevertheless, the process of displacement of farmers in border areas by Bedouins occasionally reached serious proportions. For details, see I. M. Smilianskaia, 27, 29–30; N. Lewis, 9–23.

162 M. Radziwiłł, 52.

163 M. Radziwiłł, 53, 57; Grigorovich-Barsky, 1800, 329; I. Iu. Krachkovskii, "Pis'mo G. Adama iz Venetsii," 484.

164 Grigorovich-Barsky, 1885, 298.

165 For some of the causes of Christian migration, see: B. Masters, 60.

Chapter 4: Shepherds and Flock

1 In the present study, we have not sought to analyze in detail the economic situation and professions of the Christians, because a number of publications have been dedicated to the economy of Ottoman Syria, to which we will direct the reader. On agricultural production and agrarian relations, see in particular *Agrarnyi stroi Osmanskoi imperii. Dokumenty i materialy*, compiled, translated and commented by A. S. Tveritinova; I. M. Smilianskaia, *Sotsial'no-ekonomicheskaia struktura*, 35–59, 65–83; T. Yu. Kobashchanov, 73–75.

2 With the exception of those cases where the practice of these professions was considered taboo or reprehensible by *shari'a*, such as professional money-lenders (*sarraf*), butchers, and producers of kosher products or Christian ritual objects.

3 Cohen A., 11; T. Iu. Kobishchanov, 75–108.

4 I. M. Smilianskaia, *Sotsial'no-ekonomicheskaia struktura*, 116.

5 Macarius, "Gruziia v 17 stoletii," 456. As the voivode of Kiev wrote to Prince Alexei in August 1656 the Patriarch Macarius's messages from Russia, "[We] in conversation spoke with him, how there are mulberry trees in Kiev in the merchant and in the monastic gardens, and if only there were a master and one could hope for silk seeds, then it would be possible to establish a silk workshop. And the patriarch said 'You, lords, explain how to establish a silk workshop' and he will send 'as many silk masters as is necessary from Antioch'" (RGADA, Fond 52/1, 1654, no. 21, part III, f. 279).

6 Paul of Aleppo, 1.2, 5.143, 151; *Beirut Ecclesiastical Chronicle*, 72, 74, 75; Arsenii Sukhanov, 166; G. Murkos, 221; Grigorovich-Barsky, 1800, 289, 291, 300; Sabanu, *Tarikh hawadith al-Sham wa-Lubnan*, 37.

7 A. Cohen and B. Lewis, 121.

8 "al-'Arifa … bi-intikhab Kirillus Tannas," 125–131.

9 C. Charon and L. Cheikho, "Usqufiyyat al-Rum al-Kathulik fi Bayrut," 201.

10 Paul of Aleppo. 1.1.

11 MS Damascus 289.

12 L. Cheikho, "Khabar iqunat Saydnaya," 462.

13 Melety, C. 302.

14 Porphyry Uspenskii, *Kniga bytiia moegoi*, 1.408ff.

15 Ibid., 2.274–275.

16 Volney, C. 345.

17 Melety, 134.

18 Ibid., 135.

19 A. Pachini, 260.

20 In his description of Sultan Murad IV's meeting in Aleppo with the people of the city in 1639, Paul of Aleppo says, "With him was our father His Eminence the Metropolitan, priests and other Christians, along with the craft guilds" (Paul of Aleppo. 5.192).

21 A. Cohen, 10, 12.

22 Paul of Aleppo. 5.172.

23 Ibid., 169.

24 Mikha'il Burayk, *Tarikh al-Sham*, 101.

25 Porphyry Uspenskii, *Kniga bytiia moego*. 2.210–211.

26 A. Cohen, 12–13.

27 K. A. Panchenko, "Tripoliiskoe gnezdo."

28 Regarding Yunus and the Sakruj clan, see *Beirut Ecclesiastical Chronicle*, 54, 73–78; Sabanu, *Tarikh hawadith al-Sham wa-Lubnan*, 103. Not having set for ourselves the task of delving into the topic of Christians' representation in the organs of Ottoman provincial administration, we refer the reader to the relevant chapter in the book of T. Iu. Kobashchanov (T. Iu. Kobashchanov, 109–160).

29 Mikha'il Burayk, *Tarikh al-Sham*, 39.

30 Beirut Ecclesiastical Chronicle, 85.

31 Thus, Patriarch Macarius mentions that in his day there were many rich people in Qara, Kafr Buhum, and especially in Marmarita (Mikha'il Burayk, 441). Residents of Aleppo traditionally were considered to be rich (Uspenskii, *Skazanie o Siriiskoi unii*, 501). Paul of Aleppo wrote that the residents of Baalbek were "extremely poor" (Paul of Aleppo. 5.169).

32 I. M. Smilianskaia, *Sotsial'no-ekonomicheskaia struktura*, 60–61.

33 Mikha'il Burayk, 425–426.

34 K. M. Bazili, 2007, 442.

35 Beirut Ecclesiastical Chronicle, 65, 75–76.

36 I. Luk'ianov, col. 247.

37 Grigorovich-Barsky, 1885, 289.

38 Ibid., 364.

39 Dositheus, "Gramota," 62.

40 I. M. Smilianskaia, *Sotsial'no-ekonomicheskaia struktura*, 71.

41 Iona, 21.

42 SIPPO, 1895, 542.

43 S.n., *Pravovaia organizatsiia Sviatogrobskogo bratstva*, 158.

44 Paul of Aleppo. 5.152.

45 Ibid.

46 Mikha'il Burayk, *Tarikh al-Sham*, 117.

47 For more on this see Chapter 6.

48 Beirut Ecclesiastical Chronicle up to 56.

49 At the same time, in Hawran, the annual tax to the patriarch was paid in kind even in the twentieth century (SIPPO, 1909, 128).

50 Paul of Aleppo. 5.143.

51 Ibid., 153–154.

52 Mikha'il Burayk, *Tarikh al-Sham*, 83.

53 Mikha'il Burayk, 443.

54 Paul of Aleppo, 5.191.

55 Ibid., 1.4.

56 Ibid., 5.154.

57 SPBF ARAN, Fond 1026/1, no. 246, ff. 22v–23.

58 Arsenii Sukhanov, 97

59 Mikha'il Burayk, 435.

60 Mikha'il Burayk, *Tarikh al-Sham*, 96.

61 See, for example Mikha'il Burayk, C. 431.

62 Bezobrazov, *Materialy dlia biografii Porfiriia Uspenskogo*, 2.103, 475–476; K. M. Bazili 1875, 2.209, 216, 223; SIPPO. 1891, 21.

63 K. M. Bazili, 1875, 2.209–215.

64 Ibid., 216–226.

65 For details, consult chapters 6 and 8.

66 A. N. Murav'ev, *Istoriia*, 2.269–270; A. P. Lebedev, *Istoriia*, 773; N. F. Kapterev, "Gospodstvo grekov," 198–200.

67 Maximus Simaius, 41. In this case, Maximus quotes Dositheus, whose chronicle is not available to us.

68 Cited in: K. M. Bazili 1875, 2.200–202.

69 A. N. Murav'ev, *Istoriia*. 2.270.

70 A. P. Lebedev, *Istoriia*, 773, 782.

71 Maximus Simaius, 41; N. F. Kapterev, "Gospodstvo grekov," 199.

72 Makarii (Veletennikov), "Gramota patriarkha Germana," 206.

73 A. Cohen, 12, 17.

74 N. F. Kapterev, "Gospodstvo grekov," 203

75 P. V. Kuzenkov and K. A. Panchenko, 11.

76 V. Pozniakov, 33.

77 IVR RAN Arabic MS 869, f. 135.

78 N. F. Kapterev, "Gospodstvo grekov," 209.

79 I will take this opportunity to express my sincere gratitude to the Israeli professor Amnon Cohen, who kindly provided a copy of this document, which is held in the archives of the *shari'a* court of Jerusalem (*Sijill of Jerusalem*, Vol. 58, 385). Several authors give a brief account of this document from the words of the Patriarch Dositheus: N. F. Kapterev, "Gospodstvo grekov," 82; A. N. Murav'ev, *Istoriia*, 2.273.

80 N. F. Kapterev, "Gospodstvo grekov," 202.

81 RGADA, Fond 52/1, 1636, no. 15, f. 9. See also: K. A. Panchenko, "Rossiia i Antiokhiiskii patriarkhat," 213–215.

82 On the dating of these events, see K. A. Panchenko, "Rossiia i Antiokhiiskii patriarkhat," 216–217.

83 N. F. Kapterev, "Gospodstvo grekov," 202.

84 Documents from the *shari'a* court of Jerusalem permits us to confirm the dating that we propose: on February 20, Paisius appealed to the *qadi* asking him to register the sultan's *firman* (O. Peri, 109). With this the plenary powers of Paisius were recognized, which had to be supported by the authority of the Ottoman administration in Jerusalem.

85 Maximus Simaius, 60.

86 I. I. Sokolov, "Sviatogrobskoe bratstvo," 15, 19.

87 Grigorovich-Barsky, 1885, 347.

88 Iona, 3–4; I. Luk'ianov, col. 247, 260, 331.

89 See, for example, Andrei Ignat'ev, 43; Melety, 101, 152, 179, 191, 225.

90 SPBF ARAN, Fond 1026, Op. 1, no. 246, f. 28v.

91 MS Saydnaya, 22.

92 I. Luk'ianov, col. 321. Perhaps Patriarch Dositheus, in establishing him as metropolitan of 'Ajlun, sought to institute at least some pastoral care for the Arabs of Transjordan. If what he needed was not another titular bishop, but a man who was ready at every hour to risk his life in that wild land where bands of Bedouins had more power than the Ottoman *sanjak-bey* and the local Christians were not very different in their manners than the Bedouins, the patriarch naturally had to appoint an Arab. It seems that the metropolitan did indeed stay in Transjordan. In his note, 'Isa ibn Shahin mentions the ruler of 'Ajlun. In the time of Ivan Lukyanov, however, the metropolitan of Jordan, like the other bishops, no longer lived in his diocese "out of fear of violence from the Turks and Arabs" (I. Luk'ianov, col. 314).

93 Andrei Ignat'ev, 36.

94 MS Saydnaya, 98.

95 Nasrallah, "Euthème Saifi," col. 68.

96 Porphyry Uspenskii, *Kniga bytiia moego*, 1.229.

97 S.n., *Pravovaia organizatsiia Sviatogrobskogo bratstva*, 159; I. I. Sokolov, "Sviatogrobskoe bratstvo," C. 15.

98 S.n., *Pravovaia organizatsiia Sviatogrobskogo bratstva*, 156, 157.

99 Bezobrazov, *Materialy dlia biografii Porfiriia Uspenskogo*, 2.475

100 Procopius Nazianzen, 336.

101 Grigorovich-Barsky, 1885, 363.

102 Ibid., 363–364.

103 Ibid., 365.

104 Arkhim. Leonid, "Serbskaia obshchina v Palestine," 42–53; A. Fotić, 232. In the scholarly literature, the generally accepted date is 1504, which is given in the chronicle of Dositheus. It should be noted, however, that this date may very well be provisional and approximate.

105 Trifon Korobeinikov, 98.

106 Savva Nemanich, 14, 37.

107 B. Arbel, 169.

108 In 1593, the embassy of Trifon Kolobeinikov reported on the allocation of funds to the metochion: "To the builder elder Leontius and the five brothers was given . . . 10 gold pieces" (*Posol'skaia kniga*, 159).

109 N. F. Kapterev, "Gospodstvo grekov," 209.

110 Vasilii, gost', 10.

111 *Proskinitarii 1580-x gg,* 199.

112 Ibid., 209.

113 RGADA, Fond 52/1, Book 1, f. 173; A. N. Murav'ev, *Snosheniia Rossii s Vostokom*, 103.

114 RGADA, Fond 52/2, no. 6.

115 See footnote 78.

116 Arkhim. Leonid, "Serbskaia obshchina v Palestine," 61.

117 Arkhim. Leonid, "Serbskaia obshchina v Palestine," 53.

118 V. Pozniakov, 51–53, 79; Arhim. Leonid, "Serbskaia obshchina v Palestine," 53.

119 RGADA, Fond 52/1, Book 1, ff. 148–148v.

120 M. Radziwiłł, 136; A. N. Murav'ev, *Snosheniia Rossii s Vostokom*, 147, 264; N. F. Kapterev, *Snosheniia.* 1.14–15; Arkhim. Leonid, "Serbskaia obshchina v Palestine," 54–55.

121 RGADA, Fond 52/1, 1592, no. 1, ff. 1–8; A. N. Murav'ev, *Snosheniia Rossii s Vostokom*, 261; Arkhim. Leonid, "Serbskaia obshchina v Palestine," 56.

122 V. G. Chentsova, "Gramota Ioakima VI," 294–297. See also the biographical sketch of Damaskin.

123 Arkhim. Leonid, "Serbskaia obshchina v Palestine," 58.

124 Nasrallah, *HMLEM*, 4(1).72.

125 Ibid., 59.

126 Ibid., 60–61; A. N. Murav'ev, *Snosheniia Rossii s Vostokom*, 281–299; N. F. Kapterev, *Snosheniia*, 1.15–23.

127 RGADA, Fond 52/1, 1629, no. 22, f. 6.

128 A. Fotić, 234.

129 Arkhim. Leonid, "Serbskaia obshchina v Palestine," 61–62.

130 A. Fotić, 230, 235.

131 N. F. Kapterev, *Snosheniia*, 46–59.

132 Arkhim. Leonid, "Serbskaia obshchina v Palestine," 63.

133 N. F. Kapterev, "Gospodstvo grekov," 208, 229. Arkhim. Leonid, "Serbskaia obshchina v Palestine," 63.

134 N. Khutsishvili, 126–127; A. Tsagareli, 42–57.

135 It is interesting that the Greek sources say that the Georgians rented out the Monastery of St John the Theologian, which the Franks later appropriated. The Georgian sources, however, say that the monastery was handed over to the Catholics by command of the sultan and the Georgian monks had to vacate it "after futile resistance" (A. Tsagareli, 116–118; Arsenii Sukhanov, 165; Procopius Nazianzen, 141, 164; A. Cohen, 88; N. Khutsishvili, 133).

136 N. F. Kapterev, "Gospodstvo grekov," 27; Dositheus, "Poslaniia," 172.

137 A. Cohen and B. Lewis, 88, 90.

138 Colophons from 1570 and 1572 mention Archbishops Vlas of Urbnisi and Barnabas of Tbilisi who bound old books in the Monastery of the Holy Cross (A. Tsagareli, 64, 182, 188).

139 See footnote 78.

140 Trifon Korobeinikov, 96–100.

141 Gabriel of Nazareth, 22; Iona, 14; Arsenii Sukhanov, 164.

142 A. Tsagareli, 65–66.

143 Dositheus, "Poslaniia," 170; N. Khutsishvili, 127–131, 133–134.

144 Dositheus, "Poslaniia," 157–158.

145 Dositheus, "Poslaniia," 171.

146 Ibid., 170.

147 Ibid., 160; N. Khutsishvili, 135; A. Tsagareli, 66–70.

148 A. Tsagareli, 99.

149 Arsenii Sukhanov, 175.

150 Dositheus, "Poslaniia," 160.

151 Ibid., 169.

152 Ibid., 170.

153 Gabriel of Nazareth, 22.

154 A. Tsagareli, 71–72.

155 "Inasmuch as [the money] was donated by Greek Christians (a good gift, for brothers helped brothers), we not only do not require the Iberians to repay it, but they may still return to the Monastery of the Holy Cross and the other [monasteries]" (Dositheus, "Poslaniia," 172).

156 Ibid., 169–73.

157 The most famous of these pilgrims, the archbishop and writer Timothy, was in the Holy Land in 1758 (A. Tsagareli, 82–88, 248–254; N. Khutsishvili, 129–131).

158 A. Tsagareli, 181. (A colophon left by a hieromonk in 1814.) The hieromonk Laurentius was a passionate Georgian patriot from Imereti who lived at the Monastery of the Holy Cross in the early nineteenth century. In a note he left in an ancient manuscript, he lists the Georgian inscriptions on the walls of the churches and monasteries of Palestine which, in his words, "show who did what and how much was spent and serve as evidence for the sacrifices made by our country. Whoever enters into this Monastery of the Holy Cross, let him look at the Synaxarion of Golgatha located here and, looking at the very beginning of it, understand to whom Golgotha belongs" (A. Tsagareli, 190).

159 Arsenii Sukhanov, 70; I. I. Sokolov, "Sviatogrobskoe bratstvo," 21–22.

160 N. F. Kapterev, *Snosheniia*, 1.64.

161 N. F. Kapterev, *Snosheniia*, 1.46–57, 72–73; V. G. Chentsova, *Ikona Iverskoi Bogomateri*, 112, 113, 133, 139.

162 S.n., *Patriarshie dokumenty*, 348.

163 N. F. Kapterev, "Gospodstvo grekov," 38.

164 Ibid.

165 N. F. Kapterev, "Gospodstvo grekov," 38–39; I. I. Sokolov "Sviatogrobskoe bratstvo", 9–19.

166 I. Pomerantsev, "Izbranie ierusalimskikh patriarkhov."

167 N. F. Kapterev, "Gospodstvo grekov," 201–207; I. Pomerantsev, "Izbranie ierusalimskikh patriarkhov," 209–232; A. N. Murav'ev, *Istoriia*. 2.273, 300, 318, 328; Maximus Simaius, 81, 84–85; Neophytus of Cyprus, "Dvadtsatiletie," 152.

168 Procopius Nazianzen, 139–140; A. N. Murav'ev, *Istoriia*, 2.273.

169 See Chapter 3.

170 Paul of Aleppo, 5.173, 152; Grigorovich-Barsky, 1800, 333; Mikha'il Burayk, 446.

171 Mikha'il Burayk, 425–426; Paul of Aleppo. 5.155, 171; Mikha'il Burayk, *Tarikh al-Sham*, 36; Bezobrazov, *Materialy dlia biografii Porfiriia Uspenskogo*, 2.228.

172 Mikha'il Burayk, 438–439.

173 Ibid., 439.

174 Ibid.; Paul of Aleppo, 5.190.

175 Vl. V. Polosin, "Zapiska Pavla Aleppskogo," 339, notes 18, 19.

176 Porphyry Uspenskii, "Siriiskaia tserkov'," 133; Bezobrazov, *Materialy dlia biografii Porfiriia Uspenskogo.* 2.128; SIPPO, 1913, 450–451.

177 SIPPO, 1909, 126, 128; I. N. Berezin, "Khristiane v Mesopotamii i sirii," 25; SIPPO, 1897, 630–635.

178 I. N. Berezin, "Khristiane v Mesopotamii i sirii," 25; see also SIPPO, 1909, 124.

179 SIPPO, 1913, 450

180 SIPPO, 1909, 124, 127; see also I. N. Berezin, "Khristiane v Mesopotamii i sirii," 25; SIPPO, 1897, 630–635.

181 Porphyry Uspenskii, "Siriiskaia tserkov', 134.

182 SIPPO, 1913, 450.

183 SIPPO, 1909, 128.

184 IVR RAN, MS V 1227, ff. 34–34v, 129. See also a document regarding the election of the first Uniate patriarch of Antioch: S.n. "Al-ʿArifa bi-intikhab Kirillus Tannas", 124–125.

185 *Nisba*: a family name indicating geographic origin.

186 A. Rabbat, "Al-Tawa'if al-sharqiyya," 798.

187 Paul of Aleppo. 5.153.

188 Mikha'il Burayk, *Tarikh al-Sham*, 27–29, 34–35, 76, 82–85.

189 Mikha'il Burayk, *Tarikh al-Sham*, 82–85, 87, 94–96, 100.

190 A. Rustum, 2.43.

191 Paul of Aleppo, 5.143–144.

192 Ibid., 144.

193 See also C. Walbiner, "Bishoprics and Bishops," 127.

194

Period	Major City	Medium City	Country	Greek Lands
1550–1600	2 (1)	4 (2)	6 (2)	
1600–1652	6 (4)	6 (1)	6 (1)	2 (1)
1652–1700	8 (2)	1	1	1 (1)

195 C. Walbiner, "Die Bischofs-und Metropolitensitze," 128, 133.

196 Paul of Aleppo. 5.187.

197 C. Walbiner, "Die Bischofs-und Metropolitensitze," 99–152; C. Walbiner, "Bishopics and Bishops," 128, 133.

198 See, for example, Vl. V. Polosin, "Zapiska Pavla Aleppskogo," 329–342.

199 RGADA, Fond 1608, no. 129, f. 3; D. A. Morozov, 88. The text of the document is dated 1584, but D. A. Morozov later revised this date: D. A. Morozov, "Tsifrovye sistemy v arabo-khristianskikh i grecheskikh rukopisiakh IX-XVII vv." in *Paleografiia i kodikologiia: 300 let posle Monfokona: Materialy mezhdunarodnoi nauchnoi konferentsii. Moskva 14-16 maia 2008 g* (Moscow, 2008), 116.

200 C. Walbiner, "Die Bischofs-und Metropolitensitze," 123. The metropolitan's grandson, the scribe Gabriel who lived in the 1640s, did not forget to specify his genealogy and who his grandfather was (MS Damascus, 206).

201 In addition to the previous footnote, see: MS Homs, 38; C. Walbiner, "Die Bischofs-und Metropolitensitze," 124; C. Charon, "Qara," 330; MS Vostfaka, 474.

202 I. I. Sokolov, "Antiokhiiskii patriarkh Sil'vestr," 15, 25.

203 Paul of Aleppo, 5.188.

204 S.n., *Patriarshie dokumenty*, 280–282.

205 Paul of Aleppo, 5.142–149, 154, 165–166.

206 C. Walbiner, "Bishopics and Bishops," 128.

207 Mikha'il Burayk, 435; Foma Dibu-Maluf, 336.

208 A. Rustum, 40.

209 A. Rustum, 40.

210 Paul of Aleppo. 5.65.

211 Ibid.

212 Mikha'il Burayk, 455–456.

213 Mikha'il Burayk, 425–426; Paul of Aleppo, 5.187; Nasrallah, "Chronologie, 1500–1634," 33–34.

214 In the middle of the seventeenth century, the French traveler Monseigneur Grelot reported that in the district of Jabal ʿAjlun on the canonical territory of the Patriarchate of Jerusalem, two alms collectors from the Brotherhood of the Holy Sepulchre seized an imposter posing as an alms collector sent from the Monastery of Saydnaya (Grelot, 144–145).

215 A. Rustum, 41.

216 Ibid., 41–43.

217 MS Saydnaya 156.

218 L. Cheikho, "Min Rayaq ila Hama," 951–952; P. V. Kuzenkov and K. A. Panchenko, 10–11.

219 L. Cheikho, "Kirill VIII," 628. G. Levenq, "Athanase II" in *DHGE*, II, col. 1369.

220 C. Basha, "Mulhaq li-silsilat matarinat Sur," 622; C. Charon, "Tarabulus," 406.

221 Nasrallah, *Chronologie, 1500–1634,* 36.

222 Mikha'il Burayk, 425; Paul of Aleppo. 5.187; Nasrallah, *Chronologie, 1500–1634,* 31–37; see also: K. A. Panchenko, "Tripoliiskoe gnezdo."

223 Mikha'il Burayk, 426–427; Paul of Aleppo. 5.188; Nasrallah, *Chronologie, 1500–1634,* 38–39.

224 Mikha'il Burayk, 427.

225 Mikha'il Burayk, 427–428; Paul of Aleppo. 5.187; See also: K. A. Panchenko, "Antiokhiiskii patriarkhat i Rossiia," 207–208; idem, "Tripoliiskoe gnezdo," part 1, 49–53. However, the colophon to a Syrian manuscript states that Michael died on Christmas Day 1592, surviving his rival Joachim for a short while (C. Karalevskij, col. 637; Nasrallah, "Chronologie, 1500–1634," 7, 42). In any case, by 1583 Michael, who by that time was almost ninety years old, finally retired and ceased to claim the patriarchate.

226 Mikha'il Burayk, 428; *Risala,* 357–361; Nasrallah, "Chronologie, 1500–1634," 46–48; see also: K. A. Panchenko, "Antiokhiiskii patriarkhat i Rossiia," 208; idem, "Tripoliiskoe gnezdo," part 1, 56, 58.

227 Mikha'il Burayk, 429; Nasrallah, "Chronologie, 1500–1634," 44; K. A. Panchenko, "Tripoliiskoe gnezdo," part 1, 59–62. For Anastasius's literary activities, see Chapters 9 and 10.

228 S.n., *Patriarshie dokumenty,* 281–82.

229 Mikha'il Burayk, 431; Paul of Aleppo. 5.188.

230 Mikha'il Burayk, 431–432; K. A. Panchenko, "Tripoliiskoe gnezdo," part 2, 21–23.

231 Mikha'il Burayk, 433.

232 Paul of Aleppo, 5.189.

233 Paul of Aleppo, Ibid.; Mikha'il Burayk, 432–436; K. A. Panchenko, "Tripoliiskoe gnezdo," part 2, 25–34.

234 Paul of Aleppo, 5.192.

235 Mikha'il Burayk, 436–437, 440; Paul of Aleppo, 5.191–192.

236 Paul of Aleppo, 5.194.

237 Vl. V. Polosin, "Zapiska Pavla Aleppskogo."

238 A. Rabbat "al-Tawa'if al-sharqiyya," 972.

239 Uspenskii, *Skazanie o Siriiskoi unii,* 496–497.

240 I. I. Sokolov, "Tserkovnye sobytiia," 318.

241 Mikha'il Burayk, 444; see also: Uspenskii, *Skazanie o Siriiskoi unii,* 497–499; *Beirut Ecclesiastical Chronicle,* 33; I. I. Sokolov, "Tserkovnye sobytiia," 314–330.

242 B. Masters, 83–84.

243 Uspenskii, *Skazanie o Siriiskoi unii,* 500; Mikha'il Burayk, 444; I. I. Sokolov, "Tserkovnye sobytiia," 337.

244 Uspenskii, *Skazanie o Siriiskoi unii*, 500.

245 Mikha'il Burayk, 445.

246 Uspenskii, *Skazanie o Siriiskoi unii*, 500–504; *Beirut Ecclesiastical Chronicle*, 34–36; Mikha'il Burayk, 444–446; I. I. Sokolov, "Tserkovnye sobytiia," 338–344; G. Levenq, "Athanace III," col. 1369–1374.

247 Mikha'il Burayk, 447–448; Uspenskii, *Skazanie o Siriiskoi unii*, 504; I. I. Sokolov, "Tserkovnye sobytiia," 345.

Chapter 5: Monasteries and Monasticism

1 An excerpt of this story of the Sinai Monastery of St Catherine was presented by the author in the article, "Ekateriny velikomuchenitsy monastyr' no Sinae," *Pravoslavnaia Entsiklopediia*, 18.170–184.

2 These Greek testimonies can serve as a model found in the collection RGADA, "Skaska Novospaskogo monastyria kelalia Grechenina Ioannikiia pro monastyri, imeiushchiesia v Tsar'grade, Ierusalime i vo vsei grecheskoi oblasti" (RGADA, Fond 52/1, 1629, no. 22). Ioannikii, close to Patriarch Theophanes of Jerusalem, settled in Moscow in 1619 and wrote, in particular, to the experts of the Posolsky Prikaz about the affairs of the Orthodox East. (On Ioannikii, see N. F. Kapterev, *Snosheniia ierusalimskikh patriarkhov*, 1.60). Although "The Tale" of Ioannikii is dated in the archival inventories as 1629, B. L. Fonkich has definitely proved that it should be referenced to 1619, during the visit of Theophanes (B. L. Fonkich, "Ioannikii Grek," 85–110).

3 Sometimes they were given by the same Greek informants, adding onto each other or significantly differing among themselves, thereby creating additional difficulties in the distribution of royal alms in the East. Thus, in 1624, the Muscovite envoys Kondyrev and Bormoso, having arrived in Istanbul accompanied by the metropolitan of Bethlehem who was returning from Moscow to Palestine, reported about sending money to the monastery of the Holy Cross, "According to the inventory of Moscow it was commanded to give the abbot 2 gold pieces, and a half-piece of gold to the thirty elders . . . and according to the account of Athanasius, metropolitan of Bethlehem, and the abbot Amphilophius of Jerusalem, there is now in this monastery an abbot and 40 elders"; alms were sent, based on the figure of 40 (RGADA, Fond 52/1, 1624, no. 11, f. 1).

4 If one is to be maximally accurate, one should make note of the Greek *proskynetarion*, "About the city of Jerusalem and its environs," referring to the first half of the sixteenth century. However, the list of the monasteries of Jerusalem in this short guide (which counts eleven monasteries apart from the patriarchal ones) gives the impression of being incomplete and cursory (S.n., *O grade Ierusalimei okrestnostiakh ego*, 246).

5 V. Pozniakov, 51.

6 A. N. Murav'ev, "Puteshestvie", 198.

7 Papadopulo–Keramevs, *Proskinitarii, 1608–1624*, 54.

8 A. N. Murav'ev, "Puteshestvie", 198.

9 Serapion, 92–93, 116; see also Papadopulo–Keramevs, *Proskinitarii, 1608–1624*, 54–55; I. Vishenski, 84

10 RGADA, Fond. 52/1, 1629, no. 22, f. 4.

11 Serapion, 116; I. Vishenski, 64; Melety, 28.

12 I. Vishenski, 74, 84; Varlaam, 64; M. Nechaev, 28; Serapion, 116; Melety, 244; Porphyry Uspenskii, *Kniga bytiia moego*, 2.322.

13 *Proskinitarii 1580-x gg*, 205.

14 S.n., *O grade Ierusalimei okrestnostiakh ego*, 246.

15 Trifon Korobeinikov, 97; RGADA, Fond 52/1, 1628, no. 8, f. 48; 1629, no. 22, f. 6; Iona 13–14; I. Vishenski, 84.

16 Trifon Korobeinikov, 100; RGADA, Fond 52/1, 1628, no. 8, f. 45; Arsenii Sukhanov, 164.

17 I. Vishenski, 84; Melety, 244; Porphyry Uspenskii, *Kniga bytiia moego*, 2.317.

18 Arsenii Sukhanov, 164; Trifon Korobeinikov, 100; RGADA, Fond 52/1, 1628, no. 8, f. 47; 1629, no. 22, f. 7; Gabriel of Nazareth, 9.

19 Arsenii Sukhanov, 164; Trifon Korobeinikov, 98; RGADA, Fond 52/1, 1628, no. 8, f. 47; 1629, no. 22, f. 7; I. Luk'ianov, col. 321; Hieromonk Makarii, 15; I. Vishenski, 84; Serapion, 116; Melety, 244; Porphyry Uspenskii, *Kniga bytiia moego*, 2.328.

20 I. Vishenski, 84; Varlaam, 64.

21 Serapion, 117; Trifon Korobeinikov, 100; RGADA, Fond 52/1, 1628, no. 8, f. 46; no. 23, f. 15v; 1629, no. 22, f. 8; Gabriel of Nazareth, 9; Arsenii Sukhanov, 164.

22 Melety, 244; Porphyry Uspenskii, *Kniga bytiia moego*, 2.330.

23 Arsenii Sukhanov, 164–165.

24 Grigorovich-Barsky, 1885, 320.

25 I. Vishenski, 84; Melety, 244; Porphyry Uspenskii, *Kniga bytiia moego*, 2, 320–321.

26 Grigorovich-Barsky, 1885, 333; Trifon Korobeinikov, 97; RGADA, Fond 52/1, 1628, no. 8, f. 47; 1629, no. 22, f. 7; Gabriel of Nazareth, 9; Iona, 13; I. Vishenski, 84.

27 Porphyry Uspenskii, *Kniga bytiia moego*, 1.449.

28 Porphyry Uspenskii, *Kniga bytiia moego*, 2.320; Melety, 244.

29 Grigorovich-Barsky, 1885, 357; Trifon Korobeinikov, 97; RGADA, Fond 52/1, 1628, no. 8, f. 46; 1629, no. 22, f. 8.

30 Serapion, 117; Melety, 244; Porphyry Uspenskii, *Kniga bytiia moego* 2.325.

31 Trifon Korobeinikov, 97; RGADA, Fond 52/1, 1628, no. 8, f. 47; 1629, no. 22, f. 7; Gabriel of Nazareth, 9; Iona, 13–14.

32 Trifon Korobeinikov, 100; Arsenii Sukhanov, 164; Serapion, 117. The figures of the Posolsky Prikaz (12–15 people) are unreliable and contradictory. Some refer to it as a men's monastery and others as a women's monastery (RGADA, Fond 52/1, 1628, no. 8, f. 46; 1629, no. 22, f. 7).

33 I. Vishenski, 84; Serapion, 117; Melety, 244.

34 Trifon Korobeinikov, 100; RGADA, Fond 52/2, 1628, no. 8, f. 46; no. 23, f. 17, 1629, no. 22, f. 7; Arsenii Sukhanov, 164.

35 I. Vishenski, 84; Serapion, 117 (this author mistakenly called the Lavra of St Euthymius a men's monastery); Melety, 244; Porphyry Uspensky, *Kniga bytiia moego*, 2.316.

36 Porphyry Uspenskii, *Kniga bytiia moego*, 2.327.

37 Grigorovich-Barsky, 1885, 332; Trifon Korobeinikov, 100; RGADA, Fond 52/1, 1628, no. 8, f. 46; 1629, no. 22, f. 8; Gabriel of Nazareth, 9; Arsenii Sukhanov, 164; Serapion, 116.

38 I. Vishenski, 84; Serapion, 117; Melety, 244.

39 RGADA, Fond 52/1, no. 22, ff. 7, 8.

40 Aside from the description of the embassy in 1628, drawn up on the basis of Ioannicius's report.

41 See about the history of the church of St Pelagia, Varsonofii, xvi–xviii.

42 Papadopulo–Keramevs, *Proskinitarii, 1608–1624*, 57; I. Luk'ianov, col. 321; Hieromonk Makarii, 16.

43 Grigorovich-Barsky, 1885, 318.

44 Serapion, 116–117.

45 Melety, 245.

46 A. N. Murav'ev, "Puteshestvie", 197.

47 Porphyry Uspenskii, *Kniga bytiia moego*, 2.316–330.

48 K. M. Bazili, 1875, 239.

49 Serapion, 108.

50 A. N. Murav'ev, "Puteshestvie", 150.

51 Hieromonk Makarii, 12.

52 N. P. Kondakov, photo lxii.

53 N. P. Kondakov, 198.

54 RGADA, Fond 52/1, 1649, no. 11, ff. 1-6.

55 Iona, 24; Hieromonk Makarii, 13; Varlaam, 68; Grigorovich-Barsky, 1885, 343.

56 Maximus Simaius, C77–78.

57 Dositheus, "Gramota," 41.

58 Macarius, 13.

59 Varlaam, 68; I. Vishenski, 85. In another place, this same author speaks of ninety monks of the Lavra (C. 93), but this is clearly a mistake.

60   Ignaty, 20; Volney, 2.485; Melety, 152.

61   Grigorovich-Barsky, 1885, 346.

62   Grigorovich-Barsky, 1885, 347.

63   Arsenii Sukhanov, 188; Hieromonk Makarii, 12; Varlaam, 68; Grigorovich-Barsky 1885, 348–349.

64   Grigorovich-Barsky, 1885, 350.

65   The issue of the monks' relationship with their nomadic neighbors is detailed in the article K. A. Panchenko, "Monastyri i beduiny."

66   Grigorovich-Barsky, 1885, 350.

67   I. Luk'ianov, col. 342–43.

68   Grigorovich-Barsky, 1885, 290–300, 350–351.

69   Maximus Simaius, 91.

70   Porphyry Uspenskii, *Kniga bytiia moego*, 2.139.

71   Neophytus of Cyprus, "Dvadtsatiletie," 133, 155, 168.

72   A. Tsagareli, 98.

73   Ibid., 98–103.

74   Grigorovich-Barsky, 1885, 335.

75   A. Tsagareli, C. 104–106.

76   Serapion, 114.

77   I. Luk'ianov, col. 264.

78   Melety says that the venerable fathers, killed by Arab robbers, were depicted on a fresco on the west side of the church (Melety, 297).

79   Serapion, 114; see also Grigorovich-Barsky, 1885, 335; A. Tsagareli, 100.

80   Maximus Simaius, 94, 97; Melety, 190.

81   A. N. Murav'ev, "Puteshestvie", 214.

82   K. M. Bazili, 1875, 233.

83   Daniel of Ephesus, 50–51.

84   A. Cohen and B. Lewis, 87.

85   Trifon Korobeinikov, 99.

86   Vasilii Gagara, 16.

87   Iona, 21; see also: Gabriel of Nazareth, 18–19.

88   Arsenii Sukhanov, 166.

89   Grigorovich-Barsky, 1885, 370–371. Lukyanov and Melety also wrote about church paintings (I. Luk'ianov, col. 263; Melety, 143).

90   Grigorovich-Barsky, 1885, 371.

91   Serapion, 110.

92   K. M. Bazili, 1875, 239.

93 A. N. Murav'ev, "Puteshestvie", 207.

94 K. M. Bazili, 1875, 239.

95 Gabriel of Nazareth, 20; see also the description of the monastery: *Proskinitarii 1580–X*, 225–226.

96 RGADA, Fond 52/1, 1629, no. 22, f. 9; Iona, 23.

97 S.n., *Pravovaia organizatsiia Sviatogrobskogo bratstva*, 153.

98 I. Vishenski, 90.

99 I. Luk'ianov, col. 347.

100 A. S. Norov, "Ierusalim i Sinai," 44.

101 Papadopulo–Keramevs, *Proskinitarii 1608–1624*, 68–69; Gabriel of Nazareth, 12–13; Iona, 20; Arsenii Sukhanov, 201.

102 G. Destunis, 58.

103 Daniel of Ephesus, 58.

104 *Proskinitarii 1580– X*, 218.

105 V. Pozniakov, 61.

106 Ibid., 62.

107 Arsenii Sukhanov, 79.

108 Grigorovich-Barsky, 1885, 277.

109 See also K. A. Panchenko, "Monastyri i beduiny," 96–97.

110 I. I. Sokolov, "Sviatogrobskoe bratstvo," 4–6.

111 The known texts are the charters of Patriarch Dositheos from 1683 to 1689, a number of regulations from Patriarch Chrysanthos (1707–1731) and Melitius (1731–1737) and two charters, composed by Patriarch Parthenios in 1755 and 1765. There are not significant differences in the subjects and contents of these regulations, and therefore they can be looked at as a whole for the convenience of presenting material.

112 S.n., *Pravovaia organizatsiia Sviatogrobskogo bratstva*, 146.

113 I. Vishenski, 64–65.

114 N. F. Kapterev, *Snosheniia ierusalimskikh patriarkhov*, 2.723; Porphyry Uspenskii, *Kniga bytiia moego*, 2.369; SIPPO, 1895, 52.

115 S.n., *Pravovaia organizatsiia Sviatogrobskogo bratstva*, 158, 163.

116 Ibid., 153.

117 Ibid., 158, 160–63.

118 Ibid., 157; I. I. Sokolov, "Sviatogrobskoe bratstvo," 10–11.

119 Porphyry Uspenskii, *Kniga bytiia moego*, 2.124.

120 I. I. Sokolov, "Sviatogrobskoe bratstvo," 14, 18.

121 Ibid., 15, 16.

122 S.n., *Pravovaia organizatsiia Sviatogrobskogo bratstva*, 158; I. I. Sokolov, "Sviatogrobskoe bratstvo," 11.

123 S.n., *Pravovaia organizatsiia Sviatogrobskogo bratstva*, 155.

124 Ibid; I. I. Sokolov, "Sviatogrobskoe bratstvo," 14.

125 S.n., *Pravovaia organizatsiia Sviatogrobskogo bratstva*, 155.

126 I. I. Sokolov, "Sviatogrobskoe bratstvo," 15.

127 SIPPO, 1895, 52.

128 Volney, 2.427.

129 I. I. Sokolov, "Sviatogrobskoe bratstvo," 20; S.n., *Pravovaia organizatsiia Sviatogrobskogo bratstva*, 158.

130 I. I. Sokolov, "Sviatogrobskoe bratstvo," 17.

131 I. I. Sokolov, "Sviatogrobskoe bratstvo," 14–16, 19; S.n., *Pravovaia organizatsiia Sviatogrobskogo bratstva*, 155, 157, 158.

132 Porphyry Uspenskii, *Kniga bytiia moego*, 2.325.

133 Porphyry Uspenskii, *Kniga bytiia moego*, 2.321–322.

134 Ibid., 319.

135 Ibid., 273–274.

136 Melety, 217.

137 The only successor to this theme in relation to the Christian East was the fiercely anticlerical A. E. Krymski, who wrote, however, of much more recent realities.

138 See, for example, on the Lambradis-Karakallos clan to which the patriarchs Theophanes and Paisius belonged : V. G. Chentsova, *Ikona Iverskoi bogomateri*, 112, 113, 139, 142.

139 Trifon Korobeinikov, 100.

140 I. I. Sokolov, "Sviatogrobskoe bratstvo," 18–19.

141 Arsenii Sukhanov, 60.

142 S.n., *Pravovaia organizatsiia Sviatogrobskogo bratstva*, 151.

143 Porphyry Uspenskii, *Kniga bytiia moego*, 3.623.

144 I. I. Sokolov, "Sviatogrobskoe bratstvo," 21–22.

145 Five stavropegic monasteries (directly subordinate to the patriarch)—Saydnaya, St Thekla in Maaloula, St George Humayra, St Elias, and Balamand near Tripoli; and thirteen diocesan monasteries—two in the Diocese of 'Akkar, five in the Diocese of Tripoli, and six in the Diocese of Beirut (Porphyry Uspenskii, "Siriiskaia tserkov'," 125–133).

146 Habib Zayat dedicated a special monograph to the history of the monastery which, unfortunately, has remained unavailable to us.

147   Mikha'il Burayk, *Tarikh al-Sham*, 83. Recall that the construction of churches in the Ottoman Empire could be carried out only with the permission of judicial powers, which often came with high costs.

148   Grigorovich-Barsky, 1800, 321.

149   Ibid.; Porphyry Uspenskii, "Siriiskaia tserkov'," 80.

150   Grigorovich-Barsky 1800, 321. For further descriptions of the monastery, see: I. Vishenski, 61–62.

151   I. Vishenski, 62.

152   See L. Cheikho, "Khabar iqunat Saydnaya," 461ff.; I. Vishenski, 62; Grigorovich-Barsky 1800, 323–325; Mikha'il Burayk, *Tarikh al-Sham*, 84, 99ff. The English traveler of the seventeenth century, Henry Maundrell, retells stories of the miracle-working icon painted with anticlerical pathos, in general, not surprising for a Protestant writer (Maundrell 493).

153   Mikha'il Burayk, *Tarikh al-Sham*, 96, 99.

154   Grigorovich-Barsky 1800, 322.

155   RGADA, Fond 52/1, Book 1, f. 172v.

156   K. A. Panchenko, "Rossiia i Antiokhiiskii patriarkhat," 205.

157   K. A. Panchenko, "Monastyri v Antiokhiiskom patriarchate," 92.

158   J. Nasrallah, "Chronologie, 1500–1634," 4.

159   Trifon Korobeinikov, 103.

160   Frescobaldi, 41–42.

161   RGADA, Fond 1608, no. 129, ff. 1, 5, 6, 9; no. 37, ff. 6-10.

162   RGADA, Fond 52/1, 1645, no. 9.

163   The date is not certain. What is clear is that it was before November 1643, when Moses left Damascus to collect alms (Ibid., ff. 1, 19).

164   Ibid., f. 19.

165   Ibid. It is unknown what alms Moses received in Moscow; the final part of the archival work is missing.

166   RGADA, Fond 52/1, 1654, no. 21, part 3, ff. 83, 86-87.

167   I. Vishenski, 61–62.

168   Grigorovich-Barsky, 1800, 322.

169   Ibid.

170   Maundrell, 492–493.

171   S. M. Saliba, *Les monastères maronites doubles du Liban* (Paris–Kaslik, 2008).

172   Mikha'il Burayk, *Tarikh al-Sham*, 102.

173   Porphyry Uspenskii, "Siriiskaia tserkov'," 129.

174   Ibid.

175 I. Vishenski, 62.

176 Ibid., 61.

177 Porphyry Uspenskii, *Kniga bytiia moego*, 1.228, 234.

178 RGADA, Fond 1608, no. 37, f. 7.

179 I. Vishenski, 54.

180 Volney, 277.

181 Grigorovich-Barsky, 1800, 322.

182 Maundrell, 493.

183 Nasrallah, "Chronologie, 1500-1634," 48.

184 Grigorovich-Barsky, 1800, 322.

185 Mikha'il Burayk, *Tarikh al-Sham*, 122.

186 Grigorovich-Barsky, 1800, 322–323; I. Vishenski, 62.

187 Porphyry Uspenskii, *Kniga bytiia moego*, 1.241–242.

188 Grigorovich-Barsky, 1800, 326–327.

189 Ibid., 326.

190 Ibid.; Paul of Aleppo, 5.192.

191 Mikha'il Burayk, *Tarikh al-Sham*, 47; Porphyry Uspenskii, *Kniga bytiia moego*, 1.232–237.

192 Paul of Aleppo, 5.192; Grigorovich-Barsky, 1800, 327.

193 Grigorovich-Barsky, 1800, 329.

194 Paul of Aleppo, 1.5. In his description of Syria in the 1780s, Volney mentions this monastery in passing as being inhabited (Volney, 484), which is not supported by other sources. Apparently this is some sort of error; the traveler was misled by his informants and never went to the monastery himself.

195 MS Muharrada; MS Kafr Buhum.

196 MS Mar Elias al-Homsi 36.

197 The three hours were probably by foot or perhaps by donkey.

198 In the literature, there is the erroneous date of 1603.

199 S. Slim, 23–26.

200 Macarius, 73–74; K. A. Panchenko, "Mitropolity i eparkhii pravoslavnoi Antiokhiiskoi Tserkvi v opisanii Patriarkha Makariia III az-Za'ima (1665 g.)," 139. According to the observation of C. Walbiner, Macarius's *nisba* does not come from the name for his native village, but from the word "dayr" which means "monastery" (C. Walbiner, "Die Bischofs-und Metropolitensitze," 136).

201 Grigorovich-Barsky, 1800, 295.

202 Ibid.

203 Ibid.

204 S. Slim, 27.

205 Ibid., 26.

206 MS IVR RAN D 226. See also: I. Yu. Krachkovskii, "Original Vati-kanskoi rukopisi," 476; SPBF ARAN Fond 1026/1, no. 246, ff. 21–32v. Further references to the Bible in the registry are indicated in the archival materials of I. Yu. Krachkovski. The copyist of this manuscript was long thought to be the thirteenth century scribe Pimen of Damascus, but in recent years compelling arguments have been made that Pimen's Bible was only the Vorlage for the Balamand manuscript, which itself is more likely to have appeared only in the early sixteenth century (S. A. Frantsuzov, "Pripiski k arabskoi Biblii," 38–42).

207 This refers to the first printed Arabic Gospel, published at the beginning of the eighteenth century in Aleppo under the leadership of Patriarch Athanasius Dabbas, and the publication of the press at the Uniate Monastery of St John of Shuwayr, in particular, *Kitab al-Injil al-Sharif* of 1776 (See L. Cheikho Tarikh fann al-tibaʿa, 356, 361–362).ʿ

208 SPBF ARAN, Fond 1026/1, no. 246, f. 24.

209 C. Walbiner, "Die Bischofs-und Metropolitensitze," 135–137. Balamand Monastery holds Simeon's manuscripts from 1611, 1616, and 1624 (MSS Balamand 31, 135, 157). One colophon from the manuscript of Hamatoura Monastery gives a relatively exact date for the elevation of Macarius to metropolitan (MS Hamatoura 23).

210 S. Slim, 24–25.

211 MS Balamand 31.

212 SPBF ARAN, Fond 1026/1, no. 246, f. 24; MS Balamand 11.

213 See K. A. Panchenko, "Sputniki Makariia."

214 RGADA Fond 52/2, no. 483.

215 Ibid., Fond 52/1, 1654, no. 21, part 3, ff. 146–150. Here it describes the appearance of the letters—on Alexandrian paper with a patterned border, with the tsar's name and signature inscribed in gold and golden stamps on silk ties.

216 Paul of Aleppo, 5.70–71.

217 MS Balamand 34.

218 Ibid.

219 RGADA, Fond 52/1, 1662, no. 28, f. 1. See also: K. A. Panchenko, "Monastyri v pravoslavnom Antiokhiiskom patriarkhate."

220 SPBF ARAN, Fond 1026/1, no. 246, f. 24v; MSS Balamand 150, 151, 163; MS Shuwayr 35.

221 MS Balamand 151.

222 SPBF ARAN, Fond 1026/1, no. 246, f. 32.

223 MS Shuwayr 35.

224 SPBF ARAN, Fond 1026/1, no. 246, ff. 24v, 28, 28v, 32.

225 MSS Balamand 84, 93, 98.

226 An extension to the west side of the church, part of its front entrance.

227 MS Balamand 80; S. Slim, 57.

228 Maundrell, 47–48.

229 T. Jak, 891; S. Slim, 29–30.

230 MS Balamand 108.

231 MSS Balamand 172, 192; S. Slim, 31.

232 Yu. A. Piatnitskii, "Zhivopis' siro-palestinskogo regiona," 202–203. This article erroneously gives the translation of the word "*al-ra'is*" ("abbot") as "archdiocese."

233 SPBF ARAN, Fond 1026/1, no. 246, f. 29. In the literature, one finds another date for the death of 'Abd al-Masih—the year 1718 (S. Slim, 31).

234 MS Balamand 76; S. Slim, 31. S. Slim writes that he was the head of the monastery for a long time, but does not indicate dates or sources.

235 S. Slim, 28, 58. It is true that the *fatwas* of the *qadi* of Tripoli authorizing construction are dated 1711 and 1713, so it is not entirely clear why they are associated with the figure of Michael. Perhaps construction work was completed while he was abbot.

236 Grigorovich-Barsky, 1800, 295.

237 MS Balamand 125.

238 Ibid.

239 MS Balamand 114.

240 MSS Balamand 73, 50; Farah and Qustandius also figure in colophons from 1785 (MSS Balamand 35, 36).

241 MSS Balamand 125, 41.

242 SPBF ARAN, Fond 1026/1, no. 246, f. 30v.

243 MS Balamand 106.

244 Porphyry Uspenskii, "Siriiskaia tserkov'," 126.

245 Ibid., 126–128.

246 A. E. Krymski left a colorful description of the location of the monastery: "Today I visited the left (west) ridge of the base of Shuwayr. What beauty! These pine forests, these crags, these vineyards, these winding paths, these monasteries in the surrounding monasteries (just like medieval castles), the Sannin to the north and the deep sea below to the west. I can not describe it" (A. E. Krymskii, *Pis'ma iz Livana*, 155).

247 Grigorovich-Barsky, 1800, 289.

248 MS Shuwayr 7.

249 MSS Shuwayr 24, 25, 28, 30, 33, 35, 36, 41, 51, 54.

250 MSS Shuwayr 5, 33, 36, 41, 45, 56, 63.

251 Uspenskii, *Skazanie o Siriiskoi unii*, 496.

252 A. E. Krymskii, *Pis'ma iz Livana*, 180.

253 Grigorovich-Barsky, 1800, 289; Porphyry Uspenskii. "Siriiskaia tserkov'," 128.

254 A. E. Krymskii, *Pis'ma iz Livana*, 179.

255 A. E. Krymski lived in Shuwayr for the summer of 1897, I. Yu. Krachkovsky in 1908 (see A. A. Dolinina, *Nevol'nik dolga*, 74–75).

256 See particularly, A. E. Krymskii, *Pis'ma iz Livana*, 179–184.

257 Uspenskii, *Skazanie o Siriiskoi unii*, 495; C. Charon and L. Cheikho,
"Usqufiyyat al-rum al-kathulik fi Bayrut," 197.

258 S.n. "*al-ʿArifa bi-intikhab Kirillus Tannas*," 131–132.

259 Uspenskii, *Skazanie o Siriiskoi unii*, 495.

260 MS Dayr al-Harf 5.

261 MS Dayr al-Malak Mikha'il.

262 "There even now they bury the Christians of Tripoli who so desire,"
wrote Grigorovich-Barsky (Grigorovich-Barsky, 1800, 294).

263 Ibid., 293–294.

264 C. Walbiner, "Bishoprics and Bishops," 121.

265 Grigorovich-Barsky, 1800, 293–294.

266 Porphyry Uspenskii, "Siriiskaia tserkov', 131.

267 Grigorovich-Barsky, 1800, 294.

268 SIPPO, 1897, 112.

269 Mikha'il Burayk, "Spisok Antiokhiiskikh patriarkhov," 432.

270 SIPPO, 1897, 112.

271 Grigorovich-Barsky, 1800, 294. Porphyry Uspenskii, "Siriiskaia tserkov'," 131.

272 Grigorovich-Barsky, 1800, 296; Porphyry Uspenskii, "Siriiskaia tserkov'" 131.

273 Grigorovich-Barsky, 1800, 297.

274 Ibid.

275 Ibid.

276 Macarius, 74; "Mitropolity i eparkhii pravoslavnoi Antiokhiiskoi
Tserkvi v opisanii Patriarkha Makariia III az-Zaʿima (1655 g.)," 139.

277 Macarius, 74; K. A. Panchenko, "Mitropolity i eparkhii pravoslavnoi
Antiokhiiskoi Tserkvi v opisanii Patriarkha Makariia III az-Zaʿima (1655 g.)," 139.

278 Nasrallah, *HMLEM*, 3(2).203; Wright, *Catalogue of Syriac Manuscripts
in the British Museum* vol. 1, 1870, 320n408.

279 Ibid., 298.

280 Ibid.

281 Ibid.

282 C. Charon and L. Cheikho, "Usqufiyyat al-rum al-kathulik fi Bayrut," 198.

283 Porphyry Uspenskii, "Siriiskaia tserkov'," 131.

284 Grigorovich-Barsky, 1800, 299.

285 Ibid.

286 Ibid., 300.

287 Ibid.

288 Ibid.

289 MSS Hamatoura 1, 25, 32, 38, 39; MSS Mar Yuhanna Douma, 13, 15. The priest Musa was quite active in writing books and charity, and he appears in the manuscript colophons of a few Syrian monasteries (Nasrallah, "Chronologie, 1500–1634," 4–5).

290 MS Hamatoura 25.

291 MS Hamatoura 14. See also K. A. Panchenko, "K istorii Ierusalimskoi tserkvi 16 v."

292 MSS Hamatoura 20, 24.

293 MS Hamatoura 24.

294 MS Hamatoura 29.

295 MSS Hamatoura 18, 31, 40, 46.

296 MSS Hamatoura 12, 15, 16, 46.

297 MSS Hamatoura 17, 47.

298 T. Jak, "Dayr milad al-Sayyida fi Ra's Ba'labak," 533–535. The author took four vertical lines scrawled on the wall of monastery as the date for the monastery's foundation—in 1111—forgetting that the chronology, "from the Birth of Christ" would only reach the Christians of Syria in the seventeenth century.

299 Nasrallah, "Chronologie, 1500–1634," 60; Mikha'il Burayk, 436.

300 T. Jak, "Dayr milad al-Sayyida fi Ra's Ba'labak," 535–537.

301 From the Arabic, *ahmar* ("red"). The name was given because of the color of the local soil.

302 Grigorovich-Barsky, 1800, 334; S. Solov'ev, "Monastyr' sv. Georgiia," 552–554.

303 Grigorovich-Barsky, 1800, 334.

304 S. Solov'ev, "Monastyr' sv. Georgiia," 553.

305 Grigorovich-Barsky, 1800, 332; S. Solov'ev, "Monastyr' sv. Georgiia," 555.

306 Grigorovich-Barsky, 1800, 333; Porphyry Uspenskii, "Siriiskaia tserkov'," 126.

307 Porphyry Uspenskii, "Siriiskaia tserkov'," 125–126.

308 S. Solov'ev, "Monastyr' sv. Georgiia," 550.

309   The theme of Muslim or pious caliphs' granting priviliges to some Christian monasteries and communities was fairly common in the literature of Middle Eastern Christians. As a rule, the text of these charters is apocryphal. In the case of the Monastery of St George, it is written that the letter of ʿUmar was written on thick, grey paper and this dispels our last doubts, because they did not learn to make paper in the Middle East until eight hundred years later.

310   S. Solov'ev, "Monastyr' sv. Georgiia," 553.

311   RGADA, Fond 52/1, 1654, no. 21, part 3, ff. 83 86.

312   Grigorovich-Barsky, 1800, 332–33.

313   Porphyry Uspenskii, "Siriiskaia tserkov'," 125.

314   Porphyry Uspenskii, *Kniga bytiia moego*, 3.196–197.

315   Porphyry Uspenskii, "Siriiskaia tserkov', 131–132; SIPPO, 1913, 459.

316   Porphyry Uspenskii, "Siriiskaia tserkov',"131–132; SIPPO, 1913, 459.

317   MS Dayr al-Qaddis Dimitrius.

318   MS Dayr al-Qaddis Dimitrius 15.

319   MS Shuwayr 34.

320   MSS Mar Yuhanna Douma, 2, 3, 6, 8, 9, 14.

321   MS Mar Yuhanna Douma 14.

322   Macarius, 69; K. A. Panchenko, "Mitropolity i eparkhii pravoslavnoi Antiokhiiskoi Tserkvi v opisanii Patriarkha Makariia III az-Zaʿima (1665 g.), 135.

323   On the process of urbanization for the Orthodox in the sixteenth to eighteenth centuries, see Chapter 3.

324   SIPPO, 1909, 113–114; 1913, 459–460.

325   SIPPO, 1908, 169.

326   Of these monastic representatives, whose origins are indicated in the sources, we can name Patriarch Euthymius II Karma (1633–1634), who was the son of a priest from Hamma (Mikha'il Burayk, 437). Patriarch Athanasius III Dabbas, a monk of the Palestinian Lavra of Mar Saba, managed in 1686 to obtain a *berat* from the sultan for the patriarchate with the help of his uncle, who headed, it seems, one of Damascus's handicraft corporations (Ibid., 444). But all this, we repeat, is a fragmented, disparate piece of information that does not give us the whole picture.

327   Volney, 487.

328   Grigorovich-Barsky, 1800, 333.

329   See footnote 320. To this we can add an example from the eighteenth century—the patriarchs of Jerusalem Sophronius (1770–1774) and Anthimus (1788–1808) were Arabs of Syrian origin, who in their youth became monks in the Greek monasteries of Palestine.

330 C. Walbiner, "Die Bischofs-und Metropolitensitze," 99–152; C. Walbiner, "Bishopics and Bishops," 121–134.

331 See, for example, Vl. V. Polosin, "Zapiska Pavla Aleppskogo," 329–342.

332 Constantin François de Chassebœuf, comte de Volney.

333 Volney, 487.

334 Cited in: A. A. Dolinina, *Nevol'nik dolga*, 75.

335 Much later, in 1865, the metropolitan of Beirut appointed a head abbot (*ra'is 'amm*) over four monasteries in northern Lebanon—Hamatoura, Kaftun, Nouriya, and Mar Yuhanna Douma (MS Hamatoura 13).

Chapter 6: A State Within a State: Intra-Imperial Connections in the Orthodox East

1 We refer the reader to the latest study of Russian pilgrimage traditions: S. A. Kirillina, *Ocharovannye stranniki: Arabo-osmanskii mir glazami rossiiskikh palomnikov XVI–XVIII stoletii* (Moscow: Kliuch-S, 2010).

2 V. Pozniakov, 37.

3 Melety, 224–225. It is difficult to say whether under "Syrians" the author was listing the Syriac-speaking Orthodox of Maaloula or whether he was mistakenly including the Syrian Jacobites or Nestorian Assyrians as Orthodox.

4 Christians of the Ottoman era embraced the Arab Muslim terms "hajj" and "hajji," which denote a person who has performed a pilgrimage.

5 Sixteenth-century travelers describe the magnificent Georgian pilgrimage caravans, cavalcades of horsemen with banners who entered Ottoman territory without paying a toll—an echo of the Georgians' privileged situation in Palestine under the Mamluk Sultanate. By the seventeenth century, however, these privileges were lost, as were the Georgian monasteries and sections of the holy places of Palestine. During the eighteenth century, even the intensity of Georgian pilgrimage to the Palestinian shrines decreased (A. Tsagareli, 59–88).

6 One in every five or six years, in Grigorovich-Barsky's time (Grigorovich-Barsky, 1885, 304). Vasily Gagara, who visited Jerusalem in 1635, was told by the local Greeks that he was the first Russian pilgrim to the Holy Land since Trifon Korobeinikov in 1593 (V. Gagara, 9).

7 Grigorovich-Barsky called on his compatriots to go worship in the Holy Land, putting forward the example of the Greeks who, although " … they have the king as an enemy … and are burdened by many taxes" nevertheless "like bees, they fly, and of their labor, like sweet honey, they render alms to redeem the Holy Sepulchre from the hands of the infidels and heretics" (Grigorovich-Barsky, 1885, 305). However, the journey to Palestine was much more difficult

for foreigners than for subjects of the Ottoman Empire. Many Russian pilgrims were subject to arrest and detention along the road on suspicion of spying, for the nonpayment of duties, or even for things that the pilgrims could not understand because of the language barrier. Turkish prisons are described by the pilgrimage literature in the darkest terms: "Then we suffered there great need and misfortune in prison, and I can not speak [of it]; because of all of the Turks we did not have space in the same prison; because of this we were forced to sit in a putrid corner where we had to defecate" (Serapion, 81). Even apart from prisons, a stay in the Ottoman Empire was fraught with heavy psychological stress for Russian pilgrims, especially when they were outside of areas with dense Christian populations. Arseny Sukhanov described his journey along the Nile: "Out of Misr [Cairo] came much evil and darkness and we suffered all sorts of blasphemous words from the Turks; inasmuch as it was all Turks sitting on the Egyptian boat they are deliberate people, and they were very educated in their laws and letters but there were no Christians, only us two" (Arsenii Sukhanov, 49). Such feelings were also experienced in the same places a half century later by Ivan Lukyanov: "And when we went on the ships with the Arabs, it was terribly bitter, the people there are like devils in appearance and in deeds, and we three were prisoners, we did not know the language, where they were taking us, God only knows, and whether they would sell us somewhere—for who would look for us and how?" (I. Luk'ianov, col. 234).

8   O. Peri, 163–164, 166.

9   O. Peri, p72.

10   Melety, 84.

11   Melety, 215.

12   Ibid., 110.

13   Ibid., 283.

14   Serapion, 87–88.

15   This was the route of Arseny Sukhanov (Arsenii Sukhanov, 21–31), Iona (Iona, 4–5), Makary (Hieromonk Makarii, 5–6), Ippolit Vishenski (I. Vishenski, 28–31), Varlaam (Varlaam, 56–57), Matvei Nechaev (M. Nechaev, 17–22), Serapion (Serapion, 83–88), Melety (Melety, 45–75), and others.

16   See, for example, I. Vishenski, 29; Melety, 58–59.

17   Maximus Simaius, 105.

18   Grigorovich-Barsky, 1885, 283–284.

19   See, for example, Varlaam, 5–7; I. Luk'ianov, col. 243.

20   Serapion, 125; M. Nechaev, 21–22.

21 Grigorovich-Barsky, 1885, 277; Melety, 75; Regarding the existence of a patriarchal metochion in Jaffa up to the early eighteenth century, per col. 241.

22 Grigorovich-Barsky, 1885, 279; Serapion, 89.

23 I. Luk'ianov, col. 244.

24 Grigorovich-Barsky, 1885, 283.

25 Ibid., 284; Arsenii Sukhanov, 49; Serapion, 89.

26 M. Nechaev, 22–23.

27 In describing his escape from Bedouins in the mountains near Mar Saba, Lukyanov wrote, "If you were caught by Arabs—that would be the end! Not only would you be robbed—everyone would be beaten because the animals are nomadic, not settled. When we got to Jerusalem, there we were robbed by those settled; they only rob you, they do not kill" (I. Luk'ianov, col. 339).

28 I. Luk'ianov, col. 242–248. Matvei Nechaev fell into a similar situation in 1721 (M. Nechaev, 22).

29 Grigorovich-Barsky, 1885, 296–297; See also: Varlaam, 58–59; Serapion, 89–90.

30 I. Luk'ianov, col. 251.

31 Ibid.., col. 252.

32 Ibid., col. 251

33 Ibid., col. 254.

34 S. A. Kirillina, 112.

35 Melety, 79.

36 Melety, 79.

37 See: Hieromonk Makarii, 9.

38 M. Nechaev, 11.

39 Ignaty Denshin writes that the rich would pay as much as 40 rubles for the convoy (Ignaty, 14). On the Abu Ghosh see especially K. M. Bazili, 2007, 143.

40 V. Gagara, iii-iv; Arsenii Sukhanov, 90–98.

41 K. A. Panchenko, "Pravoslavnye Araby i Kavkaz," 67.

42 Paul of Aleppo, 5.118.

43 Maximus Simaius, 99.

44 Paul of Aleppo, 5.191–192.

45 RGADA, Fond 52/1, 1653, no. 34, f. 98; K. A. Panchenko, "Sputniki Makariia."

46 Paul of Aleppo, 5.152.

47 Arsenii Sukhanov, 91–97.

48 O. Peri, 170.

49 Varlaam, 61

50 Varlaam describes the standard menu of the monastery kitchen as "they place on the table a single cup of water, boiled beans, boiled grains of wheat, rice porridge, olives, cheese, a single turnip and a single lemon for everyone; they also drink four cups of wine at the meal, but sometimes six cups" (Varlaam, 61; see also: Iona, 6–7; Arsenii Sukhanov, 52; I. Luk'ianov, col. 255–257; Varlaam, 59–61; Grigorovich-Barsky, 1885, 314–317; Serapion, 91–93).

51 Oded Peri, however, believes that the difference in taxation did not depend on the pilgrim's religious affiliation but rather on the relative remoteness of the region from which the "hajji" was coming. The more a pilgrim used the empire's roads, the more he had to pay (O. Peri, p. 165). However, in this case, it is unclear why the largest collection was levied on the Franks, who arrived in the Holy Land by sea, and why this amount was so different from the levy paid by the Balkan Greeks also arriving in Palestine by sea.

52 Gold coins minted by the Egyptian sultan Qaitbay (1468–1495) on the model of Venetian ducats (O. Peri, 164).

53 O. Peri, 162–164.

54 We recall that the Mamluks had an interest in maintaining friendly relations with Georgia, which controlled the supply route of slaves to Egypt, and Ethiopia, which controlled the upper course of the Blue Nile (O. Peri, 162–163).

55 Ibid., 163.

56 Serapion, 94; Grigorovich-Barsky, 1885, 315.

57 A. Cohen and B. Lewis, 95–96; M. Bakhit, 48.

58 Serapion, 94.

59 Porphyry Uspenskii, *Kniga bytiia moego*, 2.326.

60 Serapion, 99.

61 Grigorovich-Barsky, 1885, 319.

62 Dositheus. "Poslaniia," 170, 173.

63 Hieromonk Makarii, 10.

64 Ignaty, 15.

65 Ibid., 22.

66 Maximus Simaius, 130.

67 Serapion, 99.

68 Varlaam, 69.

69 Volney, 427.

70 Volney, 423.

71 Ibid., 427.

72 I. Luk'ianov, col. 339.

73 Ibid., col. 260.

74 Ibid., col. 262.

75 Ibid., col. 264.

76 Ibid., col. 346.

77 Ibid.

78 Serapion, 119.

79 See, for example, Arsenii Sukhanov, 78.

80 Serapion, 119.

81 Ibid.

82 Ibid., 120.

83 Grigorovich-Barsky, 1885, 374.

84 Grigorovich-Barsky, 1885, 377.

85 Serapion, 121. However, from the bulk of other evidence, it is clear that only a small part of the mass of pilgrims in Jerusalem went to the Jordan.

86 Ignaty, 21

87 Varlaam, 69.

88 Serapion, 124.

89 Ibid., 124–125.

90 Grigorovich-Barsky, 1800, 238.

91 Maximus Simaius, 99.

92 Ibid., 102–104.

93 O. Peri, 179.

94 B. Nikolaev, "Zapadnye palomnichestva," 404.

95 V. Gagara, 31; Iona, 19.

96 O. Peri, 179.

97 B. Nikolaev, "Zapadnye palomnichestva," 404.

98 I. Vishenski, 95, 98. In that year, 900 Copts came to Jerusalem to worship with their patriarch at their head.

99 Melety, 180, 308.

100 Grigorovich-Barsky, 1800, 238; Grigorovich-Barsky, 1885, 305.

101 Volney, 423.

102 Neophytus of Cyprus, "Dvadtsatiletie," 154, 158, 162.

103 Neophytus of Cyprus, "Rasskaz," 67.

104 Peri, 169–170.

105 We refer the reader to the monograph N. Iorga, *Byzantium after Byzantium* (Iasi–Ox.–Portland, 2004, and other editions).

106 See, for example, on the charity of the princes of Moldavia and Wallachia to the Monastery of Sinai in the fifteenth and sixteenth centuries: Porphyry Uspenskii, *Vtoroe Puteshestvie*, 273–279, 310–312.

107 A. N. Murav'ev, *Istoriia,* 2.274. Sophronius's presence in Moldavia in 1588 is particularly well-known (I. Malyshevskii, 327).

108 N. Iorga, *Histoire des Etats balcaniques jusqu'à* 1924, 56. The author thanks Vera Chentsova for pointing out this information.

109 *Posol'skaia kniga,* 159; Arsenii Sukhanov, 4.

110 N. F. Kapterev, *Snosheniia ierusalimskikh patriarkhov,* 93.

111 Porphyry Uspenskii, *Kniga bytiia moego,* 3.35–36.

112 Ibid., 296–298. In addition to those in Constantinople, Moldavia, and Wallachia, the Patriarchate of Jerusalem had metochia in other parts of the Ottoman Empire. Mid-seventeenth century sources mention a metochion in Silistria with a Church of the Most Holy Theotokos ("monks live there who collect alms for the Holy Sepulchre") (Iona, 3) and Rosetta, Egypt, where, according to Iona, "there are elders from the Patriarchate of Jerusalem who collect alms from boats for the Holy Sepulchre and buy provisions: sugar, wax, and fish and send it to Jerusalem" (Ibid., 5). In 1726, Grigorovich-Barsky met with Patriarch Chrysanthos of Jerusalem at the metochion of the Brotherhood of the Holy Sepulchre on Chios (Kh. M. Loparev, "Khrisanf," 26).

113 A. N. Murav'ev, *Istoriia,* 2.296.

114 Maximus Simaius, 56.

115 Ioannikii, 232–237.

116 Maximus Simaius, 60. In his letter to the Russian tsar, Paisius describes this procedure: "The entire holy council of bishops…elected and called me… the heiromonk Paisius, the former abbot of the divine and sovereign Monastery of the Ascension of our Lord God and Savior Jesus Christ, who had been living in the Moldavian lands of Iasi *at the behest of the pious sovereign…Lord Vasile* [author's emphasis], the voivodes of all the Moldavian lands, faithful friend of your great and holy kingdom…in the Divine and sovereign monastery…by the exarch of the most holy metropolitan of the holy metropolitanate of Larissa, Kyr Gregorius, and the most holy metropolitan Kyr Varlaam of the local Moldavian lands…at the behest of the Most Holy and Ecumenical Patriarch Kyr Parthenius.'" (N. F. Kapterev *Snosheniia ierusalimskikh patriarkhov,* 117).

117 N. F. Kapterev, *Snosheniia ierusalimskikh patriarkhov,* 121, 153, 160, 172–173; Maximus Simaius, 324; N. F. Kapterev, "Gospodstvo grekov," 205.

118 Paul of Aleppo. 1.104.

119 N. F. Kapterev, "Gospodstvo grekov," 203, 206; A. N. Murav'ev, *Istoriia,.* 2.318, 328.

120 N. F. Kapterev, *Snosheniia ierusalimskikh patriarkhov,* 187ff.

121 B. L. Fonkich, "Pis'mo Dionisiia Ivirita," 227.

122 Ibid., 227–229.

123 I. Pomerantsev, "Dosifei," 18–20, 23–26.

124 Kh. M. Loparev, "Khrisanf," 21–27; N. F. Kapterev, *Snosheniia ierusalimskikh patriarkhov*, 376; I. I. Sokolov, "Sviatogrobskoe bratstvo," 21–22; I. Pomerantsev, "Dosifei," 27.

125 Maximus Simaius, 84, 85.

126 Porphyry Uspenskii, *Kniga bytiia moego* 3.29.

127 Ibid., 45.

128 Mikha'il Burayk, 434.

129 Paul of Aleppo. 5.58.

130 Porphyry Uspenskii, "Vostok Khristianskii: Siriia," 112; C. Walbiner, "Pioneers of Book-Printing," 11; L. Cheikho, "Tarikh Fann al-Tiba'a," 356. See Chapter 10 for the activities of the printing press.

131 Porphyry Uspenskii, *Kniga bytiia moego*, 3.413; Mikha'il Burayk, 451, 452; *Beirut Ecclesiastical Chronicle*, 49, 52; Mikha'il Burayk, *Tarikh al-Sham*, 27, 42.

132 *Bor'ba pravoslavnykh i latinian iz-za obladaniia Sv. mestami*, 188; S.n., *Patriarshie dokumenty*, 292–297.

133 S.n., *Patriarshie dokumenty*, 298–301.

134 Ibid., 300.

135 Ibid., 302–310.

136 Mikha'il Burayk, *Tarikh al-Sham*, 39, 43.

137 Procopius Nazianzen, 202.

138 Maximus Simaius, 41–42; I. Malyshevskii, 14; Runciman, *The Great Church in Captivity*, 199.

139 Paul of Aleppo, 5.188; Mikha'il Burayk, 426.

140 Maximus Simaius, 45.

141 I. Malyshevskii, 341–355.

142 For the biography and views of Cyril Lucaris, see A. P. Lebedev, *Istoriia,* 633–673; Runciman, *The Great Church in Captivity*, 259–288.

143 I. Pomerantsev, "Dosifei," 9–12; Runciman, *The Great Church in Captivity*, 286–287.

144 For the publication of these documents, see : A. Rabbat, "al-Tawa'if al-sharqiyya," in *al-Mashriq* 1903, 971–973; 1904, 766–773, 795–803.

145 I. Pomerantsev, "Dosifei," 13–17.

146 Kh. M. Loparev, "Khrisanf," 26; I. I. Sokolov, "Tserkovnye sobytiia," 340–342 (in this article, the patriarch of Constantinople's encyclical is incorrectly dated to 1700).

147 Mikha'il Burayk, *Tarikh al-Sham*, 50–55.

148 Ibid., 72, 93.

149 SPBF ARAN, Fond 1026, op. 1, no. 246, f. 27.

150 Paisius Agiapostolites, 125; Porphyry Uspenskii, *Vtoroe Puteshestvie*, 249.

151 S.n., *Patriarshie dokumenty*, 314–316.

152 I. Malyshevskii, 174–181, 189–192; S.n., *Patriarshie dokumenty*, 316–323.

153 S.n., *Patriarshie dokumenty*, 283–288; see also: I. Malyshevskii, 444–446.

154 The future metropolitan of Rhodes (1597–1603) and author of a poetic "Description of the Holy Mountain of Sinai."

155 S.n., *Patriarshie dokumenty*, 285.

156 S.n., *Patriarshie dokumenty*, 273–277, 283–292; Paisius Agiapostolites, iv–v, 175–176; I. Malyshevskii, 630–640.

157 I. Malyshevskii, 642–644; Dositheus, "Istoriia episkopii gory sinaia," 25–27, 31.

158 Ioannikii, 210–263; Dositheus, "Istoriia episkopii gory sinaia," 34–61.

159 I. Vishenski, 43; Andrei Ignat'ev, 44.

160 Dositheus, "Istoriia episkopii gory sinaia," 111–112.

161 N. F. Kapterev, "Russkaia blagotvoritel'nost' Sinaiskoi obiteli," 385–400. For details, see Chapter 8.

162 Dositheus, "Istoriia episkopii gory sinaia," 107.

163 Dositheus. "Istoriia episkopii gory sinaia," 107.

164 Ibid., 122–130; S.n., *Patriarshie dokumenty*, 427; N. F. Kapterev, "Russkaia blagotvoritel'nost' Sinaiskoi obiteli," 398, 401; A. Voronov, "Sinaiskoe dielo," 392.

165 See Chapter 4.

166 I. Malyshevskii, 666–672; S.n., *Patriarshie dokumenty*, 264–292; N. F. Kapterev, "Gospodstvo grekov," 205. N. F. Kapterev, *Snosheniia ierusalimskikh patriarkhov*, 228.

167 N. F. Kapterev, "Gospodstvo grekov," 205; V. G. Chentsova, *Ikona Iverskoi Bogomateri*, 83, 211–215.

168 Arseny Sukhanov reported the words of his informant in Istanbul, Archimandrite Amphilochius: "Patriarch Parthenius was a good and intelligent man ... respected not just by the Christians, but also by the Turks. And now every rank grieves over him, the Greeks, the Jews, the Armenians and the infidels; for a few people did it [i.e., organized the murder of the patriarch]" (Arsenii Sukhanov, 15). Bishop Gabriel of Nazareth, one of Paisius's confidants, also wrote with indignation to Moscow about how they "put" the patriarch "to death" (RGADA, Fond 52/4, no. 42). On the Greek ecclesiopolitical groupings, see also Chapter 8.

169 N. F. Kapterev, *Snosheniia ierusalimskikh patriarkhov*, 228.

170 Robert Haddad writes that in the two centuries before 1724, there was hardly a single patriarchal tenure in the Church of Antioch that was not subject to improper interference from the Constantinopolitan Greeks (R. Haddad, *Syrian Christians*, 26). Describing Damascus in the seventeenth century, M. Bakhit complains that the sources do not give a picture of the relationship between the local parish clergy and the Greek ecclesiastical elite (M. Bakhit, 26).

171 C. Walbiner, "Bishops and Metropolitans," 585–587, and his other works. Thomas Philipp thought that Cyril Tanas (1724–1762) was the first patriarch elected by the residents of Damascus and not delivered from Constantinople. This author explains the formation of the Melkite Uniate community in terms of the struggle of the Christians of Damascus and Aleppo for autonomy and freedom from the authority of the Phanar (Th. Philipp, 18–19). In the literature, there can be found even more radical statements, like that the whole upper hierarchy of the Antiochian Church in the seventeenth and eighteenth centuries was composed of Greeks, as in A. K. Rafek (cf. Th. Philipp, 18) and Kamal Salibi (cf. C. Walbiner, "Bishops and Metropolitans," 585). Through Salibi, these views came to be popular in the literature, including in the Russian-language literature—see Hasan bin Talal, *Khristianstvo v Arabskom mire* (Moscow, 2013), 76.

172 Nasrallah, "Chronologie, 1500–1634," 28.

173 Nasrallah, "Chronologie, 1500–1634," 29; R. Haddad, *Syrian Christians*, 23.

174 Porphyry Uspenskii. "Vostok Khristianskii: Siriia," 95.

175 C. Karalevskij, "Antioche," col. 636–637.

176 Nasrallah, "Chronologie, 1500–1634," 32–33.

177 Beirut Ecclesiastical Chronicle, 32.

178 A. Papadopoulou tou Kerameos, "Katalogos ton en tais bibliothekais tes nesou Lesbou ellenikon heirografon" in *idem.*, *Maurokordateios bibliotheke etoi genikos perifgafi ƙos katalogos ton en tais ana ten Anatolen bibliothekais euriskomenon ellenikon heirografon* (Constantinople, 1884) 7–8, 171, 172. The author thanks Vera Chentsova for helping him to become acquainted with these documents.

179 I. Malyshevskii, 288.

180 See Chapter 4.

181 Mikha'il Burayk, 430; Nasrallah, "Chronologie, 1500–1634," 52.

182 Mikha'il Burayk, 432.

183 See Chapter 4.

184 K. A. Panchenko, "Rossiia i Antiokhiiskii patriarkhat," 211–212.

185 C. Walbiner, "Bishops and Metropolitans," 586.

186   MS Saydnaya 13.

187   C. Walbiner, "Die Bischofs-und Metropolitensitze," 124.

188   Paul of Aleppo, 1.14.

189   Thus, Paul stated that, "As a result of … the shortcomings and defects of the Greeks … we could find absolutely no people sympathetic to them" (Paul of Aleppo, 3.132). He spoke of the hatred for the Greeks in Moldavia and Wallachia and hostility to them in Ukraine, "While the Muscovites," wrote Paul, "only accept them out of compassion, for the sake of providing them with aid. How many of them have they sent to exile in Siberia and to the monasteries of the Black Sea!" (Ibid.) Many Greeks were given this punishment, according to Paul, for "shamelessness, wickedness and abominations"—drunkenness, fraud, infighting, and smoking tobacco (Ibid., 2.101). "In the Frankish countries," Paul continued, "they cannot hear mention of the Greeks with indifference, saying that they, through their poor governance, lost their kingdom and helped the Turks, when they conquered them, against other states. What kind of a people is this?! How detestable are their actions!" (Paul of Aleppo, 3.132).

190   Paul of Aleppo, 5.151.

191   For example, John Sakoulis, Macarius's secretary and economos of the Church of Antioch from 1656–1667, who accompanied him on his second trip to Russia (See: B. L. Fonkich, "Ioann Sakulis").

192   In one of these petitions to the tsar in 1656, Macarius mentions his representative Ivan Feodulov (as it is given in its Russified form), who lived in Constantinople "on my business" (RGADA, Fond 521, 1654, part 3, f. 83). That is, he acted as something like the patriarch's diplomatic representative in the capital.

193   See RGADA, Fond 52/2, nos. 508, 509, 512, 514, 547, 556, 561, 565, 568–570, 574, 575, 596.

194   See Chapter 8.

195   I. I. Sokolov, "Tserkovnye sobytiia," 315.

196   I. I. Sokolov, "Tserkovnye sobytiia," 319–322.

197   Mikha'il Burayk, 493–494.

198   C. Walbiner, "Bishops and Metropolitans," 586–587.

199   It is curious that the family tradition of the Syrian Dabbas clan claims that Sylvester was the previous patriarch's maternal nephew. Sylvester's mother, Photini, is said to be Athanasius's sister (A. Dabbas, *Tarikh al-tiba'a al-ʿrabiyya*, 41). In principle, there is nothing impossible about this, since Orthodox Arabs were in close contact with Greek Cypriots and intermarriages between them could well have taken place. In this case, the traditional outline of the establishment of the Greek xenocracy in the Church of Antioch falls to pieces: the first

Greek patriarch was a member of an influential Arab clan. However, chroniclers of the eighteenth century, in contrast to Arab nationalists of the following century, did not attach much importance to Sylvester's origins.

200 Th. Philipp, 15.

201 For details, see Chapter 9.

202 Mikha'il Burayk, *Tarikh al-Sham*, 87. We have no information about which side of the family the younger Sylvester, the patriarch's nephew, was from and whether he had Arab blood. At the same time, there is a very interesting Greek note made in 1760 by the Patriarch Sylvester in a printed service book addressing his nephew, who apparently received the book as a gift. In the text, there are several Arabic expressions, written sometimes in Arabic and sometimes in Greek script (MS Saydnaya, 177). It seems that both bishops were fluent in both languages and easily passed from one into the other.

203 Grigorovich-Barsky, 1800, 335. However, according to Carsten Walbiner, Timothy was installed as a metropolitan by the Patriarch Cyril and held the See of Hama from 1697 to 1720, while in 1721, Athanasius installed a new metropolitan, the Cypriot Leontius (C. Walbiner, "Die Bischofsund Metropolitensitze, 1665–1724," 63–64).

204 Beirut Ecclesiastical Chronicle, 87.

205 Mikha'il Burayk, *Tarikh al-Sham*, 84–85.

206 Ibid., 87–88.

207 Mikha'il Burayk, *Tarikh al-Sham*, 91. Different sources give different accounts of the election of the second Greek patriarch. The Beirut Chronicle says that Constantinople itself, "after long difficulties," recommended that the bishops of Syria who were gathered in Damascus elect Philemon, and that it was done at the end of April of 1766 (*Beirut Ecclesiastical Chronicle*, 64). In our opinion, the Damascene Mikhail Breik should have had more information about these proceedings. From his words, it would follow that Philemon was not only elevated to the Patriarchate of Constantinople on April 30, but also that the message of the bishops of Syria and inhabitants of Damascus with their request to install Sophronius as patriarch was only sent on June 10, and after that the Syrians were presented with the facts that a patriarch had already been chosen for them (Mikha'il Burayk, *Tarikh al-Sham*, 91; Mikha'il Burayk, 455).

208 Mikha'il Burayk, *Tarikh al-Sham*, 81–82, 85–99; Mikha'il Burayk, 445–446; Uspenskii, *Skazanie o Siriiskoi unii*, 541–544.

209 Mikha'il Burayk, 455–457; Mikha'il Burayk, *Tarikh al-Sham*, 96–100.

210 Beirut Ecclesiastical Chronicle, 64; Uspenskii, *Skazanie o Siriiskoi unii*, 544.

211 J. Neale, 193–194.

212 Ibid.

213 Mikha'il Burayk, *Tarikh al-Sham*, 100–101, 109, 116–117, 119.

214 A. Trad, 150.

215 Specifically, in December 1791 (J. Neale, 198).

216 Uspenskii, *Skazanie*, 544, 550–551; A. Trad, 152.

217 See Chapter 9.

218 Uspenskii, *Skazanie o Siriiskoi unii*, 551–552.

219 Foma Dibu-Maluf, 338; Nasrallah, *HMLEM*, 4(2).196.

220 A. Trad, 149–151; A. E. Krymskii, 333–334.

Chapter 7: The Holy Places

1 The Armenian traveler of the early seventeenth century, Simeon Lekhatsi, argues that this building belonged to the Armenians, but in 1616, the Mufti of Jerusalem confiscated it and erected a mosque with a minaret close to the church. "The sheikhs and Muslims of the city had long been jealous but they could not take [the church] away," he wrote, "for Paronter [the Armenian patriarch of Jerusalem] wrote a petition complaining to Istanbul and went to Aleppo and Damascus with bribes and saved the church. The mufti, however, took it by force … and all the Christians were greatly sorrowful" (Simeon Lekhatsi, 212). Simcon laments that he witnessed such a misfortunate. That is, he was an eyewitness to it. It is not clear how to reconcile this with the words of Mikołaj Krzysztof Radziwiłł, who already in 1583 referred to the site of the Dormition as a mosque where Christians had previously enjoyed free access, but two years earlier they had been banned from it by the *qadi* who was "very impatient with infidels" (M. Radziwiłł, 107).

2 Daniel of Ephesus, 41.

3 V. Pozniakov, 43.

4 I. Luk'ianov, col. 308.

5 Porphyry Uspenski, *Kniga bytiia moego*, 2.82.

6 Ibid.

7 Anfim Ankhial'skii, 329.

8 Melety, 107, 148.

9 Grigorovich-Barsky, 1885, 383.

10 As Serapion caustically remarked about the organ, "often the Latin priests there, in their madness, have a custom to play music" (Serapion, 95).

11 I. Luk'ianov, col. 311.

12 Mladshii Grigorovich, 74–75.

13 A. N. Murav'ev, *Puteshestvie k Sv. mestam*, 177.

14   Arsenii Sukhanov, 55–56, 64, 67–70; Parthenius the Athenian, 199, 213.

15   V. V. Bartol'd, "Karl Velikii i Kharun ar-Rashid," 345–346.

16   Agrefenii, 267–268; Ignaty Smolnianin, 18–19; Zosima, 30–31; Vasilii, gost', 9–10; Porphyry Uspenskii, *Kniga bytiia moego*, 3.256–257; M. Baumgarten, 133, 136–139; A. von Harff, 203–204; O. Peri, 43–44.

17   James of Verona, 99.

18   Agrefenii, 269; *Dushespasitel'nyi rasskaz o Sv. grobe*, 163.

19   D. Richards, 459.

20   Agrefenii, 267; Porphyry Uspenskii, *Kniga bytiia moego*, 3.256; Zosima, 31; Daniel of Ephesus, 38; M. Baumgarten, 139; D. Richards, 459–467.

21   James of Verona, 104; Agrefenii, 271; Ignaty Smolnianin, 22–23; Zosima, 37; Vasilii, gost', 8; M. Baumgarten, 134, 153.

22   James of Verona, 100.

23   A. von Harff, 189, 203; M. Baumgarten, 134–135.

24   For the bibliographical question, see: O. Peri, 43–44.

25   For a Russian translation of the texts, see: Procopius Nazianzen, C. 229–237.

26   Neophytus of Cyprus, "Rasskaz," 4–14; Maximus Simaius, 38; Procopius Nazianzen, 231–237; Dositheus. "Gramota," 2–3.

27   Kirakos Gandzaketsi, 46–47; O. Peri, 128–131.

28   O. Peri, 129.

29   N. A. Mednikov still described ʿUmar's decree in this way (N. A. Mednikov, 1.608–613), but in the late 1450s, it simply did not exist for Patriarch Athanasius (see: K. A. Panchenko, "Patriarkh Ioakim").

30   Arkhim. Makarii (Veretennikov), "Gramota patriarkha Germana," 208.

31   Maximus Simaius, 43; N. F. Kapterev "Gospodstvo grekov," 210. Notices from these sources about Germanus's renovation of the Church of the Resurrection and the Basilica of the Nativity, probably following the earthquake of 1545, as well as Patriarch Sophronius's reinforcing the collapsing church arch of Bethlehem in the late sixteenth century, do not in themselves indicate a preferential right on the part of the Greeks to possession of the major shrines of Jerusalem and Bethlehem. It may then be a question of repairing the particular Orthodox sections of these churches.

32   V. Pozniakov, 66.

33   A. Cohen, 12.

34   See note 19.

35   V. Pozniakov, 41.

36   Ibid., 25.

37 Kh. M. Loparev, "Prilozhenie," 65.

38 Neophytus of Cyprus, "Rasskaz," 12.

39 Maximus Simaius, 43.

40 Neophytus of Cyprus, "Rasskaz," 12.

41 In 1543, Germanus signed a letter from Greek bishops to Russia request-ing the release from prison of Maksim Grek (A. N. Murav'ev, *Snosheniia Rossii s Vostokom*, C. 44). In 1544 (1545) the patriarch of Jerusalem presided over a church council that elected Dionysius I as the new primate of Constantinople (I. Malyshevskii, 179).

42 Neophytus of Cyprus, "Rasskaz," 13.

43 Ibid., 13–14.

44 Neophytus of Cyprus, "Rasskaz," 14. The same pattern was described in 1583 by the Polish pilgrim Mikołaj Krzysztof Radziwiłł: the chapel of the Apparition in the northern part of the church, the high altar of the chapel of the Finding of the Cross by St Helen, the place of the Nailing to the Cross in the southern part of Golgotha, the Stone of Anointing, the Holy Sepulchre, and the altar of Mary Magdalene were all in the hands of the Catholics (M. Radziwiłł, 71–80). In Bethlehem, the Chapel of the Nativity was locked by the Catholics (possibly due to the constant presence of Muslims in the church) and the Holy Grotto could be accessed only through an underground passage from the Franciscan monastery (Ibid., 123).

45 Serapion, 116.

46 Neophytus of Cyprus, "Rasskaz,", 14–15.

47 Maximus Simaius, 47; N. F. Kapterev, "Gospodstvo grekov," 33–34; A. N. Murav'ev, *Istoriia,* 2.288.

48 *Bor'ba pravoslavnykh i latinian iz-za obladaniia Sv. mestami*, 175–183; O. Peri, 108.

49 *Bor'ba pravoslavnykh i latinian iz-za obladaniia Sv. mestami*, 185–191.

50 Maximus Simaius, 53–54.

51 *Bor'ba pravoslavnykh i latinian iz-za obladaniia Sv. mestami*, 192; Dositheus, "Gramota," 3; O. Peri, 109.

52 Neophytus of Cyprus, "Rasskaz," 16.

53 O. Peri, 134–137.

54 P. V. Kuzenkov and K. A. Panchenko, 4.

55 N. F. Kapterev, *Snosheniia ierusalimskikh patriarkhov*, 74. As mentioned, Theophanes himself was in Istanbul at the time and wrote about the miracle of the Holy Fire based on the words of pilgrims returning from Jerusalem.

56 I. Luk'ianov, col. 316–317.

57   For an analysis of the circumstances around the phenomenon of the Holy Fire in 1634 and the later existence of related legends, see P. V. Kuzenkov and K. A. Panchenko, 12–21.

58   I. Vishenski, 72.

59   Maximus Simaius, 51–53; A. N. Murav'ev, *Istoriia,* 2.291–294.

60   M. L. Zulalian, 157.

61   Procopius Nazianzen, 267–269; O. Peri, 120.

62   Neophytus of Cyprus, "Rasskaz," 6; O. Peri, 120–121.

63   Arsenii Sukhanov, 87.

64   O. Peri, 123.

65   Neophytus of Cyprus, "Rasskaz," 18–19. Neophytus erroneously attributed the story of the mitre to 1653, while it actually took place in 1657. See the details in chapter 8.

66   Maximus Simaius, 61–65; Procopius Nazianzen, 166–167; N. F. Kapterev, "Gospodstvo grekov," 30–31, 35–38; O. Peri, 112–113, 124.

67   O. Peri, 120.

68   H. Manundrell, 463.

69   H. Manundrell, 463.

70   H. Manundrell, 464.

71   I. Vishenski, 98.

72   Serapion, 122.

73   Maximus Simaius, 67–69. Maximus Simaius does not date this clash precisely, only relating it to the patriarchate of Nectarius (1661–1669). It is possible that Oded Peri discusses the same case on the basis of Ottoman court records from June 1671 (O. Peri, 116), but it is also possible that it is a different case.

74   H. Maundrell, 442.

75   Maximus Simaius, 73–74; O. Peri, 111; Dositheus, "Gramota," 62.

76   As Dositheus puts it in one of his letters, "the French wolf, the lawless ambassador of Western pridefulness" who provoked the conflict over the holy places by his arrival, was withdrawn by the Ottoman authorities in Istanbul "so that he could live in his lair like a destructive bear" (Dositheus, "Gramota," 62–63).

77   I. Pomerantsev, "Dosifei," 18–19; O. Peri, 109; Dositheus, "Gramota," 3–4, 62.

78   Dositheus, "Gramota," 63.

79   Procopius Nazianzen, 145–146; Maximus Simaius, 78; Neophytus of Cyprus, "Rasskaz," 21–22; Dositheus, "Gramota," 4–7; O. Peri, 112.

80   I. Luk'ianov, col. 261.

81 I. N. Berezin, "Pravoslavnye tserkvi v Turtsii," 34.

82 In 1700, even the Armenians attempted to achieve equal rights with the Greeks through the embassy of the Shah of Persia (Dositheus, "Gramota," 35).

83 Dositheus, "Gramota," 27.

84 Ibid., 5–7, 25–28.

85 Ibid., 86–87.

86 A. V. Lavrent'ev, 187–189.

87 Dositheus, "Gramota," 26, 38, 48, 54.

88 Chrysanthos, 129–138; Maximus Simaius, 80.

89 Procopius Nazianzen, 168; See also: M. S. Meier, 174–180.

90 Parthenius the Athenian, 191.

91 Ibid., 195–196; Neophytus of Cyprus, "Rasskaz," 25.

92 O. Peri, 130–131.

93 Parthenius the Athenian, 273.

94 Ibid., 192, 197–197, 201–211.

95 Parthenius the Athenian, 223–231; Procopius Nazianzen, 168–180.

96 Melety, 178–179.

97 A. N. Murav'ev, *Istoriia*, 2.352.

98 Neophytus of Cyprus, "Rasskaz," 23–24; Maximus Simaius, 82–83; Procopius Nazianzen, 148–150.

99 Mikha'il Burayk, *Tarikh al-Sham*, 72.

100 SBF ARAN, Fond 1026/1, no. 246, f. 27.

101 A. N. Murav'ev, *Istoriia*, 2.353; Maximus Simaius, 84; Neophytus of Cyprus, "Rasskaz," 26–27.

102 Neophytus of Cyprus, "Rasskaz," 31–32; Maximus Simaius, 182; Procopius Nazianzen, 182.

103 Procopius Nazianzen, 183.

104 Neophytus of Cyprus, "Rasskaz," 33. This was the official viewpoint of the Patriarchate of Jerusalem (N. F. Kapterev, *Snosheniia*, 515). According to the Greek chronicler Procopius Nazianzen, "Having heard this [about the power of Mustafa Bayraktar] induced the Armenians in Jerusalem to begin pointless and ungodly intrigues; and an evil spirit ignited the imagination of the worst of them, who in their demonic and ungodly thoughts decided to burn the Church of the Life-Bearing Tomb" (Procopius Nazianzen, 184). A. N. Muravyev considered the initiator of this plan to be the grand vizier who, looking for a pretext to trample on the ancient *firmans*, "inspired [the Armenians] to the criminal means that they deny" (A. N. Murav'ev, *Istoriia*, 2.367).

105 Such was the Armenian interpretation of events, voiced in the chronicle of Maximus Simaius (Maximus Simaius, 108). Muravyev presented this version of events but does not trust it (A. N. Murav'ev, *Istoriia,* 2.366). Even Maximus Simaius wrote, "The shameless, wicked and insane Armenian dragoman confessed, 'We did not expect that the fire would reach such dimensions.' He said this in the presence of the mufti and some of our people in the courtyard of the church" (Maximus Simaius, 109). If the search for answers goes to the perennial question "Who benefits?" it should be remembered that on the night of September 30, 1808, Mustafa Bayraktar was still in power and so the *firman* for the restoration of the church would have inevitably gone to the Armenians.

106 Procopius Nazianzen, 184–185.

107 Maximus Simaius, 108.

108 Procopius Nazianzen, 185.

109 Maximus Simaius, 111–126; Neophytus of Cyprus, "Rasskaz," 34–38; Procopius Nazianzen, 188–204.

110 Procopius Nazianzen, 205.

111 Neophytus of Cyprus, "Rasskaz," 39–43; Procopius Nazianzen, 205–208; Maximus Simaius, 127–130.

112 Neophytus of Cyprus, "Rasskaz," 44–47; Procopius Nazianzen, 209–217.

113 Neophytus of Cyprus, "Rasskaz," 50–57; Procopius Nazianzen, 154, 217–228.

114 Neophytus of Cyprus, "Rasskaz," 59; Procopius Nazianzen, 158–164.

115 Neophytus of Cyprus, "Rasskaz," 62–63.

116 K. M. Bazili 1875, 2.229.

117 A. P. Lebedev, *Istoriia,* 512; N. Skabalanovich, 454–458.

118 SIPPO, 1907, 320.

119 I. N. Berezin, "Khristiane v Mesopotamii i Sirii," 56.

120 Parthenius the Athenian, 258.

121 Procopius Nazianzen, 216.

122 O. Peri, 134; see also 127–133.

123 Ibid., 134–137.

124 N. Skabalanovich, 454.

125 O. Peri, 138–145.

126 Ibid., 145–149.

127 Ibid., 153.

128 In an earlier monograph, the present author attempted to highlight some of the stages of patterns in Ottoman domestic policy of the Porte's view toward the various Christian confessions (K. A. Panchenko, *Osmanskaia*

imperiia, 108–113). Years later, the observations made at that time do not seem convincing to me, although they may be considered as one possible explanation of the dynamics of the struggle over the holy places.

Chapter 8: Foreign Relations

1 Among the most recent works to address these issues, we note the monograph by Vera Chentsova, *Ikona Iverskoi Bogomateri: Ocherki istorii otnoshenii grecheskoi tserkvi s Rossiei v seredine VII v.*

2 The history of relations between the Orthodox East and Russia has continuously attracted the attention of researchers. Many have written on this subject, especially in the context of Greco-Russian relations in the sixteenth through the eighteenth centuries. Thus, it is difficult to depict the northern vector of the foreign policy of the Middle Eastern Orthodox world without excessively repeating the studies of other scholars. In any case, however, this chapter must be present in this monograph, because the foreign policy of the Levantine patriarchs is one of the brightest chapters in the history of Middle Eastern Orthodoxy in the Ottoman period. As regards this subject more than anything else, it is necessary for us to look beyond the Syro–Palestinian region because, as has been said, it is not possible to artificially separate the politics of the patriarchs of Jerusalem and Antioch from the aspirations of the other Orthodox churches of the Eastern Mediterranean, as they were so closely interrelated and interdependent.

3 Murav'ev, *Snosheniia Rossii s Vostokom*, 12–33.

4 Kapterev, *Snosheniia ierusalimskikh patriarkhov*, 6.

5 Murav'ev, *Snosheniia Rossii s Vostokom*, 34–35.

6 Ibid., 39–40.

7 Ibid., 41.

8 Archim. Makary (Veretennikov), "Gramota patriarkha Germana," 208.

9 Ibid.

10 Kapterev, *Snosheniia ierusalimskikh patriarkhov*, 8–9.

11 Murav'ev, *Snosheniia Rossii s Vostokom*, 44–45; Kapterev, *Snosheniia ierusalimskikh patriarkhov*, 8.

12 On April 4, 1543, according to Murav'ev (Murav'ev, *Snosheniia Rossii s Vostokom*, 46), or in 1545, according to contemporary researchers (Kashtanov, *Rossiia i Grecheskii mir v XVI v.*, 112n29).

13 Murav'ev, *Snosheniia Rossii s Vostokom*, 47.

14 Ibid., 48.

15 Murav'ev, *Snosheniia Rossii s Vostokom*, 56–59; Kapterev, *Snosheniia ierusalimskikh patriarkhov*, 8–9.

16 Murav'ev, *Snosheniia Rossii s Vostokom*, 74–86, 104–119; Kapterev, *Kharakter otnoshenii*, 27–33.

17 Murav'ev, *Snosheniia Rossii s Vostokom*, 88–93 (Muraviev and Kapterev date the composition of the letter and the arrival of the embassy one year earlier); Pozniakov, ii.

18 Pozniakov, ii.

19 Ibid., 6.

20 Ibid., 21–22.

21 Murav'ev, *Snosheniia Rossii s Vostokom*, 101–102

22 Ibid., 102.

23 Ibid., 100.

24 Kapterev, *Snosheniia ierusalimskikh patriarkhov*, 10–11.

25 RGADA, Fond 52/1, book 1, ff. 169v–173v; Murav'ev, *Snosheniia Rossii s Vostokom*, 102–103; Panchenko, "Rossiia i Antiokhiiskii patriarkhat," 205.

26 Murav'ev, *Snosheniia Rossii s Vostokom*, 122–127, 135–143; Trifon Korobeinikov, ii–iv.

27 Murav'ev, *Snosheniia Rossii s Vostokom*, 128–134, 146–147.

28 Ibid., 144, 148–154.

29 Murav'ev, *Snosheniia Rossii s Vostokom*, 155–162.

30 Kapterev, *Snosheniia ierusalimskikh patriarkhov*, 12–13.

31 Ibid., 13–14.

32 Concerning the activity of Joachim Daw in Ukraine, see Kartashev, *Ocherki*, 1.617; Krachkovskii, "Gramota Ioakima IV," 447.

33 Concerning Joachim's sojourn in Russia, see Murav'ev, *Snosheniia Rossii s Vostokom*, 169–179; Kartashev, *Ocherki* 2.12–16; Panchenko, "Rossiia i Antiokhiiskii patriarkhat," 206–220.

34 Kartashev, *Ocherki*, 2.16–44; Murav'ev, *Snosheniia Rossii s Vostokom*, 189–264; Kapterev, *Kharakter otnoshenii*, 34–59; Buganov and Lukichev, *Posol'skaia kniga*, 11–154.

35 Trifon Korobeinikov, v–vii, 72–103; Murav'ev, *Snosheniia Rossii s Vostokom*, 266–277; Buganov and Lukichev, *Posol'skaia kniga*, 154–168; Kartashev, 2.44–46; Kapterev, *Snosheniia ierusalimskikh patriarkhov*, 14–15; Panchenko, "Rossiia i Antiokhiiskii patriarkhat," 209. There is a letter of thanksgiving from Joachim to the tsar, signed by all Antiochian metropolitans, see Panchenko and Fonkich, "Gramota 1594 g." In our commentaries on this letter, we have suggested that it was delivered to Moscow by Trifon Korobeinikov who had made a stop in Damascus on his return trip. Subsequently, Vera Chentsova convincingly substantiated the view that Trifon was not in Damascus; see Chentsova, "Gramota Ioakima VI." In this case, in our view, it seems likely that the letter was brought by Damaskinos,

the cellarer of Mar Saba, who was just at that time heading to Moscow and clearly not without reason was mentioned in the letter of Joachim ibn Ziyada.

36 See Chapter 4.

37 Murav'ev, *Snosheniia Rossii s Vostokom*, 279–299; Kapterev, *Snosheniia ierusalimskikh patriarkhov*, 16–23.

38 Murav'ev, *Snosheniia Rossii s Vostokom*, 300–324; Kapterev, *Snosheniia ierusalimskikh patriarkhov*, 23–24.

39 Murav'ev, *Snosheniia Rossii s Vostokom*, 325–328; Kapterev, *Snosheniia ierusalimskikh patriarkhov*, 24–25.

40 RGADA, Fond 52/1, 1619 no. 2, f. 1.

41 Prokopy Lyapunov (d. 1611)—a Ryazan nobleman, who led the so-called First People's Volunteer Army, which attempted in the summer of 1611 to drive the Poles out of Moscow.

42 RGADA, Fond 52/1, 1619 no. 2, ff. 1–2.

43 Murav'ev, *Snosheniia Rossii s Vostokom*, 329–339.

44 Murav'ev, *Snosheniia Rossii s Vostokom*, 340–347; Kapterev, *Snosheniia ierusalimskikh patriarkhov*, 29; Kartashev, *Ocherki*, 2. 276–277.

45 Kapterev, *Snosheniia ierusalimskikh patriarkhov*, 30.

46 Murav'ev, *Snosheniia Rossii s Vostokom*, 348; Kapterev, *Snosheniia ierusalimskikh patriarkhov*, 30; A. Mironovich, 118.

47 See Kartashev, *Ocherki*, 1.603–604; I. Malyshevsky, Vol. 2.

48 Kartashev, *Ocherki*, 2.276–277; A. Mironovich, 119–122.

49 Kapterev, *Snosheniia ierusalimskikh patriarkhov*, 46–57.

50 Ibid., 58–68.

51 Ibid., 72–77.

52 Ibid., 78–81.

53 Kapterev, *Snosheniia ierusalimskikh patriarkhov*, 29–42; Kartashev, *Ocherki*, 2.85–94.

54 Kapterev, *Snosheniia ierusalimskikh patriarkhov*, 110.

55 Kapterev, *Snosheniia ierusalimskikh patriarkhov*, 81–82.

56 Ibid., 77.

57 Ibid., 70.

58 It is possible that he is speaking here of the very same Abaza Pasha who acted as patron of the Armenians in the struggle for the holy places and was executed in 1634 (see Chapter 7, note 61).

59 Kapterev, *Snosheniia ierusalimskikh patriarkhov*, 71.

60 Chentsova, *Ikona Iverskoi Bogomateri*, 109–113.

61 Ibid., 78–79, 85–86, 117, 122.

62 Ibid., 318. However, one may not find this explanation as completely satisfying, because such fierce opponents of Catholicism as Cyril Lucaris and Patriarch Nectarius of Jerusalem were also of Cretan origin.

63 This refers the Yedikule Fortress (Castle of Seven Towers), located in southwest part of Istanbul, near the shores of the Marmara (White) Sea. In the Ottoman period it was a prison for high-ranking prisoners.

64 Kapterev, *Snosheniia ierusalimskikh patriarkhov*, 85.

65 Chentsova, *Ikona Iverskoi Bogomateri*, 111, 112.

66 Ibid., 84, 111, 124, 125, 132.

67 Kapterev, *Snosheniia ierusalimskikh patriarkhov*, 87–90.

68 Ibid., 91–93.

69 See Chapters 4 and 6.

70 RGADA, Fond 52/1, 1634, no. 7, ff. 16–17 ; Panchenko, "Rossiia i Antiokhiiskii patriarkhat," 211.

71 For more detail, see Panchenko, "Rossiia i Antiokhiiskii patriarkhat," 212–215.

72 Ibid., 217–220.

73 Candia is the ancient name for Heraclion in Crete. The War of Candia is sometimes referred to as the War of Crete.

74 Chentsova, *Ikona Iverskoi Bogomateri*, 130–132, 136, 138, 191.

75 Kapterev, *Snosheniia ierusalimskikh patriarkhov*, 116–119.

76 Ibid., 119–120.

77 Floria, "Rossiia, stambul'skie greki i nachalo Kandiiskii voiny," 174–187. For example, in 1646, the papal nuncio in Warsaw reported on the arrival of a secret delegation to the Polish king from Eastern patriarchs and Athonite monasteries, who promised to raise a rebellion of the nations oppressed by the Ottomans if Poland began war with the Ottoman Empire (Ibid., 183).

78 Chentsova, *Ikona Iverskoi Bogomateri*, 195–198, 203, 205, 215.

79 Ibid., 137.

80 Ibid., 145; for more detail concerning Paisius's visit to Moscow, see Kapterev, *Snosheniia ierusalimskikh patriarkhov*, 121–152; Nikolaevskii, 253–265; Chentsova, "Istochniki," 153–154.

81 Kapterev, *Kharakter otnoshenii*, 353–368; Kapterev, *Snosheniia ierusalimskikh patriarkhov*, 152–160; Chentsova, "Istochniki," 155–156.

82 Chentsova, "Istochniki," 157–164; Chentsova, *Ikona Iverskoi Bogomateri*, 206–207, 232–239.

83 Zen'kovskii, 172–173; Kapterev, *Snosheniia ierusalimskikh patriarkhov*, 164.

84 Kartashev, *Ocherki*, 2.126–131.

85 Chentsova, *Ikona Iverskoi Bogomateri*, 83.

86 Arseny Sukhanov, 7–52.

87 Much to the chagrin of Arseny, one of the ships on which he sent a box of his papers was intercepted and robbed by the Franks, resulting in the loss of many records, including "sheets of drawings of different lands" (Ibid., 75).

88 In particular he wrote: "The walls are built from big stones, in thirteen rows up to the merlons … and in some places, more; there is little weaponry on the ground: sometimes there is, sometimes there is not, but even then the windows are small, suitable for hand cannons, where a big cannon will not fit…. And in order to get over the wall into the city one needs a ladder, about three *sazhens* in length, in low places. There are lots of all kind of stone near the city…. which one would need if the city is under siege…. All the city gates are firmly covered with iron boards…. Right there by the road is a tall mountain, and near it—the city itself; if one shoots from that mountain with a small-caliber gun, one can reach the city, but from a big caliber cannon one can shoot from that mountain over the wall into the city…. Here also the city wall is low, because the hill comes close to the wall" (Ibid., 134).

89 Ibid., 52–90.

90 Let us, as an example, cite his description of the Arabic liturgy in Ramla: "The priests shave almost half of their head in the front, and on the tip of their heads they shave a small tonsure. They all wear turbans, and during liturgy the priests who do not serve stand in the sanctuary in their turbans. The priests serve the liturgy in Arabic, only saying exclamations in Greek" (Ibid., 51).

91 Malyshevskii, 351.

92 Paul of Aleppo, 2.101, 188.

93 Arsenii Sukhanov, 74. It is no wonder that after Arseny's departure from Palestine (through Syria, eastern Anatolia, and the Caucasus, returning to Moscow in the summer of 1653), Patriarch Paisius hastened to hedge against possible disclosures by the Russian envoy. After seeing Arseny off from Jerusalem, the patriarch sent a denunciation letter to the tsarina (for some reason he was afraid to appeal to Aleksei Mikhailovich himself). In this letter, Paisius complains of the plotting of the "evil-tongued people," Sukhanov in particular, "for whom God only knows how we cared, and who nevertheless proved to be an ungrateful Judas." "But we rejoice when we are slandered," continued the patriarch, "because great many of the saints have been slandered unjustly and without reason. There is only one thing, my tsarina, about which we were saddened … that he deceived the just tsar and, in deceiving the tsar, deceived God…. And he was not afraid, a thrice-wretched one, that the earth would open and

swallow him up as it did Dathan and Abiram" (Kapterev, *Snosheniia ierusalim-skikh patriarkhov*, 174– 175). Dathan and Abiram were the Old Testament fig-ures who led a revolt of Jews against the authority of Moses during the sojourn in the desert. By the will of the Lord the earth was split asunder under the feet of these rebels, and they were cast into the abyss. Vera Chentsova believes that the patriarchal letter was addressed to the tsarina in the hope that it will also be perused by her father, Ivan D. Miloslavsky, whom Paisius regarded as one of his supporters in the Muscovite ruling circles (Chentsova, *Ikona Iverskoi Bogomateri*, 84).

94 Kapterev, *Snosheniia ierusalimskikh patriarkhov*, 164–171.

95 Kartashev, *Ocherki*, 2.127.

96 Arsenii Sukhanov, 55, 62, 73.

97 In his *Proskinitary* Arseny Sukhanov presents this episode: "The patri-arch arrived from St Elias for vespers and ordered a deacon to beat a Christian Arab on the cheeks and head, then to whip in the face, and threw him out of the church, and no one knows for what fault" (Arsenii Sukhanov, 65; see also ibid., 73).

98 Vera Chentsova privately speculated that the former patriarch of Constantinople, Athanasius Patelarus, who died in his prime in 1656, also fell victim to the intrigues of Paisius. The former allies could not reach a consensus regarding the quickly changing political situation in Eastern Europe. After the 1653 overthrow of Vasile Lupu, Paisius quickly found a common language with the new Moldavian ruler, who supported the geopolitical project of the patri-arch of Jerusalem. Athanasius, however, used all his capabilities to persuade the Ottoman authorities to return the Moldavian throne to Vasile. This was not part of Paisius's plan, and Athanasius died suddenly in the Lubny monastery in Ukraine. The remains of the patriarch were revered as holy relics. Later, during Soviet times, they were preserved in the Museum of Atheism in Leningrad, and now have been returned to the church. With this in mind, it is not possible in the present day to carry out a chemical analysis of the remains which could cor-roborate or disprove the possibility that Athanasius had been poisoned.

99 See further for more detail.

100 Paul of Aleppo, 1.44-111.

101 Ibid., 113–154.

102 Ibid., 2.1–93.

103 Idem, 3.2–38.

104 Ibid., 3.50–51, 137, 170–171, 181, 4.108; P. F. Nikolaevskii, 759–760; Kartashev, *Ocherki*, 2.155–160; S. Zen'kovskii, 219–222.

105 Paul of Aleppo, 4.158.

106 Ibid., 171.

107   See Paul of Aleppo, 2.100–101, 129, 165–166, 174, 188, 199, 3.3, 30, 168169, 4.142, 185.

108   Ibid., 4.158–160; RGADA, Fond 52/1, 1654, no. 21, part 3, ff. 7–14, 21–22, 37, 40, 75–76, 79–80, 86–87, 90, 93, 99, 116, 146–150, 161–166.

109   Chesnokova, 169.

110   RGADA, Fond 52/1, 1654, part 3, no. 21, f. 196–197, 208, 212, 248, 252–253, 260–275, 278–279; 1657, no. 24. ff. 1–15; Fond 52/2, no. 547–559, 561–563, 565–570, 574–576, 596; Nikolaevskii, 767–774.

111   Paul of Aleppo, 4.62.

112   RGADA, Fond 52/1, 1654, no. 21, part 3, ff. 69–72, 83, 96, 219–220, 225–240.

113   Ibid., part 2, ff. 205–221; see also Panchenko, "Sputniki Makariia."

114   RGADA, Fond 52/1, 1654, no. 24, part 3, ff. 263–265, 296–300.

115   Chentsova, "Istochniki", 168; Chentsova, *Ikona Iverskoi Bogomateri*, 253–258.

116   Paul of Aleppo, 5.7.

117   RGADA, Fond 52/2, 1658, no. 11, ff. 4-5.

118   Ibid.

119   Chentsova, "Mitra Paisiia," 14–17.

120   Chentsova, "Istochniki", 169.

121   Chentsova, "Mitra Paisiia," 11–14, 25–26.

122   Kapterev, "Gospodstvo grekov," 36–38; Neophytus of Cyprus, "Rasskaz," 18–19; A. N. Murav'ev, *Istoriia,*, 2.311–313; Chentsova, "Mitra Paisiia," 11–12, 33–35. Paisius's envoys, who arrived in Russia in 1657 with the report concerning these events and petitions for alms, were confronted with an incomprehensible boycott on the part of the Moscow authorities: patriarchal clerics stopped in Putivl and were sent back with small gifts. According to Chentsova, close contacts with Paisius, who dreamt of an anti-Catholic alliance of Orthodox and Protestant nations, no longer fit with the interests of the Moscow government, which was at war with Sweden (Chentsova, "Mitra Paisiia," 30–31).

123   Paul of Aleppo, 5.23.

124   Ibid., 80.

125   Ibid., 84–87.

126   Ibid., 92.

127   Paul of Aleppo, 5.104–146.

128   Kapterev, *Snosheniia ierusalimskikh patriarkhov*, 161; Chentsova, "Dionisii Ivirit," 58–62.

129   Kapterev, *Snosheniia ierusalimskikh patriarkhov*, 189–190; Kapterev, *Kharakter otnoshenii*, 182–195; Kartashev, *Ocherki*, 2.202–204; Zen'kovskii, 280–283.

130 N. Gibbenet, 658–659.

131 Kapterev, *Snosheniia ierusalimskikh patriarkhov*, 190–202; N. Gibbenet, 91–97, 561–696; Kartashev, *Ocherki*, 2.204–206.

132 Kapterev, *Snosheniia ierusalimskikh patriarkhov*, 203–207.

133 Ibid., 187.

134 Ioannikii/Ioannicius of Alexandria, 221–224, 230, 246, 258.

135 Ibid., 258.

136 S.n., *Patriarshie dokumenty*, 390.

137 Dositheus, "Istoriia episkopii gory sinaia," 141–148.

138 Kapterev, *Snosheniia ierusalimskikh patriarkhov*, 198.

139 Gibbenet, 718, 832–849, 895–912.

140 RGADA, Fond 52/2, 1667, no. 9, f. 41v.

141 Due to this we know the clothing sizes of the patriarchs: "Macarius, Patriarch of Antioch wears an exoriasson 2 *arshin*s [arshin = 0.71 m] and 2 *vershok*s [vershok = 4.5 cm] in length [Paisius was somewhat taller, his riasson was 2 *arshin*s and 3 *vershok*s in length] and across the shoulders and waist and hem and sleeves it is longer than that of the Alexandrian [patriarch]." In the waist, the riasson reached one *arshin* minus one *vershok*, and the sleeves were one *arshin* in length (Gibbenet, 939).

142 RGADA, Fond 52/1, 1667, no. 9, ff. 1–48v; Gibbenet, 913–962; Dmitrievskii, "Priezd v Astrakhan' vostochnykh patriarkhov," 318–335.

143 Gibbenet, 962–994.

144 Ibid., 1023–1024.

145 Paul of Aleppo, 3.145, 4.128, 169.

146 In particular, the council considered the affair of the beatings inflicted on Nikon's servant by *okolnichy* (high-ranking courtier) Bogdan Khitrovo in 1658, which was the last straw that led Nikon toward public refusal to exercise patriarchal duties. Naturally, the courtier was acquitted, and Patriarch Macarius, wishing to distinguish himself, rose and blessed Khitrovo with the sign of the cross—clearly, at his own initiative (Gibbenet, 1070).

147 Gibbenet, 999–1099; Kartashev, *Ocherki*, 2.208–212; Zen'kovskii, 290–291.

148 Kartashev, *Ocherki*, 2.177–183, 212–218; Zen'kovskii, 294–304.

149 RGADA, Fond 52/1, 1669, no. 11; Kapterev, "Khlopoty moskovskogo pravitel'stva o vosstanovlenii Paisiia," 69–81; Gibbenet, 1100–1109.

150 RGADA, Fond 52/1, 1669, no. 21, f. 17.

151 Ibid., f. 20.

152 Ibid., 1679, no. 47, f. 15.

153   RGADA, Fond 52/1, 1671, no. 25, f. 22; see more on Macarius's sojourn on the Caucasus in Kapterev, "Khlopoty moskovskogo pravitel'stva o vosstanovlenii Paisiia," 212–214; Dmitrievskii, "Priezd v Astrakhan' vostochnykh patriarkhov," 354–358; Panchenko, "Pravoslavnye Araby i Kavkaz," 65–67; idem, "Osvedomiteli," 313–315.

154   RGADA, Fond 52/1, 1671, no. 25, ff. 62–63.

155   Kapterev, "Khlopoty moskovskogo pravitel'stva o vosstanovlenii Paisiia."

156   Kapterev, *Snosheniia ierusalimskikh patriarkhov*, 239–241. See the text of Dositheus's letter to the patriarch of Moscow in "Gramota Dosifeia," 60–66.

157   Kapterev, *Snosheniia ierusalimskikh patriarkhov*, 250.

158   Ibid., 246.

159   Kapterev, *Snosheniia ierusalimskikh patriarkhov*, 235, 243–245; RGADA, Fond 52/1, 1683, no. 2.

160   Kapterev, *Kharakter otnoshenii*, 369–375.

161   Kapterev, *Snosheniia ierusalimskikh patriarkhov*, 222–224.

162   Ibid., 357.

163   Only a few Eastern patriarchs could write to their Muscovite benefactors using the same tone as Dositheus in March 1691: "You boasted many times that you wished to do this or that, and it always turned out to be just words, and as far as deeds were concerned, nothing came about. Now is the time, when all Christian rulers rose up … be watchful, work, show your zeal" (Kapterev, *Snosheniia ierusalimskikh patriarkhov*, 282).

164   Kapterev, *Kharakter otnoshenii*, 300.

165   Kapterev, *Kharakter otnoshenii*, 300–301. Kapterev, *Snosheniia ierusalimskikh patriarkhov*, 294–295.

166   Ibid., 301.

167   Ibid., 302; "Gramota Dosifeia," 13–14.

168   "Gramota Dosifeia," 13.

169   Kapterev, *Snosheniia ierusalimskikh patriarkhov*, 315–319.

170   "Gramota Dosifeia," 22.

171   Ibid., 54.

172   Ibid., 24.

173   Ibid., 44, 46, 49. In June 1704 Dositheus wrote concerning Pyotr Tolstoy: "The current ambassador of your divine majesty in Constantinople had a very good stay, for whatever he did not understand, he used to ask us, and he listened to what we used to tell him" (Ibid., 49).

174   Kapterev, *Snosheniia ierusalimskikh patriarkhov*, 335, 336.

175   As Dositheus explained his silence in one such case: "We have not written especially because we do not have the means of writing in secret code, and we were wary lest our letters fall into the wrong hands" ("Gramota Dosifeia," 46).

176 See, for example, Ibid., 39, 40, 45, 49–53: Kapterev, *Snosheniia ierusalim-skikh patriarkhov*, 337–340.

177 "Gramota Dosifeia," 59.

178 Ibid., 44.

179 Kapterev, "Kharakter otnoshenii," 299–306.

180 From the 1706 letter to Pyotr Tolstoy, the ambassador in Istanbul (Ibid., 294).

181 Ibid., 294–295.

182 The Ghassanids were one of the sixth-century Arab tribal confedera-tions, *foederati* of the Byzantine Empire who protected Syria from the desert. The Empire's termination of its alliance with the Ghassanids in the late sixth century is considered to be one of the factors that facilitated the Muslim con-quest of the Middle East. The Mardaites were a Byzantine military contingent that advanced into Mount Lebanon in the mid-seventh century to counter Arab expansion. Virtually invincible in the mountains of Lebanon, the Mardaites kept the cities and plains of the Syrian interior under attack. In the late seventh century, when the Emperor Justinian II concluded a peace agreement with the Arabs, he withdrew the Mardaites back to Cilicia, which weakened the geopo-litical position of Byzantium and earned the rebukes of later chroniclers.

183 "Gramota Dosifeia," 15–19.

184 Ibid., 29–30.

185 Ibid., 30.

186 Ibid.

187 Ibid., 64.

188 Ibid., 67.

189 Ibid., 67.

190 Ibid.

191 Loparyov, "Khrisanf," 21.

192 Kapterev, *Snosheniia ierusalimskikh patriarkhov*, 296, 300–306; Ialamas, 228–238.

193 "Gramota Dosifeia," 56.

194 Kapterev, *Snosheniia ierusalimskikh patriarkhov*, 264.

195 "Gramota Dosifeia," 42.

196 Kapterev, *Snosheniia ierusalimskikh patriarkhov*, 350–353.

197 Ibid., 30–31, 57, 70–71. It must be said that, by Muscovite criteria, the standard of living for Eastern clergy was poor and did not command respect from the Russian observers, accustomed to the sumptuous worship and high authority of the episcopal rank. A contemporary of Dositheus, the Russian pil-grim Ivan Lukyanov, wrote highly critically of the life of the clergy of Constan-tinople, saying that "[t]he Greek patriarch walks around like a simple monk and

you will not recognize that he is patriarch…. Their metropolitans … go around
the market themselves, to get something even for six coins to cover themselves"
(I. Luk'ianov, col. 151).

198 "Gramota Dosifeia," 43.

199 Kapterev, *Snosheniia ierusalimskikh patriarkhov*, 368.

200 Dositheus, "Istoriia episkopii gory Sinaia," 5. It is curious that in theory
Dositheus advocated a completely different model for a patriarch: "May the
bishops, priests, and presbyters have the ability to speak before him concerning
church matters, let him not be like a beast so that other bishops may fear him….
May he [the patriarch] not be able to speak in church anything that is alien
to the church, and may he not interfere into civil [affairs] and give orders to
the government, as Nikon did, perplexing the world" (Dositheus, "Gramota,"
42–43). On the other hand, there were the recommendations which in 1702
Dositheus gave to the tsar concerning the election of the patriarch of Moscow
and concerning the candidates' desirable characteristics. Why would Dositheus
need another Nikon in Moscow, a middle-man between him and the tsar? In no
way was Dositheus himself inferior to Nikon in the lust for power—there was
really no room for two such hierarchs in the Orthodox world.

201 Kapterev, *Snosheniia ierusalimskikh patriarkhov*, 341.

202 Ibid., 369–371.

203 Rose, 244.

204 Patriarch Macarius, "Gruziia v 17 stoletii," 115–118; Mikha'il Burayk,
399–400, 416. See also Walbiner, "Accounts on Georgia," 246; idem, " … Antiochia und der Kirche von Georgien," 437–442.

205 Paul of Aleppo, 5.196.

206 Khutsishvili, 127.

207 Ibid., 131.

208 Ibid., 130; Seleznev, 11; Dositheus, "Gramota,"158.

209 *Istoriia Gruzii*, 296–310; Rzianin; Seleznev, 43, 140, 162–169.

210 Patriarch Macarius, "Gruziia v 17 stoletii," 122.

211 Walbiner, "Accounts on Georgia," 247; Walbiner, " … Antiochia und
der Kirche von Georgien," 443.

212 Paul of Aleppo, 5.193.

213 Ibid., 3.87; see also 82–86, 171–172.

214 RGADA, Fond 52/4, no. 46. Macarius wrote also to Patriarch Nikon
concerning the same matter; see Nikolaevskii, 771.

215 Macarius, "Gruziia v 17 stoletii," 442–443.

216 Walbiner, "… Antiochia und der Kirche von Georgien," 443.

217 Seleznev, 12, 30–38.

218 Walbiner, "Accounts on Georgia," 248.

219 Macarius, "Gruziia v 17 stoletii," 67.

220 See the Arabic text and the Russian translation in Macarius, "Gruziia v 17 stoletii."

221 RGADA, Fond 27, no. 542. The text was published in N. Sh. Asatiani, ed., *Materialy k istorii Gruzii XVII veka: opisanie Gruzii, sostavlennoe Pavlom Aleppskim* (Tbilisi, 1973) [in Georgian], 69–79. See also Panchenko, "Pravoslavnye Araby i Kavkaz," 59–61.

222 Macarius, "Gruziia v 17 stoletii," 112. Because we know that Macarius spent one year and nine months in Georgia, he must have arrived there in the summer of 1664.

223 Panchenko, "Pravoslavnye Araby i Kavkaz," 61.

224 RGADA, Fond 27, no. 542, ff. 6-6v, 8.

225 Macarius, "Gruziia v 17 stoletii," 448–449.

226 Ibid., 455.

227 Ibid., 442–443, 445–446.

228 Ibid., 450.

229 Ibid., 454.

230 Ibid., 444, 450–454.

231 Ibid., 71.

232 RGADA, Fond 27, no. 542, f. 15.

233 Gibbenet, 835.

234 Kacharava; Asatiani, 101.

235 RGADA, Fond 27, no. 542, f. 13; Panchenko, 64.

236 On the geopolitical situation in the Caucasus and Georgia's efforts to break out of the enemy blockade in the direction of Volga and Astrakhan trade route, see T. D. Botsvadze, 200–210.

237 RGADA, Fond 27, no. 542, ff. 13–15.

238 Ibid., f. 11–12.

239 Ibid., f. 16–17.

240 Ibid., f. 17v.

241 Ibid., f. 18v.

242 Ibid., f. 19.

243 See Chapters 4 and 5.

244 Seleznev, 46–47.

245 Dositheus, "Epistles," 160–164, 166.

246 Ibid., 167.

247 Cited after Seleznev, 44.

248 Dositheus, "Epistles," 167.

249 Ibid., 167, 168.

250 Dositheus, "Epistles," 168; Seleznev, 44.

251 Dositheus, "Epistles," 167.

252 Ibid., 168.

253 Ibid., 162.

254 RGADA, Fond 52/1, 1683, no. 2, ff. 37–56.

255 Ibid., Fond 52/2, no. 719; Fond 52/1, 1707, no. 25.

256 Ibid., Fond 52/2, 1707, no. 19; 1709, no. 12.

257 Ibid., 1714, no. 13, f. 3v.

258 Ibid., Fond 52/2, 1662, no. 28, f. 2.

259 Fonkich, "Sinaiskii pomiannik," 259–263.

260 Loparev, "Khrisanf," 21, 22; Kapterev, *Snosheniia ierusalimskikh patriarkhov*.

261 I. Vishenski, 92; Porphyry Uspenskii, *Kniga bytiia moego*, 2.85–86.

262 Ibid., 3.175.

263 Murav'ev, "Puteshestvie," 155.

264 Andrei Ignat'ev, 36–37.

265 "Evangelia na arabskom iazyke, napechatannoe v Aleppo, 1708 goda, izhdiveniem Mazepy," *ZhMNP* 79 (1853): 47–49; Krymskii, *Istoriia novoi arabskoi literatury,* 114; Morozov, "Arabskoe Evangelie Daniila Apostola."

266 Kapterev, *Snosheniia ierusalimskikh patriarkhov*, 379.

267 Ibid., 381.

268 Ibid., 388.

269 Ibid., 398.

270 Ibid.

271 Ibid., 390–391, 394–396.

272 Ibid., 389.

273 Vishenski, 92–99.

274 Kapterev, *Snosheniia ierusalimskikh patriarkhov*, 397.

275 Semonova, *Kniazhestva Valakhiia i Moldaviia*, 292.

276 Kapterev, *Snosheniia ierusalimskikh patriarkhov*, 401.

277 Ibid., 403.

278 Loparev, "Khrisanf," 24–25.

279 Kapterev, *Snosheniia ierusalimskikh patriarkhov*, 408.

280 From the letter of Shafirov to Chancellor Golovkin on July 19, 1713 (Ibid., 405).

281 Ibid., 409.

282 In this respect, a phrase of Count Pyotr Tolstoy is very revealing: "By your order, Sovereign, I will not let Greeks go to Moscow, since, Sovereign, indeed all of them are liars, from small to great, and it is in no way possible to trust them at all" (Kapterev, *Snosheniia ierusalimskikh patriarkhov*, 413).

283 The only exceptions are the church hierarchs of Moldavia and Wallachia, but Russia was interested in them only because of their role in local politics.

284 Hopwood, 5.

285 Kapterev, *Snosheniia ierusalimskikh patriarkhov*, 414.

286 Ibid., 457.

287 Ibid., 458.

288 Ibid., 414–417.

289 Ibid., 420–422.

290 Foreign Policy Archive of Russian Empire (AVPRI), Fond 89/1 (Russo–Turkish Relations), 1732, no. 18, ff. 3, 8–11v. Kapterev mistakenly writes only about 2,000 rubles in alms (Kapterev, *Snosheniia ierusalimskikh patriarkhov*, 424–425).

291 AVRPI, Fond 87/8, no. 748, f. 75; Kapterev, *Snosheniia ierusalimskikh patriarkhov*, 473.

292 AVRPI, Fond 87/8, no. 748, f. 75–75v.

293 Kapterev, *Snosheniia ierusalimskikh patriarkhov*, 440, see also Ibid., 434–439.

294 Ibid., 442.

295 Ibid., 445–458.

296 Ibid., 459–460.

297 Ibid., 460–461.

298 AVPRI, Fond 89/1, 1745, no. 4, f. 30v.

299 AVRPI, Fond 89/1, 1745, no. 4, f. 40.

300 Diplomatic correspondence of Russian representatives in Constantinople during the first half of the eighteenth century is catalogued superficially and, most likely, is still hiding materials for many future discoveries.

301 AVPRI, Fond 90/1, no. 262.

302 Ibid., f. 4.

303 Ibid., f. 4v.

304 AVPRI, Fond 90/1, no. 262, f. 4v.

305 Ibid., f. 5.

306 Ibid., f. 5v.

307 See more on the connection between Parthenius and Russia in Panchenko, "Ierusalimskii patriarkh Parfenii."

308   AVPRI, Fond 89/8, no. 748, f. 81v.

309   Ibid., f. 82.

310   Ibid., no. 394, ff. 52–53.

311   Ibid., no. 748, f. 82–82v.

312   Ibid., f. 73.

313   AVPRI, Fond 180, list 517/1, no. 223, f. 7. I am indebted for this information to T. Yu. Kobishchanov.

314   The fact that Eastern patriarchs for decades avoided communication with St Petersburg can be possibly explained by reference to extremely strong anti-Russian sentiment in the eighteenth-century Ottoman society, especially following the treaty of Küçük Kaynarca in 1774 and the annexation of Crimea in 1783. This point of view was expressed privately by T. Yu. Kobishchanov, and it is close to Hopwood's opinion, cited earlier, concerning the reasons for the decline in Russian relations with the East.

315   Kapterev, *Snosheniia ierusalimskikh patriarkhov*, 463–465.

316   Ibid., 521.

317   Kapterev, "Russkaia blagotvoritel'nost' Sinaiskoi obiteli," 408–411; Fonkich, "Sinaiskii pomiannik," 259–263. Porphyry Uspensky has seen in the monastery library another book for the recording of donations, which was issued in the Holy Synod to the archimandrite of Sinai in 1767 (Porphyry Uspenskii, *Vtoroe Puteshestvie*, 335).

318   Porphyry Uspenskii, *Vtoroe Puteshestvie*, 332.

319   Grigorovich-Barsky, *Pis'ma*, 519, 522.

320   AVPRI, Fond 89/8, no. 748, f. 75v.

321   Thus, in January 1745 resident A. Veshnyakov reported to the emperor: "We are to follow the decree of your imperial majesty in denying admission [into Russia] to the monks who seek alms and to send [to St Petersburg] the copies from their letters" (AVPRI, Fond 89/1, 1745, no. 4, f. 42).

322   Ibid., f. 117v.

323   Ibid.

324   Ibid., Fond 89/8, no. 1056, f. 4.

325   Walbiner, "… Antiochia und der Kirche von Georgien," 449–450.

326   Ibid., 451.

327   Zayat, 105–110.

328   Mikhailova, 206–207.

329   Walbiner, "… Antiochia und der Kirche von Georgien," 451–452; Tsagareli, 251.

330   Tsagareli, 82.

331 Ibid., 248.

332 Ibid., 83, 87.

333 Porphyry Uspensky, *Kniga bytiia moego*, 2.358.

334 Walbiner, "… Antiochia und der Kirche von Georgien," 454; idem, "Accounts on Georgia," 246.

335 Kapterev, *Snosheniia ierusalimskikh patriarkhov*, 511–512, 534–536.

336 Ibid., 512–523.

337 Ibid., 524–534.

Chapter 9: The Catholic Unia

1 Interesting ethnographic observations about the Arab-Catholic relations belong to Melety (Melety, p. 129, 134, 141) and Porphyry Uspensky (Porphyry Uspenskii, *Kniga bytiia moego*, 1.412; 3.293–297).

2 Volney, 2.438–439.

3 P. V. Topychkanov, "Diamperskii sobor,'" 624–625; M. A. Rodionov *Maronity*.

4 B. Masters, 82.

5 V. N. Anichkov, 183–186.

6 Th. Philipp, 3–5, 9; B. Masters, 71–73.

7 Th. Philipp, 9–10, 16–17; B. Masters, 73–77.

8 R. Haddad, *Syrian Christians*, 30–33; R. Haddad, "On Melkite Passage to the Unia," 68; Th. Philipp, 11; B. Masters, 80.

9 Th. Philipp, 11–12, 17; B. Masters, 79–80.

10 R. Haddad, *Syrian Christians*, 31–32; B. Masters, 80–81.

11 I. N. Berezin, "Pravoslavnye tserkvi v Turtsii," 16.

12 A. P. Lebedev, *Istoriia*, 506–507.

13 Th. Philipp, 12.

14 Ibid., 12, 13.

15 R. Haddad, *Syrian Christians*, 23–25.

16 Ibid., 24–25.

17 It should be recalled that the discussion was about a mutual recognition of the sacraments and the approval of mixed marriages, while maintaining the integrity of doctrine in both communities (for details see Chapter 6).

18 Nasrallah, "Chronologie 1500–1634," 66.

19 C. Charon and L. Cheikho, "Uskufiyyat al-Rum al-Kathulik fi Bayrut," 197.

20 *Monumenta*, 1.264, 309, 312. See Chapter 4, as well as K. A. Panchenko, Triopoliiskoe gnezdo," part 1, 49–57.

21 [Giulio Antonio Santorio (June 6, 1532–May 9, 1602) —Translators' note.]

22 *Monumenta*, 1.312, 376–377.

23 Ibid., p. 332.

24 C. Karalevskij, "Antioche," col. 638–639; B. Heyberger, 232.

25 *Risala...*, 357–361.

26 R. Haddad, *Syrian Christians*, 24.

27 C. Karalevskij, "Antioche," col. 639; *Risala...* 359–360; *Monumenta*, 2.112–113.

28 *Monumenta*, 2.113.

29 *Monumenta*, 2.113; C. Karalevskij, "Antioche," col. 639; B. Heyberger, 233.

30 See in particular: Krachkovskii, "Gramota Ioakima IV," 445–454; Kartashev, *Ocherki*, 1.603–604.

31 Anastasius ibn Mujalla, f. 85; Graf, 3.89; Nasrallah, *HMLEM*, 4(1).181–183.

32 Anastasius ibn Mujalla, ff. 88v–90.

33 This work and the historical circumstances surrounding its appearance are discussed in detail in the article K. A. Panchenko, "Antiokhiiskaia pravoslavnaia tserkov' i Rim v epokhu Kontrreformatsii: Polemicheskii otvet pape rimskomu Anastasiia ibn Mudzhally."

34 L. Cheikho, "Kirill VIII," 628; G. Levenq, "Athanase II," col. 1369.

35 J. Nasrallah, *Chronologie, 1500–1634*, 55.

36 Cited after: L. Cheikho, "Kirill VIII," 629.

37 Ibid.

38 C. Karalevskij, "Antioche," col. 641; B. Heyberger, 392; Nasrallah, "Chronologie, 1500–1634," 61.

39 However, unlike many "Westerners," Karma did not feel sympathy for the European consumer material culture. Recall how he forbade the Christian women of Aleppo to "dress up in foreign obscene clothing and facial tint, as it destroys the entire soul" (Mikha'il Burayk, 438–439). By certain indecent clothes, the metropolitan meant the Frankish neckline that shocked conservative Eastern Christian clergy. Arseny Sukhanov, who saw similar outfits in Chios, wrote with poorly-concealed resentment: "Greek women ... go about in the Frankish way. They do not button their blouses, their chests are bare, their whole shoulders to their breasts are bear, and they keep clean ostensibly for their charms" (Arsenii Sukhanov, 24). The coincidence of cultural-aesthetic preferences between the quasi-Catholic in Aleppo and the Old Believers' favorite author seems typical.

40 C. Karalevskij, "Antioche," col. 641; B. Heyberger, 392–393; B. Masters, 81; C. Walbiner, "... Die Bemuhungen des Meletius Karma um den Druck arabischer Bucher in Rom," 165–174.

41 C. Walbiner, "The Christians of Bilad as-Sham: Pioneers of Book-Printing," 9, 11. According to Aurélien Girard, the cardinals sent the Greek liturgical texts that Meletius intended to publish alongside the Arabic ones to the Spanish Inquisition for examination. Many "heretical" elements were found in the books, as was generally typical of all the Greek presses in Venice. Correcting these errors would have been a very long and laborious endeavor. Rome quickly cooled to the entire project [A. Girard, "Entre crosaide et politique culturelle au Levant: Rome et l'union des Chrétiens syriens (premiere moitie du XVII siecle)" in *Papato e politica internazionale nella prima eta moderna*, edited by M. A. Visceglia. (Rome, 2013), 419–437].

42 Nasrallah, *HMLEM*, 4(1).73–74.

43 Beirut Ecclesiastical Chronicle, 32.

44 R. Haddad, *Syrian Christians*, 23.

45 The text of this letter was published in: N. Edelby, *Asaqifat al-Rum al-Malikiyyin bi-Halab fi al-'asr al-hadith* (Aleppo, 1983), 93.

46 V. Chentsova, "Le patriarche d'Antioche Macarie III Ibn al-Za'im et la chretienité Latine," in *Reduire le schisme? Ecclesiologies et politiques de l'union entre Orient et Occident (XIIIe–XVIIIe siècle)*, edited by M.-H. Blanchet and F. Gabriel (Paris, 2013), 313–335, here 326–330.

47 Ibid., 316, 327–328.

48 C. Karalevskij, "Antioche," col. 643; B. Heyberger, 393–396; B. Masters, 88.

49 Paul of Aleppo, 2.8. It is worth noting that when the *Journey of Macarius* entered into the European scholarly literature, mention of the patriarch of Antioch's "crypto-Catholicism" among Catholic writers became markedly less (see B. Heyberger, 394).

50 A. Rabbat, "Athar al-Sharqiyya," 501.

51 Ibid., 502.

52 RGADA, Fond 52/1, 1657, no. 24, ff. 6-10; P. F. Nikolaevskii, 772–774; T. A. Oparina.

53 Hilary Kilpatrick is of a smiliar opinion: "The letters, which he [Macarius] wrote to the Vatican and to the French king, are difficult to interpret, given the literary conventions of the era, including the use of sometimes hyperbolic compliments. They, as well as his relationship to the papacy, should as follows be considered in the context of his [Macarius's] financial difficulties and his direct contact with Catholic missionaries in Aleppo. He was impressed by the intellectual level of these people, and he wanted to receive books from Rome and from France ... financial support ... on the other hand, Rome had disappointed him, as his teacher Meletius Karma did not succeed in printing the

Orthodox liturgical books…. In any case, the cultural roots of Macarius were, on the one hand, in Antioch, and on the other hand, in the Byzantine and post-Byzantine world" (H. Kilpatrick, 268).

54 B. Masters, 83–84.

55 R. Haddad, *Syrian Christians*, 17.

56 Th. Philipp, 13.

57 C. Karalevskij, "Antioche," col. 645; Sokolov, "Tserkovnye sobytiia," 340–342.

58 Macarius, 68; K. A. Panchenko, "Mitropolity i eparkhii pravoslavnoi Antiokhiiskoi Tserkvi v opisanii Patriarkha Makariia III az-Zaʻima (1665 g.)," 133.

59 Latin missionaries allowed their followers fish during the fast. It was important in the coastal cities, particularly for the poor.

60 Uspenskii, *Skazanie o Siriiskoi unii*, 500–503; Mikhaʼil Burayk, 444–446; Beirut Ecclesiastical Chronicle, 34–35; Porphyry Uspenski, "Vostok Khristianskii: Siriia," July 1875, 14.

61 P. Bacel, 222–225; Nasrallah, "Euthème Saifi," col. 68–69; C. Walbiner, "Pioneers of Book-Printing," 11.

62 C. Karalevskij, "Antioche," col. 645.

63 Mikhaʼil Burayk, 446–448; Beirut Ecclesiastical Chronicle, 36; I. Sokolov, "Tserkovnye sobytiia v Sirii," 340–342; R. Haddad, "On Melkite Passage to the Unia," 68; C. Karalevskij, "Antioche," col. 647.

64 Cited in I. Sokolov, "Antiokhiiskii patriarkh Silʼvestr," 9, 20.

65 C. Karalevskij, "Antioche," col. 646.

66 Nasrallah, "Euthème Saifi," col. 68.

67 R. Haddad, "On Melkite Passage to the Unia," 76–81; Mikhaʼil Burayk, 446.

68 Mikhaʼil Burayk, *al-Haqaʼiq al-wafiyya*, 160; Mikhaʼil Burayk, 446–447; Beirut Ecclesiastical Chronicle, 36.

69 R. Haddad, "On Melkite Passage to the Unia," 84; Mikhaʼil Burayk, 447.

70 J. Nasrallah, "Euthème Saifi," col. 69–70.

71 [By Elias Miriatis, bishop of Lixouri (d. 1714). The book was published posthumously in 1718. —Translators' note.]

72 Mikhaʼil Burayk, 448–449; Beirut Ecclesiastical Chronicle, 40–41; I. I. Sokolov, "Tserkovnye sobytiia v Sirii," 342; G. Levenq, "Athanase III," col. 1371–1373.

73 B. Masters, 89; P. Bacel, 226; I. I. Sokolov, "Tserkovnye sobytiia v Sirii," 342. I. I. Sokolov mistakenly gives the date of the decision of the three patriarchs as 1700.

74 J. Nasrallah, "Euthème Saifi," col. 70.

75 Ibid.

76 Beirut Ecclesiastical Chronicle, 37–38.

77 C. Karalevskij, "Antioche," col. 647; C. Walbiner, "The Split of the Greek Orthodox Patriarchate of Antioch," 28–29.

78 G. Levenq, "Athanase III," col. 1372.

79 Mikha'il Burayk, *Tarikh al-Sham*, 19–20.

80 Beirut Ecclesiastical Chronicle, 41.

81 Cited in C. Walbiner, "The Split of the Greek Orthodox Patriarchate of Antioch," 17.

82 Beirut Ecclesiastical Chronicle, 42; Mikha'il Burayk, *Tarikh al-Sham*, 19; C. Karalevskij, "Antioche," col. 647; B. Heyberger, 398. However, French diplomacy had condemned the excessive zeal of the missionaries and French nationals, as the church of Antioch was fraught with turmoil and the deteriorating situation of local Catholics (Th. Philipp, p. 14).

83 S.n., "al-ʿArifa bi-intikhab Kirillus Tanas", 123–132.

84 Beirut Ecclesiastical Chronicle, 45.

85 Ibid., 43.

86 C. Walbiner, "The Split of the Greek Orthodox Patriarchate of Antioch," 30.

87 Ibid.; C. Karalevskij, "Antioche," col. 649.

88 I. I. Sokolov, "Tserkovnye sobytiia v Sirii," 14.

89 Mikha'il Burayk, 449.

90 Mikha'il Burayk, *Tarikh al-Sham*, 20–21; Uspenskii, *Skazanie o Siriiskoi unii*, 514; Beirut Ecclesiatical Chronicle, 46; I. I. Sokolov "Antiokhiiskii patriarkh Sil'vestr," 10.

91 I. N. Il'minskii, 372.

92 Uspenskii, *Skazanie o Siriiskoi unii*, 515.

93 Th. Philipp, 15; B. Masters, 89–90.

94 Grigorovich-Barsky, 1800, 284–285.

95 Ibid., 291.

96 Grigorovich-Barsky, 1800, 313.

97 Ibid., 317.

98 Ibid., 345.

99 Th. Philipp, 21; B. Masters, 92; C. Karalevskij, "Antioche," col. 648; B. Heyberger, 400; K. Katib, 1069.

100 Mikha'il Burayk, 449; Beirut Ecclesiastical Chronicle, 47; Mikha'il Burayk, *Tarikh al-Sham*, 22; Niʿma ibn al-Khuri Tuma, 138–140; Th. Philipp, 15; B. Masters, 90–91.

101 Grigorovich-Barsky, 1800, 354.

102 B. Masters, 91.

103 For more about him, see Chapter 10.

104 Th. Philipp, 9.

105 Beirut Ecclesiastical Chronicle, 47; Uspenskii, *Skazanie o Siriiskoi unii*, 516.

106 Mikha'il Burayk, 449.

107 I. I. Sokolov, "Didaskal Iakov Patmosskii," 337.

108 I. I. Sokolov, "Didaskal Iakov Patmosskii," 338; Mikha'il Burayk, *Tarikh al-Sham*, 22; Ni'ma ibn al-Khuri Tuma, 138–142; Grigorovich-Barsky, 1800, 354.

109 Grigorovich-Barsky, 1800, 341, 342.

110 Beirut Ecclesiastical Chronicle, 48–49; Ni'ma ibn al-Khuri Tuma, 142–143.

111 Beirut Ecclesiastical Chronicle, 57–60.

112 Hananiya al-Munayyir, 362.

113 Ni'ma ibn al-Khuri Tuma, 144.

114 B. Masters, 93.

115 Ibid., 93–94.

116 Beirut Ecclesiastical Chronicle, 59–60; Uspenskii, *Skazanie o Siriiskoi unii*, 527–532; Mikha'il Burayk, *Tarikh al-Sham*, 144; B. Masters, 94–95.

117 Grigorovich-Barsky, 1800, 396.

118 Ibid. See also Mikha'il Burayk, *Tarikh al-Sham*, 24; Mikha'il Burayk, 451–452.

119 I. I. Sokolov, "Didaskal Iakov Patmosskii," 347–348.

120 Beirut Ecclesiastical Chronicle, 50–56; Uspenskii, *Skazanie o Siriiskoi unii*, 522–523; Mikha'il Burayk, 452–454; Mikha'il Burayk, *Tarikh al-Sham*, 27–29, 34, 41.

121 B. Masters, 101.

122 Ni'ma ibn al-Khuri Tuma, 145.

123 Beirut Ecclesiastical Chronicle, 533–534.

124 Ni'ma ibn al-Khuri Tuma, 146.

125 B. Masters, 101.

126 Ni'ma ibn al-Khuri Tuma, 146–147; B. Masters, 76–77, 102.

127 Ni'ma ibn al-Khuri Tuma, 147–148; B. Masters, 102.

128 Ni'ma ibn al-Khuri Tuma, 150.

129 Beirut Ecclesiastical Chronicle, 62; Ni'ma ibn al-Khuri Tuma, 149–152; B. Masters, 102.

130 A. Trad, 78–79; Beirut Ecclesiastical Chronicle, 63; Ni'ma ibn al-Khuri Tuma, 152–153.

131 Ni'ma ibn al-Khuri Tuma, 153; Porphyry Uspenskii, "Vostok Khristianskii: Siriia," 19–21.

132 Uspenskii, *Skazanie o Siriiskoi unii*, 539; Beirut Ecclesiastical Chronicle, 64.

133 Beirut Ecclesiastical Chronicle 64; Niʿma ibn al-Khuri Tuma, 154.

134 B. Masters, 103; Th. Philipp, 19.

135 Uspenskii, *Skazanie o Siriiskoi unii*, 540–541.

136 J. Neale, Vol. 5, Appendix, 196–198.

137 The pallium is an element of liturgical vestments of senior hierarchs of the Catholic Church, a ribbon of white wool embroidered with six black crosses.

138 Aʿmal al-diwan al-sirri, 155–162; Benedict XIV, 164–166.

139 Grigorovich-Barsky, 1800, 285; C. Karalevskij, "Antioche," col. 649–650; Th. Philipp, 17.

140 At the end of the eighteenth century, for a short time there existed a third Uniate Basilian congregation at the monastery of St Simeon in Biskinta (C. Karalevskij, "Antioche," col. 650).

141 Hananiya al-Munayyir, 360.

142 Ibid., 398–402

143 Ibid., 359–360; L. Cheikho, "Nicholas al-Saʾigh," 97–111.

144 L. Cheikho, *Tarikh fann al-tibaʿa*, 360.

145 For details see Chapter 10.

146 C. Karalevskij, "Antioche," col. 649; P. Bacel, 364.

147 Mikhaʾil Burayk, *Tarikh al-Sham*, 81–82; Hananiya al-Munayyir, 362–363; C. Karalevskij, "Antioche," col. 650; G. Levenq, "Athanase IV," col. 1374, 1376.

148 Sabanu, *Tarikh hawadith al-Sham wa-Lubnan*, 12–14.

149 Th. Philipp, 25, 27–30.

150 Ibid., 11, 21, 26.

151 Ibid., 23, 35–43.

152 K. M. Bazili, 2007, 88; T. Iu. Kobishchanov, 122–124.

153 Beirut Ecclesiastical Chronicle, 77.

154 Sabanu, *Tarikh hawadith al-Sham wa-Lubnan*, 89.

155 Beirut Ecclesiastical Chronicle, 77.

156 Uspenskii, *Skazanie o Siriiskoi unii*, 548–549.

157 Beirut Ecclesiastical Chronicle, 77.

158 Ibid., 79.

159 Beirut Ecclesiastical Chronicle, 77–80; Uspenskii, *Skazanie o Siriiskoi unii*, 548–549.

160 Th. Philipp, 29.

161 Hananiya al-Munayyir, 384, 407, 439; Melety, 191; T. Iu. Kobishchanov, 124–126.

162 L. Cheikho, "Mikhaʾil al-Bahri," 10–22.

163 Beirut Ecclesiastical Chronicle, 73–75, 81–86, 89.

164 A. Trad, 128.

165 A. Trad, 126–136.

166 B. Masters, 103.

167 Neophytus of Cyprus, "Ob arabo-katolikakh," 184.

168 Ibid.

169 B. Masters, 104–106; Neophytus of Cyprus, "Ob arabo-katolikakh," 184–185; P. V. Bezobrazov, "O Snosheniiakh Rossii s Palestinoi," 24–25.

170 Sabanu, *Tarikh hawadith al-Sham wa-Lubnan*, 62.

171 Ibid., 63–64.

172 Ibid., 65–67.

173 Neophytus of Cyprus, "Ob arabo-katolikakh," 185.

174 B. Masters, 107.

175 I. Vizantiiskii, "Antiokhiiskii patriarkh Mefodii," 38.

176 Neophytus of Cyprus, "Ob arabo-katolikakh," 186.

177 Ibid., 171.

178 Ibid., 175–176.

179 Beirut Ecclesiastical Chronicle, 35.

180 Mikha'il Burayk, 448; Mikha'il Burayk, *Tarikh al-Sham*, 36–37.

181 *A'mal al-diwan al-sirri*, 158–160.

182 K. Salibi, "The Traditional Historiography of the Maronites," 213; W. Baum, "The Syrian Christian Community in India", 345.

183 This trend in the Catholic historiography reached its peak after World War I, during the era of the French mandate in Syria, when the history of the Melkite Church was represented as a continuous line from the early Christian era through the Middle Ages to the Patriarchate of Antioch of the Uniate community from the eighteenth to the nineteenth centuries, whereas the history of the Orthodox—dissenters who did not wish to be reunited with Rome—began only from 1724 ("Rum–dissidents, colloquially called *urtuduks* [Orthodox]," C. Karalevsky "Bostra," col. 1401, 1404).

184 This observation was made by Porphyry Uspensky in his preface to al-Ujaymi's Chronicle (I. Dzhemi, 387).

185 Yuhanna al-'Ujaymi, *al-Hhujja al-rahina fi haqiqat asl al-Mawarina* (Cairo, 1900).

186 See, for example, the letter of Cyril Tanas to Louis XIV (Cyril Tanas, "Risalatan," 707). See also B. Masters, 91, 92.

187 On the development of this name, see A. E. Krymskii, 351.

188 In Europe, it was Cyrille Karalevskij and many other authors of the journals *Proche-Orient Chrétien* and *Echos d'Orient*. In the East, such views were

developed by the magazine *Al-Mashriq* and its lead authors Louis Cheikho, Constantine Basha, and later Habib Zayyat.

189 B. Masters, 96.

190 Beirut Ecclesiastical Chronicle, 87.

191 C. Karalevskij, "Antioche," col. 651, 653; Nasrallah, *HMLEM*, 4(2).162, 168–169.

192 B. Masters, 87, 92, 94, 96.

193 Ibid., 92–96.

194 Th. Philipp, 18–19.

195 B. Masters, 71.

196 Ibid., 88.

197 Ibid., 87.

198 See Chapter 4.

199 B. Masters, 86.

200 R. Haddad, "On Melkite Passage to the Unia," 67–68, 78, 86–87. See also Th. Philipp, 3–11, 16, 17; Masters, p. 70, 80.

201 B. Masters, 97.

202 B. Heyberger, 149–153; B. Masters, 86–87.

203 Krachkovskii, "Puteshestvie antiokhiiskogo patriarkha Makariia," 259–260.

Chapter 10: The Culture of the Orthodox Orient

1 Folktales come down to us in pilgrims' accounts. For example, Vasily Poznyakov in his *Journey* especially highlights the story of how Patriarch Joachim of Alexandria was forced by a Muslim ruler to drink a cup of poison and remained unharmed and the miracles of St Nicholas and the Archangel Michael associated with the monasteries of Cairo and Jerusalem (V. Pozniakov., 8–14, 15–16, 51–53, 79). The legend of the miraculous appearance of the Holy Fire from the cracked columns of the Church of the Resurrection in Jerusalem enjoyed exceptional popularity (for an analysis of this legend, see P. V. Kuzenkov and K. A. Panchenko, 15–21). Many pilgrims repeated the legend of a mass martyrdom of the monks of the Lavra of Mar Saba at the hands of the infidel Turks (M. Radziwiłł, 136–138; I. Luk'ianov, col. 341–342; Melety, 154). In the mid-nineteenth century, Porphyry Uspensky collected rich ethnographic material in the Orthodox village of Taybeh north of Jerusalem. The scholar took from there multiple copies of texts in manuscripts, most of which, again, were apocryphal legends that were current in the Arab Christian environment (S.n., *Kratkii obzor sobraniia rukopisei, prinadlezhavshego ep. Porfiriiu*, 160). An analysis

of the emergence and continued existence of these and other Middle Eastern legends would be too time-consuming to carry out within the framework of this book. For such a study, someone with more literary skill is needed rather than a historian, even if these legends cannot be understood without reference to the proximate historical realities of the medieval Middle East.

2   One can cite as an example the expulsion of the Franciscan monastery on Mount Sion around 1550 (M. Bakhit, 50), the seizure of the Maronite churches of Beirut in 1570 and 1661, which were converted, respectively, into a caravanse-rai and a mosque (Ibid., 39–40), and the destruction of the Armenian Church of the Ascension in 1616 (Simeon Lekhatsi, 212). It is noteworthy that the majority of these incidents did not directly affect the Orthodox.

3   Let us recall how the construction of a tower at the Monastery of Mar Saba undermined the finances of the Serbian monastic community and the reconstruction of the Monastery of the Holy Cross bankrupted the Georgian colony.

4   Arkhim. Makarii (Veretennikov), "Gramota patriarkha Germana," 208.

5   Zuhair El-Isa, 233.

6   N. F. Kapterev, *Snosheniia*, 8–9.

7   Kh. M. Loparev, "Prilozhenie," 66.

8   N. F. Kapterev, "Gospodstvo grekov," 210.

9   Ibid.; Maximus Simaius, 64, 72.

10   See Chapter 7; see also N. F. Kapterev, "Gospodstvo grekov," 211; Maximus Simaius, 73–74, 77.

11   Chrysanthos, 131–138; Maximus Simaius, 80.

12   Maximus Simaius, 83, 85.

13   Regarding the course of the restoration work, see Maximus Simaius, 110–130; Procopius Nazianzen, 188–217; Neophytus of Cyprus, "Rasskaz," 32–48.

14   A. Fotić, 234.

15   Grigorovich-Barsky, 1885, 279.

16   Porphyry Uspenskii, *Kniga bytiia moego*, 2.204.

17   Ibid., 197; see also, 207.

18   Porphyry Uspenskii, *Kniga bytiia moego*, 1.233.

19   See Chapter 5, note 162.

20   Mikha'il Burayk, *Tarikh al-Sham*, 59, 76.

21   Beirut Ecclesiastical Chronicle, 64–65.

22   Paul of Aleppo, 5.190.

23   Ibid., 5.150–152; see also Chapter 3.

24   Maximus Simaius, 74.

25 Slim, Nassif, and Kassatly, 82–83.

26 Yu. A. Piatnitskii, "Ikona 'Sv. Ekaterina' iz sobraniia Gosudarstvennogo Ermitazha," 50, 53, 55.

27 Paul of Aleppo, 5.190.

28 Arsenii Sukhanov, 196.

29 In this regard, it is worth drawing attention to the Tripolitan icon painter of the first half of the eighteenth century, Hanna al-Qusdi (i.e., the Jerusalemite) (Yu. A. Piatnitskii, "Zhivopis' siro-palestinskogo regiona," 126–127). He represents an interesting example of a Palestinian artist working in the Patriarchate of Antioch. Another example of the artistic activity of the Palestinian Arabs is found in the collection of Greek manuscripts that Porphyry Uspensky brought back from the Middle East. It is an instruction manual for church paintings, copied from a book that belonged to an Arab Orthodox iconographer from Jerusalem (S.n., *Kratkii obzor sobraniia rukopisei, prinadlezhavshego ep. Porfiriiu*, 108).

30 There are many rare iconographic themes encountered on icons in the churches of the Lavra of Mar Saba, such as a scene depicting the Theotokos giving communion from the chalice to Sava and other monks.

31 Iu. A. Piatnitskii, "Zhivopis' siro-palestinskogo regiona," 114.

32 Melety, 307.

33 Iu. A. Piatnitskii, "Ikona 'Sv. Ekaterina'," 54.

34 Porphyry Uspenskii, *Kniga bytiia moego*, 3.212.

35 Melety, 307.

36 Volney, 420

37 H. Maundrell, 445–446.

38 Ibid., 445.

39 Volney, 426.

40 See, for example, M. Immerzeel, *Divine Cavalry*, 265–286.

41 *Icônes Arabes*, 12.

42 This also fully applies to the Copts, Syrian Jacobites, and Nestorians, who also stopped producing icons after the fourteenth century.

43 *Arabskaia Psaltyr'*, 26.

44 MS IVR RAN, A 187, 358, see A. I. Mikhailova, *Arabskaia Psaltyr'*.

45 *Icônes Arabes*, 30–31.

46 RGADA, Fond 52/1, 1654, no. 21, part 3, f. 69.

47 V. G. Briusova, 129–130.

48 Ibid.

49 Paul of Aleppo. 2.41.

50 Ibid., 4.43.

51 *Icônes Arabes*, 31.

52 Ibid., 42–43. This work can be compared to a similar icon of Simeon Stylites the Younger attributed to Yusuf al-Musawwir (Ibid., 38–39), which is a graphic novel with many dozens of characters, whose plot revolves around the central axis—the stylite's column—and which is accompanied by explanatory texts. It was with the iconographic type of the stylite saints bearing a distinct regional flavor that Arab artists were most successful.

53 *Icônes Arabes*, 50–51.

54 Ibid., 31.

55 Ibid., 73.

56 Ibid., 66.

57 Ibid., 80–81 [Translators' note: Bartolomé Esteban Murillo, d. 1682].

58 Ibid., 87.

59 Ibid., 31.

60 *Icônes Arabes*, 32.

61 Yu. A. Piatnitskii, "Zhivopis' siro-palestinskogo regiona," 111–113.

62 See also S. Slim, 95–101.

63 *Icônes Arabes*, 76–77; Yu. A. Piatnitskii, "Zhivopis' siro-palestinskogo regiona," 111–112, 126–127, 206, 212.

64 *Icônes Arabes*, 32. There are also icons attributed to the Patriarch Anthimus (1792–1813). Porphyry Uspensky mentions having seen this patriarch's icon of the Savior, dated 1810 (Porphyry Uspenskii, "Vostok Khristianskii: Siriia," 122).

65 *Icônes Arabes*, 107.

66 Ibid., 113.

67 *Icônes Arabes*, 119–135.

68 Ibid., 136–145.

69 Ibid., 209.

70 Ibid.

71 Ibid., 159.

72 Ibid., 163, 167, 169, 170.

73 *Icônes Arabes*, 171.

74 Ibid., 182–207.

75 A. S. Norov, 1878, 44.

76 Porphyry Uspenskii, *Kniga bytiia moego*, 2.141.

77 Ibid., 3.543.

78 Ibid., 3.542, 2.207, 201.

79 A *proskynetarion* of the 1580s.

80 Ibid., 199.

81 Ibid., 227.

82 Gabriel of Nazareth, ii–v; *Pravoslavnaia Entsiklopediia*, 10.206–207.

83 A. P. Lebedev, *Istoriia,* 8–9; SIPPO, 1892, 499–500; I. Pomerantsev, "Dosifei," 26.

84 Paul of Aleppo, 5.27–29.

85 MSS Balamand, 178, 179.

86 Russian translation: Kirill Lukaris, *Ispovedanie very* (St Petersburg, 2001); see also A. P. Lebedev, *Istoriia*, 633–673.

87 A. P. Lebedev, *Istoriia,* 674–695; I. Pomerantsev, "Dosifei," 9–17.

88 A. P. Lebedev, *Istoriia,* 633.

89 Ibid., 690–695.

90 In just one of Dositheus's works, the *History of the Bishopric of Mount Sinai*, we counted more than thirty sources, from Eusebius of Caesarea to Nectarius, not including the acts of local councils to which Dositheus makes reference. There survive, copied by the patriarch himself, texts of many documents on church history from the thirteenth through the seventeenth centuries that he used in his scholarly work.

91 N. F. Kapterev, *Kharakter otnoshenii*, 223.

92 Dositheus, "Neizdannye glavy," 30.

93 Ibid., 29–30.

94 It should be noted in this regard that Greek chroniclers attributed the compilation of a historical chronicle to Germanus, the first Greek patriarch in Jerusalem (Maximus Simaius, 100). However, we must question the veracity of these reports; they are simply due to poor knowledge of the realities of the sixteenth century among later chroniclers of the Brotherhood of the Holy Sepulchre.

95 Dositheus, "Istoriia episkopii gory Sinaia."

96 See Chapter 6.

97 Dositheus, "Istoriia episkopii gory Sinaia," iii.

98 D. A. Ialamas, "Gramota Dosifeia," 236.

99 D. A. Ialamas, "Gramota Dosifeia," 237.

100 Ibid.; B. L. Fonkich, "Popytka sozdaniia grecheskoi tiografii."

101 I. Pomerantsev, "Dosifei," 23–25.

102 Ibid., 28–29; I. Sokolov, "Sviatogrobskoe bratstvo," 8.

103 This feeling is reinforced by the peculiarities of the Russian translation of the *History and Description of the Holy Land*. Around 1728 a copy of this work was sent by Chrysanthos as a gift to the Russian Emperor Peter II and translated by a Ukrainian translator into the unattractive bureaucratic language of the

Petrine era, thickly interspersed with the Polonisms and Latinisms characteristic of the vocabulary of graduates from the Western Russian schools. Already in the nineteenth century, this translation was described as "literal, often obscure, sometimes nonsensical" (Kh. M. Loparev, "Khrisanf," 27).

104 About Chrysanthos, see Chrysanthos, *Istoriia Sv zemli*; Kh. M. Loparev, "Khrisanf"; *Vizanticheskii Vremennik* 1.694; 8.557–560.

105 Parthenius, "Rasskaz Parfeniia Afiniana, mitropolita Kesarii Palestinskoi, o raspriakh mezhdu pravoslavnymi i armianami" in *Materialy dlia istorii Ierusalimskoi patriarkhii XVI–XIX veka*, vol. 1 (St Petersburg, 1901), 189–275.

106 Parthenius's work is entitled "A Brief Account of the Ancient Rights of the Patriarchs of Jerusalem and the Causes of Strife Between the Greeks, Romans and Armenians." The original Greek manuscript of this work, along with copies of accompanying historical documents, is stored in the AVPRI (Fond 89/1, 1745, no. 4, ff. 53-74v. Russian translation: Ibid., ff. 75-117). An abridged translation of the "Brief Account" was published by N. F. Kapterev (*Snosheniia*, 446–455).

107 I. I. Sokolov, "Iakov Patmoskii," 501–522.

108 Bolkhovitinov, 233.

109 Bolkhovitinov, 234.

110 MS Damascus 102.

111 Maximus Simaius, 84; Nasrallah, *HMLEM*, 4(2).93–95, 196; I. Sokolov, "Didaskal Iakov Patmosskii," 507, 518; for a complete bibliography for Ephraim, see: K. A. Panchenko, s. v. "Efrem II Afinianin, patriarkh ierusalimskii," *Pravoslavnaia Entsiklopediia*, 19.69–70.

112 G. Iared, 12, 16–17, 23–24; Melety, 13–16; G. Graf, 146–148.

113 "See how clearly our Lord, in His infinite mercy and wisdom walled off ... the holy Orthodox faith ... He lifted up out of nothing this powerful empire of the Ottomans over the site of our Roman Empire, which had started to shy away from the truth of the Orthodox faith. And He raised this empire of the Ottomans higher than any other kingdom in order to demonstrate without a doubt that this happened by God's will rather than human strength ... The almighty Lord placed over us this lofty kingdom, 'for there is no authority except from God' so that it would be for the people of the West a bridle and for us, the people of the East—a means to salvation" (Cited in: B. Braude and B. Lewis, 16–17).

114 Melety, 283.

115 A fragment of it has been published in Russian translation under the title "Istoriia, Ierusalimskhikh patriarkhov ot vremeni 6 vselenskogo sobora do 1810 g." See: Maximus Simaius.

116   It seems that Maximus wrote his *History of the Patriarchs of Jerusalem* in 1801. The journal of events in Palestine from the beginning of 1802 to 1809 was a separate work, added to the *History* by later editors (Maximus Simaius, 55, 94).

117   Procopius Nazianzen, 222.

118   Ibid., 132.

119   Ibid.

120   A. S. Norov, *Puteshestvie*, 1.217.

121   Porphyry Uspenskii, *Kniga bytiia moego,* 3.559–560.

122   Ibid., 1.437, 3.623.

123   *Vizanticheskii Vremennik*, 1.683–690.

124   Arsenii Sukhanov, C. 164–165, see also 196; *Vizanticheskii Vremennik*, 1.546–554, 683–690.

125   R. Curzon, 187.

126   S.n., *Kratkii obzor sobraniia rukopisei, prinadlezhavshego ep. Porfiriiu*, 72–156; For more on the Lavra's library, see A. S. Norov, *Puteshestvie*, 1.60.

127   S.n., *Pravovaia organizatsiia Sviatogrobskogo bratstva*, 156.

128   R. Curzon, 172; See also: A. S. Norov, *Puteshestvie*, 1.217; Porphyry Uspenskii, *Kniga bytiia moego*, 2.309–315. Porphyry evaluated the contents of the patriarchate's library more modestly: over 54 parchment manuscripts, 284 paper manuscripts, and 540 printed books: a total of 878 volumes.

129   Porphyry Uspenskii, *Kniga bytiia moego*, 3.327–334.

130   Ibid., 326; *Otchet IPB*, 1899, 60, 66.

131   MSS Vostfaka, 221, 231; *Otchet IPB,* 1899, 73; MSS Saydnaya, 43, 84.

132   MSS Vostfaka, 196, 227; *Otchet IPB*, 1899, 61, 68; MS Hama 39; MS Homs 40.

133   RNB, Ar. n. s. 242.

134   Ibid.

135   S.n., *Pravovaia organizatsiia Sviatogrobskogo bratstva*, 156, 157.

136   A. Tsagareli, 168, 172, 181, 182, 188.

137   B. Heyberger, 147.

138   Krachkovskii, "Gramota Ioakima IV," 29.

139   A. Rustum, 42.

140   S.n., *Patriarshie dokumenty*, 283. Joachim, without a doubt, relied on the apocryphal Arabic text, *The Acts of the Council of Nicaea*, described by later researchers (Nasrallah, *HMLEM*, 2(2).200–201). It is possible that the patriarch sincerely believed that he was dealing with an authentic document.

141   P. V. Kuzenkov and K. A. Panchenko, 10, 23–24.

142   See Chapter 9.

143 G. Graf, 3.87–88; K. A. Panchenko, "Tripoliiskoe gnezdo," part 1, 55.

144 IVR RAN, MS V 1220, ff. 86v-104v; K. A. Panchenko, "Tripoliiskoe gnezdo," part 1, 56–57; G. Graf, 3.89; Nasrallah, *HMLEM*, 4(1).181–182.

145 G. Graf, 3.90; Nasrallah, *HMLEM*, 4(1).182.

146 G. Graf, 3.90–91. Nasrallah, *HMLEM*, 4(1).182; IVR RAN, MS V 1220, ff. 104v–124v.

147 See also K. A. Panchenko, "Mitropolit 'Isa."

148 See Chapter 4.

149 K. A. Panchenko, "K Istorii Ierusalimskoi Tserkvi XVI v."; K. A. Panchenko, s. v., "Ioakim, mitropolit Vifleemskii," *Pravoslavnaia Entsiklopediia* 23.151–152.

150 Nasrallah, *HMLEM*, 4(1).231–232.

151 For examples of this type of creative work, see F. Freijat, 30–32.

152 Nasrallah, *HMLEM*, 4(1).231–240; G. Graf, 3.91.

153 A. Baumstark, 337–338.

154 Garshuni is a type of writing in which Arabic texts are written in the letters of the Syriac alphabet. It was in use, starting from the early Middle Ages, among Middle Eastern Christians of Aramaic origin.

155 Metropolitan Simeon of Saydnaya, in 1630. RGADA, Fond 1608, no. 129, f. 1. In documents from the Monastery of Saydnaya there are different important writings in Syriac from 1608 (Ibid., f. 5) and 1628 (Ibid., f. 9).

156 K. A. Panchenko and B. L. Fonkich, "Gramota 1594 g.," 183–184. We thank D. A. Morozov for deciphering the Garshuni and indicating the spelling mistakes.

157 We know of in particular a few examples of bilingual Syriac-Arabic liturgikons in the eighteenth century (MS Damascus 305; MSS Balamand 15, 19).

158 G. Graf, 92; Nasrallah, *HMLEM*, 4(1).70–85; C. Walbiner, "Understanding of Printing," 69–70.

159 G. Graf, 92–93.

160 C. Walbiner, "Die Bemühungen des Meletius Karma um den Druck arabischer Bücher in Rom," 168, 169.

161 Mikha'il Burayk, 437.

162 Historians love to quote Paul of Aleppo's description of Macarius's audience with Tsar Alexei Mikailovich: "When [Macarius] spoke with the interpreter in Greek he would falter a little, for the Greeks speak fast, while we, because we had learned it, could not speak as fast as them for their tongue is light. So the King asked the interpreter: 'Why does he not speak fast?' and he said: 'Because he learned the language recently. But he can speak Turkish and if your Majesty so desires, he can speak it.' [The King] answered: 'No, never! Such

a saint should not defile his mouth and tongue with that filthy language!'" (Paul of Aleppo, 3.20–21; English translation by Ioana Feodorov in *The Orthodox Church in the Arab World*, edited by S. Noble and A. Treiger, 266).

163 Krachkovskii, "Opisanie puteshestviia Makariia Antiokhiiskogo," 260. On Macarius's literary activity, see: G. Graf, 3.94–110; Nasrallah, *HMLEM*, 4(1).87–127; H. Kilpatrick, 262–269.

164 Patriarch Macarius. I have prepared a Russian translation of this source: K. A. Panchenko, "Mitropolity i eparkhii pravoslavnoi Antiokhiiskoi tserkvi v opisanii patriarkha Makariia III az-Za'ima (1655 g.): Tekst i kommentarii," *Vestnik tserkovnoi istorii* N1/2 (25/26) (2013), 116–157.

165 "Gruziia v 17 stoletii po izobrazheniiu patriarkha makariia."

166 Nasrallah, *HMLEM*, 4(1).99.

167 Nasrallah, *HMLEM*, 4(1).99–114.

168 Ibid., 114–127.

169 Paul of Aleppo, 5.196.

170 Paul of Aleppo, 5.191–197; I. Yu. Krachkovskii, "Opisanie puteshestviia Makariia Antiokhiskogo," 261. We cannot agree with this assessment. There are manuscripts known to have been copied by Paul in his youth, at the age of fifteen. At that time he had clear and neat handwriting, reminiscent of typeface. Over the years, the archdeacon allowed himself more calligraphic liberties, decorated with curly letters that sometimes obscure what is written.

171 Paul of Aleppo, 5.150–174.

172 B. L. Fonkich mentioned in a private conversation the possibility that nervous overwork and heavy stress played a role in this, which Macarius and his fellow travelers managed to survive during their stay in the Caucasus fom 1668–1669 (for details, see Chapter 8 and the article K. A. Panchenko, "Pravoslavnye Araby i Kavkaz," 65–67). Patriarch Athanasius III Dabbas argues that Paul was poisoned (Athanasius Dabbas, p. 157). Joseph Nasrallah puts it on June 22 of that same year, recalling for some reason that day as marked in a letter from Macarius to Patriarch Ioasaf of Moscow, in which he remembers the death of Paul (J. Nasrallah, *HMLEM*, V. 4(1), p. 219). Nasrallah did not know of the letter from Macarius to Artamon Matveev from Tbilisi on August 24, 1669, where he gives the date of Paul's death as January 30 (in the text it is mistakenly "February"), 1669 (RGADA Fond 52/1, 1669, no. 21, f. 7. See also: B. L. Fonkich, "O date konchiny Pavla Aleppskogo," *Ocherki feodalnoi Rossii*, 13 (2009), 289-292). Vera G. Chentsova believes, however, that this is a mistake in the day and not in the month (V. G. Chentsova, "Polednie mesiatsy zhizni Pavla Aleppskogo" (in press).

173   On the biography of Paul, see Paul of Aleppo, 5.150–174, 192–197; Krachkovskii, "Opisanie puteshestviia Makariia Antiokhiiskogo," 355.

174   Paul of Aleppo, 3.30; for the education, artistic taste, and literary works of Paul, see also Paul of Aleppo, 2.41, 64, 89, 3.131–132, 149, 4.43, 47, 55, 74, 5.150–174; Krachkovskii, "Opisanie puteshestviia Makariia Antiokhiiskogo," 261, 265–267, 271; Krachkovskii, "Arabskie rukopisi Grigoriia IV," 11; G. Graf, 3.110–113; Nasrallah, *HMLEM*, 4(1).219–224; H. Kilpatrick, 269–272.

175   Nasrallah, *HMLEM*, 4(1).221–222.

176   See details in K. A. Panchenko, "Pravoslavnye Araby i Kavkaz," 59–61; see also Chapter 8.

177   C. Walbiner, "Macarius Ibn al-Zaʿim and the Beginnings of an Orthodox Church Historiography," 14–15.

178   Paul of Aleppo, 5.184.

179   Nasrallah, *HMLEM*, 4(1).222–223.

180   Mikhaʾil Burayk, 17.

181   Mikhaʾil Burayk, 418.

182   Nasrallah, *HMLEM*, 4(1).224.

183   Thus, it appears in the chronicle of Mikhail Breik, which, as was mentioned, was based on an early version of the Macarius's work. However, in the unpublished manuscript V 1227, there is preserved a later version of the treatise where the eleventh century is described in hypertrophied detail, chiefly through use of Nikon of the Black Mountain. At the same time, Macarius presents the period from the twelfth through the fifteenth century spottily. Paul of Aleppo, working in parallel to his father, was much more successful in reconstructing the Mamluk era.

184   Paul of Aleppo, 5.184.

185   Paul of Aleppo, 186.

186   Nasrallah, *HMLEM*, 4(1).224.

187   Nasrallah, *HMLEM*, 4(1).206–209; about him, see also the section on "Fine Arts."

188   Nasrallah, *HMLEM*, 4(1).249–251.

189   Ibid., 228–230; Krachkovskii, "Arabskaia geograficheskaia literatura", 681–682.

190   C. Walbiner, "Rihlat Raʿad min Halab ila al-Bandaqiyya," in *Majmuʿat abhath wa-maqalat ila al-Mutran Neophytus Edelby* (Beirut, 2005), 367–383. See also the research by this author about an anonymous journey to Sinai in 1635–1636; C. Walbiner, "Ein Christlish-Arabischer bericht uber eine pilgerfahrt von Damascus zum berge Sinai in den jahren 1635–36," in *Parole de l'Orient* 24 (1999), 319–337.

191 Nasrallah, *HMLEM*, 4(1).224–228.

192 Uspenskii, *Skazanie o Siriiskoi unii*, 496; Beirut Ecclesiastical Chronicle, 32, 96.

193 MSS Damascus 125, 212, 378.

194 MSS Hamatoura 14, 15, 18, 24, 26, 31, 40, 46, 47; SPBF ARAN, Fond 1026, op. 1, no. 246, ff. 23v-24, 27, 28, 29; MSS Balamand, 80, 89, 105, 140.

195 MS Balamand, 181.

196 Nasrallah, *HMLEM*, 4(1).234–238.

197 Ibid., 237.

198 Paul of Aleppo, 5.161–164.

199 See Chapter 4.

200 Nasrallah, *HMLEM*, 4(1).241–243.

201 On Arab Christian poetry of the eighteenth century, see Nasrallah, *HMLEM*, 4(2).268–276; on geographical literature, see also 300–305.

202 Ibid., 107.

203 P. P. Bacel, "ʿAbdallah Zakher," 370–371.

204 Krachkovskii, "Opisanie puteshestviia Makariia," 260.

205 I. Luk'ianov, col. 239.

206 Nasrallah, "Euthème Saifi," col. 68–69.

207 Nasrallah, *HMLEM*, 4(1).186, 188–192.

208 The differences between Orthodoxy and Catholicism can be reduced primarily to a number of doctrinal controversies. These include the problem of the Filioque; the question of the procession of the Holy Spirit from the Father and, in the Catholic point of view, also from the Son (the Latin *filioque* means "and from the Son"); the treatment of the sacrament of the Eucharist (whether to use leavened or unleavened bread); the doctrine of purgatory, accepted by Catholicism and rejected by Orthodoxy; the dogma of the infallibility of the pope and his primacy in the Christian world ("the primacy of the Papal See"); and, finally, the doctrine about the nature of sanctity, which, in the Catholic understanding, involves the Church's accumulation of "surplus" grace bestowed to the saints and the subsequent redistribution of it by means of indulgences.

209 Nasrallah, "Euthème Saifi," col. 71; Nasrallah, *HMLEM*, 4(1).186–187.

210 I. I. Sokolov, "Tserkovnye sobytiia," 342; see more on this treatise further in the present chapter.

211 H. Maundrell, 491.

212 IVR RAN, MS V 1227. See, for example, f. 129.

213 Nasrallah, *HMLEM*, 4(1).130–131.

214 Ibid., 135–140, 144.

215 Nasrallah, *HMLEM*, 4(1).134–135. In the 1930s, this work was printed with a Romanian translation: *Atanasie Dabbas*. The author expresses his deep gratitude to V. G. Chentsova for assistance in becoming acquainted with the contents of the chronicle.

216 In Arabic translation: Salah al-hakim wa-fasad al-ʿalam al-damim. See also: K. A. Panchenko, "Review of D. Cantemir, *The Salvation of the Wise Man and the Ruin of the Sinful World*."

217 G. Levenq, "Athanase III" in *DHEG* vol. 3. col. 1373; Nasrallah, *HMLEM*, 4(1).141–142.

218 P. Bacel, 225–226, 281–283, 367–369; Nasrallah, *HMLEM*, T. 4(2).111–138.

219 C. Walbiner, "Monastic Reading and Learning," 463, 465–466.

220 On the biography and literary works of Nicholas al-Saygeh, see L. Cheikho "Nicholas al-Sa'igh," 97–111; Nasrallah, *HMLEM*, 4(2).109–111, 268–270.

221 Grelot, 146. For some reason, European travelers believed that the liturgy of the Arab Orthodox was in Greek.

222 H. Maundrell, 406.

223 AVPRI, Fond 152, op. 505, 1765, d. 7 (vol. 2), p. 204. The author thanks Prof. S. A. Kirillina for kindly providing this information.

224 A. Peristeris, 176.

225 G. A. Murkos, 221–222.

226 I. Pomerantsev, "Dosifei," 28; I. I. Sokolov, "Sviatogrobskoe bratstvo," 8.

227 Porphyry Uspenskii, *Kniga bytiia moego*, 3.545. Many of these apocryphal texts were copied at the order of Porphyry Uspensky and are now awaiting researches in the manuscript department of the Russian National Library (See: S.n., *Kratkii obzor sobraniia rukopisei, prinadlezhavshego ep. Porfiriiu*, 172).

228 This refers to singing the Octoechos, the liturgical book with the songs for the weekday cycle, and the Menaion, a collection of religious literature (lives of saints, teachings, and so on) arranged according to the days of the month.

229 I. Luk'ianov, col. 250.

230 Ibid.

231 C. Walbiner, "Monastic Reading and Learning," 463.

232 Ibid., 464.

233 Ibid., 464; L. Cheikho, "Nicholas al-Sa'igh," 98–100.

234 L. Cheikho, "Niqulawus al-Sa'igh," 99.

235 C. Walbiner, "Monastic Reading and Learning," 466.

236 Ibid., 466

237 C. Walbiner, "Monastic Reading and Learning," 469–475.

238 Ibid., 476.

239 Ibid., 467–468.

240 Ibid., 469.

241 Nasrallah, *HMLEM*, 4(2).191.

242 I. I. Sokolov, "Didaskal Iakov Patmosskii," 343.

243 Ibid., 338–339.

244 I. I. Sokolov, "Didaskal Iakov Patmosskii," 508–511.

245 A. P. Lebedev, *Istoriia*, 414–436.

246 Ibid., 425. The notes in brackets belong to A. P. Lebedev.

247 Grigorovich-Barsky, 1800, 290.

248 I. I. Sokolov, "Didaskal Iakov Patmosskii," 507–508.

249 G. Iared, 12.

250 G. Iared, 16.

251 Porphyry Uspenskii, *Kniga bytiia moego*, 1.347–348, 300, 3.491.

252 Ibid., 1.404.

253 Ibid., 231.

254 MSS Damascus, 13, 29. See also: Porphyry Uspenskii, *Kniga bytiia moego*, 3.583.

255 Porphyry Uspenskii, *Kniga bytiia moego*, 3.446.

256 Ibid., 1.255.

257 Volney, 267.

258 The Photian Schism was an ecclesiastical conflict between Rome and Constantinople in the ninth century. It erupted around the patriarch of Constantinople, Photius, who was accused by his opponents of uncanonically seizing the throne. Photius's opponents appealed to the pope of Rome, while Photius categorically denied the right of the Roman pontiff to interfere in the affairs of other churches. Relations between the two ecclesial centers were strained to the extreme, in many ways anticipating the final divergence between the East and the West of the Christian world in 1054.

259 For more about the works and biography of Elias Fakhr, see: Nasrallah, *HMLEM*, 4(2).202–216; G. Graf, 3.134–140; A. Trad, 78–79; MS Damascus, 131, 133, 173, 193; A. B. Khalidov, V 1220, V 1222, V 1223, no. 10443–10449, 10540–10542; I. I. Sokolov, "Didaskal Iakov Patmosskii," 337–8; B. Masters, 76.

260 Nasrallah, *HMLEM*, 4(2).138–142.

261 Nasrallah, *HMLEM*, 4(2).151–155.

262 Beirut Ecclesiastical Chronicle, 88.

263 Beirut Ecclesiastical Chronicle, 88; Porphyry Uspenskii, "Vostok Khristianskii: Siriia," 120; Nasrallah, *HMLEM*, 4(2).216; A. Trad, 123.

264 Nasrallah, *HMLEM*, 4(2).154, 216.

265 Beirut Ecclesiastical Chronicle, 88; A. Trad, 123–124.

266 Nasrallah, *HMLEM*, 4(2).147, 219–221.

267 See Chapter 6.

268 Nasrallah, *HMLEM*, 4(2).195–199.

269 Ibid., 161–180.

270 K. M. Bazili, 2007, 511, 512.

271 Beirut Ecclesiastical Chronicle, 88.

272 Anastasius ibn al-Mujalla, f. 92v. At the same time, Anastasius judged and criticized the wording adopted by the Council of Florence with full knowledge of the facts.

273 Although these certificates were printed in large quantities, few have come down to us because it was customary to put the certificate in the coffin of its owner (D. F. Kobeko, 270, 278–279).

274 See, for example, K. M. Bazili, 2007, 510. An interesting, though not impartial, observation by this author concerning the religious consciousness of the Uniates in the late 1840s: "The centuries-old effort by the Roman clergy to spread Western dogmas has had hitherto little success with the Syrian Uniates," he wrote. "They do not believe in purgatory; they have an unfavorable opinion of the Roman pontiff and overall do not recognize him as the head of the church; they do not respect indulgences; they avoid the Latin church; the aspiration of the clergy and the efforts of the bishops is to gradually replace celibate clergy with married priests; the hieromonks induce discontent amongst the people" (K. M. Bazili, 2007, 514).

275 Cited in: Th. Philipp, 17.

276 K. M. Bazili, 2007, 513.

277 On him, see: Nasrallah, *HMLEM*, 4(2).200–201; A. Trad, 150.

278 Nasrallah, *HMLEM*, 4(2).231–232.

279 Ibid., 224.

280 Ibid., 225.

281 Niʿma ibn al-Khuri Tuma, 138–155; J. Manash, 396–405; Nasrallah, *HMLEM*, 4(2).307–309.

282 Sabanu, *Tarikh hawadith al-Sham wa-Lubnan*; A. E. Krymskii, 210–213.

283 Sabanu, *Tarikh hawadith al-Sham wa-Lubnan*, 14.

284 Nasrallah, *HMLEM*, 4(2).312–313.

285 Hananiya al-Munayyir, 359; Nasrallah, *HMLEM*, 4(2).316–317.

286 Nasrallah, *HMLEM*, 4(2).317–318; Hananiya al-Munayyir, 351–516.

287 C. Walbiner, "Monastic Reading and Learning," 473–474.

288 Nasrallah, *HMLEM*, 4(2).309–311. This text has not yet been published. Ironically, the only fragment of it that has been published was in Russian

translation by Porphyry Uspensky. Porphyry was able to briefly obtain a manuscript of 'Ujaymi from the abbot of one of the Uniate monasteries. Through the dragoman of the Patriarchate of Jerusalem, Porphyry managed to translate 'Ujaymi's text only up to the description of the twelfth century. Then the Uniate hieromonk demanded that the manuscript be returned, fearing trouble from his superiors because of his contacts with the Russian archimandrite (I. Jemi, 385–386). As a result, only the initial part of the chronicle was introduced into scholarly circulation in 1875. Thus, the Uniates themselves did not publish the work of the first chronicler of their community.

289 I. Jemi, 396–397.

290 Ibid., 470–472, 475, 476–478.

291 C. Walbiner, "The Split of the Greek Orthodox Patriarchate of Antioch," 19, 25.

292 In his chronicle *Tarikh al-Sham*, Breik explains that he started it in 1720 in part because, as he wrote, "I saw with my own eyes" events occurring at the time "and it is the first thing that I remember in my life" (Mikha'il Burayk, *Tarikh al-Sham*, 17).

293 Mikha'il Burayk, *Tarikh al-Sham*, 8–11, 17, 35, 38, 74–75, 77, 96, 102; Nasrallah, *HMLEM*, 4(2).316.

294 Mikha'il Burayk, 419.

295 Breik writes, "I was searching for [works] about the history of the city of Damascus and I did not find [any] except for during the time of the demise of the Patriarch Macarius of blessed memory, there was a man known as the priest Farah who wrote in brief about what happened between the Patriarchs Cyril and Neophytus and I copied it" (Mikha'il Burayk, *Tarikh al-Sham*, 17). That is, perhaps, the account of Farah that only goes up to the 1680s, not to 1724 as thought Constantine Basha. There is, however, another argument in favor of Basha's opinion. Arab Christian chroniclers used the Era of Adam, although they also used Hijri reckoning and the era of the birth of Christ, which, incidentally, Greek authors preferred for dating. The first date according to this reckoning in the *History of the Patriarchs of Antioch* is the death of the Patriarch Athanasius in 1724. The last dating according to the Era of Adam figuring in the chronicle is the death of the Patriarch Macarius in 7180/1672. This fragment of text clearly belongs to Farah, as well as the consecration of Athanasius Dabbas in 7194/1686 and the death of Cyril al-Za'im in 7228/1720. It is more likely that these topics were also described by Farah, not Mikhail Breik.

296 Mikha'il Burayk, 350.

297 Ibid.

298 C. Walbiner, "The Split of the Greek Orthodox Patriarchate of Antioch," 15.

299 In his work on Melkite literature, Joseph Nasrallah does not mention the other major Orthodox historiographers apart from Breik (Nasrallah, *HMLEM*, 4(2).305–320); see also C. Walbiner, "The Split of the Greek Orthodox Patriarchate of Antioch," 19.

300 The fate of the Beirut Ecclesiastical Chronicle in scholarship is no less remarkable than that of the ecclesiastical histories of Yuhanna ʿUjaymi and Mikhail Breik. As is the case with these two chronicles, the Russian translation of the Beirut Chronicle appeared long before the publication of the Arabic original. Porphyry Uspensky in 1874 and A. E. Krymsky in 1908 published Russian versions of the various recensions of the chronicle. An abridged Arabic version was published in 1903 and became a bibliographic rarity that is not available to most European researchers. A full scholarly edition of the Arabic text of the chronicle was only published in 2002. A. Trad.

301 Uspenskii, *Skazanie o Siriiskoi unii*, 497–544; Beirut Ecclesiastical Chronicle, 33–64; A. Trad, 31–84.

302 Uspenskii, *Skazanie o Siriiskoi unii*, 531.

303 Beirut Ecclesiastical Chronicle, 41.

304 These issues have been analyzed in the previous chapter.

305 C. Walbiner, "The Split of the Greek Orthodox Patriarchate of Antioch," 28–31; see also the previous chapter.

306 Uspenskii, *Skazanie o Siriiskoi unii*, 522–523, 544–550; Beirut Ecclesiastical Chronicle, 53–55, 64–75, 80–89; A. Trad, 61–64, 85–105, 115–125.

307 Uspenskii, *Skazanie o Siriiskoi unii* in *TKDA*, 9 (1874), 491–553.

308 Beirut Ecclesiastical Chronicle, 75–80; A. Trad, 106–114.

309 A. Trad, 138–146.

310 Ibid., 147–156.

311 Ibid., 153–158.

312 A. E. Krymskii published a fragment of the chronicle going up to 1791 ("Iz beirutskoi tserkovnoi letopisi XVI–XVIII vv." *Drevnosti Vostochnyia* Древности 3.1 (1907), 1–89).

313 C. Walbiner, "Pioneers of Book-Printing," 11, 12.

314 The first printing press in Arabic script was established in Italy already by 1514. By order of the pope, it printed prayer books that were then distributed to the Christian East (C. Walbiner, "Understanding of Printing," 66.).

315 C. Walbiner, "Understanding of Printing," 72, 76.

316 On the attitude of Macarius and Paul to toward the printed book, see ibid., 71–75.

317 Porphyry Uspenskii, *Kniga bytiia moego*, 3.329–332; I. Feodorov, "The Edition and Translation of Christian Arabic Texts," 56–57; I. Feodorov, "The Romanian Contribution to Arabic Printing," 42–45.

318 We believe it appropriate here to use the well-known term "Byzantine Commonwealth" introduced into Byzantine Studies by Dmitri Obolensky. It refers to the group of Orthodox countries during the Middle Ages that formed a unified cultural and political space gravitating toward Constantinople. In the post-Byzantine period, these cultural ties were preserved in full.

319 Porphyry Uspenskii, *Kniga bytiia moego*, 3.330–332.

320 The fate of the Arabic font made by Antim Ivireanul remains an open question. Some authors observe a difference between the Bucharest and Aleppo fonts and believe that a new font was produced in Aleppo (L. Cheikho, "Tarikh Fann al-Tibaʿa," 355–356).

321 See Chapter 8. On the typographic activity in Aleppo, see L. Cheikho "Tarikh Fann al-Tibaʿa," C. 355–356; C. Walbiner, "Pioneers of Book-Printing," 11, 24–25; Porphyry Uspenskii, *Kniga bytiia moego,* 3.322; A. Dabbas, *Tarikh al-Tibaʿa al-ʿarabiyya*, 63–81.

322 L. Cheikho, "Tarikh Fann al-Tibaʿa," 357. Porphyry gives the erroneous date of 1727 (Porphyry Uspenskii, *Kniga bytiia moego*, 3.333).

323 A. Dabbas, *Tarikh al-Tibaʿa al-ʿarabiyya*, 78–79. [Ed. Sulayman al-Aswad's Europeanized name was Solomon Negri. The Psalms and Gospel books mentioned were published in conjunction with the SPCK.]

324 Ibid.

325 L. Cheikho, "Tarikh Fann al-Tibaʿa," 357.

326 Volney, 264.

327 C. Walbiner, "Pioneers of Book-Printing," 12.

328 L. Cheikho, "Tarikh Fann al-Tibaʿa," 362.

329 Nasrallah, *HMLEM*, 4(2).143–144.

330 Volney, 266.

331 Volney, 266–267.

332 C. Walbiner, "Pioneers of Book-Printing," 12.

333 Mikha'il Burayk, *Tarikh al-Sham*, 27.

334 Some attribute the Arabic translation of Nectarius's work to the deacon and future patriarch Sophronius al-Kilizi and date it to 1733 (MS Balamand, 178). There the publication of the treatise in Iasi is erroneously dated to 1743. On the other hand, Porphyry Uspensky, seeing this book in the library of the

metropolitan of Bethlehem, reported that the translation was made by the priest Mas'ad Nashw in Cairo in 1740 (Porphyry Uspenskii, *Kniga bytiia moego*, 3.323). It is not to be excluded that both Arab writers independently translated Nectarius's work and that the translation by Nashw that was published in Iasi was mistakenly attributed to Sophronius.

335 Porphyry Uspenskii, "Vostok Khristianskii: Siriia," 119.

336 Porphyry Uspenskii, *Kniga bytiia moego*, 3.333. On Sylvester's publishing activities in Moldavia, see also: I. Feodorov, "The Romanian Contribution to Arabic Printing," 46–47.

337 Porphyry Uspenskii, *Kniga bytiia moego*, 3.334.

338 MS Balamand, 22; MS Hamatoura 8.

339 Porphyry Uspenskii, "Vostok Khristianskii: Siriia,", 119–120; Porphyry Uspenskii, *Kniga bytiia moego*, 3.328–329; L. Cheikho, "Tarikh Fann al-Tiba'a," 501–502.

340 Porphyry Uspenskii, *Kniga bytiia moego*, 3.329; L. Cheikho, "Tarikh Fann al-Tiba'a," 502.

341 *Siriia, Livan i Palestina*, 324.

342 Porphyry Uspensky described a Gospel printed in Iasi at the expense of "the glorious Daniel"—according to Porphyry's assumption, the Patriarch of Antioch Daniel of Chios (1767–1791). (Porphyry Uspenskii, *Kniga bytiia moego*, 3. 329). Only recently, D. A. Morozov proved that Porphyry was dealing with a defective copy of the Gospel published at the expense of Daniel Apostolos (D. A. Morozov, "Vifleemskii ekzempliar arabskogo Evangeliia," 645–651).

343 Porphyry Uspenskii, *Kniga bytiia moego*, 3.333.

344 *Siriia, Livan i Palestina*, 324.

Conclusion

1 He was, one might recall, a Maronite. That is, he cannot be attributed to the Melkite Renaissance.

2 *Icônes Arabes*, 13.

3 This same Porphyry encountered among them the most admired figure among the Arab Orthodox in the nineteenth century, Archimandrite Athanasius, abbot of Balamand in the 1830s. The priest Yusuf Muhanna al-Haddad, an educator, writer, and translator who was killed during the massacres in Damascus in 1860 and later canonized, was already a highly authoritative figure in the Orthodox community in the 1840s. Porphyry, someone who was not habitually generous with praise, called him "a true laborer" and a "man of God" (Porphyry Uspenskii, *Kniga bytiia moego*, 1. 255).

Appendix

1 The list of Ottoman sultans is given according to S. Len-Pul, *Musulman-skie Dinastii* (Moscow, 2004), 141. The list of patriarchs of Constantinople is given according to A. P. Lebvedev, *Istoriia*, 324. The author has corrected the dates for the reigns of the other patriarchs.

GLOSSARY OF TERMS

Agha—Ottoman honorific title.

Akçe (Turk.)—A small silver Ottoman coin. Minted from the fourteenth century, initially its weight was 1.154 grams, and was 90 percent pure. In the sixteenth and seventeenth centuries, the silver content and the weight of an akçe fell sharply (by the middle of the seventeenth century, its weight had decreased by six times and its silver content decreased to 50 percent). In 1687 the akçe, because of its extreme depreciation, was replaced by another unit, the qirsh. See *Qirsh*.

Altyn—A Russian coin worth 3 kopecks.

A'yan (Arab.)—Representatives of the regional elite of the Ottoman Empire ("notables").

Berat (Turk. "letter, certificate")—A charter issued by the Ottoman sultans to the patriarchs and metropolitans before their appointment to their sees. It contained a statement of the rights, duties, and privileges of a hierarch of the church.

Bilad al-Sham (Arab.)—Greater Syria, the historical-geographical region that includes the territories of modern Syria, Lebanon, Israel, the Occupied Territories of Palestine, and Jordan.

Chervonny, chervonets—The Russian designation for European gold coins of the highest grade, mainly Dutch ducats (3.4 grams).

Copts—A subethnicity composed of indigenous Egyptian Christians. Genetically, they trace back to the ancient Egyptians of the Pharaonic era; however, the Coptic identity and culture has nothing to do with the ancient Egyptian civilization. Their identity was formed in the first centuries A.D. under the influence of Christianity. In the fifth and sixth centuries, the Copts adopted the monophysite confession and created their own ecclesiastical structure parallel to the Byzantine Orthodox Church. During the course of the tenth to the fourteenth centuries, they underwent a process of Arabization. The Coptic language survived only as a sacred language of worship. In the Ottoman era, they constituted about 10 percent of the population of Egypt.

Dhimmi (Arab. *ahl al-dhimma,* "the protected")—A non-Muslim living in Muslim lands and of an abject social status.

Diptych—The list of people commemorated during church services.

Divan (Arab. *diwan*)—The council of senior officials under the emperor in advisory, judicial, or legislative capacity.

Dragoman ("translator")—1. An official in the patriarchate in charge of relations with the secular Muslim authorities and in charge of organizing pilgrims. 2. The grand dragoman of the Sublime Porte was a high-ranking official in the office of external relations of the Ottoman state. Until the Greek uprising of 1821, those appointed to the post were Phanariot Greeks. 3. In the diplomatic practice of the nineteenth century, an official in a consulate or embassy who as a rule was locally born and who served as a mediator for a diplomatic representative.

Druze—An extreme Shiite sect, established in the eleventh century in the Lebanese mountains. The Druze doctrine combines elements of Islam, Christianity, Judaism, and Zoroastrianism. They are perceived as heretics by Sunni Muslims. In the Ottoman period, the Druze emirs and sheikhs controlled a significant part of Mount Lebanon.

Efimok—The Russian name for a silver European thaler (28–32 grams). Since 1655, it was worth 64 kopecks.

Eyalet (*pashalik*)—The basic administrative unit in the Ottoman Empire. From the 1830s on, it was replaced by the term "vilayet."

Firman—A sultan's decree.

Grivna, grivennik—A Russian silver coin worth 10 kopecks. It was minted from 1701.

Hajj (Arab.)—A pilgrimage. The term was applied equally to Muslim and Christian visitations to holy places. The person who has made the pilgrimage added the prefix "hajj" ("hajji") to his name.

Qadi (Arab.)—A *shari'a* judge.

Kaffar—The duties levied from Christian pilgrims for traversing the Empire's roads and visiting the holy places.

Qaimaqam (Arab. *qa'im maqam* "deputy")—An officer who manages provinces in the absence of the governor.

Qassis, qass (Arab.)—A hieromonk or priest without a parish. See *Khuri*.

Khuri (Arab.)—A parish priest.

Kakhya (Turk. *kekhaya-bey*)—A chief manager, the majordomo.

Levok—The Slavicized name for the Ottoman coin called the *aslani qurush* (*esedi qurush*), literally, "lion qurush" ("lev" means "lion" in Russian). It was minted with the image of a lion modeled on Western European thalers.

Litany—A series of supplicatory petitions proclaimed in the course of church services.

Logothete—An official of the patriarchate who oversaw the church economic affairs.

Maronites—A subethnicity of Lebanese Christians who originally professed the Monothelete doctrine, and then in the twelfth to sixteenth centuries, were turned towards the union with Rome. The historical center of Maronite settlement was the northernmost foothills of the Lebanese mountains (Jubayl, Batroun, Jubbat Bsharri). In the Ottoman period, the Maronites colonized the more southern mountainous region of Lebanon (Keserwan and areas of the Chouf), and a large community of Maronites emerged in Aleppo. In contrast with the majority of other Middle Eastern Christians, the Maronites had their own military and political elite, a "feudal" aristocracy, which actively participated in the struggle for control of Mount Lebanon. The Druze Shihab dynasty, which dominated Lebanon from the eighteenth century until the first half of the nineteenth century, relied on the support of Maronite clans. In the middle of the eighteenth century, part of the Shihab clan converted to Maronite Christianity.

Monophysites (Greek. *mone physis* "one nature")—Adherents of a religious doctrine that postulates that after the Incarnation, Christ had one, composite divine-human nature. The radical form of this doctrine (eutychianism) emerged in the first half of the fifth century and was condemned at the Council of Chalcedon in 451 after which the Monophysites split from the dominant Orthodox Church of the Byzantine Empire and formed their own ecclesiastical bodies. The Armenian Apostolic Church, the Syriac Jacobite Church, Coptic, Ethiopic, and some other churches belong to the commonwealth of monophysite churches.

Monotheletes (Greek. *monos* "one single" and *thelema* "will")—Adherents of a religious doctrine adopted in the 630s by the Byzantine Emperor Heraclius with the aim of reconciling the Orthodox and the Monophysites. Monotheletes recognize the presence of two natures in Christ, divine and human, and only one divine will. This confession was condemned at the Sixth Ecumenical Council. The adherents of Monotheletism in the Syro-Lebanese region formed their own church and later formed the subethnicity of the Maronites. In the twelfth century, the Maronite church accepted the union with Rome which had finally solidified by the sixteenth century.

Mulk (Arab.)—Privately owned property.

Mutasallim (Arab. "ruler")—An Ottoman administrative position; the deputy of a *wali* in his absence; the term often was used to mean the governor of a city.

Nestorians—Adherents of a religious doctrine which formed in the beginning of the fifth century and professed the existence of two natures in Christ after the Incarnation, the divine and the human, with each one having its own hypostasis (concrete manifestation) and united in one person of Christ. After the condemnation of Nestorianism at the Council of Ephesus in 431, the Nestorians migrated from Byzantium to the Sasanian Empire, where their doctrine received support from the Christian communities of Mesopotamia. At the end of the fifth century, they united to form the self-governing Church of the East.

Para—A small silver coin, 1/40 of a qirsh. In the sixteenth century, in Syria, it was worth 2 akçe, and in the seventeenth century, it was worth 4 akçe. During the sixteenth to eighteenth centuries, the value of the para continuously fell because of inflation and the debasement of coinage. In 1689, a para in circulation had a weight of 0.689 grams (70 percent silver), and by the end of eighteenth century, the weight of a para had fallen to 0.308 and the content of silver in it was 37 percent.

Pasha—The title of the highest dignitaries in the Ottoman Empire. It was awarded to viziers and provincial governors.

Pashalik—See Eyalet.

Piaster—The same as a qirsh (qurush).

Purse—A monetary unit. In the seventeenth century, it was worth 40,000 akçe; later it was worth 50,000 akçe.

Qirsh, qurush (Arab. from the Slavic "grosh")—An Ottoman silver coin worth 40 para. In the middle of the seventeenth century, it was equivalent to 80 akçe, and at the end of seventeenth century, it was worth 120 akçe.

Raya (Arab. *ra'aya* "flock")—The tax-paying population of the Ottoman Empire. In European historiography, it was perceived as a derogatory name for Ottoman Christians.

Sanjak (Turk.)—An administrative unit of the province (eyalet). Governed by the sanjak-bey.

Sarraf—A moneychanger, banker, moneylender.

Shammas (Arab.)—A deacon.

Shari'a (Arab.)—The set of regulations in Islamic law.

Sheikh (Arab. *shaykh* "elder")—The head of a tribe or community; honorary title.

Syngelos, protosyngelos—The manager of patriarchal affairs. Often the syngeloi became the successors to the patriarchs.

Syriac Jacobites, Jacobites—The community of Syriac Monophysites. They are named for the bishop Jacob Baradaeus, the spiritual leader of the Monophysites in the sixth century. In the Middle Ages, the Syriac Jacobite community was sizable and prosperous, but in the Ottoman period, it was considerably reduced and went into a deep decline. The core settlement of the Syriac Jacobites was the hilly region of Tur Abdin with its center in the city of Mardin on the watershed in the middle of the Tigris and Euphrates. Separate groups of Syriac Jacobites lived in Aleppo, Homs, and villages in central Syria.

Thaler—The same as a qirsh, piaster, levok; a silver coin worth 40 para.

The Sublime Porte (Ott. *Bab-i 'ali*)—The name of the central apparatus of power in the Ottoman Empire.

Vizier (Arab. *wazir*)—The highest dignitary of the Ottoman Empire, a member of the apparatus of the central government with the rank of three-tailed pasha. Many provincial governors took on the title vizier. In European and Russian literature, it is often used as a synonym for the term *sadrazam* (grand vizier), the head of the apparatus of the central government.

Wakil (Arab.)—A deputy.

Wali (Arab., Turk. *beylerbey*)—A deputy, provincial governor (of an eyalet or pashalik) with the title of pasha.

Waqf—Land and other property of religious organizations given to them for charitable purposes and eligible for tax benefits.

BIBLIOGRAPHY

ARCHIVES AND MANUSCRIPT COLLECTIONS

AVPRI—Arkhiv vneshnei politiki Rossiiskoi imperii [The Archive of Foreign Policy of the Russian Empire]
  Fond 89. "Snosheniia Rossii s Turtsiei" [Russian-Turkish Relations].
  Fond 90. "Konstantinopolskaia missiia" [Mission in Constantinople].

IVR RAN—Institut vostochnykh rukopisei RAN, St Petersburg [Russian Academy of Sciences, Institute of Oriental Manuscripts, St Petersburg]

RGADA—Rossiiskii Gosudarstvennyi Arkhiv Drevnikh Aktov [Russian State Archive of Ancient Acts]
  Fond 27. "Prikaz Tainykh diel." [Office of Secret Affairs].
  Fond 52. "Grecheskie diela" [Greek Affairs].
  Fond 1608. "G. A. Murkos."

RNB—Ar. n. s. Rossiiskaia Nationalnaia Biblioteka (St Petersburg). Rukopisnyi otdel. Arabskaia novaia seriia. [Russian National Library (St Petersburg). Department of Manuscripts. New Arabic Series].

SPBF ARAN—Sankt-peterburgskii filial arkhiva Rosiiskoi Akademii Nauk [St Petersburg Branch of the Archive of the Russian Academy of Sciences].
  Fond 1026/1. Krachkovskii, I. Iu. No. 246. O rukopisakh Aziatskogo Muzeia [On the Manuscripts of the Asiatic Museum].

Anastasius ibn al-Mujalla. "The Polemical Epistle of the Melkite Bishop Anastasius ibn al-Mujalla to Pope Gregory XIII." Ms. V 1220 in the collection IVI RAN ff. 85–106v.

Balamand. *Al-Makhtutat al-ʿarabiyya fi al-adira al-Urthudhuksiyya al-Antakiyya fi Lubnan. Al-Juzʾ al-thani: Dayr Sayyidat al-Balamand*. Beirut: Markaz al-Dirasat al-Urthudhuksi al-Antaki, 1994.

Bantysh-Kamenskii, N. N. *Reestry Grecheskim dielam Moskovskogo arkhiva Kollegii inostrannykh diel*. Moscow: Indrik, 2001.

Beirut Bibliothèque Orientale—Louis Cheikho. "Al-Makhtutat al-ʿArabiyya fi khizanat kulliyyatina al-sharqiyya." *Al-Mashriq* 7 (1904): 33–38, 73–79, 122–128, 276–283, 331–336, 487–490, 676–682, 1066–1072.

Damascus. *Al-Makhtutat al-ʿarabiyya fi maktabat Batriyarkiyyat Antakiya wa-Saʾir al-Mashriq lil-Rum al-Urthudhuks*. Beirut: Markaz al-Dirasat al-Urthudhuksi al-Antaki, 1988.

Dayr al-Harf. "Wasf makhtutat Dayr al-Qaddis Jawurjiyus Dayr al-Harf." In *Al-Makhtutat al-ʿrabiyya fi al-adira al-Urthudhuksiyya al-Antakiyya fi Lubnan*. al-Juzʾ al-Awwal. Beirut: Markaz al-Dirasat al-Urthudhuksi al-Antaki, 1991.

Hama. "Mutraniyyat Hama: Makhtutat Abrashiyyat Hama." In *al-Makhtutat al-ʿarabiyya fi Abrashiyyat Hums wa-Hama wal-Ladhiqiyya lil-Rum al-Urthudhuks*. Beirut: Qism al-tawthiq wal-dirasat al-Antakiyya, Jamiʿat al-Balamand, 1994.

Hamatoura. "Wasf makhtutat Dayr Sayyidat Hamatura Kusba." In *Al-Makhtutat al-ʿrabiyya fi al-adira al-Urthudhuksiyya al-Antakiyya fi Lubnan*. al-Juzʾ al-Awwal. Beirut: Markaz al-Dirasat al-Urthudhuksi al-Antaki, 1991.

Homs. "Mutraniyyat Homs: Makhtutat Abrashiyyat Homs." In *Al-Makhtutat al-ʿrabiyya fi al-adira al-Urthudhuksiyya al-Antakiyya fi Lubnan*. al-Juzʾ al-Awwal. Beirut: Markaz al-Dirasat al-Urthudhuksi al-Antaki, 1991.

Kafr Buhum. "Wasf makhtutat Abrashiyyat Hama." In *al-Makhtutat al-ʿarabiyya fi Abrashiyyat Hums wa-Hama wal-Ladhiqiyya lil-Rum al-Urthudhuks*. Beirut: Qism al-tawthiq wal-dirasat al-Antakiyya, Jamiʿat al-Balamand, 1994.

Khalidov, A. B., ed. *Arabskie rukopisi Instituta Vostokovedeniia AN SSSR. Kratkii Katalog*. Moscow: Nauka, 1986.

Lattakia. "Makhtutat Abrashiyyat al-Ladhiqiyya." In *al-Makhtutat al-ʿarabiyya fi Abrashiyyat Hums wa-Hama wal-Ladhiqiyya lil-Rum al-Urthudhuks*. Beirut: Qism al-tawthiq wal-dirasat al-Antakiyya, Jamiʿat al-Balamand, 1994.

Macarius ibn al-Zaʿim. "Bishops and Eparchies of the Antiochian Church." Ms. V 1227 in the collection IVR RAN.

Mar Elian al-Homsi. "Makhtutat Abrashiyyat Hums." In *al-Makhtutat al-ʿarabiyya fi Abrashiyyat Hums wa-Hama wal-Ladhiqiyya lil-Rum al-Urthudhuks*. Beirut: Qism al-tawthiq wal-dirasat al-Antakiyya, Jamiʿat al-Balamand, 1994.

Mar Yuhanna Douma. "Wasf Makhtutat Dayr al-Qaddis Yuhanna al-Maʿmadan Duma." In *Al-Makhtutat al-ʿrabiyya fi al-adira al-Urthudhuksiyya al-Antakiyya fi Lubnan*. al-Juzʾ al-Awwal. Beirut: Markaz al-Dirasat al-Urthudhuksi al-Antaki, 1991.

Mhardeh. "Makhtutat Abrashiyyat Hama." In *al-Makhtutat al-'arabiyya fi Abrashiyyat Hums wa-Hama wal-Ladhiqiyya lil-Rum al-Urthudhuks*. Beirut: Qism al-tawthiq wal-dirasat al-Antakiyya, Jami'at al-Balamand, 1994.

Monastery of St Demetrius. "Wasf Makhtutat Dayr al-Qaddis Dimitriyus Kusba." In *Al-Makhtutat al-'rabiyya fi al-adira al-Urthudhuksiyya al-Antakiyya fi Lubnan*. al-Juz' al-Awwal. Beirut: Markaz al-Dirasat al-Urthudhuksi al-Antaki, 1991.

Monastery of St Michael. "Wasf makhtutat Dayr al-Malak Mikha'il Buq'ata." In *Al-Makhtutat al-'rabiyya fi al-adira al-Urthudhuksiyya al-Antakiyya fi Lubnan*. al-Juz' al-Awwal. Beirut: Markaz al-Dirasat al-Urthudhuksi al-Antaki, 1991.

Morozov, D. A. *Kratkii katalog arabskikh rukopisei i dokumentov Rossiskogo Gosudarstvennogo arkhiva drevnikh aktov*. Moscow: Arkheograficheskii tsentr, 1996.

Otchet Imperatorskoi Publichnoi biblioteka. 1899.

Saydnaya—*Batriarkiyat Antakiya wa sa'ir al-Mashriq lil-Rum al-Urthudhuks: Dayr Sayyidat Saydnaya al-Batriarki. Wasf li-l-kutub wal-makhtutat*. (Damascus: NP, 1986).

Shwayya. "Wasf makhtutat Dayr al-Nabi Ilyas al-Batriyarki Shwayya." In *Al-Makhtutat al-'rabiyya fi al-adira al-Urthudhuksiyya al-Antakiyya fi Lubnan*. al-Juz' al-Awwal. Beirut: Markaz al-Dirasat al-Urthudhuksi al-Antaki, 1991.

Sijill of Jerusalem. Vol. 58, p. 385. [An act from the Sharia court of Jerusalem on the approval of Patriarch Sophronius of Jerusalem, May 1583.]

Troupeau, Gérard. *Bibliothèque Nationale. Catalogue des manuscrits arabes*. Première partie. Manuscrits chrétiens. Paris: Bibliothèque Nationale, 1972.

S.n. *Kratkii obzor sobraniia rukopisei, prinadlezhavshego preosv. ep. Porfiriiu a nyne khraniashchegosia v Imperatorskoi Publichnoi biblioteke*. St Petersburg: Tipografiia V.S. Balasheva, 1885.

PRIMARY SOURCES

'Abdallah ibn Trad al-Bayruti. *Mukhtasar tarikh al-asaqifa alladhina raqu martabat ri'asat al-kahanut al-jalila fi madinat Bayrut*, edited by Na'ila Taqi al-Din Qa'idbayh. Beirut: Dar al-Nahar, 2002.

Agrefenii. "Khozhenie arkhimandrita Agfeniia." In *Antologiia khozhenii russkikh puteshestvennikov XII-XV veka*, edited by E. I. Maleto. Moscow: Nauka, 2005.

Andrei Ignat'ev. "Puteshestvie iz Konstantinopolia v Ierusalim i Sinaiskuiu goru, nakhodivshagosia pri Rossiiskom posslanike, grafe Petre Andreeviche Tolstom, sviashchennika Andreia Ignat'eva i brata ego Stefana, v 1707 godu: Palomniki-pisateli petrovskago i poslepetrovskago vremeni ili putniki vo grad Ierusalim, pod red. Arkhimandrita Leonida." *Chteniia v Obshchestve istorii i drevnostei rossiiskikh* (1874): 27–54.

Anfim Ankhial'skii. "Rasskazy monakha Anfima Ankhial'skogo, sekretaria Sviatogrobskogo bratstva." In *Materialy dlia istorii Ierusalimskoi patriarkhii XVI-XIX v.*, edited by P. V. Bezobrazov, 325–350. 1 Vol. St Petersburg: Tipigrafiia V. Kirshbauma, 1901.

Arculf. "The Travels of Bishop Arculf in the Holy Land." In *Early Travels in Palestine: Comprising the Narratives of Arculf, Willibald, Bernard, Saewulf, Sigurd, Benjamin of Tudela, Sir John Maundeville, De La Brocquière, and Maundrell*, edited by Thomas Wright, 1–12. New York: AMS Press, 1969.

Arsenii Sukhanov. *Proskinitarii Arsenia Sukhanova: 1649–1653*, edited by N. I. Ivanovskii. St Petersburg: Tipografiia V. Kirshbauma, 1889.

Asatiani, Nodar. *Masalebi me-17 saukunis Sak'art'velos istoriisat'vis: Sak'art'velos aghceriloba shedgenili Pavle Alepoelis mier*. Tbilisi: Mecʻniereba, 1973.

Athanasius Dabbas. "Istoria Patriarhilor de Antiohia." *Biserica Ortodoxă Română* 48 (1930): 851–864, 961–972, 1039–1050, 1136–1150; 49 (1931): 15–32, 140–160.

Baumgarten, Martyn. *Posetitel' i opisatel' Sviatikh mest v trekh chastiakh sveta sostoiashchikh, ili puteshestvie Martyna Baumgartena, nemetskoi imperii dvorianina i kavaliera v Egipet, Araviiu, Palestinu i Siriiu*. St Petersburg, 1794.

Bazili, K. M. *Siriia i Palestina pod turetskim pravitel'stvom v istoricheskom i politicheskom otnosheniiakh*. 2 Vols. St Petersburg: A. E. Landau, 1875.

Bazili, K. M. *Siriia i Palestina pod turetskim pravitel'stvom v istoricheskom i politicheskom otnosheniiakh*. Moscow, 2007.

Beirut Ecclesiastical Chronicle. "Iz beirutskoi tserkovnoi letopisi XVI-XVIII vv." *Drevnosti Vostochnyia* 3, No. 1 (1907): 1–89.

Benedict IV. "Ila al-Akh al-Muwakkar Kirillus al-Antaki al-Kathuliki Batriyark al-Rum al-Malikiyya." In *Tarikh al-Sham* by Mikha'il Burayk, edited by Ahmad Ghassan Sabanu, 164–166. Damascus: Dar al-Qutayba, 1982.

Berezin, I. N., "Khristiane v Mesopotamii i Sirii." *Moskvitianin* No. 16 (1854): 129–156; No. 17 (1854): 1–28; No. 2 (1855): 17–56; No. 3 (1855): 65–88.

Berezin, I. N., "Pravoslavie i drugie khistianskie tserkvi v Turtsii."*Biblioteka dlia Chteniia* 133 (1855): 1–70.

Bernard the Wise. "The Voyage of Bernard the Wise." In *Early Travels in Palestine: Comprising the Narratives of Arculf, Willibald, Bernard, Saewulf, Sigurd, Benjamin of Tudela, Sir John Maundeville, De La Brocquière, and Maundrell*, edited by Thomas Wright, 23–31. New York: AMS Press, 1969.

Bezobrazov, P. V. *Materialy dlia biografii episkopa Porfiriia Uspenskogo*. 1–2 Vols. St Petersburg: Imp. akademiia nauk, 1910.

Buganov, V. I., and M. P. Lukichev, eds. *Posol'skaia kniga po sviaziam Rossii s Gretsiei (pravoslavnymi ierarkhami i monastyriami): 1588–1594*. Moscow: Institut istorii AN SSSR, 1988.

Cantemir, Demitrie. *The Salvation of the Wise Man and the Ruin of the World: Salah al-Hakim wa-fasad al-'alam al-dhammim, edited, translated and annotated with editor's notes and indices*, edited by Ioana Feodorov. Bucharest: Editura Academiei Române, 2006.

Cheikho, Louis. "Risala wujhat al-Rum al-Tarabulusiyyin ila al-Baba Grigoriyus al-sadis 'ashar." *Al-Mashriq* 9 (1906): 357–361.

Chrysanthos. *Istoriia i opisanie Sviatoi zemli i sviatogo grada Ierusalima: sochinenie blazhennieshago Khrisanfa, patriarkha Ierusalimskago 1728 goda*. St Petersburg: Tip. Imp. akademii nauk, 1887.

Curzon, Robert. *Visits to Monasteries in the Levant*. London: Arthur Barker, 1955.

Cyril Tannas. "Risalatan lil-batriyark Kirillus Tannas." *Al-Mashriq* 12 (1909): 706–709.

Daniel of Ephesus. *Rasskaz i puteshestvie po sviatym mestam Daniila mitropolita Efesskogo*. St Petersburg, 1884.

Daniil. *'Khozhenie' igumena Daniila v Sviatuiu zemliu v nach. XII v*. St Petersburg: Izdatel'stvo Olega Abyshko, 2007.

Dositheus. "Istoriia episkopii gory Sinaia." In *Materialy dlia istorii arkhiepiskopii Sinaiskoi gory*. 2 Vols., 1–209. St Petersburg: Tipografiia V. Kirshbauma, 1909.

Dositheus. "Neizdannye glavy istorii Ierusalimskikh patriarkhov patriarkha Dosifeia Notara." *Soobshcheniia Imperatorskago Pravoslavnago Palestinskago Obshchestva* 7 (1896): 23–42.

Dositheus. "Poslaniia ierusalimskikh patriarkhov v Gruziiu." *Trudy Kievskoi Dukhovnoi Akademii* No. 2 (1866): 157–173.

Dositheus. "Gramota Dosifeia." In *Snosheniia ierusalimskogo patriarkha Dosifeia s russkim pravitel'stvom (1669–1707)*, edited by N. F. Kapterev, 1–91. Moscow: A. I. Snegireva, 1891.

Ernst, Hans. *Die mamlukischen Sultansurkunden des Sinai-Klosters*. Wiesbaden: Otto Harrassowitz, 1960.

Eutychius of Alexandria. *Eutychii Patriarchae Alexandrini Annales*, edited by Louis Cheikho. 1–2 Vols. Paris: C. Poussielgue, 1906 and 1909.

Frescobaldi, Lionardo. *Puteshestvie vo Sviatuiu zemliu: Zapiski ital'ianskikh puteshestvennikov XIV v.* Moscow, 1982.

Gagara, Vasilii. *Zhitie i khozhdenie v Ierusalim i Egipet kazantsa Vasiliia Iakovleva Gagary 1634–1637.* St Petersburg: Tipografiia V. Kirshbauma, 1891.

Gabriel of Nazareth/Gavriil Nazaretskii. *Povest' o Sviatykh i bogoprokhodnykh mestakh sv. grada Ierusalima, pripisyvaemaia Gavriilu, Nazaretskomu arkhiepiskopu 1651 g.* St Petersburg, 1900.

Gibbenet, N. *Istoricheskoe issledovanie diela patriarkha Nikona.* Part 2. St Petersburg: Tipografiia Ministerstva vnutrennikh diel, 1884.

Grelot, Guillaume-Joseph. *A Late Voyage to Constantinople.* London: John Playford, 1683.

Grigorovich-Barsky, Vasilii. "Pis'ma peshekhodtsa Vasiliia Grigorovicha-Barskogo 1723–1746." *Russkii Arkhiv* No. 9 (1874): 513–531.

Grigorovich-Barsky, Vasilii. *Peshekhoda Vasiliia Grigorovicha-Barskago-Plaki-Albova, urozhentsa Kievskago, monakha Antiokhiiskago, puteshestvie k sviatym mestam v Evrope, Azii i Afrike nakhodiashchimsia, predpriniatoe v 1723 i okonchennoe v 1747 godu, im samim pisannoe.* St Petersburg: Izhdivenim Imperatorskoi Akademīi Nauk, 1800.

Grigorovich-Barsky, Vasilii. *Stranstviia Vasiliia Grigorovicha-Barskago po sviatym mestam Vostoka s 1723 do 1747 g.* Part 1. St Petersburg: Tipografiia V. Kirshbauma, 1885.

Guseinov, P. A. "Iz 'Khronika' Mikhaila Siriitsa: Staty 1–5." *Pis'mennye Pami-atniki Vostoka* (1973): 26–54; (1974): 11–29; (1975): 16–33; (1976–1977): 73–91; (1978): 45–55.

Ibn al-ʿAdim, Kamal al-Din. "Slivki, sniatye s istorii Khaleba." In *Iz istorii srednevekovoi Sirii: Sel'dzhukskii period*, edited by L. A. Semenova, 104–217. Moscow: Nauka, 1990.

Ignaty Smolnianin. *Khozhdenie Ignatiia Smolnianina.* St Petersburg: Tipografiia V. Kirshbauma, 1887.

Ignaty Smolnianin. Opisanie puteshestviia ottsa Ignatiia v Tsar'grad, Afonskuiu goru, Sv. zemliu i Egipet 1766–1776. St Petersburg, 1891.

Il'minskii, N. I. "Obshchii otvet bakalavra N.I. Il'minskogo za vremia prebyvaniia ego na vostoke." In *V pamiat' o Nikolae Ivanoviche Il'menskom*, 357–386. Kazan, 1892.

Ioannikii. "Sobstvennoruchnye zapiski Ioannikii, patriarkha Aleksandriiskogo, o Sinaiskikh dielakh v Egipte." In *Materialy dlia istorii arkhiepiskopii Sinaiskoi gory*, 210–263. 2 Vols. St Petersburg: Tipografiia V. Kirshbauma, 1909.

Iona. *Poviest' i skazanie o pokhozhdenii v Ierusalim i vo Tsar'grad chernogo diakona Iony Malen'kogo 1649–1652*. St Petersburg: Tipografiia V. Kirshbauma, 1895.

al-Jabarti. ʿAbd al-Rahman al-Hasan. *ʿAja'ib al-Athar fi al-Tarajim wa-l-Akhbar*. 1 Vol. Cairo, 1879.

James of Verona. "Khozhdenie ko sviatym mestam avgustinskogo monakha Iakova Veronskogo v 1355. *Soobshcheniia Imperatorskago Pravoslavnago Palestinskago Obshchestva* 7 (1896): 94–115.

John Phocas. *Ioanna Foki skazanie vkratse o gorodakh i stranakh ot Antiokhii do Ierusalima … kontsa XII v*. St Petersburg: Tipografiia V. Kirshbauma, 1889.

Kapterev, N. F. *Snosheniia Ierusalimskikh patriarkhov s russkim pravitel'stvom*. 1–2 Vols. St Petersburg: Izdatel'stvo Imp. pravoslavnago palestinskago obshchestva, 1895–1898.

Kashtanov, S. M., ed. *Rossiia i Grecheskii mir v XVI veke*. Moscow: Nauka, 2004.

Kekelidze, K. "Novootkrytyi agiologiicheskii pamiatnik ikonoborcheskoi epokhi (Zhitie sv. Romana Novogo)." *Trudy Kievskoi Dukhovnoi Akademii* (June 1910): 201–238.

Kekelidze, K. "Zhitie Petra Novogo, muchenika Kapetoliiskogo." *Khristianskii Vostok* 4, No. 1 (1916): 1–71.

Kipshidze, I. A. "Zhitie i muchenichestvo sv. Antoniia Ravakha." *Khristianskii Vostok* 2, No. 1 (1914): 54–104.

Kirakos Gandzaketsi. *Istoriia Armenii*, translated and annotated by L. A. Khanlarian. Moscow: Nauka, 1976.

Korobeinikov, Trifon. *Khozhdenie Trifona Korobeinikova 1593–1594*. St Petersburg: Tipografiia V. Kirshbauma.

Krymskii, A. E. *Pis'ma iz Livana 1896–1898*. Moscow: Nauka, 1975.

Kuchuk-Ioannesov, Kh. "Pis'mo imperatora Ioanna Tsimiskhiia k armianskomu tsariu Ashotu III." *Khristianskii Vostok* 10 (1903): 91–101.

Kuri, Sami. *Monumenta Proximi Orientis: Palestine–Liban–Syrie–Mésopotamie*. 1 Vol. (1523–1583), 2 Vol. (1583–1623). Rome: Institutum Historicum Societatis Iesu, 1989 and 1994.

Leontius. "Iz zhitiia ierusalimskogo patriarkha Leontiia." In *Ioanna Foki skazanie vkratse o gorodakh i stranakh ot Antiokhii do Ierusalima … kontsa XII v.*, xxv–xxxvii. St Petersburg: Tipografiia V. Kirshbauma, 1889.

Luk'ianov, I. "Puteshestvie v Sviatuiu zemliu sviashchennika Luk'ianova." In *Russkii Arkhiv* (1863) No. 1 cols. 21–64, No. 2 cols. 114–159, No. 3 cols. 223–264, No. 4 cols. 305–343, No. 5–6 cols. 385–415.

Macarius. "Gruziia v 17 stoletii po izobrazheniiu patriarkha Makariia." *Pravoslavnyi sobesednik* (January 1905): 111–127; (March 1905): 441–458; (May 1905): 66–93.

Macarius. "Mitropolity i eparkhii pravoslavnoi Antiokhiiskoi Tserkvi v opisanii Patriarkha Makariia III az-Zaʻima (1665 g.). Predislovie, perevod i kommentarii K. A. Panchenko." *Vestnik tserkovnoi istorii* 1–2 (25–26) (2012): 116–157.

Makarii, Hieromonk. "Put' nam ieromonakham Makariiu i Selvestru iz monastyria Vsemilostivogo spasa Novgorodka Severskago do sv. grada Ierusalima poklonitisia Grobu Gospodniu: Palomniki-pisateli petrovskago i poslepetrovskago vremeni ili putniki vo grad Ierusalim, pod red. Arkhimandrita Leonida." *Chteniia v Obshchestve istorii i drevnostei rossiiskikh* No. 3 (1874): 1–26.

Matthew of Edessa. *Armenia and the Crusades: Tenth to Twelfth Centuries: The Chronicle of Matthew of Edessa*. Lanham, MD: University Press of America, 1993.

Maundrell, Henry. "The Journey of Henry Maundrell, from Aleppo to Jerusalem, A.D. 1697." In *Early Travels in Palestine: Comprising the Narratives of Arculf, Willibald, Bernard, Saewulf, Sigurd, Benjamin of Tudela, Sir John Maundeville, De La Brocquière, and Maundrell*, edited by Thomas Wright, 383–512. New York: AMS Press, 1969.

Melety. *Puteshestvie vo Ierusalim Sarovskiia obshchezhitel'nyia pustyni ieromonakha Meletiia v 1793 i 1794 gody*. Moscow: Tipografiia A. Rieshetnikova, 1798.

Michael the Syrian. *Chronique de Michel le Syrien*, edited by Jean-Baptiste Chabot. 3 Vols. Paris: Ernest Leroux, 1905.

Mikha'il Breik [Burayk]. "Spisok Antiokhiiskikh patriarkhov." *Trudy Kievskoi Dukhovnoi Akademii* No. 6 (1874): 346–457.

Mikha'il Breik. *Al-Haqa'iq al-Wafiyya fi Tarikh Batarikat al-Kanisa al-Antakiyya*, edited by Na'ila Taqi al-Din Qa'idbayh. Beirut: Dar al-Nahar, 2006.

Mikha'il Breik. *Tarikh al-Sham 1720–1782*, edited by Ahmad Ghassan Sabanu. Damascus: Dar al-Qutayba, 1982.

al-Munayyir, Hananiya. "Kitab Hananiya al-Munayyir al-Khati" In *Tarikh Ahmad Basha al-Jazzar*, edited by Haydar Ahmad Shihab, 351–516. Beirut: Maktabat Antwan, 1955.

Murav'ev, A. N. "Puteshestvie k sviatym mestam v 1830 godu." In *Sviatye mesta vblizi i izdaleka: putevye zametki russkikh pisatelei 1–i pol. XIX v.*, 89–233. Moscow: Shkola-Press, 1995.

Nechaev, Matvei. "Kniga Khozhdenie vo sviatyi grad Ierusalim Iaroslavtsa Tolchkovskoi slobody posadskogo cheloveka Matveia Gavrilova syna Nechaeva." *Varshavskie universitetskie izvestiia* No. 1 (1875): 1–34.

Neophytus of Cyprus. "Dvadtsatiletie, ili prodolzhenie vsego sluchivshegosia v pravoslavnoi ierusalimskoi tserkvi s 1821 g. do nastoiashchego 1841 g." In *Materialy dlia istorii Ierusalimskoi patriarkhii XVI-XIX v.*, edited by P.V. Bezobrazov, 121–170. 1 Vol. St Petersburg: Tipigrafiia V. Kirshbauma, 1901.

Neophytus of Cyprus. "Ob arabo-katolikakh, ili uniatakh." *Materialy dlia istorii Ierusalimskoi patriarkhii XVI-XIX v.*, edited by P. V. Bezobrazov, 171–187. 1 Vol. St Petersburg: Tipigrafiia V. Kirshbauma, 1901.

Neophytus of Cyprus. "Rasskaz Neofita Kiprskago o nakhodiashchikhsia v Ierusalime khristianskikh veroispovedaniiakh i o ssorakh ikh mezhdu soboi po povodu mest pokloneniia." *Materialy dlia istorii Ierusalimskoi patriarkhii XVI-XIX v.*, edited by P. V. Bezobrazov, 2–119. 1 Vol. St Petersburg: Tipigrafiia V. Kirshbauma, 1901.

Nicephorus Bryennius. *Istoricheskie zapiski Nikifora Vrienniia (976–1087)*. Moscow: Posev, 1997.

Ni'ma ibn al-Khuri Tuma. "Bayan al-mawaqi' wal-idtihadat allati jarat 'ala ta'ifat al-Rum al-Kathulikiyyin bi-Halab." In *Tarikh al-Sham* by Mikha'il Burayk, edited by Ahmad Ghassan Sabanu, 138–155. Damascus: Dar al-Qutayba, 1982.

Norov, Avraam. Ierusalim i Sinai: Zapiski vtorogo puteshestviia na Vostok A.S. Norova. St Petersburg: Izdatel'stvo Polivanova, 1878.

Norov, Avraam. *Puteshestvie po Sv. Zemle v 1835 g. Avraama Norova*. St Petersburg: Tip. III otdieleniia Sobstvennoi E.I.V. kantseliarii, 1844.

Palmer, Andrew, et al. *The Seventh Century in West-Syrian Chronicles*. Liverpool: Liverpool University Press, 1993.

Panchenko, K. A. "Mitropolity i eparkhii pravoslavnoi Antiokhiiskoi tserkvi v opisanii patriarkha Makariia az-Za'ima (1665 g.): Text i Kommentarii." *Vestnik tserkovnoi istorii* 1–2, No. 25–26 (2012): 116–157.

Papadopulo-Keramevs, A. *Muchenichestvo shestidesiati novykh sviatykh muchenikov, postravdashikh vo Sviatom grade Khrista Boga nashego pod vladychestvom arabov*. St Petersburg: Pravoslavnyi Palestinskii Sbornik, 1892.

Papadopulo-Keramevs, A. *Paisiia Agiapostolita mitropolita rodskogo opisanie Sv. gory Sinaiskoi i eia okrestnostei v stikhakh, napisannoe mexhdu 1577 i 1592 gg.* St Petersburg: Tipografiia V. Kirshbauma, 1891.

Papadopulo-Keramevs, A. I. *Opisanie sviatykh mest bezymiannogo kontsa XIV v.* St Petersburg: *Pravoslavnyi Palestinski Sbornik*, 1890.

Papadopulo-Keramevs. *Proskinitarii po Ierusalimu i prochim sviatim mestam 1608 i 1624 g.* St Petersburg: Tipografiia V. Kirshbauma, 1900.

Parthenius the Athenian. "Rasskaz Parfeniia Afinianina, mitropolita Kesarii Palestinskoi, o raspriakh mezhdu pravoslavnymi i armianami." In *Materialy dlia istorii Ierusalimskoi patriarkhii XVI-XIX v.*, edited by P. V. Bezobrazov, 189–275. 1 Vol. St Petersburg: Tipigrafiia V. Kirshbauma, 1901.

Paul of Aleppo. *Puteshestvie Antiokhiiskogo patriarkha Makariia v Rossiiu v polovine XVII veka, opisannoe ego synom arkhidiakonom Pavlom Aleppskim*, translated by Georgii Murkos. 1–5 Vols. Moscow: Izdatel'stvo Moskovskogo Univesiteta, 1896–1900.

Pleshcheev, S. *Dnevnikovye zapiski puteshestviia iz arkhipelagskogo Rossii prinadlezhashchego ostrova Parosa v Siriiu i k dostopamiatnym mestam v predelakh Ierusalima nakhodiashchimsia s kratkoiu istoreiu Alibeevykh zavoe-vanii Rossiskogo flota leitenanta Sergeia Pleshcheeva v iskhode 1772 leta.* St Petersburg: 1773.

Polosin, V. V. "Zapiska Pavla Aleppskogo o postavlenii mitropolitov antiokhiiskim patriarkhom Makariem. *Khristianskii Vostok* 2, No. 8 (2000): 239–342.

Popov, A. P. *Mladshii Grigorovich: Novootkrytyi palomnik po sv. mestam XVIII veka.* Kronshtadt: Tipografiia gazeta Kotlin, 1911.

Porphyry Uspenskii. *Kniga bytiia moego.* 1–8 Vols. St Petersburg: Izd. Imp. akademii nauk, 1894–1902.

Porphyry Uspenskii. *Pervoe puteshestvie v Sinaiskii monastyr' v 1845 g. arkhimandrita Porfiriia Uspenskogo.* St Petersburg: Tipografiia Imp. akademii nauk, 1856.

Porphyry Uspenskii. "Siriiskaia tserkov'." *Zhurnal ministerstva narodnogo prosveshcheniia* 67 (1850): 117–144.

Porphyry Uspenskii. "Skazanie o Siriiskoi Unii." *Trudy Kievskoi Dukhovnoi Akademii* 9 (1874): 491–553.

Porphyry Uspenskii. *Vostok Khristianskii: Aleksandriiskaia patriarkhiia: Sbornik materialov, issledovanii i zapisok, otnosiashchikhsia do istorii Aleksandriiskoi patriarkhii.* St Petersburg: Izd. Imp. Akademii nauk, 1898.

Porphyry Uspenskii. *Vtoroe puteshestvie arkhimandrita Porfiriia Uspenskogo v Sinaiskii monastyr' v 1850 godu.* St Petersburg: Tipografiia morskago kadetskago korpusa, 1856.

Pozniakov, V. *Khozhdenie kuptsa Pozniakova po sviatym mestam Vostoka 1558–1561.* St Petersburg: Tipigrafiia V. Kirshbauma, 1887.

Procopius Nazianzen, "Popiraemii Ierusalim." In *Materialy dlia istorii Ierusalimskoi patriarkhii XVI-XIX v.*, edited by P. V. Bezobrazov, 131–350. 2 Vols. St Petersburg: Tipigrafiia V. Kirshbauma, 1904.

Prokof'ev, N. I., "Khozhdenie Zosimy v Tsargrad, Afon i Palestinu." *Voprosy Russkoi Literatury* 455 (1971): 12–42.

Radziwiłł, Mikołaj. Puteshestvie ko sviatym mestam i v Egipet kniazia Nikolaia Khristofora Radzivila. St Petersburg: 1787.

Rozen, V. R. *Imperator Vasilii Bolgaroboitsa: Izvlecheniia iz letopisi Iakh'i Antiokhiiskogo.* St Petersburg: Tipografiia Imp. Akademii nauk, 1883.

Sabanu, Ahmad Ghassan, ed. *Tarikh hawadith al-Sham wa-Lubnan aw Tarikh Mikha'il al-Dimashqi 1782–1841 li-mu'allif majhul.* Dimashq: Dar al-Qutayba, 1981.

Savva Nemanich. *Puteshestvie sv. Savvy, arkhiepiskopa Serbskogo,* edited by Archimandrite Leonid. St Petersburg, 1884.

Serapion. "Putnik, ili puteshestvie vo Sviatuiu Zemliu Matroninskago monastyria inoka Serapiona: Palomniki-pisateli petrovskago i poslepetrovskago vremeni ili putniki vo grad Ierusalim, pod red. Arkhimandrita Leonida." *Chteniia v Obshchestve istorii i drevnostei rossiiskikh* (1874): 78–128.

Simaius, Maximus. "Istoriia Ierusalimskikh patriarkhov so vremen 6 vselenskogo sobora do 1810 g." In *Materialy dlia istorii Ierusalimskoi patriarkhii XVI-XIX v.,* edited by P. V. Bezobrazov, 1–130. 2 Vols. St Petersburg: Tipigrafiia V. Kirshbauma, 1904.

Simeon Lekhatsi. *Putevye zametki.* Translated by M. O. Darbinian. Moscow: Nauka, 1965.

Solov'ev, S. "Monastyr; sv. Georgiia v Sirii." *Soobshcheniia Imperatorskago Pravoslavnago Palestinskago Obshchestva* 16 (1905): 547–555.

Theophanes the Confessor. *Letopis' vizantiitsa Feofana ot Diokletiana do tsarei Mikhaila i syna ego Feofilakta.* Moscow: V Univ. tip. (M. Katkov), 1884.

Varlaam. "Peregrinatsiia, ili putnik, v nem zhe opisuetsia put' do sviatogo grada Ierusalima i vsia sviataia mesta palestinskaia, ot ieromonakha Varlaama, byvshago tamo v 1712 g.: Palomniki-pisateli petrovskago i poslepetrovskago vremeni ili putniki vo grad Ierusalim, pod red. Arkhimandrita Leonida." *Chteniia v Obshchestve istorii i drevnostei rossiiskikh* (1874): 55–77.

Varsonofii. *Khozhdenie sviashchennoinoka Varsonofiia ko sviatomu gradu Ierusalimu v 1456 i 1461–2 g.* Moscow: Izdatel'stvo Imp. Pravoslavnago palestinskago obshchestva, 1896.

Vasilii, gost'. *Khozhdenie gostia Vasilia.* St Petersburg: Izdatel'stvo Imp. Pravoslavnago palestinskago obshchestva, 1884.

Vishenski, Ippolit. *Puteshestvie ieromonakha Ippolita Vishenskogo v Ierusalim, na Sinai i Afon.* St Petersburg: Izdatel'stvo Imp. Pravoslavnago palestinskago obshchestva, 1914.

Volney, Constantin-François. *Puteshestvie Vol'neia v Siriu i Egipet, byvshee v 1783, 1784, 1785 godakh*. 2 Vols. Moscow: Pechatano v privilegirovannoi Tipografii u F. Gippiusa, 1793.

Von Harff, Arnold. *The Pilgrimage of Arnold von Harff from Cologne, through Italy, Syria, Egypt, Arabia, Ethiopia, Nubia, Palestine, Turkey, France and Spain, which he Accomplished in the Years 1469 to 1499*. Nendeln, Liechtenstein: Kraus Reprint, 1967.

Willibald. "The Travels of Willibald." In *Early Travels in Palestine: comprising the narratives of Arculf, Willibald, Bernard, Saewulf, Sigurd, Benjamin of Tudela, Sir John Maundeville, De La Brocquière, and Maundrell*, edited by Thomas Wright, 13–22. New York: AMS Press, 1969.

Wright W. Catalogue of Syriac Manuscripts in the British Museum. T. I. L., 1870, P. 320, n. 408.

Yahya al-Antaki. *Eutychii Patriarchae Alexandrini Annales. Pars Posterior. Accedunt Annales Yahia Ibn Said Antiochensis*, edited by Louis Cheikho. Paris: C. Poussielgue, 1909.

Zayat, Habib. "Vie du patriarche melkite d'Antioche Christophore (d. 967) par le protospathaire Ibrahim b. Yuhanna: Document inédit du Xe siècle." *Proche-Orient Chrétien* 2 (1952): 11–38, 333–366.

Zev'ulf, "Puteshestvie Zevul'fa v Sviatuiu Zemliu 1102–1103 gg." In *Zhit'e i khozhden'e Daniila, Russkyia zemli igumena 1106–1108 g*. Part 2, 263–291. St Petersburg, 1885.

Zhemi, Ioann. "Antiokhiiskie patriarkhi v arabskom spiske sviashchennika Ioanna Zhemi, 1756 goda. Vostok Khristianskii: Siriia." *Trudy Kievskoi Dukhovnoi Akademii* (March 1875): 385–480.

S.n. "Al-ʿArifa al-muqaddima lil-dawla bi-intikhab Kirillus Tanas batriyarkan ʿala yad ʿUthman Basha Abu Taʾuk wazir al-Sham." In *Tarikh al-Sham* by Mikhaʾil Burayk, edited by Ahman Ghassan Sabanu, 123–131. Damascus: Dar al-Qutayba, 1982.

S.n. "Aʿmal al-diwan al-sirri Consistoire alladhi inʿaqada fi 3 Shubat sanna 1744 li-manah al-baliyum li Kirillus Tanas" In *Tarikh al-Sham* by Mikhaʾil Burayk, edited by Ahmad Ghassan Sabanu, 155–162. Damascus: Dar al-Qutayba, 1982.

S.n. "Bor'ba pravoslavnykh i latinian iz-za obladaniia Sb. mestami v. 1631/7 gg." *Soobshcheniia Imperatorskago Pravoslavnago Palestinskago Obshchestva* 10 (1899): 171–192.

S.n. "Dushespasitel'nyi rasskaz o Sv. Grobe." In *Vosem' grecheskikh opisanii Sv. mest XIV, XV i XVI vv.*, edited by Athanasios Papadopoulos-Kerameus and V.V. Latyshev, 22–38, Russian translation 162–176. St Petersburg: Tipografiia V. Kirshbaum, 1903.

S.n. "Istoricheskoe skazanie o podvizhnichestve sviatogo velikomuchenika Ilii Novogo iz iliopolitov, postradavshchego v Damaske." *Sbornik palestinskoi i siriiskoi agiologii* 1 (1907): 49–68.

S.n. "O grade Ierusalime i okrestnostiakh ego zemle obetovannoi." In *Vosem' grecheskikh opisanii Sv. mest XIV, XV i XVI vv.*, edited by Athanasios Papado- poulos-Kerameus and V.V. Latyshev, 22–38, Russian translation 242–249. St Petersburg: Tipografiia V. Kirshbaum, 1903.

S.n. "Patriarshie dokumenty (1592–1735)." In *Materialy dlia istorii arkhiepiskopii Sinaiskoi gory*. 2 Vols., 264–442. St Petersburg: Tipografiia V. Kirshbauma, 1909.

S.n. "Proskinitarii, soderzhashchii vse chudesnye znameniia, iavlennye Spasitelem nashim v sviatom gorode Ierusalime, i opisanie mestnostei." *Vosem' grecheskikh opisanii Sv. mest XIV, XV i XVI vv.*, edited by Athanasios Papadopoulos-Kerameus and V.V. Latyshev, 22–38, Russian translation 194–291. St Petersburg: Tipografiia V. Kirshbaum, 1903.

S.n. *Siriia, Livan i Palestina v pervoi polovine XIX* v. Moscow, 1991.

S.n. "Skazanie o muchenichestve sviatykh ottsov, izbiennykh varvarami sar- atsinami v velikoi lavre prepodobnogo ottsa nashego Savvy." *Sbornik palestin- skoi i siriiskoi agiologii* 1 (1907): 1–48.

Secondary Sources

Abu-Husayn, Abdul-Rahim. *Provincial Leadership in Syria 1575–1650*. Beirut: American University of Beirut, 1985.

Anichkov, V. N. "Frantsuzskaia katolicheskaia missiia na Vostoke." *Soobsh- cheniia Imperatorskago Pravoslavnago Palestinskago Obshchestva* 17 (1906): 183–202.

Antoniia/Ravakha: Kipshidze, I. A. "Zhitie i muchenichestvo sv. Antoniia Ravakha." *Khristianskii Vostok* 2, No. 1 (1914): 54–104.

Arbel, Benjamin. "Venetian Cyprus in the Muslim Levant, 1473–1570." In *Cyprus and the Crusades*, edited by Nicholas Coureas and Riley J. Smith, 159–185. Nicosia: Cyprus Research Center and SSCLE, 1995.

Arkhim. Leonid. "Serbskaia inocheskaia obshchina v Palestine." *Chteniia v imperatorskom obshchestve istorii i drevnostei rossiskikh* 3, No. 3 (1867): 42–65.

Arkhim. Leonid. "Tri stati k russkomu palestinovedeniiu." *Pravoslavnyi Pales- tinskii Sbornik* 6, No. 1 (1889).

Arkhim. Makarii (Veretennikov). "Gramota Ierusalimskogo patriarkha Germana Novgorodskomu arkhiepiskopu Makariu." In *Ierusalim v russkoi kul'ture*, edited by A. L. Batalov and Aleksei Lidov, 205–211. Moscow: Nauka, 1994.

Atiya, Aziz. *A History of Eastern Christianity*. London: Methuen, 1968.

Bacel, Paul. "ʿAbdallah Zakher." *Echos d'Orient* 9 (1908): 218–226, 281–287, 363–372.

Bakhit, Muhammad Adnan. "The Christian Population of the Province of Damascus in the Sixteenth Century." In *Christians and Jews in the Ottoman Empire: The Functioning of a Plural Society Volume 2*, edited by Benjamin Braude and Bernard Lewis, 19–66. New York: Holmes and Meier, 1982.

Bartol'd, V. V. "Islam i melkity." In *Sochineniia*, 651–658. 6 Vols. Moscow: Izdatel'stvo vostochnoi literatury, 1966.

Bartol'd, V. V. "K voprosu o franko-musul'manskikh otnosheniiakh." *Khristian-skii Vostok* 3 (1914): 263–296.

Bartol'd, V. V. "Karl Velikii i Kharun ar-Rashid." In *Sochineniia*, 342–364. 6 Vols. Moscow: Izdatel'stvo vostochnoi literatury, 1966.

Bartol'd, V. V. "Khalif Omar II i protivorechivye izvestiia o ego lichnosti." In *Sochineniia*, 504–531. 6 Vols. Moscow: Izdatel'stvo vostochnoi literatury, 1966.

Bartol'd, V. V. "Turtsiia, islam i khristianstvo." In *Sochineniia*, 413–431. 6 Vols. Moscow: Izdatel'stvo vostochnoi literatury, 1966.

Bartol'd, V. V. "Review of Lektsii po istorii Vizantii by A. A. Vasil'ev." In *Sochineniia*, 575–594. 6 Vols. Moscow: Izdatel'stvo vostochnoi literatury, 1966.

Basha, Qustantin. "Mulhaq li-silsilat matarina Sur." *Al-Mashriq* 9 (1906): 620–625.

Basha, Qustantin, and Louis Cheikho. "ʿAbdallah ibn al-Fadl al-Antaki." *Al-Mashriq* 9 (1906): 886–890, 944–953.

Bat Yeor. *Zimmii: Evrei i khristiane pod vlastiu islama*. 2 Vols. Jerusalem: Biblioteka Aliia, 1991.

Baum, Wilhelm. "The Syrian Christian Community in India and Contacts to Europe and the Mediterranean Area before the Arrival of the Portuguese." *Khristianskii Vostok* 3, No. 9 (2001): 344–353.

Baumstark, Anton. *Geschichte der Syrischen Literatur*. Bonn: A. Marcus und E. Weber, 1922.

Bezobrazov, P. V. "O snosheniiakh Rossii s Palestinoi v XIX veke." *Soobshche-niia Imperatorskago Pravoslavnago Palestinskago Obshchestva* 22 (1911): 20–52.

Boiko, K. A. *Arabskaia Istoricheskaia literatura v Egipte IX-X vv*. Moscow: Nauka, 1991.

Bol'shakov, O. G. *Istoriia Khalifata*. 3 Vols. Moscow: Nauka, 1989–2000.

Bol'shakov, O. G. "Vizantiia i khalifat v VII-X vv." In *Vizantiia mezhdu Zapa-dom i Vostokom*, 354–379. St Petersburg: Aleteiia, 2001.

Bolkhovitinov, Evgenii. *Slovar' istoricheskii o byvshikh v Rossii pisateliakh dukhovnogo china Greko-rossiiskoi tserkvi*. Moscow: Ruskii Dvor, 1995.

Botsvadze, T. D. "Rol' Rossii v gruzino-severokavkazskikh otnosheniiakh XV-XVIII vv." In *Voprosy istorii narodov Kavkaza*, 200–210. Tbilisi: Metsniereba, 1988.

Braude, Benjamin, and Bernard Lewis. "Introduction." In *Christians and Jews in the Ottoman Empire: The Functioning of a Plural Society*, 1–34. New York: Holmes and Meier, 1982.

Brett, Michael, "Al-Karaza al-Marqusiya. The Coptic Church in the Fatimid Empire." In *Egypt and Syria in the Fatimid, Ayyubid and Mamluk Eras IV: Proceedings of the 9th and 10th International Colloquium Organized at the Katholieke Universiteit Leuven in May 2000 and May 2001*, edited by Urbain Vermeulen and J. van Steenbergen, 33–60. Orientalia Lovaniensia 140, Louvain: Peeters, 2005.

Brett, Michael. "Population and Conversion to Islam in Egypt in the Medieval Period." In *Egypt and Syria in the Fatimid, Ayyubid and Mamluk Eras IV: Proceedings of the 9th and 10th International Colloquium Organized at the Katholieke Universiteit Leuven in May 2000 and May 2001*, edited by Urbain Vermeulen and J. van Steenbergen, 1–32. Orientalia Lovaniensia 140, Louvain: Peeters, 2005.

Briusova, V. G. "Ikony russkikh ikonopistsev XVII veka na Blizhnem Vostoke." *Pravoslavnyi Palestinskii Sbornik* 31, No. 94 (1992): 129–130.

Brodel', F. [Fernand Braudel]. *Sredizemnoe more i sredizemnomorskii mir v epokhu Filippa II*. 2 Vols. Moscow: Iazyki Slavianskoi Kultury, 2003.

Brooks, E. W. "The Sources of Theophanes and the Syriac Chroniclers." *Byzantinische Zeitschrift* 15, No. 2 (January 1906): 578–587.

Browne, Laurence E. *The Eclipse of Christianity in Asia from the Time of Muhammad till the Fourteenth Century*. New York: Fertig, 1967.

Burns, Ross. *Damascus: A History*. New York: Routledge, 2005.

Burns, Ross. *Monuments of Syria: An Historical Guide*. New York: I. B. Tauris, 1999.

Charon, Cyrille. "Al-Usqufiyyat al-Manuta bi-Kursiyy Sur: Tarabulus." *Al-Mashriq* 10 (1907): 401–407.

Charon, Cyrille. "Silsilat Asaqifat al-Malikiyyin: Qara." *Al-Mashriq* 13 (1910): 328–331.

Charon, Cyrille. "Silsilat Asaqifat Dimashq al-Malikiyyin." *Al-Machriq* 12 (1909): 912–920.

Charon, Cyrille, and Louis Cheikho, "Usqufiyyat al-Rum al-Kathulik fi Bayrut." *Al-Mashriq* 8 (1905): 193–202.

Cheikho, Louis. "Bi-Ghibtat al-Sayyid al-Batriyark Kirillus al-Thamin." *Al-Mashriq* 5 (1902): 625–630.

Cheikho, Louis. "Khabar Iqunat Saydnayya al-ʿAjiba." *Al-Mashriq* 8 (1905): 461–467.

Cheikho, Louis. "Mikha'il al-Bahri." *Al-Mashriq* 3 (1900): 10–22.

Cheikho, Louis. "Min Rayaq ila Hama." *Al-Mashriq* 5 (1902): 951–952.

Cheikho, Louis. "Niqulawus al-Sayigh." *Al-Mashriq* 6 (1903): 97–111.

Cheikho, Louis. "Tarikh Fann al-Tibaʿa fi al-Mashriq." *Al-Mashriq* 3 (1900): 78–85, 174–180, 251–257, 355–362, 501–508.

Chentsova, V. G. "Dionisii Ivirit i russko-moldavskie peregovory 1656 g." In *Chteniia pamiati prof. N.F. Kaptereva: Materialy*, edited by B.F. Fonkich, 58–62. Moscow: Institut vseobshchei istorii RAN, 2003.

Chentsova, V. G. "Gramota Antiokhiiskogo patriarkha Ioakima VI 1594 g.: neskol'ko zamechanii po povodu novogo izdaniia." *Paleoslavica* 17, No. 1 (2009): 280–310.

Chentsova, V. G. *Ikona Iverskoi Bogomateri (Ocherki istorii otnoshenii grecheskoi tserkvi s Rossiei v sredine XVII veka po dokumentam RGADA)*. Moscow: Indrik, 2010.

Chentsova, V. G. "Istochniki fonda 'Snosheniia Rossii s Gretsii' Rossiiskogo Gosudarstvennogo Arkhiva Drevnikh Aktov po istorii mezhdunarodnykh otnoshenii v Vostochnoi i Iugo-Vostochnoi Evrope v 50–e gg. XVII v." In *Russkaia i ukrainskaia diplomatiia v Evrazii: 50–e gody XVII veka*, edited by B. N. Floria, 151–179. Moscow: Institut slavianovedeniia RAN, 2000.

Chentsova, V. G. "Mitra Paisiia Ierusalimskogo—ne prislannyi russkomu gosudariu venets 'tsariia Konstantina'." In *Patriarkh Nikon i ego vremia*, edited by E. M. Iukhimenko, 11–39. Moscow: Gosudarstvennyi istoricheskii muzei, 2004.

Chesnokova, N. P. "Russkaia blagotvoritel'nost' pravoslavnomu Vostoku v sredine XVII v." *Kapterevskie chteniia* 7 (2009): 163–181.

Clogg, Richard. "The Greek Millet in the Ottoman Empire." In *Christians and Jews in the Ottoman Empire: The Functioning of a Plural Society Volume 1*, edited by Benjamin Braude and Bernard Lewis, 185–207. New York: Holmes and Meier, 1982.

Cohen, Amnon. "On the Realities of the Millet System: Jerusalem in the Sixteenth Century." In *Christians and Jews in the Ottoman Empire: The Functioning of a Plural Society Volume 2*, edited by Benjamin Braude and Bernard Lewis, 7–18. New York: Holmes and Meier, 1982.

Cohen, Amnon, and Bernard Lewis. *Population and Revenue in the Towns of Palestine in the Sixteenth Century*. Princeton, NJ: Princeton University Press, 1978.

Dabbas, Antwan. *Tarikh al-Tibaʿa al-ʿarabiyya fi al-Mashriq*. Beirut: Dar al-Nahar, 2008.

Destunis, G. *Rasskaz i puteshestvie po sviatym mestam Daniila metropolitan Efesskogo*. St Petersburg: Pravoslavnyi Palestinskii Obshchestvo, 1884.

Dmitrievskii, A. A. "Drevneishie patriarshie Tipikony ierusalimskii (sviato-grobskii) i konstantinopolskii (Velikoi tserkvi). Gl. 2." *Trudy Kievskoi Dukhovnoi Akademii* (January 1901): 34–86.

Dmitrievskii, A. A. "Priezd v Astrakhan' vostochnikh patriarkhov Paisiia Aleksandriiskogo i Makariia Antiokhiiskogo i sviazannoe s nim uchrezhdenie zdes' mitropolii." *Trudy Kievskoi Dukhovnoi Akademii* (March 1904): 317–358.

Dolinina, A. A. *Nevol'nik dolga*. St Petersburg: Peterburgskoe Vostokovedenie, 1994.

Eckenstein, Lina. *A History of Sinai*. London: Society for Promoting Christian Knowledge, 1921.

El-Isa, Zuhayr. "Earthquake Studies of Some Archaeological Sites in Jordan." *Studies in the History and Archaeology of Jordan* 2 (1982): 229–235.

Eremeev, D. E., and M. S. Meier. *Istoriia Turtsii v srednie veka i novoe vremia*. Moscow: Izdatel'stvo Moskovskogo Universiteta, 1992.

Fargues, Philippe. "The Arab Christians of the Middle East: A Demographic Perspective." In *Christian Communities in the Arab Middle East: The Challenge of the Future*, edited by Andrea Pacini, 48–66. Oxford: Clarendon Press, 1998.

Feodorov, Ioana. "The Edition and Translation of Christian Arabic Texts of the 17th–18th Centuries Referring to Romanians." *Revue des Etudes Sud-Est Européennes* 43 (2005): 253–273.

Feodorov, Ioana. "The Romanian Contribution to Arabic Printing." In *Impact de l'imprimerie et rayonnement intellectuel des Pays Roumains*, edited by Elena Siupiur, Zamfira Mihail, et al. 41–61. Bucharest: Biblioteca Bucureştilor, 2009.

Fil'shtinskii, I. M. *Istoriia arabov i khalifata (750–1517 gg.)*. Moscow: Muravei – Gaid, 1999.

Finkelstein, Israel. "Byzantine Monastic Remains in Southern Sinai." *Dumbarton Oaks Papers* 39 (1985): 39–79.

Floria, B. N. "Rossiia, stambul'skie greki i nachalo Kandiiskii voiny." *Slaviane i ikh sosedi* 6 (1996): 174–187.

Foma (Dibu-Maluf). "Emesskaia eparkhiia v Sirii." *Soobshcheniia Imperatorskago Pravoslavnago Palestinskago Obshchestva* 26 (1915): 325–349.

Fonkich, B. L. "Ioann Sakulis: Stranichka iz istorii uchastiia grekov v 'Diele patriarkha Nikona'." In *Grecheskie rukopisi i dokumenty v Rossii*, 188–197. Moscow: Indrik 1997.

Fonkich, B. L. "Ioannikii Grek (K istorii grecheskoi kolonii v Moskve pervoi treti XVII v.)." *Ocherki feodal'noi Rossii* 10 (2006): 85–110.

Fonkich, B. L. "O date konchiny Pavla Aleppskogo." *Ocherki feodal'noi Rossii* 13 (2009): 289–292.

Fonkich, B. L. "Pis'mo Dionisiia Ivirita Paisiiu Ligaridu." In *Grecheskie rukopisi i dokumenty v Rossii*, 217–229. Moscow: Indrik 1997.

Fonkich, B. L. "Popytka sozdaniia grecheskoi tipografii v Moskve v kontse XVII v." *Rossiia i Khristianskii Vostok* 2–3 (2004): 465–471.

Fonkich, B. L. "Sinaiskii pomiannik." *Rossiia i Khristianskii Vostok* 1 (1997): 259–263.

Fotić, A. "Obnova srpskog manastira sv. Savve Osvećenog kod Jerusalima 1613 godine." *Balcanica* 21 (1990): 225–238.

Frantsuzov, S. A. "Pripiska Arabskoi rukopisnoi Biblii (D 226) iz sobraniia Instituta vostochnykh rukopisei RAN kak istoricheskii istochnik." *Vestnik PSTGU* Ser. III. Filologiia 3 (17) (2009): 38–57.

Freijat, Fayez. "Batarikat Antakiya al-Malikiyyun fi al-qarnayn al-Sadisa 'Ashar wal-Sabi'a 'Ashar." *al-Masarra* 84 (1998): 26–32.

Frenkel, Yehoshu'a. "Mar Saba during the Mamluk and Ottoman Periods." In *The Sabaite Heritage in the Orthodox Church from the Fifth Century to the Present*, edited by Joseph Patrich, 111–116. Leuven: Peeters, 2001.

Girard, Aurélien. "Entre croisade et politique culturelle au Levant: Rome et l'union des Chrétiens syriens (premiere moitié du XVII siècle)." In *Papato e politica internazionale nella prima eta moderna,* edited by Maria Antonietta Visceglia, 419–437. Rome: Viella, 2013.

Grabar, Oleg. *City in the Desert: Qasr al-Hayr East: An Account of the Excavations Carried out at Qasr al-Hayr East.* Cambridge, MA: Harvard University Press, 1978.

Graf, Georg. *Geschichte der christlichen arabischen Literatur.* Vol. 3. Vatican City: Biblioteca Apostolica Vaticana, 1949.

Griffith, Sidney. "Anthony David of Baghdad, Scribe and Monk of Mar Saba: Arabic in the Monasteries of Palestine." In his *Arabic Christianity in the Monasteries of Ninth-Century Palestine.* Aldershot: Variorum, 1992, Essay XI, 7–19.

Griffith, Sidney. "The Arabic Account of 'Abd al-Masih an-Nagrani al-Ghassani." In *Arabic Christianity in the Monasteries of Ninth-Century Palestine.* Aldershot: Variorum, 1992, Essay X, 331–74.

Griffith, Sidney. "Greek into Arabic: Life and Letters in the Monasteries of Palestine in the Ninth Century: the Example of the *Summa Theologica Arabica.*" In *Arabic Christianity in the Monasteries of Ninth-Century Palestine.* Aldershot: Variorum, 1992, Essay VIII, 117–138.

Griffith, Sidney. "The *Life of Theodore of Edessa*: History, Hagiography and Religious Apologetics in Mar Saba Monastery in Early 'Abbasid Times." In *The Sabaite Heritage in the Orthodox Church from the Fifth Century to the Present*, edited by Joseph Patrich, 147–169. Leuven: Peeters, 2001.

Griffith, Sidney. "The Monks of Palestine and the Growth of Christian Literature in Arabic." *The Muslim World* 78 (1988): 1–28.

Grumel, Venance. "La chronologie des patriarches grecs de Jérusalem au XIIIe siècle." *Revue des Etudes Byzantines* 20 (1962): 197–201.

Haddad, Robert. "On Melkite Passage to the Unia: The Case of Patriarch Cyril al-Za'im (1672–1720)." In *Christians and Jews in the Ottoman Empire: The Functioning of a Plural Society Volume 2*, edited by Benjamin Braude and Bernard Lewis, 67–90. New York: Holmes and Meier, 1982.

Haddad, Robert. *Syrian Christians in Muslim Society: An Interpretation*. Princeton, NJ: Princeton University Press, 1970.

Halil Inalcik, "The Status of the Greek Orthodox Patriarch under the Ottomans." *Turcica* 21–23 (1991), 407–436.

Halil Inalcik, "Ottoman Methods of Conquest." *Studia Islamica* 2 (1954), 103–129.

Heyberger, Bernard. *Les Chrétiens du Proche-Orient au temps de la Réforme catholique: Syrie, Liban, Palestine, XVIIe–XVIIIe siècles*. Rome: Ecole française de Rome, 1994.

Hitti, Philip. *History of Syria: Including Lebanon and Palestine*. London: Macmillan, 1951.

Hiyari, Mustafa, "Cruader Jerusalem 1099–1187 AD." In *Jerusalem in History*, edited by Kamil Jamil Asali, 130–176. Brooklyn, NY: Olive Branch Press, 1990.

Ialamas, D.A., "Gramota ierusalimskogo patriarkha Dosifeia ob izdanii grecheskikh knig v Moskve." *Slaviane i ikh sosedy* 6 (1996): 228–238.

Iared, G. "Anfim, patriarkh Ierusalimskii." *Strannik* (1867): 5–25.

Irwin, Robert. *The Middle East in the Middle Ages: The Early Mamluk Sultanate 1250–1382*. London: Croom Helm, 1986.

Istoriia Gruzii. Vol. 1. Tbilisi, 1962.

Ivanov, N. A. *Programa kursa "Istoriia arabskikh stran."* Moscow, s.n. 1993.

Ivanov, N. A. "Sistema milletov v Arabskikh stranakh XVI–XVII vv." *Vostok* 6 (1992): 29–41.

Jak, Timuthaus. "Al-Ruhbaniyya al-Basiliyya al-Qanuniyya al-Halabiyya al-Shuwayriya." *Al-Mashriq* 9 (1906): 891–899.

Jak, Timuthaus. "Dayr Milad al-Sayyida fi Ras Ba'labak." *Al-Mashriq* 9 (1906): 533–540.

Jotischky, Andrew. "Greek Orthodox and Latin Monasticism around Mar Saba under Crusader Rule." In *The Sabaite Heritage in the Orthodox Church from the Fifth Century to the Present*, edited by Joseph Patrich, 85–96. Leuven: Peeters, 2001.

Kacharava, Iu. "Politicheskoe polozhenie Gruzii i voprosy vzaimootnoshenii s Rossiei (2 pol. XVII v.)." PhD diss., Institut Istorii arkheologii i etnografii im. I.A. Dzhavakhishvili, 2008.

Kapterev, N. F. *Kharakter otnoshenii Rossii k pravoslavnomu Vostoku v XVI i XVII stoletiiakh*. Sergiev Posad: M.S. Elov, 1914.

Kapterev, N. F. "Gospodstvo grekov v Ierusalimskom patriarkhate s pervoi poloviny XVI do poloviny XVIII veka." *Bogoslovskii Vestnik* (May 1897): 198–215; (July 1897): 27–43.

Kapterev, N. F. "Khlopoty moskovskogo pravitel'stva o vosstanovlenii Paisiia Aleksandriiskogo i Makariia Antiokhiiskogo na ikh patriarshikh kafedrakh i o razreshenii ot zapreshcheniia Paisiia Ligarida." *Bogoslovskii Vestnik* No. 9 (1911): 67–98; No. 10 (1911): 209–232.

Kapterev, N. F. "Russkaia blagotvoritel'nost' Sinaiskoi obiteli v XVI, XVII, i VIII stoletiiakh." *Chteniia v obshchestve liubitelei dukhovnogo prosveshcheniia* No. 10–11 (1881): 363–414.

Karalevskij, Cyrille. *Dictionnaire d'histoire et de géographie ecclésiastiques*, s.v. "Antioche." 3 Vols. Paris: Letouzey et Ané, 1924. Cols. 585–703.

Karalevskij, Cyrille. *Dictionnaire d'histoire et de géographie ecclésiastiques*, s.v. "Bostra." 9 Vols. Paris: Letouzey et Ané, 1937. Cols. 1399–1405.

Kartashev, A. V. *Ocherki po istorii russkoi tserkvi*, Vols. 1–2. Moscow: Terra, 1993.

Katib, Alaksiyus. "Naufitus, Mutran Saydnana." *Al-Mashriq* 3 (1900): 1068–1072.

Kekelidze, K. "Gruzinskaya versiia arabskogo Zhitiia sv. Ioanna Damaskina." *Khristianskii Vostok* 3, No. 2 (1914): 99–174.

Khutsishvili, N. "Obrazovanie zemlevladeniia ierusalimskikh monastyrei v Gruzii." *Khristianskii Vostok* 2, No. 8 (2000): 126–136.

Kilpatrick, Hilary. "Makariyus Ibn al-Za'im and Bulus Ibn al-Za'im." In *Essays in Arabic Literary Biography II: 1350–1850*, edited by Joseph E. Lowry and Devin J. Stewart, 262–273. Wiesbaden: Harrassowitz, 2009.

Kirillina, S. A. *Ocharovannye stranniki: Arabo-osmanskii mir glazami rossiiskikh palomnikov XVI–XVIII stoletii*. Moscow: Kliuch-S, 2010.

Kobeko, D. F. "Razreshitel'nye gramoty ierusalimskikh patriarkhov." *Zhurnal ministerstva narodnogo prosveshcheniia* (Juna 1896): 270–279.

Kobishchanov, T. Iu., "Krest nad Beirutom: rossiskaia ekspeditsiia v Vostochnoe Sredizemnomor'e 1769–1774 gg. v vospriatii siriiskikh sovremennikov." *Vestnik Moskovskogo universiteta Ser. 13: Vostokovedenie* No. 1 (2009): 3–23; No. 2 (2009): 3–21.

Kobishchanov, T. Iu. *Khristianskie obshchiny v arabo-osmanskom mire (XVII– pervaia tret' XIX v.)*. Moscow: Institut Azii i Afriki pri MGU, 2003.

Kondakov, N. P. *Arkheologicheskoe puteshestvie po Siri i Palestine*. St Petersburg: Izdatel'stvo Imp. Akedemii Nauk, 1904.

Koraev, T. K. "Musul'mansko-khristianskie otnosheniia v Egipte i Sirii epokhi mongolo-mamliukskikh voin (vtoraia polovina XIII–pervaia polovina XIV v.)." *Vestnik Moskovskogo universiteta* No. 4 (2005): 37–51.

Korobeinikov, Dimitri. "Orthodox Communities in Eastern Anatolia in the Thirteenth to Fourteenth Centuries. Part 2: The Time of Troubles." *Al-Masaq* 17, No. 1 (2005): 1–29.

Krachkovskii, I. Iu., "Arabskaia geograficheskaia literature." In *Izbrannye sochineniia* 4 Vols. Moscow: Izdatel'stvo akademii nauk SSSR, 1957.

Krachkovskii, I. Iu., "Arabskie rukopisi iz sobraniia Grigoriia IV, patriarkha Antiokhskogo (Kratkaia opis')." In *Izvestiia Kavkazskogo Istoriko-Arkheologiskogo instituta*, 1–19. 2 Vols. 1917–1925.

Krachkovskii, I. Iu. "Gramota Ioakima IV, patriarkha Antiokhiskogo, l'vovskoi pastve v 1586 godu." In *Izbrannye sochineniia*, 445–454. 6 Vols. Moscow: Izdatel'stvo akademii nauk SSSR, 1960.

Krachkovskii, I. Iu. "Opisanie puteshestviia Makariia Antiokhiiskogo kak pamiatnik arabskoi geograficheskoi literatury i kak istochnik po istorii Rossii v XVII v." In *Izbrannye sochineniia*. 1 Vols. Moscow: Izdatel'stvo akademii nauk SSSR, 1955.

Krachkovskii, I. Iu. "Original Vatikanskoi rukopisi arabskogo perevoda Biblii." In *Izbrannye sochineniia*, 472–477. 6 Vols. Moscow: Izdatel'stvo akademii nauk SSSR, 1960.

Krachkovskii, I. Iu. "Pis'mo G. Adama iz Venetsii." In *Izbrannye sochineniia*, 478–476. 6 Vols. Moscow: Izdatel'stvo akademii nauk SSSR, 1960.

Krivov, M. V. "Araby-khristiane v Antioii X-XI vv." In *Traditsii i nasledie Khristianskogo Vostoka*, edited by D.E. Afinogenov and A.V. Murav'ev, 247–255. Moscow: Indrik, 1996.

Krivov, M. V. "Otnoshenie siriiskikh monofizitov k arabskomu zavoevaniiu." *Vizantiiskii Vremennik* 55 (1994): 95–103.

Krymskii, A. E. *Istoriia novoi arabskoi literatury*. Moscow: Nauka, 1971.

Kulakovskii, Iu. A. *Istoriia Vizantii*. 3 Vols. St Petersburg: Aleteiia, 1996.

Kuzenkov, P. V., and K. A. Panchenko, "'Krivye Paskhi' i Blagodatnyi ogon v istoricheskoi retrospektive." *Vestnik MGU, Ser. 13 Vostokovedenie* No. 4 (2006): 1–29.

Lavrent'ev, A. V. "Kovcheg E.I. Ukraintseva iz sobraniia GIM." In *Rossiia i Khristianskii Vostok* 1 (1997): 185–196.

Le Strange, Guy. *Palestine under the Moslems: A Description of Syria and the Holy Land from AD 650–1500*. Beirut: Khayats, 1965.

Lebedev, A. P. *Istoriia greko-vostochnoi tserkvi pod vlastiu turok: Ot padaniia Konstantinopolia (1453 g.) do nastoiashchego vremeni*. 1–2 Vols. Sergiev Posad: Tipografiia A.N. Snegirevoi, 1896, 1901.

Levenq, G. *Dictionnaire d'histoire et de géographie ecclésiastiques*, s.v. "Athanase II." 3 Vols. Paris: Letouzey et Ané, 1924. Col. 1369.

Levenq, G. *Dictionnaire d'histoire et de géographie ecclésiastiques*, s.v. "Athanase III." 3 Vols. Paris: Letouzey et Ané, 1924. Cols. 1369–1374.

Levenq, G. *Dictionnaire d'histoire et de géographie ecclésiastiques*, s.v. "Athanase IV." 3 Vols. Paris: Letouzey et Ané, 1924. Col. 1367–1374.

Lewis, Norman. *Nomads and Settlers in Syria and Jordan, 1800–1980*. Cambridge: Cambridge University Press, 1987.

Loparev, Kh. M. "Ierusalimskii patriarkh Khrisanf (1707–1731) i ego otnoshenie k Rossii." *Trudy vos'mogo arkheologicheskogo sezda v Moskve* (1890): 20–27.

Loparev, Kh. M. "Prilozhenie." In *Khozhdenie kuptsa Vasiliia Pozniakova po sviatym mestam Vostoka 1551–1561 gg*. St Petersburg: Tipografiia Kirshbauma, 1887.

Loparev, Kh. M. "Vizantiiskie zhitie sviatykh VIII-IX vv." *Vizantiiskii Vremennik* 17 (1911): 1–223; 18 (1911): 1–147; 19 (1912): 1–151.

MacAdam, Henry Innes, ""Settlements and Settlement Patterns in Northern and Central Transjordania, ca 550–750." *In The Byzantine and Early Islamic Near East: Land Use and Settlement Patterns*, edited by Averil Cameron and G.R.D. King, 49–94. Princeton: Darwin Press, 1994.

Malyshevskii, I. I. *Aleksandriiskii patriarkh Meletii Pigas i ego uchastie v dielakh russkoi tserkvi*. Kiev: Tipigrafiia Kievopecherskoi lavry, 1872.

Manash, Jirjis. "Ni'ma ibn al-khuri Tuma al-Halabi al-sha'ir al-nathir." *Al-Mashriq* 5 (1902): 396–405.

Masters, Bruce. *Christians and Jews in the Ottoman Arab World: The Roots of Sectarianism*. Cambridge: Cambridge University Press, 2001.

Matveevskii. "Ocherk istorii Aleksandriiskoi tserkvi so vremen Khalkidonskogo sobora." *Khristianskoe chtenie* (1856): 188–271, 358–419.

Mednikov, N. A. *Palestina ot zavoevaniia ee arabami do krestovykh pokhodov*. 1–2 Vols. St Petersburg: Izdat'elstvo Imp. pravoslavnago palestinskago obshchestva, 1897–1903.

Meier, M. S. *Osmanskaia imperiia v XVIII veke: Cherty strukturnogo krizisa*. Moscow: Nauka, 1991.

Meinardus, Otto, "Coptic Christianity Past and Present." In *Christian Egypt: Coptic Art and Monuments through Two Millennia*, edited by Massimo Capuani, 8–20. Cairo: American University of Cairo Press, 2002.

Mets, Adam. *Musul'manskii renessans*. Moscow: Nauka, 1973.

Mikhailova, A. I. "Litsevaia arabskaia rukopis' perevoda grecheskogo khronografa XVII v." *Palestinskii Sbornik* 15, No. 78 (1966): 201–207.

Mironovich, A. "Deiatel'nost' ierusalimskogo patriarkha Feofana III v Rechi Pospolitoi." *Kapterevskie chteniia* 7 (2009): 115–128.

Moosa, Matti. *The Maronites in History*. Syracuse: Syracuse University Press, 1986.

Morozov, D. A. "Arabskoe Evangelie Daniila Apostola." *Arkhiv Russkoi istorii* 2 (1992): 193–203.

Morozov, D. A. "Vifleemskii ekzempliar arabskogo Evangeliia Daniila Apostola." *Arkhiv Russkoi istorii* 8 (2007): 645–651.

Müller, Christian, and Johannes Pahlitzsch, "Sultan Baybars I and the Georgians in the Light of New Documents, Related to the Monastery of the Holy Cross in Jerusalem." *Arabica* 51, No. 3 (July 2004): 258–290.

Murav'ev, A.N. *Istoriia sviatago grada Ierusalima, ot vremen apostol'skikh do nashikh*. 1–2 Vols. St Petersburg: V Tip. III. otdiel. sobstv. E.I.V. kantseliarii, 1844.

Murav'ev, A.N. *Snosheniia Rossii s Vostokom po dielam tserkovnym*. 1 Vol. St Petersburg: Tip. III Otdieleniia Sobst. E.I.V. Kantseliarsii, 1858.

Murkos, G. A., "O rukopisnom sbornike XVII v. na raznykh vostochnykh iazykakh iz sobraniia grafa A.S. Uvarova." *Drevnosti Vostochnye* 1, No. 2 (1891): 212–222.

Nasrallah, Joseph. *Chronologie des patriarches melchites d'Antioche de 1250 à 1500*. Jerusalem: s.n., 1968.

Nasrallah, Joseph. *Chronologie des patriarches melchites d'Antioche de 1500 à 1634*. Jerusalem: s.n., 1959.

Nasrallah, Joseph. *Dictionnaire d'histoire et de géographie ecclésiastiques*, s.v. "Euthème Saifi." 16 Vols. Paris: Letouzey et Ané, 1967. Cols. 64–74.

Nasrallah, Joseph. *Histoire du mouvement littéraire dans l'Église melchite du Ve au XXe siècle: Contribution à l'étude de la littérature arabe chrétienne*, Vols. 2.1–4.2. Louvain: Peeters, 1979–1989.

Nasrallah, Joseph. *Souvenirs de St. Paul*. Damascus: s.n., 2001.

Naumov, E. P. "Osmanskoe gosudarstvo i serbskaia pravoslavnaia tserkov'." In *Osmanskaia imperiia: Sistema gosudarstvennogo upravlenniia, sotsial'nye i etnoreligioznye problemy*, 117–135. Moscow: Nauka, 1986.

Neale, John Mason. *A History of the Holy Eastern Church: The Patriarchate of Antioch*. London: Rivingtons, 1873.

Nicol, Donald M. "The Confessions of a Bogus Patriarch: Paul Tagaris Palaiologos, Orthodox Patriarch of Jerusalem and Catholic Patriarch of Constantinople in the Fourteenth Century." *Journal of Ecclesiastical History* 21, No. 4 (October 1970): 289–299.

Nikolaev, B. "Zapadnye palomnichestva vo Sv. zemliu v sredine veka." *Soobshcheniia Imperatorskago Pravoslavnago Palestinskago Obshchestva* 25 (1914): 291–407.

Nikolaevskii, P. F. "Iz istorii snoshenii Rossii s Vostokom v polovine XVII stoletiia." *Khristianskoe chtenia* (1882): 245–267, 732–775.

Oparina, T. A. "Grecheskii chin priema katolikov v pravoslavie v serbskikh i ukraino-bielorusskikh pamiatnikakh i ego vliianie na russkuiu traditsiiu." *Vestnik tserkovnoi istorii* 1–2, No. 17–18 (2010): 215–231.

Pacini, Andrea. "Socio-Political and Community Dynamics of Arab Christians in Jordan, Israel and the Autonomous Palestinian Territories." In *Christian Communities in the Arab Middle East: The Challenge of the Future*, edited by Andrea Pacini, 259–285. Oxford: Clarendon Press, 1998.

Pahlitzsch, Johannes. "Athanasios II, a Greek Orthodox Patriarch of Jerusalem (c. 1231–1244)." In *Autour de la première Croisade: actes du colloque de la Society for the study of the crusades and the Latin East, Clermont-Ferrand, 22–25 juin 1995*, edited by Michel Balard, 465–474. Paris: Publications de la Sorbonne, 1994.

Pahlitzsch, Johannes. "Georgians and Greeks in Jerusalem (1099–1310)." In *East and West in the Crusader States: Context, Contacts, Confrontations. III, Acts of the Congress Held at Hernen Castle in September 2000*, edited by Krijna Ciggaar and Herman Teule, 35–52. Leuven: Peeters, 2003.

Panchenko, Constantin. "The Antiochean Greek-Orthodox Patriarchate and Rome in the Late 16th C. A Polemic Response of the Metropolitan Athanasius Ibn Mujalla to the Pope." In *Actes du symposium international Le Livre. La Roumanie. L'Europe. 4-eme édition. 20–23 Septembre 2011. T. III. Section III. Latinité Orientale*, 302–315. Bucharest: Editura Biblioteca Bucureştilor, 2012.

Panchenko, Constantin. "When and Where 'The Melkite Renaissance' Started? Metropolitan Uwakim of Bethlehem, a Forgotten Arab-Christian Scholar of the Late 16th Century." In Travaux de symposium international Le Livre. La Roumanie. L'Europe. Troisieme édition—20 a 24 Septembre 2010. 4 vols. 469–481. Bucharest: Editura Biblioteca Bucureştilor, 2011.

Panchenko, K. A. "Antiokhiiskaia pravoslavnaia tserkov' i Rim v epokhu Kontrreformatsii: Polemicheskii otvet pape rimskomu Anastasiia ibn Mudzhally" in *Pravoslavnye araby: put' cherez veka*, edited by K. A. Panchenko, 292–322. Moscow: Izdatel'stvo PSTGU, 2013.

Panchenko, K. A. "Antiokhiiskii patriarkh Khristofor (um. 967 g.): lichnost' i epokha." In *XIV Ezhegodnaia bogoslovskaia konferentsiia PSTBI: Materialy*, 216–234. Moscow: Pravoslavnyi Sviato-Tikhonskii Bogoslovskii institute, 2005.

Panchenko, K. A. "Greki vs. Araby v Ierusalimskoi tserkvi XIII-XVIII vv." In *Meyeriana: Sbornik statei, posviashchennyi 70–letiiu M.S. Meiera*, 7–50. 2 Vols. Moscow: Institut stran azii i afrikii pri MGU, 2006.

Panchenko, K. A. "Ierusalimskii patriarkh Parfenii (1737–1766 gg.) i Rossiia: neponiatii soiuznik." *Vestnik tserkovnoi istorii* 3–4, No. 19–20 (2010): 271–285.

Panchenko, K. A. "K istorii Ierusalimskoi tserkvi XVI v. Nesostoiavshaiasia arabskaia al'ternativa grecheskoi ksenokratii ili Kogda i gde nachalsia Mel-kitskii Renessans?" *Pravoslavnyi Palestinskii Sbornik* 107 (2011): 271–284.

Panchenko, K. A. "K istorii pravoslavnogo letopisaniia v Khalifate (Istochniki khroniki Agapiia Manbadzhskogo)." *Vizantiiskii Vremennik* 60, No. 85 (2001): 109–120.

Panchenko, K. A. "K istorii russko-vostochnykh sviazei 70–x gg. XIV v. O datirovke i obstoiatel'stvakh palomnichestva arkhimandrita Agrefeniiia i pervogo priezda na Rus' blizhnevostochnykh mitropolitov." *Kapterevskie chteniia* 7 (2009): 5–20.

Panchenko, K. A. "Kosta ibn Luka (830–912) i ego mesto v arabo-khristianskoi istoriografii." *Pravoslavnyi Palestinskii Sbornik* 100 (2003): 153–163.

Panchenko, K. A. "Mitropolit 'Isa i pervoe arabskoe opisanie Moskovii (1586 g.)." *Vestnik MGU, Ser. 13 Vostokovedenie* (2007): 87–95.

Panchenko, K. A. "Monastyri i beduiny v osmanskoi Palestine i na Sinae (XVI-pervaia pol. XIX vv.)." *Vestnik Pravoslavnogo Sviato-Tikhonskogo Gumanitar-nogo Universiteta: Ser. Filologiia* 1, No. 7 (2007): 68–98.

Panchenko, K. A. "Monastyri v pravoslavnom Antiokhiiskom patriarkhate XVI- nach. XIX vv." *Vestnik MGU, Ser. 13. Vostokovedenie* (2004): 89–113.

Panchenko, K. A. *Osmanskaia imperiia i sud'by pravoslaviia na Arabskom Vostoke.* Moscow: Institut Azii i Afriki pri MGU, 1998.

Panchenko, K. A. "Patriarkh Ioakim mezhdu Kairom, Rimom i Moskvoi: K istorii russko-palestinskikh kontaktov XV v." In *Russkaia Palestina: Rossiia v sviatoi zemle*, edited by E. I. Zelenev, 228–239. St Petersburg: Izdatel'skii dom SPbGU, 2010.

Panchenko, K. A. "Podzhog Kaira 1321 g. i problema khristianskogo terrorizma v Mamliukskom gosudarstve." *Vestnik PSTGU: Ser. "Filologiia"* 4, No. 26 (2011): 96–124.

Panchenko, K. A. "Pravoslavnye araby i Kavkaz v sredine XVII v." *Vestnik MGU. Ser. 13 Vostokovedenie* (2000): 56–70.

Panchenko, K. A. "Pravoslavnye Araby-osvedomiteli rossiiskogo Posol'skogo pri-kaza v XVII v." *Arabskie strany Zapadnoi Azii i Severnoi Afriki* 4 (2000): 307–317.

Panchenko, K. A. "Problema religioznykh gonenii v osmano-pravoslavnykh otnosheniakh v Siri ii Palestine (1516–1831)." *Vestnik MGU, Ser. 13. Vostoko-vedenie* (1995): 25–38.

Panchenko, K. A. Review of *The Salvation of the Wise Man and the Ruin of the World: Salah al-Hakim wa-fasad al-'alam al-dhammim, edited, translated and annotated with editor's notes and indices*, edited by Ioana Feodorov in *Vestnik Moskovskogo Universiteta Ser. 13 Vostokovedenie* (1995): 117–122.

Panchenko, K. A., "Rod Ioanna Damaskina i stanovlenie khristianskoi elity v khalifate." *Vestnik MGU, Ser. 13. Vostokovedenie* (2002): 88–99.

Panchenko, K. A. "Rossiia i Antiokhiiskii patriarkhat: nachalo dialoga (konets XVI – pervaia polovina XVIII v.)." *Rossiia i Khristianskii Vostok* 2–3 (2004): 203–221.

Panchenko, K. A. "Sputniki antiokhiiskogo patriarkha Makariia v ego pervom puteshestvii v Rossiiu" in *Pravoslavnye araby: put' cherez veka*, edited by K. A. Panchenko, 348–367. Moscow: Izdatel'stvo PSTGU, 2013.

Panchenko, K. A. "Tripoliiskoe gnezdo: Pravoslavaia obshchina g. Tripoli v kul'turno-politicheskoi zhizni Antiokhiiskogo patriarkhata XVI – pervoi poloviny XVII v." *Vestnik PSTGU: Ser. III "Filologiia"* 1, No. 15 (2009): 41–64; 3, No. 17 (2009): 19–37.

Panchenko, K. A. "Vospriiatie istoricheskogo protsessa arabo-khristianskimi khronistami." In *Religii stran Azii i Afrikii: istoriia i sovremennost': Nauchnaia konferentsiia Lomonosovskie chteniia. Aprel' 2001. Tezisy dokladov*, 82–86. Moscow: Institut stran azii i afrikii pri MGU, 2002.

Panchenko, K. A. "Zabytaia katastrofa: K rekonstruktsii posledstvii Aleksandriiskogo krestovogo pokhoda 1365 g. na Khristianskom Vostoke" in *Pravoslavnye araby: put' cherez veka*, edited by K. A. Panchenko, 202–219. Moscow: Izdatel'stvo PSTGU, 2013.

Panchenko, K. A., and B. L. Fonkich, "Gramota 1594 g. antiokhiiskogo patriarkha Ioakima VI tsariu Fedoru Ivanovichu." *Monfokon: Issledovaniia po paleografii, kodikologii i diplomatike* (2007): 166–184.

Peri, Oded. *Christians under Islam in Jerusalem: The Question of the Holy Sites in Early Ottoman Times*. Leiden: Brill, 2001.

Peristeris, Aristarchos. "Literary and Scribal Activities at the Monastery of Mar Saba." In *The Sabaite Heritage in the Orthodox Church from the Fifth Century to the Present*, edited by Joseph Patrich, 171–177. Leuven: Peeters, 2001.

Petra Kapitoliiskogo: Kekelidze, K. "Zhitie Petra Novogo, muchenika Kapetoliiskogo." *Khristianskii Vostok* 4, No. 1 (1916): 1–71.

Philipp, Thomas. *The Syrians in Egypt, 1725–1975*. Stuttgart: Steiner, 1985.

Piatnitskii, Iu. A. "Ikona 'Sv. Ekaterina' iz sobraniia Gosudarstvennogo Ermitazha." *Palestinskii Sbornik* 32, No. 95 (1993): 49–56.

Piatnitskii, Iu. A. "Zhivopis' siro-palestinskogo regiona." In *Xhristiane na Vostoke: Isskustvo mel'kitov i inoslavnykh khristian*, 108–135. St Petersburg: Slaviia, 1998.

Piccirillo, Michele. "The Christians in Palestine during a Time of Transition: 7th–9th Centuries." In *The Christian Heritage in the Holy Land*, edited by Anthony O'Mahoney, 47–56. London: Scorpion Cavendish, 1995.

Plank, P. "Pravoslavnye khristiane Sv. Zemli vo vremena krestovykh pokhodov (1099–1197)." *Al'fa i Omega* 4, No. 26 (2000): 180–191.

Pomerantsev, I. "Ierusalimskii patriarkh Dosifei II (1669–1707)." *Soobshcheniia mperatorskago Pravoslavnago Palestinskago Obshchestva* 19 (1908): 1–32.

Pomerantsev, I. "Izbranie ierusalimskikh patriarkhov v XVII i XVIII stoletiakh." *Soobshcheniia Imperatorskago Pravoslavnago Palestinskago Obshchestva* 18 (1907): 209–232.

Popov, Aleksandr. *Latinskaia ierusalimskaia patriarkhiia epokhi krestonostsev*. St Petersburg: Pechatnia S.P. Iakovleva, 1903.

Popović, Svetlana. "Sabaite Influences on the Church in Medieval Serbia." In *The Sabaite Heritage in the Orthodox Church from the Fifth Century to the Present*, edited by Joseph Patrich, 385–407. Leuven: Peeters, 2001.

Potulov, V. "Maronitskaia tserkov' v V-IX vv." *Soobshcheniia Imperatorskago Pravoslavnago Palestinskago Obshchestva* 23 (1912): 32–52.

Rabbat, Antun. "Al-Tawa'if al-sharqiyya wa-bid'at al-Kalwiniyyin fi al-jayl al-sabi' 'ashar." *Al-Mashriq* 6 (1903): 971–973; 7 (1904): 766–773, 795–803.

Rabbat, Antun. "Athar al-sharqiyya fi makatib Baris." *Al-Mashriq* 6 (1903): 85–90, 501–510.

Raymond, André. "Une communauté en expansion : les chrétiens d'Alep à l'époque ottomane (XVIe–XVIIe siècles)." In *La ville arabe, Alep, à l'époque ottoman (XVIe–XVIIIe siècles)*, edited by André Raymond, 351–372. Damascus: Institut français d'études arabes de Damas, 1998.

Reifenberg, Adolf. *The Struggle between the Desert and the Sown: Rise and Fall of Agriculture in the Levant*. Jerusalem: Publication Department of the Jewish Agency, 1956.

Richard, Jean. *Latino-Ierusalimskoe korolevstvo*. St Petersburg: Evrasia, 2002.

Richards, Donald S. "Arabic Documents from the Monastery of St. James in Jerusalem including a Mamluk Report on the Ownership of Cavalry." *Revue des Etudes Arméniennes* 21 (1988–1989): 455–469.

Rodionov, M. A. *Maronity: Iz etnokonfessional'noi istorii Vostochnogo Sredizemnomor'ia*. Moscow: Nauka, 1982.

Romana Novogo: Kekelidze, K. "Novootkrytyi agiologiicheskii pamiatnik ikonoborchesko epokhi (Zhitie sv. Romana Novogo)." *Trudy Kievskoi Dukhovnoi Akademii* (June 1910): 201–238.

Rose, Richard B. "The Native Christians of Jerusalem, 1187–1260." In *The Horns of Hattin: proceedings of the Second Conference of the Society for the Study of the Crusades and the Latin East, Jerusalem and Haifa, 2–6 July 1987*, edited by Benjamin Z. Kedar, 239–249. London: Variorum, 1992.

Runciman, Steven. *A History of the Crusades, Vols. 1–3*. Cambridge: Cambridge University Press, 1968–1975.

Runciman, Steven. *The Great Church in Captivity*. Cambridge: Cambridge University Press, 1968.

Runciman, Steven. *The Historic Role of Christian Arabs of Palestine*. London: Harlow, Longmans, 1970.

Runciman, Steven. *Vostochnaia skhizma: Vizantiiskaia teokratiia*. Moscow: Nauka, 1998.

Rustum, As'ad. *Kanisat Madinat Allah Antakiya al-'Uzma*. 1–3 Vols. Beirut: al-Maktaba al-Bulusiyya, 1988.

Rzianin, A. A. "Gruzinskii vopros vo vneshnei politike Moskovskogo tsarstva v 1 pol. XVII v. (1613–1652)." PhD diss., Tbilisi, 1955.

Saliba, Sabine Mohasseb. *Les monastères maronites doubles du Liban: entre Rome et l'Empire ottoman (XVIIe–XIXe siècles)*. Paris: Geuthner, 2008.

Salibi, Kamal. "The Traditional Historiography of the Maronites." In *Historians of the Middle East*, edited by Bernard Lewis and P. M. Holt, 212–225. London: Oxford University Press, 1962.

Schick, Robert, "Luxuriant Legacy: Palestine in the Early Islamic Period." *Near Eastern Archaeology* 61, No. 2 (June 1998): 74–108.

Seleznev, M. "Puteshestvie patriarkha Dosifeia, s religioznym i politicheskim sostoianiem Gruzii do XVII veka." *Rukovodstvo k poznaniiu Kavkaza* 1 (1847): 1–178.

Semonova, L. E. *Kniazhestva Valakhiia i Moldaviia kon. IV–nach. XIX v.: Ocherki vneshneppoliticheskoi istorii*. Moscow: Indrik, 2006.

Sharon, Moshe. *Corpus inscriptionum Arabicarum Palaestinae*. Vol. 3. Leiden: Brill, 2004.

Shestopalets, D. V. "Svedeniia arabskikh istochnikov ob islamizatsii khristian Blizhnego Vostoka v XIII-XV vv." In *Problemy istoriografii, istochnikovedeniia i istorii Vostoka*, 151–161. Lugansk, 2008.

Skabalanovich, N. "Politika turetskogo pravitel'stva po otnosheniiu k khristianskim poddanym i ikh religii." *Khristianskoe chtenie* (1878): 423–464.

Slim, Souad, Ra'if Nassif, and Houda Kassatly. *Balamand: Histoire et patrimoine*. Beirut: Dar an-Nahar, 1994.

Smilianskaia, I. M. "Osmanskoe provintsial'noe upravlenie i obshchestve-nye instituty v Sirii XVIII v." In *Gosudarstvennaia vlast' i obshchestvenno-politicheskie struktury v arabskikh stranakh*, edited by I. P. Ivanova, M. B. Piotrovskii, and I. M. Smilianskaia, 51–80. Moscow: Nauka, 1984.

Smilianskaia, I. M. *Sotsial'no-ekonomicheskaia struktura stran Blizhnego Vostoka na rubezhe Novogo vremeni*. Moscow: Nauka, 1979.

Sokolov, I. I. "Antiokhiiskii patriarkh Sil'vestr (1724–1766)." *Soobshcheniia Imperatorskago Pravoslavnago Palestinskago Obshchestva* 24 (1913): 3–33.

Sokolov, I. I. "Didaskal Iakov Patmosskii: Ocherk iz istorii dukhovnogo pros-veshcheniia v Siri ii Palestine v XVIII veke." *Soobshcheniia Imperatorskago Pravoslavnago Palestinskago Obshchestva* 20 (1909): 321–351.

Sokolov, I. I. "Sviatogrobskoe bratstvo v Ierusalime." *Soobshcheniia Imperator-skago Pravoslavnago Palestinskago Obshchestva* 17 (1906): 1–22.

Sokolov, I. I. "Tserkovnye sobytiia v Sirii v kontse XVII i v nachale XVIII v." *Soobshcheniia Imperatorskago Pravoslavnago Palestinskago Obshchestva* 23 (1912): 312–346.

Solov'ev, S., "Monastyr' sv. Georgiia v Sirii." *Soobshcheniia Imperatorskago Pravo-slavnago Palestinskago Obshchestva* 16 (1905): 547–555.

Swanson, Mark. "The Christian al-Ma'mun Tradition." In *Christians at the Heart of Islamic Rule: Church Life and Scholarship in ʿAbbasid Iraq*, edited by David Thomas, 63–92.

Todt, Klaus-Peter. "*Notitia* und Diozesen des griechisch-orthodoxen Patriarch-ates von Antiocheia im 10. und 11. Jarhundert." *Orthodoxes Forum* 9 (1995): 173–185.

Todt, Klaus-Peter. *Region und griechisch-orthodoxes Patriarchat von Antiocheia in mittelbyzantinischer Zeit und im Zeitalter der Kreuzzüge (969–1204)*. Wiesbaden, s.n., 1998.

Tsagareli, A. *Pamiatniki gruzinskoi strany v Sviatoi zemle i na Sinae*. St Petersburg, 1888.

al-ʿUjaymi, Yuhanna. *Al-Hujja al-rahina fi haqiqat asl al-Mawarina*. Cairo: Maktabat Sharikat al-Tamaddun, 1900.

Uspenskii, F. I. *Istoriia Vizantiiskoi Imperii*. 1–3 Vols. Moscow: Mysl, 1996–1997.

Uspenskii, Porphyry. "Vostok Khristianskii: Siriia." *Trudy Kievskoi Dukhovnoi Akademii* (July 1875): 1–32; (August 1875): 33–48; (October 1875): 49–64; (November 1875): 65–80; (December 1875): 81–96; (March 1876): 97–125.

Veselovskii, A. N. "K skazanniiu o prenii zhidov s khristianami." In *Zametki po literature i narodnoi slovesnosti*, 14–33. St Petersburg: Tip. Imp. Akademii Nauk, 1883.

Vizantiiskii, I. "Antiokhiiskii patriarch Mefodii (1823–1850 g.)." *Soobshcheniia Imperatorskago Pravoslavnago Palestinskago Obshchestva* 16 (1905): 28–42.

Voronov, A. "Sinaiskoe dielo." *Trudy Kievskoi Dukhovnoi Akademii* (1871): 330–401.

Vyronis, Speros. *The Decline of Medieval Hellenism in Asia Minor and the Process of Islamization from the Eleventh through the Fifteenth Century*. Berkeley, CA: University of California Press, 1971.

Walbiner, Carsten-Michael. "Accounts on Georgia in the Works of Makarius Ibn al-Za'im." *Parole de l'Orient* 21 (1996): 245–255.

Walbiner, Carsten-Michael. "'Und um Jesu willen, schickt sie nicht ungebunden!' Die Bemühungen des Meletius Karma (1572–1635) um den Druck arabischer Bücher in Rom." In *Studies on the Christian Heritage*, edited by Rifaat Ebied and Herman Teule, 163–175. Leuven: Peeters, 2004.

Walbiner, Carsten-Michael. "Bishoprics and Bishops of the Greek Orthodox Patriarchate of Antioch in the 16th and 17th Centuries." In *Tarikh Kanisat Antakiya lil-Rum al-Urthudhuks: Ayya Khususiya?* 121–134. Tripoli, Lebanon: Balamand University, 1999.

Walbiner, Carsten-Michael. "Bishops and Metropolitans of the Antiochian Patriarchate in the 17th Century." *ARAM* 9–10 (1997–1998): 577–587.

C. Walbiner, "Ein Christlish-Arabischer bericht uber eine pilgerfahrt von Damascus zum berge Sinai in den jahren 1635–36," in *Parole de l'Orient* 24 (1999), 319–337.

Walbiner, Carsten-Michael. "Die Beziehungen zwischen dem Griechisch-Orthodoxen Patriarchat von Antiochia und der Kirche von Georgien vom 14. bis zum 18. Jahrhundert." *Le Muséon* 114 (201): 437–455.

Walbiner, Carsten-Michael. "Die Bischofs-und Metropolitensitze des griechisch-orthodoxen Patriarchats von Antiochia von 1665 bis 1724 nach einigen zeitgenossischen Quellen." *Oriens Christianus* 88 (2004): 36–92.

C. Walbiner, "Macarius Ibn al-Za'im and the Beginnings of an Orthodox Church Historiography," 14–5.

Walbiner, Carsten-Michael. "Monastic Reading and Learning in Eighteenth-century Bilad al-Sham: Some Evidence from the Monastery of al-Shuwayr (Mount Lebanon)." *Arabica* 51, No. 4 (2004): 462–477.

C. Walbiner, "Rihlat Ra.ad min Halab ila al-Bandaqiyya," in *Majmu.at abhath wa-maqalat ila al-Mutran Neophytus Edelby* (Beirut, 2005), 367–383.

Walbiner, Carsten-Michael. "Some Observations on the Perceptions and Understanding of Printing amongst the Arab Greek Orthodox (Melkites) in the Seventeenth Century." In *Printing and Publishing in the Middle East: Papers from the Second Symposium on the History of Printing and Publishing in the*

Languages and Countries of the Middle East, Bibliothèque nationale de France, Paris, 2–4 November 2005, edited by Philip Sadgrove, 65–76. Oxford: Oxford University Press, 2008.

Walbiner, Carsten-Michael. "The Christians of Bilad al-Sham (Syria): Pioneers of Book-Printing in the Arab World." In *The Beginning of Printing in the Near and Middle East: Jews, Christians and Muslims*, edited by Klaus Kreiser et al., 11–29. Wiesbaden: Harrassowitz, 2001.

Walbiner, Carsten-Michael. "The Split of the Greek Orthodox Patriarchate of Antioch (1724) and the Emergence of a New Identity in Bilad al-Sham as Reflected by Some Melkite Historians of the 18th and Early 20th Centuries." *Chronos* 7 (2003): 9–36.

Wright, William. *Kratkii ocherk istorii siriiskoi literatury*. St Petersburg: Tip. Imp. akademii nauk, 1902.

Zanemonets, A. V. *Gennadii Skholarii, patriarkh Konstantinopolskii (1454–1456 g.)*. Moscow: Bibleisko-bogoslovskii Institut sv. Apostola Andreia, 2010.

Zayat, Habib. *Khaza'in al-Kutub fi Dimashq wa-Dawahiha*. Cairo: al-Ma'arif, 1902.

Zen'kovskii, S. A. *Russkoe staroobriadchestvo*. Moscow: Tserkov', 1995.

Zeyadeh, Ali, "Settlement Patterns, An Archeological Perspective: Case Studies from Northern Palestine and Jordan." In *In The Byzantine and Early Islamic Near East: Land Use and Settlement Patterns*, edited by Averil Cameron and G. R. D. King, 117–132. Princeton, NJ: Darwin Press, 1994.

Zhuze, P. "Eparkhii Antiokhiiskoi tserkvi." *Soobshcheniia Imperatorskago Pravoslavnago Palestinskago Obshchestva* 22 (1911): 481–498.

Zulalian, M. K. "Obstoiatel'stva vosstania Abaza-pashi v Erzerume po armianskim istochnikam." In *Srednevekovyi vostok: Istoriia, kul'tura, istochnikovedenie*, edited by G. F. Girs, 151–157. Moscow: Nauka, 1980.

S.n. "Pravovaia organizatsiia Sviatogrobskogo bratstva v Ierusalime." *Soobshcheniia Imperatorskago Pravoslavnago Palestinskago Obshchestva* 23 (1912): 145–175.

INDEX

ACKNOWLEDGMENTS

The author expresses his deep gratitude to all those who, through their advice and wishes, contributed to the creation of this book. First of all, the author is deeply grateful to M. S. Meyer, director of the Institute of Asian and African Studies at Moscow State University, for his many years of support, interest, and help in the work on this monograph. A special word of thanks goes to F. M. Atsamba for his abiding interest in the author's research and for enriching it with many valuable suggestions. At an intermediary stage of the writing of this monograph, T. A. Konyashkina and T. Yu. Kobischanov made many important suggestions and observations that substantially corrected and completed the range of topics covered in this study. The author is equally grateful to L. O. Basheleishvili, V. V. Orlov, D. R. Zhantiev, G. G. Kosach, D. A. Morozov, Yu. N. Emelyanov, and S. A. Frantsuzov for their critical comments and assistance in acquainting me with a number of sources. In working on topics in this monograph that lie on the junction between Byzantine, Oriental, and Slavic studies, the author received the selfless help and assistance of experts in these fields, B. L. Fonchik and V. G. Chentsova, as well as P. B. Kuzenkov and T. A. Oparina. The author also benefited from highly fruitful collaboration with foreign scholars, especially in the form of longstanding discussion with Europe's leading specialists in the history of the Arab Orthodox in the Ottoman Period: Carsten-Michael Walbiner, Hilary Kilpatrick, Ioana Feodorov, Suad Slim, Herman Teule, Amnon Cohen, and Nikolai Serikov. The author likewise wishes to thank the staff of libraries in Moscow and St Petersburg and all those who took part in the editing and publishing work in bringing this monograph to print. This work would never have seen the light of day without the constant attention and support of my parents, Galina Tikhonovna and Alexandr Ivanovich Panchenko.

Finally, I would like to express my particular gratitude to my teacher S. A. Kirillina, because it was her energetic assistance and mentoring that made possible not only the appearance of this work, but also the formation of the author as a scholar and historian.

Constantine A. Panchenko